APPLIED MODELING
AND SIMULATION:

AN INTEGRATED APPROACH TO
DEVELOPMENT AND OPERATION

SPACE TECHNOLOGY SERIES

This book is published as part of the Space Technology Series, a cooperative activity of the United States Department of Defense and the National Aeronautics and Space Administration.

Wiley J. Larson
Managing Editor

From Kluwer and Microcosm Publishers:

Space Mission Analysis and Design, Second Edition by Larson and Wertz.

Spacecraft Structures and Mechanisms: From Concept to Launch by Sarafin.

Reducing Space Mission Cost by Wertz and Larson.

From McGraw-Hill:

Understanding Space: An Introduction to Astronautics by Sellers.

Space Propulsion Analysis and Design by Humble, Henry, and Larson.

Cost-Effective Space Mission Operations by Boden and Larson.

Fundamentals of Astrodynamics and Applications by Vallado.

Applied Modeling and Simulation: An Integrated Approach to Development and Operation by Cloud and Rainey.

Future Books in the Series

Human Space Mission Analysis and Design by Giffen, Humble, and Larson.

Risk Strategies for Space Systems by Reeves and Larson.

APPLIED MODELING AND SIMULATION:
AN INTEGRATED APPROACH TO DEVELOPMENT AND OPERATION

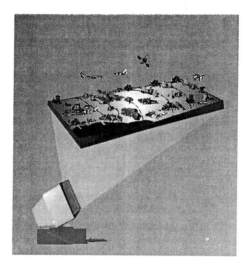

Edited by
David J. Cloud
United States Air Force Academy

Larry B. Rainey
The Aerospace Corporation

*This book is published as part of the
Space Technology Series, a cooperative activity
of the United States Department of Defense and the
National Aeronautics and Space Administration.*

The McGraw-Hill Companies, Inc.
Primis Custom Publishing

*New York   St. Louis   San Francisco   Auckland   Bogotá
Caracas   Lisbon   London   Madrid   Mexico   Milan   Montreal
New Delhi   Paris   San Juan   Singapore   Sydney   Tokyo   Toronto*

McGraw·Hill

A Division of The McGraw·Hill Companies

APPLIED MODELING AND SIMULATION:
AN INTEGRATED APPROACH TO DEVELOPMENT AND OPERATION

1 2 3 4 5 6 7 8 9 0   DOC DOC   9 0 9 8

ISBN 0-07-228303-3
Library of Congress Catalog Card Number: 98-66611

Publisher: M.A. Hollander
Cover Design: Marsha Taylor
Text Design: Anita Shute
Technical Editor: Perry Luckett
Printer/Binder: R. R. Donnelley & Sons Company, Inc.

Table of Contents

List of Authors and Editors

Emily B. Andrew. Major, United States Air Force, Project Integrator, Mission Oriented Information Technology Resources, Ballistic Missile Defense Organization, Washington, D.C. M.S. (Electrical Engineering) Colorado Tech University. B.S. (Electrical Engineering) University of Colorado at Denver. B.S. (Biology) University of Connecticut. Chapter 13—*Establishing Standards and Specifications.*

John M. Barry. Program Development Manager, The Boeing Company, Seal Beach, California. M.S. (Computer Science) Northrop University. M.S. (Logistics Management) Air Force Institute of Technology. M.S. (Systems Management) University of Southern California. B.S. (Multiple Science) LeMoyne College. Chapter 7—*A Conceptual Approach to Developing Models and Simulations.*

Kirstie I. Bellman. Principal Director, Aerospace Integration Sciences, The Aerospace Corporation, El Segundo, California. Ph.D. (Neuropsychology) University of California. Chapter 8—*Designing Models.* Appendix B—*Software Design.*

Bart E. Bennett. Senior Operations Research Analyst, RAND Corporation, Santa Monica, California. Ph.D. and M.S. (Mathematical Sciences) Johns Hopkins University. B.S. (Math and Computer Science) University of California at Los Angeles. Chapter 9—*Producing and Managing Data.*

Ronald J. Berdine. Senior Associate, Air Academy Associates, Colorado Springs, Colorado. Ph.D. (Statistics) Texas A&M University. M.S. (Operations Research) Stanford University. B.S. (Mathematics) Iowa State University. Appendix C—*Statistical Analysis and Experimental Design.*

David J. Cloud. Visiting Professor, United States Air Force Academy, Colorado Springs, Colorado. Ph.D. (Engineering Science) Oxford University. M.S. (Aeronautical and Astronautical Engineering) Stanford University. B.S. (Mathematics and Engineering Science) United States Air Force Academy. *Editor,* Chapter 1—*Introduction to Modeling and Simulation.*

Michael D. Crumm. Assistant Program Manager, Command Technologies, Inc., San Antonio, Texas. M.S. (Computer Management) Webster University. B.S. (Computer Science) Rollins College. Chapter 1—*Introduction to Modeling and Simulation.*

David S. Eccles. Director, Modeling and Simulation Department, The Aerospace Corporation, El Segundo, California. M.S. and B.S. (Civil Engineering) Brigham Young University. Chapter 14—*Adapting to Changing Technology.*

Tom Fall. Principal Systems Engineer, Lockheed Martin Western Development Laboratories, Sunnyvale, California. Ph.D. (Mathematics) and B.S. (Chemistry) University of California. Chapter 10—*Implementing Models and Simulations in Hardware and Software.*

David E. Gobuty. Technical Consultant, Lockheed Martin Western Development Laboratories, San Jose, California. J.D. (Law) Golden West University, M.S. (Computer Science) and B.A. (Psychology) California State University. Chapter 17—*Information Security in Simulator Design and Operation.*

Brian Goldiez. Deputy Director and Manager R&D, University of Central Florida, Institute for Simulation and Training, Orlando, Florida. M.S. (Computer Engineering) University of Central Florida. B.S. (Aerospace Engineering) University of Kansas. Chapter 12—*Integrating and Executing Simulations.*

Richard Hillestad. Senior Systems Analyst and Manager, Management Sciences Group, RAND Corporation, Santa Monica, California. Ph.D. (Engineering) University of California. M.S. and B.S. (Electrical Engineering) University of Wisconsin. Chapter 9—*Producing and Managing Data.*

David A. Hollenbach. Associate, Booz-Allen & Hamilton, Inc., Colorado Springs, Colorado. B.S. (Engineering Mechanics) United States Air Force Academy. M.S. (Systems Engineering) Air Force Institute of Technology. Chapter 2—*Systems Science and Systems Engineering.*

Mark J. Kiemele. Senior Associate, Air Academy Associates, Colorado Springs, Colorado. Ph.D. (Computer Science) Texas A&M University. M.S. and B.S. (Mathematics) North Dakota State University. Appendix C—*Statistical Analysis and Experimental Design.*

Christopher Landauer. Aerospace Integration Science Center, The Aerospace Corporation, Los Angeles, California. Ph.D. (Mathematics) Caltech. Chapter 8—*Designing Models.* Appendix B—*Software Design.*

Jerry W. Lawson. Director of Research and Development, The Peak Technologies Group, Inc., Englewood, Colorado. B.S. (Math) Milligan College. Chapter 6—*Developing an Acquisition Strategy;* Appendix A—*Estimating Cost and Schedule.*

Gordon Alfred Long. Information Engineer, Computer Sciences Corporation, Colorado Springs, Colorado. M.S. (Chemical Engineering) University of California. B.S. (Military Engineering) United States Military Academy, West Point. Chapter 9—*Producing and Managing Data.*

Dale K. Pace. Principal Professional Staff, The Johns Hopkins University Applied Physics Laboratory, Laurel, Maryland. Th.D. (Theology) Luther Rice Seminary. B.D. (Theology) Capital Bible Seminary. Chapter 11—*Verification, Validation, and Accreditation.*

J. Mark Pullen. Associate Professor, Computer Science, George Mason University. Director, Simulation and Networking Laboratory, Center of Excellence in Command, Control, Communications, and Intelligence, George Mason University. M.S. and B.S. (Computer Science) The George Washington University. Chapter 15—*Network Issues in Distributed Simulation.*

Larry B. Rainey. Senior Project Engineer, The Aerospace Corporation, Colorado Springs, Colorado. Ph.D. (Systems Engineering) The Union Institute. M.S. (Industrial and Systems Engineering) The Ohio State University. M.S. (Operations Management) Northrop University. B.S. (Mechanical Engineering) The University of Colorado. *Editor,* Chapter 1—*Introduction to Modeling and Simulation.* Chapter 2—*Systems Science and Systems Engineering.*

Steve Rapp. Principal/Senior Program Director, Computer Sciences Corporation, Consulting and Systems Integration, Waltham, Massachusetts. M.S. (Operations Research–Advanced Modeling) United States Naval Postgraduate School. B.S. (Engineering and Finance) United States Naval Academy. Chapter 5—*Creating a Modeling and Simulation Baseline.*

Stephen R. Schmidt. Senior Associate, Air Academy Associates, Colorado Springs, Colorado. Ph.D. (Applied Statistics) University of Northern Colorado. M.S. (Operations Research) University of Texas. B.S. (Mathematics) United States Air Force Academy. Appendix C—*Statistical Analysis and Experimental Design.*

Martin R. Stytz. Lieutenant Colonel, Air Force Institute of Technology, Wright-Patterson Air Force Base, Ohio. Ph.D. (Computer Science and Engineering); M.S. (Computer Information and Control Engineering) The University of Michigan. The University of Michigan. M.A. (Political Science) Central Missouri State University. B.S. (Political Science) United States Air Force Academy. Chapter 16—*Interactive Simulation: Inserting Humans into Distributed Virtual Environments.*

William Tucker. Manager, Modeling and Simulation Technology, The Boeing Company, Huntsville, Alabama. B.S. (Electrical Engineering) Wichita State University. Chapter 4—*Defining the Need for Models and Simulations.*

Bernard P. Zeigler. Professor, Department of Electrical and Computer Engineering, University of Arizona, Tucson, Arizona. Ph.D. (Computer/Communication Science) University of Michigan. M.S. (Electrical Engineering) Massachusetts Institute of Technology. B.S. (Engineering Physics) McGill University. Chapter 3—*A Framework for Modeling and Simulation.*

Preface

Better! Cheaper! Faster! We've all grown accustomed to these watchwords as we strive to create new capabilities with limited budgets. Whether identifying needs, designing, acquiring, operating, or training, we must develop and use tools that improve our abilities and help us achieve objectives without increasing cost. Modeling and simulation (M&S) has long been part of the arsenal supporting this effort, but the explosion in computing power over the past few decades has led to more comprehensive computer models and simulations. We can now use virtual, not physical, prototypes to examine how we analyze, design, acquire, operate, train, and make decisions. The result: more iterative development and earlier changes that dramatically reduce costs and significantly compress schedules.

Most people familiar with M&S will readily admit that, until now, the M&S community has been segmented and disorganized. We know developing and building models and simulations has been "ad hoc"—relying almost exclusively on the expertise of those chosen to develop and operate the products. People who need the results are often asked simply to "trust" the experts. More and more, however, we see models and simulations used naturally in developments across diverse fields of application. This effectiveness and range demand that we unify the community by capturing and emphasizing the discipline's fundamental characteristics. Using these fundamentals, we can replace small groups of trusted experts with strong, effective teams of developers, users, and sponsors. These teams can produce thoughtful "standard" approaches and replace "ad hoc" M&S development with well planned, cost-effective results.

Although any M&S application contains unique elements, basic concepts and principles apply to and benefit all potential applications. This book focuses on these concepts and principles and organizes them into a useful and practical approach for designing, developing, and operating M&S support that must meet broad, often poorly defined objectives for systems and missions. We present you with the big picture of M&S development and operation and enough details to create an effective, top-level strategy for carrying it out. We emphasize using sound principles from systems engineering to create the required M&S support; describe the processes, tools, and information you'll need to tackle these tasks; and provide the broad insights and general approaches you must understand to apply M&S activities creatively in your discipline. At the same time, you'll learn what can and can't be done with M&S, as well as how to communicate system structures and behaviors across the complete range of development activities.

With the help of this text, you'll be able to establish a coherent, integrated plan for developing and operating models and simulation—a plan that

- Identifies workable objectives and defines meaningful requirements
- Translates objectives and requirements into cost-effective concepts and good preliminary designs early enough to save money and time, as well as to trade on the future

- Captures how you'll develop, verify, and test your system, with criteria for judging the success of each step
- Attends to details throughout the effort and documents compliance with requirements
- Ultimately, develops M&S "systems" that work at the lowest possible cost

To get this job done, we've focused on creating a practical, experience-based guide instead of a theoretical treatise on the discipline. We assembled a strong group of experts from across industry, government, and academia and asked them to record their experiences, insights, lessons learned, and recommendations for future improvements. With a firm editing hand, we've tried to make their wisdom concise and well-organized. Obviously, with this many authors, opinions differ and ideas conflict. In many cases, we decided to leave these differences in the book to provide food for thought as you apply these concepts and principles to your activities. This is one way to ensure it will help the entire M&S community. Another is to make sure its material applies to a broad range of potential activities. To do this, we've tackled critical issues at the level of detail we believe to be appropriate for the broad audience we're trying to reach and avoided excessive technical detail. If you want to see a more rigorous treatment, consult the references for further study.

We believe you're reading a reference that clearly and logically lays out the principles, concepts, and guidelines for developing and operating models and simulations. We recognize that developing models and simulations is complex. It runs parallel to developing "real-world" systems, with potentially many M&S "systems" floating through a program's lifecycle. We also readily admit that a book is a tough way to capture many of the feedback and iteration loops that are so important to successful M&S products. To capture this complexity, we've divided this book into parts that address different elements of the development effort and routinely refer you forward and backward to other sections whenever we need to emphasize how concepts interconnect.

Part I (Chapters 1-3) provides a motivational foundation for M&S development, describes the relationships that must exist to generate effective M&S support, and establishes a framework for M&S development based on sound systems-engineering principles.

Part II (Chapters 4-6) presents a conceptual framework that enables you to organize for effective modeling and simulation. Key questions we answer include: How do we structure and characterize "real-world" development activities? Which of these activities will benefit from modeling and simulation? Where, when, how, and why should modeling and simulation be used to support these activities? How are appropriate modeling and simulation objectives and requirements generated? What alternative M&S approaches are available and how do we evaluate them? What does an effective baseline strategy for producing required M&S

tools look like? How do we promote integration and reuse of M&S products across the program's lifecycle and among functional areas? What technical and managerial techniques should we employ to establish appropriate priorities and ultimately get what we need?

Part III (Chapters 7–12) and Part IV (Chapters 13–17) transition from the "macro" perspective of defining processes to the "micro" perspective of carrying them out. Here, we focus on the details associated with designing, developing, creating, operating, and maintaining M&S tools. In Part III, we cover activities normally associated with developing useful M&S tools (designing models; producing and managing data; implementing designs in hardware and software; verifying, validating, and accrediting models; and executing and integrating simulations). We also provide managerial guidance and technical information to help you do them. In Part IV, we tackle other important elements you should consider while designing, developing, and building models and simulations to produce tools you can use effectively in all potential applications.

Finally, three appendices present short tutorials on particular areas of interest. These tutorials don't comprehensively discuss these topics; they simply introduce them, so you can apply them to concepts, ideas, and guidelines presented elsewhere in the book.

We organized these parts so you can focus more easily on elements of M&S development and operation that apply to your activities. For a more detailed roadmap of the text and how you can use it, see the end of Chap. 1.

This book is designed for widely varying individuals and groups. It you're an engineer or manager, you'll find the information you need to work effectively with M&S designers and developers and to get the products you need to do your job. If you're a policymaker, decision maker, or other end-state user (operator or researcher), you'll find guidelines that make sure you get what you need and understand what you have once it's delivered. As an experienced M&S manager or member of an M&S development staff, you'll see a sound "big-picture" perspective. This view allows you to interact with users to structure M&S activities effectively and create the "right" M&S products. Finally, this book is a compendium of corporate memory. If you're just entering the discipline or a student (graduate or advanced undergraduate) with little or no M&S background, it offers guidance you'll need to apply this knowledge and climb the steep learning curves required to become productive. With the information and guidelines presented here, you should be able to generate and operate models and simulations with greater abilities and more opportunities for interoperability and reuse. These improved tools should, in turn, help you improve and accelerate system analysis and design, acquisition, operation, and training to produce better decisions, better products, and better skills at reduced cost.

As with any effort of this size, it's especially important to recognize the many organizations and individuals who made it all possible. Leadership, funding, and support essential to developing the book were provided by Air Force Phillips Laboratory, Air Force Space Command, Air Force Space and Missile Center, the Defense Advanced Research Projects Agency, Goddard Space Flight Center, and NASA Headquarters. Getting money to develop much-needed reference materials is always difficult and demanding. We're deeply indebted to these sponsoring organizations, particularly Col. Bob Reddy and the Defense Advanced Research Projects Agency, for their support and their recognition of the importance of projects such as this one.

This book is the result of three years of effort by a dedicated team of government, industry, and academic professionals. The Department of Astronautics at the United States Air Force Academy provided unwavering support for the project. Robert B. Giffen and Michael L. DeLorenzo, Department Heads, furnished the time, encouragement, and resources necessary to complete the book. Perry Luckett carefully reviewed our grammar, improved figures and tables, and heroically turned "engineerese" into English. Joan Aug and Connie Bryant cheerfully handled the huge administrative burden at the Academy, while many faculty members and staff graciously sacrificed their time to provide assistance and comments. OAO Corporation, Colorado Springs, Colorado, provided exceptional contract support for the project. Ed Warrell, Rich Poturalski, and Sandy Welsh were particularly helpful throughout the entire development. We especially want to thank Anita Shute, who devoted countless hours to changing "chicken scratch" into competent drafts and camera-ready copy for the entire volume. In addition, we want to thank Dr. Paul Davis, Dr. Rich de Jonckheere, Dr. Mike Proctor, and Dr. Andy Sage for the time they took out of their busy schedules to review this book for technical content and accuracy. Finally, we'd like to thank our families and each other for the patience and understanding so important to making such a demanding effort successful.

We've tried hard to eliminate ambiguities and errors and are committed to improving this work, so please send any errors, omissions, corrections, or comments to us at the address below. We sincerely hope you'll be able to use this book in your daily activities.

David J. Cloud   *Department of Astronautics*

Larry Rainey   *HQ USAFA/DFAS*

                          2354 Fairchild Hall, Suite 6J71

                          USAF Academy, CO 80840-6224

                          Fax: (719) 333-3723

CHAPTER 1

Introduction to Modeling and Simulation

Larry Rainey, *The Aerospace Corporation,*
David J. Cloud, *U.S. Air Force Academy,*
Michael D. Crumm, *Command Technologies, Inc.*

From conceiving state-of-the-art systems to producing piece parts and training workers on the assembly line, we must make informed decisions and create realistic, yet safe, practice situations to improve skills. Policy-makers, managers, engineers, analysts, and teachers (among others) are continually looking for ways to represent "real-world" systems, so they can generate information or create scenarios needed to make informed decisions and get the job done.

In many special cases, engineers and analysts have relied on computers as artificial "laboratories" to describe, investigate, and understand a system's behavior. They've mathematically characterized selected attributes and relationships and transformed these mathematical representations into computer software that captures scenarios and conditions. As a result, they have produced valuable information to support a broad range of decisions for development and operation.

Although these modeling and simulation (M&S) activities have been around for many years, they've only recently become practical for many settings. As a result, the desire to use them and the areas in which they're being applied have grown dramatically. Simulations now help doctors test and practice new surgical techniques without endangering human life. They capture details of factory production lines to help managers identify changes that will increase production or reduce the risk of injury. Imagine being able to enter a virtual factory. Before construction begins, you could examine every element of the plant—"seeing" and "touching" parts to determine if they all work together. Time after time, managers and designers who have previously invested a lot of time and money into prototyping or trial and error are discovering that M&S can economically solve increasingly complex problems.

In part, the increased emphasis on M&S depends on evolving computer hardware, software, and information technologies. The costs for hardware drop daily while processing speed increases almost hourly. Millimeter-size microchips containing over a million circuits have replaced room-sized computers. Home computers now have more computing power and storage than the mainframes of the 1970s, at a fraction of the cost. With this new computing ability comes greater demands for smaller, less costly, and more powerful machines. Rapidly improving graphical interfaces are making it possible to transform pages of numerical data and crude line graphs into informative, three-dimensional images. Animations can focus attention on how parts perform and on the relationships that are so critical to describing the entire system's behavior.

Computer software has advanced just as rapidly and is demanding more performance from hardware while decreasing its cost and size. Computing languages have evolved from assembler code, through languages such as COBOL, FORTRAN, PASCAL, ADA, and C, to modern languages such as C++, Smalltalk, Visual Basic, JAVA, VRML, and J++. Today's software engineer can concentrate on tasks and applications while letting the computer system deal with software interfaces and operating-system functions. User-friendly operating systems with graphical interfaces have produced many simple tools that make it easy to handle hardware and communication interfaces, thus cutting the time required to develop input and output routines.

M&S is also evolving because information is now more available and transportable. Compact disks; high-density tapes; pocket-size, removable hard drives; optical hard drives; and other reusable media are making information more available. The internet and the distributed interactive simulation network are breaking down barriers to acquiring knowledge and significantly improving our ability to share information, tools, and methods. Researchers can often "surf the net" instead of traveling to libraries. Virtual conferences are substituting for expensive, time-consuming, face-to-face meetings to exchange ideas and decide issues. We're also readily accessing shared libraries of software tools that have been tested, verified, and validated. Thus, we can select, tailor, and apply these tools with few changes to support designers, researchers, developers, decision makers, and everyday users.

Today, as managers, analysts, or engineers, we must

- Solve increasingly complex problems with reduced budgets, fewer resources, and shorter schedules

- Examine in detail nearly every aspect of design, development, production, and operation
- Quickly generate information to support solutions that minimize program risks
- Transform this information into formats that concisely portray key concepts and approaches decision makers need

That's why people are rapidly discovering and becoming excited about M&S, which helps them attain their goals on time, on target, and under budget. The result is obvious: dramatically increased demand for and application of M&S, including all types and levels of users. Indeed, "Why use M&S?" has abruptly changed to "Why aren't you using M&S?"

This explosive growth recognizes how M&S can help solve complex problems by providing cost-effective ways to investigate alternatives and demonstrate envelopes of operation. This boundless potential applies to various disciplines and a wide range of tasks. In fact, M&S transcends disciplines and applies within each discipline to many activities, from early planning and analysis, through acquisition, to testing, operations, and training. This flexibility accentuates its power but also dictates effective planning and organizing to get the highest benefit while avoiding the pitfalls that inevitably arise in rapidly expanding fields.

A key part of M&S planning is coordination among large groups of people (with widely differing perspectives) who define, develop, and operate models and simulations. For example, end users want effective, "real-world" abilities and the support they need to use them. Program managers, technical managers, and subject-matter experts must define, size, and structure solutions to these "real-world" problems. M&S managers, designers, developers, integrators, and testers must create models and simulations that support decisions and help create appropriate solutions. You can quickly see the challenges:

- Define these widely varying expectations and fully express them
- Carefully determine how decisions to start and develop models and simulations will affect real-world systems
- Make sure everyone with a stake in the effort soundly understands the steps involved in defining, designing, acquiring, operating, and maintaining these models and simulations

Meeting these challenges requires a reasonable understanding of the discipline. You must consider early in design and development what it can do, who will use it, what is required, when it's needed, and how you will do it. Decide early whether to use M&S and how to integrate it with other program activities. Use this book for descriptions of M&S activities and for guidelines on defining, organizing, developing, acquiring, and maintaining cost-effective models and simulations. These simulations will be flexible enough to use, and reuse, across a system's lifecycle or throughout a program's evolution. Whether you're a developer or user of M&S, you'll find technical details clearly explained so you'll be better prepared to apply M&S when and where you need it.

1.1   Applying Models and Simulations

Let's begin by examining the roles and areas of application for M&S within a system's development lifecycle. This introduction will give you a broader perspective on using M&S, so you can see how models and simulations improve decisions for many activities in system development.

1.1.1   Roles for M&S

Why is M&S key to enhancing decisions? First, it allows us to ask and answer questions. It helps remove doubt, second guessing, and the unknowns associated with a project or a task. If designed properly, models and simulations can identify important performance and cost parameters, which you can compare to solidify your understanding of a problem. Second, the M&S process eliminates many flawed solutions, thus saving a lot of money you might otherwise spend on them. You can also use M&S to construct potential solution spaces, "tradespaces," or "operational envelopes" that define performance and cost for proposed new systems or enhanced current systems. In these tradespaces, you can apply constraints to a range of potential solutions in order to determine which are feasible and which aren't. In general, models and simulations can provide valuable quantitative information that can clear up uncertainty, focus attention on key elements of decision making, and help justify decisions.

M&S applications are primarily designed to describe system behavior—either deterministic or probabilistic. Tools that represent deterministic systems characterize stable problems with well-defined inputs and known data and assumptions. Tools that represent probabilistic systems characterize complex phenomena that change over time. In this case, inputs, data, and assumptions are unknown and must be described stochastically. Both descriptions can be used for researching, designing, planning, observing, explaining, analyzing, and even operating systems. Although applications are limited only by our imaginations, we can start with six roles for M&S, as shown in Table 1.1.

In all phases of a project, M&S products can help us describe or define problems and learn how systems designed to solve them behave. Applying M&S in the early stages of system development gives us the greatest return on investment in this area because it allows us to investigate concepts and recommend whether to proceed with a project before committing resources to it. As an example, M&S helped evaluate alternative avionics suites during the early development stages for the F-16 fighter. Limited space within the cockpit made this evaluation necessary. Models and simulations helped evaluators investigate the performance of alternatives, evaluate the contribution of each to the weapon system's operational effectiveness, and trade capability with projected cost. Program managers used the studies to make key decisions without having to build costly prototypes.

Analyzing focuses on determining the critical measures of merit and issues that need more clarification or research during system development. It can exist within any phase of a project and is similar in many ways to explaining and

Table 1.1.   **Potential Roles for Models and Simulations.** M&S can be used in a variety of activities. Pritsker (1995) identified six categories to help structure the potential applications of M&S.

Role	Description	Examples
Explore alternatives	Describe system operation in context of operational scenarios and environments	Limited space in the cockpit of F-16 fighter aircraft required evaluation of alternative avionics suites against mission objectives
Analyze measurements	Evaluate changes in measures of merit (MOMs) against system requirements and mission objectives	Missile detection and warning from ground- and space-based perspectives produce different MOMs that must be evaluated against mission objectives.
Assess designs	Evaluate proposed designs against operational scenarios and environmental conditions	Space Shuttle investigations of operational flight hardware would have shown design deficiencies
Predict performance	Evaluate systems' operational potential and limitations against mission objectives	Simulation studies of HH-53 radar's performance before installing clearance software to ensure proper operation
Train operators	Simulators help users become proficient in operating real-world systems through practice in simulated environments	Space Shuttle simulators prepare astronauts and ground controllers for missions
Educate and market	Describe system applications to users	Simulations help describe the use of space systems to warfighters

exploring. As an analyst, you identify theories and concepts to understand system operation and sensitivities. Then, using M&S tools, you produce accurate data that can confirm or deny these hypotheses and generate the results needed by decision-makers and end users. Consider ground-based versus space-based detection of missiles. What are the key parameters and how do they differ among the possible alternative solutions? For performance, probability of detection and warning time are critical. On the cost side, lifecycle costs of development and operation are good candidates. Using models and simulations, you can evaluate how well detection systems operate from the ground and from space. You can determine the measures of performance and key costs for development and operation. Analyzing cost versus benefits or operational effectiveness is key to defining cost-effective solutions. If you expand the problem to include several alternatives and various parameters of performance and cost, your analysis and evaluation can quickly become so complex and intense that no-one can grasp the many relationships and trade-offs you must examine to make effective decisions. In these situations, M&S can characterize the solution space and show how parameters interact, thus clarifying the effectiveness of alternatives.

To help assess designs, M&S can synthesize and evaluate proposed solutions and investigate envelopes of operation. Virtual worlds, which M&S is now beginning to address, show how humans and machines interact and allow predictions that before weren't thought possible. For example, using virtual people, developers can evaluate human-machine interfaces (e.g., can a human change an engine's spark plug without being a contortionist or having to remove half the engine?). In product development and operation, M&S can help ensure parts match, study how proposed designs will work, and investigate potential failure modes before accidents occur. For example, using visual inspections and post-accident analyses, NASA recreated Space Shuttle Challenger's explosion, from the initial O-ring failure to the solid-fuel booster's burning into the liquid-fuel tank. M&S activities could (and should) have taken place before launch to identify these kinds of potential catastrophes. The value of M&S to system safety is obvious.

Prediction—forecasting and helping to plan future development—is another potentially valuable role for M&S. Managers must understand a system's operational potential and limits. Sensitivity analyses using simulations can help by describing the system's behavior over time, under different operating conditions, and in different environments. But predictors are only as good as the information used to create them. We can't rely on them to produce "the answer"—only to help us understand operational abilities, limits, and other helpful information. An example is using computer simulation to predict the accuracy of the set clearance for the Terrain Following Radar onboard the HH-53 rescue helicopter, Pave Low III. Before developers installed software and did test flights, simulation studies made sure the helicopter would clear the terrain at 200-, 400-, and 1000-foot set clearances, within stated limits of accuracy. But remember, test flights still confirmed performance.

Training is perhaps the most visible use of simulation, mainly because flight simulators are so common. Training simulators mainly try to help users learn how to operate real-world systems through practice in a simulated environment and to better handle anomalous conditions. Simulators offer two key advantages. First, the experiences in a simulation can expose operators to a much wider range of situations than they can achieve in "real-life" training. Using simulation gives them a chance to operate systems at the "edge of the envelope" or in other dangerous and potentially life-threatening situations. Substituting training simulators for expensive training hardware with huge operating costs can also save a lot of money. Creating a realistic training environment is the key to training simulators and is the driver for most of the dramatic technological improvements we've observed in the simulation community.

Education and marketing are the last roles in the list. In many cases, M&S can educate managers, staffs, or users on the application of systems. A good example is showing warfighters how they benefit from using space systems that are normally transparent to them. Similarly M&S can sell technical concepts or processes that are otherwise too difficult to explain.

1.1.2   Areas of Application

As shown above, models and simulations play various roles in system development. The next obvious question to ask is, "Where should I consider applying different M&S products to support real-world development?" As you'll see below, the answer to this question is across the system-acquisition lifecycle—from concept exploration and definition; through demonstration and validation, engineering and manufacturing support, and production and deployment; to operations and support.[*]

Concept exploration and definition is the first phase of acquisition. It involves basic research for important activities: concept development and system planning. This research focuses on examining theories and new ideas to solve stated problems. Here, the computer becomes an "artificial laboratory" to investigate and understand the behavior of actual systems in new roles or hypothesized systems under different operating conditions. As exploratory devices, models and simulations can highlight the abilities of alternative concepts and flush out those which promise to solve a problem. M&S products can also help define initial performance requirements during system planning by showing how systems will be fielded, tested, and operated. In addition, you can use them for sensitivity analyses that evaluate how imposed constraints affect cost and schedule as you prepare for system development.

Demonstration and validation, the second phase of acquisition, is the stage for defining preliminary concepts, developing alternatives to satisfy the need, and assessing these alternatives. As part of this activity, you want to observe the behavior of systems operating under different scenarios and attempt to explain it. Defining and assessing systems means understanding how they'll work under real-world conditions and when pressed to their limits. At the same time, you must develop test plans with stated objectives and measurable criteria (e.g., measures of merit) to ensure you can evaluate the system once it is developed. Prototypes to show how the proposed system will work are a valuable part of this effort, and M&S can help by providing early analyses that relate system performance to objectives and requirements. In addition, models and simulations can predict and help assess the operational envelope before testing the prototype. The HH-53's terrain following radar, mentioned previously, highlights the use of M&S to evaluate performance and safety before testing.

Engineering and manufacturing support is the next phase in acquisition. It focuses on detailed system design and planning for manufacturing. During detailed design, the baseline system identified during demonstration and validation must be studied, designed, developed, and tested under potential operating conditions to determine if it will meet requirements. M&S is a key to assessing your design during this phase. You can use models of components to evaluate the system's performance and the effectiveness of interfaces. System simulations can generate information to measure performance against requirements and to highlight changes you must consider to meet objectives. Simulations can also address human factors to ensure the current design is useable once it's manufactured. As you plan for manufacturing, models and simulations

---

[*] The five acquisition phases identified here are the traditional ones used by the Department of Defense to describe the acquisition lifecycle. Although organizations may divide and name the phases differently, the activities are common to all acquisition programs.

can help investigate production options. You can use them to evaluate alternative plant layouts and analyze different resource allocations to identify promising, reasonably priced options.

During production and deployment, you allocate resources to the production line and field the operational system. Here, you can use M&S tools to identify and eliminate potential choke points and other production problems before they occur and to develop and evaluate contingency plans. M&S can help you keep production moving and resources flowing during peak production. Analysis also applies to systems you deploy to their operating locations. Here too, you can use models and simulations to evaluate alternatives for delivering a system cost-effectively and on time.

Operations and support, the last acquisition phase, involves daily operations, planning and rehearsing missions, assessing readiness, maintenance, logistics support, and developing doctrine and tactics. Improving operational skills through training is probably the most visible role for M&S during this phase. For example, realistic flight simulators allow pilots to practice operational procedures and exercise contingencies. But managers can also use training simulations to plan for missions and rehearse strategies. For logistical planning, M&S can help determine the best Integrated Logistics Support Plans (e.g., plans to support a system throughout its lifecycle). M&S can also help us place real-world systems in various scenarios, evaluate their ability to meet operational objectives, and investigate possible changes to doctrine and tactics that can make them more effective. We can also explore new technologies to identify new concepts of operation and develop new doctrines and tactics. At the same time, the information from these models and simulations can feed into other lifecycle phases to support decisions on developing future systems.

Table 1.2 summarizes the potential roles and areas of application for M&S. To use M&S effectively across this broad range of activities, you must understand the implications of using, developing, and operating models and simulations. Table 1.2 begins to identify what M&S can do in the various phases of the acquisition cycle, but it's not comprehensive. Use it as a starting point from which you can expand your investigations as needed.

1.2   What to Expect from Modeling and Simulation

As shown above, you can apply models and simulations in various ways across all phases of the acquisition lifecycle. But, it isn't a panacea. It can't solve every problem. Before jumping into M&S, you must carefully consider both its benefits and limitations. For example, you have to weigh application and function against cost and development time to make sure M&S will be an effective option.

1.2.1   Benefits

Pritsker (1995), Adkins (1977), McHaney (1991), and Neelamkavil (1987) have identified many potential benefits of M&S, including its ability to

Table 1.2.   **M&S Roles Versus Phases of Application.** M&S can apply variously across a spectrum of activities to support system development. This table identifies some representative examples of the ways you can use M&S inside a framework that helps you identify M&S's potential to support your specific activities.

M&S Roles	Phases of Application				
	Concept Exploration & Definition	Demonstration & Validation	Engineering & Manufacturing Support	Production & Deployment	Operations & Support
Explain & Explore	defines requirements	identify deficiencies			develop doctrine and tactics
Analyze	cost & schedule system performance	design tests plan tests	production limitations	schedule decisions	assess readiness
Assess Designs			assess performance of components evaluate interfaces		
Predict		assess effectiveness	predict faults	choke points in manufacturing	rehearse missions
Train					individual and collective skills staff training

- Test concepts before using them
- Develop a more complete understanding of system behavior
- Improve analysis
- Enhance creativity
- Increase user readiness
- Reduce development costs

Testing concepts gives us a way to detect unforeseen problems and to flush out a design before "bending metal." During the earliest stages of system development, the many unknowns make anticipating outcomes nearly impossible. M&S can support rapid prototyping, which allows us to explore widely varying concepts and avoid troublesome situations. Representing alternative designs in software enables managers to predict performance and make better decisions on what to do next. For example, while planning for developmental and operational testing of the HH-53, managers used M&S to rule out test missions because they didn't satisfy realistic test objectives.

Thoroughly understanding a system's behavior will help you evaluate operating strategies or options throughout its development. Models and simulations can support this effort in three ways. First, you can examine alternative designs without spending money on hardware prototypes by developing computer-based models instead. Second, you can use models and simulations of operational systems to provide information whenever experimenting with the systems would be too costly or dangerous. Finally, you can use models and simulations to test a system's operating limits whenever hardware testing would destroy the system. In all three cases, models and simulations can better define the system by establishing a common, easily understood perception of its behavior and limits.

Improved system analysis is a third potential benefit of modeling and simulation. Using computer-based models and simulations as a "risk-free" laboratory, you can do more complex studies than would be acceptable using real hardware. Computer speed also reduces the time these studies require and allows you to do more investigations within tight schedules. These attributes allow you to improve performance evaluations and provide feedback on program objectives to decision makers. M&S also enables you to analyze the sensitivity of input parameters and model variables, which clarifies the limits on a system's operational performance.

Another benefit is enhanced creativity. M&S allows developing, testing and evaluating of ideas never thought possible. For example, virtual-reality technology has opened opportunities, such as realistic flight training, that before had been only dreams.

Models and simulations can also improve user skills and increase readiness. Wherever safety concerns seriously limit "real-life" training, simulators can help operators maintain or increase proficiency without risking their lives or equipment. Simulators can reduce overall training time and overcome practical limitations and environmental restrictions. Indeed, some commercial airlines now certify their pilots based on simulator experience instead of check-out flights in the actual aircraft.

Finally, M&S support can save money. In most cases, developing models and simulations costs less than building a hardware prototype. Similarly, as shown by the use of distributed interactive simulation in several wargames, replacing hardware with simulations for training can save a lot of money and decrease wear and tear on actual systems. The abilities of M&S are increasing while costs of computer software and hardware are dropping. Furthermore, as software libraries, repositories, and reusable development tools become more available, we can hold down the cost of developing software. That means future models and simulations will be even less expensive.

1.2.2   Limitations

Despite these benefits, as Adkins (1977), McHaney (1991), and Neelamkavil (1987) correctly point out, you must also weigh the limitations of M&S:

- The effect of hidden critical assumptions
- Difficulties in collecting good data
- Deficiencies in technology
- Long development times
- Large resource requirements

Not identifying or misunderstanding key assumptions can cause simulation results to diverge from reality. You can't capture every reality in models and simulations, so you must make assumptions that limit their application. If you don't pay attention to these assumptions, you may produce incorrect solutions and conclusions. Yet, even in these situations, M&S results can "look" real, so it's easy to accept them as "the truth." Carefully identify and understand all assumptions for the tool you're using. Even then, always use your common sense and experience to assess the results, recognizing that they only approximate the real world so you can better understand a system's "operational envelope."

Data may also limit your application because it may require a lot of time and money to collect, develop, or interpret. In some cases, you may not be able to get the data needed to create a model or simulation that will satisfy objectives. Thus, you must accept limited results or spend the time and money to collect data that will produce the desired M&S product.

Technology may still limit your application, despite the dramatic growth in computer processing. Some modeling relationships are extremely difficult or impossible to capture in software. In particular, combining various levels of abstraction (as required in many wargames) remains a challenge. "Seamless operations or representations" still present hurdles that M&S must clear to yield valuable results.

Two other important limitations of M&S are its potentially long development times and large resource requirements. If not done properly, software development can eat up time and money at a tremendous rate. Effective development plans and tight controls must be in place to produce these tools on time and within budget. In addition, the right combination of expertise and resources must be available to get the job done. Even then, you're not home free. Complex tasks can consume much more time and money, easily stretching even the largest budget. M&S development can be expensive. If done well, benefits outweigh these costs. If not, you'll quickly find yourself wondering why you started it in the first place.

1.3 Developing and Operating Models and Simulations

Clearly, models and simulations can help you design, develop, and deploy systems, as well as make decisions throughout the development lifecycle. But developing and operating M&S tools to support this full range of activities are potentially complex, ranging from creating simple spreadsheets to developing detailed, "end-to-end" system simulations. Figure 1.1 suggests that the problem becomes even more demanding when we consider developing multiple M&S products simultaneously at any stage of system development or a single product that evolves into a family of related products. To this challenge, we must add an array of players—end users, program managers and system designers, M&S managers and development staff—and their different perspectives on the problem. It's easy to see that producing the right M&S tools requires a sound, disciplined approach that emphasizes why you're developing them, creates a solid set of requirements, and establishes a way to trace activities back to these objectives and requirements.

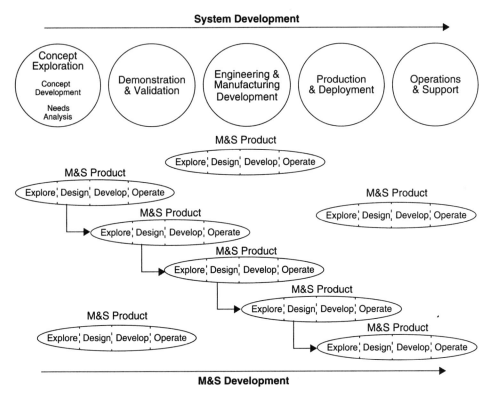

Fig. 1.1.   **Developing and Operating M&S Products through the System-Development Lifecycle.** Multiple M&S development activities can occur simultaneously at any stage of the system-development lifecycle. Without a well formulated approach to M&S development and operation, each of these activities can quickly take on a life of its own. The result can be disastrous. We want to create cost-effective tools that support system development and that can interconnect and be reused to enhance understanding and improve decision making; instead, we may get stand-alone products with limited applicability that can't interact with other products when needed.

Throughout this book, we establish a process to effectively develop and apply models and simulations across the development lifecycle and present practical guidelines to carry it out. Table 1.3 (located at the end of the chapter) summarizes the steps that create the M&S products you'll need. The first six steps present concepts that allow you to plan for the effective use of modeling and simulation to support program objectives. How you form and develop "real-world" abilities to meet mission requirements is closely related to the process you should use to create appropriate M&S products that support these activities. Before undertaking M&S activities, you must answer some key questions: How do I structure and characterize "real-world" development activities? Which of these activities will benefit from modeling and simulation? Where, when, how, and why should I use modeling and simulation to support these activities? How do I generate appropriate objectives and requirements for modeling and simulation? What alternative M&S approaches are available and how do we evaluate them? What does an effective baseline strategy for producing the required M&S tools look like? How do I promote integrating and reusing M&S products across the program's lifecycle and between functional areas? What technical and managerial techniques should I employ to make sure my team establishes appropriate priorities and ultimately gets what we need?

The second part of the process (Steps 7 to 11) transitions from the "macro" perspective associated with planning to the "micro" perspective associated with building simulations. Here, we focus on the normal activities needed to develop useful M&S tools—designing models; producing and managing data; building hardware and software; verifying, validating, and accrediting systems; and running and integrating simulations. We provide managerial guidance and technical information (in appropriate detail) to tackle these steps and answer the question: "How do I design, develop, build, and operate the individual models and simulations defined during planning?

Glancing again at Table 1.3, you'll quickly recognize that many activities associated with developing and operating good models and simulations must occur simultaneously. In addition, information generated at different stages gives you feedback that allows you to iterate towards more complete, effective solutions. Unfortunately, it's often difficult to capture feedback loops and iteration activities in a reference text without a clear map of where you're headed. We've divided this book into parts to help you organize for the journey ahead, and Fig. 1.2 provides the roadmap you'll need to use this reference effectively.

The rest of Part 1 lays the foundation for the information to follow. Chapter 2 provides the principles from systems science and systems engineering which underpin the M&S planning activities described in Chaps. 4 through 6. It provides an outline we'll fill in as we discuss the need to structure the "real-world" problem, describe how M&S supports this structure, and create a baseline strategy (both technically and programmatically) for developing and building the defined M&S products. Chapter 3 focuses on modeling and simulation as a discipline. It defines key concepts for M&S development in a structured way, so you can go to the detailed chapters in Part 3 with an understanding of the principles that underlie the discipline. It also provides a rationale for the structure we've adopted and a template you can use consistently to develop models and simulations.

The next three chapters examine planning. Chapter 4 looks at the real-world problem we must solve. It captures early activities and the information needed to form a plan for effective M&S. Then, it focuses on associating M&S tasks to defined mission areas. Where and why do you need M&S? What guidelines are available to help define the potential applications for M&S within the given structure? What are the pros and cons of using M&S for the identified applications? In Chap. 5, we use the information from our "real-world" application to create M&S objectives, requirements, and constraints, which will help us define appropriate tasks and develop operations concepts for M&S products. We present ways to investigate

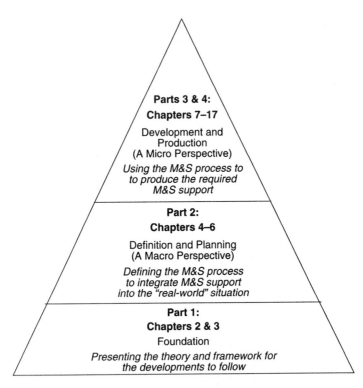

Fig. 1.2.   **Organization of this Book.** The text is divided into parts to organize the process of defining, designing, and developing effective models and simulations. The pyramid presented here provides a roadmap to the details presented in the following chapters.

alternative strategies and analyze abilities. How do you assess deficiencies and propose ways to overcome them? How do you decide whether to use existing models and simulations or develop new ones? How can you develop and evaluate options to meet the specified requirements and constraints, while emphasizing the importance of interoperability and reuse? Then, in Chap. 6, we formalize an acquisition strategy to help you get the products you've identified. We suggest how to estimate size, cost, and schedule, as well as how to determine the resources you need to tackle the job. We also highlight ways to prioritize tasks and develop technical and programmatic metrics you can use to assess progress throughout an M&S development.

Part 3 (Chaps. 7 through 12) addresses core techniques for building models and simulations; Part 4 (Chaps. 13 through 17) highlights other techniques you may need for your applications. Here's where we tackle the details. How do you abstract from reality to create models that will generate the needed information? How must you produce and manage data to describe a model of the system under investigation? How do you transform this model into operating hardware and software? How do you integrate and test the simulation's hardware and software? How can you validate and verify your operating model's performance? How do you use the product and analyze results to produce information that supports the real program or mission? What must you consider when you integrate the product with other models and simulations? We'll finish by looking at how standards and specifications help development and how you can prepare to adapt to changing technologies. We'll also highlight some of the most important issues associated with networks for distributed simulation, interactive simulation, and information security.

We finish the book with three tutorials which introduce the basics of estimating cost and schedule, designing software, and using statistical analysis and experimental design in M&S activities. These tutorials aren't comprehensive; instead, they introduce topics that support earlier discussions and supply references in case you want more information.

The information presented here captures the wisdom of people experienced in modeling and simulation to give you a solid grasp of processes and important relationships. Their observations will help you overcome common difficulties and take advantage of exciting new technologies and rapidly expanding abilities to handle complex problems. They also create a common starting point for organizations who are trying to work together to produce M&S support that applies throughout a system's lifecycle. After reading this book, you should be able to shed any perception that M&S development takes too long and costs too much. Instead, you can embrace the reality that M&S is a cost-effective tool for understanding complex behavior and supporting key decisions during system development and operation.

Table 1.3.   A Process for Developing and Operating Models and Simulations.

	Step	Considerations	Reference
M&S Planning	1. Define the system problem	• Characterize the "real-world" problem in terms of objectives, requirements, and constraints; what must be done; and systems to be developed • Define the information you need to develop a mission or system • Establish the foundation for developing M&S support	Chap. 4
	2. Determine if M&S applies	• Decide whether M&S is acceptable for solving your problem • Select the parts of your problem that will benefit from M&S support and drop those that won't	Chap. 4
	3. Define the M&S problem	• Identify the high-level scenario or part of reality to capture • "Quantify" the resolution, detail, and fidelity required • Characterize the system's components, variables and interactions, and data requirements • Examine and characterize external and environmental factors • Determine the need for real-time operation or geographic separation	Chap. 5
	4. Establish alternative methods for solution	• Examine formalisms, interactivity types, and application levels • Consider distributed vs. centralized operation • Investigate using legacy products vs. developing a new system • Decide whether you need families of models to capture different levels of fidelity	Chap. 5
	5. Evaluate alternatives and establish a baseline approach	• Examine risks associated with required capabilities, complexity, cost, and schedule • Establish metrics to evaluate risk and reward • Provide a baseline approach for creating M&S products to solve the problem	Chap. 5
	6. Formalize an acquisition strategy	• Identify limits on cost and schedule and required deliverables • Estimate size, cost, and schedule of your development effort • Establish metrics for tracking and overseeing your project • Create procedures and policies to manage requirements, manage configurations, and ensure quality • Identify maintenance needs and establish maintenance procedures	Chap. 6

Table 1.3.   **A Process for Developing and Operating Models and Simulations. (Continued)**

	Step	Considerations	Reference
M&S Implementation	7. Design models	• Select important phenomena to model and characterize the model's properties (scope, scale, entities, relationships) to place limits on model design • Construct initial high-level models • Divide your models into parts with explicit roles and responsibilities • Evaluate choices to see if they meet modeling goals • Analyze effects of model choices and optimize design • Define interfaces, connections, and operation between components; integrate component models	Chap. 8

	8. Produce and manage data	• Design a "strawman" data architecture and identify authoritative data sources based on knowledge of the proposed M&S application
		• Coordinate with developers, customers, users, and sponsors and quantify relationships between customers' needs, M&S requirements, and data architecture
		• Build the architecture and populate it with data
		   – Standardize formats and procedures
		   – Ease access to information repositories and data
		• Test to ensure the model works and iterate until conflicts are resolved
		• Archive information and refine repositories to allow growth and operation with other models
			Chap. 9

	9. Design and build the simulation in hardware and software	• Characterize the context for creating your simulation • Assess and evaluate methods for building the simulation • Evaluate and select software structures • Evaluate and select programming languages • Select appropriate hardware • Maintain integrity, manage configuration, and assess and document progress	Chap. 10
	10. Verify, validate, and accredit the models and simulations	• Verify and validate the M&S concept and the quality of the design before building the simulation • Develop a detailed plan for verification and validation • Verify the design and model as built • Validate simulation results • Do an accreditation review	Chap. 11
	11. Operate and integrate the simulation	• Receive and inventory the simulation • Study simulation documents and operate the simulation to learn the product's purpose and context • Identify simulation components and external elements to assess compatibility • Create and carry out an integration strategy • Develop and use an operation plan • Gather and analyze data; assess your simulation's performance	Chap. 12

References

Adkins, Gerald and Udo W. Pooch. 1977. "Computer Simulation: A Tutorial." *Computer*, 10, No.4.

McHaney, Roger. 1991. *Computer Simulation: A Practical Perspective*. New York, NY: Academic Press, Inc.

Neelamkavil, Francis. 1987. *Computer Simulation and Modeling*. New York, NY: John Wiley and Sons.

Pritsker, Alan. 1995. *Introduction to Simulation and SLAM II*. New York, NY: John Wiley and Sons.

CHAPTER 2

Systems Science and Systems Engineering

Larry Rainey, *The Aerospace Corporation*
David A. Hollenbach, *Booz·Allen & Hamilton, Inc.*

In the previous chapter, we introduced modeling and simulation (M&S): its purpose, roles, general uses, application areas, advantages, and disadvantages. In this chapter we address two major concepts associated with M&S: systems science—the theoretical foundation which establishes basic concepts and principles for developing and operating models or simulations, and systems engineering—a basis for creating a rigorous process for developing models and simulations.

Just as engineering has its theoretical foundation in physics, so M&S has a theoretical foundation. In this chapter, we show that the source of basic concepts and principles for M&S is systems science or systems theory. According to Zadeh (1962), systems theory concerns itself with the mathematical properties of systems and not their physical form. What matters are the mathematical relations between the variables which describe the system's behavior. Later in the same article, Zadeh states that systems theory contributes "concepts and mathematical techniques to systems engineering and operations research, but is not a part of these fields, nor does it have them as its own branches." Thus, we study systems theory to understand the concepts and principles that underlie the M&S discipline; and we investigate systems engineering because it provides a sound process for developing M&S products.

2.1   Basic Concepts and Principles

The word "system" or "systems" is part of our daily speech. But what does this word really mean and how does it relate to M&S? A composite definition based on Webster's dictionary (1964), as well as the definitions of systems scientists such as Beer (1979) and Buckley (1968), establishes a system as a "collection of objects, living or not, which are related in a way that helps them work together to perform some intended function."

What is the relationship of a "system" to M&S? First, "the system" is what M&S studies. Through M&S we try to understand the system's operation so we can predict behavior, explore, analyze, and assess designs, and train operators, as stated in Chap. 1. Typically, we try mathematically to characterize selective attributes and their relationships in a process known as modeling. Then, we make the system "go" by capturing the mathematical model in a computer language and letting the computer exercise it. This process is known as simulation. In simulations, we also specify the scenarios and conditions in which we want the system to operate. Together, modeling and simulating help us understand a real system's operation without having to deal with it directly. You'll find these general definitions compatible with the formal definitions of modeling and simulation in Chap. 3.

The second relationship of M&S to the word "system" is that M&S products are systems themselves. Systems engineering is a way to develop real products, such as aircraft and spacecraft. But applying it to M&S produces another system that consists of models and simulations.

Now let's look at systems science and see how it applies to M&S. Science typically refers to the physical and social sciences. In the first category, we usually think of physics, biology, and chemistry. In the second, we usually think of economics, sociology, and psychology. Each of these areas is a discipline that attempts to explain the world through the filter of its own laws and principles. But systems science differs from these traditional disciplines, as Klir (1991) points out, because "systems science is a science whose objects of study are systems." Specifically, its "domain of inquiry consists of those properties of systems and associated problems that emanate from the general notion of systemhood."

To understand this difference, we must understand the notions of thinghood and systemhood. Systemhood properties address parts in relation to one another, so the whole is greater than the sum of the parts. Thinghood properties are individual properties of the parts, such as mass, weight, or volume. One example is an organization. An organization consists of people, machines, and other resources to carry out a given mission. But as a system, the organization depends on the way these elements interact, or synergize, so it becomes more than the "things" and "thinghood properties" that go into it. A second example is an automobile. The thinghood properties of an automobile are defined by its parts, such as the engine, powertrain, or tires. But its systemhood depends on the relationships among its parts, which act together to create the automobile.

Although systems science operates across and above the boundaries of classical science, it shares the key characteristics of any discipline (Klir 1991):

- A body of knowledge regarding its domain
- Methods for acquiring new knowledge
- Methods for dealing with relevant problems
- "Metamethods" for characterizing and examining methods and their relationships to problems

In Fig. 2.1 you can see how systems science developed from other disciplines we're familiar with and how it relates to other system-oriented disciplines. In the next three subsections, we'll introduce some basic concepts from systems science, which are fundamental to developing and operating models and simulations.

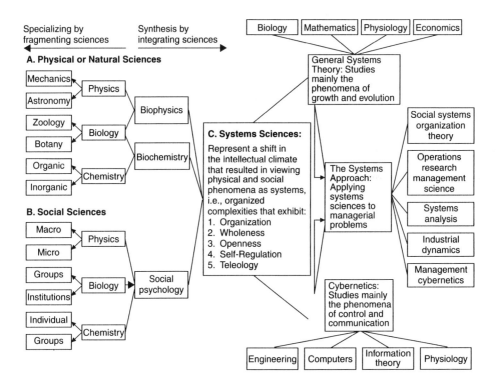

Fig. 2.1.   **The Origins and Development of the Interdisciplinary Movement.** This chart shows the development of systems science and its relationship to other disciplines. (Taken from *Management Systems: Conceptual Considerations* by P. Schoderbek, et.al. and published by Business Publications, Inc. Permission to reproduce granted by Dr. Asterios G. Kefalas, University of Georgia.)

2.1.1   Variety as a Measure of Complexity

A characteristic of all modern systems is complexity, which means the number of interactions among components or elements of a system. How do we describe a system's complexity? We must

1. Select which variables to describe.
2. Decide which relationships, among the variables, to portray.
3. Determine how to model these variables and the associated relationships.
4. Develop the simulation.
5. Consider baselines, test cases, and scenarios.

Mix in the subjective judgements of many players in an M&S project and you'll have an idea how tough it can be to get a handle on complexity. But one way is to follow Beer (1979), who states that, "the measure of complexity is called variety." He goes on to define variety as "the number of possible states of whatever it is whose complexity we want to measure." The number of possible states is something we can count, so the measure will be a pure number. This means, for example, that we can compare the complexity of one company with another even though everything else about the two companies is different. Thus, variety makes unlike things measurable.

In addition, Beer (1979) states that it is "the observer who defines the system, its nature, purpose, boundaries, and (it turns out) its variety." Let's examine this idea and find out how this is true. Consider the question: What are the possible purposes—and their inherent variety (V)— for the exhibit in Fig. 2.2?

Fig. 2.2.   **Example of Variety.** This diagram displays a system whose purpose can vary depending on the perception (e.g., nature, purpose, and boundaries) of the observer [Beer 1979]. (Reproduced with permission from *The Heart of Enterprise* by Stafford Beer. Copyright John Wiley and Sons, Limited.)

Possible answers include:

*   The exhibit's purpose is to tell us what a cross looks like. It gives us several examples of a cross, so we won't misunderstand. A cross is one distinctive mark selected from a huge range of distinctive marks. A cross has no other possible state than to be itself, so variety is:

$$V = 1$$

- The exhibit intends to show what is meant by "number." It's a kind of diagrammatic abacus on which we may count from one to seven, and we may fix its state according to the population we're counting. The abacus also permits us to see the advanced notion of "nought," corresponding to a zero population. Thus,

$$V = 8$$

- The purpose is to mark seven locations, at each of which—as the system develops in time—something may or may not happen. For instance, these may be seven lights, any combination of which we may light at any time. In this case,

$$V = 2^7 = 128$$

- The purpose is to exemplify a system consisting of seven interacting elements. The number of possible states depends on the number of possible connections between the elements. Therefore,

$$V = n(n-1)/2 = 7 \times 6/2 = 21$$

- The purpose is similar to the one just above, but we must recognize that a relationship between any two elements may be directional. To connect A to B is not necessarily to mark the same relation as in connecting B to A. (That is, for example, an uncle is different from a nephew.) Taking this directional quality into account gives

$$V = n(n-1) = 7 \times 6 = 42$$

- The purpose of the exhibit is to show a dynamic system in which, at any time, any one of the directional relationships between elements may or may not be active. The variety of this much more complex system is:

$$V = 2^{42} = 4{,}398{,}046{,}511{,}104$$

In summary, depending on the perception of the observer, the exhibit in Fig. 2.2 can display a variety ranging from 1.0 to 4.4×10^{12}.

We could come up with more answers, but these six show that the observer determines a system's variety and that systems may encompass a broad range of complexity. In particular, the last answer demonstrates the explosion of variety once we see a system as richly interconnected and dynamic. Simulations must account for these interactions, the varying perceptions of users and developers, and the levels of fidelity for various purposes.

2.1.2   Law of Requisite Variety

In the above section we defined variety as a measure of complexity. Now we want to explain the governing principle for variety. An English physician named W. Ross Ashby is the source of this law, which states that analysts must be able to take at least as many actions (as great a variety of countermeasures) as the observed system can exhibit [Hare 1967]. Similarly, Beer (1979) has suggested, "The regulator has to be capable of generating a variety equivalent to the variety that has to be regulated—or the regulator will fail."

What does this really mean? Consider a system which has from 1 to m possible states or alternatives (S_1, ..., S_m) and a regulator which has from 1 to n possible states or alternatives (R_1, ..., R_n). (For this discussion, regulators may be people, who manage the outcomes of an organization or process through the decisions they make, or computers that monitor and correct a process or operation.) Ashby's Law indicates that the number of alternatives available to the regulator (n) must be at least equal to the number of alternatives the system may exhibit (m) to effectively control the system. In reality, n should exceed m to allow reserves for given problem areas and unexpected situations, but we must consider costs associated with building this extra capability before deciding to add it. To illustrate, consider Fig. 2.3, which displays all possible combinations of system and regulator states for this example. Requisite variety corresponds to the situations along the diagram's main diagonal, where the numbers of system and regulator states are equal. For these cases and all those to the right of this main diagonal, the regulator has enough variety to adequately control the system. Situations to the left of the main diagonal violate Ashby's Law, so the regulator can't effectively control the system.

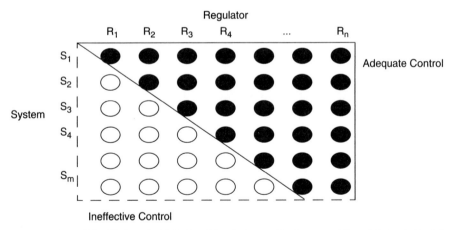

Fig. 2.3.   **Requisite Variety for Relationships between Systems and Regulators.** Ashby's Law dictates that a regulator must have at least as many states (or alternatives) as the system to effectively control the system's behavior.

Although a relatively simple concept, Ashby's Law is an elegant and powerful tool for system analysts and designers because [Hare 1967]

1. It establishes an upper limit to the amount of control we can exert in a given case or a minimum we must meet.

2. It tells us we can adjust our ability to control a system in only two main ways: increase the controller's variety or reduce the variety of the system to be controlled.

3. It permits us to approach complex, large-scale systems with a proper sense of proportion and to adjust realistically our strategies for defining, analyzing, and improving the system.

4. It directs our attention, as students of systems, to studying two types of methods: those which increase the possible variety of actions available to us and those we use to simplify, restrict, partition, or otherwise cut system variety as the need arises.

To illustrate this law, let's consider three examples:

Example: A biological organism is able to counter changes in the environment, such as moderate changes in humidity, temperature, and oxygen content of the air, but it can't handle all possibilities. To survive, the organism must restrict the range of its environment. Thus, we don't take baths in liquid nitrogen, reside in furnaces, or confer at the tail end of a jet engine. We eliminate impossible rows from the outcome table by avoiding them and thereby restricting the conditions our control function must face. Or we add more columns to provide new actions that offer more choices in the outcome table. If we must confer at a missile launch, we do so in the block house.

Example: Physicians aren't expected to cure simultaneously all of a patient's ills—social, economic, psychological, or even medical. They restrict their attention to the few critical symptoms and ills they can control. Physicians must follow Ashby's law.

Example: Traffic directors of large cities don't try to regulate the precise movement of each vehicle. They work to control the general traffic flow by introducing restrictions (one-way streets, limited access roads) and by increasing the variety of their control actions (computer controls on traffic lights based on various area traffic flows). They can't do otherwise.

Why is the Law of Requisite Variety important to M&S? Basically, simulations are tools that managers or decision makers can use to evaluate their systems. To be in control, managers or decision makers must develop contingency plans for every possible negative action their systems may generate. Simulations generate these "what ifs," and managers tap their resources to develop contingency plans for every negative case. Stated another way, simulations increase the managers' variety. The other side of this coin is, of course, to limit or reduce the variety the system can generate. For the Law of Requisite Variety to hold in a given situation, we must determine what variables and relationships to model and simulate, as well as what type of models or simulations to develop.

2.1.3 Conant-Ashby Theorem

This theorem relates the Law of Requisite Variety to modeling and simulation by stating that "every regulator contains a model of whatever is regulated" [Beer 1979]. But we'll temper this theorem by saying every regulator

should contain or require a model of whatever is regulated. Beer (1979) also says this model "must have requisite variety. If it had less variety than the system under regulation, that system could undertake activities that were incomprehensible to the regulator."

The Conant-Ashby Theorem relates directly to the next section, in which we discuss how the computer serves as a laboratory for managers and analysts. In other words, a simulation on the computer allows managers and analysts to experiment with the system without interrupting its actual operation. That is, they can use simulations to generate "what ifs" for contingency plans, as stated above, and hence increase their variety.

Chapter 1 covered the roles of M&S, which included explanatory devices, analytical vehicles, design assessors, and predictors. The Conant-Ashby Theorem suggests another role—what Beer (1966) calls controlling operations. In this context, Beer suggests models of regulators contain two submodels—structural models and parametric models. Structural models are the "equations of motion" of the real-world situation but don't contain numerical data. Parametric models quantify structural models by including actual quantities that describe the real-world situation—the coefficients and other numerical values of key parameters. Chapters 8 and 9 will treat these ideas in detail by discussing how we develop models and acquire and manage data, respectively.

2.2   The Computer as a Laboratory

With some basic notions about systems science in hand, we can now explore how we gain knowledge about a system [Klir 1991]. Of course, we typically aren't able to exercise systems in the real world to gain this knowledge. Instead, we acquire it mathematically or experimentally. Mathematical system theories apply to associated categories of systems. Examples are theorems pertaining to controllability, stability, state equivalence, information transmission, decomposition, homomorphism (similarities in appearance or size), self-organization, and self-reproduction [Klir 1991]. But we want to focus here on experimenting to gain systems knowledge—especially by simulating systems on computers and thereby combining mathematics and experimentation. This link allows us to investigate problems we can't solve analytically—in a sense, to make the system look real. Therefore, we can examine or experiment with the simulation to discover or validate hypotheses just as traditional scientists do in their laboratories. In fact, computers become our laboratories, often allowing us to acquire knowledge otherwise unobtainable [Klir 1991].

Computers can serve as laboratories in which we

- Simulate an element of reality
- Explore systems that may model a real phenomenon
- Investigate hypotheses mathematically
- Discover or validate laws of systems science

- Discover methods for establishing methods of inquiry

Let's look at each potential application in more detail.

The first and most obvious case is that of computer simulation, in which we simulate a system that models reality so we can generate scenarios under various assumptions about the system's environment and using various system parameters. Simulations are particularly effective when we must analyze the results of projected policies and decisions [Klir 1991]. An example would be evaluating alternative systems for public transportation to serve a given metropolitan area.

A second, closely related use of the computer is to explore various systems as prospective models of real-world phenomena, based on hypothetical explanations of the phenomena. These systems are like the first case but differ in the values of selected parameters. We simulate the systems and compare their operating schemes with that of the real phenomena until we determine the values for which the operating scheme of the model is closest to the real phenomenon [Klir 1991]. For example, if a system for public transportation is already in place, what alternative upgrades might be as capable?

In the third case we use the computer to simulate many applicable examples of systems so we can look for regularities that support a mathematical conjecture. Once the support is adequate, we must prove the conjecture formally, but regularities observed from many generated examples may inspire construction of a formal proof. In either case, the computer amplifies intuition by allowing the mathematician to examine many more examples than might otherwise be possible [Klir 1991]. An example might be developing alternative mathematical formulations of a transportation system for a metropolitan area to certify that it will always meet the agreed-on measures of effectiveness.

The fourth case is discovering or validating the laws of systems science. Unlike the laws of nature associated with traditional science, which characterize objects or groups of objects, the laws of systems science characterize the properties of system categories. Systems scientists experiment on the computer with many systems of the same type to discover characterizing properties or, at least, validate some hypotheses about that category [Klir 1991]. An example might be considering alternative models of various transportation systems, all of which address the degree of complexity required for a given metropolitan area. Clearly, we'd have to specify the measures of complexity, so we could quantify them. In this case, they may be measures of performance rather than effectiveness.

Finally, we can use a computer as a laboratory to gain knowledge about alternative system methods, so we can see how they will operate on a given type of system problem. In this case, we select, apply, and document the result of using sets of methods until we've exhausted all the desired possibilities [Klir 1991]. An example might be examining to what extent we can observe and control a transportation system.

Having shown how systems science contributes to developing and operating models and simulations, we can now talk about how systems engineering gives us the process for developing them.

2.3   Systems Engineering Defined

Practitioners often disagree on what "systems engineering" means. Some think it's the process by which people design and create communication networks. Others believe it's the practice by which experts in the "ilities" (reliability, maintainability, etc.) make sure these engineering disciplines get into product design. Still others equate it to industrial engineering or refer to engineering generalists who make subsystems work together. In a sense, they're all correct!

Systems engineering is the organized process by which various specialized fields of engineering (and other specialties) combine to design products. It's based on a communicative approach that focuses the design team on meeting the user's needs. The essence of systems engineering is a holistic view of the system. Traditional engineering activities, such as analysis, research, and design, aren't ends in themselves; instead, they're a means for ultimately satisfying people's needs for products or services. Thus, systems engineering concerns itself with engineering **and** the needs of people [Blanchard 1990].

Systems engineering is perhaps the most important "engineering" function in developing any product, including models and simulations. Although universities turn out experts in one field or another, clearly, the process that manages requirements and integrates these specialties is most important to creating something useful. Of course, design teams must also be solidly grounded in the engineering disciplines to make the systems-engineering approach effective.

2.3.1   Systems Engineering and M&S

M&S applies the computer-as-a-laboratory concept to provide information that helps us make better decisions and leads to products that are cheaper, have higher quality, and are faster to design and produce. M&S allows us to examine how changes in one subsystem can affect the whole. It especially takes advantage of two principles in systems theory:

- The whole is greater than the sum of the parts
- Optimizing all subsystems (suboptimizing) doesn't always lead to the best system

Systems engineering manages how we divide systems into their basic parts, but it requires practical methods for understanding the effects of subprocesses or components on one another. M&S gives us this ability. For instance, looking solely at a rocket engine's parts reveals only how each works alone—control the mass flow rate of fuel and oxidizer, pump the fuel into the combustion chamber, store the fuel, exit the exhaust gases, etc. But until we model the way these parts work together, we can't readily study their contribution to the whole. When the parts of a rocket engine are assembled and work together, they produce enormous thrust and can propel a satellite into orbit around the Earth. Similarly, "best-in-class" tires, suspensions, engines, doors, and so on won't always produce the best sports cars when assembled because, although designed for optimal performance, they may miss the mark when manufactured and measured against total system performance (cost, reliability and comfort). Clearly, M&S can help the systems engineer design the best overall system to meet clearly defined requirements.

Modeling and simulation open engineers' eyes to what is happening to the overall system, rather than just seeing their own small stake in it. For instance, because high performance is often the objective of space system engineering, much effort and many resources go into building propulsion systems that will lift every additional ounce of cargo into space. Additionally, engineers often try to squeeze many extra years of on-orbit life out of components even though a satellite's fuel supply may last only a few years. Unfortunately, costs skyrocket for marginally better performance. This "suboptimizing" is costly and can actually reduce overall performance. Optimal systems result from optimal integration of subsystems, and getting the best service from the whole system may involve complex interrelationships, which only a computer model crunching a lot of data can readily solve. Even then, "optimal" solutions may not always produce the best results—for some users, a mathematical optimum is often only a starting point towards fielding the best system.

Although M&S is a key tool for systems engineering, it also can benefit from adopting systems engineering for its own design. However, we haven't taken advantage of these benefits because hardware- and software-development paradigms are different. Software systems are abstract, and hardware and software engineers have very different backgrounds. But, like any product, M&S has customer requirements it must satisfy, constraints to identify, concepts to evaluate, and optimizing to perform. Engineers must deal with these elements, whether they're designing a model to simulate automobile traffic flow in a large city or building a dam to manage regional water usage. In the rest of this chapter, we'll focus on the history of systems engineering, its process, and how it relates to M&S product design. Table 2.1 lists chapters in this book that cover certain steps in systems engineering for M&S.

Table 2.1.   **Where to Find Discussions of Systems Engineering for Modeling and Simulation.**

Systems-Engineering Steps	Chapter
Define the problem	5
Design the value system	5
Synthesize the system	8, 9, 10, & 11
Analyze systems	8, 9, 10, & 11
Optimize	12 & Appendix C
Decide	12

2.4 Evolution of Systems Engineering

Before the industrial revolution in the United States, crafters were the main providers of finished goods. They specified designs orally to their apprentices and tailored products for each customer. As a result, products weren't very uniform but they still usually met users' needs and expectations. As mass production gained steam and products became more uniform and complex, the crafter era waned and managers of the new "mechanized companies" looked for principles of management and engineering to help them control the uniformity of products, increase efficiency, reduce waste, and get the most out of people and machines.

In the early 1900s, Frederick Taylor, a management consultant and engineer, devised a production method by which engineers designed a product and the production managers ensured it was manufactured as designed. Everything focused on increasing efficiency. This "scientific management" also fostered the development of independent, specialized, non-communicative organizations within the company. Taylor believed observation, measurement, classification, and the principles derived from empirical studies should apply to all managerial problems. He said managers should use the same kind of investigation to determine how work was to be done and to "scientifically" select, train, and develop workers so their individual productivities could be measured and increased [Grolier 1995].

Layers of management developed the rules and procedures needed to manage these complex new organizations. As a natural by-product, "stovepipes" and bureaucracy arose in the organizations, which eroded communication and synergy in design and manufacturing. At the same time, mass production was coming of age, and American business began to thrive as exports increased. "Made in the USA" was the international symbol for quality after World War II. Taylor's system gained momentum because of its huge temporary success and the growing global demand for goods after the war.

Today, the system that made the United States the market leader has become somewhat outdated and obsolete. Throwing the design over the wall into the manufacturing department and expecting the manufacturing engineer to get it right (like an automaton) doesn't work well enough any more because many off-shore competitors have found ways to do it faster, better, and cheaper. Essentially, manufacturing organizations (and the groups within them) became too specialized, focusing on organizational efficiency and losing sight of user requirements. Engineers tried to design the best subsystems with little regard to their effects (in terms of cost, quality, and performance) on the entire system. Systems engineering began as a way to develop the best system at the best possible price. It is the next logical step towards increasing quality of goods and services.

M&S development is also moving away from a "crafter era" into using recognized, standardized, proven methods to create our products. Thus, we want to describe a design process in the rest of this chapter that helps develop well engineered models and simulations by using an "industrial" method—one that is repeatable, has standards and methods, and results in high-quality products [Jacobson 1995].

2.4.1   The Design Process

In traditional design, if we design and build a system that meets users' requirements, we consider the design successful. The dilemma has always been to discover the best way to fold a customer's needs into designs, translate them to the manufacturing floor or into lines of computer code, and ultimately, make them into a useful product the customer can afford. The design processes and tools employed by world-class manufacturers and software developers have several common threads. First, they're totally committed to meeting the customer's needs. Second, they use techniques and repeatable ("industrial") methods to ensure they address these needs at every level of design and manufacture. Third, they strongly emphasize continuing improvement of the processes used and products created.

Systems engineering answers the design dilemma. "Total quality control," "concurrent engineering," "off-line quality control," or other variations bring together all functional specialties as early as possible in the design cycle. The systems-engineering process provides a rational structure to guide the design team through user requirements and arrive at a product design (and eventually a product). The design should account for every measurable system characteristic, and the product should be manufactured with as little variation as possible from the design. In Chap. 5 you'll see how to get the most from several design processes working in parallel. Figure 2.4, below, shows how traditional methods and systems engineering compare in terms of the time and resources required to produce a product [King 1989].

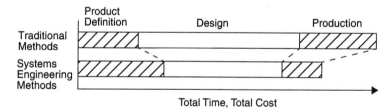

Total Time, Total Cost

Fig. 2.4.   **Comparison of Traditional Methods and Systems Engineering.** Traditional design cycles take longer and cost more because expert knowledge is lost in the rush to "hack out" a product. Systems engineering, which requires more time to define the product, ultimately saves time and money because it generates expert knowledge "up front," requiring fewer changes and less rework downstream.

The traditional method defines the product faster but takes much longer to design, redesign, and produce it. The systems-engineering approach takes more time to define and design the product, but because there are fewer subsequent problems in production (where costs are large compared to design), it produces a higher-quality product in a shorter time and at lower costs than the traditional method.

Some managers and engineers resist systems engineering because early costs are high, it appears to take a long time, and measuring progress is difficult. In the traditional approach, the team is "bending metal" earlier, but then it has to re-bend more metal more often to reach the same result as systems engineering. One of the most frequent engineering mistakes is starting production too soon (sometimes in parallel with defining requirements), which allows the product to take on a life of its own. Eventually, as issues and problems arise in schedule, requirements, or system integration near the end of the effort, engineers sadly recognize they can't influence the design in time to fix all of these problems, even though their team knowledge of the system is greatest at that point.

2.4.2   Systems-Engineering Methods

Systems-engineering methods used today in world-class manufacturing organizations were first developed in the United States. Dr. W. Edwards Deming, who applied statistical and managerial methods to reducing variation of products and improving quality, implied that we need to communicate differently in his ninth "Point for Management." He said, "Break down barriers between functional areas. Teamwork among different departments is needed" [Deming 1986]. Teaming is also essential to creating a credible design—going it alone is a recipe for failure [Katzenbach 1994]. Although the principle appears very simple, carrying it out can be complex and challenging. We have to translate complicated and sometimes ambiguous user requirements for a product or service and then deliver what the user needs.

Although Deming, a mathematician, never discussed or espoused "systems engineering," Arthur D. Hall did. Hall applied detailed methods to "breaking down the barriers" in his "Three-Dimensional Morphology for Systems Engineering" [Hall 1969]. Hall's thesis was that design teams could work together to divide (and subdivide) all projects into basic tasks and subsystems, creating knowledge that allows them to agree on customer requirements, rank alternatives, and ultimately make better design decisions. To create this knowledge, he suggests structured methods that help us integrate subsystem models into an overall system model. The process improves design by promoting communication and traceability among engineering specialties, thereby increasing the likelihood of a complete, high-quality design. In the rest of this chapter, we'll use some of Hall's and others' methods, as well as some practical tools, to illustrate the design process.

2.5   The Form and Structure of Systems Engineering

In 1969, Hall presented a comprehensive three-dimensional framework for systems engineering—his Morphology for Systems Engineering [Hall 1969]. *Morphology* is the study of form and structure, and Hall's morphology provides an effective way to divide a problem into its basic variables so we can eventually solve it. As Fig. 2.5 shows, Hall's morphology, or framework, has three dimensions:

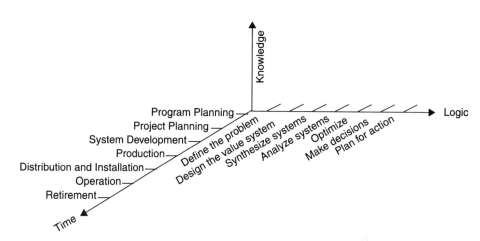

Fig. 2.5.   **Morphological Box for Systems Engineering.** The three axes of systems engineering represent the framework within which we can dissect and solve any problem.

- A *logic axis*, which details the steps carried out in each phase of systems engineering
- A *time axis*, which represents the natural phases of a system's lifecycle and includes program planning, project planning, system development, production, distribution and installation, operation, and retirement
- A *knowledge axis*, which refers to the specialized fields, professions, and disciplines applied during the process, such as law, management, science, and engineering

As we apply systems engineering to M&S development, we'll examine only the logic and time axes. The knowledge axis represents all the disciplines in Fig. 2.1— too much ground to cover here.

The logic and time axes combine into an "activity plane" that is the basis of systems engineering. This plane represents seven activities applied *appropriately* within the seven phases of a program's lifecycle. For instance, in retirement (on the time axis), you're unlikely to use optimizing techniques (on the logic axis), but in system development (on the time axis), you must optimize the design before moving into production. Thus, we see that, when finished with the Plan for Action step in Program Planning, we're ready to move on to the Define the Problem step in Project Planning. This is a general model of systems engineering. Most projects will require the team to tailor all or part of it for their use. Experience shows that, if teams don't use a systematic approach, they will most likely produce traditional results.

Progress through Hall's process is like moving on a spiral (see Fig. 2.6), in which the cycle iterates through the series of activities on the logic axis over time [Hall 1969]. Each trip through the cycle refines the system being designed. The first lap through might be simply to develop and select a concept, whereas subsequent iterations will prove out detailed technologies and designs to support the concept.

The number of iterations through the systems-engineering cycle depends on the system's technical complexity and how large and dispersed it must be. Shanhar and Bonen (1997) classify systems based on complexity and scope and offer management techniques based on these characteristics to ensure project success. Other commercial and government models of the systems-engineering process have heritage from the Department of Defense's (DOD), Military Standard 499B model, shown in Fig. 2.7.

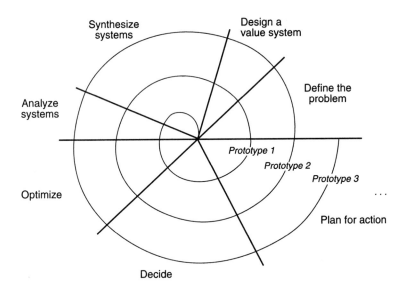

Fig. 2.6.   The Spiral Model for Systems Engineering. This model, a combination of Boehm's (1986) and Hall's (1969) ideas, shows how the design team moves forward in well-planned, incremental, repetitive steps over time. The process allows designers to develop new versions, prototypes, or subassemblies as the system becomes more mature. Understanding of the design increases with each pass, and design fidelity increases with each revolution. This model also supports continual improvement through built-in refinement as a key to effective systems engineering, and relies on interacting often with users to be most effective.

2.5.1   Phases on the Time Axis

The phases of Hall's time axis represent the natural phases of a system's lifecycle. We define and select programs during Program Planning, then identify specific projects to be carried out in Project Planning. In System Development, we create projects necessary to develop the system and plan for production; while in Production, we produce the system and plan to install it. The system is installed for operation in the Distribution phase and serves its intended use in the Operations phase. In Retirement, the system is withdrawn from use and is replaced by a new system, modified, or destroyed.

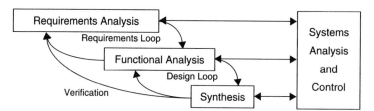

Fig. 2.7.   **The DOD's Model of the Systems-Engineering Process.** Many commercial and
government organizations use the DOD Military Standard 499B. The similarities to Halls'
model include the interative nature of systems engineering and the sequence of
activities. The differences include the lack of explicit steps for defining the problem and
optimizing. This model also places less emphasis on traceability, prototyping, and cross-
functional team involvement.

2.5.2   Steps on the Logic Axis

The *Problem Definition* step of Hall's activity matrix for systems engineering
aims to describe fully (in history and data) how a problem came to be a problem.
The design team identifies users, captures their requirements, and develops design
alterables. The purpose of *designing a value system* is to match alterables (the
"hows") to requirements, develop system functions, and develop the team's
knowledge about the system by creating and examining target objectives and
performance measures. *Synthesizing systems* means developing concepts which
might allow us to meet requirements and identifying the components that make
up these concepts. We then *analyze the systems and components* using models
that will help us develop insight into their interrelationships, behavior, and
characteristics (in terms of performance measures and alterables). *Optimizing*
means fine tuning the design—selecting parameters and coefficients that will
allow each proposed concept to best satisfy the performance measures. Then, we
choose one or more concepts worthy of further consideration, based on system
constraints and requirements. In *planning for action* (the next phase), we revisit
the previous six steps so we can begin the next phase. Each of these steps is
iterative, and we can continually refine the output of any step based on results of
preceding steps [Sage 1977].

2.5.3   Using Quality Function Deployment (QFD) and Matrices in Systems
Engineering

Whether developing an aircraft or an M&S product, moving from one step to
the next without a clear process can cause us to become confused, lose focus, and
abandon sound design concepts—traditional methods leading to traditional
results. Quality Function Deployment (QFD) is one method that can help uncover
the user's needs, produce design knowledge and traceability, and provide a
framework to design and construct a system based on those needs [King 1989].
QFD provides a process and the tools to link the user's requirements to the final

design. It's well-suited to looking at an entire system or subsystems, including M&S products. Several QFD approaches are commonly applied to developing hardware, but they can also help develop models and simulations. In fact, QFD has recently been applied to developing software products [Thackeray 1989], and Bob King (1989) shows how it can cut time and cost from typical designs. We'll rely on some of King's methods to investigate the process.

The heart of QFD is developing the "house of quality" matrix. Matrices provide an intuitive and systematic way to define and trace all linkages and better understand how parts of a system interact by helping design teams attack "bite-size" pieces instead of becoming overwhelmed by the entire problem. In this way, design teams can develop, highlight, and store all information. The way we arrive at a set of matrices is the real essence of systems engineering. Dr. M. James Naughton (1989) suggests that the key to developing these kinds of matrices is not necessarily in the matrices themselves, but in the "expert knowledge" the design team gains while using this technique. Traditional engineering teams believe they can get by without a systematic process; yet, they often miss even the obvious requirements. Hall (1969) also says that a structured process for developing requirements "helps find more solutions than could be found merely by listing them." Figure 2.8 summarizes the process.

QFD matrices unify the system by highlighting self interactions and cross interactions among entities. By identifying these interactions, matrices help us track where changes to one part of the system impact requirements and vice versa [Jacobson 1995]. (See Sec. 2.8 at the end of this chapter for more detail.) Using matrices may be cumbersome, time consuming, and unpopular among managers and engineers, who believe time would be better spent "making something." But the time invested in developing matrices is usually well spent. To translate users' requirements into usable systems, many organizations resort to writing lengthy requirements documents, writing (and re-writing) multiple specifications, and adopting a "fix it later" or firefighting mentality to meet project milestones and ensure product quality. This takes less effort in the beginning, but the costs to fix the design later in the lifecycle almost always outweigh savings from shoddy design work. Unfortunately, simply satisfying *user-stated* requirements doesn't guarantee we'll meet all of their needs—uncovering and deciphering the hard-to-quantify needs increase the chance of high returns on investment.

2.5.4 Decomposing Systems Reveals Similarities in Hardware and Software

Recall one of the two principles of systems engineering—the whole is greater the sum of the parts—which assumes we understand how the parts fit ʋogether into a system and, conversely, how to break the system into manageable pieces. System decomposition is the "hierarchical, functional, and physical partitioning of any system into hardware assemblies, software components, and operator activities that can be scheduled, budgeted, and assigned to a responsible manager" [Motorola 1992]. Good systems engineering always starts by defining the problem (deriving the user's requirements) and then partitioning it into

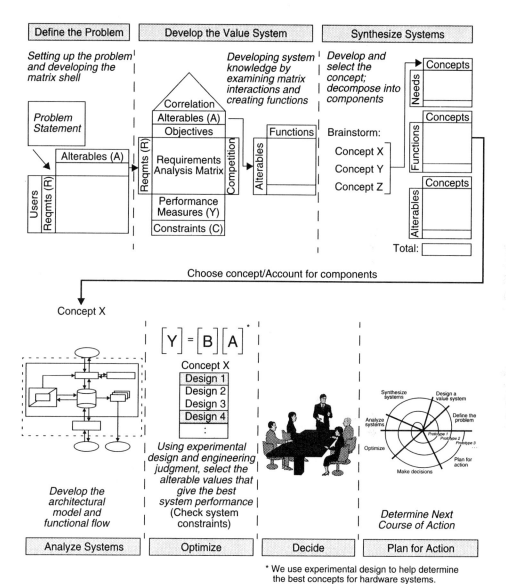

Fig. 2.8.   Using Modified QFD for Systems Engineering. This systematic approach guides the design team through design by focusing it on user requirements and determining the best solutions to the problem.

subsystem requirements, until we can understand and act on a manageable ("bite-size") set of requirements. Decomposition is as important and applicable to developing computer models and simulations as it is to developing any other system (see Fig. 2.9).

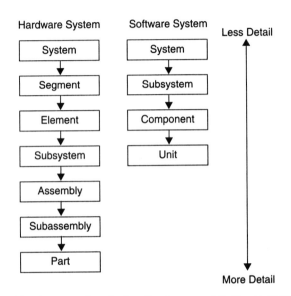

Fig. 2.9.   **Similarities between Developing Hardware and Software Systems.** The systems-engineering model has typically applied only to hardware projects. Now, using decomposition in systems engineering, we see similarities in developing hardware and software. The aim is to break the system into manageable subsystems and tasks. This allows the engineering team to work on "bite-sized" pieces.

2.6   Steps in Systems Engineering

In each of the remaining sections, we'll discuss processes and display results in matrices or graphs. We'll develop a conceptual design to illustrate how systems engineering works. For best results, the team that starts the systems-engineering process must stay involved in every step. Otherwise, you'll lose knowledge, and you may lose sight of requirements as emphasis shifts to meeting cost and schedule objectives later in development and production. The recent trend of "job-hopping" from one employer or product to another can destroy product quality because the "experts" take critical, sometimes irreplaceable, knowledge with them. And it's difficult to recover from these disruptions because of tight schedules for design and production.

2.6.1   Define the Problem

Defining the problem involves identifying users, describing its nature, assessing requirements, and establishing alterables. Key to this step are collecting and analyzing the user's requirements and transforming them into measurable, controllable, and actionable design criteria.

Identifying Users

Users (or customers) of a system define the problem to be solved and requirements to be satisfied. Their voices must be the driving force and be traceable through program planning, system development, and operations to ensure the system meets all requirements.

A good rule of thumb to identify users is to determine whom the product or service best serves and then assess their "stance" or perspective in using it [Lendaris 1986]. We can also add to this list people who think about, study, use, or pay for the system. People who directly use the system are called *primary users*; those responsible for system maintenance, production, etc. are called *secondary users*. Identifying primary and secondary users is critical to considering properly all user inputs to system development. But systems engineering is concerned with producing the best overall system rather than just the best subsystems. Thus, maintainability and producibility are nearly as important to the system design as are primary user requirements, such as ease of use and cost. In some cases, the needs of the primary and secondary users overlap; in other cases, their needs are contradictory, calling for breakthroughs and tradeoffs to find the best compromise.

In our spacelift-scheduling example, we identified the following users:

Primary
1.   Analyst: Person using the tool
2.   Decision Maker: Person using the model's results to make decisions
3.   Launch Director: Person using schedules to marshal resources to support a particular launch

Secondary
1.   Maintainer: Person maintaining the model and software
2.   Data Provider: Person providing the data for use in the model
3.   External Decision Maker: Person who uses schedules to decide on budget, acquisition, or other issues

Defining the Problem Statement

To be effective, the problem statement requires

- A description explaining the nature of the problem and how it became a problem
- The problem's environment
- History and data

- Limits of the system to be developed: the problem boundaries, within which our design should focus

Like all steps in systems engineering, the design team should develop the problem statement because many opinions and ideas lead to good team education and consensus building during this step. Brainstorming sessions among the design group are a useful way to begin. They help the team generate many creative ideas quickly; they also prove that the whole is greater than the sum of the parts because individual ideas build on each other to start solving the problem. Goal/QPC, a firm dedicated to helping industry focus on developing quality products through better management, offers a useful approach and guidelines for brainstorming [Brassard 1989].

The problem statement below should give you a reasonably good idea of what is involved: it contains the nature of the problem, the environment, an historical perspective, and boundaries.

Sample Problem Statement

> In the past, a space launch was treated as a one-time event or experiment with little attention to repeatable processes and dependable schedules. Schedulers used rules of thumb, personal opinions, convenient field data, and other information to schedule activities at the launch base. With the increasing emphasis on using space to collect and distribute information, this policy is evolving. National policies identify the need to ensure critical space abilities are available for space missions as a key concept which supports national doctrine. Therefore, there is a need to forecast and plan launch schedules and supporting resources which ensure the efficient use of national spacelift capabilities to satisfy all users of space-based systems.

Assessing Requirements

After listing the primary and secondary users and defining the problem, identifying requirements is perhaps the most labor-intensive activity early in design, but it may offer the greatest return on time invested. User requirements are the result of a stimulus or deficiency—users alone define needs and deficiencies relative to the way the system is used. Unsatisfied requirements result in poor-quality systems; visible, driving requirements implemented in the design help produce high-quality systems. Organizations that best meet these requirements create good products and get repeat business.

Several studies illustrate that errors made while gathering requirements are extremely expensive to repair. If such errors were infrequent, they wouldn't cost much; but they're the most frequent type of error in complex software projects. In a study of a U.S. Air Force project, Sheldon (1992) found requirements errors comprised 41 percent of discovered errors, compared to only 28 percent for design-logic errors. The other 31 percent included documentation and human errors, as well as errors caused by the environment, data, and interfaces. Other studies show similar percentages [Yates 1990]. Because of their magnitude, finding and fixing requirements errors can consume 70 to 80 percent of costs for project rework.

Given the inherent problems of poorly defined requirements, we must understand the user at the beginning of the development cycle. Letting an organization design a product in a vacuum (without involving users) usually doesn't produce the best results. At the same time, although customers may always be right, uncovering what they really need is difficult. Surveys and interviews may help, but as King (1989) says, "customers don't tell you everything. Also (they) ignore the fact that company specialists know the possibilities that customers may never have considered." Let's explore one proven way to help drive out what users really want.

Again, we must assemble a creative, open-minded team with various skills to assess needs. This is critical because knowledge and communications must transcend the marketing, engineering, sales, accounting, and manufacturing departments. Second, the team must ask the appropriate users what they need in a system through market research, interviews, and surveys. This is called capturing the "voice of the customer." Getting a consensus can take weeks and even months of hard work.

Brainstorming, affinity diagrams, and tree structures (see Sec. 2.8) are also particularly useful at this stage to group the requirements and to determine the appropriate level of detail required for the process [Brassard 1989]. Requirements should stay focused on what the user wants, not how the design team is going to implement them. Otherwise, solutions (or concepts) narrow down prematurely, and the program may fail if it can't overcome these solutions' inherent technological or physical risks. Systems engineering provides for this narrowing down later in the process.

Requirements should also be stated in language that is positive, simple, easy to understand, and conceptual rather than numerical. For example, "highly reliable" is a good example of a need, whereas "doesn't malfunction more than two percent of the time" isn't as good because users generally aren't able to understand what a 98-percent reliable product really means. It's better to let the engineering team define the precise reliability target.

Table 2.2 illustrates a generic set of requirements for a system—note that requirements may (and usually will) outnumber users. It's also useful to attach the identified users to their sets of requirements. Once we've identified the requirements, we can finish defining the problem by developing alterables.

System and Subsystem Alterables

How do we account for requirements? Developing system alterables (also called design variables or system attributes) is the next key step in producing the problem-definition matrix. The alterables (A) are what we eventually use in modeling the system while trying to choose the best design. Alterables answer the

Table 2.2.   **Example of a Matrix for User Requirements.** Primary and secondary users of the system have many requirements that have to be understood and satisfied in order to produce the best system for both. (Note that n, for requirements, doesn't have to equal m, for users.)

Primary and Secondary Users	Requirements
User$_1$	R$_1$
User$_2$	R$_2$
:	:
User$_m$	R$_n$

question "How?" They derive directly from the requirements discussed in the previous section. Again, affinity and tree-structure methods are powerful ways to derive alterables.

The most important consideration in establishing alterables is making sure we can act on, control, evaluate, test, measure, and most importantly, manage them. A "thought algorithm" is also helpful in starting to develop alterables. It allows us to systematically build a tree of alterables that addresses each requirement by actually substituting the requirement phrase into the algorithm—e.g., "How can we affect the requirement Produces Schedules Quickly (R4)?" or "If I control A$_n$ *(one of the measurable quantities or controllable characteristics of the product)*, I'll meet the requirement for producing schedules quickly." Using the tree diagram, with the requirement as the origin, ensures traceability and completeness. Once the alterables are defined, we can move to the next step in the process. Figure 2.10 shows the matrix that summarizes the problem-definition step.

2.6.2   Develop the Value System

Developing a value system is critical to systems engineering because it allows us to weight the correlation between requirements and alterables and systematically fill out the relationships in the requirements-analysis matrix created during problem definition. It's also the place where we develop target objectives, performance measures, functions, and constraints to help us understand the alterables and relate them to requirements through cross-interaction matrices. A "complete" cross-interaction matrix means the alterables address all the requirements.

Develop Target Objectives

Target objectives (O) show the direction (increase or decrease) in which we should focus the alterables and act as goals for trade studies. Usually, they're obvious, but systematic exercises to arrive at them are useful to help focus the design team. Using arrows to show direction is an easy convention to use and remember. Figure 2.11 shows how they're used. In this example, we want to reduce the time to develop schedules (A1) and increase the number of standard modules (A9).

User	No.	Requirement	A1 Time to Develop Schedules	A2 Time to Update Model	A3 Time to Learn to Use	A4 Time to Enter Data	A5 Time to Install	A6 Software Types	A7 Stability of Software	A8 Scheduler Type	A9 Standard Modules	A10 Portability	A11 Number of Data Types Used	A12 Number of Reports	A13 Tailorability of Reports	A14 Flexibility of User Interface	A15 Statistical Accuracy	A16 Variability Measurements	A17 Version Update Frequency	A18 Security Features	A19 Staff Required to Run	A20 Fault Checking
Analyst	R1	Consistent Inputs/Outputs																				
Analyst	R2	Doesn't hang																				
Analyst/Decision Maker	R3	Standard operating system compatible																				
Analyst	R4	Produces schedules quickly																				
Analyst	R5	Runs in time to answer real time what-if's																				
Analyst	R6	Looks friendly																				
Decision Maker	R7	Looks professional																				
Analyst	R8	Standard look and feel																				
Maintainer	R9	SEI Compliant																				
Analyst	R10	Compatible with existing computer systems																				
Analyst	R11	Exportable/Electronic outputs																				
Analyst	R12	Calendar style output																				
Analyst	R13	Easy to read/project/publish																				
Analyst	R14	Transportable outputs																				
Analyst	R15	Provides schedule confidence values																				
Decision Maker	R16	Graphical output																				
Analyst	R17	Accounts for historical data																				
Analyst	R18	Forecasts delays																				
Analyst	R19	Calculates Frequency of delays																				
Analyst/Decision Maker	R20	Accounts/Notifies of Resource Conflicts																				
Analyst/Decision Maker	R21	Models Launch Processes																				
Analyst Decision Maker	R22	Models Major Operations																				
Decision Maker	R23	Good ability to forecast																				
Analyst	R24	Updates schedule based on daily progress																				
Analyst	R25	Easy to learn																				
Maintainer	R26	Easy to maintain																				
Analyst	R27	Advanced degree analyst not required																				

Fig. 2.10. **Defining the Problem: First Step in Systems Engineering.** This critical phase results in "expert knowledge." Users, requirements, and alterables can be set up to later develop relationships between them. (Note: The requirements-development tree used to derive requirements, Fig. 2.21, is in Sec. 2.8.)

Alterables (Objective):

- A1 (↑) Time to Develop Schedules
- A2 (↑) Time to Update Model
- A3 (↑) Time to Learn to Use
- A4 (↑) Time to Enter Data
- A5 (↑) Time to Install
- A6 (↑) Software Types
- A7 (↑) Stability of Software
- A8 Scheduler Type
- A9 (↑) Standard Modules
- A10 (↑) Portability
- A11 (↑) Number of Data Types Used
- A12 (↑) Number of Reports
- A13 (↑) Tailorability of Reports
- A14 (↑) Flexibility of User Interface
- A15 Statistical Accuracy
- A16 Variability Measurements
- A17 Version Update Frequency
- A18 Security Features

If I control → (Alterable) Then I'll meet (Requirement)

No.	Requirement	A1	A2	A3	A4	A5	A6	A7	A8	A9	A10	A11	A12	A13	A14	A15	A16	A17	A18
R1	Consistent Inputs/Outputs	3	1	9		1	1	3	3	3	1	1	3	1	3	1	–	–	–
R2	Doesn't hang	1	1	1	1	1	3	9	1	3	3	3	1	1	3	–	–	–	–
R3	Standard operating system compatible	–	–	1	–	9	9	9	–	–	–	–	–	–	–	–	–	3	–
R4	Produces schedules quickly	9	3	3	3	3	1	–	3	–	–	–	–	–	3	–	–	–	–
R5	Runs in time to answer real time what-if's	9	9	–	9	1	1	1	–	–	–	–	–	–	1	–	–	–	–
R6	Looks friendly	–	–	–	–	–	9	–	–	–	–	1	3	3	9	–	–	–	–
R7	Looks professional	–	–	–	–	–	9	–	–	–	–	1	3	3	9	–	–	–	–
R8	Standard look and feel	–	–	–	–	1	3	–	–	1	–	–	–	–	3	–	–	–	–
R9	SEI Compliant	–	–	–	–	–	9	–	–	–	–	–	–	–	9	–	–	–	–
R10	Compatible with existing computer systems	–	–	1	–	9	9	1	–	–	3	–	–	–	–	–	–	9	–
R11	Exportable/Electronic outputs	–	–	–	–	–	9	–	–	3	–	–	–	1	–	–	–	–	–
R12	Calendar style output	–	–	–	–	–	–	–	9	–	–	–	9	9	1	–	–	–	–
R13	Easy to read/project/publish	–	1	1	1	–	–	1	9	–	–	1	–	9	3	1	–	–	–
R14	Transportable outputs	–	–	–	–	–	–	–	–	–	–	–	–	1	1	1	–	–	–
R15	Provides schedule confidence values	–	–	–	–	–	–	–	9	–	–	–	3	3	1	9	3	–	–
R16	Graphical output	–	–	–	–	–	–	–	3	–	–	–	3	3	–	–	–	–	–
R17	Accounts for historical data	–	3	–	–	–	–	–	9	–	–	–	1	–	–	3	3	–	–
R18	Forecasts delays	–	–	–	–	–	–	–	9	–	–	–	1	–	–	3	9	–	–
R19	Calculates Frequency of delays	–	–	–	–	–	–	–	9	–	–	–	1	–	–	3	3	–	–
R20	Accounts/Notifies of Resource Conflicts	–	–	–	–	–	–	–	9	–	–	–	1	–	–	3	3	–	–
R21	Models Launch Processes	–	3	–	–	–	–	–	9	–	–	1	–	–	–	–	–	–	–
R22	Models Major Operations	–	3	–	–	–	–	–	9	–	–	–	–	–	–	–	–	–	–
R23	Good ability to forecast	–	–	–	–	–	–	–	9	–	–	–	–	–	–	–	–	–	–
R24	Updates schedule based on daily progress	–	9	–	9	3	–	–	–	–	–	–	–	–	–	–	–	–	–
R25	Easy to learn	–	–	9	–	–	–	–	–	–	–	–	3	–	–	1	–	–	–
R26	Easy to maintain	–	3	–	–	3	9	9	–	–	9	–	–	–	–	3	3	9	–
R27	Advanced degree analyst not required	1	–	9	–	–	–	–	9	–	–	3	3	1	9	–	3	–	–
	TOTAL	23	36	34	23	40	63	33	109	10	18	11	33	37	54	27	28	21	–
	Performance Measures	Run time	Update time	Learning time	Data entry time	Installation time	Complexity	No. crashes per/hr	Complexity	Percent object oriented	Networking (Y/N)	Complexity	Number of reports	Reporting flexibility	Use flexibility	•	•	•	•
		Y1	Y2	Y3	Y4	Y5	Y6	Y7	Y6	Y8	Y9	Y6	Y10	Y11	Y12	•	•	•	•
	Constraints	5 min.	3 min.	2 days	10 min.	10 min.	1.00	0.001	1.00	90%	Yes	1.00	13	Yes	Yes	•	•	•	•

Note: The interactions between requirements and alterables are classified as strong (9), medium (3), or weak (1). A dash (–) represents no interaction.

Fig. 2.11.   Designing a Value System: Second Step in Systems Engineering. The value provides the "glue" between all the entities discussed to this point. To produce a good design, we must ensure there is "sufficient" linkage between all parameters [ASI 1989]. (See pages 8–64 in ASI for a definition of sufficiency.) In this example, A8 is the most important alterable.

Develop Performance Measures

Performance measures (Y) help us determine how well the alterables have been satisfied. They should be measurable because we'll use them to evaluate the goodness of the design. Too often, a design team defines alterables without determining how to measure their accomplishment. Once again, a proven method for developing measurement criteria is the tree method, with the alterable as the origin. An example of performance measures for a launch base scheduler and simulator might be its

Y1)	Run time	Y7)	Number of crashes per hour
Y2)	Update time	Y8)	Percent object oriented
Y3)	Learning time	Y9)	Networking
Y4)	Data entry time	Y10	Number of reports
Y5)	Installation time	Y11)	Reporting flexibility
Y6)	Complexity	Y12)	Use flexibility

Through matrix development, these measures link not only to the alterables but ultimately back to the user's requirements. You'll recognize this common theme of traceability throughout systems engineering.

Develop Functions vs. Alterables

Functional analysis identifies things the product should do which the user may not know about. Up to this point, the design has primarily reflected the "voice of the customer." Functional analysis inserts the "voice of the engineer" into the design [King 1989]. While users normally state their requirements based on how they plan to use the product, engineers can add "excitement" features to the design that make it even more appealing and useful. In most cases users wouldn't think of these features. But once they have them, they can't live without them.

Functional analysis is a top-down approach to analyzing requirements and dividing them into discrete tasks or activities. Brainstorming system or subsystem functions and using a block diagram to represent how the product works are recommended ways to develop a set of functions. Again, we can use the matrix format to present the functions logically and make sure none are missed. The matrix also identifies functions for which there are no alterables and vice versa, so it provides one more check to help us ensure the alterables are complete.

The key to developing functions is to keep them at the appropriate level of abstraction for the current design level and iteration. For instance, if we're trying to design a computer model for scheduling launch processes, one function (F) might be F1) to produce readable schedules, but another might be F2) to pass error messages from the algorithm engine to the report-generator engine. This is clearly an example of non-parallel levels of abstraction. Functions in our model for launch processing and scheduling might include

F1)   Help schedule current launch operations

F2)   Help deconflict scheduling issues

F3)   Support "what-if" scheduling analysis

F4)   Capture historical statistics for launch operations

F5)   Produce scheduling and analysis reports

F6)   Product work-around options for launch anomalies

F7)   Provide a standard method for long-term forecasting

Establish Constraints

Constraints (C) are criteria that remain constant or identify a minimum or maximum boundary for the performance measures. They define system limits, design feasibility (hit or miss, fail or pass, etc.), and possibly goals we must consider to produce the best design. These goals could be determined from marketing studies to determine who is the best in the field or as an exercise in continuing improvement. Often constraints are external to the system, but we must consider them to make sure the system doesn't violate laws, customs, or physics. For instance, constraints (C) on developing a new model for space-launch processing and scheduling might include

C1)   Run time in less than <u>five minutes</u>

C2)   Update time in less than <u>three minutes</u>

C3)   Learning time in less than <u>two days</u>

C4)   Software complexity factor less than <u>1.00</u>

C5)   Data entry time less than <u>ten minutes</u>

C6)   Installation time less than <u>ten minutes</u>

C7)   At least <u>90%</u> object-oriented software

C8)   Reports output of <u>13 or greater</u>

C9)   Ability to configure reports (<u>yes</u> or <u>no</u>)

C10) Standard user interface (<u>yes</u> or <u>no</u>)

Other constraints on software development might be a mandatory environment for building it—programming language, operating system and environment, component libraries, memory limitations, user expertise, design-staff talent, etc.

If we're re-engineering a system (instead of building a new one), constraints may also be subsystem interfaces we can't violate for economic or other reasons, or manufacturing limitations we can't overcome in time for system development. While ignoring constraints may seem to be a simple way for us to "hedge" the process, the price of not understanding limits can be severe, as the accident to the space shuttle *Challenger* illustrates. A design constraint on the shuttle's solid rocket motor limited safe operations to temperatures much higher than the outside air temperatures on that fateful day.

Building Matrices that Assess Market Competition

Unless the M&S effort is the final product (in a competitive procurement), competition probably doesn't affect systems engineering. However, with the increasing emphasis on M&S products in the marketplace, it's worth mentioning here. Assessing competition is useful whenever the product needs to stand out to gain a market edge [King 1989]. To be most effective, marketing and research departments should help do this assessment. The analysis examines how well your competition measures up against requirements. If the competition fares better than you (perhaps they added excitement features you didn't think of or did a better job analyzing requirements), you have more work to do. If not, your team may have discovered something about your customer that your competitors have overlooked—a powerful advantage.

Building Matrices that Examine Correlations

The correlation matrix is a self-interaction matrix examining the relationships between the alterables—dependence or conflicts. This matrix is developed to capture interactions that may be overlooked—a major problem in design [King 1989]. Positive correlations show one entry supports another. An example might be in the two alterables, A3 and A14. Positive interactions identify places where there may be synergy between several entries, and we don't have to duplicate our effort to achieve the same results. Perhaps more importantly, negative interactions show where two or more entries conflict. These conflicts identify the important design trades and research and development actions (breakthroughs) we must perform to obtain the best overall system. An example of negative interactions includes the two system alterables: A3 and A12; the more reports you produce, the longer users take to learn the system. Figure 2.11 summarizes the results of designing a value system. Note, again, that this example is incomplete, but it does illustrate the concepts we've described.

2.6.3 Synthesize Systems

During this step, we develop and select concepts for further study. This is where we develop ways to address the requirements developed earlier. Matrices to capture all relevant information are again particularly useful. Now, we're ready to ask "What are the possible ways to satisfy the user?"

Develop Concepts

As designers, we use brainstorming techniques to develop candidate concepts based on our practical experience, as well as on what we learned in defining the problem and designing the value system. We shouldn't reject unpopular or technically unlikely candidates too early and we should remain properly sensitive to the user's biases. Too much attention to these biases can lead to an expensive product; not enough attention can create a product no one will use. Though time consuming, following the right steps will allow us to choose the best concepts for further exploration and design.

When possible, competing concepts should incorporate architectures that efficiently use commercial off-the-shelf (COTS) hardware and software, which reduces cost and risk and helps control the schedule. Using different technologies for competing concepts is also useful because each technology carries different risks, pros and cons, and economics that we can study further while exploring concepts. For example, a new space-launch system might pit bimodal propulsion against traditional chemical propulsion. Or, we might consider using C++ or Ada as the programming language to develop our launch processing and scheduling model.

In our launch processing and scheduling problem, we reassemble our team and brainstorm the following concepts: develop a network-type queuing model, use a COTS project scheduling program, or develop a general set of algorithms and use them in an interactive spreadsheet program.

Two Ways to Select Concepts

To select concepts for a set of requirements, you can develop models of the concepts you want to evaluate and use experimental design (see App. C) to rank the concepts based on the performance measures, alterables, and constraints identified previously. But if you aren't going to build working models of the products, you'll have to use the requirements, functions, and alterables to better evaluate the concepts. Then, you can determine which ones to pursue based on a summary of advantages and disadvantages. Evaluate hardware concepts using either method; but, evaluate software concepts using only the second approach. As you read further, you'll also see that concept selection using experimental design blurs the line between Systems Synthesis and Systems Analysis. For completeness, we'll show both methods here—the first approach further illustrates how computer models can be used in the "laboratory." New research may help develop a more rigorous process that applies experimental design to help evaluate and select software concepts.

The Experimental Design Method. Experimental design allows us systematically to review the concepts we've compiled using performance measures, alterables, and constraints. The experimental design creates a relationship between performance measures and alterables and takes the form of an objective function (also called a "prediction model"):

$$Y_i = B_1A_1 + B_2A_2 + ... + B_nA_n \tag{2.1}$$

where

Y_i = vector of performance measures
B_n = constant coefficients
A_n = vector of alterables

The process then consists of

1. Setting up an orthogonal designed experiment by setting the alterables to their appropriate levels for the experiment—levels determined using engineering judgment and other information available to the team.

2. Running each experiment and recording the results in terms of the performance measures.

3. Throwing out concepts that violate the system constraints and selecting the best overall concept.

A quick example will help illustrate this process. Let's assume a design team must design a new casing for the rocket motor of an air-to-air missile. Based on its requirements assessment and value system, this team brainstorms three competing concepts: using a new plastic casing, improving the existing steel casing, or developing a new propulsion system that doesn't need a casing. At this point, they must decompose the missile system into its key components and consider developing subsystem models to simulate the mechanical, guidance, and propulsion systems for each concept, as well as heat transfer and aerodynamic characteristics, accuracy, polymer manufacturability, supportability, and cost. These subsystem models were chosen because they represent a way to describe completely all alterables and performance measures. *The subsystem models must account for all.* Depending on the number of programmatic constraints (usually program schedule and budget), the team can use standalone or interconnecting simulations. Whether to link or "sneakernet" the models depends on the design team's proficiency and limits on time. Usually, inexperienced teams should run their models independently to establish a process for trading data with the other teams before going to the effort of linking the models; however larger experiments may warrant as much automation as possible.

The team then runs the experimental design for each concept by varying the alterables through a predefined range—for instance, varying the missile's dimensions, material, propulsion type, guidance package, fin size, and logistics concepts according to engineering judgment and the processes discussed in App. C. Without violating system constraints, the experiment outputs a vector of performance measures (one for each experimental run) containing:

$$Y_i = [P_k; M; R; C; G; SF; Mfg] \tag{2.2}$$

where

P_k = Probability of "kill"

M = Max mach number

R = Reliability

C = Cost

G = Max "g" load

SF = Supportability factor

Mfg = Manufacturability

For the fourth run, the vector may be

$$Y_4 = [0.97; 1.4; 0.93; \$380,\!000; 9.2; 0.98; 0.91]$$

Once the team has the results from the experimental design's runs (as vectors of performance measures), it ranks them and decides which one(s) to develop—a difficult task. The team can decide better if they select a concept with a technique such as the Pareto optimum: for each Y_i, let greater values be more preferred and assume that no other information on the preference is available or established. Then, we will prefer one solution over another if, for components, $Y_i \geq Y_{i+n}$ for all i ($n \neq 0$). Basically, this means that any movement away from the best concept solution (in the solution space) results in a less acceptable system to the user [Smale 1981].

Results of the Pareto analysis indicated that the team should use the plastic casing (with associated dimensions, material, propulsion type, guidance package, fin size and logistics concepts) because it showed the best overall performance. Although team members originally felt the steel missile was the "best bet," the process showed that the plastic casing concept had a higher overall score and greater promise of meeting *all* user requirements. Continued iterations through this process (on key subcomponents that require more attention and refinement to satisfy user requirements) will rely on further system decomposition and experimental design on components at lower levels.

An Alternative to Experimental Design. Unfortunately, the experimental-design approach described above isn't particularly useful for evaluating software concepts whose foundation lies in logical sets of instructions, not physics. In these situations, we can use the following steps to determine which concepts are best for a given set of requirements.

Step 1: Match Concepts to Requirements

You should begin selecting the concept by investigating the interactions between concepts and requirements. When developing a new product, you will naturally want to do this before you design the value system. Instead, try to wait until you begin synthesizing the systems. By waiting, you can avoid limiting your thinking to known technologies or selecting a design solution too early (as in the traditional approach). If you're re-engineering a product, you should probably investigate these interactions while defining the problem because you already understand the problem and recognize the constraints and boundaries defined by the rest of the system. Matching concepts to requirements allows us to better define and rank the design concepts. Figure 2.12 shows how to analyze concepts against requirements.

Step 2: Match Concepts to Functions

An important part of concept selection is identifying system-level functions: what the system or subsystem does. Like the process used to evaluate requirements versus concepts, this matrix shows how concepts relate to product function. A winning concept will provide advantages over the benchmark while introducing minimal new shortfalls (see Fig. 2.13).

No.	Requirement	C1 Real-time and Stochastic Model	C2 Spreadsheet Model	C3 Benchmark	C4 Project Scheduler
R1	Consistent Inputs/Outputs	+	–		+
R2	Doesn't hang	+	+		+
R3	Standard operating system compatible	+	+		+
R4	Produces schedules quickly	+	+		+
R5	Runs in time to answer real time what-if's	+	+		+
R6	Looks friendly	+	+		+
R7	Looks professional	+	+		+
R8	Standard look and feel	+	+		+
R9	SEI Complaint	+	+		+
R10	Compatible with existing computer systems	–	+		+
R11	Exportable/Electronic outputs	+	+		+
R12	Calendar style output	+	–		+
R13	Easy to read/project/publish	+	+		+
R14	Transportable outputs	+	+		+
R15	Provides schedule confidence values	+	–		–
R16	Graphical output	+	+		+
R17	Accounts for historical data	+	–		–
R18	Forecasts delays	+	–		–
R19	Calculates Frequency of delays	+	–		–
R20	Accounts/Notifies of Resource Conflicts	+	+		+
R21	Models Launch Processes	+	+		–
R22	Models Major Operations	+	+		–
R23	Good ability to forecast	+	+		–
R24	Updates schedule based on daily progress	+	+		+
R25	Easy to learn	–	+		+
R26	Easy to maintain	–	–		+
R27	Advanced degree analyst not required	+	+		+
	Total (+)	24	20	--	20
	Total (–)	3	7	--	7

Fig. 2.12. **Matching Concepts to Requirements.** This step, developed by Stuart Pugh, determines which concepts are the most promising for continued design [King 1989]. The column marked "benchmark" is a standard to compare with different concepts. In this case, the benchmark is the existing tool for creating launch base schedules. Add the total (+) and (–), but don't cancel out the two because both (+) and (–) values are important. The (–) scores represent where a concept falls short of the benchmark. Once you select a concept, you should revisit the (–) scores and develop an action plan to improve these shortfalls. Blank values represent parity between the candidate concept and the benchmark. Experienced engineers can also weight interactions instead of using a single (+) or (–).

No.	Functions	C1 Real-time and Stochastic Model	C2 Spreadsheet Model	C3 Benchmark	C4 Project Scheduler
F1	Help schedule current launch operations	+	+		+
F2	Help deconflict scheduling issues	+	−		+
F3	Support what-if scheduling analysis	+	+		+
F4	Capture historical statistics for launch operations	+	+		−
F5	Produce scheduling and analysis reports	+	+		+
F6	Produce workaround options for anomalies	+	+		+
F7	Provide a standard method for longterm forecasting	+	+		+
	Total (+)	7	6	--	6
	Total (−)	0	1	--	1

Fig. 2.13.   Mapping Concepts to Functions. This matrix identifies which concepts best support the user's functions for the M&S product. In this case, all the concepts are much better than the benchmark [King 1989].

Step 3: Match Concepts to Alterables

Before selecting a concept, you must analyze how proposed concepts stack up against alterables (see Fig. 2.14). Add the (+) and (−) totals to determine which concept will most strongly support M&S alterables without introducing deficiencies [King 1989].

Step 4: Select Concepts

After completing the first three steps, you can fully assess which concepts best meet the requirements, functions, and alterables—they have the fewest minuses and the most pluses (see Fig. 2.15). The minuses identify candidate areas for further study and required technological breakthroughs.

No.		C1	C2	C3	C4
No.	**Alterables**	Concept / Real-time and Stochastic Model	Spreadsheet Model	Benchmark	Project Scheduler
A1	Time to develop schedules	−	+		+
A2	Time to update model				
A3	Time to learn to use	+	+		+
A4	Time to enter data	+	+		+
A5	Time to install				
A6	Software types	−	−		−
A7	Stability of software				
A8	Scheduler type	+	+		−
A9	Standard modules				
A10	Portability	−	−		−
A11	Number of data types used	−	−		−
A12	Number of reports	−	−		−
A13	Tailorability of reports	−	−		+
A14	Flexibility of user interface				
A15	Statistical accuracy	+	+		−
A16	Variability measurements	+	+		−
A17	Version update frequency	+	+		+
A18	Security features	+	+		−
A19	Staff required to run	−	−		−
A20	Fault checking	+	−		+
	Total (+)	8	8	--	6
	Total (−)	7	7	--	9

Fig. 2.14.   **Matching Concepts to Alterables.** This matrix helps the design team assess which concepts best meet alterables. Again, blank values represent parity between the benchmark and the given concept.

Summary		Real-time and Stochastic Model	Spreadsheet Model	Benchmark	Project Scheduler
	Total (+)	39	34	--	32
	Total (−)	10	15	--	17

Fig. 2.15.   **Selecting Concepts.** Stuart Pugh observed that engineers sometimes hold on to their favorite engineering solutions. Concept selection helps engineers review concepts more objectively and select the concepts with the largest number of pluses (+) and smaller number of minuses (−) [King 1989]. Although the realtime and stochastic model has some serious negatives, overall it appears to be the best choice in meeting the user's requirements. The negatives highlight where the concept is worse than the benchmark and focus the team on the need to improve this concept during the iterative product design process.

Step 5: Divide the System into Components and Design the Architecture

While still synthesizing the system, you want to flow concepts to the next lower level of detail. For example, we might have decided to use a real-time, stochastic model for our space-launch processing and scheduling model. Using system decomposition (Sec. 2.5.4), its major components (Comp) might be

Comp 1)   Graphical user interface
Comp 2)   Report generator
Comp 3)   Long-term data storage device
Comp 4)   Stochastic modeling engine(s) [long term]
Comp 5)   Communication system
Comp 6)   On-line applications to help users
Comp 7)   Computer operating system
Comp 8)   The user (In some systems, the user is part of the system. In others, the user is the stimulus.)
Comp 9)   Engine for near-term scheduling

Step 6: Match Components to Functions

By analyzing these components versus previously identified functions (see Fig. 2.16), we can determine which module does what (design-team accountability) and which modules are most difficult to design and complete (resource assignment and schedule planning). These steps should lead to a successful development effort.

In hardware development, you should determine which subcomponents are the most critical to satisfying the user's needs and then focus your design efforts on them. For software development (especially in M&S activities), it's hard to identify which modules or objects are more important than others. That's because failure (from poor design or development) of any module or object can hinder operations of the entire M&S product. Clearly, a sound algorithm "engine" is critical, but a user interface can make or break the product as well.

Now that you've narrowed your set of concepts and established the key components for development, you can move on to the next phase of the process, where you'll build a model of the concept using the components you've just identified.

2.6.4   Analyze Systems

According to Hall (1969), systems analysis involves systematically determining how the system behaves against our performance measures. To do this for M&S products, we must model the system and its subsystems using a different method than that for hardware.

As mentioned earlier, in M&S applications, building a model to simulate the logical interworkings of each module or block is either very difficult or not worth the effort. Instead, we recommend building a graphical model or architecture

No.	Function	Comp1 Graphical user interface	Comp2 Report generator	Comp3 Data storage device	Comp4 Stochastic modeling engine	Comp5 Communications system	Comp6 Help application	Comp7 Operating system	Comp8 User	Comp9 Real-time modeling	
F1	Help schedule current launch operations	3	9	3	--	9	1	--	3	9	
F2	Help deconflict scheduling issues	3	9	1	--	3	1	--	9	9	
F3	Support what-if scheduling analysis	1	3	3	3	--	1	--	3	3	
F4	Capture historical launch operations statistics	3	--	9	--	1	--	--	1	--	
F5	Produce scheduling and analysis reports	--	9	--	--	--	1	--	--	3	
F6	Produce work-around options for anomalies	3	3	1	--	--	1	--	3	9	
F7	Provide a standard method for longterm forecasting	9	--	1	9	--	1	1	3	--	
	Component weight	22	33	18	12	13	6	1	22	33	160
	Component percentage	14%	21%	11%	7%	8%	4%	1%	14%	20%	100%

Fig. 2.16. **Matching Components to Functions.** This synthesis activity identifies which components relate most to key functions and ensures all components are in place before modeling them. In this example, the key components are COMP2 and COMP9. This tells us that most resources need to be dedicated to making these components work.

(a representation or abstraction) of how the actual system will work. At a top level, architectural design may focus on the individual modules that make up a large system, showing control hierarchy and interfaces. Here, we model the system's structure in the form of data-flow diagrams and schematics. The advantage of our extended method over the traditional method is evident here because we have a complete set of modules that comprise the concept design—all linked back to requirements.

For M&S applications, these models may be composed of "blocks," which actually are an abstraction of the design [Jacobson 1995]. We call the module level of programming language an "object module." These blocks are analogous to the subsystem models developed for hardware. Although we'll eventually link them, they encapsulate functions into a manageable object. Jacobson claims:

The blocks are actually an abstraction mechanism for the source code. By speaking in terms of blocks we can discuss the system on an overview level and understand the architecture of the system. Through this abstraction mechanism, we reduce the complexity radically, which means that it is easier to build a correct system that will avoid errors caused by complexity. It has been noted...that it is qualitatively better to avoid construction errors by reducing complexity at an early stage than to search the system for faults when it is completed and to correct each error. The latter variant is (unfortunately) often typical of today's traditional system development [Jacobson 1995].

Figure 2.17 shows the architectural model for the launch base scheduler. Figure 2.18 illustrates the functional flow of the stochastic modeling engine. With these models, we can then use software optimizing techniques to evaluate how the concept stacks up against our performance measures.

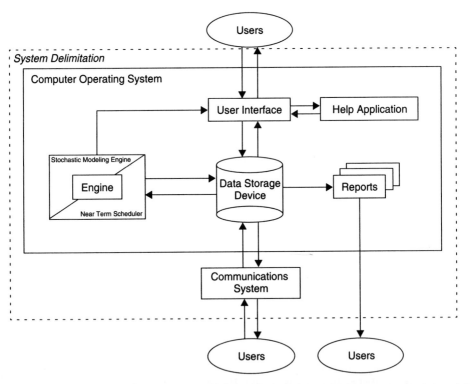

Fig. 2.17.   **Architectural Model for Launch Scheduling.** We have to build a representative model of the hardware or software system to help us better understand the system and determine how it stacks up against our performance measures. This architecture accounts for COMP1 through COMP9.

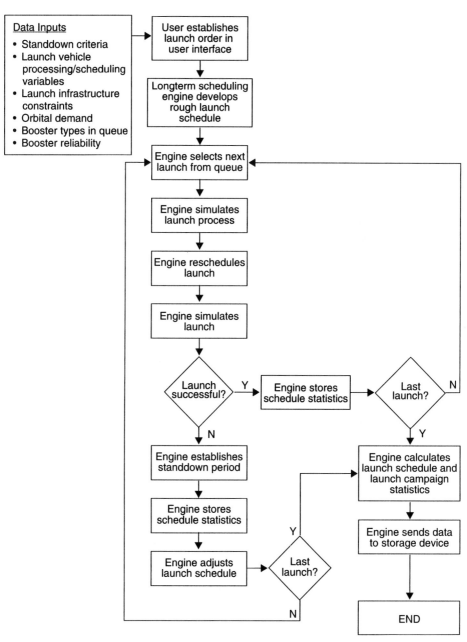

Fig. 2.18.   **Diagram of Functional Flow for the Stochastic Modeling Engine.** This diagram describes the logical functions in the engine for long-term stochastic modeling. As we identify more information about the system, we can provide more detail in the model by creating blocks within each block.

2.6.5   Optimize

Optimizing—the next step along the Logic axis—is refining the best overall design concept so it satisfies or exceeds the requirements. Designing the best complex systems used to require a lot of time and resources, as well as the ability to process large amounts of numerical data. The technological revolution in computers and advanced M&S techniques have greatly reduced design time and associated costs. The benefit to engineering is obvious—we can refine different concepts (or even subcomponents) in a relatively short time and finish the design activity sooner. As with systems synthesis and analysis, optimizing works differently for hardware and software.

Designing the Best Hardware Systems

Finding the best overall design hinges on creating a model of the system and finding where it performs best within system constraints. As you'll soon see, our analysis matrices build up to this step. Having already chosen the concept, we can now start to look at making the best overall system.

It's difficult to find the best solution when the number of alterables increases, but mathematically, any "problem in which certain parameters need to be determined to satisfy constraints can be formulated as an optimum design problem" [Arora 1989]. Often, some alterables have unknown interactions and canceling effects on others. In these cases, we have to adjust the alterables to a level that best satisfies the performance measures. Unfortunately, this stage of systems engineering is often overlooked because it's human nature to "hack" out a solution, field it, and then work to refine it by "tweaking" the alterables in subsequent designs and deliveries. (Recall Fig. 2.4 for the results of this practice.)

Traditional experimentation varies one alterable at a time to determine its effect on the performance measures. This approach is costly and may not allow the experimenter to see interactions between different alterables. But experimental design takes advantage of orthogonal design and allows experimenters to assess the average change of the performance measures over far fewer simulation runs. It's relatively easy to see how to use experimental design to design a sports car engine for highest speed and lowest fuel consumption. It means setting the alterables to different levels, analyzing key performance measures (e.g., RPM, gear ratio, fuel efficiency) as outputs from the computer simulation in the virtual laboratory, and choosing the appropriate settings for the alterables. In this case, we might also use a physical model if resources permit. In M&S, however, we can optimize certain performance measures only through design iteration and engineering judgment. See App. C for more information on systems optimization and experimental design.

Designing the Best M&S Products

It's generally difficult to develop a comprehensive list of performance measures for M&S products. Usually, model speed, ease of use, output accuracy, and format of the output data are good examples. Because we usually model M&S products in graphical form instead of building an actual computer model, we must use more traditional methods to get the best design.

In most cases, we need something to measure in order to correctly optimize M&S performance. Because we have nothing to measure until we build the M&S system, we can't find the best solutions early on. One way of avoiding this dilemma is to prototype incrementally so we can see what the system should look like and make incremental improvements (recall Fig. 2.6). A good design team will develop a matrix of performance measures and alterables for iterative prototypes to record the results of their efforts. This matrix logs their activities and confirms that they're moving in the right direction.

Unfortunately, the process of optimizing M&S products is still new, and we need more thought and research to develop "industrial" techniques for this stage of M&S development. Until we do, the one-at-a-time varying of alterables still appears to be the best method available.

2.6.6   Make Decisions and Plan for Action

The next step in the process is to retrace our steps iteratively (recall Fig. 2.6). We know the system requirements, and we've chosen the resulting concepts, developed the system model, and optimized the system design. Now, we need to add more detail to the design by driving out lower-level requirements for lower-level components and ultimately developing more refined models of the subsystem components. This iteration continues until seasoned engineers and managers determine the system is adequately defined and manufacturing starts.

Although the systems-engineering process helps us select the best concept and optimize its design, other factors not in the system model will always affect the finished design. Risks complicate our decisions. Examples include new technology, program schedule, design complexity, and even the risk of making a wrong decision in a highly charged political situation. We can quantify and analyze risk by using different risk models, but decision making will still require the opinions of experienced engineers and managers [Hill 1972].

A Summary of the Systems-Engineering Process

Systems engineering has developed as a way to plan, design, and construct "large-scale systems that may involve both machines and human beings" [Flagle 1960]. Engineering today can't be just analysis, research, and design in a vacuum—instead, it needs to become a team activity involving all disciplines, recognizing the interactions between these disciplines, and using structured communications (linkage) as a means of tracking and satisfying user requirements. Quality function deployment (QFD) provides a structure for M&S development and neatly fits into Hall's morphology of systems engineering. This and other methods will continue to improve the way we develop M&S products.

Based on the process we've laid out here, you may get the impression that it's easy to implement systems engineering. Unfortunately, it's not. Developing any product is incremental and iterative—with many refining steps needed to make something that works the way it's supposed to. The process we've defined provides the foundation, logic, and timing for a solid, disciplined approach to design. It has built-in assurance of traceability to user requirements and uses optimizing to provide the best overall product. But you'll still have to add hard work, experience, and engineering sense to make your design a success.

2.7 Summary

In this chapter, we addressed two related subjects: systems science and systems engineering. Key concepts in systems science such as complexity, the Law of Requisite Variety, and the Conant-Ashby Theorem, lay a strong foundation for modeling and simulation. With this foundation, we can use the computer as a laboratory to evaluate system complexity and alternative system behaviors, to create information required to make better decisions, and to design and manufacture high-quality products quicker and cheaper. Systems engineering provides a sound process for developing effective M&S products, including identifying requirements and constraints, evaluating concepts, optimizing and ultimately, meeting customer needs. The seven steps we've highlighted in the systems-engineering process should give you a good starting point for investigating the detailed M&S activities discussed in the rest of this book.

References

American Supplier Institute (ASI). 1988. *Total Quality Management: Variability Reduction and Tools for Implementation.* Dearborn, MI.

Arora, Jasbir S. 1985. *Introduction to Optimum Design.* New York: McGraw-Hill Book Co.

Beer, Stafford. 1966. *Decision and Control.* New York, NY: John Wiley.

Beer, Stafford. 1979. *The Heart of Enterprise.* New York, NY: John Wiley.

Blanchard, Benjamin S., and Walter J. Fabrycky. 1990. *Systems Engineering and Analysis.* Englewood Cliffs, NJ: Prentice-Hall, Inc.

Boehm, B.W. 1986. "A Spiral Model of Software Development and Enhancement." Found in *Object Oriented Software Engineering* by Ivar Jacobson, 1995. Wokingham, England: Addison Wesley Publishing Company.

Brassard, Michael. 1989. *The Memory Jogger Plus+TM.* Metheun, MA: GOAL/QPC.

Buckley, W. 1968. *Modern Systems Research for the Behavioral Scientist.* Chicago, IL: Aldine Publishing Co.

Deming, W. Edwards. 1986. *Out of the Crisis.* Cambridge, MA: MIT—Center for Advanced Engineering Study.

Flagle, C.D., et al. (eds) 1960. *Operations Research and Systems Engineering.* Baltimore, MD: The John Hopkins Press.

Grolier Encyclopedia, 1995. CD ROM Multimedia Version 7.02.

Hare, Jr., Van Court. 1967. *Systems Analysis: A Diagnostic Approach.* New York, NY: Harcount, Brace and World, Inc.

Hall, Arthur D. 1969. "Three-Dimensional Morphology for Systems Engineering." *IEEE Transactions on Systems Science and Cybernetics.* Vol. SSC-5.

Hill, J. Douglas and John N. Warfield. 1972. "Unified Program Planning." *IEEE Transactions on Systems, Man, and Cybernetics.* Vol. SMC-2, No. 5.

Jacobson, Ivar. 1995. *Object Oriented Software Engineering.* Wokingham, England: Addison-Wesley Publishing Company.

Karnopp, Dean C., Donald L. Margolis, Ronald C. Rosenberg. *System Dynamics-A Unified Approach.* New York, NY: John Wiley.

Katzenbach, John R. and Douglas K. Smith. 1994. *The Wisdom of Teams.* New York, NY: Harbor Business Press.

King, Bob. 1989. *Better Designs in Half the Time: Implementing QFD.* Metheun, MA: GOAL/QPC.

Klir, George J. 1991. *Facets of Systems Science.* New York, NY: Plenum Press.

Lendaris, George G. 1986. *IEEE Proceedings: Systems, Man, and Cybernetics.* Vol. SMC-16.

Motorola. 1992. The Systems Engineering Process Handbook. Chandler, AZ: Motorola, Inc. Satellite Communications Division. (Developed by The Center for Systems Management, Inc., Santa Clara, CA.)

Naughton, M. James. 1989. *Developing Tree Structures that Include Qualitative Characteristics.* Expert Knowledge Systems, Inc.

Sage, Andrew P. 1977. "A Case for a Standard for Systems Engineering Methodology." *IEEE Transactions on Systems, Man, and Cybernetics.* Vol. SMC-7, No. 7.

Schmidt, Stephen R. 1989. *Understanding Industrial Designed Experiments.* Longmont, CO: CQG Ltd. Printing.

Schoderbek, Peter P., G. Kefalas Asterios, and Charles G. Schoderbek. 1975. *Management Systems: Conceptual Considerations.* Dallas, TX: Business Publications, Inc.

Shanhar, Aaron J. and Zeev Bonen. 1997. "The New Taxonomy of Systems: Toward an Adaptive Systems Engineering Framework." *IEEE Proceedings: Systems, Man, and Cybernetics.* Vol. 27.

Smale, S. 1981. in *Handbook of Mathematical Economics*, Vol. I, edited by K. Arrow and M. Intriligator. Amsterdam: North-Holland.

Webster's New World Dictionary of the American Language. 1964.

Yates and Schaller. 1990. "Reliability Engineering as Applied to Software." Reliability and Maintainability Symposium Proceedings. Found in *Knowledge Based Management* by Stephen R. Schmidt, Mark J. Kiemele, and Ronald J. Berdine. 1996. Colorado Springs, CO: Air Academy Press.

Zadeh, L.A. 1962. "Circuit Theory to Systems Theory." *IRE Proceedings*, 50.

2.8   Postscript: A Few Special Topics

2.8.1   Using Matrices

Interaction matrices (see Figs. 2.19 and 2.20) show how one entry depends on, or conflicts with, another entry (objectives to objectives or alterables to alterables). Positive correlations are those in which one entry supports another. An example might be in the two programmatic objective (O) statements: O4) to spend the taxpayer's defense dollars more efficiently, and O3) to reduce the lifecycle costs of a space-launch system. Positive interactions identify places where there may be synergy between several entries, so we don't need to duplicate effort to achieve the same results. Negative interactions are those in which two or more entries conflict. These conflicts are extremely important because they identify important trades and research and development opportunities (breakthroughs) we must consider to get the best system, which usually results from many design trades. The two statements—O1) Carry more payload to orbit and O2) increase the margin of safety—provide an example of negative interactions.

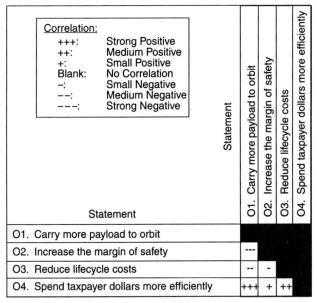

Fig. 2.19.   Example of a Self-Interaction Matrix. This matrix provides information on dependencies or interactions between entries.

The information in a cross-interaction matrix provides a "cross-check," allows the design team to thoroughly evaluate all relationships, and usually results in a more complete design. Figure 2.20 is an example of a requirements-analysis matrix.

	Alterables	A1. Propulsion system reliability	A2. Orbital accuracy	A3. Structural system reliability	A4. System MTBF*
Relationships: +++: Strong ++: Medium +: Small					
Requirements					
R1. Doesn't break often		+++		+++	+++
R2. Launches on time					
R3. Costs less than competitors		+			++
R4. Performs adequately		+	++	+	

* MTBF = mean time between failures

Fig. 2.20.   Example of a Cross-Interaction Matrix. This matrix provides a way to evaluate relationships between different entries.

Examine the example requirements (R), like R1) Doesn't break often, against a series of controllable factors, or alterables, (A), like A1) Propulsion-system reliability and A2) Orbital accuracy. Comparing R1 to A1, we see an intuitive strong, positive relationship whereas there is little or no relationship between R2 and A3. The interaction or "linkage" between two groups indicates a relationship. Intersections of blank rows are places where no relationships exist.

2.8.2   Using Tree Structures

While constructing entities (programmatic objectives, requirements, constraints, etc.), we often find they fall into different logical levels or groupings. We can define a relationship, or set of levels, whenever we must complete one entity to achieve another. In this case, the entity responsible for completing another related entity is termed "subordinate." Developing a "tree" or relationship diagram of subordinate entities is very useful to design because we find a particular level of the tree is appropriate to the design. Usually, constructing three layers of entities to bound the appropriate level (top and bottom) helps drive out non-parallel entities [Naughton 1989]. The tree exercise also fosters creativity, creates a broad perspective, and stimulates associative memory [Naughton 1989].

In constructing an entity tree, we must decide where to start. Determining the tree's origin automatically establishes a logical framework. After establishing the origin, we can create the subordinate levels by asking ourselves: "What is the most immediate way to achieve the origin?" One useful method is to have the design team use an "affinity-diagram" exercise—brainstorming to develop and organize a lot of information. Section 2.8.3 discusses this process. After completing an affinity diagram and developing logical, tiered connections, we can insert the information into lower levels of the tree. An example of a tree diagram is in Fig. 2.21. Then, we can insert this information into a matrix for use in the systems-engineering process.

2.8.3   Using Affinity Diagrams

Affinity diagrams group ideas or objects that are naturally related and identify one concept that describes and unifies the group. They are useful whenever the systems-engineering team is wading through a large volume of ideas (perhaps consumer needs) and can't agree on direction and content.

To use affinity methods [Brassard 1989], you must

1. Develop a general statement for the team to focus on. Too detailed a statement could narrow or prejudice the team in the wrong direction. An example might be: "customer requirements for a new space-launch system."

2. Brainstorm and record ideas. Naughton (1989) uses an approach in which all team members brainstorm and write ideas down on cards or 3M Post-It Notes™ and then affix them to a flip chart or wall. This allows the team to move and group information as they see fit.

3. Organize cards by like categories.

4. Generate a category title for each set of groupings. This statement summarizes all the ideas in the grouping.

Figure 2.22 is an example of an affinity diagram for one attribute ("operability") of a space-launch system.

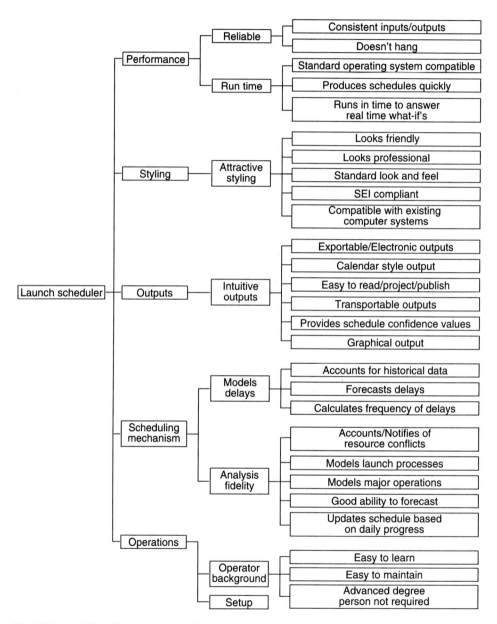

Fig. 2.21.   **A Tree Diagram.** A tree diagram allows the design team to take a lot of information and assimilate it into a logical, connected structure. The tree ensures that all items are connected and complete. It often results in a more complete and parallel set of requirements. This exercise creates the first-level requirements for a tool to schedule space launches.

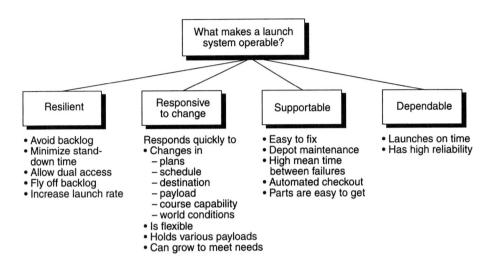

Fig. 2.22.   Affinity Diagram for Requirements of a Space-Launch System. Affinity diagrams group ideas or objects that are naturally related and identify one concept to describe or unify the group.

CHAPTER 3

A Framework for Modeling and Simulation

Bernard P. Zeigler, *University of Arizona*

In this chapter, we'll start by reviewing a systems framework to establish continuity with Chapter 2. Then, we'll reinterpret these concepts in terms more applicable to modeling and simulation (M&S). This reinterpretation, called the systems-specification hierarchy, is the basis for an M&S framework, which sets forth the basic entities and relationships of M&S. Based on this framework, we'll outline the issues and problems you'll encounter in the rest of the book. Terms such as "model" and "simulator" are often loosely used but have very precise meanings in the framework we will discuss and maintain throughout the book. So it's important to understand what the definitions include and exclude. (This is especially true if you have some experience in M&S and are likely to associate [or prefer] meanings different from those developed here.) Please refer to the Glossary at the end of the book for a complete list of framework terms. For more information, visit the World Wide Web at www-ais.ece.arizona.edu.

3.1 Review of a Systems Framework

As shown in Table 3.1, George Klir (1991) has identified four basic levels of knowledge about a system. At each level we know some important things about the system that we didn't know at lower levels. The *source* level identifies a part of the real world that we wish to model and the means by which we are going to observe it. The *data* level is a database of measurements and observations made for the source system. When we get to level 2 (*generative*), we can recreate this data using a more compact representation, such as a formula. Of course, many formulas typically generate the same data, so choosing a particular formula or approach constitutes knowledge we didn't have at the data level. Whenever people talk about models for simulation, they're usually referring to generative concepts— programs to generate data. At the last level (*structure*) we have a very specific generative system. In other words, we know how to generate the data observed at level 1 in terms of interconnected components, whose interaction accounts for the observations made. When people talk about systems, they're often referring to this level of knowledge. They think of reality as being made up of interacting parts so that the whole is the sum (or sometimes more or less than the sum) of its parts. Although some people use the term "subsystems" for these parts, we call them component systems (and reserve the term subsystem for another meaning; see the glossary at the end of the text).

Table 3.1. **Klir's Levels of System Knowledge.** This table shows the ways we can know about a system—ordered as levels of increasing knowledge.

Level	Name	What we Know at This Level
0	Source	What variables to measure and how to observe them
1	Data	Data collected from a source system
2	Generative	Means to generate data in a data system
3	Structure	Components (at lower levels) coupled to form a generative system

As we have suggested, Klir's terms are by no means universally known, understood, or accepted in the M&S community. However, his framework is a useful starting point because it unifies what are usually considered to be distinct concepts. From this perspective, systems create only three basic kinds of problems, which involve moving between the levels of system knowledge (Fig. 3.1 and Table 3.2). In *systems analysis*, we're trying to understand the behavior of an existing or hypothetical system based on its known structure. Whenever we don't know what this structure is, we do *systems inference*—trying to guess this structure from observations we can make. Finally, in *systems design*, we're investigating the alternative structures for a new or redesigned system.

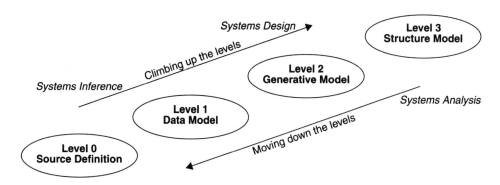

Fig. 3.1.   **Moving Up and Down Levels of Knowledge.** This figure portrays how systems problems involve transitions between levels of system knowledge.

The central idea is that whenever we move to lower levels we don't generate any new knowledge—we only make explicit what is implicit in the description we already have. One could argue that making something explicit can lead to insight, or understanding, which is a form of new knowledge. For example, we may use computer simulations for systems analysis to generate data under instructions a model provides. Although the results may reveal interesting system properties, Klir wouldn't consider this subjective (modeler-dependent) knowledge to be "new."

Table 3.2.   **Klir's Fundamental Systems Problems.** This table shows how the fundamental problems in M&S involve moving between the levels of knowledge.

Systems Problem	Does the Data Source Exist? What Are We Trying to Learn About it?	Which Level of Transition is Involved?
Systems Analysis	The system being analyzed may exist or may be planned. In either case we are trying to understand its behavioral characteristics.	Moving from higher to lower levels—using generative information to generate the data in a data system.
Systems Inference	The system exists. We are trying to infer how it works by observing its behavior.	Moving from lower to higher levels—having data and finding a means to generate it.
Systems Design	The system being designed doesn't exist in the form we're thinking about. We are trying to come up with a good design for it.	Moving from lower to higher levels—having a means to generate observed data, and synthesizing it with components taken off the shelf.

On the other hand, systems inference and systems design involve climbing up the levels. In both cases we have a low-level system description and wish to come up with an equivalent higher-level one. For systems inference, the lower-level system is typically data we've observed from the source system. We are trying to find a generative system, or even a structure system, that can recreate the observed data. In M&S, this is usually called *model construction*. In the case of systems design, the source system typically doesn't exist; our objective is to build one that does what we want it to do. Typically, we want to come up with a structure system whose components are technological—can be obtained off-the-shelf (or built from scratch). When these components are interconnected, as specified by a coupling relation for the structure system, the result should be a real system that behaves as desired.

3.2 Hierarchy of Systems Specification

About the same time (early 1970s) that Klir introduced his epistemological (knowledge) levels, I formed a similar hierarchy for M&S. This framework employs the concept of a dynamical system and identifies useful ways in which such a system can be specified. These ways of describing a system can be ordered in levels, as in Table 3.3. Just as in Klir's framework, at each level the specification provides information that can't be derived from lower levels. Because this hierarchy is so useful for M&S, we're strongly recommending it—and using it throughout this book.

Table 3.3. **Relation Between the System-Specification Hierarchy and Klir's Levels.** This table defines levels of system specification oriented toward M&S and relates them to Klir's framework.

Level	Specification Name	Corresponds to Klir's	What We Know at This Level
0	Observation Frame	Source System	How to stimulate the system with inputs, what variables to measure, and how to observe them over a time base.
1	I/O Behavior	Data System	Time-indexed data collected from a source system; consists of input/output pairs.
2	I/O Function	--	Knowledge of initial state; given an initial state, every input stimulus produces a unique output.
3	State Transition	Generative System	How states are affected by inputs; given a state and an input, what the state is after the input stimulus is over and what output event a state generates.
4	Coupled Component	Structure System	Components and how they are coupled. The components can be specified at lower levels or can even be structure systems themselves—leading to hierarchical structure.

As you can see in Table 3.3, these levels roughly correspond to those of Klir's framework. The major difference is that our system-specification hierarchy recognizes that simulation deals with dynamics—the ways systems behave over time. Therefore, time orders all events. We also view systems as having input and output interfaces through which they can interact with other systems. As illustrated in Fig. 3.2, systems receive time-ordered stimuli through their *input ports* and respond on their *output ports*. The term "port" signifies a specific means of interacting with the system, whether by stimulating it with inputs or observing its outputs (see Glossary). The time-indexed inputs to systems are called *input trajectories*; likewise, their time-indexed outputs are called *output trajectories*. Ports are the only channels through which one can interact with the system. This means that systems are modular (see Glossary). Although Klir's framework can include dynamics, input/output ports, and modules, it doesn't concentrate on these concepts. Yet, understanding these concepts is critical to solving problems in M&S.

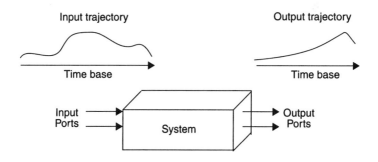

Fig. 3.2.   **Input/Output System.** This figure illustrates a system initially specified at level 0 as an Observation Frame in which input and output trajectories have been observed (level 1).

As an example, Fig. 3.3 shows a forest subject to lightning, rain, and wind— modeled as input ports, with smoke produced from fire represented as an output port. This is a level 0 or *Observation Frame* specification. Note that we could have chosen different variables and orientations. For example, we could have included an output port to represent heat radiation. Moreover, each variable can have an array of values distributed over space. Such choices depend on our modeling objectives and are specified through experimental frames, a concept to which we'll return shortly.

Fig. 3.3.   **Forest System.** This figure represents a forest specified as an Observation Frame (level 0).

Figure 3.4 shows some examples of input and output trajectories. The input trajectory on the lightning port shows a bolt occurring at time t_0. Only one such bolt occurs in the time period shown. The smoke-output trajectory, at the top, depicts a gradual buildup of smoke starting at t_0 (presumably caused by a fire the lightning bolt starts). The possible values taken on by smoke, called its *range*, would result from some appropriate measurement scheme, such as measuring the density of particulate material in grams/cubic meter. The pair of input and associated output trajectories is called an ***input/output (I/O) pair***. Figure 3.4 also displays a second I/O pair with the same input trajectory but different output trajectory, showing that the same stimulus may cause many responses. In the second case, lightning didn't cause a major fire because the one that broke out quickly died. Multiple output trajectories (for the same input trajectory) are characteristic of knowledge at level 1. At the next level, we'll know how to distinguish these output trajectories.

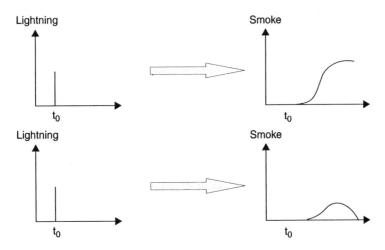

Fig. 3.4.   **Some Input/Output Pairs for the Forest System.** This figure shows two I/O pairs that might be observed in the frame of Fig. 3.3.

The collection of all I/O pairs gathered by observation is a system's *I/O behavior*. As you can see in Table 3.3, this represents a system specification at level 1. Now suppose we can uniquely predict the response of the smoke output to a lightning bolt. For example, suppose we know that if the vegetation is dry, a major fire will ignite, but if the vegetation is moist, any fire will quickly die. This knowledge of the *I/O function* is at level 2. Here, we add initial states to lower-level information in the specification—when the initial state is known, input and output trajectories have a functional relationship. In other words, the initial state determines the unique response to any input (Fig. 3.5).

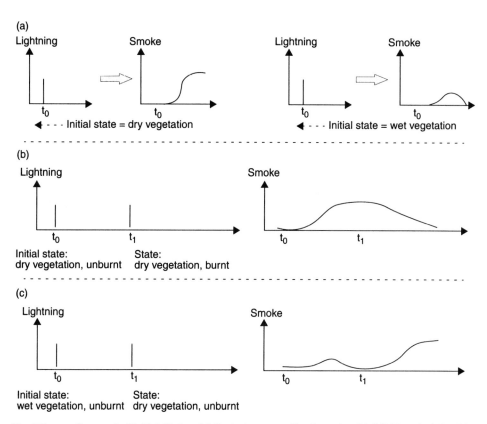

Fig. 3.5.   **Concept of Initial States.** (a) illustrates a specification at level 2 (I/O Function), in which we know a forest's initial states. (b) and (c) highlight the specification at level 3 (State Transition), where we now know how the state changes as the system responds to inputs.

At the next level of system specification (*state transition*), we can specify not only initial state information but also how the state changes as the system responds to its input trajectory. Figure 3.5(b) and (c) illustrate this important concept. Figure 3.5(b) represents an unburned forest with dry vegetation when a lightning bolt occurs at time t_0. But at time t_1, when a second bolt occurs, the forest is in state (dry vegetation, burnt), showing that a fire has ignited. Because the forest is in a different state, the effect of this second bolt is different from the first. Indeed, the second bolt has no effect because there's little left to burn.

In contrast, Fig. 3.5(c) represents a forest that is wet and unburned when the first bolt occurs. It doesn't cause a major fire, but it does dry out the vegetation, so the resulting state is (dry, unburned). Now the second bolt produces a major fire, just as the first bolt did in Fig. 3.5(b)—because both the state and subsequent input trajectory are the same, the response of the system is the same.

At the highest level of system specification (*coupled component*), we can describe more of the system's internal characteristics. At first, it was a black box, observable only through I/O ports. Subsequently, we were able to peer inside and observe its state. Now, at this level, we can specify how the system consists of interacting components. For example, Fig. 3.6 illustrates how a forest system could contain interacting cells, each representing a region, with adjacent cells interconnected. The cells are modeled at level 3: their state-transition and output-generation definitions are used to act on inputs from, and generate outputs to, other cells. In other words, the output ports of each cell are coupled to the input ports of its neighbors.

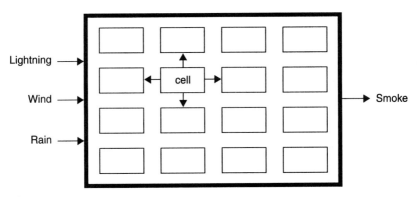

Fig. 3.6.   **Specifying the Component Structure for the Forest System.** This figure illustrates a system specification at level 4 (Coupled Component) which describes how components connect to form a larger system.

At this point we've seen two related frameworks for organizing the state of our knowledge about a system. The systems-specification hierarchy provides five ways to specify a system, each capturing what we know about it. We now turn to a framework for modeling and simulation that identifies the key elements and their relationships and is based on this systems-specification hierarchy. For example, we use specifications at different levels to characterize the different elements. For more detail on the systems-specification hierarchy, see [Zeigler 1976, 1984, 1991].

3.3   Framework for Modeling and Simulation

Figure 3.7 establishes entities and relationships that are central to M&S. Understanding these concepts will improve how analysts, programmers, managers, and users of a simulation-modeling project carry out their tasks and communicate with each other. The entities are *source system, model, simulator,* and *experimental frame;* their relationships are *modeling and simulation relationships.* Table 3.4 defines the entities, with corresponding levels of knowledge from the system specification. The level of knowledge is an important feature for distinguishing between the entities, which are often confounded in the literature. You can return to Fig. 3.7 and Table 3.4 to keep an overall view of the framework as we describe each of the components.

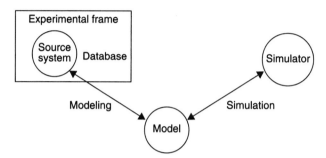

Fig. 3.7.   **Entities and Relationships in the Framework for Modeling and Simulation (M&S).** This figure shows how sources, models, and simulators are interdependent and are based on the experimental frame we establish for observing a system.

Table 3.4.   **Defining the Basic Entities in M&S.** This table defines the basic entities and indicates the level at which they reside in the specification hierarchy.

Basic Entity	Definition	Related System-Specification Levels
Source system	Real or artificial source of data	Known at level 0
Behavior database	Collection of gathered data	Observed at level 1
Experimental frame	Specifies the conditions under which the system is observed or experimented with	Constructed at levels 3 and 4
Model	Instructions for generating data	Constructed at levels 3 and 4
Simulator	Computational device for generating the model's behavior	Constructed at level 4

3.3.1   Source Systems

The *source system* (we'll omit the "source" qualifier, when the context is clear) is the real or virtual environment we want to model. It is viewed as a source of observable data, in the form of time-indexed trajectories of variables. The data we've gathered from observing or otherwise experimenting with a system is called the *system-behavior database*. (Chapter 9 describes the critical role of this database for modeling and simulation activities.) As shown in Table 3.4, this concept of system is a specification at level 0 (Klir's source system), and its database is a specification at level 1 (Klir's data system). This data is viewed or acquired through experimental frames of interest to the modeler.

Applications of M&S differ with regard to how much data is available to populate the system database. Data-rich environments give us abundant information from prior experiments or from convenient measurements. In contrast, data-poor environments offer meager amounts of historical data or low-quality data (which may not represent the system). In some cases, it's impossible to acquire better data (for example, of combat in real warfare); in others, it is expensive to do so (for example, topography and vegetation of a forest). In the latter case, modeling can direct us to acquire data that most strongly affects the final outcome of our current project.

3.3.2 Experimental Frames

An *experimental frame* is a specification of the input, output, and operating domain conditions under which we observe or experiment with the system. An experimental frame is the operational formulation of the objectives that motivate a modeling and simulation project. For example, out of the many variables that relate to a forest, the set {lightning, rain, wind, smoke} is a choice motivated by an interest in modeling the way lightning ignites a forest fire. A more refined experimental frame would add the moisture content of the vegetation and the amount of unburned material as variables. Thus, we can form many experimental frames for the same system (both source system and model) or apply the same experimental frame to many systems —depending on our objectives.

Two views of an experimental frame are equally valid. One views a frame as a definition of the type of data elements that will go into the database. The other views a frame as a system that interacts with the source system to obtain needed data under specified conditions. In this second view, the frame is implemented as a measurement system or observer, typically having three parts (as shown in Fig. 3.8): a *generator* that creates inputs to the system, an *acceptor* that monitors an experiment to make sure it meets the desired experimental conditions, and a *transducer* that observes and analyzes the system outputs. Section 3.5.4 on model validation will say more about these components.

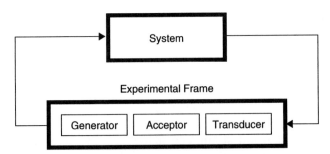

Fig. 3.8.   **Experimental Frame.** The three major parts of an experimental frame create inputs (generator), monitor the experimental conditions (acceptor), and analyze system outputs (transducer).

Objectives and Experimental Frames

Objectives for modeling relate to the role of the model in systems design, management, or control. The statement of objectives focuses model construction on particular issues. It's crucial to agree on this statement as early as possible in development, so project leaders can control the team's efforts. Once we know the objectives, we can develop suitable experimental frames. Remember, such frames translate the objectives into more precise experimental conditions for the source system or its models. A model is expected to be valid for the system in each frame. Having stated our objectives and established the right experimental frames, we should be able to answer questions at the appropriate level of abstraction.

Figure 3.9 shows how we can transform objectives into experimental frames. As will be discussed in Chaps. 4 and 5, modeling objectives typically concern system design. Here, we must measure how effectively a system meets our requirements in order to evaluate the design alternatives. To compute these *outcome measures*, the model must include and compute the values of suitable *output variables* when it's run. During execution, the transducer part of the experimental frame maps the observed trajectories of these output variables into outcome measures. Often, more than one layer of variables may intervene between output variables and outcome measures. In military simulations for example, *measures of performance*, such as the success of a missile in hitting its target, are output variables that typically judge how well parts of a system are operating. Such measures factor into outcome measures, often called *measures of effectiveness*, which assess how well the overall system goals are being achieved. An example might be how many battles are actually won by a particular combination of weapons, platforms, and people [Pinker 1994]. The implication is that components must perform well and be coordinated to achieve the goals of highly effective systems.

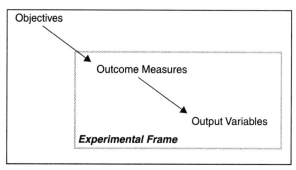

Fig. 3.9. **Transforming Objectives to Experimental Frames.** We must first decide on outcome measures that represent the modeling objectives and then define appropriate output variables. In a simulation run, the transducer component of the experimental frame will observe the trajectories of the output variables and compute the outcome measures from these observations.

Throughout this book, we'll apply modeling and simulation (M&S) techniques to forest-fire management, which includes fighting fires when they break out and trying to prevent them from breaking out in the first place, or at least minimizing the damage when they do. Modeling these two objectives leads to different experimental frames.

In the first frame, real-time interdiction (on-the-spot fire fighting) requires accurate predictions of where the fire will spread within hours. These predictions are used to allocate resources, so they'll be most effective. The great danger to people demands highly reliable, short-term predictions. A typical question would be: is it safe to put a team of fire fighters on a particular ridge within reach of the current fire front for the next several hours? Data from satellites may improve the model's accuracy by updating its state so it corresponds better with the real fire.

The experimental frame for interdiction calls for a model whose initial state includes all known prevailing fuel, wind, and topographic conditions. The output we want is a detailed map of fire spread after, say, five hours within the region of interest.

On the other hand, fire prevention or damage control isn't interested in accurate, short-term prediction of spread. Instead, it emphasizes answering "what-if" questions for planning. For example, land-use planners might ask what should be the width of a fire break (area cleared of trees) around a residential area bordering a forest so there is less than 0.1% chance of houses catching fire. Here, the model must be able to work with a larger area of the landscape and rank alternatives without necessarily producing highly accurate fire-spread behavior.

The experimental frame for prevention requires wider scope and lower resolution (see Abstraction for Model Construction in Sec. 3.5.1). It represents the landscape in a way that allows us to input a range of expected lightning-strike, wind, rain, and temperature regimes. The model may then use different states corresponding to alternatives for prevention or damage control, such as different fire-break regions. The output for a particular run might be as simple as a binary variable indicating whether or not the residential area was engulfed by fire. The output summarized over all runs might be a rank-ordering of alternatives according to their effectiveness in keeping fire from spreading to the residential area (e.g., the percent of experiments in which flames didn't engulf the residential area).

3.3.3 Models

In its most general guise, a *model* is a system specification at any of the levels defined in Table 3.3. However, in traditional M&S, the system specification is usually at levels 3 and 4, corresponding to Klir's generative and structure levels. Thus, **a simulation model is a set of instructions, rules, equations, or constraints for generating I/O behavior.** In other words, we write a model with a state-transition mechanism (level 3) to accept input trajectories and generate output trajectories depending on its initial state setting. Such models become part of more complex models which couple them to form a specification at level 4, as in Fig. 3.6. This coupling is very important for reusing models as components in larger models as shown in Sec. 3.5.6.

The word "model" can take on many meanings. It often refers to any physical, mathematical, or logical representation of a system, entity, phenomenon, or process. In contrast, our concept of "model" is much more restrictive: it is a system specification, usually at level 3 or 4. Defining "model" in terms of system specifications is advantageous because it has a sound mathematical foundation and definite semantics that everyone can clearly understand. Although it doesn't capture every dictionary meaning, it does cover the concepts most useful to M&S.

3.3.4   Simulators

As a set of instructions, a model needs an agent, or simulator, that can obey the instructions and generate behavior. A *simulator* is any computation system (such as a single processor, a processor network, or more abstractly, an algorithm) that can run a model to generate its behavior. It may be special-purpose or general-purpose, depending on the range of models it can execute (see Sec. 3.5.2), and can be built in hardware, software, or both. In addition, it can run in—or much faster or slower than—real time. Two key issues for designing and building a simulator are its ability to operate correctly on its own and with other simulators.

3.3.5   Relationships

The entities—system, experimental frame, model, simulator—take on real importance only when properly related to each other. For example, we build a model of a particular system for some objective—only some models, and not others, are suitable. Thus, certain relationships must hold for M&S to be successful. Two of the most important are *validity* and *simulator correctness* (see Table 3.5).

Table 3.5.   Basic Relationships Among M&S Entities. This table summarizes the basic relationships among framework entities and their corresponding level of system specification.

Basic Relations	Definition	Related Level of System Specification

Validity
 	
  Replicative
  Predictive
  Structural
	Concerned with how well model-generated behavior agrees with the system's observed behavior	
		
		Comparison is at level 1
		Comparison is at level 2
		Comparison is at level 3,4

Simulator correctness	Concerned with ensuring that the simulator correctly carries out the model instructions	Basic comparison is at level 2; involves homomorphism at levels 3 or 4

Model Validity

The basic modeling relation, *validity*, refers to the relation between a model, a system, and an experimental frame. Validity is often thought of as the degree to which a model faithfully represents a system. But it's more practical to match the model only to the system behavior required by the simulation study's objectives. In our formulation, validity tells us how closely the model matches the system in our experimental frame. The most basic concept, *replicative validity*, is affirmed if, for all the *experiments* possible within the experimental frame, the observed behaviors of the model and system agree within acceptable tolerance. In other words, replicative validity means we can match the data observed from the real system with that from the model—so the system and model agree at the I/O relation (level 1) of the system-specification hierarchy.

Predictive and structural validity are stronger forms. In *predictive validity* we require replicative validity plus the ability to predict future or unobserved system behavior. We must be able to set the model's state so it corresponds to the system's and correctly predict the system's outputs given specified inputs. Thus, predictive validity requires agreement at the next level of the system hierarchy—I/O function, level 2. Finally, *structural validity* requires agreement at level 3 (state transition) or higher (coupled component): the model must replicate the system data and mimic how the system does its transitions (step-by-step, component-by-component).

Often, the term accuracy replaces validity. Another term, fidelity, is often used to combine validity and detail (see Sec. 3.5.1). Thus, a high-fidelity model may be highly detailed and valid (in some understood experimental frame). The assumption seems to be that a lot of detail automatically ensures high fidelity and validity. In fact, a very detailed model may be very much in error, simply because some of the highly resolved components work differently from their system counterparts. I'll come back to correlating validity and level of detail when we discuss model abstraction in Sec. 3.5.1.

Simulator correctness

Simulator correctness relates a simulator to a model. A simulator *correctly simulates* a model if it faithfully generates the model's output trajectory given its initial state and its input trajectory. Thus, simulator correctness requires agreement at the I/O function, level 2. In practice, simulators execute not just one model but a family of possible models, so we can use them for a range of applications. In such cases, we must establish that a simulator will correctly execute a particular class of models. Because the structures of the simulator and model are at hand, we may be able to prove correctness by showing that a homomorphism relation holds (see Table 3.6). A *homomorphism* is a correspondence between simulator and model states that is preserved under transitions and outputs. I'll discuss the homomorphism concept further in Sec. 3.5.3.

Table 3.6.   Other M&S Relationships. This table shows other relations among the entities that are especially important when dealing with a family of models.

Relationship	Definition
System 1 is homomorphic to System 2	System 1's internal structure mirrors System 2's
Experimental frame applies to a model	The model can enforce the conditions on experimentation that the frame requires
Model accommodates experimental frame	Frame applies to the model
Experimental Frame 1 is derivable from Experimental Frame 2	Any model that accommodates Experimental Frame 2 also accommodates Experimental Frame 1

Other Relationships

Relationships that order models and experimental frames are also important to understanding modeling and simulation. I've already mentioned homomorphism, which is a relation between two systems described at level 3 or higher. In addition, it's often critical to know whether applying a given experimental frame to a model makes sense. This relation is called *applicability*, and its converse is called *accommodation* (see Table 3.6).

Notice that, if a model in a particular experimental frame is to be valid, it must accommodate the frame. Assume we have a repository of models and experimental frames that have been built up over years of experience (Sec. 3.5.6). If so, we must be able to ask whether any of the experimental frames meet our current objectives and whether any models can accommodate this frame. Only those models stand any chance of validly answering our questions.

The *derivability relation* formulates the degree to which one experimental frame is more restrictive in its conditions than another. A more restrictive frame leaves less room for experimentation or observation than one it derives from. So, as Fig. 3.10 shows, we define the *scope frame* of the model to represent the most relaxed conditions under which it can be experimented with (clearly a characteristic of the model). Then a frame applies to a model if we can derive it from the model's scope frame. This means a repository of models need only answer derivability queries, as long as each model has an associated scope frame.

Figure 3.11 illustrates the interplay of these relationships. Derivability orders experimental frames. Frames get less restrictive as we move up the figure—lower frames can derive from higher frames. Similarly, homomorphism orders models. Models higher in the figure can represent reality better than lower ones. Applicability is a relationship between experimental frames and models. **Given an experimental frame, we want to find a model that accommodates it. We also usually want the lowest model of all that accommodate the frame.** In other words, we want the smallest model (typically measured by number of states) that matches our experimental objectives and is valid under the given conditions. Finding this model is not as straightforward as it may seem because we may try to

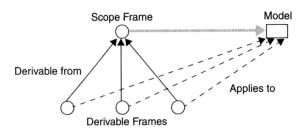

Fig. 3.10. **Experimental Frames Must Be Derivable and Applicable.** Experimental frames apply to a model if we can derive them from a model's scope frame.

include lots of detail in a model, producing one that is too complex to be practical. A key problem is reducing this detail while still obtaining a homomorphic image of the original model that can accommodate our frame of interest. I'll address it in Sec. 3.5.1.

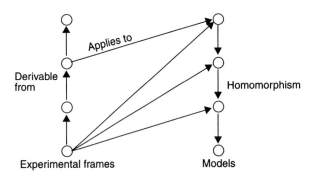

Fig. 3.11. **Interplay Among Important M&S Relations.** Derivability orders experimental frames; homomorphism orders models. To get the right model for an experimental frame, we find the lowest model from all that accommodate the frame.

3.4 Dimensions of Modeling and Simulation Activities

Once we understand basic entities and relationships for M&S, we must elaborate our conceptual framework to develop and deploy simulations. Figure 3.12 shows three major dimensions that can help us categorize M&S activities.

Formalisms are the basic symbolic and mathematical languages in which models are expressed:

- Differential equations for continuous systems
- Difference equations and state machines for discrete-time systems
- Event and process descriptions for discrete-event systems

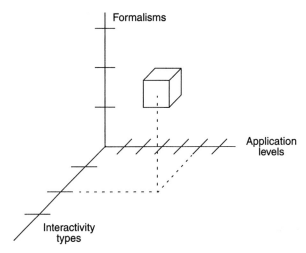

Fig. 3.12.   Dimensions of M&S Activities. M&S concepts and activities can be described by the way they're expressed (formalisms), the way their elements interact (interactivity types), and the contexts within which they apply (application levels).

Interactivity types are the ways in which humans, equipment, and simulators interact:

- Constructive—all action takes place within the computer
- Virtual—humans or equipment interact with the computer environment as if it were real
- Live—real entities, such as tanks, are part of the simulation exercise

These types aren't meant to be exclusive; they merely suggest the kinds of interaction that can take place.

Application levels are the technological, operational, and managerial contexts for application.

We'll highlight key concepts associated with each of these dimensions here. Chapter 5 will show how these dimensions help determine the nature of the M&S product to be developed.

3.4.1   Formalisms

Formalisms, or mathematical languages, enable us to conveniently describe models to the computer for simulation and other manipulation. They're a shorthand means of specifying a system.

Figure 3.13 differentiates the major formalisms in terms of a framework's basic entities (Fig. 3.7). Each formalism assumes certain background conditions that enable it to efficiently specify a system.

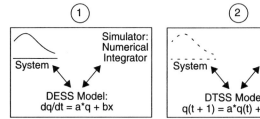 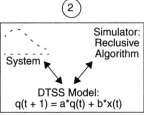 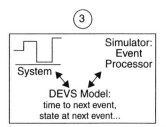

System Specification:

DESS: Differential-equation system specification
DTSS: Discrete-time system specification
DEVS: Discrete-event system specification

Fig. 3.13. **System Specification Formalisms.** This figure depicts the three basic ways to specify dynamic system models.

The *differential-equation system specification (DESS)* assumes that the time base is continuous and that the trajectories in the system's database are piecewise continuous functions of time. The models (system specifications) are expressed as differential equations that specify rates of change of state variables. The corresponding simulation concept is numerical integration.

The *discrete-time system specification (DTSS)* assumes the time base is discrete, so the trajectories in the system database are sequences anchored in time. The models are expressed as difference equations that specify how states transition from one step to the next. A forward-marching, time-stepping algorithm is the associated simulator.

The *discrete-event system specification (DEVS)* assumes the time base is continuous and the trajectories in the system's database are piecewise constant. In other words, the state variables remain constant for variable periods of time. The jump-like state changes are called events. The models specify how events are scheduled and what state transitions they cause. Associated simulators handle the processing of events as dictated by the models. For more detail, please refer to Zeigler (1976, 1984, 1991).

Often, valid representations of a system require us to use combinations of these formalisms. For example, combining continuous- and discrete-event formalisms allows us to represent physical elements with classic differential equations while representing decision making with formalisms that combine artificial intelligence and discrete-event dynamics. For more detail, please refer to Zeigler (1990, 1991), Fishwick (1994), and Elzas (1986, 1989).

3.4.2 Interactivity Types

One of the main dimensions of M&S for military applications is the nature of the participants in a simulation exercise. As Fig. 3.14 shows, the terms constructive, virtual, and live often describe the human, software, or hardware components in a simulation exercise, especially for training or system testing. Although the boundaries between these terms are vague, they provide a starting point for dealing with interactivity. *Live* participants are real systems, people, and physical environments. For example, in training exercises, people interact with real entities almost as if they are engaged in real warfare (except that the ammunition is harmless). *Virtual* simulators are intended to be highly realistic, as perceived by human, or even non-human, participants. For example, consider that Human-in-the-loop (HIL) simulations run with virtual simulators, whose multisensory responses make infantry students think they're in real combat. Similarly, in Hardware-in-the-loop (HWIL) simulation exercises, a virtual simulator accurately responds to hardware being tested, so the hardware undergoes the sorts of stresses it would encounter in operation. *Constructive* participants are simulators that employ models which aren't intended to support "virtual reality," such as those for analysis or design. However, we can also make them interact with live and virtual participants.

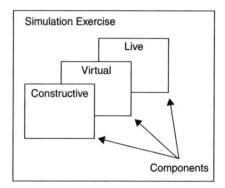

Fig. 3.14.   Potential Interactive Participants in a Simulation Exercise. A simulation exercise may include live, virtual, and constructive components, but not all are present in many kinds of applications. Distributed Interactive Simulation has made possible training exercises that bring together these components in realistic, yet simulated and safe, battle scenarios.

3.4.3   Application Levels

M&S may occur at various application levels, which in turn drive the objectives for development or training [Committee on Technology 1997]. Table 3.7 shows typical application levels in system analysis and design for military combat [Davis 1995a, b]. Also shown are the issues or questions typical of these levels. Corresponding levels of application arise in the commercial world. For example, industry might focus on

- Interaction between firms (competition, cooperation)
- The firm itself
- Individual departments
- Teams
- Individuals

Table 3.7.   Application Levels for M&S Systems. This table shows levels for applying M&S and how they relate to typical questions in military analysis and design.

Level	Description	Key Analytical Issues
War	Possibly global with multiple campaigns	Force structure and allocation
Theater	Single campaign	Force structure and allocation
Battle	Many-on-many	Force employment and operational concepts over large scope
Mission	Few-on-few	Force employment and operational concepts over small scope
Engagement	One-on-one encounters System configurations	Engineering and component performance; system design

3.5   Problems and Issues

The framework for M&S provides the entities and concepts we need to discuss the basic problems of real simulations. Our goal is to focus attention on the concerns associated with trying to develop M&S products. Here, we'll discuss

- Model Construction
- Simulator Construction
- Verification
- Validation
- Quality Assurance
- Repositories and Model Integration

In each case, I'll outline the key problems and current solution methods and technologies. I'll also briefly highlight costs, benefits, and tradeoffs for these solutions. The remaining chapters will address these concerns in much greater detail.

3.5.1   Model Construction

Model construction means developing models for simulators to execute. A disciplined approach to model construction based on concepts and formalisms presented earlier in this chapter is essential (see Chap. 8 and Zeigler [1976, 1984, 1991] for further detail). It's benefits include

- Better linkage to the applications context
- Greater control of M&S development
- Improved documenting and communicating of model assumptions
- Greater portability of models
- Better support of model abstraction through aggregation and other simplifying procedures in formalisms rather than in code
- Greater reuse of results from previous developments
- Longer life because models can survive technology changes

Although these benefits seem compelling, practitioners have been slow to adopt disciplined approaches because M&S development based on systems theory requires more training and more formal methods and documentation that don't contribute immediately to coding. Many M&S shops are unwilling or unable to incur these costs, but competition and the benefits of tools that make disciplined approaches affordable will eventually drive organizations to adopt them.

Abstraction for Model Construction

Abstraction is a method or algorithm applied to simplify a model while preserving its validity in an experimental frame. The time and money constraints on project budgets require working with models at various levels of abstraction. More detailed models are more difficult to develop and demand more computational resources from simulators and more time and money from the development team. The amount of detail in a model depends on its structure and, as Fig. 3.15 shows, we can characterize it as the product of the model's scope and resolution. *Scope* refers to how much of the real world it represents, and is typically measured by how many variables it employs. *Resolution* refers to the precision, or granularity, of the model's variables. As the number and required precision of these variables increase, the amount of detail (and the demand for computational and developmental resources) grows.

Fixed resources (time, space, people, etc.) may require us to limit a model's complexity by trading off scope against resolution. We may represent only a few components very precisely to focus on certain aspects of a system or try to capture all components at relatively low resolution to obtain a comprehensive view of the system. Abstraction is a general process that includes simplifying approaches such as those outlined in Table 3.8.

Most abstraction methods work on the structure of a base model to achieve a valid lumped model. Thus, they work at levels 3 and 4 of the specification hierarchy, which support state and component descriptions. Homomorphism then gives us criteria for valid simplification. If a model isn't perfectly homomorphic, it may contain errors. But the abstraction may still be valid if the errors don't exceed the tolerance for goodness of fit (see Sec. 3.5.3). In some cases, we may be able to build only relatively abstract models because we lack data or are uncertain about it. When this occurs, there may be no "official" base model to simplify, but a

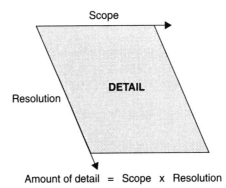

Amount of detail = Scope x Resolution

Fig. 3.15.   **Model Complexity.** A model's complexity, which depends on its detail, drives up the need for computational and developmental resources. Detail is the product of the model's *scope* (breadth in the figure) and its *resolution* (depth in the figure).

Table 3.8.   **Ways of Simplifying a Model.** Various methods can be used to reduce the resources required to simulate a model. The challenge is to simplify while preserving a model's validity with respect to its counterpart real system in desired experimental frames.

Simplifying Method	Brief Description
Transforming formalisms	Mapping from one formalism to another more efficient one; e.g., mapping differential-equation models into discrete-event models
Aggregating	Combining groups of entities into a single entity that represents their combined behavior when interacting with other groups
Omitting	Leaving out entities, variables, or interactions
Replacing deterministic or stochastic descriptions • Deterministic → Stochastic • Stochastic → Deterministic	Replacing algorithms having many factors with samples from easy-to-compute distributions Replacing a distribution of sampled values with a constant value—the mean of the distribution

conceptual base model may constrain the structure of the models we build. In addition, there are advantages to postulating more detailed models than the current data justifies (as discussed under Predictive and Structural Validation in Sec. 3.5.4).

Besides reducing complexity, abstract models also help us

- Keep costs low while analyzing rapidly
- Do quick "first cuts" (innovating, exploring, etc.)
- Improve comprehension (seeing the forest rather than the trees)
- Support decisions

- Apply modeling to different situations
- Constrain the calibration of more detailed models

On the other hand, more detailed models

- Help us understand phenomena
- Achieve realism (e.g., in virtual simulation exercises)
- Calibrate or inform less detailed models

Abstraction may also

- Decrease fidelity (validity)
- Require more effort to produce valid simplifications
- Demand more model management to cross validate and synchronize models at different levels of abstraction

Modelers must trade off the advantages of model abstraction against the costs. For example, as abstract models decrease runtime and memory requirements, they may also reduce predictive accuracy. Ideally, as illustrated in Fig. 3.11, we try to construct the least complex model that still accommodates our experimental frames of interest with the accuracy an application requires.

3.5.2 Simulator Construction

Choosing how to construct a simulator for a model depends on what kinds of behavior we want the simulator to generate (requirements) and how well we can configure real computing devices to do it (implementation). Under requirements, we'll discuss

- Special versus general purposes
- Real-time versus non real-time execution
- Dispersed versus localized sites
- Computational demands
- Ability to operate with other systems

Under implementation, we'll consider whether to use serial or parallel/distributed platforms and whether to simulate with hardware or software.

Requirements for Simulators

The first issue is how diverse a family of models the simulator should support. The more general purpose a simulator is, the more types of models it can execute. As simulators move from specific to general purposes, they can

1. Be dedicated to a particular model or small class of similar models.
2. Accept all (practical) models from a wide class, such as an application domain (e.g., communication systems).

3. Be restricted to models expressed in a modeling formalism, such as models using continuous differential equations.

4. Accept models having components from several formalism classes, such as continuous and discrete-event.

Good general-purpose simulators are independent of, and easily portable to, various platforms. Clearly, the more portable software is, the more flexible its application.

The next issue relates to how close to real time we want the simulator to operate. *Real-time simulation* requires that the simulated model's time base corresponds identically to the actual time on a wall clock. Such simulations must provide the correct logical results of computation in a timely fashion. Real-time simulation is desirable in virtual and live simulations, for which participants shouldn't be able to distinguish the responses of real and simulated entities in all aspects including their timing. But real-time execution doesn't apply to constructive simulations. Indeed, in many analytical, design, or control studies, we want the simulator to grind out model behavior much faster than it occurs in reality. This contrasts with some scientific applications, in which the simulator might operate much more slowly than the underlying reality—simulating the behavior of a sub-atomic model, for example.

M&S resources (humans, hardware, software) are usually dispersed among many physical locations because not everybody can be expert in, or own, everything. Sharing such resources, if possible, may greatly benefit the project. *Advanced Distributed Simulation* is the name given to linking geographically dispersed simulators for a common simulation objective and also presenting a common view of the results. Information and data must pass among sites using predefined protocols. The sites can be anywhere in the world, in any number, and operate with different hardware and software.

Simulations with a large scope and high resolution demand a lot of computation to speed processing, manage databases, and provide graphics. In addition, geographically dispersed simulations require very high communication bandwidths for sharing of information and data. These demands have been moving the preferred platforms from single to multiple processors.

The ability to operate with other simulators is important because a simulator often must work with existing systems, such as databases. This requirement may greatly constrain the simulator's design. Unfortunately, many designs haven't considered the need to interact with add-ons. Newer standards and open architectures may alleviate many of these problems. The Defense Modeling and Simulation Office has accepted the *High Level Architecture (HLA)* standard to make models and simulators operate better together in distributed simulations. This standard is driving simulations for the Department of Defense.

Possible Implementations for Simulators

Simulator architectures can use single or multiple processors. A single *serial processor* (conventional workstation) is most convenient to carry out simulations of models requiring fewer computations and to develop the code for more complex ones. But even the most powerful single processors may not be able to do all the computations for complex simulations.

Multiprocessor architectures connect serial processors to coordinate how they handle and share data. Having many processors enables us to distribute simulation execution among them so they work concurrently. In a *heterogeneous architecture*, the processors differ in type. For example, they may be of different manufacture, have different internal architectures, or be specialized for different types of processing, such as graphics or data handling.

Multiprocessor architectures come in three flavors:

1. *Networks of workstations:* Local Area Networks (LANs) connecting workstations with Ethernet or other network protocols commonly support distributed computing. These networks for loosely coupled clusters of workstations have long latencies and low communication bandwidths compared to tightly coupled supercomputers (below). But they'll become a better alternative as hardware and software improve because they can evolve from single workstations while keeping costs low.

2. *High-performance supercomputers:* Supercomputers are state-of-the-art, high-performance, parallel machines. Supercomputers usually compute quickly; have fast, large main and secondary memories; and use parallel structures and software extensively. They cost a lot for setup and maintenance.

3. *Distributed heterogeneous environments:* As mentioned, advanced distributed simulation requires networking of geographically dispersed simulators. Because these simulators can use workstations, network clusters, or supercomputers, the resulting multiprocessor architecture is (geographically) distributed and heterogeneous.

Multiprocessor simulators give us higher performance through

- Increased speed—if done right, adding processors can proportionately reduce the time required for a simulation run
- Bigger models—by using the combined memory capacity of all processors
- Greater capacity for handling data using specialized nodes
- Better graphics using specialized nodes

Parallel/distributed architectures carry certain costs:

- Development environments aren't as user-friendly as for conventional workstations
- Simulator correctness is more difficult to achieve

- More dollars are needed for technology
- Vendors are more likely to go in and out of business

Choosing hardware or software depends on whether we're focusing on speed or flexibility. Software is more flexible than hardware, but hardware designed for an application can run faster than equivalent software. Thus, the larger our intended class of models, the more likely we'll use software to simulate them. The more speed we require, the more likely we'll use hardware. Yet, because hardware and software are ever improving, we should always mix them in the best possible way to handle the class of models we're considering at the time. Chapter 10 discusses simulator construction in more detail.

3.5.3   Verification

Verification is the attempt to make sure a simulator correctly executes a model. Or, if the simulator can execute a class of models, we want to guarantee that it can execute any one correctly. Homomorphism, as Fig. 3.16 shows, is the basic concept for establishing correctness. When a model should go through a state sequence (such as a,b,c,d), the simulator should go through a corresponding state sequence (say A,B,C,D). Typically, a simulator has a lot of apparatus, represented in its states, to accommodate the class of models rather than a single one. Thus, we don't assume a simulator's states and a model's states are identical—only that there is a predefined correspondence between them, illustrated by the dotted connecting lines in the figure. For this correspondence to be homomorphic, whenever the model specifies a transition between states (e.g. from state b to state c), the simulator must transition between the corresponding states (B and C). Typically, the simulator takes a number of computation steps (microstate transitions) to transition from B to C. If a simulator designer can show that such a homomorphism holds, the simulator will properly reproduce any state trajectory in the model.

As already indicated, we can also use homomorphisms to determine whether two models share the same behavior. I'll return to this point in a moment when I discuss model validation.

Verification takes two general approaches: formal proofs of correctness and extensive testing. Formal proofs employ mathematical and logical formalisms underpinning the systems-specification concepts to rigorously establish a homomorphism. Unfortunately, such proofs are difficult or impossible to carry out for large, complex systems. They may also be prone to error because humans ultimately have to understand the symbols and manipulate them. On the positive side, more automated tools are becoming available to relieve some of this burden.

In the absence of once-and-for-all proofs, we must test extensively to make sure test cases cover all conditions that could arise in simulator operation. Time and other resources limit the amount of testing we can do. But even if we don't use formal proofs, homomorphisms come in handy because they help us lay out the combinations of inputs and states for thorough, yet efficient, testing.

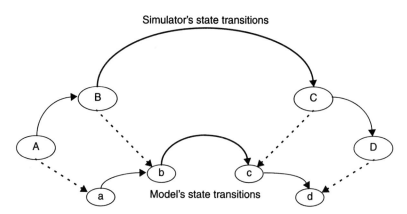

Fig. 3.16.   **Homomorphism Concept.** Homomorphism requires a simulator's state transitions (A, B, C, D) to mirror a model's state transitions (a, b, c, d).

3.5.4   Validation

Validation is the process of testing a model for validity (as defined in Sec. 3.3.5). Figure 3.17 shows that the experimental frame is critical to validating a model. The frame generates input trajectories to the source system and the model under test. The corresponding output trajectories of the model and system feed back into the frame. Validity—whether replicative, predictive, or structural (Table 3.5)—requires these trajectories to agree within a desired tolerance.

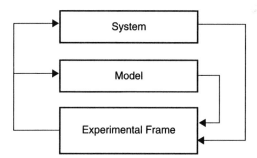

Fig. 3.17.   **Validation within the Experimental Frame.** For a model to be valid, the trajectories an experimental frame feeds into the model and source system must *equal* the output trajectories which the model and system feed back into the frame.

How Elements of the Experimental Frame Affect Validation

Recall from Fig. 3.8 that the frame has three parts: generator, acceptor, and transducer. Table 3.9 presents some generator, acceptor and transducer behaviors typically specified for continuous, discrete-time, and discrete-event systems. Remember that a *generator* stimulates the system with input trajectories. In continuous systems such trajectories take the form of aperiodic functions, such as steps and ramps, or of periodic functions, such as sine waves or square waves. In discrete-event systems, events (such as jobs for processing) may arrive periodically or stochastically (randomly). In the latter case, we need to specify the probability distribution (e.g., uniform or exponential) of the arrival times. The type of processing required (workload) is also part of the generator specification.

Table 3.9. Typical Parts of an Experimental Frame. This table shows what components of the experimental frame typically do in the context of system-specification formalisms. Continuous and discrete-time formalisms often have similar experimental frames.

System Formalism	Typical Generator	Typical Acceptor	Typical Transducer
DESS (Continuous Systems) and DTSS (Discrete Time)	Aperiodic: step, ramp Periodic: sine wave, square wave	Transient Steady state	Rise time Final value
DEVS (Discrete Event)	Periodic arrivals Stochastic arrivals Workload characteristics	Small queues Large queues	Throughput Turnaround time, use of resources Failure rate, blocking rate

We often distinguish between the transient and steady-state characteristics of a system's behavior. The *acceptor* is the slot in the experimental frame where we can specify conditions limiting the observation of behavior, such as steady state versus transient. For example, if transient behavior is specified, as in Fig. 3.18, the frame would extract only the parts of the trajectories shown within the corresponding box.

The *transducer* processes the output trajectories. This post-processing may range from none at all (trajectories directly observed) to very coarse summaries, which extract only certain features of interest. For example, for transient conditions, we may be interested in the rise-time (time to adjust to change). On the other hand, for steady-state conditions, the final value may be of interest. In discrete-event systems, we may want to know the turnaround times required to process jobs or the throughput (rate of job completion). Or, we may want to know about the use of resources and occurrence of special events such as failure or blocking.

Usually, the many numbers produced are summarized into statistical quantities such as the average, maximum, or minimum. Data may also be grouped into classes called quantiles with associated breakpoints. For example, the *median* separates the data into two classes of equal sizes.

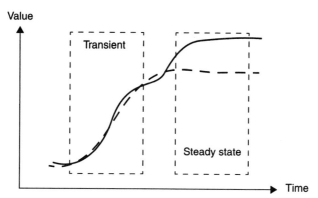

Fig. 3.18.   **Transient Versus Steady-State Conditions.** An acceptor limits the observation of system behavior. For example, it might focus on different parts of a model trajectory having to do with transient (changing) or steady-state (unchanging) behavior, respectively.

I've mentioned only some of the many features we can formulate in experimental frames. Also, features associated with continuous systems or discrete-event systems often may apply to both.

Replicative Validity: Quantitative Comparison

Recall that validation requires us to compare the behavior of models and source systems under the experimental conditions specified in the frame: the input trajectories created by the generator, the control conditions checked by the acceptor, and the output summaries done by the transducer. Figure 3.19 shows how we compare summaries of the transducer outputs from a model and a system. In the conventional approach, comparison requires a *metric* and a tolerance. The metric provides a numerical basis for measuring goodness-of-fit. Typical metrics are the familiar distance measure in Euclidean space (square root of the sum of squared differences), largest absolute difference, and "city block distance" (sum of absolute differences).

The *tolerance* is a positive number that determines when the fit is good enough. When the fit is outside of tolerance, the model isn't valid within that frame because its trajectory isn't close enough to that of the system. On the other hand, if the fit is within tolerance, the model's validity is confirmed. But it's not established because we still need to compare an infinite number of possible trajectories.

If we assume the processes are stochastic, we must also consider how well the observed samples represent the underlying spaces. Then, we use statistical techniques to judge significance in terms of the number of samples observed and the variance in their values. But be careful with statistical techniques. They often assume the data sources have particular stochastic characteristics, such as normal distributions. These are themselves models and may not be valid!

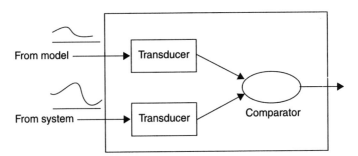

Fig. 3.19.   Comparing Trajectories. We must compare the transducer outputs of a model and a system to determine replicative validity.

In doing such comparisons, we may easily forget that choosing what to observe can have as much, or more, bearing on validity judgments as the metrics and statistical procedures. For an example, let's return to Fig. 3.18. The two curves shown are very close (under most reasonable metrics) in the transient behavior but far apart in the steady-state region. Thus, a model might be valid in a frame which focused on transient behavior but not in a frame that looked at steady-state behavior. Or, a model might agree well in the steady-state region but not in the transition to it. Indeed, typically, it's easier to accurately model a real system's steady-state behavior than to represent its transient behavior. Unfortunately, many processes are never in a steady state!

Replicative Validity: Qualitative Comparison

Although quantitative comparison provides an objective basis for validation, it may miss more qualitative discrepancies or agreements that humans can detect if provided the right perspectives by methods such as visualization and animation. *Visualization* attempts to map complex numerical data into graphics that humans can more readily understand.

Animation presents a model's simulated state behavior in a "movie" that corresponds to the underlying physical reality. For example, a simulation of manufacturing might show parts moving from one workstation to the next on conveyor belts. *Virtual reality* goes further by making us feel we're **in** the simulation. Validation methods can profit from such presentations because humans can recognize events or configurations that seem to conflict with everyday experience. Neural nets or other artificial recognizers of patterns can also "learn" to do this detection.

Predictive and Structural Validation

As noted earlier, predictive and structural validity correspond to higher levels of knowledge in the specification hierarchy. For *predictive validity*, we must be able to infer the proper initial state of a model from past system observations. For *structural validity*, we must also be able to infer that the model's structure is the only one consistent with the observed data. Certain conditions justify such inferences [Zeigler 1976; Zeigler 1984], but we need more work and better computerized tools to help determine whether the justifying conditions hold in real applications. Usually, the issue is ignored at the cost of overconfidence in a model's predictive ability. Roughly put, if we can't show a model is structurally valid, any other model structure consistent with the observed data could represent the real system. Thus, further experiments may prove our model poorly captures the system's structure.

Improving the predictive and structural validity of our models requires us to determine appropriate values for their unknown parameters. This is a difficult problem, commonly solved by calibration—adjusting parameter values so the model best fits the observed system data. Unfortunately, just because we can make a model fit past data doesn't guarantee that it will fit future data. In other words, parameters that replicate don't necessarily predict.

We can become more confident in the uniqueness of predictions by assessing their sensitivity to perturbations. One approach that sometimes works is to try to locate all, or at least many, of the parameter assignments that result in a good fit. We can then assess how much model predictions vary over the range of these parameter assignments.

Another possibility is to assess the sensitivity of model predictions to variations in the assumptions made in its construction—for example, by adding in greater detail. In this case, we're investigating how predictions vary over a family of more detailed models that each map to the original model.

Local or Global Validation across Models

Relations between high- and low-detail models lead us to distinguish between *local validation*, which applies to the model in focus, and *global validation*, which applies between models at different levels of resolution. Global cross-validation more strongly constrains model calibration because the parameter values must be consistent with related ones in other models. For example, if we've validated a high-detail model and are very confident in its parameter values, we should check the parameter values in a low-detail model for consistency. In other situations, low-resolution models can constrain the parameters of models with a higher resolution [Zeigler 1984; Davis 1993].

3.5.5 Quality Assurance in Developing M&S Software

M&S involves many development activities for hardware and software, all of which require some process to ensure their quality. Clearly, verification and validation are part of quality assurance. Verification seeks to ensure the simulator's correctness, whereas validation seeks to ensure the model's accuracy. However, software may be developed for other activities such as defining the experimental frame, checking the model's structure (e.g., agreement of message types in output-to-input connections), and giving the model access to the source system's database (see Oren [1984] for more details). All such activities should follow one of the disciplined methods for developing software, such as waterfall, incremental, or spiral. These methods include quality-assurance procedures to make sure requirements are satisfied.

Chapter 11 describes verification, validation, and accreditation (VV&A) as parts of quality assurance for M&S. It uses the term conceptual model to include the M&S product's data, assumptions, algorithms, and intended uses. Table 3.10 shows how these terms correspond to parts of the framework.

Table 3.10. **How Framework Concepts Correspond to Terms in Conceptual Models.** This table shows how quality-assurance terms in VV&A literature correspond to the framework in this chapter.

This Part of a Conceptual Model	Refers to this Part of the Framework	And Means
Data	Source-system data	
Assumptions	Model	Constraints placed on an assumed, more refined model to derive this one through abstraction
Algorithms	Model	The instructions, rules, or constraints that define the model
Intended uses	Experimental frame	Modeling objectives captured by intended experiments within an experimental frame

3.5.6   Repositories and Model Integration[*]

Up to now, succeeding generations of simulations have routinely and wastefully restarted from scratch. But recent advances in object-oriented design and programming now support repositories of reusable objects that may eliminate this waste. Figure 3.20 shows the objects and activities that can make this happen. Models reside in a database called a *model base*. If we need to construct a new model for given objectives, we can retrieve models from the model base to serve as parts of the new model. Then, we appropriately couple these components to *synthesize* the new model. When validated, verified, or otherwise properly accredited, the new model is stored in the model base so we can reuse it (see Zeigler [1990] for more details).

Unfortunately, this scenario is easier to describe than to bring into common practice. Some of the issues include:

- How can a modeler discover models that meet a project's objectives?

---

* The material in this section is reprinted with permission from Technology for the United States Navy and Marine Corps, 2000–2035: Becoming a 21st-Century Force. Vol. 9: Modeling and Simulation. Copyright 1997 by the National Academy of Sciences. Courtesy of the National Academy Press, Washington, D.C.

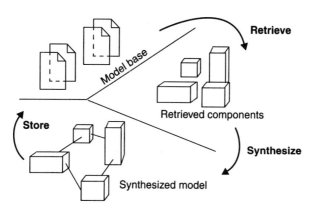

Fig. 3.20.　　**Concept of a Model-Base Repository.** This figure shows how we can retrieve models from a repository, synthesize them for a new project, and store the synthesized model for reuse.

- How can models be designed so they can serve their current purposes and anticipate future needs?

- How can models be partitioned so their parts can remain in the model base and recouple later in different configurations? (This problem is worse for dispersed geographic simulations, which can distribute models over computers in many locations.)

None of these problems is easily solved, but the modeling and simulation framework provides some starting points:

- Index models by the experimental frames that capture project objectives (as in Fig. 3.11)—if we can find frames in the model base that are closely related to the frame we need for the new project, potentially relevant models will automatically be available.

- Construct models from hierarchical modules—to be reusable, models must be self-contained, with input/output ports as we have assumed in the system specification. A model synthesized from them must also be modular, so we can use it as part of still larger models.

- Design building blocks for a family of applications—rather than focus entirely on the models needed for a particular project, designers "regress" to a lower layer and search for good "primitives" they can synthesize into models that span the application domain.

- Provide coupling templates—going hand-in-hand with the building blocks are standardized ways to couple them. To use these templates, designers must give the building blocks input and output ports that match.

Costs, Benefits, and Trade-offs

Reusability has obvious benefits: millions of dollars potentially saved through faster project completions and more reliable results using fewer programming hours. But repository-based M&S demands careful design and maintenance, as suggested above. Because no individual project requires these extra activities, they're likely to be considered burdensome overhead. Given limited time and resources, managers may be much more interested in completing their current projects than in laying the basis for completing future ones. But a long-term perspective trades off the extra overhead for the first few projects to reap the tremendous potential benefits. For advanced distributed simulations, several organizations may develop the models, so reusability may be more difficult. But the increased payoff should make this added effort worthwhile.

Integrating Legacy Models

We can couple models developed from systems concepts into larger models because they have identified input and output ports. But we may also want to reuse models developed before object-oriented concepts took hold. Unfortunately, interoperating or integrating these "legacy" models creates formidable hurdles because

- They may have been developed for disparate objectives, often not clearly stated
- Their assumptions are often undocumented and may be inconsistent
- They may have varying levels of detail (resolution and scope)
- They may use disparate coded forms (languages, operating systems, etc.)
- Worse still, the experimental frame and simulation features may be entangled with the model itself

In contrast to the forward design of reusable, object-oriented repositories, retrofitting legacy models may cost more than it's worth. Sometimes, we can "wrap" a legacy model within an object interface so it can properly interact with other objects, but the problems mentioned above may make wrapping ineffective. Integration may work if we use the outputs of models only to initialize the states or parameters of other models, rather than feeding these outputs to the other models' input ports. In this case, the legacy models aren't components of a larger coupled model, so they don't have to meet the stronger requirements for consistent time advance and input/output compatibility.

3.6   Roles and Responsibilities

To get comfortable with M&S activities, shown in Table 3.11, you should know who carries them out and how these people relate to one another. The ultimate customer, who will pay for the desired system, has needs based on the current system's limitations, failures, drawbacks, etc. This is the starting point for system

Table 3.11.   Roles and Responsibilities in an M&S Project. This table outlines some of the roles and responsibilities in an M&S project created to support systems design.

This Person or Group	Takes This Input	And Turns It into an Output that	To Be Used by
Ultimate customer		Identifies needs	System designer
System designer	Ultimate customer's needs	Provides the current source system and the control, management, or redesign problem	Developer of the M&S project
Project developer	Current source system and problem	Forms the experimental frames and desired alternatives that will be evaluated in these frames—what's required of the M&S product	Project planner Model designer Simulator designer
Project planner	M&S product requirements (experimental frames and "to-be" alternatives)	Estimates the resources required to develop the M&S product and forms a plan for using these resources	Project manager
Project manager	Estimated resources and project plan	Establishes the resources and carries out the project planner's plan	Model designer Implementor Tester Analyst
Model designer	Requirements for the M&S product	Translates the requirements into specifications for the experimental frames and family of models in the M&S product	Integrator Validation tester
Simulator designer	M&S product requirements	Translates the requirements into specifications for the simulator in the M&S product	Integrator Verification tester
Integrator	Specifications for the M&S product	Integrates M&S product specifications coming from designers of the model and simulator	Implementor
Implementor	Integrated specifications for the M&S product	Implements the specifications as executable software or hardware, or both	Validation tester Verification tester Analyst
Validation tester	Specifications for the M&S product	Develops and applies tests for model validity within the experimental frames with respect to the source system	Feedback upstream
Verification tester	Specifications for the M&S product	Develops and applies tests for simulator correctness with respect to the specified family of models	Feedback upstream
Analyst	Executable M&S product	Draws conclusions concerning the cost and benefits of the desired alternatives	Reporter
Reporter	Conclusions of the M&S study	Translates conclusions into understandable recommendations	System designer Ultimate customer

design. The system-design team characterizes the current system and forms the general alternatives for controlling, managing, and redesigning it to meet the customer's needs. The output of the system-design team is the starting point for developing the M&S project, which goes through several phases before it returns to the system-design team with some recommendations. These phases include planning, executing, and conveying the results of the project to the design team and the customer. The project itself involves the coordinated efforts of various types of people.

As detailed in Table 3.11, the activities of these individuals or teams apply to the entities and relationships discussed in this chapter. They don't necessarily represent any particular project nor exhaust the range of possibilities. In practice, the same person may assume various roles. For example, the project leader may also be the "reporter" who interfaces with the customer or even the "chief analyst" or "model designer."

References

Committee on Technology for Future Naval Forces, N.R.C. 1997. *Technology for the United States Navy and Marine Corps, 2000–2035: Becoming a 21st-Century Force. Volume 9: Modeling and Simulation.* Washington, D.C.: National Academy Press.

Davis, P.K. and R. Hillestad. 1993. "Families of Models that Cross Levels of Resolution: Issues for Design, Calibration, and Management." *1993 Winter Simulation Conference.* IEEE Press.

Davis, P.K. 1995a. "Distributed Interactive Simulation in the Evolution of DOD Warfare Modeling and Simulation." *Proceedings of the IEEE*, 83 (8), pp. 1138–1155.

Davis, P.K. 1995b. "An Introduction to Variable-Resolution Modeling and Cross Resolution Model Connection." *Naval Logistics Journal.* 42 (2), pp. 151–182.

Elzas, M.S., B.P. Zeigler, and T.I. Oren. 1986. *Modelling and Simulation Methodology in the Artificial Intelligence Era.* Amsterdam: North Holland Publishing Company.

Elzas, M.S., B.P. Zeigler, and T.I. Oren. 1989. *Modelling and Simulation Methodology: Knowledge Systems Paradigms.* Amsterdam: North Holland Publishing Company.

Fishwick, P.A. 1994. *Simulation Model Design and Execution: Building Digital Worlds.* Englewood Cliffs, NJ: Prentice-Hall.

Hillestad, R., L. Moore, and B. Bennett. 1995. *Modeling for Campaign Analysis: Lessons for the Next Generation of Models.* Santa Monica, CA: RAND, DRR-1088-AF.

Klir, George J. 1991. *Facets of Systems Science.* New York, NY: Plenum Press.

Oren, T.I., B.P. Zeigler, and M.S. Elzas.1984. *Simulation and Model based Methodologies: An Integrative View.* New York, NY: Springer Verlag Publishing Company.

Pinker, A., A.H. Samuel, and R. Batche. 1995. "On Measures of Effectiveness." *Phalanx.* Vol. 28, No. 4.

Zeigler, B.P., G.J. Klir, M.S. Elzas and T.I. Oren. 1972. *Methodology in Systems Modelling and Simulation*. Amsterdam: North Holland Publishing Company.

Zeigler, B.P. 1976. *Theory of Modelling and Simulation*. New York, NY: Wiley Publishing Company. Reissued by R.E. Krieger Publishing Company, Malabar, FL: 1984. Revision for second edition to be published by Academic Press, 1998.

Zeigler, B.P. 1984. *Multifaceted Modelling and Discrete Event Simulation*. Orlando, FL: Academic Press.

Zeigler, B.P. 1990. *Object-Oriented Simulation with Hierarchical, Modular Models: Intelligent Agents and Endomorphic Systems*. Orlando, FL: Academic Press.

Zeigler, B.P. 1991. "Object-Oriented Modelling and Discrete Event Simulation." *Advances in Computers*. Ed: M. Yovitz. 1991. Boston: Academic Press. Vol. 33, pp. 68–114.

CHAPTER 4

Defining the Need for Models and Simulations

William Tucker, *The Boeing Company*

The focus of this chapter is on the "real-world" application of modeling and simulation. The purpose is to help program managers establish the need for M&S and to determine the kinds they need. Projects can successfully apply a number of development processes, and a rich variety of modeling and simulation tools are available to support them. Chapter 3 thoroughly covers the basic differences among model types. This chapter describes the potential program lifecycles within which these models can be applied, as well as how a specific project might determine the objectives, requirements, and alternatives for applying M&S. I'll also broadly identify the types of models that apply to elements of a program and provide examples of their application to lifecycle phases. Following chapters will describe the tasks needed to apply these models.

Of course, M&S never provides a "silver bullet." Modeling and simulation can predict and analyze system performance and other attributes, but it consumes a project's resources. Thus, we should use M&S only to the extent that it helps us evaluate and reduce a program's risks and cost, and we must recognize that models and simulations are products with their own lifecycles. They must be planned and paid for as described throughout this book. Reusing models and data reduces the cost of M&S, and therefore increases its utility, so I strongly emphasize reuse in this chapter. Models commonly used within a lifecycle phase are typically incompatible with each other and are almost always incompatible with models used in any preceding or following phase. Models are an investment in system knowledge, so we must plan carefully to retain this knowledge as the program proceeds.

It's critically important that all simulations and data be sufficiently verified, validated, and accredited (or certified) to fit their intended purpose. But this topic is an aspect of a simulation's lifecycle, rather than of the system, so it's discussed in Chap. 11. In this chapter, I'll discuss:

1. Common system lifecycles
2. How M&S types support each phase of a typical lifecycle
3. Practical implications of using models in these applications, including:
   - Types of tools available
   - Reapplying models and data later in the system lifecycle (downstreaming)
   - Reusing models and data developed for other applications

4.1   Lifecycle Model

To understand how to apply modeling and simulation to system development, we must first understand how systems are developed through a system lifecycle—events that describe how systems come to be created, used, maintained, and eventually disposed of. Lifecycle models simply pattern how organizations work while developing, using, and disposing of a system. Models often represent intent more than an organization's present reality. In this section, I'll briefly introduce the more popular lifecycle models and show how they affect modeling and simulation.

The United States' Department of Defense (DOD) has successfully used a common lifecycle to procure complex systems for many years. Figure 4.1 shows the phases of this lifecycle, the milestones that demonstrate compliance with the requirements of each phase, and the metrics we must evaluate to support each milestone. It also briefly suggests the types of models we can use to evaluate those key metrics. This lifecycle has been designed to dramatically decrease the risk and cost of committing a complex defense system to development, to production, to deployment, and finally to retirement.

As shown in the figure, M&S tools help analyze and support each lifecycle phase. A major milestone at the end of each phase demonstrates that the previous phase is complete and that the costs and risks of the following phase are well understood. Because this process flows from one complete step to the next, it's often called a *waterfall*. A waterfall process is an excellent one to use whenever the system requirements are well understood and stable, and the program doesn't require any unusual technology. In general waterfall development (of which the DOD's model is a special case), the need for a system is first carefully expressed in the language of its user (the ultimate customer). When this task is complete, the system enters a phase called requirements specification, during which the user's need statement is analyzed and re-expressed in detail. These specifications are further refined and broken down until they describe the technical and design requirements for nearly all parts of the system and plans for the implementation

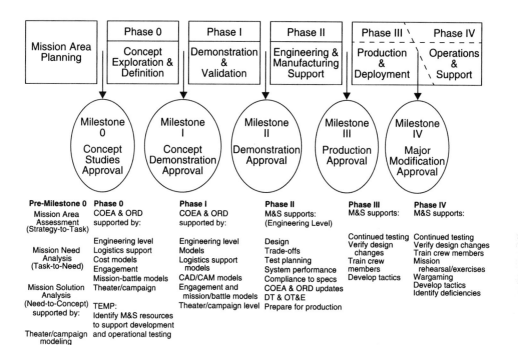

Fig. 4.1.   M&S Support to the Lifecycle of DOD System. M&S supports every phase of the basic lifecycle for DOD systems.

and verification of the requirements. This detailed description of system requirements is called a preliminary design. The next phase, detailed design, captures these detailed requirements in design documents that define the system's components and their relationships for manufacture. In succeeding phases, the system's components are manufactured, then integrated into an operational system, tested as a system, and delivered to the customer. Although the waterfall's main feature is its one-way flow from one phase to the next, the steps can overlap while preserving the lifecycle's essential character. For example, with only modest risk, detailed design can often start before preliminary design is complete. Despite this slight potential overlap, the lifecycle has an intuitive tidiness in that we finish a task and fully define the system at each level of detail before moving on to the next task.

The waterfall lifecycle model discussed here is appropriate whenever there is, or will shortly be, agreement on the need a system will meet. Under these circumstances, the system development may proceed uniformly through the phases, with little need to revisit previous phases. But the need often isn't clear, especially for software-intensive systems. In this case, using the waterfall lifecycle may be difficult, and a few of these difficulties are worth noting here.

First, customers for very large systems are under increasing cost pressures. In the past, developers emphasized function over cost. For example, at the height of the Cold War, national security needs for strategic weapons overwhelmed cost and environmental concerns. But this is no longer the case, so today we must procure such systems under tight cost constraints. However, because the cost of such large projects is notoriously hard to estimate beforehand, the waterfall model doesn't work well.

Second, computing technologies and needs often don't match—one typically outstrips the other. When technology outpaces concepts, systems may become obsolete on or before delivery. If the system's needs are too ambitious, as recent history has shown, systems fail because critical technology isn't ready. The waterfall model doesn't readily address these problems.

Finally, development periods for large systems are so long that the customer's needs may change by the time the system is delivered. In fact, when systems take decades to develop, changes in needs and requirements are likely. Yet, the waterfall model assumes we can freeze agreement at the end of each phase before proceeding to the next.

4.1.1   Spiral Development

Many organizations have responded to the problems of the waterfall lifecycle by modeling their system development as a spiral. Figure 4.2 illustrates this model. In this approach, developers cycle through a series of mini-waterfalls focusing on some parts of the system while temporarily neglecting others. They defer examining system components that are most subject to changing requirements, changing technology, or other risks until later in the development process. This approach seeks to build robust depth into subsystems while sacrificing breadth. Unfortunately, this lifecycle model can easily lose cohesion in the system as a whole.

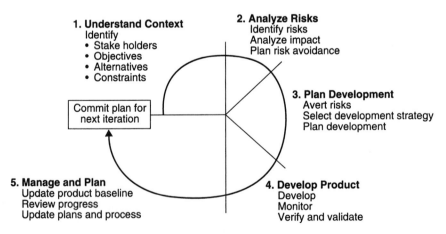

Fig. 4.2.   **Illustration of Spiral Development.** Spiral development reduces risk in developing systems with poorly understood requirements.

A spiral model for the development lifecycle creates new challenges for modeling and simulation. By representing the non-developed systems, modeling and simulation should overcome the loss of cohesion. But because these simulations can be based only weakly on real requirements, developers of "real" components may distrust them.

4.1.2   Evolutionary Development

One response to spiral development's shortcoming is an evolutionary approach (sometimes called incremental development). Figure 4.3 illustrates this lifecycle model. Like spiral development, the evolutionary approach uses several passes through traditional development processes (a series of mini-waterfalls). Unlike the spiral approach, however, the evolutionary approach continues to seek breadth across the entire system before depth in a few subsystems. Each incremental release provides an operational system with increased capability. This approach can be especially effective for environments in which the entire design team follows the product through its lifecycle. Difficulties with it include determining the number of increments required and planning the abilities and features of each increment.

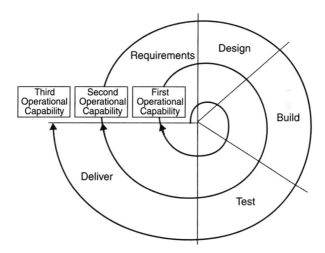

Fig. 4.3.   **Illustration of Evolutionary Development.** Evolutionary development provides a sequence of prototypes with increasing capability.

Concurrent engineering is a special case of evolutionary development. Using this technique, we process successive increments of the spiral, with requirements development, design, and test occurring simultaneously. It keeps each group challenged with new issues, but makes managing configurations more complex and amplifies communication problems.

Evolutionary development presents a special opportunity for modeling and simulation because developers often include with each increment a simulation of what the next increment will provide. Simulations allow them to evaluate the risks and requirements for the next increment. Evolutionary development also encourages reusable models because successive increments can use them again.

4.1.3   Rapid Prototyping

Rapid prototyping speeds up development by leveraging a project's special circumstances against standard operating procedures to reduce development time. Rapid prototyping goes beyond doing normal development tasks faster and more efficiently. Although all organizations try to streamline development, standard operating procedures often add unnecessary steps. In these cases, organizations may try rapid prototyping, only to discover they reduced development time because they identified and eliminated inefficiencies in the normal process. This discovery, if used effectively, can speed up all future developments within the organization (even when they don't use rapid prototyping).

For specific development efforts, true rapid prototyping can speed up the process even more by leaving out additional steps when circumstances make them unnecessary (as shown in Fig. 4.4). We can see the potential for rapid prototyping more clearly if we consider an organization whose normal development process is at or near top efficiency. In this case, rapid prototyping can benefit the organization if it relaxes some of the project's requirements—the well-known "ilities": functionality, maintainability, availability, reliability, supportability, and so forth. For example, for a proof-of-concept system, reliability may not be particularly important, so the requirements related to reliability can be less strict. If we understand the relationship between particular steps of our development lifecycle and certain groups of requirements, rapid prototyping can produce substantial benefits.

Modeling and simulation offers help to organizations who want to use rapid prototyping. First, the relatively new field of process simulation offers a way for organizations to study the likely impact of proposed changes in their development processes and to determine if the gain will justify the change. Second, organizations may use simulation to avoid neglecting relaxed requirements. For example, a project with relaxed supportability requirements may use simulation to estimate logistics for various system configurations, without the expense of a formal logistical analysis. The danger, of course, is that such simulations can at best only approximate the real situation—a caveat that all too often is lost in the pressure to complete the project.

4.1.4   Virtual Prototyping

The recent emergence of virtual environments has suggested a lifecycle model that centers on simulation. All other lifecycle models pick out and build a single system design. Alternative systems may be explored in the concept phase, but only

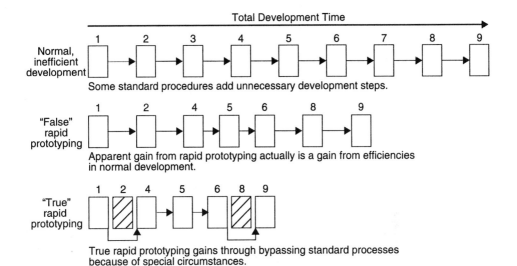

Fig. 4.4. **Illustration of Rapid Prototyping.** True rapid prototyping takes advantage of reduced requirements and skips development steps to complete projects faster.

notionally and at a high level of abstraction. Virtual prototyping overcomes this limitation by creating several alternative system configurations within a virtual environment. In exercising this environment, the customer and system developer can virtually "fly off" competing ideas. This approach is particularly helpful when constructing alternative prototypes is prohibitively expensive. Figure 4.5 shows how to apply virtual prototyping to the concept phase. Of course, virtual prototypes can also be used to evaluate system risks during later development phases.

Modeling and simulation is an enabling technology for virtual prototyping, which is becoming more common for large-scale, complex systems. As an example, consider how the U.S. Department of Defense (DOD) selects an aircraft design. In the competition to build the Advanced Tactical Fighter (F-22), the competing development organizations were funded to develop functional prototypes of the system. The DOD directly compared these prototypes against the range of system requirements. But just a few years later, the DOD relied heavily on simulation to compare competing designs for the Joint Strike Fighter. Chapter 7 investigates virtual prototyping in more detail.

4.1.5 Dual-Lifecycle Models

The marketplace for large-scale, complex systems consists of providers of systems to end users and providers of system components. Those providing components, which range from individual integrated circuits to entire subsystems, make a living by supporting many different systems. Because they understand their product line, they're able to manufacture components so economically that

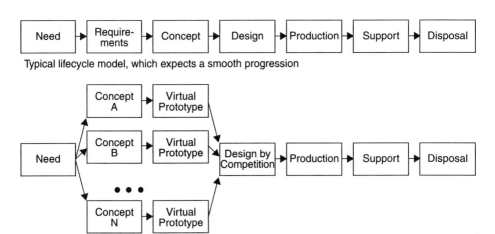

Typical lifecycle model, which expects a smooth progression

Virtual-prototyping model, which leverages competition and experimentation

Fig. 4.5. **Illustration of Virtual Prototyping.** Virtual prototypes allow users quickly to explore alternate approaches. Prototyping different concepts may occur in parallel, as shown here, or in series.

system integrators find it easier to buy them than to construct them. Because organizations typically build a series of related products that capitalize on their experience, system integrators could find similar economies of scale within their own product lines.

The Defense Advanced Research Projects Agency (DARPA) has explored this approach through the Software Technology for Adaptable, Reliable Systems (STARS) project. STARS aimed at advancing the management, quality, adaptability, and reliability of the DOD's software-intensive systems. Over the years, the STARS project gradually focused on enabling the DOD to shift to megaprogramming, or development of a software product line. Megaprogramming focuses on developing software using a two-lifecycle process (see Fig. 4.6). The first lifecycle (domain engineering) develops reusable assets, such as coarse- or fine-grained elements of a system or process, for use across a product line. The second lifecycle (application engineering) applies these reusable elements to the development of a particular product within the product line. This approach should lead to a lot of leveraged reuse—adapting software components to multiple products.

A two-lifecycle model raises challenges for system design because a product line must be useful over a series of systems. Research has shown that, if we can construct components to be useful for three systems, the additional cost of domain engineering will be recouped and the total costs will decline. Thus, organizations can focus their investment on domains that hold this promise. Simulation itself is such a domain, and this lifecycle holds much promise for reusing M&S, as discussed in Sec. 4.3.

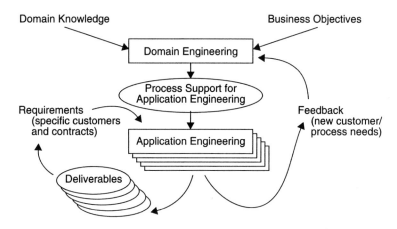

Fig. 4.6.   **Illustration of the Two-Lifecycle Model.** The two-lifecycle model develops reusable components separately from new products that apply those components.

4.2   Applying M&S to Lifecycle Phases

We've discussed several lifecycles: waterfall, spiral development, evolutionary development, rapid prototyping, and virtual prototyping. Each can apply within the DOD lifecycle, has strengths and weaknesses, and is supported by M&S in a slightly different way. I'll introduce a generic lifecycle, depicted as a "V," which provides a useful, but not prescriptive, framework for a discussion of M&S applications. By expanding and simplifying the standard "waterfall" lifecycle and bending it into a "V," I'm able to show design refinement down the left side, with system assembly and testing up the right. (See Fig. 4.7).

The "V" shape emphasizes that each step down the design side corresponds to an evaluation step on the manufacturing, assembly, and test side. For example, the conceptual design meets a user's top-level need. As the figure shows, the actual system can't be tested against these requirements until all other steps are complete (meaning the system has been built and delivered and much money has been spent). If a simulation represents the conceptual system well enough, users can evaluate it against their needs. Thus, a simulation can lower risk by changing our basic question from, "Is this proposed system likely to meet the user's needs?" to "Does this simulation accurately reflect the probable capabilities of the proposed system?"—before we've spent much money. By reducing risk, we power the drive toward ever better M&S. The top of the "V" deals with more abstract risks: "are we building the right system?" The lower levels of the "V" address more concrete risks: "are we building the system (or subsystem, or component) right?" Each program phase has characteristic risks, which M&S can help us evaluate and decrease.

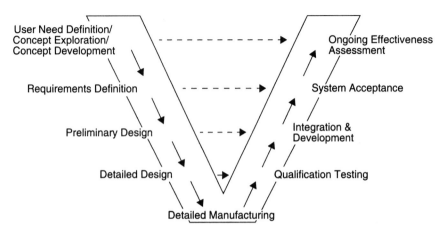

Fig. 4.7.   **System Lifecycle Model.** The simplified "V" model shows the relationship between design and verification steps as system development flows down the left and up the right side.

This lifecycle is like the waterfall because it assumes each phase is essentially complete before the next phase begins. The process starts with a clearly articulated set of user needs and a conceptual approach to meet those needs—often considered the system-acquisition phase of system development. The next step is to translate those needs and concepts from the users' domain into the developer's domain and express them as requirements. This step begins the development phase of the project, and the supporting simulations are often called engineering simulations. In the same way that the user's need corresponds to the effectiveness assessment, developing system requirements corresponds to acceptance testing. Applying modeling and simulation at this point might be best described as comparing the specification's requirements section (carrying out a design concept) to its test section (describing how those requirements will be tested). In the same way, simulation of preliminary design, which breaks the system into its subsystems and assemblies, predicts the test results for these partially integrated elements. Finally, simulating detailed design predicts how components will perform and meet their detailed tests.

The final steps of system development (climbing up the right side of the "V") are the integration and testing activities that verify how well the system meets requirements. Modeling and simulation support tests by providing test harnesses and other synthetic representations of the environment. Perhaps the most powerful application of M&S to test is using test results to validate simulations and then using these simulations with high confidence to predict a system's performance in untestable domains.

In other words, models and simulations can answer specific questions about proposed systems by evaluating metrics that relate to identified risk areas. In the following paragraphs, I describe how certain types of models support analysis in each phase of a system's lifecycle while specifying the risks appropriate to each phase. For example, weight is important to design risk for many types of systems (aircraft, submarines, missiles, satellites, automobiles, etc.). Therefore, models that can represent weight and answer questions about weight and balance are used throughout the development of these types of systems.

4.2.1   Defining User Needs, Exploring and Developing Concepts

Because this phase is dedicated to developing and evaluating high-level system concepts, very little of the system design is known. The user's high-level needs or functional requirements characterize the system. Modeling covers every variable relevant to the domain of interest. For an aircraft, lift and drag are computed as a function of general airfoil shapes, then combined with other gross factors of the conceptual design to compute range and capacity. Analytical models can support selection of the best design concepts to satisfy a set of requirements. These models are often in the form of spreadsheets containing heuristic-based algorithms. The algorithms generate curves showing tradeoffs between performance characteristics and design features. Or they may optimize design features against these curves. Large spreadsheet programs may even represent complex analytical models, such as the Quantified Judgment Model. Spreadsheets are very powerful tools that allow non-programmers to manipulate and visualize very complex interactions. But despite their popularity, these models are difficult to maintain and reuse, particularly when they become very large. Also, the data in this type of model is often difficult to extract for use later in the lifecycle—it doesn't move downstream well. Other kinds of models are available that reuse data better. For example, the U.S. Air Force at Wright Patterson AFB has developed the DATCOM program to predict aerodynamic performance data for conceptual systems.

Whatever modeling technique analysts use, they try to accurately predict a conceptual system's ability to meet a set of high-level requirements. Typical performance metrics include measures of outcome—did the system affect the outcome of a situation in some positive way?—or measures of effectiveness—was this system concept more effective than others in some measurable way? This comparison shows the significance of the "V" shape. We evaluate the projected system's abilities against the users' needs, just as we'll eventually test the completed system against these same needs. A weapon system is evaluated using a series of models that consider

- Measures of performance—predicted performance of each system
- Measures of effectiveness—in engagements of one against one, or of many against many
- Measures of outcome—the system's effect on the combat's overall outcome

Non-combat systems are evaluated in terms of their ability to integrate into and improve their intended application. For both, we want to bring the humans who will use the system into the evaluation as early as possible to determine if the conceptual design works. These applications best leverage M&S because they accurately measure very abstract metrics and help reduce the worst possible program risk: building the wrong system!

Because cost is important in nearly every project, we often use models to try to predict a system's cost relative to previous systems, based on a set of parameters. Typical parameters used in cost-prediction models include weight, software size, and maturity of technology. COCOMO is a popular software model that uses historical data on software projects to predict the cost and schedule of any new software project. To arrive at its prediction, COCOMO uses the new project's key parameters, such as size, complexity, and the development environment.

4.2.2   Defining Requirements

This program phase starts with functional requirements and system concepts and ends by establishing firm performance requirements and allocating them to the major subsystems. Here, we extend the system's architecture to describe the operations and interactions of these subsystems. The objective is to precisely meet the need at the lowest practical cost and risk. In this phase, M&S can help identify the requirements needed to carry out the customer's concept, measure the relative cost and value of specific requirements, monitor requirements stability, or refine high-level functional requirements into detailed performance requirements.

One approach to defining requirements is to synthesize a system as a set of high-level functions and then determine if it will work, based on broad criteria such as cost, schedule, or existing technology. The models for this type of activity usually depend on key system characteristics such as payload, range, or known characteristics from past systems. They focus on meaningfully identifying and capturing the system requirements and then applying the requirements to the model to generate results. Once we determine the requirements will work, we can analyze certain requirements to determine their relative cost or value. If a requirement is driving up system cost, we can run other requirements against the model and see what happens. We can also apply tolerances for requirements using fuzzy logic. For example, an upper weight limit of 150 pounds may be established for a certain system because the customer wanted two soldiers to be able to lift it. But if we allow the system to weigh 155 pounds, another material or a different design might meet the functional requirements at a much lower cost, and the lifting requirement might not be needed.

Various modeling tools can help us trace requirements and compute compliance of systems and subsystems as requirements become more defined— even for this type of fuzzy tradeoff. Once we've established the requirements model, we can use it for the rest of the development effort to trace requirements to the design, investigate and refine lower-level requirements for components, and investigate design alternatives. The modeling that first occurs in this phase simply represents the integrated subsystems to show that, when working together, they still meet all requirements. All of the modeling activity previously described continues for the system and its subsystems.

4.2.3   Preliminary Design

The preliminary design phase provides an opportunity to apply traditional engineering M&S to predict a system's performance and compliance. Here, M&S can compare the validity of competing subsystem-design concepts, refine the system architecture, develop and test interfaces among system components, and refine and allocate detailed design requirements. The goal is to develop a robust system design that meets the customer's requirements and can be produced safely within the constraints on cost and schedule. During preliminary design, project teams design the overall system, allocate requirements to hardware and software, develop and define a detailed system architecture, define interfaces between system components, and refine detailed requirements. M&S can help teams develop all these products.

During this phase we model the system in much more detail, paying attention to components and interactions that make a system work well. We can model how system components communicate with commercial software programs that represent data flow or specific interfaces such as an Ethernet or 1553 bus. Using typical products such as Computer-Aided Design/Computer-Aided Manufacture (CAD/CAM), or other types of languages and tools, we can develop software to represent these components as simple black boxes that deal with inputs and outputs or as complex mechanical systems. During this process design, these modeling tools support trade studies to select hardware components, materials, and processes.

As the design progresses, the design model can be periodically reassessed against the requirements model to effectively score how well the design meets the requirements. This information can help us determine where the system may be over- or under-designed and correct it. As the design matures, we can enhance the requirements model to include detailed requirements for components, which helps us with the detailed design.

4.2.4   Detailed Design

Modeling and simulation in detailed design is a natural extension of our efforts during preliminary design. In this phase, we can use M&S to validate the final design against detailed performance requirements, plan for testing, define test equipment and procedures, identify and commit resources to production, and do integration planning. The key question here is, "Will the components meet their specified requirements?" The design is documented in a vast amount of detail (sufficient for production), and M&S predicts the performance of given designs. For example, if we model a detailed design for an electrical system using computer-aided design, M&S can very accurately predict the design's performance.

During detailed design, our models are more accurate because the system data is becoming very real and exacting. As the system design matures, the models can be updated and enhanced to include more faithful representations of the components and sub-components, which allow for a more complete test of the design against the system requirements. This result can be especially attractive when many of the components are commercial off-the-shelf (COTS) products or developed by subcontractors. By this phase of the program, the purchased COTS products are usually available for use, enabling the developer to test the actual products for compatibility with the interface and performance against the rest of the system. For subcontracted development efforts, the subcontractor's detailed design model can be used to assess system-level compatibility and progress as thoroughly as in traditional critical design reviews.

Once the detailed design is essentially complete, we can also use the models to start testing and evaluation. For example, they can help us develop and dry run system test procedures, plan tests by analyzing how long and complex they must be, and define the suite of test tools. In many cases, validated models of the system can support stand-alone testing of system components, thus adding to their value.

Designs that can meet the customer's requirements must also be producible. Some may be too expensive to produce due to selection of materials, manufacturing steps, special tooling, or incompatibility with the company's existing production assets. Once we've tested the detailed design and baselined it against the requirements, we can use the models to conduct producibility studies that will

- Ensure the end design is producible
- Suggest the best way to build the design
- Help us select cost-effective materials
- Define special tooling requirements
- Support production planning

Once these studies are complete, the company can baseline the final design and start building the system. It will then use significant resources to produce and deliver the product. A proven, producible design will sharply reduce costs and help avoid production risks later in the development lifecycle. To get value from producibility models, the design and manufacturing organizations must cooperate because producibility trades can strongly affect design choices. These models must accurately reflect agreement about the relative cost of competing designs and manufacturing approaches.

4.2.5   Detailed Manufacturing

Once the design is complete—actually well before—the factory must be set up to produce the system. Factory planners have long used modeling and simulation to choose equipment and processes that will produce the best products at a reasonable cost. For example, they may use classic queuing theory for factory planning: how many machines do I need and how should I arrange them to best support this production process? Or, models can help them visualize more advanced, complex applications: how can I most efficiently machine this shape or how can I lay out this complex flat pattern to efficiently use the material? Key metrics to predict for manufacturing include rates for cost, schedule and rejection, scrap, and waste. At this point, we've hit the bottom of the "V" and the lowest level of abstraction in the lifecycle. Our knowledge about the system's construction is complete and based on solid, measurable, concrete facts, but our knowledge of the system's performance derives entirely from the models' predictions. The metrics taken in these and following phases are compared with the predictions made by the models earlier in the project. Comparisons increase our confidence in these predictions and improve the accuracy of our models based on current experience. Design for manufacturing, complete with M&S support, is actually part of the design process.

4.2.6   Qualification Testing

Here, as we leave engineering development and enter testing, we see the first practical tests of the system's ability to meet the developed requirements. Individual components are tested against their requirements. Simulations provide realistic stimuli to support this effort. Models may simulate the interfaces of interacting components that aren't yet available. We use the test results to calibrate system-level simulations that we're still running to predict the completed system's performance. Simulation can predict the performance of the system and subsystems far more cheaply and safely than actual tests, but the simulations themselves must be designed and tested with great care to ensure valid results. We must run at least enough physical tests to validate the models.

4.2.7   System Integration and Development

The system-integration phase gathers the tested components into assemblies, subsystems, and finally, an integrated whole. Tests at each stage of integration measure how well the system's elements meet requirements. Increasingly complex environmental models stimulate the system-element test so we can verify the full array of performance requirements. Examples of highly complex test environments include the huge chambers used to test extreme weather at Eglin Air Force Base, Florida, and the anechoic test chambers that are part of the Radio Frequency Simulation System at Redstone Arsenal, Alabama. Increasingly sophisticated software models of system performance are becoming available to allow system testers to use such complex facilities more efficiently.

M&S can make system integration and developmental testing much more efficient. We can use it to better control system integration, to evaluate and validate the system's performance step-by-step, and to immerse and test the entire system in a synthetic environment.

Controlled system integration is key to successful development, and a robust system model that follows the system architecture helps make it possible. As system components are produced, we can add them to the simulation in place of their respective models. This "hardware-in-the-loop" approach allows us to test each component against the entire simulated system. Or we can combine other developed, COTS, or subcontracted system components and simulations. This method of integration supports acceptance and integration of system components that subcontractors have developed, especially if the simulation is available to the subcontractors for their own testing. This flexible method allows for all or part of the system to be simulated or "real" at any time. It also allows us to effectively troubleshoot test and integration problems.

We can also use this process earlier in the development cycle to evaluate the system and validate performance. Once a system component is designed and a model reflecting that design is available, it can be integrated into the system baseline to determine how well the component matches system requirements and interfaces to other components in the system. We can also make sure the component works as designed with other system components. This type of developmental testing is used to identify inconsistencies that have crept into the design during manufacture and assembly. It saves money and time during this critical stage of the project. At the same time, the results of developmental testing further validate the model set.

Once all system components are tested and integrated, we must test the whole system to ensure that it works as the user intended. In some cases, we may be able to immerse the entire developed system into a synthetic environment and test it. This final task of the integration effort is sometimes the last step before formal system testing. It allows the developer to "dry-run" the test procedures on the final configuration to make sure it's ready for testing.

4.2.8   System Acceptance

This phase evaluates the integrated system's ability to meet the total performance requirements established at the requirements phase—the performance specification. Because the system is complete, simulation now provides synthetic environments (both natural and tactical) for system evaluation, supports training of test system operators and maintainers, develops and validates test scenarios, and supports test planning. Test-planning support is needed to plan and test instrumentation and even to schedule scarce test resources. The characteristic questions for this phase are the same as for the requirements phase, plus those concerning the pragmatic problems of supporting and operating the physical system. The test data from acceptance testing finally validates the models, so we can downstream them into operational support. At the end of this phase the system is complete, and we've found that its designed performance abilities meet requirements. In other words, the "system has been built right." The remaining question is, "was the right system built?"

4.2.9   Deployment—Assessing Ongoing Effectiveness

Most fielded systems undergo periodic modifications and upgrades. Because each modification has its own product-development cycle, I won't treat them here. The models for fielded systems support operator and maintainer training, plus planning for operations, routine support, and system effectiveness. The system is continually measured against an ever-changing environment to make sure it meets the user's current needs. The questions asked of the system models here are the same as those asked during the conceptual phase: "Is this the right system?" "Is this the right way to use this system?" Of course the models are maintained with data from the field. For example, the supportability models are updated to account for using spares. Effectiveness and survivability models are updated to reflect any deployment experience available. And performance models, particularly those used in training systems, are maintained to predict actual performance.

4.2.10   Summary

Table 4.1 identifies the types of models I've discussed for the lifecycle phases. This list isn't exhaustive but it does indicate a rich variety of potential modeling support.

In summary, we've explored the application of M&S to system lifecycles at a very high level. In any of these lifecycles, a system becomes progressively more defined as it passes through each phase. Similarly, supporting models must grow in level of detail. When the system definition is very abstract, the models used to articulate and evaluate that design are abstract. When the system is more fully defined, the supporting models must be highly refined, detailed, and precise. Figure 4.8 illustrates this concept.

4.3   Reuse in Simulation and Modeling

Repeatable production of quality systems begins with process. Obviously, one way to get high-quality systems is to use the best components, and the easiest way to do that is to reuse components from earlier successful applications. This reuse allows us to retain the investment we've made in the information content of simulations. The Virginia Center of Excellence has proposed a reuse maturity model, similar to the various Capability Maturity Models from the Software Engineering Institute. The reuse maturity model specifies five levels of maturity to organizational reuse: (a) ad hoc, (b) opportunistic, (c) integrated, (d) leveraged, and (e) anticipated. Ad hoc reuse is the incidental reuse that occurs mainly through the natural movement of people between organizations. Opportunistic reuse occurs when organizations take advantage of reuse opportunities discovered in the natural process of design. Integrated reuse occurs when organizations begin to seek out such opportunities as a required part of their development process. Leveraged reuse assumes that a given product is actually a member of a product family, the members of which have something in common. Organizations attempting leveraged reuse construct domains that take in the product family. Anticipatory reuse means constructing domains that anticipate needs.

Modeling and simulation can benefit from advanced techniques for reuse in two ways. Models and simulations developed for one project can be useful on the next similar project—an example of leveraged reuse. But the changing nature of system development also means opportunities for reusing simulation models within a project. For example, simulations constructed during concept exploration, if correctly designed, could be reused in requirements analysis, design, and so forth. Obviously, for such downstream reuse to work, initial models will need to be built to more exacting specifications—an example of anticipatory reuse. Figure 4.9 shows the chances for reuse in the system lifecycle.

Table 4.1.   Summary of Model Types for Phases of System Development.

Model Type	Questions Answered	Data Used	Applicable Phase
Lifecycle cost	How much will it cost?	System parameters	All
Performance	How well will it perform?	Models based on mathematics or physics plus system descriptions	All
Human systems integration	How will it work with people?	Data on the system and human behavior	Preliminary and detailed design
Technology	Is the technology appropriate and available in time?	Data on the technology and the system	Conceptual
Supportability	How much will it cost to support the system?	System parameters	All
Producibility	How difficult is the system to build?	System parameters	Conceptual to detail design
Effectiveness	How effective is the system when operationally employed?	System parameters	All
Requirements	Do the requirements consistently and completely cover the situation?	Descriptions of requirements and the system	Requirements
Architecture	Can this architecture meet the requirements?	Architecture description	Conceptual
Interface	Do these interfaces fully support all required functions?	Descriptions of functions and interfaces	Requirements and preliminary design
Training simulations	How does the trainee perform?	Details of system and performance	Operational
Computer aided design	What are the design details and how do they interact?	Design details	Preliminary and detailed design
Simulations to validate designs	Does this design meet its specifications?	Data from computer-assisted design	Detailed design
Hardware in the loop	Does this subsystem meet its performance requirements?	Description of subsystem interfaces	Integration
Synthetic environment	N/A	N/A	N/A

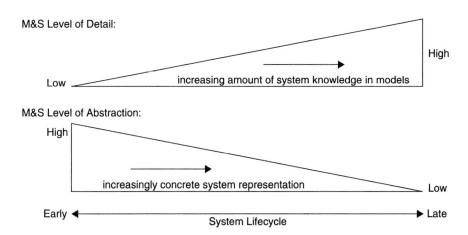

Fig. 4.8.   Relationship of Model Levels of Abstraction and Detail to the System Lifecycle. Later phases of a system's lifecycle require more detailed models.

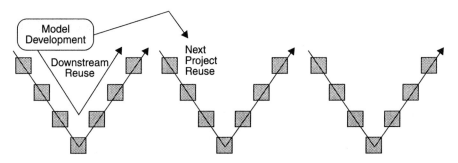

Fig. 4.9.   Reuse of Modeling and Simulation in the System Lifecycle. Reuse of modeling and simulation helps retain system knowledge.

The F-22 fighter program has successfully applied process and planning to reuse of M&S. In this program all potential users of certain aircraft-system models agreed on the requirements for those simulations very early in the program and cooperated in their development. Examples were engineering and training systems' cooperative requirements for propulsion or aerodynamics. This early agreement guaranteed that the model could be downstreamed from one user to the next in the same program, thus increasing its credibility and reducing cost. But even this significant accomplishment involved essentially similar models, all involving real-time simulation of selected aircraft systems. Of course broad-based reuse requires more than program process and planning. One of the lifecycles discussed earlier was the two-lifecycle model. This model contains the concept of a product line, a series of products built on the same architecture with some common design elements. Because these product lines may span many military and commercial projects, no individual program manager can influence all of the model users in their project to enable 100% downstreaming of data or 100% reuse between projects.

Chapter 1 emphasizes the need to manage investments in M&S. Effective reuse promises to deliver the benefits of M&S at an affordable price. The Defense Modeling and Simulation Office is sponsoring efforts to increase interoperability in defense simulation. These efforts are widely supported by industry and academia. They focus on a basic approach to data reuse, called the common model of the mission space, and a major initiative called the High Level Architecture (HLA). This initiative strives to build on previous successes in simulator operability—Distributed Interactive Simulation (DIS) and Aggregate Level Simulation Protocol (ALSP)—combining their strengths into new common and reusable architectures and processes. The goal is to produce consensus-based industry standards to improve operability among simulators and reuse of models and data. The overarching aim is to increase the credibility and utility of M&S while reducing the cost. Obtaining wide agreement on an architecture and on data representation can significantly increase the reuse of M&S between and within projects. Well-planned reuse will increase the quality of M&S while reducing its cost. These results will enable a program manager to more broadly, confidently, and efficiently apply modeling and simulation in order to reduce program risk and cost.

Modern system development depends on processes that lifecycle models describe in an organized way. Each of these lifecycle models has strengths and weaknesses. The basic historical model is the waterfall, but other commonly used lifecycles include spiral development, evolutionary development, rapid prototyping, virtual prototyping, and dual. M&S can do much to support the phases of whatever lifecycle you select for a project, but you must plan carefully to make it cost effective. Good planning can promote reuse of models and data and preserve the investment made in the information content of M&S. The DOD is working to improve interoperability and reuse of models and data by providing common architectures and data.

References

Blanchard, B. S. and W. J. Fabrycky. 1990. *Systems Engineering and Analysis*. 2nd Ed. Englewood Cliffs, NJ: Prentice-Hall.

Blyskal, J. et al. 1991. *Evolutionary Spiral Process Guidebook*. Herndon, VA: Software Productivity Consortium.

Boehm, B. and B. Scherlis. 1992. *Megaprogramming Process*. DARPA Software Technology Conference. Arlington VA: Meridan Corporation.

DOD High Level Architecture http://www.dmso.mil/projects/hla/

Institute for Simulation and Training, Standard for Information Technology. 1993. Protocols for Distributed Interactive Simulation Applications, Version 2.0, Third Draft. Orlando, FL: University of Central Florida.

McCabe, R. et al. 1993. *Reuse Driven Software Processes Guidebook.* Herndon, VA: Software Productivity Consortium.

Piplani, L. K., J. G. Mercer and R. O. Roop. 1994. *Systems Acquisitions Manager's Guide for the Use of Models and Simulations.* Fort Belvoir, VA: DSMC Press.

Rhoads, D. I. 1983. *Systems Engineering Management Guide.* Fort Belvoir, VA: DSMC Press.

Schach, S. R. 1990. *Software Engineering.* Homewood IL: Aksen Asken Associates Inc.

Wymore, A. W. 1993. *Model-Based Systems Engineering.* Boca Raton, FL: CRC Press.

CHAPTER 5

Creating a Modeling and Simulation Baseline

Steve Rapp, *Computer Science Corporation*

In this chapter, we'll present a process to select a baseline approach for modeling and simulation. This process captures how a program manager and a technical manager must interact to develop an M&S program plan. Chapter 6 then develops the acquisition strategy to execute it. Ideally, for the relationship and process to work best, the program manager should have experience in M&S, and the technical manager should be a senior engineer with detailed experience in M&S. By carefully following the steps depicted in Fig. 5.1, we can take customer requirements and create a detailed program plan to describe the baseline approach to M&S development. This chapter also will concentrate on how to create the right relationship between the customer and the team who will build the model or simulation. Cost overruns, poor engineering design, and project failures almost always point back to a bad start, with improperly defined requirements and alternatives. Without the correct definition of, and concurrence on, requirements, the technical team can't know what the operational problems are.

The "Process"

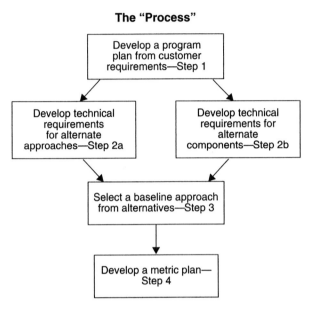

Fig. 5.1.   Selecting a Baseline Approach for Simulation. Developing a program plan, assessing technical requirements for alternatives, selecting a baseline approach, and establishing metrics to determine a simulation's effectiveness are the four steps that lead to effective models and simulations.

5.1   Develop a Program Plan

When starting any M&S program, program managers must know the problem and the available sources of funding. To establish a basic program plan, managers must understand several things. First, is this a major new development or is it an upgrade? New developments are more risky, although reusing existing products to supplement the development can greatly reduce this risk. Second, does this development support a broader R&D effort? If so, the entire M&S team must track its subprogram inside that effort. Third, will the simulation only prove a concept or must it be completely validated and verified? A complete system will usually cost ten times as much. Finally, will any part of this project become part of a repository? The answer here will increase documentation for the effort.

The technical manager's responsibility is to validate the customer's requirements, derive the simulation's technical requirements, and then update the basic program plan. The dilemma for any program is that good cost and schedule estimates aren't possible until technical requirements are clear. At the same time, the program can't develop technical requirements or more detailed functional specifications without having a funding mark. Thus, program managers, technical managers, and customers must talk to one another a lot in order to develop a solid program plan. In other words, they must work in parallel to create the plan, a process called concurrent engineering. To avoid inevitable conflicts that arise while working in parallel, they should use a control tool such as Quality Function Deployment (QFD) to develop, baseline, and control requirements. Figure 5.2 summarizes the interactions that must occur to develop a sound program plan.

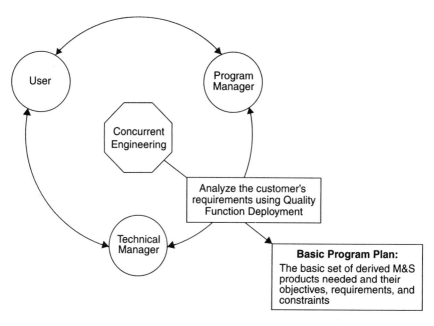

Fig. 5.2.   **Develop the Program Plan from Requirements.** To establish an effective program plan, program managers must interact with technical managers and users to derive M&S objectives, requirements, and constraints from established customer requirements.

Requirements can be confusing because no standard terms exist to categorize them. We'll divide requirements into two general categories: customer and technical requirements. Customer requirements are generally referred to as business requirements in the commercial world and operational requirements in the government world. As shown in Fig. 5.3, these requirements follow a natural hierarchy based on missions and objectives. Technical requirements can be derived from customer requirements and also follow a natural hierarchy as shown in Fig. 5.3. If we have a simple system to model, general technical requirements and functional specifications are typically the same. For complex systems, we must first derive general technical requirements, then translate them into intermediate technical specifications, and finally decompose them into functional specifications.

As we begin to develop a program plan, we'll run into two key problems with requirements. First, the customer won't know all of the requirements and won't understand the trade-offs needed to develop a cost-effective technical solution.

Second, modelers or engineers—especially inexperienced ones—typically will know how to solve problems only if they're stated technically. Customers and modelers must work together to create a common and well understood blueprint, so they can arrive at a mutually satisfactory solution.

Dedicated use of concurrent engineering creates the environment for learning and team building throughout the development. It coordinates and combines requirements definition, prototyping, and production, instead of moving through these phases sequentially. It also creates a dynamic development environment that takes into account evolving requirements discovered during prototyping and early production. Concurrent engineering isn't perfect, but it has provided cheaper, more reliable products that better satisfy customers.

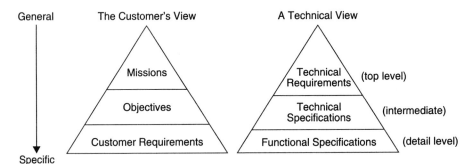

Fig. 5.3.   **Different Views of Requirements.** Customer requirements and technical requirements follow a natural hierarchy from general to specific. Technical requirements derive from customer requirements and, for complex systems, must be decomposed into finer and finer detail.

Production in simulation normally consists only of code unless you're building a hardware simulator. Every stream requires concurrent action from the program manager, technical manager, technical team, and customers. Figure 5.4 shows how these tools relate in a simulation program plan.

5.1.1   Determine the Customers' Requirements

Customers focus on the business or operational problem. They usually know what needs solving and are the starting point for developers to model the system using systems engineering (Chap. 2). But customers may not know the technical solutions or the cost and quality tradeoffs of these solutions. Even if customers do understand the problem technically, they count on the developer to define it because they can't take time away from their business or operational work. Otherwise, they wouldn't be in the market for simulation services. On the other hand, developers are experts on the value of each technology that could solve customers' problems or, at least, they know how to develop and find a solution. But they may know little about the customers' needs. Also, customers and

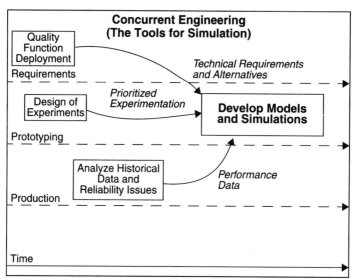

Fig. 5.4.   **Concurrent Engineering for Modeling and Simulation.** Concurrent engineering combines requirements definition, prototyping, and production to create a dynamic development environment for creating effective models and simulations.

developers want to get on with the work. In their haste, they may never truly pass on to each other what they need to work the problem together. The biggest dilemma in any simulation development is: Are customers and developers synchronized with the requirements? In this section we'll explore how to determine customers' requirements and how to help them understand the developers' continual tradeoffs between technical solutions.

5.1.2   Discover the Assumptions

As a program manager, you should first develop a statement of intended use to synchronize the customer with the developer. This statement creates a common focus on the project and guides expectations throughout the effort. Unmanaged expectations produce unmanaged costs. The next step is to agree on a characterization of the final product. The definitions shown in Table 5.1 are a starting point. Then, you must understand cost and quality. Cost falls into four categories:

- Direct dollar outlays (money directly funded for the project)
- Indirect dollar outlays (money expended or funded outside the project which you can leverage)
- Measurable costs (things you can value, but not in dollars)
- Unmeasurable costs (things you can't value or can't get agreement on how to measure)

Quality for simulations should focus on how easily customers can determine the cost tradeoffs from a simulation's results. The deeper issues of technical quality, such as "the goodness of the simulation's basis in math and physics," must match a customer's understanding. History is rife with examples of sophisticated and mathematically correct simulations that customers discarded because the simulations were obtuse, were impossible to understand, or answered fascinating questions that weren't asked.

Table 5.1.   **Important Characteristics of Models and Simulations.** This list of characteristics identifies the details you must define to describe the models and simulations that must be developed to reach your goals. It provides a starting point for translating desires into estimates of required cost and quality.

Characteristics	Meaning	Explanation
Intended use	The *why* of the model	Defines the model's main purpose in terms of what questions it's intended to address.
Scope	The *breadth* of the model	The subset of reality that the model tries to represent.
Resolution	The *depth* of the model	The precision, or granularity, of the variables in the model. The model's resolution characterizes its ability to differentiate a system's features and effects. It encompasses the *entities* (the objects manipulated by the model), their *attributes*, and the system's *functions*.
Detail	The *range* of the model	The product of scope and resolution—the broader the scope or the greater the resolution, the more detail in the model. Detail indicates how much information about the system a model is using or addressing.
Fidelity	The *how well* of the model	The degree to which a model accurately reproduces the effects of a system's functions.
Approach	The *how* of the model	Describes the model's implementation. The modeling approach used by a tool most affects the types of questions a model can address.
Data	The *substance* of the model	Data is the fuel that the model's engine runs on. A model generally represents a system's response to events—data makes it specific. Too often, little or no attention is placed on the availability and quality of the data a model will use.

The above cost categories are in priority order. For customers, direct dollar outlays determine what can and can't be funded, so they essentially drive simulation development. The second category is almost as important because it provides the greatest leverage to the technical team. Business and government have "sunk costs" in many parallel programs. The bigger the organization, the more likely you can find and leverage these sunk costs or use organizational resources funded through other channels. If you're a technical manager, you should aggressively search for these leverage points. The third category— measurable costs—relates to customers' subjective sense of value. For costs in this category, customers can define choices and may even be able to describe which ones are better. They just can't quantify how much these choices will cost. The fourth category—unmeasurable costs—can't be adequately defined or quantified, but they're vital to the project's value. Even though costs in this fourth group aren't measurable, you must document them in case future understanding makes them measurable—worth considering if you upgrade the simulation.

Of course, all assumptions don't relate to cost, but not understanding cost will give us the wrong assumptions. Remember, we're talking about more than just dollar outlays. For instance, how many total dollars are available? Can sunk costs from this and other projects be leveraged? What are the physical, chemical, and engineering constraints? What do the minimum technical requirements mean to the model itself and to development costs? For instance, in our simulation of firefighting, can we assume fires move with linear speed (easier and cheaper to model) or must we have a more costly, non-linear model? If we use the linear model and misjudge a fire's speed, would firefighters be in more danger? This is an example of the third cost type. More danger is worse—we can measure it but not in dollars. How about letting more forest burn to improve the firefighters' safety? For example, we won't allow firefighters into a particularly dangerous area, but they must eventually accept some risk or the whole forest will be destroyed. Directly modeling the firefighters' safety (their lives) against acceptable forest destruction not only would be difficult but also may be politically inappropriate. Most of the time, we won't directly model assumptions based on trading off this type of cost; instead, they'll be part of the analysis and output. For instance, we may do twenty simulation runs at one safety level and twenty others at another safety level. We may halve each set to measure different rates of fire expansion. But customers must determine the value of each mix. As developers, we simply ensure the runs for each mix are statistically significant. The customers and technical team must concurrently agree to and list all assumptions with customer requirements.

Even quality can be a costing expression. Quality is the value that customers and developers assign to what—and how well—a simulation performs. But they can agree on this value only if they concur on the requirements, objectives, and solutions. Quality Function Deployment maps all processes, so concurrence and joint understanding can develop and remain throughout the project.

5.1.3   Developing the Program Plan's Objectives from the Customer's Macro View

The program plan's objectives are simply the customers' requirements restated in simulation terms. They are key to translating customer requirements into technical requirements. Remember, a simulation's program plan may address only a subset of customer requirements, so the program plan's objectives must state clearly which ones will be addressed. Program managers work with technical managers to establish a program plan that covers a set of customer requirements the simulation can satisfy. Using these objectives, the entire technical team can create simulation requirements before determining technical or functional specifications.

For our fire management example, we can capture the customer's mission in one statement: improve fire management across four elements—detection, attack, fuels management, and prevention. A customer requirement might be to do so while keeping firefighters reasonably safe. Simulations will train firefighters in fire management, so a program plan's objectives might include

1. Creating a fire-detection simulation that enables assessing new detection technologies and training fire-watch crews
2. Creating a fuels-management simulation that has high-resolution physics models for accurate fire movement and speed but is easily integrated in real time to the fire-management wargame
3. Creating a training simulator for the fire crews that includes ground and air attack and that correctly models fuel consumption

5.1.4   Tools to Determine Technical Requirements

How well we derive the technical requirements from customer requirements and prioritize them ultimately determines a customer's satisfaction. To do so, we need effective tools, including quality function deployment, multi-attribute scoring, design of experiments, and statistical process control.

Quality Function Deployment

Quality Function Deployment (QFD) for general development is a structured approach by which we can identify and rank technical solutions or design characteristics against a customer's requirements. That allows us to derive parameters for products and processes. QFD also allows us to determine what each design characteristic contributes to fulfilling the customer's requirements. By identifying design targets and comparing processes, we can consider earlier manufacturing, test, and inspection, thus focusing development.

The main sequential activities of QFD are product planning, product design, process planning, and process-control planning (see Fig. 5.5)

1. Product planning—correlate customer requirements with the technical requirements in a matrix called a "house," which has led to calling QFD the "house of quality."
2. Product design—correlate prioritized technical requirements with part characteristics.
3. Process planning—correlate prioritized part characteristics with process characteristics.
4. Process-control planning—correlate prioritized process characteristics with process-control methods to rank order these methods.

These activities, done thoroughly and correctly, reveal the priorities for each development phase and shape our ideas about what kind of simulation to build.

QFD for simulation development differs from the general model because simulation programs don't involve hardware except for simulators of aircraft,

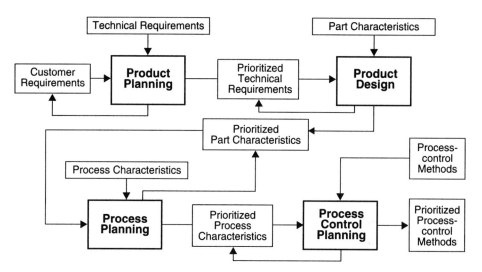

Fig. 5.5.   **The General Flow for Quality Function Deployment.** Quality Function Deployment provides a structured approach to identify and rank technical solutions or design characteristics against customer requirements. It helps relate design characteristics to customer requirements and focuses development activities on key quantities much earlier in the development process.

tanks, and other vehicles. For simulations, the four steps become analyzing requirements, designing the architecture, assessing technology, and planning for implementation (see Fig. 5.6).

This process is easy to learn, but using it improperly can produce bad results. It requires your team to hear and understand the customer's true requirements. Also, technical managers and teams must not leap to implementation planning when designing the architecture. If you do QFD well, you can clearly map resources to customer requirements. The more complex your development, the more you need this kind of requirements control.

QFD's benefits are tremendous. It can

- Reduce cost tenfold whenever it moves a design change into the requirements phase from the prototyping phase
- Reduce cost at least one hundred fold whenever it moves a design change from the production phase back to the requirements or the prototyping phase
- Drop engineering changes, design cycles, and start-up costs by 40%
- Document more systematically our engineering knowledge
- Make pricing more competitive by keeping R&D costs low
- Result in more satisfied customers
- Produce a more accurate and understandable model

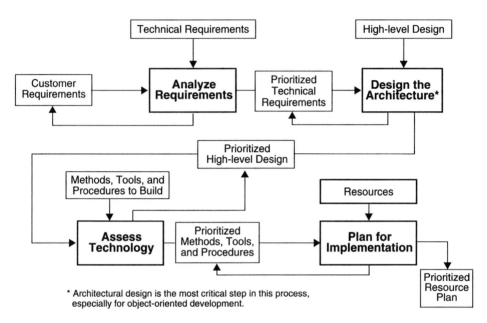

Fig. 5.6.   **Steps in Quality Function Deployment for Modeling and Simulation.** Quality Function Deployment can be adapted to modeling and simulation activities that don't normally require hardware development. The steps here provide a structured approach that matches design characteristics to customer requirements.

Multi-Attribute Scoring

Doing a matrix correlation of the inputs inside each QFD house depends on a scoring mechanism—linear, non-linear (based on gaming principles from Japanese horse racing), or some substitute. Linear and non-linear techniques usually work well enough, but you may want to use a more mathematically rigorous approach, such as multi-attribute scoring. As an example, the analytical hierarchical process smoothes out and corrects inconsistencies that result from scoring attributes one by one.

Design of Experiments

This technique depends on analyzing inputs to generate output responses (see App. C for discussion). It provides the key factors you must model and therefore will help you find the best experimental design. It saves money on hardware and software prototypes and is the main concurrent-engineering tool for controlling experiments in this phase. Information from design of experiments can feed back to the original requirements analysis for Quality Function Deployment. Use it to update the houses of QFD.

Statistical Process Control

This method uses basic graphical and statistical tools to analyze, control, and reduce process variance. You can use its information directly in analyzing a new system's reliability. Or you can generate Monte Carlo elements for a new simulation based on this information. It's also useful in defining requirements. Derived control information, with the system required to maintain that control, helps bound costs and development needs (See App. C for more detail.) You may also use it to update the houses of QFD.

5.1.5   Creating Prioritized Technical Requirements

Turning Missions and Objectives into Customer Requirements

Our fire-management example has a single mission—best manage fires across detection, attack, fuels, and prevention. One objective might be to do so while keeping firefighters safe. From this mission statement and objective, we can group the customer's requirements, such as:

1. Use the most appropriate detection equipment available from the ground, air, and space
2. Exchange information between assets
3. Create fused detection data to reduce false alarms
4. Develop command and control with state-of-the-art computers at a centralized building
5. Create a center for command and control that can be set up and operational anywhere in North America in less than eight hours
6. Create a national database for logistics support from all fire-management agencies
7. Enact memoranda of agreement among all these agencies to share logistics support and to agree on common deployment schedules
8. Create a database of all assets for search and rescue owned by fire-management agencies and the DOD
9. Enact agreements between all these agencies on using and deploying these assets
10. Make identifying fire trouble spots automatic to reduce labor costs
11. Maintain a backup with a human in the loop to identify trouble spots
12. Improve weather-prediction models to help study controlled burns
13. Automate these designs and analyze their effect
14. Nationally integrate fire-management training for all agencies
15. Write memoranda of agreement regarding national training
16. Improve the simulation for managing core fuels to better model a fire's intensity and rate of spread

17. Better describe humidity, precipitation, and temperature to simulate fuels management

18. Improve early warning on the probability of natural lightning strikes

19. Develop a surge plan to enhance national awareness before the fire season starts

Notice we've just gone from one mission statement, with four objectives, to nineteen customer requirements. This is normal. Also recognize that some or many of these requirements may have little to do with the simulation effort. Remember, the M&S program plan must identify the requirements it will address. But we still have to consider all of them because the forest service's budget depends on Congressional limits, so each competing priority affects the simulation effort. We'll correlate them against the technical requirements in Quality Function Deployment, but we'll address only the relevant ones for the simulation (see Table 5.2).

Table 5.2.   Effects of Operational Requirements on the Fire-Management Simulation. Operational requirements derived from mission objectives may or may not directly affect the models and simulations developed to meet stated goals.

Customer Requirements for the Fire-Management Simulation																		
1	2	3	4	5	6	7	8	9	10	11	12	13	14	15	16	17	18	19
Direct Effect on Simulation: X(1) X(2) X(3) X(4) X(5) — — — — X(10) — X(12) X(13) — X(15) X(16) X(17) —																		
Indirect Effect on the Simulation: — — X(3) X(4) X(5) X(6) X(7) X(8) — X(10) — — X(13) X(14) — — — — X(19)																		

Direct Effect on Simulation: columns 1, 2, 3, 4, 5, 10, 12, 13, 15, 16, 17 marked X.

Indirect Effect on the Simulation: columns 4, 5, 6, 7, 8, 9, 11, 13, 14, 19 marked X.

Turning the Customer's Requirements into Technical Requirements

Modelers must consider all the customer's requirements initially and then focus on the ones to be addressed in the program plan. Normally, several technical requirements will stem from each customer requirement, as listed earlier. For this example, we'll look only at

3 – Create fused detection data to reduce false alarms

5 – Create a center for command and control that can be set up and operational anywhere in North America in less than eight hours

For customer requirement three, some technical requirements might be

1. Identify all data types and formats to be fused
2. Develop software for communication that accepts these data types
3. Develop fusion algorithms for this data
4. Test fusion algorithms with the data

For customer requirement five, some technical requirements could be

1. Catalog all supplies and equipment required for a mobile command and control center
2. Ensure total supplies and equipment stay under the C-130's weight limits
3. Integrate all software and hardware into as few platforms as possible
4. Develop plan for human resources and for operations
5. Test operational choices using a simulation to determine the center's most effective layout

Notice, the technical requirements are still broad. Your first matrix under Quality Function Deployment (QFD) will rank order the technical requirements based on customer priorities and the correlation of technical requirements to these priorities. Remember, QFD will allow you to go deeper and deeper into the requirements hierarchy (see Fig. 5.6). A successful simulation takes into account the customers' beliefs about a simulation's operational value and relevance. If you don't plan for these beliefs, you won't develop a simulation that satisfies them and you won't be able to place a true value or cost on your simulation effort.

Flowing Assumptions and Costing to Simulation Constraints

Our assumptions about a simulation flow directly from the technical requirements. For example, consider technical requirement 4 from customer requirement 3: Test fusion algorithms with the data. Let's assume we want to develop a test that shows different kinds of fused data so the forest service can decide which is best for their purposes. This problem has two extreme solutions. The first is that we show all data and do no fusion whatsoever. This means that, if all the sensors pick up a fire, the display will show a mark for each contributing sensor and a single fire may be interpreted as several fires—as many as one per sensor. The other extreme is that we use the most sophisticated algorithms possible to correlate each sensor so only one mark appears on the display—a computationally expensive solution. To avoid these extremes, we may want to test several proposed fusion architectures, each having its own set of assumptions. For example, one assumption that will vary inside the fusion algorithm is the allowed geographical error for each sensor's mark of the fire location. Given enough error, the fusion algorithm may reject one fire location and show two fires close to each other. Table 5.3 below shows the assumption set for fusion in the fire-management example.

Table 5.3.   Assumptions for the Fire-Management Example.

	Fusion Architecture		
Assumption	**No Correlation**	**Correlation for Proximity**	**Correlation to Reduce Matrix Errors**
Allowed geographical error per fused mark	No fusion, no error tracking	2 km for space-based sensors; 500 m for air-based sensors	500 m off x-axis and 1 km off y-axis for space-based sensors; 200 m off vector centerline

The simulation's constraints flow directly from the assumptions. With no correlation, the simulation would have no constraints on displaying simulated marks from the sensors. In correlation for proximity, two space-based sensor marks within 2 km of each other would appear as one mark, and two air-based sensor marks more than 500 m apart would show as two marks. A space-based sensor and an air-based sensor mark would use the more conservative 500-m constraint. Additional simulation constraints would apply depending on the model we choose to mimic the architecture types. For instance, a "cookie cutter" radar model may not provide the sensor accuracy to simulate a radar properly in the correlation algorithm for proximity. We must tell customers that choice of models makes a difference. A less detailed model may not have the accuracy to predict how the system will respond.

Ranking Requirements

The technical approach includes all the simulation tools you have to answer the technical requirements. You must choose the best tools while controlling cost, so you need to use Quality Function Deployment or another analytical tool to rank the technical requirements against the customer requirements. Then, map each technical approach against the technical requirements it is supposed to answer. Table 5.4 shows how you might rank the customer's requirements and the (top 5) technical requirements from our example.

Table 5.4. Ranking Operational and Technical Requirements. Prioritizing operational and technical requirements can help define options, describe assumptions, and establish constraints.

Operational Requirements

Rank	Customer Requirement Number	Description
1	5	Create a command and communication center that can be set up and operational anywhere in North America in less than eight hours
2	3	Create fused detection data to reduce false alarms

Technical Requirements

Rank	Description	Reference to Operational Requirement
1	Test operational choices in a simulation to determine most effective layout of the center	#5
2	Develop input/output software for communications	#3
3	Test fusion software with all data types	#3
4	Ensure that all supplies and equipment are under a C-130's weight limit	#5
5	Catalog all data types and formats	#3

From these prioritized technical requirements, engineers can now roughly estimate the cost of the simulation and present options. The entire team's assumptions will then allow for a final cost estimate. Table 5.5, below, shows some general technical approaches—in priority order—you can use to satisfy the five technical requirements.

Table 5.5.   **Approaches to Satisfy Technical Requirements.** This table describes representative technical approaches you might consider to meet the technical requirements listed in Table 5.4.

Technical Approach	Description	Answers Technical Requirement
1	Operations-center simulation from the U.S. Navy • Will require modification and a communication interface to the Forest Service's fire-propagation models	1
2	Fusion algorithm for sensor data from the Drug Enforcement Agency and Department of Defense • No modification needed	3
3	C-130 logistics model from the U.S. Air Force • No modification needed	4
4	Five different commercial databases can provide differing levels of interface between the models	2, 5

Mapping Assumptions and Constraints

Assumptions are the most critical part of simulation development. After customers, managers, and engineers baseline the requirements, they're ready to derive assumptions. The available technical approaches and resources may force certain assumptions: increasing the simulation's fidelity reduces what you can assume and calls for better and more mathematically intense models. The engineers will of course want to use better models, as will your customer (until they understand how high the cost is). At this point, customers want to relax their requirements to fit the cost. Without an open dialogue, managers tend to alter models based on what makes customers happiest and best fits their project schedule, with little regard for engineering dilemmas. The baseline itself becomes irrelevant if you don't state and get agreement on assumptions that balance cost and performance. Remember, assumptions and requirements are complementary. Altering one always affects the other.

Notice from Table 5.5 that some of the technical requirements could be answered with only one model choice or would require a complete build from scratch. That's often true. Also, we may have several choices available—in this case, databases. Your engineers determine the technology tradeoffs between selections; your customers can then decide how accurate the model can be within cost constraints. At this point, you can calculate project costs.

Any government agency or corporation building a simulation can carry out the steps described here in three ways: do all the work internally, pay a contractor or consultant to do the design work and then competitively bid some or all of the engineering effort, or mix these approaches. Additionally, the government has available unique organizations called Federally Funded Research and Development Centers. They don't have to compete for contractual work, so they can develop high-risk simulations that wouldn't be efficient or profitable if contracted to industry. They can provide "honest-broker" modeling and project-selection support to the government, whereas a contractor may have a vested interest in particular choices that support its objectives at the expense of the government. As a program manager, you'll have to weigh these choices but usually a mixed approach is best because most research and development requires high- and low-risk efforts. You can mix their strengths and weaknesses to provide higher quality at lower cost. But make sure the government agency or corporation shoulders the burden of creating the project baseline before you contract with them. If necessary, consult experts to create the best request for proposal or contract!

For a commercial agency, the procedures are about the same as for the government but with notable exceptions. The commercial sector isn't as constrained by budget requirements and can develop projects quicker. But they can get into disastrous R&D failures faster than the government. That's why private industry created concurrent engineering to provide control and adherence to the customer's requirements. Also, many large software firms are trying to adopt standard techniques and specifications to help develop and control baselines. The ISO 9000/9001/9002 standards and the Software Engineering Institute's model are key controls that fit well with concurrent engineering when you construct your baseline.

As you map assumptions against available time, people, and money, the resource constraints naturally fall out. Use project-management tools to test your project's relationships, physical constraints on the real world, and control constraints on your simulation.

Physical constraints are those nature imposes on the real-world system. They include allowable interaction of time and space, force equations, chemical equations, gravity or magnetic force equations, nuclear interactions, biological interactions, and entropy relations. Your assumptions will determine how accurately you must model these physical constraints. Remember that higher fidelity increases the model's complexity and the project's cost.

Control constraints deal with only the "rules" your simulation must follow to mimic the real world. They reflect your choices of modeling type, level, and formalism. For example, choosing discrete-event modeling constrains your simulation's future-event queue; choosing continuous modeling requires you to set a cycle for updating the clock that governs differential-equation control of state elements.

5.1.6   Document Results in a Program Plan

QFD correlates the customer's requirements with the derived technical requirements to rank order the technical requirements for program and technical managers. The technical manager and technical team continue QFD to translate these ranked requirements into a preliminary design and define software methods, procedures, tools, and finally a prioritized resource plan. The result is a baseline program which also provides a starting point for developing and considering alternatives as needed.

5.2   Apply Technical Requirements to Identify Alternatives

Figure 5.7 shows how concurrent engineering works for Step 2. During this step, program managers work with technical managers at the same time that the latter consult with their teams. With a sound program plan in hand, program managers will understand their problems better and can more clearly establish program costs. Remember, customers "know it when they see it." Feedback from concurrent engineering allows them to say "that's not it" and to say what they want. This step is a continuous conversation—each element can occur several times until program managers, technical managers, and teams agree on the baseline and alternatives. Because of the technical nature of these choices, technical managers are the central players in this second step.

The key difference between these two substeps is the level of detail. Technical managers and program managers talk about broad issues, whereas technical managers and teams hash through details. Of course, I'm generalizing—some managers are fascinated with details. But most program managers will operate at a more abstract level than the technical team.

5.2.1   System Dimensions Drive Model Alternatives and the Baseline

Simulation development includes many dimensions. Selecting elements within each dimension creates a unique development path, and each path leads to an alternative approach that the technical manager and team must define for the program manager.

Choosing Formalisms to Develop Simulation Models

Formalisms are mathematical languages, so choosing one directly affects the type of software code we use and how we package it. Table 5.6 summarizes the key elements of each formalism. To determine which formalism to use, you must be able to identify system events and things that affect or trigger other events.

Step 2a: Developing Alternative Approaches

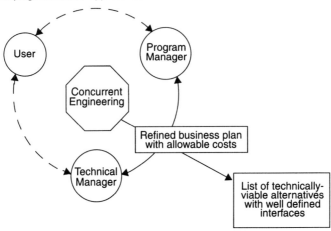

Step 2b: Developing Alternative Components

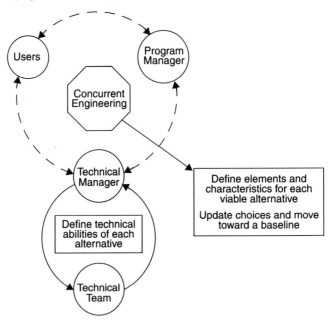

Fig. 5.7.   **Applying Technical Requirements to Develop Alternatives.** Program managers, technical managers, and technical staffs are all actively involved in translating technical requirements into viable alternatives. Technical managers are the focal points for these activities. They interact with program managers to make sure problems are understood and costs are clearly identified, while working closely with the technical team to make sure all technical details are carefully considered.

Table 5.6.   Summary of Formalisms for Modeling and Simulation. Understanding the key elements of each formalism is important to choosing the right one for your application.

Formalism	Characteristics	Applications	Issues
Discrete Event	The model is based on a state machine—tracking only events that affect the system's state. Time is advanced based on the time of the next state change (event). Most efficient if the number of events is not too large.	Used for process-related systems (such as a job-shop) or event-oriented systems (such as the packet flow through a communications network).	Complex systems may contain discrete elements that can use this formalism
Differential Equations (Continuous)	The state of the system varies continuously as a function of time.	Used for systems that respond continuously (such as guidance and control systems or sensor systems).	Very computationally expensive. Doesn't scale well to large systems.
Discrete Time (Time-stepped)	Simulation time is advanced in fixed and even increments. At each increment, the state of the system is evaluated.	Used for systems that depend on time.	Can be slow if there are long periods of little simulated activity.
Real Time	Simulation time is periodically synchronized with "wall-clock" time, so events occur as they would in the "real world," as perceived by a viewer.	Used for human-in-the-loop and hardware-in-the-loop simulations.	Time synchronizing can be complicated.

1. Determine your system's purpose while recognizing it can have several objectives, some of which may conflict. Quality Function Deployment, with or without the analytical hierarchical process, helps you and your customer define purpose. It's also excellent in resolving conflicting objectives and logic.

2. State the objectives of your study and simulation. These flow directly from the customer's mission and operational requirements.

3. Qualitatively and quantitatively design the experiments you want your simulation to do. Design of experiments is an excellent tool for analyzing alternatives and finding the best solution.

4. Identify the resident and transient entities in your system. What are their important attributes? Statistical process control and reliability analysis may help you.

5. Identify the system dynamics and the circumstances that cause your system to change. These elements are your events.

The following discussions provide additional insights for each formalism.

Discrete-Event Simulations. In a discrete-event simulation, time advances in discrete steps to the next state change. The time steps are variable and often of random length. This simulation skips over the time during which no events are occurring rather than tracking detailed system dynamics. This means it can model very large systems, such as factories, communications networks, medical systems, and logistical systems. It maintains a particular state by numerically valuing its attributes and future schedule. Changes in the state, called events, change one or more of the state variables. As events occur, they spawn future events stored in a list. A communications system might include a message-finishing transmission, a message arriving into a queue, a communications link failing, or a link being repaired.

If you can cast your system in terms of states, discrete-event simulation works fine and is usually fast. But make sure your simulation can afford the time jumps. If you want to analyze results and don't have to track detailed system dynamics or live in real time, discrete-event simulation is good. It can run hundreds to millions of times faster than real time, allowing for many runs in testing and analysis. It can distinguish between time-invariant (resident) and time-varying (transient) entities in your system. In the fire-management example, the aircraft and spacecraft providing fire-warning messages would be resident entities, whereas the messages themselves would be transient. In an assembly line, the machines are resident; the parts being manufactured and combined to form components and completed systems are transient.

Differential-Equation Simulations. These simulations are used in science and engineering to study such things as stress on airplane wings, astronomical events, orbit propagation, molecular interactions, societal models, and economic systems. They assume time is continuous and state variables change differentially. The time steps are identical and don't vary. Differential equations model the state variables' instantaneous rates of change, which may depend on time or the state variables. Normally, the differentials are calculated recursively in the computer to approximate state changes over the time steps. Usually, a continuous-time model will have several state variables coupled in dynamic time. This means we must know the state variables' values to calculate changes and the changes (differentials) to calculate the state variables' values. In other words, the equations must be solved at the same time, which normally involves approximations. As a result, continuous-time simulations accumulate errors, which we can solve in only two ways:

1. Reduce the time step. Problem: it takes longer to run.
2. Design algorithms more carefully. Problem: it takes longer to run.

Thus, although continuous-time simulations free you from having to live with discrete events, approximations to model state changes carry errors that can accumulate. Fixing those errors drives up cost.

Discrete-time Simulations. These simulations differ from discrete-event simulations because they assume a consistent, discrete time base. In discrete-event models, one event may occur at five seconds and the next at ten minutes. In discrete time, a two-second step means we measure the state every two seconds. The algorithm marches forward at consistent intervals but not necessarily at real time or clock speed.

Real-time Simulations. We can develop these simulations from any of the above formalisms. For example, a discrete-event model can link a time clock to the future-events list. As the computer clock catches up to the time for the future event to occur, it allows the event to be processed. A discrete-time model set for real time could require its time steps to synchronize with an actual clock. A differential-equation model could measure and map its differential equations and rates of change to steps in real time.

Interestingly, heavy processing causes the same problem for all formalisms: the simulation may fall behind as the real clock advances. The heavier the computing requirements (added realism and chaos), the worse the problem, which makes errors, system crashes, and bad analysis more likely. To help solve this problem, you can

- Add a catch-up algorithm
- Add internal abilities for parallel processing
- Distribute the simulation over multiple platforms

Unfortunately, these solutions add their own problems—typically, with internal synchronizing. In the fire-management example, the simulation may deploy a firefighting unit to stop a fire that was actually out because the process hadn't caught up yet or was out of view of the event scheduler in a parallel or distributed process. For real-time simulations, you must carefully code the software to synchronize these events.

Human-in-the-loop models, wargames, and trainers typically use real-time simulations with significant analog components to eliminate continuous-time errors. In most cases, we can integrate these hybrid systems with other simulations. They're made for testing and training, but we may also have to use them for analysis while developing and upgrading a system.

Distributing Simulations over Networks

Wide-area networks (WAN) and local-area networks (LAN) can make simulations faster and more accurate, particularly for real time, by distributing the processing load over several machines. Having workstations share the computing requirements allows bigger simulations, as well. But they require more sophisticated algorithms for communication and time synchronizing. Bandwidth requirements also have grown. Simulations now need better imagery, graphics, and communication interfaces.

Requirements for speed and communication can easily increase the cost of a simulation ten-fold.

Software Design Alternatives to Develop Simulations

Your software design will depend on the formalism (mathematical language) you use in your simulation. In fact, software logic has improved with demands for better simulation development, languages, and formalisms.

Modular (Traditional). Classic software logic achieved its highest mark in modular design, which uses subroutines and blocks of code in modules that carry out tasks (or events). Reusing code consists of cutting and pasting modules into other programs and then fixing incompatibilities between names, declarations, and lengths in the transplanted module and the new program. This overhead increases geometrically as programs become more complex. Most discrete-event simulations today are modular, with events stacked together and connected just as in other modular programs.

Object Orientation. More of today's software uses object orientation—a more free-flowing approach that looks at program elements as objects which interact. The focus in object-oriented design is to govern the attributes that control the object interactions. Adding more objects is simple, even though the overall logic can be complex. Once we've created an object-oriented program, we can more easily maintain, upgrade, and export it across platforms. Continuous, real-time simulations are easier to design and develop with object-oriented programming. But modular design is probably better for basic analysis because it doesn't have to consider object interactions and is therefore faster.

Rapid Prototyping. Remember, whenever we start developing a prototype, we mainly want to move the customer from concept to product. The simulation itself should find the design problems and then show how to correct them and build a hard prototype, if required. Thus, we're not oriented toward developing the system's actual hardware or software. Reusing code is important, but not at the expense of rapid prototyping. Remember, in concurrent engineering, the requirements are evolving and the production plan is moving forward. In most cases, you'll rapidly create a crude prototype and then refine it as the customer plays with it and adds insights. This means you need to consider code generators, so you can keep the model in abstract logic and generate the code from this model. If you use automated tools, you'll save a lot of time and money on finding and correcting syntax errors or "bugs." In turn, this means you can focus on proper logic. And you can more easily handle the customer's inevitable changes. An alternative to code generators is to use a very high-level language that automatically does strong checking, which provides essentially the same effect. Bottom line: use automated coding techniques, even though they're usually hard to get used to.

5.2.2   Partitioning Problems into Models and Simulations

Identify Key Characteristics for Each Interactivity Type, Application Level, and Formalism

When considering interactivity type, remember that the state space varies with human involvement in the simulation. For instance, constructive simulations have little or no human involvement during the simulation run, whereas live simulations have operators directly involved and interacting with a simulation's elements and objects. As these simulations become more realistic, the participants can't differentiate between the simulation's synthetic environment and the real world. The simulation's visual, aural, and other sensory inputs are so realistic that people begin to interact with the simulation elements as if they are real.

When considering formalisms, keep in mind that the state space varies with how the model lives in time. Discrete-event simulations consider time only for tracking events in the event queue. But continuous simulations differentially relate their system interactions to time and live in time. Real-time simulations are also continuous and are locked into the standard clock. They regulate their simulation resolution based on the time clock's refresh rate.

For application levels (hierarchies), the state space varies with player involvement and required resolution. At one end of the spectrum are engineering models that require incredibly detailed information at the physics level. One step up are engagement models, which require only the resolution necessary for people or other systems to interact with each other. At the far end of the spectrum are wargames or models of campaigns and theater operations. Here the interaction is very broad, and one-to-one actions aggregate at this highest hierarchy. Thus, interaction resolution is very low in a theater-level model. At the same time, these models consider hundreds and thousands of engagements and missions.

Combine Types, Levels, and Formalisms to Achieve the Best System

When comparing types to formalisms, remember you're associating human involvement to how the formalism considers time. Because humans live in time, live and virtual simulations will almost always be continuous and real-time. A constructive simulation can be event-driven or continuous, but because operators don't interact with it, real time usually isn't necessary.

When comparing types to levels, you're associating human involvement in the simulation to the hierarchical level of analysis or training required. Engineering models rarely require live or virtual involvement, so engineering models are almost always constructive. Interestingly, because models for campaigns or theater operations are used for strategic analysis and training, they often require constructive and live simulation. Thus, they usually have a selector switch to allow them to run in either mode. Engagement and battle simulations tend to require living in real time, so they're almost always live, although battle simulations may also have a selector switch to analyze battles constructively.

When comparing formalisms to levels, you're associating how the formalism considers time with the hierarchical level of analysis or training required. Discrete-event simulations tend to be complex in setting up the model process and don't live in time, but they have exact and discrete measurements at the events. Continuous simulations live in time but carry all the round-off error associated with differential measurements. Engineering models can be discrete-event or continuous depending on how changes in system state occur. Engagement and mission models usually have real-time requirements, so they tend to be continuous. But you can force discrete-event models to live in real time by coupling the real-time clock to the events list. Discrete-event models orient to process and not training, so if they're used for engagement or mission levels, you'll normally combine them with some continuous model that will regulate the live and virtual interactions. Models of campaigns, theater operations, and battles are also more concerned with process interactions but may require real-time modeling. Most of these models combine elements of discrete-event and continuous formalisms.

Choose Mathematical and Analytical Approaches

Mathematical modeling usually follows four steps:

1. **Determine the objective.** In simulation, this is an abstract statement based on the customer's mission and requirements. Restate the objective to include as much mathematical language as possible. If you must optimize, state separately how you'll produce the best system.
2. **Determine the assumptions.** The simulation's variables, constraints, and events will reflect these assumptions. Still, it makes good sense to list the model assumptions for the work itself, as well as for later analysis and formal verification, validation, and accreditation of the model.
3. **Determine the variables and constraints.** Define three kinds of parameters: those that identify basic scenarios and the entities' abilities (e.g., fuel capacity), those that identify the current state of the scenario or entity (e.g., 1000 pounds of fuel), and random variables that identify the results of random events.
4. **Combine the model elements into mathematical statements and create a simulation.** In other words, develop the software. After creating the mathematical statements, code the model and start basic testing to ensure the model doesn't violate fundamental scientific laws. If the model will be used for more than analysis, do formal alpha and beta testing as well as independent verification and validation.

Once you've done the mathematical modeling, use it for statistical analysis. Apply your informal or formal (design of experiments) test plan to the statistical modeling, which must include at least five steps:

1. Develop hypotheses—determine success criteria for each test.
2. Analyze sensitivity—run multiple simulations by altering the objectives, assumptions, variables, and constraints. Key point: design of experiments is useful because it describes the acceptable state space for model testing. Without a formally designed experiment, sensitivity analysis may go out of bounds.
3. Test hypotheses—assemble data from the simulation runs to determine the results and their confidence levels. See any basic book on statistics for ways to test hypotheses.
4. Track metrics—save all values of measures of effectiveness and measures of performance for each simulation run and model variation.
5. Develop statistical graphics—when the data is complex, plotting it often provides an easy way to identify trends and structure.

Decide Whether to Distribute Your Simulation

Today, many simulations are distributed. As systems become more complex and our ability to model interactions grows, processing spreads out over many machines networked together. Although we must still centrally control events and time, new systems allow simulations and their objects to interact as never before. Players and environments can now match computer platforms to nearly any resolution. But we still need improved technology to support better bandwidth and message movement between processes and players, master control of time and events, and aggregate interactions between simulation levels. Read Chap. 15 for more detail on considerations for distributed networks.

5.2.3 Decide on a Modeling Approach (Identify Elements)

Identifying elements means determining which alternatives are easier to carry out and which ones will better satisfy the customer's objectives and requirements. The modeling approach you decide on for your baseline should guide the technical team throughout the development.

Design the Model

Consider your simulation's purpose and your customer's mission and operational requirements. The three big issues for design are whether your model

- Requires human interaction—and how much
- Has specific fidelity, detail, or accuracy requirements
- Will be used for analysis or training

Build Data

To build data for your development, you must ask:

- What type of data?
- What accuracy or resolution? How much round-off is allowed?
- What data do metrics require? (This is the ultimate driver of data.)

Perhaps the biggest error simulation developers make is to build data before they know what the simulation is going to measure. That's why building data depends on concurrent engineering that gives us a plan to allow for shifting requirements, which drive changes in metrics and corresponding data requirements.

Develop Software

Approaches to software development depend mainly on how players and objects will interact. More interaction should move you toward object-oriented programming. Also, the more uncertain a customer's requirements, the more likely you'll use object-oriented code because it's easier to modify. If analytical accuracy and speed are crucial, modular programming still has its place. Hybrid, distributed models that use multiple levels, types, and formalisms will need modular and object-oriented approaches. Subdivide your development to look at interactions of elements and analytical requirements. Most legacy code is modular, but if you use object orientation for your overall development, you can describe each legacy piece as a standalone object.

Design the Experiment

As stated earlier, you must consider the experiment design while you're establishing the overall requirements. The experiment design can itself affect software development, so you need to be sure it passes the parameters, variables, and metrics to the software-development team. Each team needs people working both efforts to ensure cross pollination.

Verify, Validate, and Assess (VV&A) Your Simulation

VV&A is directly tied to model building and software development, but it's distinct and independent. You don't necessarily need different people to do VV&A, but it must start early and run distinctly throughout the simulation development. Alpha and beta testing of the code relate to VV&A because it's the testing needed to complete VV&A of the simulation software. See Chap. 11 for more details.

5.2.4   Evaluate Existing Models and Simulations

As soon as you've roughly decided on your technical requirements and alternative approaches, look at existing M&S products to answer the problem. They can be less costly to integrate than new development. Many simulation programs have wasted their resources by developing abilities identical or similar to other programs. However, you should carefully assess reuse before committing to it.

Check Sources for Models and Simulations

Catalogs of models and simulations are at the Joint Staff, Advanced Research Projects Agency, and each of the individual service's modeling and simulation management offices. The first step you should take with your customer is researching reusable modules, libraries, and modeling tools to help clarify what you want to achieve. Also, industry maintains marketing information on all their COTS packages, but remember they're selling, not informing. Most M&S organizations in the DOD are creating world wide web pages on the internet, so make them your first pass in researching current sources. As an example, the Air Force has created a Modeling and Simulation Repository that is accessible on the internet. It is basically a "card catalog" of existing M&S products, but it also includes a collection of future requirements for M&S products. The Army and Navy have similar repositories you should investigate.

Assess Models

Assessing models depends on your customer's objectives and scope of effort. Although you must always consider availability, cost, development time, and VV&A requirements, the overriding criterion tends to be cost. The harder the cost constraints, the more solid your assessment must be. You must at least assess models before starting a project. In today's tight fiscal environment, you may have to do this first assessment with internal resources. As the industry becomes more and more commercial, marketing materials are capturing much more information on models, even for the DOD's off-the-shelf models. Use the internet first and then check traditional sources for verification. If the customer insists on customized, cutting-edge development, your model assessment will be unique and more costly. But even in this case, research the open sources.

5.2.5   Identify M&S Abilities You Could Develop

If M&S abilities don't exist or would cost more to integrate than new code, your technical team must identify requirements for new abilities.

Justify New Development

The boundaries continue to blur between developing new models, upgrading old models, and integrating models. Although advances in physics and mathematics are fueling new advances in algorithms, you won't need new, improved core code for most models. More and more, we're modeling systems made up of complex systems. Upgrades also may not touch core abilities, but rather multiply and integrate new abilities, particularly in graphics, sights, and sounds. You'll need to justify new development by dividing it into components and then subdividing them into true new development, system upgrades, and system integration. Base your justification on assessment and risk criteria.

Develop Assessment Criteria

As we become more sophisticated in development and integration, we're building more accurate assessments. Automated coding, computer-aided development, CASE tools for correcting bugs, and general advances in software engineering are reducing the risk of software development. This reduced risk makes it easier to estimate and reduce software-development costs. As a project leader, you must still gather a team of engineers and operations experts to do project estimates, but you can now place greater confidence in these estimates. You must again consider availability, cost, development time, and VV&A requirements, but now in the light of how they will affect new development. You must also think critically about how well you can maintain, port, and reuse the software with regard to expanded use and upgrade costs. You can't tell how well your model will be accepted and if the acceptance will drive expanded use. These criteria cost almost nothing to consider in the beginning, but not considering them can destroy a project.

Consider Engineering Cost and Risk

Consider engineering cost needs from two perspectives. First, look at the dollar cost per hour to do each planned sub-task. Engineers, customers, and managers need to come to a team decision because customers want to pay as little as possible, engineers want all the money in the world to ensure success, and managers are trying to balance these and other competing interests. Quality Function Deployment creates the right environment in which you can hammer out requirements and address risk. Second, examine the cost of design changes. Although focusing on dollar costs per hour is important, particularly for developing the baseline and alternatives, ignoring this second perspective will result in cost overruns and increased risk. Design errors caught early on in the requirements phase cost very little. Design errors caught during prototyping cost up to ten times as much but are inexpensive compared to errors that carry into production, which cost up to 100 times as much as errors caught in the requirements phase. These risk costs have often been neglected or overlooked in the haste to get to production. Many of the U.S. auto industry's problems in the 1970s arose from neglecting to get customers, marketers, managers and engineers on the same sheet of music.

Engineering estimates are best made by a 4- to 6-member design team that includes people from all of the development's technology areas. Train your people on effective meetings before you form the team. For the actual estimation, use the three-point PERT process with Beta function for the most likely estimate. Do an optimistic, average, and pessimistic estimate and let the Beta function provide the most likely estimate. Then, enter it into project-planning software. Figure 5.8, below, ties the requirements process for Quality Function Deployment (presented in Step 1) to the engineering estimates required to develop new simulations. This subprocess is key to trading off risk and cost.

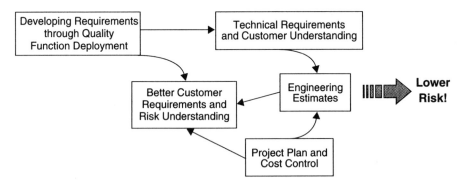

Fig. 5.8.   Doing Better Engineering Estimates, through Quality Function Deployment, Reduces Risk. Evaluating alternatives for new M&S development requires good engineering estimates of cost and risk. Quality Function Deployment generates a thorough understanding of requirements and creates the right environment for making good estimates.

Share Technology among the Government, Academic, and Commercial Sectors

Technology sharing is much easier today because R&D is much more expensive for hard prototypes and computers have reduced the cost of simulation. Thus, after defining requirements, ask: Is someone else working this project? Years ago, the DOD and its federally funded research and development centers led much of the United States' high-tech development; today, industry leads in many areas. The recent ascendance of U.S. technology results directly from global industrial competition. Additionally, industry and academia have forged alliances to increase industrial competitiveness and academic funding. San Francisco and Massachusetts are the best examples. Silicon Valley (with Stanford and the University of California—Berkeley) and Boston (with the Massachusetts Institute of Technology and Harvard) are leading the way. To optimize the cost of simulation activities, you should explore all current research before translating your requirements into costs. Many times, you'll find a technology you need already available in open-source materials.

5.2.6   Reuse Legacy Models

On the surface, using legacy code is cheaper than developing a new simulation, but improved algorithms and object-oriented languages can make it more expensive in the long run.

Ask two key questions before you reuse models. First, have basic math and physics algorithms changed since the legacy system was created? Second, is it easier to recode the legacy model than to code a specialized communications interface for the model? If the legacy model's core algorithms are still accurate enough and if the communications interface is ten times less expensive, it makes sense to reuse the legacy system.

Also consider these tradeoffs:

1.   If the model is slated only for short-term use, reuse it; don't rebuild.
2.   If the model is slated for long-term use, do a new development or a complete upgrade.
3.   If the core model has state-of-the-art algorithms that use the faster modular design, try a combination approach: reuse the algorithms but build the communications interface and object interactions from scratch.

5.2.7   Determine Needs for Logistics and Training

If logistics and training cost much more for one system than for another, even if that system is technically innovative, most likely you'll have to reject it.

Logistical Support

You must consider logistics in the planning stage of the planning, programming and budgeting system. Improving logistics while reducing cutting-edge improvements typically lowers long-term cost. Of course, this support will vary depending on the mix of commercial off-the-shelf, government off-the-shelf, and custom code. Your best bet is commercially available software because industry shoulders the logistical support (in exchange for maintenance contracts). But this approach can backfire if the company supporting its product goes out of business or decides to orphan its software. Government packages are the second best choice. The sponsoring government agency shoulders the logistics support and rarely charges its government customers fees, but upgrades tend to be slower. Also, decreased DOD budgets have orphaned many software packages. The third choice—custom code—is least attractive. But if it's unique and you can show how the package supports requirements, you can get budget support to maintain the code over the long term. Thus, it will change from custom to government off-the-shelf. Avoid the "hobby-shop" approach—creating software without any planned logistical support or formal development.

Maintenance Support for Commercial Software

Maintenance contracts typically include fixing software problems, automatic upgrades, and toll-free support hotlines—all advantages for using commercial software in your development. Remember though, your integration must follow the commercial company's rules for using its software. In the worst case, you're on your own if you don't get prior approval to change or use the software in non-standard ways.

Training Support

Many developers also ignore training support. As with logistics, the federal budgeting system now mandates planning for training support as do many corporations' information-systems departments. You should form an additional team of operators, trainers, and engineers to develop training requirements. As with logistical support, simplifying the system for easier training—even if it reduces some of the technically interesting features—usually saves a lot of money over time and increases customers' acceptance of your software.

5.3   Combining Models And Simulations

As we consider competing alternatives, we may want to change our program plan's baseline. Options that combine models and simulations can significantly affect the baseline.

5.3.1   Simulation Links

Whenever you combine simulations to create bigger and more realistic ones, consider their levels of operation and the formalisms they use to make sure the new system will work. If human involvement is an issue, also consider the simulation type. Normally, you'd combine systems to add realism and training value or to build larger simulations for analysis and training. New hybrid systems may also combine real and virtual elements. If so, you must be concerned with communication between these elements. Depending on how critical the system is and on the complexity of its human-machine interface, passing events from the synthetic world to the real world could cause major security problems—which may be the Achilles heel for future distributed, hybrid systems. For example, say a wargame simulation determines an aircraft crew is neutralized and shuts off communication to the aircraft. Does the aircraft automatically switch over to its real communication environment? How seamless is the switch? Does it affect the aircraft subsystems regulating human health? If the transfer from synthetic environment to real world isn't worked out in detail for every possible interaction involving the crew, serious problems could result, whether the aircraft's flight is real or simulated.

Controlling Simulation Levels

Hierarchical control over different levels occurs in two directions: aggregation for going up a hierarchy and de-aggregation for going down a hierarchy. The DOD maintains a working group and simulation protocol for controlling simulation levels: the Aggregate Level Simulation Protocol (ALSP). Aggregation is technically easier than de-aggregation. For example, let's say that we have fourteen tank simulators representing a tank company—Charlie Company. We can aggregate individual information on health, location, and engagements into a company report (just as in real life) and send it up the chain of command. In this case, it may be a campaign model that wants to be accurate only at the company level. Going down (de-aggregation) is a different matter. Let's say the campaign model generates a 75% loss of Charlie Company. Down at the tank-simulator level that means a binary decision—dead or alive for each crew. The de-aggregation must also include a mechanism to translate broad information into realistic, specific information. At the simplest level, it could consist of randomly rolling dice to determine who lives. Or it could use a sophisticated analytical model. The problem is that a sophisticated model slows down processing and communication because of the large amount of data associated with it.

A related, but subtle, problem involves differences in underlying assumptions between models. Most often, these differences occur in the assumptions about the perceived environments within which the models' entities operate. For example, two models for orbital mechanics may use identical equations to propagate orbits but assume different shapes for the Earth—one spherical, the other oblate. When final coordinate transformations are made, the two models will produce different latitude, longitude, and altitude coordinates for the same point in inertial space.

Combining Simulations With Different Formalisms

Connecting discrete-event simulations to continuous simulations can be easy if the discrete-event simulation runs very quickly. In this case, we can slow it down to execute its events only when the time clock reaches the event time. But if the discrete-event simulation can't execute its events quickly and falls behind, the combined simulation's output will at least be suspect. Most likely the output data will be inaccurate, and the combined system may even crash during a run. When discrete-event simulations can't keep up, connecting these simulations becomes much more difficult. We must add a second, sophisticated mechanism to control events—a "catchup" algorithm. This algorithm must queue up events to feed the discrete-event simulation correctly and wait for empty time blocks to catch up. Additionally, cascading effects from the slower running "discrete model" may have to erase events in the continuous model while catching up. For example, let's say we have a fire-analysis model that is discrete event and is doing heavy analysis (running slower than real time) on a controlled burn. The model may determine that a controlled burn is the best option, but the continuous model may have already deployed 2,500 firefighters to stop the fire instead of letting it go to the fire break. If the information from the "slower" discrete model supersedes the "faster" continuous model because the information is better, you must change the simulation and its current state in mid-stream. And you must erase events in the continuous model and make them look as if they never happened. In this example, you'd change the deployment of the firefighters and the simulated quantity of burned area and fuels to match the new simulation state.

If discrete-event and continuous models don't have to interact, you can use a simple event-queuing mechanism to link the models analytically. First, run the scenario on the discrete-event model and store the output analysis. Then, use a simple communications program to queue the output data into the continuous simulation when needed. In this case, the data can run at any continuous time basis, as long as the models don't need to interact.

Handling Human Interactions in Different Types of Simulations

There is no easy way to connect live to constructive simulations. Remember that constructive simulations are coded for little or no human interaction. But live simulations focus on human interface and reaction. Normally, live simulations run in real time and may sacrifice some accuracy to maintain real-time interaction. In most cases, you'll have to extensively recode constructive simulations to enable interactions with live simulations. Also, if the live simulation itself isn't built for interaction, you'll need to upgrade the communication interface.

Connecting Real Objects to Synthetic Objects

In the movie *Lawnmower Man*, the lead character, a mentally disabled man, gains power and intelligence as his mind interacts more deeply with simulations of virtual reality. In real life, virtual reality can't directly manipulate the brain . . . yet. Instead, we simply try to get operators to suspend disbelief. Virtual reality is a group of fancy sensory inputs to trick people into believing they're "somewhere else." Connecting real objects to synthetic objects in a simulation only requires proper communication protocols. The DOD maintains a new standard called the Distributed Interactive Simulation protocols to do just that. For example, a real radar display can show both real and simulated aircraft on the same scope. These distributed-simulation protocols formalize and standardize the message types, called protocol data units, so many different systems and simulations can communicate. The key concern in connecting real to synthetic objects deals with blurring reality and simulation. For example, it's okay to have simulated firefighters perish in a simulated fire, but it's catastrophic if firefighters in real life deploy into the middle of a hot area because a simulation says it's clear. Connecting real systems to simulations in life-and-death scenarios is still only in discussion and testing.

Calibrating One Model with Another

It's often difficult and expensive (in computing power and human resources) to use detailed models with high fidelity. In many cases, you can use these models effectively to calibrate faster, cheaper models that repeatedly perform specific analyses. One example is using a complex engagement model with six degrees of freedom to create a look-up table for probability of kill. The table decreases run time during real-time exercises in which speed is more important than precision.

5.3.2   Moving From Legacy Systems To Today's Systems

Incompatibility Between Legacy and New Systems

Using legacy software faces problems with software languages and the lack of standards found in older systems. The greatest advances in software over the past several years have been in communication and graphics. A whole new software-development paradigm, object orientation, has arisen to deal with these heavy communication requirements. Thus, we must answer certain questions when connecting or moving from legacy to current simulations:

1. Does the legacy core software require recoding into a new language?
2. Are the core algorithms still mathematically correct?
3. Does the legacy system require upgrading to pass new standards?
4. Does the legacy code require a new graphics user interface or communications interface?
5. Will the new system require distributed interaction between several systems?
6. If yes, will the legacy system require a new object orientation to interact appropriately?
7. If object orientation is the paradigm for the new combined system, can you view the legacy model (if modular) as one object in the combined system? If yes, you can save a lot of money in the short term.
8. Can the legacy model operate on a local-area or wide-area network? If not, how much recoding will you need to do?

Remember, that legacy simulations tend to be written in FORTRAN, PASCAL, BASIC, ADA, C, or special simulation languages such as SIMSCRIPT, GPSS, or SLAM. The legacy models usually aren't standard, and they stand alone. They're analytical, limited in their communication interfaces, and modular in design.

Modern simulations are written in C++ (object-oriented C) or object-oriented ADA. They also use special CASE and automated coding tools. Modern simulations usually try to follow standards under ISO 9000/9001/9002 and the Software Engineering Institute, which cover communication and graphical interfaces, as well as other general requirements. Even though the legacy model often has exceptional abilities, you'll need to recode to match it with new systems. The DOD also has several current programs trying to build integrated environments for modeling, simulation, and analysis. They provide standard interfaces to graphically build and connect diverse simulation models.

Trading Off Realism and Speed

Adding realism or fidelity to models continues to strain resources. Fortunately, today's personal computers are more powerful than yesterday's mainframes, and today's mainframes and supercomputers have made similar advances. Higher-order simulations, such as wargames, aren't as accurate as analytical models, but they run much faster. Adding high-resolution graphics and other sensory inputs can make analytical models cumbersome. You must trade processing power against bandwidth if you intend the new system to run in real time. Improving either increases the overall cost. Each simulation project has a best balance between speeding up processing or expanding bandwidth. See Fig. 5.9.

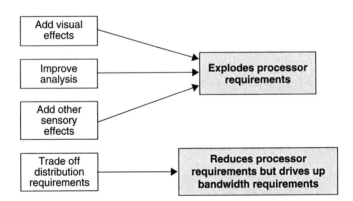

Fig. 5.9.   **Communications Effects.** Adding realism to models and simulations can dramatically increase the demand for computer resources. Distributing computations can reduce this demand at the expense of increased bandwidth. Trades between processing power and bandwidth must be considered to achieve the best balance.

To balance these competing characteristics, ask yourself some key questions:

1. How realistic must the visual inputs be and how fast must their refresh rates be?

2. How accurate must analysis be?

3. How much processing ability must you add if you improve sensory and analytical abilities?

4. Can you distribute the simulation to deal with requirements for more computations?

5. If yes, what communication bandwidth and speed do you need to maintain real-time interaction?

6. How is the database modeled? Can you distribute it?

5.3.3 Handling Communications

Simulation Databases

Beyond the communication requirements for models to interconnect through proper data formats is the database question. How will the simulation's subsystems interconnect and read and write to a common database? The common database can be complex. It may include ground geography, science, player controls, weather, current location, velocity, acceleration, and forces. Some of this data may be so massive that the database is actually a system of workstations and smaller databases.

Constructing modern databases depends on relational and object-oriented paradigms that have moved from general coding into database development. Relational databasing is sophisticated in that it governs interactions between users and data based on the declared data relationships. If you want to allow or negate data interactions, you change the relationships. Adding object orientation enhances this sense of relationship by forcing the data and relationships to be viewed as objects.

A data warehouse is a specialized, read-only database that has been scrubbed considerably to control quality. In the commercial sector, these warehouses are typically used by analysts to run business scenarios and simulations. They are particularly useful for simulation because they can be used to pull out real information without affecting ongoing operational use.

Older simulations won't have relational or object-oriented data. This is another hurdle to overcome in moving from legacy to modern systems. A possible work around is using a structured query language. Modern databases, such as DB2, use it to query old and new databases. As with any program, ask yourself: "Must I recode to support the structured query language?" and "What's the cost difference if I just start from scratch?"

Database Communications

You must consider not only the communication across a simulation's local- and wide-area networks but also the internal communication protocols. We discussed Aggregate Level Simulation Protocal and Distributed Interactive Simulation as external communication protocols. The databases on a simulation network maintain their own requirements for communication. Normally, in real life, the latest record is best. Sometimes, we keep multiple copies of a database to track the changes or allow for a refresh if an operator was wrong on the update. In simulation, the dynamics are more critical. Data may change several times a second in high-resolution simulations. The database must be open for change and very fast. Thus, you'll often have to alter a commercial package so it will work with simulations.

5.4   Specify Risks and Define Evaluation Criteria

Now that we've explored the possibilities for developing feasible alternative approaches for simulation, let's look at how you can create options of varying ability and complexity, evaluate alternatives for cost and risk, and finalize the baseline for an M&S program plan. (See Fig. 5.10)

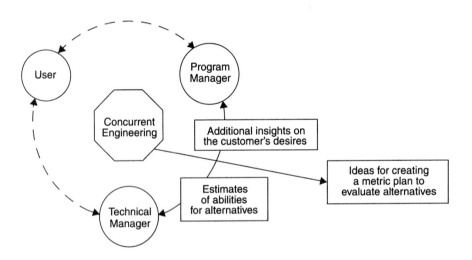

Fig. 5.10.   Selecting a Baseline from Alternatives. Step 3 in selecting a baseline approach for simulation establishes the abilities of identified alternatives and assesses their differences in risk and cost. Again, feedback to customers helps reduce the chances of overlooking or misunderstanding their needs.

5.4.1   Control Risks

Risks include required ability, complexity, cost, and schedule. Ability relates to people, hardware, software, general systems, logistics, and training. Complexity relates to the interaction of everything you need to accomplish the simulation's objectives. Cost is usually the #1 risk; it's the money required to buy what you need to complete the project. Schedule means mapping the time to build all planned components. You may equate schedule and cost in some instances, but they're essentially different.

You Must Control Cost to Establish a Proper Baseline

Although time and people are important, they're normally secondary to cost. In fact, they depend on dollars available for the project. In the long term, you can shorten or "crash" a project timeline by increasing the labor, assuming you can give the new team members work space and access to computing equipment. But in the short term, crashing is harder to do, particularly for M&S projects. New team members won't have enough background, and everyone tends to get in each other's way until you figure out "who is doing what." Over the short term, throwing more money and labor at a project actually increases costs and reduces effectiveness.

In reducing the budget, you must transfer people and extend timelines, which drives up long-term costs. Short-term cuts look good on paper, but changes to an established baseline always cost more. Of course, you can control this cost better if you have a flexible baseline with alternatives. (See Table 5.7 to review these relationships.)

Table 5.7.   Controlling Project Costs. To effectively control costs, you must understand the relationships among cost, schedule, and labor.

Budget	Time	People
Spend more	Can accelerate delivery over the long term	Can hire more people
Reduce budget	Delivery time lengthens	Must reduce staffing

Note: Reducing budgets, if drastic enough, may destroy the project. Priorities for reducing personnel costs are: #1 – Management hours, #2 – Admin/Graphics hours and then #3 – Engineer hours.

Project-management tools allow you to develop a proposed project baseline and then run alternatives against it. After evaluating these alternatives, you'll select from them to establish the project baseline. Most project-management tools allow you to maintain cost and schedule data directly in their project models (files), but they don't include the simulation's abilities and complexity. Your baseline will usually be moderately priced and have some cost flexibility to accomplish the simulation's basic objectives. Your secondary alternatives will cost more but can do more. Finally, you must prepare a bare-bones, lowest-cost model, with little or no cost flexibility, so you have a "we can't do it for less" cost boundary. Your customer must agree on the risk and cost tradeoffs for alternatives. Additionally, you should maintain separate program plans for each alternative.

5.4.2   Manage Your Engineering Project

Project management helps you control risks (capability, complexity, cost, and schedule) in an integrated environment. First, you create project models to baseline the simulation effort and to describe alternatives or excursions the customer and engineer may want to take. PERT/CPM is the main analytical tool to control schedule. Your project manager must display PERT and Gantt charts, handle work breakdown structures, and trace human resources to accomplish the mission. In this chapter, I'll talk only about the basic charts. Chapter 6 covers the details. Another important feature is the ability to maintain a file structure that saves the original baseline model and any major changes to the model as the project moves to completion. Balancing cost, schedule, abilities, and complexities (as you clarify requirements) will force you to change the project. A good file structure allows you to refer to these changes as you travel down the project timeline and to justify your actions when the project is complete. Maintaining a solid development baseline and historical record saves time and money when the final report rolls around.

5.4.3   Revisit the Tools of Concurrent Engineering

Our focus in Step 3 is to document what the baseline and alternatives can do by assessing their differences in risk and cost. Remember that concurrent engineering and its tools—Quality Function Deployment, Design of Experiments, and Statistical Process Control—directly help reduce risk. Using concurrent engineering to clarify requirements improves how you carry out your project. The original results and any updates from quality function deployment will track directly into the project and help you develop the simulation. As the simulation project runs, it should feed the hard prototype development (if the simulation project isn't software only or is part of a bigger R&D effort). Thus, computer-assisted elements should overlap and run concurrently with the simulation effort, particularly for initial design. These computer-assisted activities provide nice feedback to your simulation effort. Although they don't give you a hard prototype to compare against the simulations, you can use them to confirm basic designs and mathematics.

You must plan for reliability and build it into your simulations—typically by using automated coding, ISO 9000/9001/9002 standards, and the Software Engineering Institute's (SEI) Capability Maturity Model. Chapter 6 deals with this issue directly. Additionally, the ISO and SEI models directly help you plan for reliability, select from available models, determine development time and VV&A requirements, and make sure your software is maintainable, portable, and reusable.

The baseline and alternatives you derive for your simulation program (synthetic environment) directly affect the master program for research and development—usually as a key subset or an entry phase to determine whether or not to build the actual system. Sometimes, you'll build a simulation to train operators or provide insight into a system. In either case, the simulation is a virtual extension of the master system it is modeled from and can't be divorced from it.

5.4.4   Establish Training Requirements

You must build in requirements from the start for standards, evaluations, and training. Coordinate operational requirements that include training with other operational demands that drive your technical requirements. Also, subdivide the training requirements between what the simulation supports (real world) and what you need to maintain and improve the simulation (synthetic environment).

Include Training Requirements in the Original Control Document

As simulations become more virtual, regardless of hierarchical level, we can more easily determine and include requirements for real-world training, but the original control document still must provide a baseline for the training system. In the DOD, this document is the operational-requirements document; in commercial projects, it may be missing or included in the requirements section of what is commonly called the conceptual-design document. Because this is a control document for the entire project, the project manager for the simulation program must track it and pass it on to the technical manager for consideration in all the steps. Current simulation developments don't integrate training and logistics requirements, but in the future, project and technical managers will have to create simulations with ease of training in mind.

Using concurrent engineering will make this integration easier. Add a new task to develop training concurrently and include trainers in initial quality function deployment, requirements definition, production, and testing. Usually, customers will train their own people. In this case, developmental feedback from the simulation will help them design and develop the training system. This system may require follow-on development of training simulators and wargames that would use the first simulation as a baseline.

Use Feedback Loops

Concurrent engineering—especially quality function deployment—provides immediate feedback to customers. As modelers propose technical solutions that answer the customers' prioritized requirements, the customers will learn more about what they need to train on the new or modified system. Simulation runs themselves can help customers create learning objectives as operators interact in the synthetic environment. As a result, customers may change operational requirements based on these new insights, often making up for the engineers' tendency to overlook or misunderstand training needs.

5.4.5   Provide Logistical Support

Include Logistics Requirements in the Original Control Document

As above, when simulations become more virtual, regardless of hierarchical level, you can more easily determine the logistics requirements—especially if you use computer-assisted tools to diagram the quantities and substances of system parts. The original control document also provides a baseline for the logistics system you must track and coordinate with your technical manager and team.

Use Feedback Loops

Concurrent engineering and quality function deployment also give customers immediate feedback on logistical requirements. Making logistics less complex results in more reliable simulations.

Simulate Logistics Separately whenever Necessary

If you have to develop a logistics simulation, you can probably use an existing program and simply feed in new data. A separate logistics simulation is sometimes necessary because its unique perspective adds to the operational simulation's value.

Provide Logistical Support for the Simulation Itself

Logistics for the simulation itself boils down to choosing commercial or government software off the shelf or developing new code. Commercial software may not answer all the requirements, but industry shoulders the logistical support. If the technology area that the commercial packages come from is rich enough to have several developers competing for your business, the entire industry and customer base bear the logistics expenses. Commercial developers also view product support as key to keeping your business. Weigh the total cost of commercial software against the requirement for government software to provide program support. Perhaps the greatest cost for new code is in alpha and beta testing. Industry does this by providing the new code to their users either free or at low cost, expecting them to provide feedback. Those who do respond get the fully tested code later at no or low cost again. Most importantly, users who are familiar with the alpha and beta releases have a competitive advantage over those who don't participate in the testing. The government does alpha and beta testing by paying a contractor to do it, which costs more but involves far fewer people.

5.4.6   Use Effective Controls for Upgrades

The military has a formal upgrading process called the Planned Program Product Improvement Cycle. Commercial industry calls it upgrading. Although the process varies widely, it has some common features. Upgrading normally shortens development and often gears it toward better integrating parts of a system. When the development isn't integration, it concentrates on redesigning, replacing, or fixing one or more sub-components. If a simulation was originally built for a complex system, the simulation upgrade will concentrate on recoding only the objects or subroutines associated with the real world's upgraded components or system integration. Thus, upgrades should be faster than original development for real-world systems and accompanying simulations.

As any core system upgrades, we must upgrade the simulation at the same time. For example, upgrading an M1 tank to an M1A1 consisted of replacing a rifled 105-mm main gun with a smooth-bore, 120-mm. Because the larger round is more lethal, has different ballistics, and requires larger storage, simulating an M1A1 differs from that for the M1. Even though we may only need to change data, we still have to review the simulation model and upgrade it.

An interesting problem occurs when managers or marketers use upgrading to develop new software or extensive upgrades. It may be politically unacceptable to build a new system or it may be easier to fund a new system using funding for upgrades. Engineers don't care what the process is called. But if the upgrade is actually a new development or close to it, we must very carefully test integration of the subsystems. A classic example of this is the Marine Corps' upgrades of the Cobra helicopter. In response to the increasing threat, Cobra upgrades increased the firepower initially. This put more weight on the helicopter and slowed it down, so it needed more engine power. This increased power added torque and greater long-term stress, which ultimately resulted in some helicopters falling apart earlier than expected. An effective upgrade tests all new parallel interactions between the old and new subsystems.

5.5   Define and Document the Final Baseline

The baseline strategy includes all model components, the customer's requirements, the derived technical requirements and specifications, and the program plan. The baseline must have documented, derived controls: an approach for the technical solution (described by type, level, and formalism); model assumptions; constraints; variables; and object controls (if the simulation is to be object oriented).

5.5.1   Maintain Alternatives

Resist the common tendency to discard alternatives after choosing a baseline, especially for research efforts. Remember, research dynamics may force later changes that require you to reconsider what you discarded. If you must, archive your alternative strategies, but keep them around. At best, you should let early research help you decide which alternative to take. Unfortunately, accounting and budget controls work against these "open" decisions. Still, the greater the risk, the more you need to maintain alternatives.

In government developments, you'll have exploratory and development phases. Although both phases follow this book's development process, the exploratory phase determines the baseline for development. This phase helps reduce risk.

Commercial developments follow the same process but with more dynamic budget approval and a stronger possibility of killing the project in mid-stream. Because of the painstaking nature of government budgeting, an approved, funded government project is unlikely to be canceled. In private enterprise, marketing, production, engineering, and budgeting more dynamically influence each other. Thus, the private sector tends toward more flexible but also more volatile development.

5.5.2   Update Your Baseline

As unforeseen changes occur, you must update your baseline. It's important to revisit regularly all requirements and solution approaches. The program plan correlates the use of time, people, and money to the project and, once in place, should be easy to change as the baseline shifts. This is especially important as we manage changes and document them for costing.

5.5.3 Start Early to Write Your Final Report

If you don't plan for the final report from day one, it can end your project poorly and cost a lot of money. Many fine simulations have vaporized because the project teams didn't have a good plan in place for the final report. Concurrent engineering gives you plenty of exceptional, automated support. Quality function deployment documents and rank orders all missions, objectives, requirements, and approaches. Design of experiments shows your experimental development, selection of the best experiment set, and analytical results. You can place much of this information in your analysis appendix. The project plan provides all the timeline interactions and tells the project's story. Project-management tools usually allow you to generate final reports. Thus, you should see the final report as a concurrent effort throughout your project.

You can use the report itself to see how the project is going if you create a final-report shell at the beginning—listing what questions will be answered. Fill in the answers as you go along. Then, as problems arise, you and your team can better react and push through them. This final-report process is a management tool that supports your project plan—the main control and information tool for customers, management, and engineers.

5.6 Develop a Metric Plan

Your metric plan flows directly from the previous steps. Break out your metrics to match the hierarchical structure of ranked requirements and the broad missions and objectives. Figure 5.11 describes the elements needed to create the metric plan.

5.6.1 Metrics—What Are They?

Today, we have two basic types: (1) measures of effectiveness, which measure a system's effectiveness based on customer requirements and (2) measures of performance, which measure the system's performance based on the technical requirements.

Using Measures of Effectiveness

Measures of effectiveness evaluate the customer's bottom line. In typical wargames, this would include numbers of tanks, planes, and ships destroyed or disabled. In commercial activities, it would include changes in price/earnings ratios, market share, competitor viability, and stock value. As different scenarios run, customers can determine the best strategy and tactics. Effectiveness measures establish how well the simulation meets missions, objectives, and the customer's broad requirements. For our fire-management example, these measures might include

1. Number of acres destroyed in a given scenario or fire season (less is better)
2. Numbers of firemen and civilians lost or injured in a given scenario or fire season (less is better)
3. Percent of fires caused by humans (less is better; measures effectiveness of training and prevention techniques)

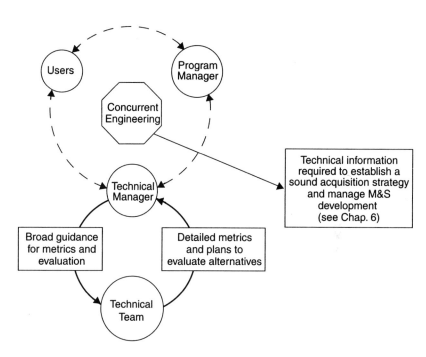

Fig. 5.11. **Develop Your Metric Plan.** Interaction between the technical manager and the technical team yields detailed metrics and plans to evaluate available alternatives. This step finalizes the technical information required to establish an acquisition strategy for M&S development and to manage these activities as they proceed.

In business, they would measure changes in revenue, profit, stock value, and market share for the given scenario.

Using Measures of Performance

Performance measures typically cover such things as the communication system's speed and carrying capacity; the accuracy of command, control, and computations; and the performance of specific systems. They measure how well the simulation meets more detailed operational requirements and their derived technical requirements. For our fire-management example, typical measures of performance would be

1. The firefighting teams' average time of response to fires (less is better).
2. Time for the system to alert the command and control center of fires (less is better).
3. Average time to deploy the mobile command and control center (less is better).
4. Accuracy of fused data in percent (more is better).

Your Simulation's Purpose Affects Metrics

For human-in-the-loop simulators, also known as trainers, you want to provide a virtual, synthetic environment to train pilots, armor crew, police, firefighters, special forces, and other operators. These specific, single-purpose simulations require greater resolution, which translates to very specific measures of effectiveness and performance. On the other end of the simulation spectrum are wargames. These simulations train and develop grand strategy. They don't show or allow individual action and are highly aggregated. Thus, their metrics are also less specific. Our fire-management example might require these simulation types:

1. Training Simulators—Hook-and-ladder actions, C-130 drops of chemical fire suppressants, or operations at the fire-watch console
2. Mid-level Crew Trainer—Simulates fire control for fire chiefs
3. Wargame Level—Wargame for national fire management

Allowing for Chaos

Nearly all simulations incorporate some form of interaction probabilities. Human-in-the-loop simulators (trainers) have fewer of them because they're oriented to react to an operator's actions. Some trainers have none. Wargames have many—variously called Monte Carlo elements, chance, or dice rolling. Engineers use these elements to mimic the real world's interactions and the chaotic elements that humans call chance.

But nothing is truly left to chance if we can know and see all the possible interactions. As our knowledge of math, physics, and chemistry expands, fewer outcomes are left to chance. Thus, many simulations are highly accurate predictors and require fewer Monte Carlo elements to mimic real-world systems. Unfortunately, as we increase a simulation's sophistication to allow for greater chaos and reduce the dice rolling, computations may increase geometrically.

As a result, engineers must cautiously create highly accurate simulations that allow for greater chaos. Customers want everything (highest fidelity) but never have the dollars to pay for it. Engineers and customers must agree to trade off fidelity and cost. This is why concurrent engineering is so important. Without it, customers never understand the technology trade-offs, and engineers never truly simulate the customers' requirements.

Allowing chaos means metrics will differ over each simulation run depending on random number seeding and human interaction. Your metrics must be averaged results from multiple runs over the entire system, because individual results may be misleading.

5.6.2 Metrics—Keeping Customers and Developers Close through Concurrent Engineering's Approach to Total Quality

Metrics—especially feedback to customers from measures of effectiveness—determine if everyone agrees. We develop simulations to define and measure possible technology choices or to learn about and train on a particular system. Figure 5.12, below, shows how concurrent engineering applies to creating metrics.

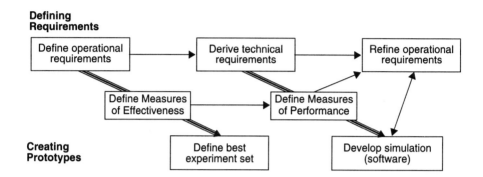

Fig. 5.12.   Flow for Creating Metrics through Concurrent Engineering. Concurrent engineering provides an effective framework for creating metrics from operational and technical requirements to help refine these requirements and develop appropriate models and simulations.

5.6.3   Applying Metrics in the Real World—a New Communication System

Recently, the military needed to test (simulate) how a new communication system could speed critical targeting data to its strike aircraft on combat air patrol. Because the targets were mobile, the data had to move quickly. One broad measure of effectiveness registered total number of targets destroyed. The baseline model used a real data set and ran excursions off the baseline wherever the communication architecture included different amounts of this new communication system. The broad measures of performance logged time through the command, control, and communication system for battle management. After all the excursions ran, the performance measures showed dramatic improvements in message time proportional to how much of the new system was in the architecture. Interestingly, the measure of effectiveness changed little. Obviously, another performance factor was more important to successfully striking these targets. Evaluators discovered that decision makers and human checkers of data took much more time than the communication network did. Thus, the customer learned the new communication system was incredibly successful in quickly passing data, but increased combat kills depended more on new streamlined decision making and human processing of this data.

As you can imagine, this discovery opened a political "can of worms." Most military services maintain rules of engagement that actually depend on slowdowns in decision making and data checking. In this case, a simulation could only provide analysis for leaders to discuss the options. Another key point is that the effectiveness measure—numbers of targets destroyed—wasn't sophisticated enough to deal with the political requirement to maintain rules of engagement. This is a clear-cut example of costs that are unmeasurable and must be determined in advance. We can measure the new communication system, weapons platforms, and targets as direct dollar costs. We can also measure the value of defending lives and property (less destroyed is preferable). However, evaluating rules of engagement is subjective. Politicians want them tight so there are fewer incidents, and the military services want them loose in combat so they can efficiently neutralize targets.

The fire-management problem would raise similar issues. More quickly communicating the locations of potential fire breakouts may increase the number of false alarms. How many can we allow before the fire-management system becomes too costly? (Remember, each deployment of a fire-response team immediately costs money.) How tight are the rules of engagement or deployment to be? As shown in the example above, a simulation could help us decide by showing what we can analyze in trying to determine total cost.

5.6.4   The Value of Metrics

The original metrics described and developed in this chapter measure how well the simulation answers questions and customer's expectations, as well as how "real" the model is. These metrics must be relevant across all excursions, so they can support your choice of a development as your baseline.

Answering Questions about Operational Effectiveness (Measures of Effectiveness)

Remember, measures of effectiveness directly answer the customer's operational questions, so customers will key on them to evaluate your proposed alternatives. In the fire-management example, measuring improvements in loss of life and property are much more significant to customers than a measure of performance that documents reduced communication time for sensor messages. Engineers must describe how performance measures tie into and feed the measures of effectiveness. In our example, reduced time for communicating suspected fire locations (the supporting performance measure) directly correlates to reduced loss of life and property (the effectiveness measure).

Start creating measures of effectiveness as soon as you begin defining requirements. Ask

1. What criteria are most important to the customer that I can measure across the baseline and all alternatives?

2. Can I translate these criteria into measures of performance and effectiveness?

When engineers understand what the customers want to measure, they can more easily create the supporting performance measures—as well as the code required to make both kinds of measures work.

Answering Analytically How Well the Simulation Performs (Measures of Performance)

Although measures of performance are less visible to customers, they're the analytical core for evaluating the modeled system. They're also easier to define and more readily accepted. They analytically clarify what may be a rather abstract, or even political, measure of effectiveness. Once you've decided on a baseline, you'll start generating metrics at a faster pace. Make sure the measures of performance are relevant across all of the potential model excursions.

References

Fisher, Gene H. 1974. *Cost Considerations in Systems Analysis.* New York, NY: American Elsevier Publishing Company, Inc.

Mattison, Rob. 1996. *Data Warehousing: Strategies, Technologies, and Techniques.* New York, NY: McGraw-Hill, Inc.

Thackeray, Ray J. and George Van Treeck. 1989. *Quality Function Deployment for Embedded Systems and Software Product Development.* Boston, MA: Digital Equipment Corp.

CHAPTER 6

Developing an Acquisition Strategy

Jerry W. Lawson, *The Peak Technologies Group, Inc.*

The M&S baseline created in Chap. 5 produces a set of critical M&S requirements. Now, the procuring agency must develop an acquisition strategy that will create the M&S products needed to meet these requirements. Acquisition begins after a need is established and continues from identifying a qualified contractor through actually developing the models or simulations and creating a maintenance contract.

This chapter establishes processes to acquire models and simulations that will satisfy the needs of the system architecture. To use these processes, we must have

1. A defined need for one or more models or simulations

2. A completed concept definition that specifies the requirements

If we properly apply the processes defined in this chapter, we'll end up with

1. One or more contracts to develop and carry out the models or simulations specified by the concept definition

2. Procedures for managing the defined models or simulations

3. Procedures for technically implementing the defined models or simulations

Successful acquisition consists of defining, managing, and implementing a project. Table 6.1 details these processes, which I'll explain in the following sections of this chapter.

Table 6.1.   How to Acquire Models and Simulations. Successfully acquiring models and simulations depends on three main steps:

Project Step	Elements
1. Defining	Determine cost limits for identified models or simulations Determine scheduling constraints for identified models or simulations Establish the project's structure
2. Managing	Plan the development effort Establish metrics for tracking and overseeing development Create procedures and policies for managing requirements Create procedures and policies for managing configurations Create procedures and policies for quality assurance Use procedures and policies for sub-contracts
3. Implementing	Monitor implementation Accept delivered product Establish maintenance needs Create a maintenance contract

6.1   Defining Project Requirements, Limits, Structure, and Responsibilities

As highlighted in Chap. 5, to start acquiring models or simulations, we must establish a need and then define a system concept that requires M&S. Concept definition begins by defining system requirements to address a real-world problem and developing a solution to satisfy these requirements. At this stage, we don't specify how to solve the problem. Instead, we state what the project team needs to accomplish and what must happen to make M&S work.

6.1.1   Develop a Solution that Meets Requirements

Once we establish system requirements, it's time to begin acquisition by obtaining possible solutions. Developers use the system requirements to guide their proposed solution and typically recommend three uses for the types of models and simulations identified in Chap. 5.

First, developers may propose using prototypes or existing models and simulations to help define the final solution. Prototype models and simulations usually apply to exploratory research or become a foundation for the final solution. Models and simulations for exploratory research are built quickly to help analyze the problem domain; we don't expect to use them by the end of the project. But sometimes, cost and schedule constraints cause exploratory prototypes to become building blocks for the final solution, even though they're not based on sound technical solutions. If we use them in this way, we're engaging in a contradiction.

Prototypes are supposed to prove concepts and solve potential high-risk technical issues. They're rarely thorough or expandable enough to provide a solid technical foundation. Thus, using a prototype model or simulation as a foundation ultimately creates a system that can barely satisfy the current requirements, much less allow for future growth at reasonable cost. Prototypes should only help us define some of the actual models and simulations in the final solution.

The second and most common use of M&S is to provide pieces of the overall solution to the real-world problem. These models and simulations need to be well defined and built to meet the user's present and future needs.

Finally, one or more models and simulations may solve the entire problem. This scenario is more typical of smaller projects; for larger or more complex projects, models and simulations are more likely to be pieces of the overall solution.

No matter what kind of M&S a project may need, we must clearly define what we need to build and what the project expects us to deliver. This is true for subcomponents, components, and the overall project. Whether the M&S is simple or complex, successful acquisition critically requires clearly defined expectations and responsibilities. The basic steps in defining an acquisition strategy are determining cost and schedule limits and creating a program structure to respond to these constraints.

6.1.2 Determine Limits on Cost and Schedule

Needs must always match money available or accessible for development, so we always have to analyze costs. Even if we have plenty of money, staying on schedule still requires models and simulations that will be done on time. Cost and schedule can severely constrain the development of models and simulations. Two scenarios exist for establishing these constraints. In the first, a critical need drives acquisition, so it overshadows current budgets. The procuring agency establishes a cost target and creates a schedule that will meet this critical need. Then, it gets the money and makes plans to meet the established constraints. In the second scenario, predefined budget and schedule limits drive requirements. In this case, the procuring agency must plan to tailor requirements so they fit the budget and schedule. It may initially trim down its requirements or implement only the most critical ones and plan to meet others later on, when it gets more money. Regardless of which scenario applies, the procuring agency must be aware of these limits and create a project structure that responds to them, so the required M&S products will be done on time and on budget.

6.1.3 Establish Project Structure

Creating M&S applications is a discipline, but so are overseeing and managing projects. Passive project structures commonly lead to failed projects. Reactive, crisis management is common, even though industry has established the basic concepts of a sound project structure. Development teams too often assume they can skip proper planning and initial definition, only to discover (too late) that these steps save—rather than cost—money. Sound project development depends on clearly identifying needs, expectations, roles, and how the elements fit together.

Prepare for Development

Any business transaction—commercial or government—works more effectively when expectations are clear from the beginning. Otherwise, we typically have to restart and reshape development (which costs more money) when needs are finally determined. Before beginning development, we must clearly understand all requirements and restrictions.

Requirements establish high-level expectations and underpin the development items we'll deliver. Next to the actual system itself, the set of established requirements is most critical to our success. Usually a requirements document captures them. The contract between a procuring agency and one or more developers will typically specify the project deliverables and due dates, along with a high-level set of requirements the system must meet. But the detailed requirements usually wait until after a contract is awarded. At least 5% to 10% of the total M&S effort goes into completing lower-level system requirements, which is often part of the overall development contract. On rare occasions, the procuring agency may choose to buy a detailed definition of requirements before awarding a contract. Although this approach allows for more accurate bidding, it also provides an unfair bidding advantage to the contractor who specifies the lower-level requirements.

The detailed requirements document is the single most important deliverable other than the actual system itself for two main reasons. First, the requirements document is a hidden contract between the development engineers and users of the M&S application. The developers and users usually have some voice in developing, reviewing, and approving this document. And the approved requirements establish a binding agreement on what the system must actually accomplish.

Second, the requirement specification establishes the functional baseline—a concept originally established in DOD-Std-2167A (1988). The developer builds functionally according to this specification, which also determines if additions or changes are in or out of scope according to the statement of work. In-scope changes should cost no more money, but out-of-scope changes usually mean the procuring agency must pay more to cover costs.

In addition to requirements, an M&S development will also have restrictions, of which four are most common:

1. Applicable Standards—The development may need to adhere to government or commercial standards imposed by the procuring agency, mandated by industry (such as the handling of hazardous waste), or required for quality control. Of course, more standards mean higher cost.

2. Cost Restrictions—which must be clear before development begins. Development teams need to establish solutions that account for these restrictions.

3. Period of Performance—or schedule restrictions that require special planning.

4. Accreditation/Certification—based on official procedures for government or industry.

Determine Deliverables Required from Development

The system and its hardware and software are obviously part of the specified deliverables. Requirements should be documented and delivered. Procuring agencies must establish formal criteria for accepting the developed models and simulations, including tests that verify they meet the conceptual design and established requirements. A formal method should also validate that the models and simulations represent the real world and, if required, ensure they receive accreditation or certification. Refer to Chapter 11 for detailed discussions on verification, validation, and accreditation.

Projects must also require training and user manuals to help ensure users can operate the delivered system. Training and documentation are critical because project success depends largely on users accepting the system. Without their acceptance and understanding, even the most sophisticated and powerful M&S applications will gather dust.

Some likely deliverables are the

Integration Plan—Systems consisting of various models and simulations need an integration plan specified as a deliverable. This plan should detail how and when the models and simulations will be delivered and what is required for each one to work alone and as part of the system.

Data Dictionary—Closely related to the integration plan, a document (or a software program) should define and control all interfaces and database items between the system's components. This allows all systems and sub-systems to follow a master plan that incorporates changes to one part of a system flow into other parts.

M&S Data—Many models and simulations depend on historical or algorithmic data to populate them. Who gets this data and populates the model should be part of this deliverable.

Source Code—Large systems will certainly be expected to have a long shelf-life, so the procuring agency will most likely want to own the source code. Once the system is installed and running, they'll need the source code to maintain the models and simulations. They'll also want a maintenance suite, including hardware-development equipment, plus software-development tools such as compilers, linkers, tools for developing the graphical user interface, and all other tools required to maintain the software.

Documentation for Design, Test, and Verification, Validation, and Accreditation (VV&A)—The procuring agency may decide to maintain the software or pay an outside agency (such as the original developers or other qualified engineering organizations) to maintain it. The larger the system, the more documentation they'll need on design, test, and VV&A. Design documentation may include descriptions of top-level and detailed design. Test documentation may include test plans and procedures that allow regression testing with little difficulty, whereas VV&A documentation may include detailed VV&A plans and procedures.

Reviews—The larger the system the more a procuring agency will want to check progress. Periodic and lifecycle reviews will maintain communication among all parties. Periodic Project Management Reviews will establish the developers' progress and identify and assess risks. Periodic Technical Interchange Meetings should discuss technical development and progress. Reviews of the system and subsystem requirements will make sure the system built meets the buyer's needs and contractual direction. Design reviews will verify the planned M&S is realistic and reasonably safe. Whether (and how often) we need these periodic and lifecycle reviews depends on the size of the M&S effort.

The length of a project also influences the need for periodic reports. Monthly progress reports, as well as monthly schedule and cost reports are typical of projects that last a year or more. One common format for progress reports is the P3 report, which has three parts—progress for the reporting period, plans for the upcoming reporting period, and problems encountered or expected.

6.1.4   Understand Roles and Responsibilities

Roles and responsibilities are distinct and important to developing an M&S project. Major players represent a system of checks and balances that help develop a quality product within the program's schedule and cost constraints. In Chap. 3, we introduced the people who conduct M&S activities and how they relate to one another. Let's now detail how they must interact to establish the acquisition strategy that will produce the desired M&S products. Managers, agents, developers, integrators, and users contribute equally to acquiring, developing, and deploying an M&S product.

At the outermost level, the procuring agency essentially manages an M&S application. They dictate who gets the contract and (depending on the contract's structure) approve the

- Overall system requirements
- Detailed sub-system requirements
- Top-level and detailed designs
- Test plans and procedures
- Final system acceptance, including VV&A
- Work changes resulting from changed or added requirements.

Thus, they can assess progress and direct the development—otherwise known as managing the effort. A closer examination of the procuring agency and the development-contract team shows that both manage three distinct areas—the contract, the project (or program), and technical development.

The procuring agency needs someone to manage the contract—from their own staff or from an outside agency. The contract administrator ensures that all interactions—including changes, clarifications, and revisions—are legal, as defined in the contract. The developer and sub-developers must also have contract administrators who ensure they act within the legal contractual framework.

Project management mainly involves overseeing the development's budget and schedule. Again, the procuring agency should have representatives who manage the project and gain insight into the contractors' development effort.

This helps protect the procuring agency's interest—especially if the contract is "Cost Plus." The most common ways to gain insight are status reports and program reviews of cost and schedule information. The procuring agency manages the program at a high level, whereas the prime contractor and subcontractors manage daily development.

The prime contractor's program manager controls the pulse and synergizes the "worlds" of the entire development effort. The dynamics of this position make it one of the most critical to M&S development. The program manager manages the project daily, usually under the eye of the developer's corporate management, which oversees various projects for all or part of the corporation. As Fig. 6.1 shows, oversight from the procuring agency's project manager and the contractor's corporate management check and balance the program manager's actions.

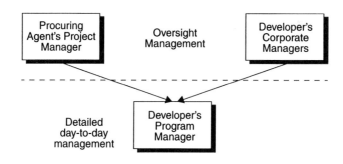

Fig. 6.1.   Checks and Balances in Program Management. Management organizations of the buyer and the developer create an effective way to monitor the program manager's actions.

Overseers review and guide how the program manager plans activities, tracks progress, and corrects problems. At the same time, the prime contractor's program manager—along with the sub-contractor's corporate management—oversees the sub-contractors' program managers. These lower-level program managers plan activities, track progress, and correct problems related to the sub-contractors' tasks.

Although having management organizations with slightly different roles establishes a system of checks and balances, this system has drawbacks. The various players may have different agendas—hidden within the obvious agenda of delivering a quality product on time and within budget. For example, corporate management may be driven by profit to assign their best people to some other project that is more important to the corporate plan. This can be true for the prime contractor and the subcontractors. Another agenda may involve managers who are next in line for promotion and who decide on short-term progress that risks long-term disaster. Sometimes even inherent checks and balances counteract the intended objective.

These potential traps may seem difficult or even impossible to combat, especially when only 16% of software-development efforts are considered successful [Comaford 1995]. But good project planning, tracking, oversight, and other management techniques to reduce risk can greatly improve this success rate. A development's program managers are the cornerstones of program management. Figure 6.2 shows that program managers consider, filter, and distribute issues to the right people. They are the contact point for problems and the orchestrators of solutions and action plans.

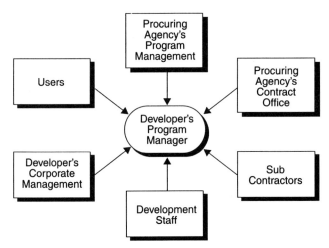

Fig. 6.2.   The Developer's Program Manager is the Hub of Program Management. All program participants look to the program manager to address issues and resolve problems.

Sometimes one player's issues may directly contradict another player's goals and objectives. For example, the development staff needs urgent training to solve a technical problem, but the procuring agency usually doesn't pay for training. Yet, when the program manager asks for money from corporate management, he or she finds corporate training funds at zero. The procuring agency and the development staff both want the training; corporate management hopes the staff can find a solution without spending more company money. In reality, program managers don't always find such solutions. Most solutions satisfy some, but rarely all, of the players.

As you can see, the development's program manager is critical to a project's success. Good organizations clearly define management processes to help this critical position, so procuring agencies should read carefully the management descriptions included in proposals from potential contractors.

Procuring agencies often retain special agents to provide expertise the agency lacks—typically in management or technical oversight. If possible, management agents should have experience as development program managers, so they'll have insight into common problems and give the procuring agency more knowledgeable and understanding oversight. They should understand sound management techniques, as discussed in Sec. 6.2. They must make sure developing organizations establish sound techniques for project planning, tracking, and oversight; requirements management; quality assurance; configuration management; and sub-contract management. Once these processes are in place, management agents should oversee them for the procuring agency.

Technical agents may help the procuring agency review and approve the developer's technical products:

Requirements—The technical agents may help create or write all the system-level requirements—or, at least, review and approve them. They may also help in, or be responsible for, reviewing and approving all lower-level requirement specifications.

Designs—The technical agent may help review and approve the top-level and detailed designs. This would involve the preliminary and the critical design reviews, along with the top-level and detailed design documents.

Testing—The technical agent may help review and approve testing of the delivered models and simulations, including test plans, test procedures, criteria for final acceptance tests, and the actual final acceptance tests.

Verification, Validation, and Accreditation—The technical agent may perform some of the VV&A activities detailed in Chap. 11, which can include the requirements, design, and testing activities described above.

Depending on the system's size and complexity, more than one developer may build the models and simulations or the components and sub-components. Although procuring agencies may directly contract the individual developers of components or sub-components, they normally hold one prime contractor responsible for developing, integrating, and completing the system, as well as making it work.

Those who will operate and use M&S applications (users) may or may not directly associate with the procuring agency, so their needs may not synchronize. In these rare cases, the developing organization carries an extra burden—making the application successful to users. An application that meets all of the procuring agency's requirements still isn't successful if it makes users unhappy.

6.2 Managing Acquisition Activities

Once a project is under way, we must make sure proper management techniques are in place before we start developing the technical application. The most common mistake project teams make is assuming the technical development is more important than project management. The reverse is actually true. Proper management leads to effective planning, lower risk, and successful technical development. When management takes a backseat, it becomes reactive—falling into a trap commonly known as crisis management.

6.2.1   Use Standard Processes that Reduce Risk

M&S development has often been late or over budget—either of which can disappoint customers and decrease profits. Few projects can afford to miss the targeted budget or the scheduled delivery. Thus, the prime contractor's proposal should demonstrate a standard way to manage systems that will produce consistent results.

Without this standard process, the development team often rushes madly to complete a development only to start another project with the same demands, expectations, and likelihood of success. A cycle (and a process) is established—but will it produce better-quality products, better estimates of M&S efforts, the best return on investment for the company, and confidence that the system will be delivered on time and within budget? Many contractors determine that, to stay competitive, they can't afford to miss schedules and budgets, exhaust or burn out employees, and continually reinvent the wheel. The Software Engineering Institute (SEI) has developed the Capability Maturity Model (Fig. 6.3) to help procurement agencies determine contractors' ability to deliver on their proposals. This model promises finally to tame the software-development beast.

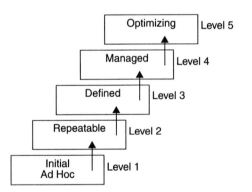

Fig. 6.3.   **The Software Engineering Institute's Capability Maturity Model [Paulk 1993].** This model helps identify qualified developers by defining different levels of effectiveness and describing the characteristics of the developer associated with each level.

Why is process maturity attractive? It allows two major goals to emerge. First, standardizing should eliminate much of the guesswork in developing cost and schedule estimates—allowing accurate bids with reasonable chances of success. Standard estimates protect profits and ensure the company can repeat its performance—regardless of who does the work. Second, established processes can grow, mature, and become more efficient, which means future software will develop faster and cheaper. They also allow engineers to work smarter, not harder. Typical results should be better processes and the ability to design and write reusable software—further lowering the cost of future development.

If standardizing processes is so attractive, why isn't it already at every software-development house across the country? Cost and government regulations are two main reasons. Some government agencies are starting to require developers to obtain accreditation from SEI before bidding on contracts, and that can be costly. Sometimes companies can't afford to invest in SEI's accreditation—yet, they can't afford not to invest. The challenge becomes how to use standard processes to develop M&S software without over-investing in them.

If a procuring agency requires contractors to get SEI's accreditation, the list of capable and accredited firms becomes very short, very fast. Fortunately, some basic standard processes can be developed without huge corporate investments— a good compromise for many contracts. In these cases, a procuring agency can look at the management and technical sections of a contractor's proposal to see if they meet the intent of SEI's Capability Maturity Model. If so, there is a good chance the contractor can deliver within budget and on schedule.

A good project-management approach would be one that meets the intent of Level 2 of SEI's Capability Maturity Model—repeatability. It gives us confidence that programs will be completed within the anticipated schedules and budgets. Repeatability consists of

- Planning the program
- Tracking and over seeing the project
- Managing requirements
- Managing configuration
- Ensuring quality ("quality assurance")
- Managing sub-contracts

6.2.2   Plan the Development

Planning is the first element of repeatability under Level 2 of SEI's Capability Maturity Model. Although developing software is somewhat of an art, project planning consists of three straightforward steps—estimate the size of the effort, determine the cost of the effort, and create a schedule that shows how the work will be done.

Developing M&S applications requires planning. "Rapid prototyping," "hacking," and "rapid applications development" have tried to convince the technical community that software can be developed without forethought and design. But these practices work only with very small development efforts, never with large projects. A plan is simply a set of logically connected goals created from human estimates. Because people must carry out these plans, few of them turn out the way we intend. That being true, why plan? Because project planning isn't about creating an exact roadmap to follow. Our plan should allow course corrections, so we can gently pull straying efforts back into alignment. As long as the work is productive, most managers can modify the plan to include what actually happens and steer the effort towards successful completion.

A plan, therefore, is simply a measuring stick for progress, by which we can redirect work to ensure it's done. Executing a plan and accomplishing a plan are two different things. Executing a plan means following it as designed, and this rarely happens in software development. But accomplishing a plan means meeting the critical milestones so pieces of the puzzle fit together at the right times. To create a good plan, we must first size the effort that the plan must model.

How to Size a Development Effort

How do we accurately estimate the size of an M&S effort? A common approach is the "engineering estimate," but it's often the worst method available. It suggests the engineer hasn't done this before and doesn't know anyone who has—so the estimate is simply a best guess. Is anyone ever comfortable doing something on a best guess?

Instead of guessing, estimates must have a proper basis. The soundest estimate derives from having done a similar development before. If an engineer took ten days to create a user interface with ten screens, a similar user interface with 15 screens should take 15 days. Circumstances could change the estimate. For example, if five of the screens from the previous effort were reusable, the 15-screen project might take just ten days. This type of logic establishes a real basis for the estimate and avoids mere guesswork.

Most basis of estimates combine many smaller elements—some sound and some having variations that result in engineering estimates. The key is to reduce the number of engineering estimates. One useful approach is to break the elements that require engineering estimates into smaller sub-elements. Many of the resulting sub-elements may qualify for a sound basis of estimate instead of an engineering estimate, thus reducing overall risk.

A true basis of estimate doesn't result in units of work, such as X hours or days. Rather, it should measure work elements to be accomplished, such as screens, communications drivers, lines of code, function points, etc. By translating work elements into engineering hours, we can establish the development cost. Thus, developing bases for estimates gives us our first insight into potential cost risk. Refer to App. A for detailed information on the basis of estimate.

How to Cost a Development Effort

To estimate cost, we apply productivity factors to the work elements mentioned above in order to arrive at a number of engineering hours required for each element. Developers must base their productivity factors on some work history—such as one screen per day or one line of code per hour. Tracking each development effort allows companies to compile these productivity factors. If they don't have them, however, they can use software estimating tools (App. A) to develop a cost estimate if they know the size of the effort. Developers who use neither performance metrics nor estimation models must rely on their best guesses, which reveals a flawed management philosophy and quality.

Once companies know the amount of work through proper bases of estimates and derive productivity factors from past performance or estimation models, they can apply the productivity factor to the work estimates and who will do the work. The result is total engineering hours by labor category. With total hours in hand, companies can calculate their total dollar cost per engineering hour per labor category to arrive at a final cost. These cost estimates add to the list of potential cost risks developed from the bases of estimates. Refer to App. A for details on determining project costs.

How to Create a Detailed Schedule

Many project-scheduling tools are available to automate scheduling, and most use Gantt or PERT charts. But no matter the tool or method, creating a useable schedule involves four basic steps:

1. Define the tasks that need doing
2. Allocate the required hours and assign who will do the work for each task
3. Establish the dependencies between the various tasks
4. Establish the created schedule as a baseline (against which to measure cost and schedule variances)

Although this process appears straightforward, it's really iterative and challenging. The first schedule may not meet contractual milestones or deliverables. Other passes won't schedule work evenly among the resources, and still others may show whether you need more staff. Thus, laying out a schedule with automated scheduling tools may still be difficult, but imagine doing the work without a schedule.

During scheduling, companies determine schedule risks and add them to the cost risks established during estimation. This scheduling process will also result in a staffing profile to use during development. Refer to App. A for details on preparing a schedule.

6.2.3   Establish Metrics to Track and Oversee Development

The established plan is the foundation for repeatability—Level 2 of SEI's Capability Maturity Model. It provides critical data for three of the four key elements in project tracking and oversight (see Fig. 6.4), which is the second requirement for repeatability.

A well-maintained project plan gives us the information we need to manage risks in the program's costs and schedule. Managing risk means periodically reviewing this data along with other known technical or associated risks. In turn, properly tracking and overseeing a project requires us to monitor the four elements of cost, schedule, trends, and risks against our baseline plan. Charting variances results in trends that can trigger corrective action when needed. This approach allows us to track the progress of a project, but in itself tracking is passive management. It's better than crisis management, in which managers act only when a crisis arises, but active management means identifying risks and creating

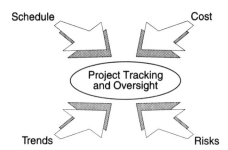

Fig. 6.4. **Key Elements of Project Tracking and Oversight.** Tracking and overseeing project costs, schedules, and trends allow us to monitor identified risks and implement corrective actions.

contingency plans that will kick in if things don't work as planned. As Fig. 6.5 shows, active management combines tracking of costs, schedules, and trends with risk management.

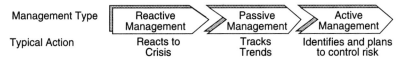

Fig. 6.5. **Active Versus Reactive Management.** Successful projects require active, not reactive, or passive management.

Cost, schedule, trends, and risks must be actively managed because cost, schedule, and function are interdependent: a change in one will probably result in similar changes for all. To illustrate this interdependence, let's suppose we need to build interface screens in order to control three separate simulations. Each simulation requires three screens: start-up and execute, a raw data dump, and charting. Thus, we need a total of nine interface screens, each of which requires four days of engineering. Finally, if we have one engineer to do the work, our schedule would be 36 days (4 days per screen × 9 screens).

The most obvious dependency is between required function (number of screens) and cost and schedule. Demanding more screens would increase the overall costs or schedule. For example, suppose we add a fourth simulation. That means we must produce 12 interface screens instead of the original nine. If we still use only one engineer, the schedule would increase by 12 days (three more screens at four days per screen). Adding staff would retain, or even shorten, the original schedule. However, adding staff reaches a point of diminishing returns. It may be logical to say that, if one engineer can do something in 20 days, two engineers could do it in ten and 20 engineers could do it in one, but it isn't realistic.

If we need to reduce overall cost, we must decrease functional requirements. For example, suppose operating one of the simulations doesn't depend on having a screen for a raw data dump, and a second simulation doesn't need a charting screen. That means we can drop two screens, which cuts eight days from our schedule *cost*. Of course, the *overall* schedule could remain at 36 days depending on how we allocate engineering staff to this project.

Shortening the schedule means we must modify functions or staffing. If one engineer must produce only ten screens instead of 12, we can shorten the schedule and reduce cost. If we can add engineering staff (without diminishing returns), we can shorten the schedule while possibly keeping overall cost the same (if we also reduce functionality).

The interdependencies between cost, schedule, and function mean we must control all three. That means we must plan carefully, track trends, and actively manage our development effort to build an application within budget and on schedule.

Analyze Cost

Most project-management tools (App. A identifies some of the more common ones) enable us to create a plan and then establish it as a baseline. As status is updated and work recorded, these tools show cost variances for individual line items, groups of sub-tasks, or any item considered a summary task. Most tools provide a line item for the planned cost of the work done—usually known as the budgeted cost of work performed. Another line item is known as the actual cost of work performed. The difference between actual and budgeted costs for the planned and actual work done is the cost variance. We can express this relationship as

Cost Variance = Actual cost of work performed – Budgeted cost of work performed

For example, if the project has completed $65,000 worth of work while spending only $45,000, it has a $20,000 cost variance (is $20,000 under budget). But watching only the overall cost variance can make us complacent because cost variances of individual components have a way of balancing out. Allowing cost overruns on components is passive management. Instead, we must examine the cost variances of all components so we can identify and address problem areas that would otherwise drive up project costs.

Analyze the Schedule

Project-management tools also provide a line item for the current cost of the work scheduled: budgeted cost of work scheduled. Comparing this line item to the budgeted cost of work performed gives us a schedule variance. Thus,

Schedule Variance = Cost of work scheduled – Budgeted cost of work performed

For example, if the project has scheduled $75,000 worth of work and completed $65,000 worth of work, it has a $10,000 schedule variance (is $10,000 behind schedule). Table 6.2 summarizes the analysis of cost and schedule for our example project.

Table 6.2. **Summary of Cost and Schedule Variances for an Example Project.** If we had scheduled $75,000 of work to be complete by a certain date, but had done only $65,000 of the work for an actual cost of only $45,000, our project would be $10,000 behind schedule and $20,000 under budget.

Budgeted Cost of Work Scheduled	Budgeted Cost of Work Performed	Actual Cost of Work Performed	Schedule Variance	Cost Variance
$75,000	$65,000	$45,000	$10,000 (behind schedule)	$20,000 (under budget)

Again, just as for costs, properly analyzing a project's schedule means analyzing the schedule variances of individual components. We can then identify problem areas and solve them before they harm the project.

Analyze Trends

Analyzing cost and schedule variances of components will help identify and correct problem areas. But knowing particular variances gives us only part of the picture. By also analyzing trends in these variances, we can see the "big picture" more clearly. For example, suppose a project stayed well under budget during the first stages of the effort but is now only slightly under budget. A current snapshot shows a healthy project (slightly under budget); yet, trend analysis shows a monthly 5% overrun for the past six months. We must detect this downward trend and act on it; otherwise, in several more months, the overall project most likely will be over budget.

Analyze Risk

Analyzing cost, schedule, and trends identifies problem areas, which also become areas of risk. Merely identifying risks is passive management. Active risk management requires us not only to define and track known risks but also to build contingency plans for unexpected or growing risks. We must examine management, technology, and staffing to identify areas that may go astray and then develop our contingency plans. Whenever variances from the original baseline plan become unacceptable, we have to carry out these contingency plans and resolve problems.

To summarize, we actively manage a project by using cost, schedule, trend, and risk analyses—measuring variances against our established plan. Measuring variances and identifying risks lead to contingency plans and corrective actions, which result in successful projects (putting us in the 16% success rate we discussed earlier).

Periodically Review Costs, Schedules, and Trends

Reviews give us the means to assemble data about cost, schedule, trends, and risks so we can make required management decisions. For example, the procuring agency should require program managers to periodically review the project's status, problem areas, and plans for corrective action. Figure 6.6 shows typical data used for these reviews.

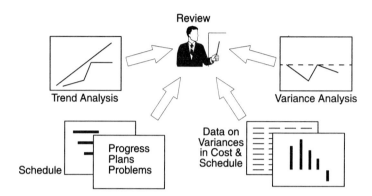

Fig. 6.6.   **Material Needed for Periodic Reviews.** Successful reviews examine information on, and analyses of, cost, schedule, trends, and risk.

Periodic reviews of this data give us a context for tracking and overseeing a project, which in turn meets the second requirement for repeatability in SEI's Capability Maturity Model.

6.2.4   Follow Policies and Procedures for Requirements Management

Managing the contracted requirements is a third characteristic of repeatability—and is critical for the procuring agency and the developer. The defined requirements establish what the contractor will develop and deliver and, equally important, what the procuring agency can expect. Requirements management is necessary because it monitors and accounts for changes. It's fairly simple and is actually part of good configuration management. At the highest level, requirements describe what the contractor must provide to the procuring agency. At the next level, we allocate requirements to components. Once developed, these components undergo acceptance tests to show they meet each requirement.

The developer must clearly map the acceptance tests to the requirements being demonstrated and provide this map to the procuring agency. The procuring agency then makes sure the developer has met every requirement with a working model.

Besides tracking established requirements to completion, requirements management also means controlling changes, which usually leads to contract modifications. Inadequate control of changes often hurts the developer because added requirements typically translate into more work and, if not paid, lower profits. Out-of-scope requirements must be identified; otherwise, developers can only cover their costs (when the contract is "cost plus") but never collect a fee for the extra work. Thus, developers must take charge of controlling all modifications to the requirements.

6.2.5   Follow Policies and Procedures for Configuration Management

Configuration management is the fourth characteristic of repeatability, under level 2 of SEI's Capability Maturity Model. Through configuration management, developers identify, control, account for, and audit system items in three categories: documentation, software, and hardware. [Ayer 1992]

Documentation includes

- The requirements documents that specify what the system must do (the functional baseline)
- The requirements documents that allocate lower-level requirements to system components (the allocated baseline)
- The design documents that specify the top-level and detailed designs for the system, software, and hardware
- Documents that specify the as-built product (the final product baseline)
- Documents that specify test criteria
- Other deliverable documentation such as user's manuals, programmer's manuals, interface-control documents, software-development plans, and quality-assurance plans

Software includes

- Source code
- Executable binary code
- Program design language
- Pseudo-code
- Media that contains the code and documentation for these media

Hardware includes

- Descriptions of hardware components
- Configuration information
- Schematics for all custom-built hardware

Controlling system items means maintaining copies of all deliverable documentation and code, whether procured or newly-developed. Above all, it means overseeing and controlling all changes to any deliverables (software, hardware, and documentation) so only approved changes to a baseline are incorporated. Accounting for items means making sure all changes to software, hardware, and documentation are traceable. As a system's complexity and size increase, so does the importance of identifying, controlling, and accounting for configurations. Most M&S applications are large and complex enough to require sound configuration management.

6.2.6 Follow Policies and Procedures for Quality Assurance

Quality assurance is the fifth characteristic of repeatability. It covers examinations, inspections, and reviews of system software, hardware, and documentation throughout development.

Successful quality assurance requires independent people who aren't involved in developing the items they're examining, inspecting, or reviewing [DOD-Std-2168 1988]. Independence means having the authority and freedom to objectively evaluate programs and recommend corrections. But members of development teams can still handle quality assurance; for example, software developers can review code for other software developers.

Good quality-assurance practices help us detect problems early in development. The later problems are identified, the more costly they are to correct; hence, the cost and time required for quality assurance are easily justified because early detection and correction save money.

6.2.7 Follow Policies and Procedures for Subcontract Management

Subcontract management is the sixth aspect of repeatability under level 2 of SEI's Capability Maturity Model. Its objective is to ensure that all subcontractors deliver quality products on time and within their established budgets. Whenever the developer hires a subcontractor, they should have the same relationship as the one between the procuring agency and the developer. The contractor, in essence, becomes the procuring agency and is buying products from the subcontractor. Thus, the contractor should reasonably expect the same kind of project planning, project tracking and oversight, requirements management, configuration management, and quality assurance.

6.3 Developing, Testing, and Maintaining M&S Systems

Implementing a project—the final acquisition activity—refers to actual technical development. By actively managing this technical development, we can identify areas needing adjustment, alternative approaches, or added resources. But implementation itself consists of applying a methodology to the development lifecycle. Software methods have undergone two major changes in the last 30 years. First, structured decomposition applied "encapsulation" to break apart and group what must be done to accomplish some actions. Then, object-oriented approaches took the concept one step further. They grouped the data and actions into encapsulated units called classes and objects. These units can reuse some or all code (through inheritance) and simplify (through polymorphism) how to represent similarly different objects that do similar things.

These two changes have tied software more closely to the concept of components traditionally associated with hardware. Many different types of analysis help developers apply structured decomposition and object-oriented concepts to the development of models and simulations. But they all tend to follow an age-old philosophy, or lifecycle, of problem solving.

Figure 6.7 illustrates the four basic steps of technical development:

- What needs doing (What)
- How to do it (How)
- Carrying it out (Do)
- Testing what's been done (Test)

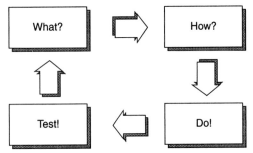

Fig. 6.7.   Lifecycle for Technical Development. What, how, do, and test—the basic steps in all development lifecycles.

The waterfall, spiral, and incremental lifecycles discussed in Chap. 4 are simply variations on the theme of what, how, do, and test. Even prototyping informally moves through the same steps. While small development efforts may emphasize a single lifecycle, larger efforts may use several lifecycles at the same time to handle multiple models or simulations.

Perhaps the best formal and detailed description of what, how, do and test was in the Department of Defense's DOD-STD-2167A, later replaced by MIL-STD-498 (1994). DOD-STD-2167A implied, but didn't require, a waterfall lifecycle. MIL-STD-498 is much more explicit about using many lifecycles. In June of 1994, Secretary of Defense William Perry directed using performance and commercial specifications instead of military specifications—except as a last resort, and then only with a waiver. But using commercial specifications hasn't changed the four development steps that are an informal or formal part of all lifecycles.

Figure 6.8 illustrates the major phases, activities, reviews, and documentation deliverables typical of full development. Again, it shows distinct stages that we can associate with what, how, do, and test. Regardless of the lifecycle selected, a developer will always solve a problem by analyzing and designing, coding and testing, and then integrating the tested components.

Each stage of any software lifecycle requires a corresponding review and expected documentation, as described in the following sections.

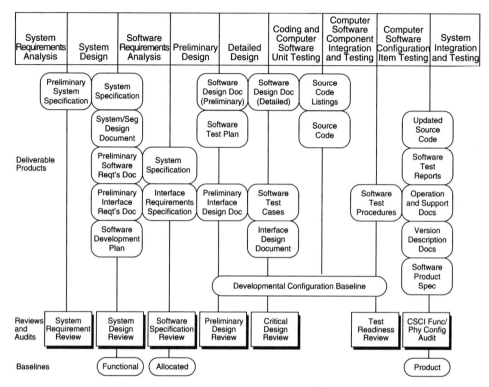

Fig. 6.8.   **A Representative Software Lifecycle.** DOD-STD-2167A established the software lifecycle shown here. It formalized the what, how, do, and test of technical development into requirements analysis, design, coding, and testing.

6.3.1   Monitor Implementation

The main lifecycles all use the same basic development phases. After defining the system, we establish requirements and allocate them to various components. These hardware and software components go through the stages of design, implementation, test, and finally, integration with other components. Incremental and spiral lifecycles will repeat these stages. In the following paragraphs, I describe the reviews expected for each stage. Smaller projects may tailor and simplify these phases and reviews but should keep their intent.

Define System Requirements

Larger M&S applications will consist of several smaller models or simulations. By defining and then reviewing the system requirements during a Systems Requirements Review, contractors can refine and stabilize the general requirements stated in the Request for Proposal. During this phase, contractors may propose enhancements and changes to the requirements in order to take advantage of current technology, improved operations, or special cost-saving techniques. Contractors can express ideas here that normally wouldn't be appropriate in their proposals. The procuring agency can consider these ideas and determine whether they warrant changing the requirements. The end result of this phase is for the contractor and the procuring agency to agree on a specific set of high-level requirements.

Design the System

The System Design Phase, concluded by a System Design Review, allows contractors to propose an overall approach for meeting the defined system requirements. This phase defines the hardware and software components and allocates each high-level requirement to one or more of them. At this point, requirements and system design have clearly defined what the system must do, so completing this phase typically establishes the functional baseline. In addition, documents describing the requirements and design should go under configuration control, and the program- and contract-management staffs should carefully control any changes to them.

Depending on the system's simplicity and how complete the high-level requirements are (in the Request for Proposal), this phase and review are often combined with the definition and review of system requirements discussed above.

Analyze Software Requirements

Contractors should analyze software requirements and review software specifications for each system component. During this phase, they break out high-level requirements for each component into detailed requirements at lower levels. Upon approval by the procuring agency, these requirements establish the allocated baseline for each component. Again, the documents describing the allocated requirements for each component should go under configuration control, and the program- and contract-management staffs should carefully control any changes to them.

Do Preliminary Design

Contractors should do a preliminary design, review this design, and prepare documentation for each system. They may combine reviews and document preparation to save money, as long as they stay on schedule. During this phase, they develop and document the top-level design for each component and an overall approach to testing the entire system. The documentation should be under configuration control. Most likely the designs will change as the development progresses; however, these changes shouldn't change the allocated baseline. Thus, the development organizations (not program or contract management) should control these documents. This phase should produce top-level designs and interface definitions.

Do Detailed Design

Contractors should do a detailed design and a critical design review for each system component. They may combine reviews and associated design documentation to save money and stay on schedule. During this phase, they develop and document the detailed design for each component, the detailed interface definitions, and preliminary procedures for testing components. These designs will change as the development progresses, but these changes shouldn't change the allocated baseline. Thus, the development organizations should also control these documents. This phase should result in detailed designs and interface definitions, along with top-level testing procedures.

Write, Compile, and Test the Code Modules and Units

During this phase, software developers write and compile all code. Then, the contractor tests the coding modules, combines these modules into larger units, and tests each unit.

Integrate Units into Components and Test Each Component

During this phase, contractors integrate units into complete components and carefully test each component. A Test Readiness Review follows this phase to determine if the detailed testing procedures clearly demonstrate the component will meet its allocated requirements. These test procedures may change before final acceptance, but not so they alter the allocated baseline. Thus, again, the development organizations should control these documents.

The terms I've used to describe levels of complexity for software—modules, units, and components—aren't set in stone. Neither are the names for process phases. But the process itself *is* set: 1) create and test small elements; 2) combine elements into larger units and test the units; and 3) build units into fully functioning components and test the components.

Test Component Configurations and Functions

Component testing shows that the component works correctly and meets all allocated requirements. During a Functional and Physical Configuration audit, the procuring agency witnesses tests and examines all documentation for each component. Depending on the complexity and contractual deliverables, the documentation would include such items as the source code, the results of component-level tests, operational and support documentation, a version description, and the final as-built design and interface documents. At this point, the component is no longer under development; it goes under configuration control as the product baseline.

Integrate and Test the System

During system integration and test, contractors combine and demonstrate all components of the system. The procuring agency should now have a full system that works as specified by the functional baseline.

6.3.2   Accept Delivered Product

A formal and specified acceptance test is critical at system delivery because it verifies that the system does what the procuring agency has contracted. The requirements document specifies what the system must do; individual acceptance tests show that the system meets each requirement or set of requirements. Again, the hidden contract surfaces—if developers can show the procuring agency they've fulfilled all requirements, they've met their obligation. If requirements aren't fulfilled, developers must redeliver when the product meets specifications. Conversely, if the procuring agency requires deliverables not specified in the requirements specification, it must pay for them. Figure 6.9 shows how acceptance tests correlate with requirements to verify that a system works as contracted. At the same time, the procuring agency must make sure the M&S applications are valid—and, if necessary, accredited—meaning that they sufficiently represent the real world being modeled or simulated. Refer to Chap. 11 for details on verifying, validating, and accreditating M&S applications.

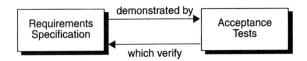

Fig. 6.9.   Making Sure the System Works as Contracted. Acceptance tests demonstrate, and therefore verify, requirements.

6.3.3   Establish Maintenance Needs

Maintenance, especially for M&S applications, is critical but often overlooked. Having defined and built a working system, developers often assume users will be content. But two scenarios describe how the end of development may be only the beginning of a major effort.

First, large M&S applications will continue to uncover problems. The larger and more complex the application, the more likely problems will surface as time passes. Acceptance testing may not have detected mistakes that were just overlooked or were hard to find because user options and configurations are so complex. Sometimes, an algorithm isn't specified properly, or a requirement is overlooked. For whatever reason, these mistakes and problems require correction.

Second, as users exercise the system, they'll discover better ways to do their jobs and use the models and simulations to answer pending questions. They'll continually request minor enhancements.

Although developers need not "fix" requested enhancements, what about problems such as incorrect algorithms, improperly stated requirements, and outright programming mistakes? Shouldn't developers be accountable for those mistakes?

Unfortunately, when procuring agencies accept the system, they accept it as is. Sometimes, especially in the commercial sector, a warranty period is provided— similar to a warranty provided with a new automobile. But we can't expect contractors to be accountable forever. This is why requirements management is vitally important to procuring agencies, who must depend on clearly stated requirements that are demonstrated at acceptance. Otherwise, they'll be stuck with a system that doesn't work according to their expectations.

What Maintenance Costs

Maintaining an M&S system is more expensive than one would expect, consuming as much as 60% to 80% of the total cost [Schrank 1995] to correct problems and add minor enhancements. This cost shows why we must stress flexibility and easy improvement during definition and implementation. Spending more money to design and implement a flexible system will pay us back during the maintenance phase.

What the Development Must Produce

The larger and more complex M&S applications are, the more procuring agencies should require documentation that will help maintenance contractors do their job. Examples would be design documents, test documents, source code (mandatory), program design language listings, programming manuals, interface documents, and regression-testing procedures and tests.

The more learning or "up-to-speed" time required for maintenance, the more costly the effort. Remember, it's much easier, quicker, and more cost effective for the engineers who create the system to document it than for another contractor to decipher the as-built system.

How to Handle a Maintenance Contract

Although M&S development usually occurs under "cost plus" contracts, maintenance is more suited to "time-and-materials" contracts. That's because the cost of maintaining a system is much less predictable than the cost for development. It's hard to predict what problems will arise and what minor enhancements users will request. On the other hand, major enhancements should occur under a "fixed-price" or "cost-plus" contract.

6.4　Summary

Using a qualified developer who employs sound management and technical processes will help ensure delivery of an M&S application within the required budget and schedule. Qualified developers should employ sound project planning, project tracking and oversight, requirements management, configuration management, quality assurance, and subcontract management. They should also follow established development lifecycles so they can actively manage all models and simulations. Of course, they can use different lifecycles for different parts of a system, depending on delivery needs. Developers should establish clear, detailed requirements, and procuring agencies must have these requirements clearly demonstrated during acceptance testing, as well as making sure the models and simulations meet appropriate standards for verification, validation, and accreditation. Qualified developers, watchful procuring agencies, and sound processes give us the best opportunity to build M&S systems within budget and on schedule.

References

Ayer, Steve J. and Frank S. Patrinostro. 1992. *Software Configuration Management.* New York, NY: McGraw Hill, Inc.

Comaford, Christine. 1995. "What's Wrong with Software Development?" *Software Development Magazine*, November.

Department of Defense. 1988. *Defense System Software Development.* DOD-Std-2167A.

Department of Defense. 1988. *Defense System Software Quality Program.* DOD-Std-2168.

Department of Defense. 1994. *Software Development and Documentation.* Mil-Std-498.

Paulk, Mark C., Bill Curtis, Mary Beth Chrissis, and Charles V. Webber. 1993. *Capability Maturity Model for Software.* Pittsburgh, PA: Software Engineering Institute, Carnegie Mellon University.

Schrank, Michael J., Glenn W. Boyce, Jr., and Carolyn K. Davis. 1995. "Ada In the Maintenance Arena." *AdaIC Report*, The MITRE Corporation.

CHAPTER 7

A Conceptual Approach to Developing Models and Simulations

John M. Barry, *The Boeing Company*

The conceptual approach in this chapter stems from the Department of Defense's (DOD) acquisition process. Called the Promotional-Visual-Operational-Requirements (PVOR) process, this approach bridges the gap between engineering planning (Chaps. 4–6) and creating a product (Chaps. 8–12). See Fig. 7.1 for a graphic of how we'll create this bridge by focusing on PVOR. I'll describe a way to create an M&S system and provide you with the building blocks to translate plans and ideas into the beginning of this system. To do so, you must

- Determine the system's operation, applications, and users

- Interview users to establish requirements

- Feed back these requirements to the M&S team

- Picture the system and represent what it does, so users and developers can decide if anything needs changing

202

Finally, I'll suggest techniques that will help you prepare to design a prototype and the final simulation. We'll make these concepts more concrete by using a problem in managing warfighting information to describe how to build a virtual prototype and a firefighting example to describe how to develop a script, which is central to the virtual prototype.

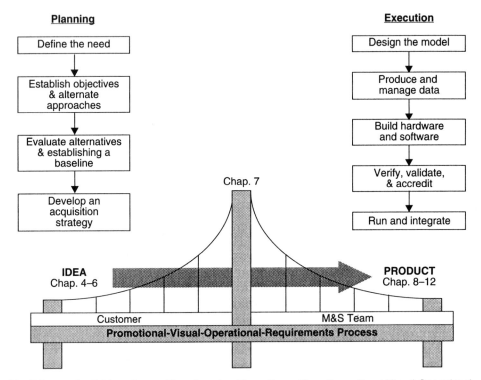

Fig. 7.1. **A Bridge from Planning to Execution.** The Promotional-Visual-Operational-Requirements (PVOR) process underpins M&S development. It transports developers from planning to execution and bridges the typical gap between customers and M&S teams.

As described in previous chapters, a key benefit from modeling and simulation is being able to see how a real system will work before committing to expensive hardware. The whole M&S team—project planners, system designers, analysts, reporters, and customers—must determine and act on a design. The translation from planning to design can't be static. It must evolve through the system's lifecycle of concept studies, demonstration, production, and deployment, and it must involve the M&S team at all stages. The DOD's acquisition cycle provides insight into development and decisions for most projects.

7.1 The Concept of Simulate Before You Buy for Acquisition

The Strategic Defense Initiative launched the concept of simulating before buying, which the Department of Defense (DOD) now requires for many systems. During this era, computer programs simulated and displayed early concepts in how to detect, identify, and destroy missiles, so the United States could combat a pre-emptive launch from the former Soviet Union. Simulation gained wide acceptance because live testing of these abilities was impractical and expensive Simulations allowed analysts to depict, virtually test, verify, and display results of many scenarios based on hardware and orbital characteristics.

The National Test Bed (now the National Test Facility), an organization devoted to simulating concepts in missile defense, was born in this era. Its staff developed several large simulations and campaign models to ensure that missile-defense concepts could be effective before going from Milestone 0 into Phase 0 (Concept Exploration) and from Milestone 1 into Phase 1 (Demonstration and Validation) of acquisition (see Fig. 7.2). During this era, several programs and parallel "horse-race" contracts moved from Phase 0 to Phase I based on simulations and testing of subsystem hardware.

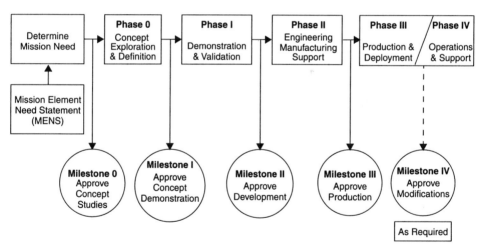

Fig. 7.2.   Traditional Phases for Acquiring Defense Systems. Using a process for acquisition introduces many opportunities to employ models and simulations while investigating concepts, reducing cost, and mitigating risk.

When the Berlin Wall came down and the Soviet empire started to dissolve, massive cuts in the military budget actually boosted reliance on simulations. The threat and its scope changed from massive missile attacks originating in one country to a global, uncertain threat. Additional military budget cuts accelerated hardware buys because the military couldn't afford the traditional process depicted in Fig. 7.2

for every weapon system. (It often required 10–15 years.) The new process—Advanced Concept Technology Demonstration (ACTD) (Fig. 7.3)—reemphasizes simulating before buying. It tests and demonstrates technology operationally without going through all the long, expensive steps in traditional acquisition.

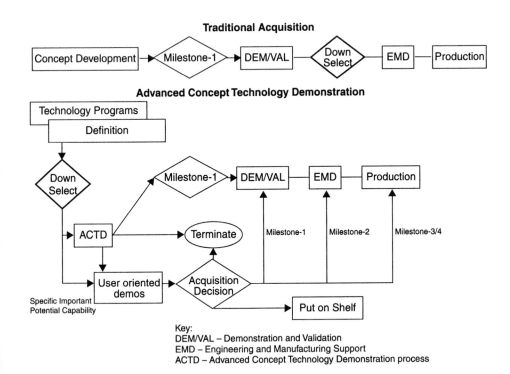

Fig. 7.3.   Advanced Concept Technology Demonstration. This process reemphasizes simulating before buying. It employs prototypes and demonstrations to reduce development time and cost for systems needed immediately.

The process for Advanced Concept Technology Demonstration employs prototypes, hardware and software simulations, and user-oriented demonstrations. It reduces the acquisition cycle and costs for systems that provide a specific important ability to meet an immediate need. In other words, systems developed using this process must support warfighters' near-term needs, such as those evolving from the 1990 Gulf War. Getting users involved changed traditional acquisition, which often didn't show hardware to users until the end of Phase III, when operational problems required expensive retrofits. This process also can allow contractors to select subcontractors sooner than the traditional point—the end of Phase II. Users can apply results to bypass traditional acquisition and make one of three decisions: 1) go directly to demonstration and validation, engineering and manufacturing support, or production; 2) end the program; or 3) put the system "on the shelf." Ending a program early saves the expense of stringing along one or more contractors through Phase I, as is typical of the traditional system. "Putting systems on the shelf" captures the technology and delays the cost of new systems until they are needed. Therefore, this new acquisition process takes advantage of the benefits of prototyping: early user involvement and participation, low cost, and rapid feedback.

The Defense Department has found the process for Advanced Concept Technology Demonstration so useful that it has authorized $277 million for 18 of these packages in fiscal year 1997. The Department's former Acquisition Chief, Paul Kaminski, stressed the concept's importance by stating: "Advanced Concept Development allows technologists and operational users to work together as a team to assess the usefulness of mature technologies. These demonstrations also provide experienced military commanders with an opportunity to develop the operational concepts that address current and future military needs prior to major acquisition decisions and large dollar commitments."

Whether a system goes through traditional acquisition or Advanced Concept Technology Demonstration, all projects still must have a mission element need statement, which operators and users develop to describe a requirement. For example, the need for battlefield information on moving tanks under all kinds of weather and in real time could generate the need for an airborne or spaceborne radar that can "see" moving targets. To "sell" the need, a system designer must demonstrate the concepts, objectives, and strategies earlier and relate them to the customer's requirements. These concepts will evolve throughout the acquisition cycle as threats and missions change.

7.2   Transitioning from Planning to Execution

Even before Advanced Concept Technology Demonstration, as customers develop need statements, they're demanding to see how the concepts being proposed will work. They're asking complex questions about how weapons and systems for command, control, and communications can integrate and interact. High-fidelity models and simulations can answer these questions by depicting the systems and their relationships. Designing and revising these models can be time-consuming and expensive. Under the Strategic Defense Initiative, large simulations were common, and some of them are still being used and modified today. Some are extremely complex and still consume enormous computing resources. They also suffer from "spaghetti code"—massive lines of code that violate principles of software engineering and object-oriented coding. Designing the simulation while getting feedback from customers complicates these problems because it has led to continual design, demonstration, and redesign. This cycle is costly, time-consuming, and contrary to sound configuration management.

Even today, M&S teams tend to start immediately, designing and coding the simulation. This approach costs time and money because we must convince users of the simulation's value, understand and demonstrate their perspectives, rehearse for the demonstrations, and recode based on the customers' feedback. In the past, designers could avoid some of this expense by presenting concepts to customers in viewgraphs. But today's customers don't have the time to wade patiently through hundreds of viewgraphs containing wiring diagrams of the simulation's design and operation. Concepts are useless unless your team can translate them into preliminary products which meet requirements and demonstrate them early and throughout the system's lifecycle.

This need for "early demonstration" has encouraged "simulate before you buy." Today's "systems of systems" require sophisticated simulations to show how they'll apply, integrate, and operate before anyone commits to a major procurement. In the DOD's product lifecycle (see Fig. 7.2), you should begin demonstrating as soon as your customer develops its need statement. Start before designing the model and continue throughout the system's lifecycle.

This book's process for developing and operating models and simulations (see Chaps. 8–12) requires you, as a system designer, to iterate and communicate evolving requirements from users to the rest of your M&S team. These evolving requirements will cause your M&S system to change throughout its lifecycle. Your initial challenge, then, is to depict the system when you haven't started designing the model. The answer to this challenge is a computer display program—the virtual prototype. This prototype is a quick, inexpensive computer program that displays the interaction of the user interface, model operation, pictures, animations, and videos of the model or system you'll create. It dynamically represents how the system is supposed to work and starts carrying out the process for developing models and simulations. It's similar to developing and distributing to customers a "demo disk" that advertises and promotes software or games, except you use it to get direct feedback from your customers. It promotes models, helps you develop them, and improves your team's interaction. The virtual prototype helps translate "blue-sky" ideas from planning to a first product before you start building the model or simulation. At the same time, it makes the proposed concept come alive in the minds of your M&S team and the users.

To develop a virtual prototype, I recommend the Promotional-Visual-Operational-Requirements (PVOR) process (see Fig. 7.4). By promotional I mean using the prototype to show and propose the M&S product to your customer before designing it, so you can gain feedback and acceptance. The visual part of PVOR creates an early "picture" of the product, which helps your M&S team transition from planning to development. It also gives you an inexpensive opportunity to feed planning results back to your customer. The operational part refers to seeking out and incorporating feedback from the operators who will eventually use the system. Requirements simply means capturing the requirements in your prototype. PVOR requires several key steps:

1. Develop a scripted, virtual prototype (see Sec. 7.3)
2. Ensure the prototype satisfies the planned baseline, including the need, objectives, and strategy developed in the idea phase.
3. Get feedback from the customer and incorporate changes
4. Start designing the model

Be sure the virtual prototype reflects any changes in the final M&S product. By keeping the prototype current, you'll have a fast, inexpensive, portable, effective way to keep the program sold through demonstrations to customers. You'll also have a "visual testbed" to incorporate new and changing requirements, as well as to communicate them to the customer.

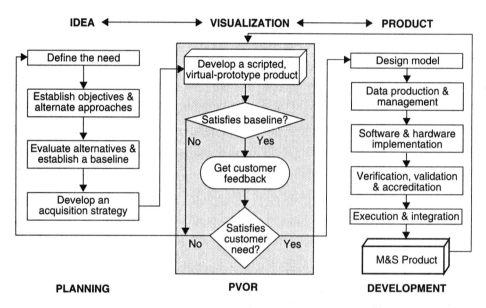

Fig. 7.4.   The Promotional-Visual-Operational-Requirement (PVOR) Process. You can use this process to create a virtual prototype of the desired models and simulations. It helps link the planning and development activities associated with creating M&S products to reduce cost and risk.

"Customers" may be one person, several people, or entire organizations. They're people in the acquisition agency but also include people who define requirements, domain experts, and "ultimate customers"—the people whom the model is supposed to support. If your M&S effort is on contract, your customers normally are well defined or specified in the contract. However, if you're trying to sell a concept or prepare for a contract, customers may be numerous and diverse. For example, I had to help sell the need for and define an integrated system to manage information that would aid military planning, training, and operations. Because this was a new idea, no group of people or set of defined requirements could provide all the feedback we needed to develop a model. Various people (see Fig. 7.5) interacted and actually helped modify the virtual prototype so we could move the idea from planning to production.

We needed feedback from all these people because they required different information to fight their part of the war. For example, people responsible for

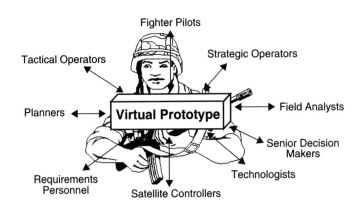

Fig. 7.5.   **Customers Can Provide Feedback.** Feedback is crucial when developing an effective virtual prototype. The virtual prototype built to define the need for an integrated system that would manage space information for warfighters relied on feedback from many sources.

requirements wanted to display as much data as could be collected. They thought it would better inform pilots during operations. But the pilots were already overloaded with information in the cockpit, so they wanted only a color change overlaid on the weapons stores part of their heads-up display to show whether space information was available for using their weapons. One color on the displayed weapons meant information was available; another color meant it wasn't. A similar difference occurred between satellite controllers and analysts in the air operations center, who did air-battle planning and tasking. The satellite operators wanted to see data on the performance of critical satellite systems and satellite-orbit curves that supported the battle zone. However, the analysts needed to see only the areas of coverage and outage of satellite communications and imagery projected on global and local maps. Senior officers wanted to see the quality of satellite information overlaid on the air and ground battle. The actual virtual prototype ended up displaying fused information that customers could select from.

Even considering all the customers' perspectives, we had to keep in mind that the ultimate objective was to provide enough timely information to support warfighters—in this case the ground troops who must occupy territory to carry out and end the war. That's why Fig. 7.5 has a ground soldier in the background. We developed the prototype so different warfighters (e.g., pilot, analyst, satellite operations controller) could see the relationship between the simulation and battlefield operations. We demonstrated the virtual prototype to these people and then followed up with field exercises that involved military planners, analysts, and decision makers.

If feedback satisfies your customer, your team can start designing the model. If your customer recommends changes, your team must revert to examining the need, the alternatives, and other planning functions. Virtual prototypes are inexpensive tools to reiterate requirements between users and M&S development teams. Changes during the execution phase of M&S development are more costly if you bypass the virtual prototype. And, if customers don't "buy" the system, you can stop your project before spending more money on design.

7.3   Virtual Prototyping

Developing virtual prototypes (see Fig. 7.6) consists of acquiring and organizing information, designing displays, and integrating displays and information into an operational prototype. Storyboards, scripts, and templates are the main parts of the virtual prototype. To organize information, start by refining the operational concept, which your team produced when you evaluated alternatives and established a baseline. Refining this concept involves examining the communications, data flows, information, integration, and interactions of the real-world system your simulation will portray. Then, develop the storyboard by creating and organizing charts that depict words or pictures to describe and visualize the simulation system. With your storyboard in place, identify basic requirements and sources for information. This step is similar to—and will help later in—the execution phase, when you produce data to develop the model. Next, partition the information and activity flows by determining where the information comes from, where it goes, and where it will be presented or displayed. The source for this information can be the customers you interviewed, such as those for warfighting in Fig. 7.5.

After partitioning, you can start designing the virtual prototype, considering such things as the appearance and order of the displays. Your script will integrate design details with the results of flowing information and activities. Then, check to ensure the displays agree with the operational concept. If they agree, proceed to integration. First, separate the display products so you can design templates that will show the data, pictures, and animation the prototype will need. Then, sandwich these displays into your prototypical M&S system (see Sec. 7.3.1). Order and animate the displays according to the script you developed in the display phase. Finally, run the virtual prototype and test to see if it operates according to the script you developed earlier. If it does, it's ready to take to your customers.

7.3.1   Animating Virtual Prototypes

To animate your virtual prototype, you can use one of many software packages for demonstration and development, such as Astound™, Compel™, Asymetrix Toolbook™, and Macromedia's Director™ and Authorware™. Animation packages include Autodesk's Animator Pro™, NewTek's Lightwave 3D™, and Electromagic's Broadcast™. You can even create simple demonstrations of a virtual prototype with Microsoft's PowerPoint™. Some of these programs allow you to package the prototype on several kinds of computer platforms. A couple notes of caution. First, prototypes can easily reach 15–20 megabytes in size. At that size, you may want to use a portable 100-megabyte drive or a direct cable

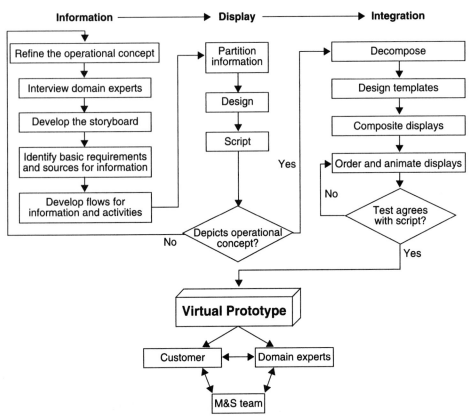

Fig. 7.6.   **Developing a Virtual Prototype.** The steps shown here provide a structured method to develop an effective virtual prototype that enhances the integration and presentation of information.

connection to transfer the program to another computer. Second, although manuals accompanying the software describe how to develop slide shows, none describes how to organize and display information to mimic the way a complete simulation operates (see Fig. 7.7 for this process).

To organize and display information, divide it into the message, template, and animated displays. First, develop a briefing which sells the program in words and pictures, describes the requirement or need, statically depicts the forthcoming displays, and orders the presentation. Then, arrange pictures, animations, data, and controls on displays that simulate your model. Follow sound practices in human-factors engineering when you allocate and place this information on the display. Next, develop the templates, which are like stencils that you'll reuse to display data, pictures, and animations against common backgrounds. These templates will help your team design human-computer interfaces for the actual

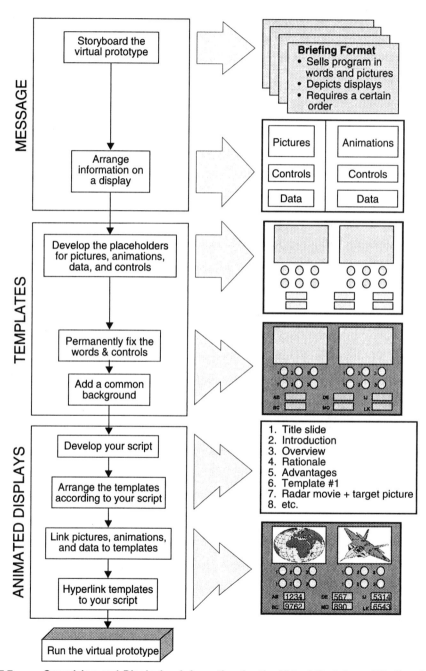

Fig. 7.7.   Organizing and Displaying Information for the Virtual Prototype. Effective virtual prototypes must organize and display information as shown here to mimic the way a complete simulation operates.

simulation. Because templates are so important, I describe how to develop them in Sec. 7.3.2. For now, I'll simply point out that they require three main steps: 1) develop placeholders for the pictures, animations, data, and controls; 2) permanently affix words; 3) add a common background. Templates used to require a lot of coding; now, you can do them with graphical design and scripting tools in the demonstration software noted earlier in this section.

Finally, you must add, reference, and index the pictures, animations, and data to actions controlled by the template. Link your script to the templates and displays, arrange the templates to match the scripts, and link the pictures, animations and data to the templates. Finally, hyperlink the template's controls to the same flow in the script. When you're done, you'll have organized and displayed information for your virtual prototype as shown in Fig. 7.7. Now, you need to test it against your baseline and show it to your customer for feedback. This feedback is important to the promotional aspect of PVOR, as well as to your eventual design.

7.3.2   Creating a Template

Without a template, as shown in Fig. 7.8, PVOR would be very expensive. You'd have to program the human-computer interface; the pictures, animations, data, and controls; and the algorithms and control statements. Templates are reusable electronic "stencils"—the human-computer interfaces, minus the pictures and animation. These stencils have "holes" or placeholders into which you insert information that portrays parts of the simulation. These inserts follow your script, which sequences displays of information and the hypertext locations referred to by the controls. After designing the templates, you construct separate pages on which you strategically place the animations, pictures, and other information. Then, you "sandwich" these pages into the order of the scenario your template's controls are activating.

7.3.3   How Prototyping Helps Concept Development

Actual prototypes are original models on which something is patterned, so they can help M&S teams and customers develop concepts. Prototyping has five key features: learning, short intervals, user involvement, low cost, and rapid feedback. Learning occurs whenever we can design systems iteratively and put prototypes into users' hands for feedback. Short intervals are necessary to speed prototype development and prepare teams and customers for the final product. The DOD's process—Advanced Concept Technology Demonstration (described earlier)—uses short intervals very effectively to accelerate acquisitions. User involvement helps turn around changes rapidly and inexpensively. Eventually, that reduces system costs and development timelines. User involvement was the main reason the Strategic Defense Initiative called for so many prototypes. Keeping costs low (compared to building the actual product or a major simulation) allows us to "experiment" with several variations before developing the final simulation.

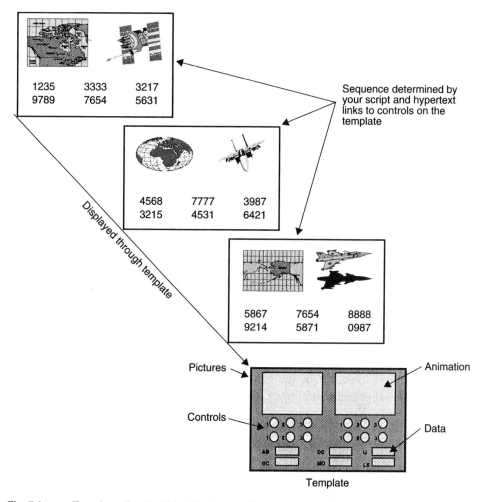

Fig. 7.8.   **Templates for the Virtual Prototype.** Developing cost-effective virtual prototypes relies on using templates, or electronic "stencils," to create the desired human-computer interfaces.

Actual prototypes are either rapid (disposable) or evolutionary, as shown in Fig. 7.9. Rapid prototypes are part of a pilot test program that helps us better understand a system's performance and users' requirements with little documentation or configuration discipline. The aerospace industry has used them extensively since the 1930s to save money and time while demonstrating a product meets requirements. Rapid prototyping occurs during the Demonstration Validation Phase (Phase 0) of traditional acquisition. The federal government funds aircraft prototypes from competing companies as precursors to the production plane (known as "fly before you buy"). This approach decides the best design between competing companies, reduces risk, and lowers cost. It also applies to large simulations. In theory, the prototype flushes out problems in design and operations early, before committing to large production buys. Problems are less expensive to correct in the prototype. Once a pilot test is done, companies often discard the prototype and begin to design the selected vehicle using configuration management.

The evolutionary approach (Option 2 in Fig. 7.9) starts with a small system and refines it over a long period, possibly even throughout the entire acquisition cycle. Simulations for the Strategic Defense Initiative were often evolutionary. Many of these prototypes took advantage of the "quick and inexpensive" features of prototyping but paid little attention to managing software and configurations in ways this book recommends. Thus, prototypes often didn't have sound documentation, configuration, and design. They simply became bigger, costlier, and more difficult to understand and validate. What can you learn from this experience? Don't use prototyping as an excuse to short circuit sound steps for designing and developing software. By-passing these steps could negate the advantages of prototyping.

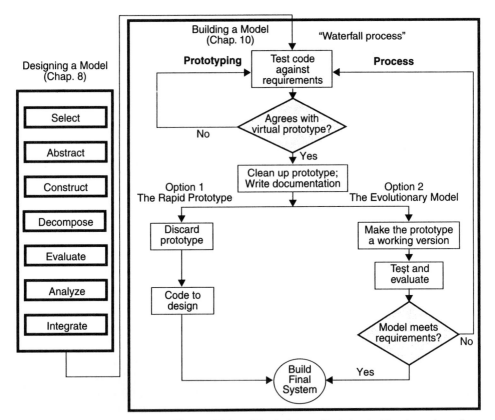

Fig. 7.9.   **Developing Rapid (Disposable) and Evolutionary Prototypes.** The steps shown here are an essential part of the "simulate before you buy" process.

One way to manage simulation prototyping is to follow some of the concepts this book introduces. Instead of rushing right into designing, demonstrating, and redesigning your prototype, first follow the design steps described in Chap. 8. These steps start with selecting a reference architecture and model by integrating component models. After you've followed this design process, you can start prototyping using a spiral or waterfall development. After coding and testing your prototype, compare it with your virtual prototype to make sure it meets your customer's requirements. If it agrees with the virtual prototype, clean up the documentation. Then, decide whether to discard the prototype and start building the final model or develop an evolutionary model. For an evolutionary model, your prototype becomes the working version.

While testing your evolutionary prototype, manage its configuration, verify and validate it, manage its databases, and build software and hardware for it according to the principles in later chapters of this book. Also consider these principles while developing your prototype if the effort is significant (relative to the final model) in terms of lines of code, expense, and operating platforms. Consider the configuration decisions required to transition from your prototype to the final system, as noted in Fig. 7.10. A prototype is truly evolutionary if it's scaleable, compatible, traceable, transferable, and relateable to the final model.

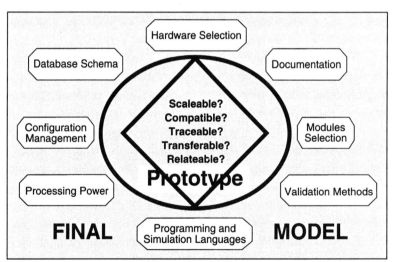

Fig. 7.10.   Building an Evolutionary Prototype. The decisions made while building the prototype influence the design of the final simulation.

These precautions for a common-sense approach to design can save time and money. For example, if your team decides to use the prototype as an evolutionary model, you would select a database scheme that can satisfy the final model's requirements. Similarly, you must make sure you select hardware and an operating system for the prototype that is scaleable to the final model. I'm aware of several model developments for the Strategic Defense Initiative in which the prototype started out on mini-mainframes with their own operating systems and grew until it required a Cray computer to operate. In fact, mapping from the prototype to the final product became questionable because of the programming, timing, and communication differences between the mini-mainframes and the Cray. These transitions required recoding programs and databases, revising documentation, redesigning modules and communication parameters, and deriving new validation methods. The development team could have avoided or reduced many of these effects by adhering to the configuration elements (see Fig. 7.10) needed for a final model. Instead, these expensive transitions negated the normal benefits of prototyping. Today, an M&S team often faces the opposite challenge because many customers want to run models on workstations and even portable personal computers. But this "downsizing" also requires sound software design and configuration management to move from a prototype to a final model.

7.4   Applying the Process

7.4.1   Translating Real-World Mechanics, Operations, and Processes into Simulated Actions

To visualize concepts and operations, models must portray conditions or actions based on real processes and scientific principles. We can't depict the origin and spread of a forest fire just by showing any picture or animation in a virtual prototype. Nor can we track, predict, and suggest a response to fighting that fire without knowing the abilities and locations of firefighting equipment, location and spread rate of the fire, current and predicted weather conditions, and status of firefighting and fire-causing supplies. For example, we can characterize a forest fire with algorithms that use variables to predict the fire's propagation pattern and speed. Typical variables are class of fuels, air temperature, dew point, humidity, wind speed and direction, and type of terrain. These equations were developed using multivariate regression analysis on empirical data related to these variables or sensed from wildfires or experiments. A virtual prototype won't contain or compute these equations, but it can display the results of scripted operations and predetermined scenarios. It can also display some pre-defined cases using different variables to predict fire propagation and suppression under varying conditions. This is one of many approaches that contribute to designing and building a model (see Chaps. 8–12).

Other approaches to model development theorize that the spread of fires depends on certain cause-effect relationships. A high-level conceptual model (Chap. 8) is necessary in this case before we can form algorithms. The virtual prototype can display parts of this conceptual model and animate their interactions as an introduction to scripted scenarios. Words or algorithms can capture the causal relationships that create and spread a fire. For example, we can assume temperature is directly related to fuel flash points. Fire is more likely with higher temperatures and lower flashpoints. We often diagram the flow of this kind of process. Displaying these diagrams in the virtual prototype is instructive to users and M&S teams.

7.4.2   Considering Multiple Perspectives—Firefighting Example

Before building models and simulations, you must consider the perspectives of all players (as for the warfighter in Sec. 7.2), including users, operators, developers, and supporters. You need all perspectives because they'll vary in the same way that witnesses of an identical event or accident will report different views. As an example, let's examine the varying perspectives of people who fight forest fires.

Let's assume we need a simulation to help develop fire-fighting procedures which use the least possible resources. In this case, headquarters management wants to assess status, predict the resources required, and determine how best to deploy resources for certain classes of fires. Before the fire, this information helps them develop cost-effective procedures and predict future expenses. During the fire, managers will use it to command and control firefighting forces. Finally, it's needed after the fire to determine how to distribute money to the agencies who fought the fire. Regional managers deploy resources to a fire zone, so they want to know about the organizations, people, and equipment deployed. They also need to know how the firefighting effort is progressing, predict the fire's size and direction, and forecast when the fire will be out. This information is necessary to direct state, local, and federal fire-fighting resources and satisfy the media. Managers in the field want to know what resources they have and can call on, where people and resources are, and the fire's intensity, direction, and spread rate. The unit is more concerned with minute-by-minute fire fighting. They want to know the fire's type, intensity, direction, and speed—not how to develop future strategies or efficiencies. Thus, each firefighting group needs different information from the simulation.

The basic question remains: "Who is the customer and how do we design the M&S system? Do we include the features everyone suggests or needs, or do we select the best features? We've all seen models that try to do everything, take a long time to run, and produce results that are difficult to understand and trace. Eventually, no one uses them because of their complexity, many inputs, and slow turnaround time. But we've also seen models so specific that their results aren't useful outside a single case or when interacting with other models. Just as no approach or model is "best," no perspective is "correct." However, you must always ask who the customers are and what is important to them.

For the firefighting example, are customers the managers at headquarters, in the field, or in units? Are they the firefighters or the taxpayers? As the ultimate customers, taxpayers want firefighting, prevention, and prediction to use tax money efficiently. But taxpayers don't develop objectives or want to see the virtual prototype, actual prototype, or final simulation. As a result, you'll probably aim a simulation at the firefighters. After all, every action being simulated and acted on ultimately benefits firefighters who, like warfighters, must "take ground" to win the battle against fire. You must balance requirements and objectives by weighing all perspectives before building a simulation.

As you consider multiple users, you'll find they all want to easily use a simulation's products. If they're using it for different information, you'll need a distributed interactive system. Furthermore, the input devices and user friendliness of the system must accommodate both types of users. A computer terminal and a program with various abilities and inputs may be necessary (and possible) for analysts who operate the system in air-conditioned offices. But firefighters in the field need simplified inputs through hand-held communication devices that don't interfere with their duties. For basic information—the wind's direction and speed, the fire's location and spread rate, or availability of resources—firefighters don't need the analysts' computing power, options, or outputs. Commanders of firefighting battalions want to see graphical representations of the fire's location, intensity, and spread in their command posts, so they can consider how to direct resources and fight the fire. The skill levels or positions of people who will operate and maintain your system help determine how you'll package the product. A simulation program and its packaging can be more complex and less robust for analysts than they are for firefighters. Finally, the amount of money available to develop the system will help determine its nature. You'll need money to add "bells and whistles" that make it more friendly to users and provide sophisticated graphical inputs and outputs.

7.4.3   Scripting for PVOR Helps Plan and Do Firefighting

To evolve an idea from paper to product, you must consider how it will flow through the simulation's lifecycle. Scripting to develop the virtual prototype, as described in this chapter, supports the logic for designing the simulation and helps you and your team understand how to flow and control its modules. A process's linearity (or lack of it), parallelism, and flow influence the model design. If the process is linear (one event follows another), problem analysis is fairly straightforward, and you can depict it in simple diagrams. However, if the problem isn't linear or has several dimensions, your analysis and problem description are more complex. For the firefighting system, a linear problem involves the steps needed to knock down the fire and direct control of the firefighting effort, as shown in Fig. 7.11. This linear flow influences how you would script the virtual prototype (as discussed in this chapter) and design the model (as described in Chap. 8).

These steps suggest the logic for building displays in a virtual prototype. Eventually, they guide the design for controlling the simulation modules you need to identify the fire's location, type, and spread, as well as to direct firefighting resources. If the process was linear, you could step through the effects of denying the fire of conditions that promote it, based on fuel and weather conditions. But firefighting has several events occurring simultaneously, so it requires cooperative inputs from various entities, parallel processing, and, therefore, a much more complex virtual prototype and simulation. For example, after locating a fire, managers must locate, coordinate, and direct firefighting resources; get these resources to the right location; and minimize the risk to firefighters and equipment. Thus, your analysis can range from simple to complex. Also, once you've established a flow, you must integrate it into timelines for the visual prototype.

Fig. 7.11.   Linear Flow for Fighting Fires. The description of real-world activities influences how you script the virtual prototype and determines the flow of the simulation.

7.4.4   Scripting the Firefighting Example

Scripting means presenting parts of the virtual prototype in a certain order. To script the firefighting example, we must examine the effect of time, the schema, and communication. Capturing timelines and displaying their relationships is important to analyzing a problem because simulations must move through time just as real situations do. Timelines reveal a problem's dimensions. For example, if two events occupy the same time, you'll need parallel processing in the simulation. You can then do bubble diagrams to capture inputs, outputs, how long events last, and how they move through time in the problem space. For example, firefighting usually requires several units to deploy at the same time and often contains fires in some locales before others. Also, containing fire in one area often depends on how fire in other areas stops or spreads. As a result, your simulation will need at least multiple clock events and parallel activities, so similar modules will run at different programmed clock speeds to model the real fire and its propagation. As discussed further below, you must also time communications about the fire's progress, the availability and consumption of resources, and the environmental conditions. Accounting for this timing helps simulate the fire's progress and the communication flows for command and control.

Correct timing depends strongly on how you script the schema for your virtual prototype. The schema maps the virtual to the real world by capturing the subsystems, their definition, the way they're connected and related, and how they communicate. It consists of entities, attributes, and relationships that describe the logical organization and use of data to meet stated objectives. Examples are provided in Fig. 7.12. In modeling and simulation, we model these objectives to predict outcomes based on various inputs. To adapt your schema to the world it is trying to model, you must determine whether its processes are distributive or iterative. A distributive process refers to a structure in which information and control are dispersed to the elements of the schema regardless of their type. An iterative process means repeatedly refining the information and control provided to the elements until you achieve the desired outcome.

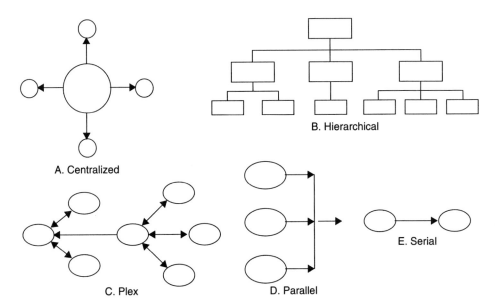

Fig. 7.12.   Types of Schema for a Virtual Prototype. Schemas map the virtual world to the real world and influence the structure and design of a virtual prototype.

Your schema may involve some, all, or combinations of these processes, depending on your analysis of the problem. For example, firefighting suggests a centralized and distributive schema. It needs a cohesive, centralized source of information which dictates how managers disperse and use resources. At the same time, firefighting calls for a distributive schema because field units need to coordinate and interact, often in real time, to fight the fire. This combined schema would lead you to model a hybrid (centralized and distributed) process. Because M&S should improve designs, you must reexamine any schema that doesn't better satisfy the measures of effectiveness for your simulation. If the schema is flawed, redesign it and alter your script, no matter what stage of development it's in.

In addition to effective timing and schema, all simulations need a communication flow to meet their objectives. Flowing information for command and control and moving resources characterize a firefighting system. You must account for these flows in developing a simulation concept. If you ignore them, the simulation won't correctly model the reality it's trying to represent. Communication can range from simple to complex—one to one, one to many, or many to many (see Fig. 7.13). In fact, simulations typically combine these processes. By knowing how communications and resources flow through the system's products or nodes, you'll be able to capture the information needed to build your simulation.

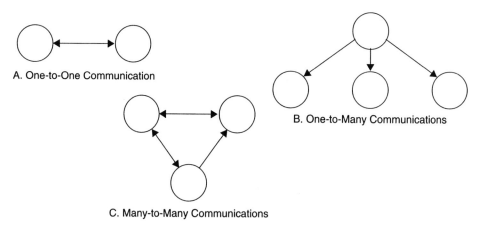

A. One-to-One Communication

B. One-to-Many Communications

C. Many-to-Many Communications

Fig. 7.13.   Communication Flow in Real Systems. Knowing how communication flows through your system's products or nodes will influence the design of your simulation.

Fighting fires involves several types of communication. Individual firefighters communicate results to each other one to one. Whenever a battalion commander issues or broadcasts orders to individuals or units, we have one-to-many communication. Finally, several units sharing information are communicating from many to many. These types of communication occur among individuals, units, and processes. For example, systems for fire propagation and decision support must transfer information to command posts and units in order to suggest or determine actions under certain conditions.

7.5   Summary

I've focused on presenting ways to visualize processes you need to transition from planning to building models and simulations. These methods bridge from previous chapters (engineering background and planning) to developing and carrying out an application for users. First, we translated requirements, paper and "blue sky" concepts, and alternatives into a preliminary framework that can unite users' requirements with the M&S team's products. This framework is what I call the Promotional-Visual-Operational Requirements (PVOR) process. It results in a virtual prototype that captures requirements and operational scenarios, as illustrated in examples for warfighting and firefighting. This prototype represents the simulation's look, feel, and operation. You can use it to construct an actual prototype, which can be temporary or evolutionary. It transports your team from planning to execution and prepares them to start designing the model. The virtual prototype, actual prototype, and final model all have an important place in modeling and simulations, as recapped in Table 7.1.

Table 7.1.   **Attributes of Virtual Prototype, Actual Prototype, and Final Models.** The attributes described here help determine when to use each kind of prototype.

Attribute	Virtual Prototype	Actual Prototype	Final Model
Scenario generation	Scripted only	Limited	Unlimited
Programming required	None	Yes	Yes
Documentation required	Minimal	Minimal	Full
Complexity	Minimal	Full	Full
Development cost (% of dollars)	1–5%	10–15%	80%
Development time	Very short	Longer	Longest
Portability	Excellent	Poor	Poor
Traceability	Good	Better	Excellent
Requirements definition	Good	Better	Best
Turnaround for changes	Very fast	Fairly fast	Slowest

CHAPTER 8

Designing Models

Kirstie L. Bellman, *The Aerospace Corporation*
Christopher Landauer, *The Aerospace Corporation,*

Let's say—based on reasons from Chaps. 4 through 6—your organization has agreed that modeling would be beneficial, estimated how much they're willing to spend in time and staffing, and started detailing the model's purpose. This chapter answers "now what?" by taking you through the modeling process, identifying key decisions at each stage, and helping you build models that can adapt to changing requirements, technology, and applications.

We'll concentrate on technical issues about models, systems of models, and model integration. Our approach is to describe what we know about the application domain, so computer programs can process or at least organize and maintain this knowledge. Other parts of this book discuss issues critical to building the simulation. (For example, Chaps. 9 and 10 describe how to build simulation programs; Chap. 7 discusses the development of simulation systems; and Chaps. 5 and 6 focus on designing simulation projects.) Turning models into computer programs and other kinds of instructions is a separate issue. We can usually reuse modeling processes and results but often can't reuse programming results. Modeling is difficult, but a good process is important because it simplifies future development activities.

Since our earliest history, humans have built models of clay, straw, pigment, and stone, mostly to capture the superficial, easily visible features of natural phenomena. But like us, these early model builders built their models to increase human understanding and, if they believed in magic, to control the world around them. Over the last eight thousand years, we have enhanced our model-building materials with mathematics, computers, and an increasing depth of knowledge and theory. But our models have the same purpose. Of course, controlling the world around us now involves designing and building artifacts our ancestors never dreamt of. Unfortunately, many model developers have focused too much on making better models out of better "stuff" (mathematics and computers instead of clay and straw). As a result, they've neglected the modeling process, which allows us to build, use, and further develop models.

Emphasizing and investing in frameworks and infrastructure for modeling won't seem justified unless we understand this need for process (Lajoie, 1994; Shaw, 1995a). Let's expand on this idea with an example from the last chapter. Chapter 7 depicts iterative prototyping—the first step is understanding the system's needs and matching them to a set of initial requirements, which often involves the first system models. These models typically combine basic conceptual models of mission or system objectives and possible solutions with more detailed models of systems, components, and computational models that use cost and reliability databases. For a large system, even at this initial stage, tradeoff studies and early feasibility analyses will begin. If we learn anything from our models (that's why we build them), we'll be deepening our understanding of requirements, possible solutions, and inevitable tradeoffs among the requirements, user populations, costs, and benefits. This means "updating" the model with what we now know about a system and also rethinking our goals for using that model within the developing system. Examples include new kinds of information the model could provide us and new ways we might use the model to fit new system goals or to manage the monitoring or analysis of the system over its lifetime. The example for the prototyping process in Chap. 7 shows that our models—even "perfect" models—at the requirements stage must be able to develop with new ideas for a system. Otherwise, we could use them only once, and they'd be dead weight or even obstacles to iterating through prototyping.

8.1   Steps in Modeling

As implied in the brief example above, modeling is iterative. A lot of the instrumentation, configuration management, and infrastructure discussed later in this chapter are created to manage the products of this iteration. Modeling follows three main steps, which we'll discuss in more detail in the following sections. For now, let's simply outline the key decisions in preparing to build models, building them, and evaluating and analyzing results. These three steps will change in detail and completeness as you repeat the modeling process.

Step 1: Preparing to Build Models

Preparation includes three highly interrelated decisions: establishing intent, choosing a focus, and deciding what abstractions or representations to use. By intent, we mean NOT what the models do, but what humans are trying to do with them. Choosing a focus means deciding what parts of the real world you're going to represent and reason about. Selecting abstractions or representations includes selecting suitable mathematical or formal spaces and associated methods and analyses.

Step 2: Building Models

Constructing models involves four key decisions: building an initial, high-level, conceptual ("overall") model that includes the context of the problem; dividing this overarching conceptual model into component models (or elaborating it as a single model); selecting or adapting legacy models; and choosing and maintaining an integration framework. A common problem in building models is quickly focusing on the object being built or designed, or the immediate problem, and not spending enough time making the context explicit and processible. Yet, the context information often allows us later to evaluate how well the model works or fits its requirements and to reuse it for appropriate problems. Context for a given model may include background information, requirements, desired outcomes, scenarios of use, models of the user, general domain knowledge, and global system attributes such as cost, reliability, and risk. For example, in space systems, context may be the operating environment for a satellite or the receivers on the ground; in medical training, context may include the medical training scenarios; for guidance systems, context may be models of ambient noise, whether intentionally induced by jamming or natural.

By dividing into components, we mean identifying which representational structures mirror which real-world phenomena. Obviously, this division continues the abstraction decisions started in Step 1, but at a more concrete level. Also, when appropriate, you'll decide at this point how many sub-models to build.

Major modeling projects typically use pre-existing models. Hence, construction includes selecting and adapting legacy models. Also, as we'll emphasize repeatedly, the successful models you're building now will become the legacy models of tomorrow. So, from the beginning, you must create the type of models and follow the development process that will make your models easily reusable.

Finally, your documentation and integration framework will organize the modeling project:

- How you're documenting the reasons for your decisions
- What standards or conventions you've adopted to coordinate the project's sub-components or to relate your model to existing computer resources
- Status of and methods for evaluating the project

Step 3: Evaluating Models

This step includes the analyses that will show how well the model accomplishes your goals and criteria, as well as the feedback for refining it.

8.2   Step 1: Preparing to Build a Model

Many people will ask you to start with "just one model." However, as we'll see shortly, when you set out to model anything, you must **decide** whether to build one model or a single framework with many component models. Intent and focus are often confused or intermingled in modeling efforts. Intent is "what do we, as developers or users, want to do with the model?"—train soldiers, answer a question about scientific research, control a navigation device, and so forth. Focus is "what do we want the model to do?"—model the spread of fire or a cardiac patient's distressed breathing.

Intent

The most important question you can ask about a model is what do the developers and users intend to gain from the modeling activity? What kinds of problems will they study? What questions will they ask during the modeling activity? What will they do with the results?

The goal for scientific modeling is often to gain understanding or to advance or refute a theory. The goal for engineering modeling is often to solve a particular problem or to control a process. For design modeling, the goal is often to experiment with the subject matter, study tradeoffs, rationalize choices, and develop a sense of the solution space. The KEY thing that expert modelers do is spend enough time (and draw on considerable experience) to define what they're trying to achieve. The more specifically you can define the goals and intent of the modeling activity, the better your choices will be on scope, representation (notation), associated analyses, content, and criteria for successful completion and good behavior.

Developing the goals for your modeling activity will help determine the types of models you'll be building. For example, detail and scope distinguish models. Whether you're building a higher-level conceptual model to "sketch out" a new system or a very detailed model for analysis will determine many of your decisions on scope and level of precision and detail. You need to define a model's entities and relationships well enough to form the right questions but not in so much detail that they harm the reliability of the results. Other distinctions are a model's:

- Role within a system, such as an "oracle," advisor, or part of some converging evidence in a voting scheme
- Place in the system, such as part of the user interface, visual display, statistical analysis, or animator
- Viewpoint, such as the user's viewpoint in a training environment or a device's point of view in a large system model that includes many models

Some of these examples may seem very odd; we've chosen them deliberately to make you aware of how differently and widely models are used nowadays.

For example, we can use models for designing a new space system to help compare different design decisions or operational environments. Then, we can apply these comparisons to plans for building the space system and identify problems that may occur. In addition, we could use models for analyzing an upgrade to a space system. The models would allow us to compare the system's behavior or use in different operational environments or to design experiments the actual system could carry out. Models can also help us predict how the space system will behave, either as is or with some proposed changes in structure, behavior, or environment. Alternatively, we sometimes want to use models to control the space system. In this case, they'd help us predict behavior and then correct it or direct it into other paths. Finally, models can "stand in" for a space system as a resource for battlefield information during a conflict. This use makes the subject a background or context for some other activity of interest. This kind of model is very prominent in simulation for training applications.

Of course, you may be able to use a model for more than one of these application styles, but don't do so without carefully studying the model. Ideally, the model should have been developed for these multiple purposes. We'll say more about the problems of managing multiple uses for a model in Sec. 8.5, but in a nutshell they are 1) consistently updating the map of its goals, its current uses, and the protocols that integrate it with the rest of the system, such as the user interface, processing programs, or libraries, 2) controlling unexpected side-effects when the models are used for different purposes or new problems.

Other questions that are important to forming a modeling problem are: What do I know about the problem and the possible solutions? What are the important aspects of the phenomenon? What is it supposed to do? How do we handle different populations of users and types of data? As we scope the modeling activity, what can we simplify and what level of detail and precision is required? When we envision the use of a model, how will it interact with its environment? How will its users (if any) interact with it during processing? Lastly, how will its users determine (or measure) what it does and whether it is successful?

You should answer these questions, at least partly, before any modeling takes place. Some may have more than one answer in a single modeling project, especially when you're studying several interacting hypotheses, so you must allow for this multiplicity. Answers to these questions help you make many design choices in constructing the models, as we show in this chapter's examples. Whenever you prepare carefully enough, the modeling process becomes straightforward, though it may still be hard to carry out.

For example, let's consider a goal of one of the projects for which we built an environment and tools. The Debris Analysis Workstation (DAW) supports studies of the hazards of space debris for operational space systems in orbit. It aims at two levels of users: scientists and analysts who develop and evaluate models of the space-debris environment and program managers who operate space systems or other space test programs. Like many other complex tasks for simulation and analysis, no single analysis or model can address space-debris problems. They need a collection or library of tools and models. However, unlike many other modeling environments for special applications, DAW seeks to do more than provide a basic library of tools and models, accessible through a common user interface. DAW provides users with "intelligent support functions" that help them select, adapt, and integrate the diverse software and modeling resources required for debris studies. In addition, the environment was developed to run different models concurrently and compare them explicitly. DAW considers three categories of space-debris problems: analyzing on-orbit events, predicting intercepts, and predicting the long-term flux-density of debris.

DAW's goal was to help expert analysts study space debris, using any observational data available (there is very little), and addressing the three main problems mentioned above. Its simplifications have to do with the very complex shape of debris clouds; we don't know the actual incidence angles for collisions or the weakened structure for explosions, so the best our models can do is a random value or a value representing an assumed uniform distribution.

Let's examine a second example: the Integration Concept Evaluator (ICE) program, which combines three stand-alone simulations for a tactical warning situation. Each program was written and used for other purposes before integration began. The problem scenario is rather simple: a tactical military situation that ground-based sensors can view. The sensors detect the threat and use a communication satellite to relay information back to the U.S. The relayed information is in the usual format but goes through the Satellite Control Network, the world-wide communication system used by the U.S. military to monitor and control all its satellites. Appropriate warning information relays back through that satellite to a ground commander who isn't close enough to the sensors to access them directly. The questions asked were: How fast can the warnings be relayed from the sensor to the commander? How does using part of the Satellite Control Network affect its use for other satellites? How does the Network's usual traffic affect the warnings, and vice versa? The ICE's goal was to demonstrate how organizations who must upgrade the Network can use simulation to study integrated models of it. Simulations allow them to use many models and data sets in order to provide information for planning decisions.

The last important question for modeling—how users will determine a model's success—may have very different answers depending on which user population we're asking. When the developers are the users, as is true in many small modeling applications, this issue becomes less of a problem in the short-term; however, part of the problem of "legacy code" is that users other than the original developers need original decisions and intentions documented. Note that "successful" means not only "getting the right answer" but also "learning enough to improve the model." For the DAW example, the users will determine what the model does by comparing its predictions to the measured effects of known space events, and then comparing the results of the program with the observed results of the event. Examining the differences will discover information that improves the models. For the ICE example, the users determined what it did by using it to examine changes in the use of the Satellite Control Network. It showed the effects of a few scenarios, which proved this kind of integration can be effective.

Many projects have invested in modeling only to have these efforts undermined because of poor understanding of the project's intent and not documenting the arguments for early decisions. An interesting example of a modeling failure at this stage occurred in a particular space system's solar panel, which is a rectangular array of active elements glued onto a substrate. After several successful deployments of satellites with these solar panels, suddenly the solar panels on new satellites in the series began to fail. Many examinations of the design and, finally, of the manufacturing process itself discovered a problem with procedure. A new person on the construction crew tried to be extremely neat, carefully wiping away excess glue from around the sides of the elements. In space, sunlight got into the sides and degraded the glue enough to loosen the elements and ruin the panel. The previous worker had been sloppy: leaving extra gobs of glue all around the sides protected the elements from the sunlight.

This example is partly about a modeling failure because nobody had thought of modeling the effects of side radiation—the kind of omission that certainly happens in many complex modeling problems. This is part of the reason we say models must change to match changes in situations. However, this example also illustrates a failure in using models because, when the solar panels worked, nobody identified the right reasons. Thus, we must not only know something works; we have to know why it works and be able to demonstrate it.

Some common attitudes about modeling are falsely "pragmatic." For example, the project leader of a very large, expensive simulation testbed said: "We've been fooling around modeling for too long and gotten nowhere. I'm tired of it; let's just build it." But modeling helps us determine whether we know enough to build something, and whether it will be the right something. If we can't finish modeling a large system, we certainly don't know enough to build it. In this example, the simulation testbed was supposed to support an expensive and technically challenging military capability. It involved many cooperating computers, which ran hundreds of simulations and emulations written by diverse groups across the country. The overall modeling effort for this testbed was unsuccessful because there was never a clear idea of what each model element was supposed to produce and how the information would help the organization decide to carry out its goals. We believe the team needed an explicit testbed model with clearly defined roles for the models, simulations, and interfaces within it. Such a model would have provided a sound first step towards creating a testbed that could answer sophisticated design questions and adapt to changing policies and new missions. Instead, the simulation testbed required so many design decisions up front that it could study only the most trivial design excursions. The mission and policy changes since it started have made it an expensive mistake.

Focus

By definition, any model only partly represents a subject, so it always emphasizes some things and omits others, depending on what we want the model to do. The key to good modeling is ensuring the model emphasizes what is most important in the phenomenon of interest. During this step, we want to develop a rationale for the model's focus.

In modeling, we try carefully to specify problems about some situation of interest, so we can use analytical methods and carry the results back to the original system and environment. Therefore, we ask 1) What to model, or how to choose the important aspects of a system? 2) How to select the appropriate partial models of behavior for the system and its environment? Providing this type of information allows developers and users to reuse their models for new problems because it allows us to determine how the model maps to the problem, the context for the modeling activity, and the criteria for evaluating modeling results.

Whenever we're trying to decide how to focus a modeling effort, a common mistake is to take the most general available model. This general model requires too much specifying to define how it maps to any given example problem, or else it needs too much interpretation to understand its results. Because the most general model is seldom the right choice, we must try to choose the "right" specialized model (which may be hard) or at least a "good" specialized model (which is not as hard). A good model must

- Account for the behavior that is important to the problem
- Provide ways of learning what it does and how it works
- Need no more detailed information to run or to explain than the level of detail for the problem

Other important questions that help us focus the models: 1) What are the problem's important phenomena?, 2) How flexible and variable must the model be? 3) What are the sources of relevant data and their models? To determine the problem's important phenomena requires some knowledge of the problem domain. This is one of the main functions for the "reference model" discussed in Sec. 8.3.4. Many of the entities and interactions are already part of a simulation's problem statement, so their choice is determined. But we also need to choose parts of the environment that might affect the model's behavior or constrain possible courses of action.

Determining how much and what types of flexibility or variability the models need is more difficult. First, by flexibility and variability we mean much more than the range of values that given parameters are allowed to take on; we mean flexibility in all of the model's behaviors: the ways a model can process information, use different methods, interact with a user, display results, or relate to other models. The model should at least be able to handle a class of problems. Using multiple models as a library of resources for modeling often allows us to improve the versatility and the range of problems a model can gracefully handle. It also allows individual models to be more specialized and vary less.

One of the major decisions while focusing a modeling activity is whether or not you have enough good information to represent a desired feature of the subject domain. Sometimes, the first choice of focus in a model is not possible because of the limitations in the quality or availability of information, so you must realistically assess these potential compromises at the start of the project. Identify every source of simulation data, the data models, plus meta-knowledge about the data or its sources (information about credibility and certification is particularly important here).

Carefully evaluate the identified data and map it to your choices as you choose entities, relationships among those entities, actions they can do, and events they can cause or be subject to. You must also understand what causes events and actions. Watch for and analyze "imbalances" (almost an aesthetic quality here)—having some entities with very well-determined behavior provided by good data or deep theoretical models coupled with other entities with sparse or poor data and sketchy theoretical foundations. One of the advantages of modeling is the ability to combine different kinds of data and information resources within a common model; however, you must carefully examine your assumptions and techniques for combining this information.

For the ICE example, we chose three programs because they covered an interesting problem area and were available (we could access the developers). We had to decide what the corresponding models were and how much detail to provide in them. We chose a very superficial view, considering only the data to be exchanged, because the example was intended to show integration of programs. Similarly, for the DAW example, we were given the programs and their models. In this case, we had to model the interactions among those programs and the problem domain thoroughly enough to express relevant interactions among the programs.

Abstraction

Before we discuss how to choose the representations for a given modeling project, it's important to understand the diversity of existing modeling representations and formal methods. Becoming an expert on these representations isn't important (or practical), but being aware of this diversity will help you seek out expertise when you need it. Reason through and document all choices. Unfortunately, too many project managers make this very critical decision based on the experience of a key developer and not on the pros and cons of using that representation to support the modeling project's goals.

Modeling Styles and Formal Spaces. For our purposes, the term "model" is the most general term; a simulation is a kind of model. Any model represents—in a formal or computational space—some objects or phenomena of interest (the "subject" phenomena). Models can be as elaborate as multi-network simulations or as simple as a table of values. For now, we'll simply list some of the kinds of models you'll need to consider, deferring further discussion until after we describe the different kinds of problems a model can be used to study:

- High-level conceptual models (usually pictures or text)
- Architectural models (usually diagrams, hierarchies, or networks)
- Prototype models (physical or device models)
- Other diagrammatic models
- Procedural models (cookbook "recipes," algorithms, etc.)
- Rule sets (heuristics, decision tables)
- Equational models (possibly dynamic)
- Simulation models

This list is purposely broad to familiarize you with the variety of existing models. A model includes some context: assumptions (we must know before applying it), goals, intended applications, definitions of terms, references (including sources, annotations, etc.), and possibly other things. Many types of models refer to variable parameters whose values are determined by many sources—equations, rules, tables, simulations, programs, and functions. For many purposes, we must have definitions, assumptions, and additional information about these parameters. Later, we can use these annotations for better understanding and for tracing model derivations. This information, called "meta-knowledge," is essential for all processes associated with models [Kiczales 1991; Maes 1988; Landauer 1996a]. To use a model correctly and to get correct, valid results, you must properly account for its assumptions. Later understanding or proper reuse of a model depends on retaining the assumptions under which it was constructed.

The spaces in which models exist are as varied as the modeling styles. We use a formal or computational space so we can find out what happens to the models, either by prior analysis (usually mathematical) or by elaboration and observation (usually computational). Modeling spaces for simulation include static structures, such as sets of equations or conceptual models that use boxes and lines to represent a connection architecture or generic relationships. Other useful spaces incorporate dynamic behaviors, such as interactions and simulations with differential equations, simulation languages, or state machines. There are many others, some of which we'll use in our example models.

Some models contain only data. They may be theoretical, empirical, or hypothetical. A theoretical model represents some scientific theory, with structure and behavior that conforms to that theory. An empirical model is simply an observation of data. It describes a set of numerical data according to some measure of fit and (often) a measure of simplicity among explanatory models. Existing theories may or may not justify a hypothetical model. Actually, most simulation models combine these types. However, it's easier to define, explain, analyze, and maintain a model if it's limited to one type of modeling style. If that's not possible, the goals, expectations, and rationale for including each of several modeling styles must be carefully defined so you can effectively combine them without unintended side effects or errors.

Considering Which Modeling Style to Use. We listed above some of the different model types you may need to consider for your applications. As you may have guessed, deciding which styles to use for your problem is still an art. But, good modelers consider certain issues as they make these difficult choices. You must pay special attention to the kinds of phenomena that are relevant to your goals and the formal spaces in which you can model the processes, behavior, entities, and relationships that define the subject phenomena. Mathematically or computationally different models require and produce different kinds of information, so they apply best to particular kinds of modeling problems. For example, computational and dynamical models require reasoning from theory to produce equations that define the model. They usually rely on intensive computation for their results, which are used to describe continuous activity, such as motion of physical objects, flows of physical media, and other physical processes. They may have rules as summaries or shortcuts, and usually have well-specified search spaces, because they're mainly mathematical.

Every model that elaborates some physical process needs space and time models, because the process must occur somewhere over some time. But keep in mind that the "time" or "space" in the model isn't physical reality. It's a model of the aspects of space and time that are important to the modeling problem. Careful treatment of this point saves trouble later on because it makes explicit the assumed properties. Many models in certain applications describe the behavior of particular kinds of physical devices, such as a computer processor, radio, truck, or missile. These models often have a dynamic component that uses differential equations and a computational component that uses some kind of program or rule. Quite often, especially in simulations of device designs, rules summarize complex phenomena, generate hypotheses, or quickly compute behavior anomalies, which we can display (given fault hypotheses) for fault diagnosis and recovery.

Many scientific and engineering disciplines have no theoretical models for some phenomena; they have only empirical models based on observed data. Similarly, we must often make our own empirical models because data is sparse. In this case, it's important to know where the models are valid, which is sometimes hard to determine. When we make our own empirical models, we need to infer structure from appropriate statistical methods, not simply rely on having many parameters to make the fit good. Heuristics are rules of thumb we can't prove helpful for certain situations, but they do help in practice. Many "educated guesses" fall under this heading, so you must recognize their importance while trying to improve your model by looking for more provable characteristics.

We want models to have some mathematical rigor in their expression because it clarifies how we can apply them. Sometimes, rigorous expression is easy: certain assertions can be proven about the situation being modeled that lead directly to equations or other mathematical expressions. But over the last few years modelers have learned that some situations are difficult or impossible to model as we'd like using conventional mathematical techniques. We've discussed this issue elsewhere [Landauer 1993b] and asked people to study hard questions on using mathematics for modeling [Landauer 1995a]. Along these lines, we often use rules as summaries or shortcuts for calculations because only the derived quantities are important to using the model. For example, in many atmospheric models, pressure is a modeled quantity. We all know that pressure derives from the motions and collisions of many gas particles, but that level of detail is irrelevant for most models and it's certainly too time-consuming to compute for almost any application. Thus, we find precision is often a trap—attractive but not necessary.

Models fall into many classes, or families, related by methods, applications, uses, and so forth. While choosing the correct formal spaces and mapping between a problem and that formal space, you may concentrate on a single model, but you're always defining a family of possible models. One of the hardest jobs here is to make explicit some of your preliminary ideas: notions of what you're looking for in this class of models, why you're leaning toward using this or that formal space, and how you're distinguishing models in this family. Some questions can help you bring out these distinctions and ideas and build them into explicit arguments: What is relevant about using this class of models for this problem? How do I define models in the class? How do models in the class pass information in and out? How can I tell if two models in the class are compatible? How do I use information to refine models in the class? How can I tell if one model refines another? How do I separate models from the class and then identify entities, relationships among them, and behaviors?

Document Your Choices, Reasoning, and Assumptions. During this stage of modeling you'll try to capture the reasons for your choices of different modeling abstractions. The right choices will actually limit later efforts by eliminating unnecessary detail and variables. So, it is important to document your reasons even if they are based on only intuition or someone's advice. First, write down the assumptions under which the selected model simplifications are valid. As discussed above, you want to state clearly why you're choosing certain representations and methods; this includes writing down limits and expectations for the representations. This process usually continues because you won't recognize some assumptions until much later. Corresponding to each assumption are criteria to determine if it's no longer valid. Check these criteria occasionally and every time you use certain software to carry out the model.

Next, determine the boundaries of applicability. A model always omits some features and emphasizes others, so make sure it's reasonably scoped and define clearly what it can't do. Scope is related to these boundaries: it defines the range of phenomena that the model is expected to represent. It is often used for numerical parameters, in which case it defines an interval of possible values for the parameter. Another boundary is for resolution, which means the level of detail in a model. For numbers, it is the smallest irrelevant difference between two numbers, which is the same as the precision of the numerical computation required. Trace descriptions of resolution limits and simplifications to design decisions, so the simulation system can evolve during development and use. Also, monitor the descriptions for errors while running or refining the system; document and maintain them as development artifacts.

Appropriate units and dimensions for numerical parameters should also be documented. We've already mentioned extent (range, scope) and detail (granularity, resolution), which relate to the numerical values themselves. In addition, time, space, and other physical or engineering units relate to the meaning of the numbers. Physical units are the simplest and perhaps best known examples of meta-knowledge. In fact, we can derive some basic physical formulas solely from knowing the units of their terms.

For each model parameter, you must choose an appropriate measurement scale from four types:

- Nominal, whenever you can distinguish measurement values from each other but they have no particular order (a set)

- Ordinal, whenever you can place the measurement values in a linear order (a sequence)

- Interval, whenever differences of measurement values make sense, as in temperature (an ordered group)

- Ratio, when quotients of measurement values make sense, as in weight (an ordered ring)

These scales are the standard set discussed in many books on measurement theory. Another commonly used scale is the circular scale, which occurs in clock time and longitude (latitude is different).

Your choices at this stage will determine some of the performance and error models when you pick hardware and software for the project. For example, different hardware platforms will constrain the choice of programming languages, so using certain types of representations or formal spaces will be difficult or impossible. Model implementations must also include software and hardware probes to catch or "trap" conditions that lead to unintentional side effects in programs. These conditions include problems that tend to occur near the boundaries of a computational process; the "exceptions" that exist in some programming languages (e.g., division by zero, array subscript out of bounds); and other unique conditions that are invalid only for a particular model. For example, in most cases, a numerical variable may be positive or negative. But in the context of a particular model that contains system weight as a variable, negative values will produce error conditions one of these probes could catch.

Finally, and perhaps most importantly, define the uncertainty models that describe the limits of your knowledge about the model. Uncertainty models range from so-called "confidence factors" to belief functions, empirical probabilities, chaos, "colored noise," and fuzzy sets. Random distributions are most common by far, but they may not be best for your problem.

It's also important to know how to act when you don't know what to do. If there is no accepted model in a problem domain (a common situation), you'll have to make one yourself. Meta-models can be very helpful here. They allow you to carefully and explicitly organize what is known and not known about a given problem domain. You will combine submodels (see mini-models in Sec. 8.3.2), based on strong conventionally derived information and techniques, with submodels representing your best current strategy for handling unknown parts of the problem. Document goals, assumptions, and limits for each submodel. In this way, you can use new information and techniques to replace the weaker parts of the overall meta-model with better submodels as well as better ways to relate the known and unknown parts of the problem. This approach is extremely powerful, and we strongly advocate using it throughout the modeling process for complex applications [Bellman 1991; Landauer 1993a].

8.3   Step 2: Building a Model

8.3.1   Building Initial Context Models

Context information has always been a big part of any modeling project. Often, appropriate context information has led to understanding what parameters could vary, how to display information, and how computer programs embodying the models interacted with their users. We must make these decisions about contexts (operational, theoretical, scientific, or organizational) explicit and processible so we can evaluate the effectiveness and appropriateness of the resulting models and maintain and develop them over their lifetime. To do this, we're going to describe several different levels of context because entities and models are embedded in these levels, and we may need to model each level to some extent depending on the project.

Model variables and factors always can be either the subject of a modeling effort or the context for some other modeling objective. Examples include weather, background radiation in space, jamming, level of user expertise, risk, cost, and movement of opposing force troops. Furthermore, any of these subjects could contribute to the modeling project—as either subject or context—at several levels. For example, in Firewatcher, weather strongly affects the spread of fire, so we'd expect to see parameters for weather conditions in the body of the model—either as a separate, detailed model or as parameters in the fire-propagation model. But the interface or display may present and explain the results differently for users with different levels of weather expertise. In other words, the interface contains the decisions on how human users expect to use the information gathered during context modeling. Lastly, if the intent was to deploy the resulting modeling system so it could be used "in the trenches" as well as in the home office, weather conditions become part of the robustness requirements for the operational system. Hence, in this example, weather variables require three types of context information: the types of problems for which human users would use the information, the levels of expertise in different users, and the actual operating environment for the deployed system. This may sound like only hardware and software issues until we recognize that models need to be built so they can be reliable under different external conditions. For example, a model deployed in space with background radiation knocking out random bits or on earth in a dirty environment may need extra components for instrumentation, self-monitoring and self-correction, or techniques to check automatically on degradation of results.

In the previous section, we distinguished what we intend to do with a model from our goals for focusing the model—both of which contribute different levels of information to context modeling. You'll use the decisions and information resulting from the first modeling stage to help you decide:

- The scope of the background modeling
- What you can assume about the different levels of context
- Which parts of the context are most relevant and which you can largely ignore
- How you'll represent the context information in the modeling project

When you're finished, the context information may well appear as documentation, as separate models integrated with the models of the project's main focus, or as attributes, factors, or parameters within a single model. It could also be part of the user interface or visual display, a set of scenarios, or a set of test cases. Often, it may appear in all of the above. Document your decisions during context modeling and, whenever you've created artifacts (models, user interfaces, data sets), map the choices and assumptions for context to these artifacts.

Context modeling is often implicit in an architecture for the problem domain that becomes a reference for a family of applications. This reference architecture describes the phenomena that are important in the domain, the ways in which they interact, and the ways in which they could affect (or be affected by) the kinds of model you're trying to build. [For more about reference architectures, see Balzer, (1993), Garlan (1995), Shaw (1995b), Terry (1994), Tracz (1992), and Wile (1983).] The context information has often implicitly defined why different subcomponents and relationships among components were selected to be part of the reference architecture. You must make this information explicit so you can evaluate whether or not the reference architecture is still relevant, appropriate, and useful when new problems arise. Furthermore, this reference architecture should be almost independent of the immediate modeling problem you're trying to solve; it models the problem domain, which you need to build using the same steps as for any model. An appropriate reference architecture helps you identify how to customize models and select the right components for your specific problem or application. Over the long term, especially in application areas that have repeated modeling problems, it will help models in that domain operate together.

The context for every model and simulation includes who builds the models, who builds the simulations, and who uses them. Thus, we can now use some of the project plans developed in Chaps. 4–6 to consider the cost of producing and maintaining the models, as well as the test and evaluation processes we must use and support. The cost considerations require tradeoffs against several technical aspects of models: How much detail and how many levels of detail do the models require? [Davis 1993; Hillestad 1996; Landauer 1993a] How much testing is appropriate? How important is it that the models be defensible technically and politically?

As to the first question, we noted before that models should be detailed enough to answer the questions of interest, but no more. In managing your own project, note that extra detail means extra time for modeling, longer schedules, and extra sources of (often) nearly untraceable errors, which require more testing and more dollars.

Testing the models is almost always more important and time-consuming than expected (or even desired). Verification, validation, and accreditation should take place throughout development; most projects allocate time for them only at the end and then shorten or drop them as schedule delays and costs first approach and then exceed the original plans. Here again, the development context makes a difference. If your organization intends to use these models over time, any testing and careful validation up front will save enormously later on.

The last question above is the most difficult. Some models are made to try out certain technical choices. Others are made to prove certain politically sensitive results. Far too many models are made without keeping track of their assumptions, which makes them automatically impossible to justify and their results hard to believe. As long as you retain these assumptions, others can study alternative sets of assumptions and compare their effects.

The context of a model's intended uses determines the relative importance of several development properties

- How much instrumentation should the model have?
- How flexible should the model's structure be?
- How important is it for the model to be general enough to use again?
- How much meta-knowledge should be developed for its use?
- How much domain knowledge should the model represent?
- How independent of the execution environment should the model be?

The answer is "almost always more than expected," but let's describe some choices for each question.

In the first question, about instrumentation, we're trying to determine how much of the model's internal structure needs to be available to the rest of the system outside it. For some purposes, especially in development, many details are needed to help verify that the model is doing what it is expected to. While using a model during production, however, we want only a little instrumentation (mainly to diagnose faults), so it will work efficiently.

The next two questions are related: models need flexibility and generality only to allow reuse in different situations, or to allow different aspects to be studied in different contexts. For example, we must allow certain constants to vary, but not others. The speed of light is a constant that changes with different units, but the number of feet in a mile is a constant that won't change. On the other hand, configuration parameters—such as the number of copies of gizmo X in mechanism Y—should always be variable, usually even at run time, so we can examine different choices directly.

Meta-knowledge is very important to model development [Kiczales 1991; Maes 1988; Landauer 1995b]. By this we mean information collected about its intended use, expected context, assumptions, limits, other model requirements, and products. Meta-knowledge is our way of recording what a modeling system must know about a model, so others can use it appropriately and its results safely. (See Sec. 8.3.4 on integration for more on this issue.)

8.3.2   Dividing a Model into Components

Matching representational structures in the formal space to real-world phenomena continues our abstraction decisions during preparation. But it becomes more concrete during construction. In this modeling step, we divide a model into its important components and, when appropriate, separate them into smaller interacting models. To build on the reference architecture started during context modeling, we also need to partition the subject system into models.

As you'll see throughout this chapter, we strongly suggest breaking the large modeling activity into sub-models. Smaller models are often more clearly scoped, specified, and evaluated because we can't attach too many goals and accomplishments to them. Small models also specify proper relationships, roles, and handoffs of information or services and avoid side-effects. Thus, they handle complex activities, making them visible and hence more accessible for integration. Some developers have mistakenly thought that small models are tougher to integrate, but relating sub-components is just as complex if we hide them inside one big model or develop lots of little models. Also, developing sub-models has nothing to do with how we create them in computer programs. We can place many sub-models into one large computer program or implement one large model as several computer programs. But putting models into several smaller computer programs has the same advantage as developing sub-models: better specification, evaluation, and maintenance.

Some people confuse the number of models with the scope of a modeling activity. Scope DOESN'T equal the number or size of models. A single model can be superficial and broad (as in a battlefield model), or many models can analyze a single effect, such as wind shear on an airplane wing.

You'll need experts on a domain to define aspects of the system and its parts, [Terry 1994] plus knowledge of modeling techniques to separate a model into useful parts. Don't allow computer programmers to partition the model based on the constraints of old software. If you don't have domain experts for a project, you should build the model as a combination of "mini-models" [Walter 1990] that capture what is known about restricted domains which relate to the problem of interest. Without an over-arching model of all phenomena, you have a nearly undefined search space, so you must take great care at the boundaries of the mini-models. Actually, most of these combination models are formally inconsistent because the mini-models make different and conflicting assumptions. Still, this inconsistency usually leads only to imprecise, not incorrect, results.

The fidelity question is one common stumbling point for complex models. [Davis 1993; Hillestad 1996; Landauer 1993a] Suppose you assume that modeling can produce only one level of detail and that everything you know about the problem may be relevant. In this case, you'll tend to produce just one detailed model. Such models are notoriously slow, difficult to validate, and cumbersome to change. We solve this problem by allowing multiple models of the same phenomena at different levels of detail. Then, having very detailed models becomes interesting rather than necessary because we can study many of the requirements with less detail. For example, wargame models at the corps level almost never need individual combatant models, because it's so hard to give scenarios the right amount of detail and to relate this detail to the entire corps' behavior. Similarly, in the ICE example, we wanted to model expected detection delays and probabilities, as well as message transmission, not a particular satellite constellation.

Each model must provide certain information or services to other models or to the system's user. Thus, determining roles for component models also requires separating these responsibilities and assigning them to the components. We've found it useful to emphasize the "roles" models play in a given modeling project because it keeps us focused both on what the model does and on what we are trying to do with the model, as we discussed in the "Intent" part of Sec. 8.2. A properly defined "role" for a modeling component expresses the information or service it produces, the target (end users and other programs) for that information or service, and the system-level goals for the component (e.g., the background terrain in a training simulator, the results that rationalize a design decision, or an input to an assembly-line controller).

For example, Firewatcher has several component models. During the early stages of modeling, we would carefully document our reasons and decisions (mustering our arguments) for including different components. It's never obvious, even with a very specific task, what components to include. For example, you could well argue the benefits of including models of satellite constellations so you could use data from existing satellites for controlling a fire. In this case, you'd need to determine what information the model needs for its computation or other behavior, what information or behavior it produces, and what context requirements must be met for it to be valid.

Another kind of model provides roles and responsibilities for other component or interaction models. For example, a generic constellation model that contains the satellites' visibility and coverage requirements for firewatching would make a good specification model. It would provide roles which particular constellation models can fill and responsibilities against which the particular models can be tested. In the DAW example the application-domain experts had already specified the problem for us; the Integration Concept Evaluator (ICE) involved a kind of directed decomposition because we already knew from the program developers what we could expect the programs to compute.

8.3.3   Adapting or Selecting Legacy Models, Systems, and Data

There is no such thing as a throw-away model. People use models repeatedly for different kinds of problems if they can and, unfortunately, often when they shouldn't. Therefore, we must try to retain enough information about the models to make their reuse more appropriate and more likely to succeed [Gamma 1995; Shaw 1995b]—to create the legacy models of tomorrow. The main questions about a legacy model are what can we study with it and how can we use it?

Both questions require collecting and generating appropriate meta-knowledge. For example, a coverage problem for a satellite configuration involves computing how many satellites can effectively see a particular area of interest on the ground. We can study this issue using averages and distribution assumptions or more detailed orbit models for each satellite. Unfortunately, the most common distribution assumptions aren't true, so we must study special coverages, such as how many satellites can effectively communicate with a particular ground station, using the more detailed model. The ICE project used a generic model for "background" traffic on the SCN rather than a time-specific traffic model. This capacity model didn't address the local bursts of traffic in most communication networks, but because the problem parameters were also generic, that was acceptable. We can't conclude from the ICE models that our delay measurements will apply to all traffic situations.

Few models have this level of meta-knowledge, which is why our discussion of legacy models is so much shorter than those of legacy programs or data. To remedy that situation, we provide ways to collect and retain meta-knowledge about the models for current and future use. [Landauer 1995c; Landauer 1996] Because we consider meta-knowledge such an essential part of creating the integration framework for a modeling project, we'll talk more about it under integration. Even more common, and even more difficult to use, are the large numbers of "legacy" software systems in place. The important questions for legacy software are almost the same as for models: What can we study or do with the system? How can we use it?

Here, too, it's important to collect and generate appropriate meta-knowledge. In fact, a burgeoning industry is trying to "re-engineer" legacy systems using many different methods. The most successful extract the models from the systems and then either rewrite the software from the new models or find a way to use the models directly [Kiczales 1991; Garlan 1995; DeRemer 1976]. In the first approach, developers extract the models and meta-knowledge as much as possible, go back to the modeling stage, and then build software to carry out the models. We can also often collect meta-knowledge about using software that allows us to use the legacy system directly, but certain programming languages make this more difficult. For example, Prolog requires a unique access mechanism, and others, such as Visual Basic, require physical actions by the user. These languages are fine for stand-alone programs but are very hard to use in a larger system.

For example, in the space-debris problem, we began with nicely structured analysis programs and access to most of the program developers, so extracting and describing the model were relatively easy. They had also been thinking about how to use the programs together, so it was fairly easy to collect the meta-knowledge that allowed our Debris Analysis Workstation (DAW) to combine them automatically for many problems. For the Integration Concept Evaluator (ICE), we had three programs to integrate: a threat simulator, a network-traffic simulator, and a scheduler for the Satellite Control Network (SCN). We developed one of the simulations and could occasionally access the developers of the second. For the third one, we communicated only through well structured files.

Finally, "legacy data" can be a problem because it may dictate model choices. For example, on ICE, certain satellite information was classified, so we couldn't access some of the traffic sources and had to rely on averages or other "pretty good" estimates of their effect on the system. Thus, our results were only approximate. In other cases, measurement data may be available only as averages, with no hint of variability, or as a mean and standard deviation, with no hint of testing the normality assumption. Perhaps some characteristic now known to be important simply wasn't measured. The models need to take these problems into account. Chapter 9 discusses this problem in more detail.

8.3.4   Integrating the Model

This step brings everything together into a full system model, so it's a systems view of all the artifacts and processes created by the modeling activity [Shaw 1995b; Zimmer 1995]. For example, the artifacts may include text products such as specifications, standards, contracts, user manuals, papers about the models and algorithms, special hardware interfaces, or robots. The processes may include agreements on subdividing labor among developers and users, testing procedures, usage scenarios, and schedules for building and revising the models. Clearly, we'll attend most to organizing and integrating the models, whether they're in paper, software, or hardware.

Depending on the purposes identified in the task analysis during step 1, we'll vary how much effort we put into

1. The main focus (e.g., building a space system, analyzing telemetry data in a ground station, controlling a robotic arm).

2. The context information. For example, to design a satellite system, we'll model background radiation, perhaps other satellites in the constellation, ground stations, and so forth.

3. The global properties and evaluators at a system level. Often, such properties as cost, reliability, and risk are substantial modeling activities in their own right.

In any major modeling activity, you'll build a number of models which you must manage and integrate into an overall system. To do so, you'll build a conceptual model that includes all the information needed to determine the purposes for each component model and its contribution or role in the modeling system, the relationships among component models, and the criteria for good performance. This information will determine the types of instruments you'll put into developing the models, so you can monitor their performance and examine their behavior.

Recognizing that you're building a system of models will strongly influence your design of single models. You'll choose the scope of a model so it accomplishes its defined role within the system and interacts properly with other models. You'll choose the notations and formal spaces so you can integrate a model with other models in the system. Lastly, you'll develop the instruments and performance analyses that monitor how a model behaves alone and when other models use it. Use architecture models to define how component models connect and operate together. Then, use corresponding interface definitions to ensure the component models can request and provide computations.

Many kinds of standards can help you, including:

- Communication protocols to pass the byte stream (these are relatively well known [Hoare 1985], and almost all are in many commercial tools)

- Object-management protocols for the data structures and interactions (commercial tools exist, but only a few are good)

- Graphics standards for certain kinds of displays (many are available, but typically you'll have only one choice for each configuration of hardware and operating system)

Here also, for large heterogeneous systems, we can apply different theories of integration. "Wrapping" depends on meta-knowledge about system resources and their use and on algorithms that process this information to build system configurations at run-time [Landauer 1996a; Landauer 1996b]. We can also use "design patterns" [Martin 1995; Soukup 1995], weaves [Gorlick 1991], and many other interesting and new approaches [Goguen 1986; Balzer 1993]. Integration was our main involvement for DAW and ICE. We had just completed a version of the theoretical underpinnings for integration, so we used a wrapping structure to show how integration could work.

We emphasize again that collecting and managing meta-knowledge is key to developing integration frameworks. Knowledge "about" the models and modeling domain helps us understand the context and use of models, the way models fit together, the way they over-simplify some aspects of the problem, and anything else that helps us choose what to do with the models. For example, the source of each model is important meta-knowledge that helps determine its reliability or credibility and allows us to choose from many, possibly contradictory, sources of information when making decisions. Choosing well is especially important in the Firewatcher example because, during crises, we often have too much information rather than too little. Scenarios also typically need more information then simple input files can provide. Scenarios are situation models of what "will" have happened before the simulation starts and of what "should" happen during the simulation run. So they should start with models of entities, interactions, constraints, relationships, and historical context (the background or environment of the problem) and then be able to discover current events and adjust themselves accordingly (feedback).

Languages and Software Programming

Let's consider how architectures and integration infrastructures apply to software. (See Chap. 10 for other issues concerning software.) Our approach is to provide an integration infrastructure that allows models to remain the same for various applications, using support software to connect the model's software to different interfaces according to context. For small problems, this infrastructure may be too expensive, but for large ones, it's essential. We'll have more to say about this infrastructure later.

You might imagine that constructing models means simply generating them from the requirements (and many books talk about model construction that way), but you'll almost never know all the requirements in advance. Instead, you'll learn them throughout the modeling process. We recommend focusing your early models on requesting and providing information services from and to other models, so you can examine their information interactions first. Then, when you translate concepts into models and algorithms, you can focus on the model's environment and information requirements. In our ICE and DAW examples, the mathematical models were already constructed, as were the programs. We made conceptual models that held enough information so we could organize the data interchanges needed to combine the programs.

Certain well known problems have plagued (and continue to plague) almost all development projects for complex systems. They've led to risk-management and damage-control techniques called "software engineering." But these problems result mainly from failures of systems engineering, not of software development. Many would disappear if we had adequate models of the system, so we could compute tradeoffs and "what-ifs" in advance. The community needs systems-engineering environments that allow these "meta-models" to be built and examined very early in design.

The code should be the least important part of a computing system because all important system knowledge should be imbedded in the models. Models that specify what the code should be can apply in different environments and include different mixes of hardware and software. We believe model languages eventually will be translated directly into executable code, bypassing detailed coding altogether [Balzer 1993; Tracz 1992]. The approach we describe here is a way to achieve that goal. The key is to develop models that properly capture a system's behavior. Of course, software also models the computational processes we want, but the application problem drives the development of models and software, so many considerations apply to both.

We won't try to say which of the programming languages is best for writing simulation programs because that depends on the problem you're studying, the models, the programmers' experience, and the available hardware, operating system, and software library. But we can give some advice about how to select an appropriate programming language. No modeling language will prevent bad models or keep models from being turned into bad programs. That said, some things will make the models and programs easier to read. Most modern languages allow very complex control structures and multiple statements on a single line. Don't use either one, except in well-defined situations and in a very stylized way. Unless control structures are thoroughly described, you'll find it hard to untangle the interactions. Also, explaining what all the conditions are is often more difficult than programming them separately, and most modern compilers optimize better than most people do.

While transforming models into code, make sure the code refers to the models: the way you construct the models links them, and therefore the code, to all other relevant information. Chapter 10 says more about this point, so here we'll only mention that you should pay special attention to the way you've expressed algorithms, the environment these algorithms need, time and space requirements, and so forth. Whenever you create models in software, especially if they are to run as parts of simulation programs, you'll need software-integration expertise to determine how the execution environment and its intended use affect the software's structure.

Finally, let's talk a little about notations, languages, and software-implementation issues pertaining to meta-knowledge. Although rule bases are the most common kind of meta-knowledge in simulations, meta-models that describe relationships among other models are becoming more popular. For example, often a collection of rules summarizes a model's effects or implications. Meta-models are an important kind of meta-knowledge because we can use them to verify the rules. Notice, we don't use the models directly and skip the rules. Rules can abstract a model's behavior without the computing burden. They're often simple and clear because they state the intended implications. Finally, we can almost always interpret rules faster than we can run the models.

Because integration was our major focus in the Integration Concept Evaluator (ICE) and the Debris Analysis Workstation (DAW) efforts, let's examine these two projects.

Integrating DAW—A Special Case

For DAW, the concepts were mostly integration concepts because, when we began, the following computing programs were already written:

- IMPACT—for explosions and collisions that produced debris clouds of various forms
- DEBRIS—for debris cloud expansion and propagation
- LIFETIME—for the amount of time debris clouds would remain in orbit
- FOOTPRINT—for the expected area of earth on which the debris falling out of orbit would land

The developers had already been thinking about combining the programs for some uses, so we had utility programs that would convert the debris-cloud output from IMPACT to the proper form for input to DEBRIS and LIFETIME. All of these programs were written in Fortran. Figure 8.1 shows the initial architectural model that described how the programs were expected to interact.

Translation was relatively easy in this case because the program writers had made many of the modeling choices. We were trying to model integration concepts, such as common data formats for object descriptions, so programs could automatically use results from another program. Other important concepts included ways of automatically invoking the programs in a suitable order and of combining pre- and post-processing and presentation programs to satisfy users' requests. The modelers had already considered this path in part because they were doing conversions and combinations by hand.

After developing the overall architectural model, we helped create several models that combined the existing programs to accomplish different studies for the users. Such models included a model of collision situations describing the position and velocity vectors of both target and projectile, their relative masses, and some energy-coupling coefficients used to determine how much of the collision energy was dissipated as heat. Also, if the two masses were very different, a parameter determined what fraction of the target's mass was knocked off into

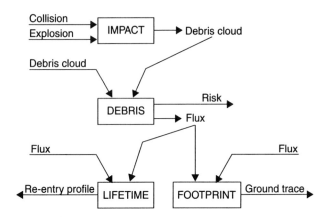

Fig. 8.1.   **Architecture of the Debris Analysis Workstation (DAW) from a User's Viewpoint.**
Debris analysts view the DAW system as a way of using specific programs to investigate
questions about space debris. In this diagram, inputs represent questions, outputs show
the form of the results, and rectangular boxes show the programs used.

particles and assumed the rest would remain with the original target object. An
explosion model had parameters similar to the target's, including a kind of
efficiency fraction that determined how much of the target mass was turned into
dust and no longer accounted for, so that the rest would be turned into particles.

Collision and explosion models used a model for distributing particle mass
that determined the masses of the resulting particles. A cloud-formation model
assumed the particles to be isotropically arranged around the center of gravity.
This model had a velocity vector computed from the projectile's and target's
masses and velocities (for collisions), and from the original object's velocity (for
explosions). The debris-cloud model was a gradually expanding density shell,
assumed to be spherically symmetrical at first, with research determining a better
shape as the cloud is pushed and pulled into whatever kind of orbit it would take.

Integrating ICE

Programs also existed for the integration concept evaluator (ICE); we wanted
to combine them in our model to answer the main questions. The programs were

- SLADE—tactical threats
- FLOW—communication networks as information flows
- ASP—scheduling of the ground stations in the Satellite Control Network
- SCAT—an intelligent interface for ASP that allowed users to construct
  graphical scenarios for input and had many interesting summary displays
  for output

SLADE and ASP were written in Fortran, FLOW in C, and SCAT in C++. We also
used several different user interfaces. Again, we started with an initial

architectural model, and Fig. 8.2 shows the resulting architecture. The developer's view presented here shows the infrastructure explicitly. (The user's version would show only SLADE and FLOW interacting, then some of the resulting files sent off to SCAT.)

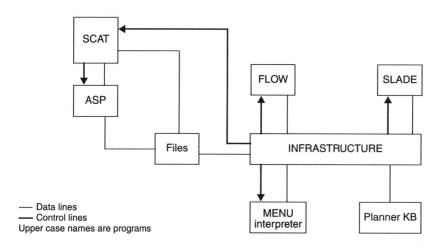

Fig. 8.2.   **Architecture for Integration Concept Evaluator (ICE) from the Developer's Viewpoint.** The ICE component integrators view the system as a way to use explicit infrastructure to put together the given component programs (SCAT, ASP, FLOW, and SLADE) and to provide users with a method for managing the transitions from user problems to coordinated use of the program.

In this case, the only modeling problem was the program-interaction model. It amounted to defining a collection of messages each program needed to generate and a corresponding collection they needed to understand and reply to. The infrastructure had a planner knowledge base that it used to determine which program would be interested in which message. All messages were sent directly from the programs to the infrastructure, which used the planner knowledge base to route them. For example, the tactical simulation SLADE needed to send a start message when it began, a message containing its idea of the current time every two simulated seconds, messages for each threat detection, and a message when it stopped. It needed to accept a message identifying the delay time for the threat information to be converted into a warning by the command center, so it could delay the warning event by an appropriate amount of time. Although we took several months to interview developers and to understand the intent of the effort in enough detail to design the overall architecture and capabilities for ICE, we took only a few weeks to write the initial software in an explicit, easily changeable form. Taking the time to design the framework for the modeling activity before developing software will usually result in this kind of cost and time savings.

8.4   Step 3: Evaluating and Analyzing a Model

In this step we begin to learn about the effects of our model choices. We compare alternative designs and design choices to determine if important aspects differ significantly. During this activity, we construct a mathematical space (or set of "satisficing" configurations) that will be suitable for the model's intent, focus, and performance requirements and that we compare by different evaluation criteria. We also

- Identify and explore configurations of design choices, so we know which designs can satisfy the constraints
- Study and evaluate the system requirements
- Examine the constraints to evaluate whether or not the requirements are design drivers and how they affect performance and cost. This evaluation determines whether they're workable and appropriate for the modeling problem

We want to identify constraints we need to keep, would like to keep (if we can afford it), and can't keep (because of inconsistencies or implications for performance or project management). We can also start optimizing the design according to our evaluation criteria.

We need to evaluate all choices about constructing models to make sure they're appropriate, typically using methods for verification and validation. To evaluate a model, declaring what it's expected to do is crucial. Verification means "does the model work correctly"—is it internally consistent and complete in the way it's expressed and structured? Validation means "does the model address the right problem"—is it appropriate given the goals, intentions, and conditions under which it will be used. Evaluation also includes testing, which involves setting up problems the model should answer and determining whether or not it does so correctly. It may also include verification proofs—mathematically formal proofs that a model structure satisfies its specification (this latter step is hard, but occasionally useful).

For ICE, we didn't expect to use analytical results because we were more interested in technical integration than in results from the application and because only program connections were validated—not the programs themselves. We evaluated ICE using our own methods [Landauer 1990; Bellman 1995; Landauer 1996a]. In DAW, the developers validated models before the project started. The results are being used to plan space events, and domain experts are extending the models.

Finally, if we make models to learn something, we ought to consider what and how we learn from a model. Analysis and elaboration are the two ways to learn. Analysis means proving some properties of models from their descriptions alone, if they're detailed or specific enough. Elaboration means we have to "watch" models operate (simulation) and statistically analyze the simulation's output. Although analytical results are more reliable and are therefore preferable to simulation, most interesting models are too complicated to understand without at least some elaboration. Usually, we learn that the models are incorrect because they've left out some interaction effect or overly approximated a known effect. Analysis or simulation can discover either of these possibilities, but simulation is often more immediate because it can animate the behavior and make it more apparent.

After modeling is complete, the developers should have interacting models that explain the application problem, describe the proposed solution, and include enough detail so the programs can be written to implement the models. In all this description, the key question is, "what is enough information to go on to the next step of refinement or development?" We take this up next as we discuss how to monitor the process, given your goals and evaluation criteria. Monitoring the development of a complex computing system isn't magical, whether it's a simulation or not. The single most important activity is paying attention to issues the developers have decided are important. In fact, the purpose of all development methods is to encourage careful attention to these issues. The model-based approach in Sec. 8.5 shows us how the eventual simulation will work and how development itself is proceeding.

To make these results (artifacts) meaningful, several decisions must occur early in design. The designers must choose the criteria and expectations for stages of the process and for the products of each stage. Machines must be able to process this information so we can assess it. These decisions may be overkill for small or medium projects, but they're essential for very large ones. You'll find some artifacts listed in Sec. 8.5.2. The ones particularly suited to change and reuse are the models and meta-knowledge, the architectures with their roles and responsibilities for other models, and the integration models that define how models interact.

If we learn anything from our models, we'll want to change them. Therefore, we must track lines of development and retain prior models (with their assumptions) so we can examine and compare them.

8.4.1   Assessing Progress

For small to medium simulations, one person may be able to keep the entire process together and drop the coordination artifacts we've described. However, for most medium and all large simulations—even for small ones because they never stay small—we recommend keeping track of your progress.

Early in modeling we must choose to monitor progress; here, we'll consider what we need to know and what we can know. That's because progress is very irregular in large simulations. The development steps overlap and occasionally interfere with one another (we can't choose an architecture until we know the components). Sloppiness isn't the reason for this irregularity (though it can make the problem worse); it occurs because modeling is hard, and people often have to live with a design problem for a while before some of the design decisions can even be identified, let alone solved.

We need to know what must be done, what is already done, and what is hard to do. At first, we can know only what is scheduled to be done, but as we refine our models and study their interactions, we gradually learn what is needed. Then, it becomes much easier to recognize what we don't need to revisit. Good modeling includes the ability to map the problem into what is needed, model what we need (enough models), and prevent needless effort (not too many models). Thus, we must learn to identify "hard" modeling problems as they occur. Confusing models warn us of hard problems; so do confusing descriptions of entities and relationships. We're also likely to have problems whenever we're troubled about model boundaries, what to model, or even whether to model some possibility.

For example, our ICE integration had a hard modeling problem: reducing interactions between SLADE and FLOW. They have different time models and very different control structures, and we didn't want to rearrange either program very much to fit the other. We settled on having SLADE announce its idea of the current simulation time, so FLOW could simulate the advance of its event schedule and update its own simulation clock. This decision did require a change in FLOW, so it could restart an ongoing simulation after it had run to a specified simulation time. That change was very small—about ten or fifteen lines of code out of several thousand—and easier because we had developed and written the program over more than ten years and knew its structure well.

If you can't know everything about a project's progress, how do you account for the uncertainties in assessment? We believe simply extending the idea of stub functions will make this much easier: the sooner a simulation runs end-to-end (at any level of detail), the sooner you can "see the whole picture" and let your intuition about a problem suggest improvements or corrections. Then, as the domain models become more refined, you can relate them to the less detailed models, perhaps even formally, and thereby refine the end-to-end model. In this context, you can validate models through simulation and observation and validate rules using models.

8.4.2   Verifying and Validating Models

Models play several roles in systems: supporting computations, helping us assess development, and sometimes applying only to a particular problem. Each kind of model requires a different kind of validation. We'll briefly describe them here, but you can find more detail in Chap. 11.

For computational and dynamic models, we must reason from theory to produce equations that define them. Validating the model is part of the scientific or engineering theory, and shortcut rules describe special cases. Domain experts must assess these rules and check special cases. And we must check models that apply a special-case rule to be sure they conform to the special case's conditions.

Each model in a combination of "mini-models" must be validated separately against theory or observations because we have no general model of the entire collection. We can use some general principles at the overlaps, but they can't replace common sense about the situation being modeled. In this case, "sanity checks" are important model constraints (for example, times and temperatures are always sensible values, the number of items of each kind is zero or higher, etc.) Usually, we check space and time models against a reference geographical or dynamic model, or against some observation of the actual space modeled (for example, direct observations often validate maps).

You may be able to validate device models and other simulations by comparing them to the device's real or expected behavior. If the device is being constructed, however, you may have no reference, so you must use the expected behavior. This brings up a tricky point: how do you specify the expected behavior? Of course it's a model, but then how do you distinguish the model of expected behavior from the device model you're trying to validate? Usually the difference is that the model of expected behavior is treating only the device's superficial characteristics—those visible to other models in the device's operating environment. The device models are usually trying to find or design a mechanism that produces this behavior; in this case, the distinction is clear. If the device model is being used in a larger simulation model, the external behavior may be all that matters; in this case, you don't need a detailed model.

For models based on empirical data, you have to validate the original data, and the methods used to infer structure for the data. You may document only the empirical model's source if it's common to an application domain, such as the extra coefficients for certain simple models of orbits. Any class of model can fit any kind of data if it has enough parameters; a good fit isn't a valid explanation of the phenomenon, though it is a valid observation of the phenomenon.

Heuristics offer another approach to validation. They are the qualitative principles or rules of thumb gleaned from strategies, simplifications, and experts' experience, all of which help narrow the search through a solution space. They are often coded as "rules" that control the performance of algorithms, numerical processes, or decision aids in the information sciences. They're very difficult to validate, although they can be verified to a certain extent using their internal consistency as a criterion. In a sense, they are automatically valid because they don't try to guarantee anything. The more important question is how much they help in modeling, which can only be answered by using a heuristic and watching its effects [Rechtin 1991]. Initially at least, there are no good criteria for what makes a good heuristic—its "goodness" depends on human intuition and common sense.

We want models to be mathematically rigorous because that makes the validation problem easier. Mathematical rigor doesn't mean formulas. It means all terms and relationships are well defined and consistently used, relationships are justified for use (if not for correctness), and the model is valid and applicable over a stated range of problems. Meta-models are as useful for validation as they are for modeling because they can abstractly model inferences. When there are no subject models, we use meta-models and rule-base correctness to provide criteria for assessing rules. [Bellman 1990a; Landauer 1990]. Another use of meta-models is to diagnose problems. Models can help us infer observable symptoms from potential system faults and explain the observed symptoms. Internal and external monitors can be organized in this way.

We don't always have the meta-models we need for validation. What makes an adequate model depends on the problem. Because we can't cover all important aspects of a system's behavior and meaning, we try instead for good partial models and descriptions of the important interactions. When there is no natural model, we have to rely on "generic models" (independent of domain), such as incidence matrices, graphs, and other "weak" models [Landauer 1996a]. We've developed validation techniques that apply esthetic criteria to detect anomalies mapping the entity we're trying to validate into some other formal spaces (these mappings produce generic models of the entity).

In general, every system description in any collection of descriptive languages has certain common features:

- Symbols, which capture scope
- Uses of symbols (use)
- Definitions of symbols (defn)
- Units of the system (compatible with scope units)

We can then build "rules" for each such unit, such as:

$$use\ use\ use\ \rightarrow\ defn\ defn\ defn$$

We're not assuming causality or dependence in these rules, which simply means that the uses occur with the definitions (that the definitions may depend on the uses). Now we can do all our usual analyses of the incidence matrix to learn something about the consistency, completeness, redundancy, connectivity, and distribution properties of the system units [Bellman 1995; Landauer 1996a].

For example, in an application to get the best machine design, uses could be design specifications or requirements, definitions could be designs, and relevant resources would then be the required materials and processes. This approach generalizes to other kinds of resources and producer-consumer descriptions: first, we model the resource producers and consumers; then, we use the descriptive model for analysis. In general, information processing in systems is sequential because some parts produce resources and others use them. That means the boxes and lines in models of the data-flow architecture need to have a time order. Although validating generic models depends strongly on the particular problem, even superficial models have been extremely useful in applications [Bellman 1995; Kiczales 1991].

8.5   Principles of Model-Based Design

Let's focus now on model-based design and how we build models that can evolve. Model-based design is based on the notion that almost all hard problems lie in developing the models, not the computer programs, and that trying to solve modeling problems in the code is unproductive and can be misleading. By the time you complete this section, you should know why evolvable models are important and how meta-knowledge, architectures, and design environments help produce them. [Shaw 1995a; Zimmer 1995] We advocate building simple models of behavior and interaction, so you can combine flexibly and more easily understand and validate their behavior [Allen 1994; Findler 1979]. Multiple models are necessary for any complex system, with each model simplifying some part of the system's behavior. This kind of modeling requires much more attention than usual to how models interact, as well as knowing what connects the models and allows them to interact.

Figure 8.3 shows multiple models for a complex phenomenon, with each regular model imaging part of the phenomenon in a formal space (drawn as regular figures). Note that none of the regular models captures all of the complex phenomenon, and they all overlap with each other. Figure 8.3 also incidentally highlights the importance of relating different formal models to each other because they all purport to model the same phenomenon. This mapping of information among formal models is a hard problem, which we're trying to address with our initiative on new mathematical foundations for computer science [Landauer 1995a].

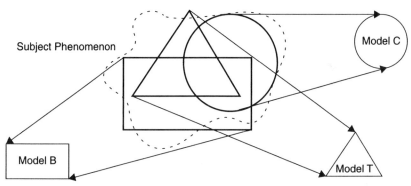

Fig. 8.3.   Complex Systems Require Multiple Models to Capture their Behavior. No single model can represent all aspects of a complex phenomenon or system. Different models emphasize different aspects of the subject domain; each model focuses on the information and attributes of the subject domain we can represent by whatever formal space we selected for that part of the modeling.

Complex problems may require complex models to study all important influences and effects, which usually means many interacting models of different entities and influences in the system. Thus, the simulation system itself requires us to develop complex software—often building models of the simulation program before developing detailed application models so we can guarantee the program will be consistent and complete. Even though people are most concerned about the models in the application domain, we also must model parts of any complex simulation system and their interconnections, so we can study the simulation program's architecture before it's built. In Sec. 8.2, we gave an example of a huge failure in simulation (the simulation testbed) that we attribute to poor models of the simulation program itself, and we have seen others.

The very popular notion that "object-oriented" design or modeling will solve all or even most design problems is a trap because it assumes a method can make up for deficiencies in modeling [Lajoie 1994; Harrison 1993]. It can't. Of course, object-oriented design is still important and useful, but it should apply mainly to models—not to code—because models are more likely to be reused. In addition, the modularity of object-oriented design may not always be the right choice, especially in simulations. Interaction effects are often important and are almost always difficult to model. Most complex simulations have global effects that pervade the system. An object-oriented approach can handle both considerations when applied properly. The issue, as always, is to choose representations that make it as easy and straightforward as possible to represent our modeling subjects.

8.5.1   Mapping Models and Rules

The sort of system flexibility we're looking for requires small pieces with clear mechanisms for integration. The variety of pieces and the different uses of these integration mechanisms provide variability and interesting behavior. For example, component-based architectures require connections (the architecture must be one of the components) [DeRemer 1976; Garlan 1995]. In this context, an architecture is a model of the system. It describes connections among the system's parts and, usually, what information or controls occur across the connections. We imagine this model is used in a hierarchical way with other models of other smaller parts of the system, and the architecture model specifies some constraints on interactions of the models that are to be combined. To distinguish these component models from their places in the architecture models, we call those places "roles" and treat a role as a kind of specification, containing constraints on the models that can "fill" the role.

We can take this separation of roles from the models that might fill them even further. Any model can contain one or more roles for other models. An important advantage of this separation is that we can use alternative models for the same role or allow the same model (such as a search strategy) to fill several roles. It also shifts the focus from the functions being modeled to the models, as well as to the processes that collect models and determine whether or not they are appropriate for particular roles in a larger model. It also makes models into units we can reason about.

For example, in the architecture pictures for the Integration Concept Evaluator (ICE) and the Debris Analysis Workstation (DAW), the boxes would normally represent actual system components, and the lines would represent information or control connections between them. But if we view them in terms of models and roles, we'll read them "top down"—as specifications of the roles that models must play and the interconnections that must occur among them if an architecture is to meet the specification imposed by the picture. Then, different models could fill each of those roles, and part of refining the picture is to make more precise the conditions and constraints we place on the models filling each role. One way this approach helped us while developing ICE was that the user interfaces (shown in the more elaborate architectural models of ICE that we developed during the project) became just another role—presenting various models results—that we could fulfill in various ways. This led to a system implementation that more easily combined user interfaces with special graphics programs on three different platforms: an Apple personal computer, a Sun workstation, and a Silicon Graphics machine.

8.5.2   Configuration Management

Through configuration management we organize the artifacts produced during a software project, maintain them and their relationships, and make them available through records or displays. Model-based design provides artifacts that show how the simulation will work and how development itself is proceeding. If we learn anything from our models, we'll want to change them, and configuration management is essential to coordinate change and reuse. It allows us to proceed simultaneously along several lines of development and to keep prior models with their assumptions, so we can compare them to newer ones.

The artifacts include all machine-readable products of the development phases. Of course, models, meta-knowledge, scenarios, and experimental designs are among these products. But so are structure diagrams, descriptions of algorithms and process or data relationships, architectures, and every other part of the system description. (For many of us in Department of Defense programs, briefing charts are often an unmonitored and subtle pressure that changes the definition and expectations for modeling projects—especially as the charts are rewritten for different audiences.) All software-development methods have their own set of artifacts, and usually all are adequate. Just be sure to make them all machine-readable and keep them all around.

Managing the configuration of complex software is difficult because these systems contain many artifacts: descriptions of program architecture (often vague), design notes, software modules, documentation, associated models, test plans, syntactic (assembly) and semantic (integration) definitions of interfaces, and history of use. As these artifacts change during development, you may have to manage many different versions. Having many artifacts and multiple lines of development makes this effort more complex than what software developers normally think of as configuration management—updating or replacing different versions of the same module within the same architecture. Software modules are certainly part of configuration management. But we prefer to think of the wider problem because systems development often founders on controlling these other artifacts, even when configuration management of software modules is well defined.

Artifacts for Model-Based Design

In addition to information about the process, artifacts include the software that monitors, alerts, and informs the user or manages these tasks. Make sure this software is machine-readable so you can get automatic help. For example, a monitor might include a database of design considerations, into which designers occasionally place notes about what they studied, with corresponding results or decisions. Other designers can see what was and was not considered as they work on their part of the design, and the monitor can tell them if they missed a consideration. The designers can then revisit or rescind a decision.

Another example is the notion of probes placed dynamically or in advance [Gorlick 1991]. A probe observes certain event classes or data structures in the models, gathers statistics about the models' execution, and either reports to the user what it sees or checks for compliance with particular constraints and announces failures. Many programming languages allow such probes, though almost all of them require probes to be defined before run-time or run as part of a "debugger." [See Gorlick (1991) for an exception to this rule—an approach that allows run-time insertion of probes.]

8.5.3   Software to Track Model Development

We advocate using many models of various sizes, but keeping track of them requires careful bookkeeping that a computer can manage most conveniently. Software can help us organize how we create, manage, analyze, and integrate models; import legacy models; do reverse engineering; verify and validate models; and handle many other tasks described in this section. We won't try to survey existing programs because they'd be obsolete in a few months. Instead, let's look at features we believe such systems must have by seeing how a system we built—VEHICLES—fits many of these features together. Although our work on VEHICLES is by no means "The Solution" for modeling environments, it does suggest what these environments will need to do the job right.

The VEHICLES System: Features for Model-Development Software

We put some of our notions about the types of flexibilities and integrative mechanisms needed to develop large software programs into VEHICLES, which is a system-engineering environment that supports conceptual modeling of space systems [Bellman 1990b; Bellman 1993]. This environment has many types of resources, including databases, analysis programs, user interfaces, knowledge bases, and models. We can vary many of these parts—much more than most design-support systems can. VEHICLES also handles multiplicity because its parts are written in several different programming languages.

Conceptually Designing Space Systems. Defining new space systems and analyzing new space missions require concept-exploration studies that use diverse models, including simulations, analytical equations, and other software programs. To model effectively in this context, we need a software environment that supports flexible use of widely varying models to help pose and answer (or at least study) questions. Thus, we have to incorporate many heterogeneous methods and software resources, including analysis tools, external programs, datasets, and models. In turn, variety and flexibility drive the need for rapid integration of models and other resources.

The VEHICLES system helps us design and analyze complex systems by providing many tools to analyze system models, including those for comparing different models, trading off performance variables, parametrically studying relationships among variables, and analyzing the sensitivity of equational models. Because of its many analysis tools and its support of flexibility and integration, VEHICLES has recently been used for rapidly prototyping modeling and analysis environments beyond conceptual design of spacecraft (its original application).

Examples are environmental testing satellites (shake, bake, rattle, and roll tests before launch), analyzing space-debris hazards (the DAW effort mentioned above), and evaluating architectural concepts for the Integrated Satellite Control System (for the ICE example mentioned above).

The abilities and types of information required of a system that supports conceptual design and planning are numerous, varied, and complex. Designers and planners of space systems work from many points of view and at different levels. Mission requirements, technological advances, and constraints on cost or other resources all influence design decisions. So design tools must be flexible enough to work at any level, without needing to be immediately aware of everything a design decision affects. By operating in this way, the VEHICLES system allows designers to address many different design problems, from defining mission requirements to scheduling effective environmental testing. Within the VEHICLES system are general analysis tools that do trade studies at any stage of the design and in any context. We can use these tools in various ways because of their flexibility.

With VEHICLES, we can start designing with broad mission goals and then work down by interpreting how mission requirements will affect subsystem requirements. We can also start with a given subsystem, work only on sizing it, and analyze its effect on other subsystems. We can even start with a given component and study how its design influences higher-level requirements and performance. As an example of the VEHICLES system's ability to support design diversity, some projects may begin by trying to determine how a new technology might affect the performance of a known space system and requirements on other subsystems. Other design projects may begin with defined requirements for the payload and mission, intending only to integrate multiple subsystems or compare several design concepts.

With possible design solutions in hand, we can compare designs and evaluate their relative merits. VEHICLES has moved strongly toward faster creation of "families" of workable designs, rather than single-point solutions. In addition, because designers often want to add their own analytical abilities and access their own databases, we've linked VEHICLES to other programs.

Analyzing Tasks. A major objective of the VEHICLES project is realistically analyzing the problems faced by designers and planners during the early phases of design. Several designers have spent a lot of time explaining how designs are created, what is involved, and what is important in a system that will support design. We've also worked on specific applications, so we might better understand these issues.

The first thing our users (analysts, designers, and planners) taught us is that conceptually designing space systems runs into two main problems: (1) a human, or group of humans, is exploring and creating something new; (2) the design involves a complex system with many components and considerations. Thus, study and design rely on many sources of information (such as text, simulations, databases, and human experts). This information will come from existing computer programs and new programs, from well-established and highly speculative models, and from deterministic and probabilistic models. In addition, various processing styles will be applied to this information. For example, information may come from detailed simulations of events, numerical analysis, databases (processed through queries), and knowledge bases (processed through rules).

Faced with these information sources and processing methods, designers worry about "credibility," which drives careful documentation, traceability, and the types of analyses that will help justify the results. The best analyses place point solutions in contexts and help us study how certain assumptions, models, or methods affect design. That's why we emphasize understanding tradeoffs among critical factors and generating families of designs.

Closely aligned with credibility is model integration. In fact, in many ways they're inseparable. All modeling methods project some of a system's important features into a formal space for study. Different formal spaces allow certain methods or operations. The more a system "fits" the formal space (meets its assumptions), the more the system under study can benefit from the associated operations. To say that each representation or method maps to a formal modeling space doesn't imply that all the different sources of information are equally rigorous; on the contrary, part of the difficulty in integrating these formal modeling spaces is that some of them contain incomplete information. Our ability to use different sources of information and methods depends on how well we can integrate these formal spaces, which determines how credible we find the results.

Developing Tools and Capabilities. Because of the above issues, designers say they need tools to support model development and integration, trade studies, and documentation and traceability. For integration, they want help in integrating and combining models and associated methods, as well as in analyzing the relationships among models to see how well they're integrated. This includes the need to

- Monitor the interactions and interdependencies in design, performance, and costing
- Evaluate, compare, and rank design solutions
- Gauge the impact of different assumptions

To do so, they must integrate models horizontally and vertically. That is, they want analyses to move beyond local models to integrated systems.

Designers also need help in studying trades and characterizing solutions for complex design problems. Thus, they need to represent and analyze what is most critical to a design (the "design drivers"), tradeoffs among these drivers, and families of possible solutions. They may also have to revisit and relax requirements.

Finally, designers need sophisticated bookkeeping to deal with the complexity of information and processing sources:

- Tracing the effect of design decisions throughout the design
- Clarifying motivations and problem-solving approaches
- Stating what information sources led to what decisions
- Tracking versions of the models

Other Important Features of Development Systems

Based on our experience, we'll list some of the software flexibilities we've found necessary to modeling. In the VEHICLES environment and in our other prototypes of modeling environments, we're gradually finding better ways to achieve flexibility and integration. Each flexibility in the software system is a way of using its diverse sources or types of processing. From VEHICLES, we've learned that each type of flexibility requires a corresponding "integrative mechanism" to help users manage diversity. This environment requires flexibility at many levels and in many forms. For example, one type of flexibility is to have components that allow us to vary a model's detail for different studies, so we can use less precise (and therefore less time-consuming) components whenever possible. To manage this flexibility, we can build a library of models at different resolutions and then use meta-knowledge to select the right one for a particular context or problem domain. Or we can use prototyping languages or automatic code generation [Balzer 1993] to change simulator configurations automatically (or nearly so) for a given problem.

To reconfigure components rapidly, we must have flexible interfaces. That means we have to manage component interactions and (for example) record summary data, so monitors can determine what the system was doing. Engineering databases, modular interconnection languages, and other higher-level specification languages can automatically generate required interfaces. [Lajoie 1994; Terry 1994]. Integration flexibility includes the ability to handle diverse types of information sources and processing abilities, as well as to extend to new sources and processing types. For flexibility in developing models, we must be able to form and compare alternative models and study architectural choices. Comparing models involves terms used in the model, constraints, context, numerical or simulation methods, and so forth.

We want the system to provide many kinds of flexibilities at these levels:

- Languages for descriptions and definitions (for resources, knowledge representations, data-transfer formats, etc.)
- Resources for each application (multiple tools, with selection criteria, and user screens that include menus and other user interface languages)
- Basic processing functions
- Functions that process and organize system resources—planning and problem solving, accessing and interpreting knowledge bases, and distributing messages [Bellman 1993]

Another important principle of flexibility is that models must be explicit and that we describe them in ways the environment can process. We've studied a form of this integration infrastructure for several years and have developed "wrappings," an approach to integrating complex systems that we've focused on in recent research [Landauer 1995b; Landauer 1996a]. Wrappings use machine-processable descriptions of all system resources to help select appropriate tools, models, or other resources, adapt them to the study context, and interpret their results. In our view, all system components are resources. These include external programs and data files, user interfaces, computational tools, databases, libraries of functions that support simulations, and complete simulation programs. They also include rule bases and inference engines (systems to manipulate symbolic formulas); scripts that refer to other resources (e.g., plans); and analysis tools that refer to other resources (e.g., parametric study).

8.6   Applying Model Design to Firewatcher

We've described some of the key considerations and processes for designing models, using our own examples. Now, let's take the Firewatcher example, which appears throughout this book, and show the modeling design steps as one continuous story. We need to address two critical issues for Firewatcher. The first broadens and deepens the task analysis you've read about in the earlier parts of this book.

Ranking Tasks

Previously, we've emphasized that a task analysis defines more than a model's content and functions, although those are usually emphasized. It also guides the types of associated programs, infrastructure, and choices for building the model. As you can see from Chapter 5, once a task analysis starts, the wishlist of needs for any system can become staggering. It is large because of the number of different users, viewpoints, possible uses, and levels in any system attempting to address real problems at a significant size. Therefore, our key concern at this stage is to rank and focus tasks—possibly beginning with intuition but always ending with justification. That is, we can't be satisfied if a customer intuitively buys off on a set of priorities. Instead, we must capture the reasons for the priorities and build a case for them with analyses, if necessary. We want to capture the rationale for the priorities in a machine-processable form, but whatever its form, it must exist by the time we finish model design.

Of course, in many projects, we don't know why a model focuses or works the way it does. That unfortunate truth is a terrible problem if anyone wants to use the model in the future. Not knowing why its designers selected the current functions first hampers its further development. Not having expectations clearly stated undermines its verification and validation. And both problems often make it impossible to maintain. Although stating reasons for building a model in a certain way can be hard, people are used to doing so. Often their justification harkens back to unspoken design choices. We must be able to answer WHY questions about all modeling choices. If we can't say why, we're not ready to specify a model further or to build it. We also need to know our expectations for the model. Because all modeling consists of representation and decisions, if we have no reasons, we have no justifiable model.

Let's go back to the scenario described in Chap. 5. That scenario seems to call for a highly classical simulation that reflects a fire's rate of movement, based on the type and combustibility of fuel and other variables, such as terrain, wind, and humidity. The highest level need that task analysis has uncovered is to provide users with an information aid that will help them understand the fire's position, its rate of spread, and its likely movement. The simulation must also show where fire-fighting resources are deployed to combat it and—at its most sophisticated level—give us a library of models that capture methods to combat fires of different types. If we look more deeply at what is implied here, we can imagine people who expect to use the system interactively, in real time, and at different levels of fidelity. They may also need it distributed to organizations doing different things at different places. This last need brings to the forefront a very different set of needs having to do with communicating and coordinating among deployed forces.

For this model, we must first find a starting point that will allow us to unravel the complex problem into individual models. We look for some "nugget" among the expressed needs that can give us this starting point. That way, we can do several things at once:

- Incrementally design and build the model

- Lower risk by allowing early assessment of whether we can do the project, manage it, and fit it to users' needs and tradeoffs of cost and performance

- Get some early capability to our users while we're completing the always too ambitious "whole project"

Let's talk more about the first task. Looking for a nugget doesn't mean we're developing a single piece and not paying attention to the system's architecture and framework. On the contrary, starting with a nugget allows us incrementally to recognize that a proposed framework will work. Because we consider this nugget critical, we carefully determine how it depends on other pieces. This architectural effort therefore becomes much more than an intellectual exercise. Instead, it's deep enough to develop a buildable project and to uncover flaws and gaps in our early concepts.

For Firewatcher, one such nugget is building a basic "fire model." That is, given the local geography, fuels, and weather, determine where—and how fast—the fire is moving. We can clearly justify picking this model first, based on the experts' description in Chaps. 5 and 6—this fire model will address the most crucial questions for the firefighters and is also essential to several other models. Hence, after building the fire model, we imagine developing models that expand our ability to model what affects the fire's growth, including special effects in that region (such as an oil spill). Other models will capture techniques for diminishing the fire. We also imagine eventually developing a class of models that reflect the differences in techniques among different organizations. These models could help organize the fire response and stop incompatible activities—for example, by showing how organizations communicate, pass off responsibilities, and work together.

Sketching the System

Let's say the customers have bought our rationale for ranking tasks and focusing the system. We now have a fire model and a rationale (that we'll continually add to) for selecting that focus. Next we need to concentrate on defining more deeply how the three additional classes of models and needs would relate to the nugget we've selected. That is, we're beginning to define the architecture for our modeling system. We now start detailing our technical nugget—our modeling focus. But note that we've also sketched out a possible embedding framework because the nugget design must fit the eventual system. In other words, the model design must account for all information and functions the model will handle for the rest of the system. We must at least put in the hooks (places to access the information interface). Because of our incremental development, we'll specify and build only a subset of the system's information and functions at any time. Still, the rationale and vision for the rest must be there to avoid locking the model away from changes to meet unforeseen uses.

This vision and its outcomes greatly affect the design of Firewatcher. For example, suppose we choose to distribute the fire model to several organizations, instead of building it for one organization that distributes results to others. Distributed simulation drives certain choices in our model design. We must determine what parts of the model are the same and can be shared, such as the terrain and weather models. But we also have to discover what parts are different and "owned" (updated and controlled) by local organizations, such as specialized fuel models.

As another example, suppose we make the fire model a basis for a library of fighting-technique models owned by different organizations. In this case, we must design it so very different models can receive data from it and provide data to it. This isn't just about software—choosing this or that language to build the model. Rather, it's a matter of designing the fire model so it expects and provides its information without limiting how we generate and use that information.

Applying Model Design to Firewatcher

Step 1: Preparing to Build Firewatcher

Preparing to model includes three highly interrelated decisions: establishing intent, choosing a focus, and deciding what abstractions or representations to use. By intent, we mean what the organization or the developers are trying to accomplish by modeling. Focus means our decisions on what to model given our intentions—what parts of the real world are we choosing to represent and reason about. Choosing abstractions involves selecting representations and formal spaces for the models. By formal spaces, we mean the types of mathematical notations or other modeling representations, plus associated methods and analyses.

These choices are much like those for our nugget, but they're more detailed. They help us determine what we want from the model, our rationale and expectations for it, and what the fire model really means. Also, during this step we translate concepts into models, which takes us from our goals for models of real-world phenomena to what they'll do for us (relating to the real world, we hope). This translation also gives us something to write down and check within a formal model, using formal relationships. For example: an increase in wind velocity increases fire movement, except in special terrain that causes eddies. In other words, we write down important properties and map our measurements into a formal space. We also set up constraints and criteria for our choices in the formal space: the names of the variables, the properties we want to capture, and the behaviors we want to define. This step will allow us to chose what formal space we want for this problem—in what formal mathematical space our variables will have the right attributes and operations. Building the model then becomes building an object in that formal space. For example, the fire model would probably use differential equations because they're one of the most effective ways of quantifying dynamic behavior. Cellular automata could also work because it would discretely model very local behavior.

Step 2: Building Firewatcher

Constructing the models involves four key decisions: building context models, dividing the system into component models, selecting or adapting legacy models, and choosing and maintaining an integration framework. Context for a given model may include background information, requirements, scenarios of use, models of the user, general domain knowledge, and global system attributes, such as cost, reliability, and risk. By dividing into components, we mean what structures in the formal space represent what phenomena. Also, when appropriate, we'll decide how many sub-models to build. Typically, we must select and adapt legacy models because few major projects can get along without them. Finally, the integration framework will embody the project's overall organization.

Building Firewatcher—as for all models—is iterative. For example, choosing a formal space in which to map our model selects a particular element of that formal space. Once we've chosen differential equations to create the fire model, we can collect terrain models, plug them into our equations wherever appropriate, and use them with other sub-models. The result would be very precise information on a fire's behavior in particular locations. Dividing a model into components depends on how we expect to use these models. Firewatcher has models for terrain, wind, rain, fuel, and countermeasures. We expect to use them either separately or together, depending on how much abstraction we need. Decomposing a model into sub-models often gives us some flexibility in putting those pieces together and in substituting new pieces. But building those pieces so others can use them and integrating them takes time and effort. We'd trade off these choices based on the schedule and resources allocated to our project. We believe this "extra effort" becomes more worthwhile as simulations grow larger.

After building the fire model, we must integrate it into a wider context. We describe how to use the model in machine-processable form and start connecting it to other models. This process includes making larger architectural models that describe the role of the fire model and producing constraints and requirements for the other models with which it will interact. For Firewatcher, we'll need models for the organization, political information, satellite and sensors, passing information, and applying countermeasures.

Step 3: Evaluating Firewatcher

This step will include the analyses that show how well the model is accomplishing our goals and criteria. It also will include the feedback for refining our models. Here we try to validate our model choices—with actual data whenever possible, but with experts and other knowledgeable sources whenever there is little or no data. The models' shortcomings and failures then feed back to adjust and refine our selection criteria. In the fire model, we could imagine having some empirical data about fire propagation and comparing it with the results of our proposed differential equation model. We also consider how—and how easily—the model can be used. Doing so can involve formal testing or simpler (and less reliable) informal analyses, such as design reviews or walk-throughs. While analyzing and evaluating the model, we'll also try to employ it in some initial demonstrations and uses. For example, firefighters at one organization's headquarters could start using Firewatcher off-line, before we extend it to other organizations and to the field.

8.7   Summary

In the first part of this chapter, we described several stages and decisions in building any model. Step one, preparing, includes establishing intent, choosing a focus, and deciding what abstractions or representations to use. The second step, building the model, contains four key actions: building context models, dividing a system into component models, selecting or adapting legacy models, and choosing and maintaining an integration framework. The final step, evaluating, involves more than traditional verifying and validating. It includes how we can better monitor, access, and record progress on model development. In the second part of the chapter on model-based design, we examined how using design environments, architectures, and meta-knowledge can help us build models that are more easily adapted and evolved. Throughout the chapter, we have detailed a process for developing and integrating models, based on our research in integration technologies. We emphasize the importance of modeling before programming (whenever possible), as well as how models and other meta-knowledge allow much more effective reuse than simply reusing code. We expanded on these themes by showing examples from two major modeling projects (ICE and DAW), as well as the shared example of Firewatcher.

Throughout the chapter, we've repeatedly emphasized vast changes in using models, types of representations and formal spaces, and ways of building models. This diversity is a two-edged sword: you have a better chance to carry out your intentions for a modeling project by using the many methods for modeling and building models, but the previous wisdom of the field may no longer apply. Thus, increasingly, you must build explicit arguments and documentation for your modeling choices. Although we've strongly recommended certain tools and procedures for building these arguments, a little thoughtfulness and discipline will go a long way toward improving modeling practices. Also, make sure you have the expertise you need for advice on new uses or modeling paradigms. In the future, few groups will have all the expertise needed for large projects.

References

Allen, Robert and David Garlan. 1994. *Formal Connectors.* Carnegie-Melon University, School of Computer Science, Technical Report CMU-CS-94–115.

Balzer, Robert and K. Narayanaswamy. 1993. "Mechanisms for Generic Process Support." *Proceedings of the First ACM Symposium on the Foundations of Software Engineering.* pp. 21–23.

Bellman, Kirstie L. 1990a. "The Modeling Issues Inherent in Testing and Evaluating Knowledge-based Systems." *Expert Systems With Applications Journal.* Vol. 1, pp. 199–215.

Bellman, Kirstie L. and April Gillam. 1990b. "Achieving Openness and Flexibility in VEHICLES." pp. 255–260, *Proceedings of the SCS Eastern MultiConference,* 23–26 Apr. 1990, Nashville, TN: Simulation Series, Vol. 22, No. 3, SCS.

Bellman, Kirstie L. 1991. "An Approach to Integrating and Creating Flexible Software Environments Supporting the Design of Complex Systems." pp. 1101–1105, *Proceedings of WSC '91: The 1991 Winter Simulation Conference,* 8–11 Dec. 1991, Phoenix, AZ. Revised version: Kirstie L. Bellman, Christopher Landauer. 1993. "Flexible Software Environments Supporting the Design of Complex Systems." *Proceedings of the Artificial Intelligence in Logistics Meeting,* 8–10 Mar. 1993, Williamsburg, VA: American Defense Preparedness Association.

Bellman, Kirstie L., April Gillam, and Christopher Landauer. 1993. "Challenges for Conceptual Design Environments: The VEHICLES Experience." *Revue Internationale de CFAO et d'Infographie,* Hermes, Paris.

Bellman, Kirstie L. and Christopher Landauer. 1995. "Designing Testable, Heterogeneous Software Environments." pp. 199–217 in Robert Plant (ed.). Special Issue: Software Quality in Knowledge-Based Systems, *Journal of Systems and Software,* Vol. 29, No. 3.

Davis, Paul K. and Richard Hillestad. 1993. "An Introduction to Variable Resolution Modeling and Model Families." *Society for Computer Simulation, Winter Simulation Conference,* San Diego, CA.

DeRemer, Frank and Hans H. Kron. 1976. "Programming-in-the-Large Versus Programming-in-the-Small." *IEEE Transactions on Software Engineering.* Vol. SE-2, No. 2, pp. 80–86.

Findler, Nicholas V. (ed.). 1979. *Associative Networks: Representation and Use of Knowledge by Computers.* Academic Press.

Gamma, Erich, Richard Helm, Ralph Johnson, John Vlissides. 1995. *Design Patterns.* Addison-Wesley.

Garlan, David, Dewayne E. Perry (eds.). 1995. "Special Issue on Software Architecture." *IEEE Transactions on Software Engineering*. Vol. SE-21, No. 4 (Apr. 1995).

Gillam, April. 1992. "A Knowledge-Based, Extensible Architecture for Space System Design." AIAA Paper 92-1115, *AIAA 1992 Aerospace Design Conference*, AIAA.

Goguen, J.A. 1986. "Reusing and Interconnecting Software Components." *Computer*, 19(2), pp. 16–28.

Gorlick, Michael M. and Rami R. Razouk. 1991. "Using Weaves for Software Construction and Analysis." *Proceedings of the 13th International Conference on Software Engineering*. pp. 23–34. IEEE Computer Society Press.

Harrison, William and Harold Ossher. 1993. "Subject-Oriented Programming (A Critique of Pure Objects)." pp. 411–428 in Andreas Paepke (ed.), *OOPSLA 1993: Proceedings of the Eighth Conference on Object-Oriented Programming, Systems, Languages and Applications*, 28–30 Sep. 1993, Washington, D.C.

Hillestad, Richard J. and Louis Moore. 1996. *The Theatre-Level Campaign Model: A New Research Prototype for a New Generation of Combat Analysis Models*. RAND Institute Report MR-388-AF/A.

Hoare, C. A. R. 1985. *Communicating Sequential Processes*. Prentice-Hall.

Kiczales, Gregor, Jim des Rivieres, Daniel G. Bobrow, 1991. *The Art of the Meta-Object Protocol*. MIT Press.

Lajoie, Richard, Rudolf K. Keller. 1994. "Design and Reuse in Object-Oriented Frameworks: Patterns, Contract, and Motifs in Concert." *Proceedings ACFAS: Colloquium on Object Orientation in Databases and Software Engineering*, Montreal.

Landauer, Christopher. 1990. "Correctness Principles for Rule-Based Expert Systems." *Expert Systems With Applications Journal*. Vol. 1, pp. 291–316.

Landauer, Christopher, and Kirstie L. Bellman. 1993a. "Integrated Simulation Environments." (invited paper), *Proceedings of DARPA Variable-Resolution Modeling Conference*, Herndon, VA: Conference Proceedings CF-103-DARPA, published by RAND; shortened version in Christopher Landauer and Kirstie Bellman. "Integrated Simulation Environments." *Proceedings of the Artificial Intelligence in Logistics Meeting*, 8–10 Mar. 1993, Williamsburg, VA: American Defense Preparedness Association.

Landauer, Christopher and Kirstie L. Bellman. 1993b. "The Role of Self-Referential Logics in a Software Architecture Using Wrappings." *Proceedings of ISS '93: The 3rd Irvine Software Symposium*, U. C. Irvine, CA.

Landauer, Christopher, Kirstie L. Bellman, and April Gillam. 1993c. "Software Infrastructure for System Engineering Support." *Proceedings AAAI '93 Workshop on Artificial Intelligence for Software Engineering*, Washington, D.C.

Landauer, Christopher and Kirstie L. Bellman. 1995a. *New Mathematical Foundations for Computer Science*. Initiative announcement available via anonymous ftp from "aerospace.aero.org," in directory "/pub/newmath," in file "workbook.html," and from www at URL "http: //www.cs.umd.edu /~cal/ newmath.html," original (Jul. 1994), rev. 1.4 (Feb. 1995) (availability last checked 23 Jun. 1996).

Landauer, Christopher and Kirstie L. Bellman. 1995b. "The Organization and Active Processing of Meta-Knowledge for Large-Scale Dynamic Integration." p. 149–160, *Proceedings 10th IEEE International Symposium on Intelligent Control*, Workshop on Architectures for Semiotic Modeling and Situation Analysis in Large Complex Systems, Monterey, CA.

Landauer, Christopher and Kirstie L. Bellman. 1995c. "Active Integration Frameworks." p. 199–206 in *Proceedings IEEE International Conference on Engineering of Complex Computing Systems*. Ft. Lauderdale, FL.

Landauer, Christopher and Kirstie L. Bellman. 1996a. "Knowledge-Based Integration Infrastructure for Complex Systems." *International Journal of Intelligent Control and Systems*, Vol. 1, No. 1, pp. 133–153.

Landauer, Christopher and Kirstie L. Bellman. 1996b. "Integration Systems and Interaction Spaces." pp. 161–178 *Proceedings of FroCoS '96: The First International Workshop on Frontiers of Combining Systems*, Munich, Germany.

Landauer, Christopher and Kirstie L. Bellman. 1996c. "Constructed Complex Systems: Issues, Architectures and Wrappings." pp. 233–238 *Proceedings EMCSR 96: Thirteenth European Meeting on Cybernetics and Systems Research*, Symposium on Complex Systems Analysis and Design, Vienna, Austria.

Maes, Pattie and D. Nardi (eds.). 1988. "Meta-Level Architectures and Reflection." *Proceedings of the Workshop on Meta-Level Architectures and Reflection*, Alghero, Italy, North-Holland.

Martin, Robert. 1995. "Discovering Patterns in Existing Applications." Chap. 19, pp. 365–393 in James O. Coplien and Douglas C. Schmidt (eds), *Pattern Languages of Program Design*, Addison-Wesley.

Rechtin, Eberhardt. 1991. *Systems Architecting: Creating and Building Complex System*. Prentice-Hall.

Shaw, Mary and David Garlan. 1995a. *Software Architecture - Perspectives on an Emerging Discipline*. Prentice Hall.

Shaw, Mary, Robert DeLine, Daniel V. Klein, Theodore L. Ross, David M. Young, and Gregory Zelesik. 1995b. "Abstractions for Software Architecture and Tools to Support Them." pp. 314–335 in David Garlan and DeWayne E. Perry (eds.), Special Issue on Software Architecture, *IEEE Transactions on Software Engineering*, Vol. SE-21, No. 4.

Soukup, Jiri. 1995. "Implementing Patterns." Chap. 20, p. 395–412 in James O. Coplien and Douglas C. Schmidt (eds), *Pattern Languages of Program Design*, Addison-Wesley.

Terry, A. et al. 1994. "Overview of Teknowledge's Domain Specific Software Architecture Program." ACM SIGSOFT Software Engineering Notes. James O. Coplien and Douglas C. Schmidt (eds), *Pattern Languages of Program Design*, Addison-Wesley.

Tracz, W. and L. Coglianese. 1992. *DSSA Engineering Process Guidelines*. Technical Report ADAGE- IBM-92-02A, IBM Federal Systems Co.

Walter, Donald O. and Kirstie L. Bellman. 1990. "Some Issues in Model Integration." pp. 249–254 *Proceedings of the SCS Eastern MultiConference*, Nashville, TN: Simulation

Series, Vol. 22, No. 3, SCS.

Wile, David S. 1983. "Program Developments: Formal Explanations of Implementations." *Communications of the ACM*, 26 (11).

Zimmer, Walter. 1995. "Relationships Between Design Patterns." Chap. 18, pp. 345–364 in James O. Coplien and Douglas C. Schmidt (eds), *Pattern Languages of Program Design*, Addison-Wesley.

CHAPTER 9

Producing and Managing Data

Bart Bennett and Richard Hillestad, *RAND Corporation*
Gordon Long, *Computer Sciences Corporation*

Simulations critically depend on data. Experience and technology have solved many data problems, but producing and managing data is still a formidable effort. Models often fail not because the model's structure or methods are flawed but because data is limited—or, more precisely, because of a poor or limited model design with regard to data. In many instances, the distinction between the data and the model (meaning the algorithms, processes, or functions) is unclear. You must carefully plan how to produce and manage data from the start of a study or a simulation development, particularly if the model is to serve many purposes. As an example, consider this imaginary but not uncommon scenario.

The fire-management study was to last six months. Its goals and objectives were to review how well the local fire department fought fires and recommend the type and quality of equipment they should maintain or buy under a constrained budget. Although ambitious, it was thought doable because of the study team's combined talents and the availability of critical resources, including most of the general-purpose models needed to do the quantitative assessments. Study leaders laid out the problem statement, high-level objectives, research plan, and tasks. The team divided into groups to look at scenarios, prevention, monitoring and detection, deployment and manpower, command and control, attack, engineering and technology, and cost. They decided to emphasize staffing and systems that could save lives, property, and the environment.

One month into the study, the scenario team had derived a matrix of various fire threats, which included forest type, terrain type, accessibility, weather conditions, available firefighting resources, available firefighting consumables, and nearness to populated areas. One member of the team felt these groupings were too broad. For example, prevention and firefighting depend strongly on specific weather conditions, such as humidity, wind speed and direction, and historical rainfall. The scenario team hashed out whether scenarios should be "generic," matched to historical cases, or based only on the last great fire or two that had been fought. Recognizing that tens, perhaps even hundreds, of scenarios were possible, they decided to focus on the last two great fires and to include other fires as lesser cases. Doing so would at least try to reduce data gathering.

After two months, the modelers on each of the teams had run some test cases to get up to speed. Some models needed very important enhancements. Also, the study required other models to complement ones the team was familiar with. The modelers ran a survey, requested the most promising models, adapted old model databases from previous studies, and filled in or adjusted numbers to their best judgment as they awaited results from the other groups, particularly the scenario group. They expected to get a tailored list of data they could easily manage and manipulate to form critical parts of the model data. Instead, they received a high-level descriptive document of the possible scenarios and conditions. An appendix provided some of the necessary data from the last two great fires but had too little detail. In particular, they recognized the tremendous gap between the scenario descriptions and the technical data needed to drive some of the model algorithms— movement rates, decision times, containment rate by fire intensity and firefighting resources employed, effect on fighting fires with aircraft only, and the value of command and control systems. The modelers turned to the other teams for these answers.

The mid-term review to the client was long on potential and short on results. The teams scrambled to find reliable data, not just to feed the models, but to understand the problem better. For example, the command and control team had found an almost bottomless pit of thorny issues and procedures while trying to connect the diverse systems brought in from several counties or states by fire units that would deploy to fight a great fire. Of particular difficulty was getting effectiveness numbers for two similar systems that would fight future fires. The engineering and technical team felt the numbers contractors quoted were too optimistic. In interviews with operators of current systems, the team collected far more pessimistic "expert opinions" on these future systems. They decided to run the models based on the range of values they received to see how sensitive the results would be. The results were sensitive—very sensitive—to the effectiveness values. So, they decided to wait for the government's official validation of these values.

At month four, the new models needed for the study arrived. Most came without databases or only test cases. Requests went back for full databases, but some were denied for proprietary reasons. The client was brought in to help resolve this problem and to speed getting the effectiveness data through the government review. Letters and memos were written, but no data arrived. Meantime, one set of model runs had many anomalies. The team determined that a scaling factor used to represent the density of forest undergrowth was too high. No one could determine who had set this value or when it was set. Perhaps it had been set years ago to test the original algorithm. Or had the anomalies occurred because the modeling team had changed some of the metrics in the model? They set the number to a more reasonable value and then wondered what to do about the several hundred runs they had already made. They also wondered about the effect of this scale factor on previous studies.

Month five began with the realization that time would no longer permit carrying out the experimental design created for the study. Critical data was still missing. The team decided to rely on *data from other models in the community, but they quickly found they couldn't use it. For example, deployment rates used in one community model included inappropriate assumptions they couldn't remove for the new algorithms. Also, enhancements to the model had drastically changed the input and output files for some of the models. As a result, the pre- and post-processors (including user interfaces, data management, and graphics tools) were no longer working properly. Runs had accumulated to create a sizeable backlog. Output data files filled most of the disk space with few tools to help examine them and only a simple, sometimes inconsistent, file-naming convention for configuration management. No one had tried systematically to capture how the data had changed over time. Team members quickly analyzed recent runs to build a case for their recommendations.*

As the last slides were being printed for the final client briefing, the validated effectiveness data arrived. The study team scanned it for consistency with, or explainable differences from, the numbers they had assumed. The approved data set contained 2,000 values conditioned on multiple dimensions for weather conditions, crew training, fire type, and ways of using the system. The team was concerned about how to reduce this data to a more manageable size for comparison, but on closer examination found that all the values were exactly the same—0.85.

This scenario is contrived, but it closely resembles our experience with problems in producing and accessing data for new or enhanced simulations. To help solve these problems, we recommend considering the main issues listed at the start of the chapter and discussed below. Notice that even this simple list contains many interactions. For example, balancing databases and model structures may depend on available and accessible data. Notice also that we're emphasizing much more than building data-processing tools that are more comprehensive and easier to use. You must also work hard to deal with the physical and contextual interactions between the data and the model. Handling, organizing, manipulating, configuring, and understanding large amounts of diverse information are very challenging tasks.[*] You must carefully choose the form of architecture—or management structure (both hardware and software)—within which you'll store, manipulate, access, and archive the data. In our experience, data issues have included doing basic research to develop scenarios and types of data that match analysis needs, as well as generating model inputs from more detailed models—creating a linked family of models. In this chapter, we address these data issues and suggest ways to manage them.

Because we'll focus on large-scale simulations with megabytes or more of data, our comments may seem overstated for much smaller ones. But you may run into the same problems in smaller simulations, and the topics we discuss relate to both. Smaller models will make some of the issues easier to deal with, although exactly how much easier and for which issues depends strongly on what your modeling effort involves. We can't presuppose the relative importance of topics or recommendations without understanding your project's requirements, so we'll cover many topics and ask you to decide what applies.

---

[*] In this chapter, we sometimes interchange "data" and "information." To be precise, data deals with values used in a calculation or resulting from a measurement or calculation. Information represents knowledge, thus adding interpretation to the data. Later in this chapter, we use these words more precisely.

9.1   Data Processes

Data is essential to modeling in three areas, as shown in Fig. 9.1. First, it's significant for defining and developing the simulation. Second, the model needs data to work: input data for calculations and output data to show results. Third, data from the "real world" must verify and validate the model. Often model designers are so focused on developing models that they don't carefully integrate data needs into modeling activities.

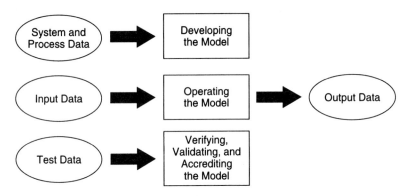

Fig. 9.1.   **How Data Affects Modeling.** Data has a significant role in development, execution, and verification and validation.

9.1.1   Considering Data while Developing the Model

As discussed in Chaps. 7 and 8, we start creating a model by establishing its purpose. What do users of the model need to do? What should we represent in the model? What should we not represent? What will the model calculate? How much detail must it have and in what areas? At first, modelers and potential users may want to capture many systems, interactions, and settings in great depth. Without considering data, designers may only slightly constrain the model, but data issues may limit model development by showing what's possible.

Figure 9.2 depicts the data processes associated with model development: (1) defining the context of the simulation in scenarios, (2) collecting data on individual systems, (3) exploring the interactions between systems, (4) focusing on the decision processes within and among systems, and (5) deciding on how to deal with external influences. (Although these steps are numbered sequentially, each one may be revisited based on results generated later in the process. For example, developing system interactions may alter certain system descriptions, or the defined decision process may affect the scenario definition.) While developing the model, you must decide what algorithms will represent and what data will represent within each algorithm. Although we focus on data here, you must consider simultaneously the implications of these five processes on the model.

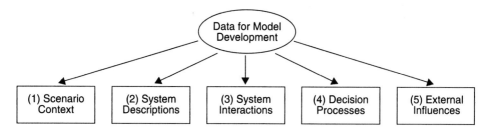

Fig. 9.2. **Data Interactions in Model Development.** In model development we must have data to define the overall context of what it will represent, the individual systems within the simulation, the interactions among systems, decision processes, and how to deal with external influences.

Starting with the scenario context, we look from the top down at what data is needed to describe the setting in which we do calculations. We may ask questions about who and what is involved—as well as where, when, and why—to define this data. Environmental information, such as terrain and weather, is also part of the scenario context.

In the second step we list the "things" or systems we intend to represent within the overall context and define their characteristics and functions by asking

- What characteristics of the system do we wish to represent?
- What do we know about each system?
- What can we measure?
- What system characteristics will simple data values represent?
- What system characteristics can or must algorithms represent?
  - What mathematical functions or relationships represent these characteristics?
  - What data values do we need to define these mathematical relationships?
- What is the system sensitive to?

This last question leads us to the third step: exploring the interactions between systems. We can ask similar questions about these interactions, which should include those between one system and another, as well as the synergistic effects of multiple systems working together. Step four focuses on the decision processes within and among the systems. We highlight these processes in the design phase, because the associated data requirements tend to be ultimately the most difficult to resolve. Here, we ask:

- How are decisions made?
- What information do these decisions require?
- Will some decisions be based on partial or inaccurate information?

- Will decisions be constrained by time or biased by skill level, workload, or emotions such as fear?
- Must the data reflect specific decision rules?

These first four steps may result in a large, perhaps overwhelming, amount of data, which requires complex, often automated methods to obtain, create or manage. Remember, we've purposefully taken these steps early in development so producing and managing data can truly affect the model design. This leads us to step five, in which we decide how to deal with things outside the model's scope. For example, a designer may well feel that a complex representation of weather in the model would require too much data collection or other efforts. But can we ignore weather in a model that assesses firefighting ability? Probably not. Therefore, we must compromise—allowing weather to affect the model but not requiring the costly data gathering and other tasks needed to represent how it works. In this case, we simplify how weather is modeled (capturing some of its effects) rather than creating a detailed model (representing processes or functions). Because the first four steps often levy heavy requirements, we may decide to include simple models of some of the elements we had hoped to capture completely. Whenever you decide to simplify, you must document this decision.

These five steps can take place in any order and will likely require several iterations. In any case, though, using them will ensure you consider data production and management in the initial steps of design. As you better understand data requirements, you'll more clearly see how to design the model and to choose ways of supporting data management.

9.1.2   Considering Data while Running the Model

As discussed in Chap. 12, data requirements don't just end with creating the model. To understand how data affects the way a model runs, we must think through how customers will actually use the model. As a simple metaphor, we can think of model users as skilled artisans, the model as their tool, and the data as the materials they will shape and transform.

To see this relationship better, refer to Fig. 9.3, which depicts the model user's perspective in relation to the path data takes into and out of the model. Simulation users typically want to do three things. First, they need to manipulate source data into a form and context consistent with the way the model works. Second, they want a way to control and manage how the model runs. They usually want to run many cases for a single study, as well as to use the model for various studies. Finally, because model outputs are often not in a form users want, they need a way to transform this data into the final products required for analysis. The bottom of Fig. 9.3 shows the data path, with a dashed line indicating that one model's output often becomes another's source data. Between the users' needs and this data path is a wide gulf that is usually bridged only by long, tedious efforts to bully the data down the path. As a model designer, you should help users by automating ways to manage and manipulate the data. Furthermore, it's prudent to question the appropriateness of the data supplied to the model. Does the data match the context in which it will be used?

You can answer this question by investigating data quality—verifying and validating what the data represents in the real world and how it is used in the model. The formal process to establish data quality (known as verification, validation, and certification or VV&C) divides naturally into three steps, which we'll describe briefly here. You can get more information on data VV&C by visiting the Defense Modeling and Simulation Office's website, http://www.dmso.mil, or consulting the Department of Defense's Modeling and Simulation Master Plan [DOD 1995], the Defense Modeling and Simulation Office's document on Data Verification, Validation, and Certification [DMSO 1997], or Rothenberg, et. al (1997a, b).

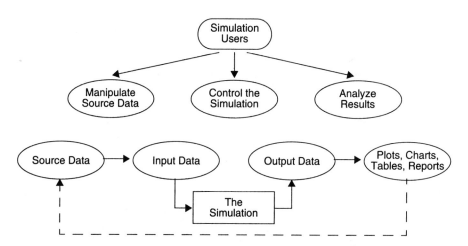

Fig. 9.3. **Data Interactions while a Model Runs [Bennett 1989].** Simulation users want to manipulate source data into a form and context consistent with the model, control how the model runs, and transform the data into the final products required for analysis. Users need automated support for this tedious, time-consuming, and often error-prone handling of data in its raw form.

Source data for the model may come from various places, in different formats, and with different contextual interpretations. It may be critical to correlate data from independent data sources, such as the transportation, map, and infrastructure databases in the firefighting example, in order to achieve consistency. Furthermore, users must often manipulate source data into a different format or combine it with other data to make it suitable for a particular model. As a wise model designer, you'll recognize that a successful model allows users to manage, process, and understand the source data. Include ways to identify sources; store formats, metrics, distribution restrictions, and meanings of the data; correct erroneous data; and fill in missing data. Much of this can be achieved using industry-standard methods to establish data quality and to define, manipulate, and interpret "metadata"—the information that describes the data itself and helps manipulate the original model data or outputs using a variety of automated techniques. See AT&T Quality Steering Committee (1992a, b, c), Blazek (1993), Galway and Hanks (1996), Loudon (1986), Redman (1992), or Wang, et. al. (1992a, b) for more information on data quality and how it relates to the verification, validation, and accreditation of models.

The second step is to control how the simulation runs. Within a single run of the simulation, various data is often necessary to set the internal controls, such as the simulation duration, input files to be read, algorithm options, and types of output. Typically, users want to run the simulation as a computing experiment, which means they must set up various cases to examine options, test hypotheses, or establish statistical significance. Setting up data for these cases can be laborious and susceptible to error. Here again, you should consider ways, perhaps external to the model, to help users create, run, and archive these cases.

Model output, in its initial form, is seldom ready for decision makers or even analysts. The output data always needs processing—often a lot of processing—to get it into the desired plots, charts, tables, or reports. At the design stage, allow for producing output data that summarizes calculations and adds information to verify these calculations. Create some kind of post-processing mechanism to transform model outputs to consumable products. Spreadsheets and other commercial off-the-shelf software provide generic tools for manipulating statistics and tabulating and graphing data; consider providing data interfaces from the model to these general-purpose tools. Finally, note that there is a natural feedback loop from one model to the next. If you want your model to operate with others, design conceptual and physical data links between models. Later in this chapter, we'll suggest various ways to improve data management and processing.

9.1.3   Considering Data while Verifying and Validating the Model

As described in Chap. 11, a model's accuracy, range of application and credibility depends on verification and validation. We're now talking about establishing the credibility of the model itself, not of the data for the model. What role does data play in this process? Recall that verification seeks to determine if we've correctly built the conceptual model. Validation tries to ascertain if the conceptual model adequately represents the real world based on the model's purpose. Figure 9.4 shows one way to verify and validate a model by testing how we represent and create it in three distinct ways: each object within itself (intra-object testing), the interactions of objects among themselves (inter-object testing), and the full operation of the model (end-to-end testing).

Intra-object testing examines the characteristics of each object in detail. Most of the data for this type of testing arises from closely examining the object itself. Collecting data for object characteristics can include the system's physical attributes; number, type, and composition of the object's parts; where the object is and how it behaves; how the object interacts with the world around it; how the object processes information; the range of actions the object might take; and how the object determines what action to take. Often, simulations include future systems or wish to examine notional changes to some object characteristics. Also, to operate precisely,

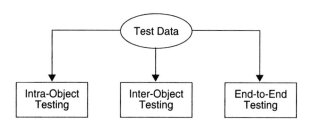

Fig. 9.4.   Data Interactions while Verifying and Validating the Model. Data is especially important in verifying and validating the model. In particular, data allows us to test the intra-object, inter-object, and end-to-end functions of the model.

many systems rely on a complex physical theory (that may not be well understood) or on specifying initial conditions with detailed data that is difficult to capture. Determining correct values for these systems or characteristics is more of an art than a science, but it cannot be arbitrary and often relies on the VV&C process for the data. Intra-object testing ensures that each object is properly set up (initialized) at the beginning of the simulation and accurately represented throughout.

Inter-object testing investigates how objects relate. Although some data on object relationships can be observed in historical events, training exercises, or testing, we usually have to calculate or specify it for the full range of possible interactions. This testing must also consider how objects interact with the environment around them. Collecting data on the interactions between objects can include how objects affect each other and the environment (creating, altering, or destroying object characteristics) and organizational relationships (command and control). Communication data is also important: what messages tag along as the object moves through the environment and zones of influence—areas around the object in which its interactions occur. Inter-object testing adds to verification and validation by showing how the overall simulation will work, but it requires comparing data from the real world with data from the model describing how objects relate. Collecting data for inter-object relationships among many, disparate objects may be very difficult. Their interactions may mask what each object contributes and how to generalize beyond a single observation.

End-to-end testing checks to ensure that intra-object characteristics and inter-object relationships combine appropriately. Often, we can define plausible intra- and inter-object relationships, but simulating many of them simultaneously may lead to inaccurate or unjustified results. End-to-end testing examines the high-level outcome measures from the simulation, particularly those the model was supposed to capture in the first place. Collecting data for end-to-end testing must rely on baseline cases derived from real-world occurrences or experiments. We must be able to calibrate these cases to get the inputs right and to observe them long enough to have representative outputs. We can then use the inputs to compute simulation results and compare them with the observed results. This benchmarking of end-to-end performance underpins the model's overall credibility.

Considering how to verify and validate a model and certify key inputs early leads you to collect enough test data and to provide the kind of model outputs that will permit effective comparative testing. You need to plan for producing and managing the test data and model outputs that will support intra-object, inter-object, and end-to-end testing.

9.2   Defining Data Items and Model Interactions

Let's discuss what data is and how it interacts with the model, as well as how to categorize data or information we usually must assemble for analysis. These categories are particularly relevant for scenario-based analysis and come mainly from our experience in combat modeling. We recognize that simulation outputs are also part of the data and should include many of the same considerations as inputs. We also have to balance system representations between algorithms in the simulation and in the supporting data. You'll note that this balancing requires us to consider the conceptual and physical relationships between the simulation and the data, what is unknown in these relationships and potentially unknowable, and the ultimate need to "validate" or credibly apply the simulation and its data. Also, well before we begin to collect and store data, we must size, categorize, and price the hardware and software architectures that will maintain it—especially the network connections with other related data repositories and remote users. Timely retrieval of the most current data is at least as important as the ability to aggregate, store, and update. Thus, we must use advanced methods of transaction processing, which protect individual data elements from becoming corrupted during access and update. Data production and retrieval systems must be carefully designed, as described below, to perform complex, interrelated functions.

9.2.1   Types of Input Data

To classify a simulation's input data (the data required to run the model as described in Sec. 9.1.2), we take the perspective of the simulation's users. Analysts must deal with widely varying data and contextual information that allows them to abstract reality, create parameters, calculate measures, and interpret results. Our categories, shown in Fig. 9.5, represent what we want to capture in the simulation. Within the broad types described, we include example data items that might be necessary to study forest management. Table 9.1 summarizes these data types. Use this scheme to develop similar categories for your mission and study.

- **Contextual information.** This data describes the "who," "where," and "when" of the mission scenario. Much of this data will be external to what the model represents but is essential to make the assumptions built into other data items described below. For the forest-management study, it could include the locations, time (current or future), and organizations the study will consider. This often descriptive, subjective data starts focusing the analysis on specific goals and ways to achieve them. But you must further refine this contextual data until it's detailed enough for successful quantitative analysis.

Input Data

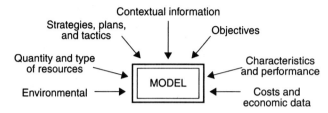

Fig. 9.5. **Categories of Input Data.** The input data to a model consists of many categories which describe the model's context, objectives, parameters, and how it should operate, including desired outputs.

Table 9.1. **Classes of Input Data.** Separating input data into classes helps simulation designers understand the full range of data requirements and focus on items which may be difficult to define, assess for quality, or find.

Data Class	Definition	Examples
Contextual information	The "who," "where," and "when" of the scenario	• Location of fires • Timing • Organization to be assessed
Objectives	The "why" of the scenarios	• To put out fires as rapidly as possible • To save lives, property, and the environment
Strategies, plans, and tactics	The "how" of the scenario, including behaviors	• Strategy for observing forested areas with limited resources • Plan for allocating firefighting units • Tactics for fighting the fire
Quantity and type of resources	The "what" of the scenario	• Quantity, type, and location of engine companies, ladder companies, and emergency medical units
Characteristics and performance	An extension of the "what" used to describe a system's abilities	• Travel speeds for various systems • Pumping rates and water availability • Decision delays • How workload and fatigue degrade performance
Environment	The interaction between systems and nature	• Undergrowth density • Winds • Terrain
Costs	Resource expenditure including money, time, and people	• Cost of acquiring a system • Costs of manpower and training • Budget over time

- **Objectives.** This data drives the simulation and answers why it's developed in the first place. Objectives rigorously quantify what users value, such as saving lives and property or protecting the environment. They range from specific thresholds to desirable goals and are often captured by more quantifiable measures, such as acreage destroyed. Objectives create a demand in the system being modeled that requires a solution. In the forest-fire example, the users' objective is to put out the fire, but you may phrase the demands in terms of the fire's timing, size, and intensity.

- **Strategies, plans, and tactics** for allocating resources to accomplish missions and study objectives, plus player "behaviors" and other human factors. This data describes the "how" of the scenario. It may be partly outside the model or database but still helps determine elements in other data categories, such as quantity of resources available over time. In older models, the simulation's logic incorporates this data, typically in lengthy sets of "if-then-else" statements. More recent models often extract the conditions and actions as data items, then use expert systems, decision tables, or other means to better handle strategies, plans, and tactics. For the forest-management study, such data could include the strategy for observing the forest area with limited resources; plans for allocating resources when a fire breaks out, including mobilizing air assets and units outside the forest service's immediate jurisdiction; and tactics for fighting the fire, such as determining which units will protect specific areas, set fire breaks, and warn or evacuate populated areas or deciding how to rotate resources over time.

- **Quantity and type of resources.** This data describes the "what" of the scenario. Often, you can start with this explicit data in determining what the database contains. In many databases, these resources are coded with numbers (system type 1, 2, and so forth) or obscure abbreviations (system type EG2B), with little description to help analysts. More recent databases include better descriptions. For the forest-management study, such data could include the number and location of different types of engine companies, ladder companies, emergency medical units, command units and vehicles, aircraft, water pumping stations, chemical supplies, and other resources.

- **Characteristics and performance.** This data extends the "what" of the scenario used to capture system parameters in simulation algorithms. Tradeoffs occur at this level between the representations in the model and the data. For example, simulating combat attrition precisely can require detailed data to support algorithms that include detection, tracking, firing doctrine, fly-out, vulnerability, and lethality. Or you may build a very simple algorithm that combines these interactions into a single data item for probability of kill. You can sometimes derive this data using engineering measurements, calculations, or estimates, but it may depend on many factors, including some external to the simulation. We don't want you to think characteristics and performance data are entirely objective. All too often, subjective data, such as estimates of the ability to integrate information and act on it, dominate the simulation. It's also important to capture uncertainties in probability distributions or statistics. For the fire-management study, such data could include the travel speed of various systems, communication and transportation networks, pumping rates, carrying capacities, decision delays, and how workload and fatigue degrade performance.

- **Environmental data.** This information describes the terrain, weather, treatment of time, and other natural phenomena. It extends the scenario's contextual "who," "where," and "when" information and establishes parameters for interactions between systems and "nature." From a functional point of view, it usually looks like characteristics and performance data, but it represents a very different kind of data—outside the system's control or definition.* Tradeoffs also occur here between the representations in the simulation and in the data. For example, to simulate detection, you can use detailed data to support algorithms that model cloud cover, smoke obstruction, atmospheric attenuation, heating, and clutter. Or you may represent detection using simple scaling factors for various extreme conditions (cloudy or clear, smoke or no smoke, etc.). In addition, some well-established relationships in nature require constants to represent, for example, the speed of light or the acceleration due to gravity. Because these constants rarely, if ever, change, we prefer to think of them as part of the model, not as environmental data. Although environmental data is "scientific," analysts often must do basic research to understand some critical phenomena. Indeed, we find much here that is unknown or unknowable (a subject we'll say more about below), or for which there are more "exceptions" than "rules." For the fire-management study, such data could include undergrowth density, winds, transitions from day to night, terrain, fire speed and spread rates, likelihood of (or conditions leading to) a fire escaping, and environmental effects of firefighting techniques.

- **Direct and indirect costs.** Data on resources such as money, time, people, and economics. Simulations that include costs are often separate from those which estimate benefits. Simulations that treat cost and benefits often don't take into account the full implications of cost. For example, sometimes they consider only acquisition costs. Excluding operation and maintenance costs may unduly favor a "status quo" solution whose acquisition investment is long since done. Lifecycle cost is a better way to compare competing options or systems, but you must still consider the

---

* You might say "nature" itself is a system and include environmental data with information on characteristics and performance. Conceptually, you may be right, but we deliberately differentiate them because simulations often try to capture natural phenomena for which there is no "unifying theory" and hence, no simple way to produce data.

mission context, including all dependencies and interactions. For example, in adding a new aircraft to the firefighting systems, you shouldn't just compare it with the lifecycle costs of other systems that do the same thing. Buying the new aircraft will inevitably change what other systems you'll keep, how you'll use some of them, how the new system will fit in, and what additional synergism among systems will occur—in terms of resource costs. For the fire-management study, such data could include costs for acquisition, staffing, training, operations, and maintenance; savings obtained by combining resource needs with other systems, budget availability over time, and phasing purchases to match budget limits.

These categories interact a lot. For example, to determine how to deploy systems (part of strategies, plans, and tactics), you must know their quantity and type. Likewise, the number and types of systems available at any particular place and time depends on how the systems are deployed. Remember, we're not trying to provide independent classes of data or to suggest this is the only way to categorize. Instead, we want to show you a structure in which you'll be able to consider the full range and depth of data for a particular mission or study. We've tried to create as few classes as possible while retaining the essential context of the mission we're representing. The physical layout may also use these categories as the top-level means of organizing the actual data files.

How does organizing input data fit into the three areas described in Fig. 9.1? Much of the structuring helps in model development, but it is equally essential in model execution and VV&A. Model users must develop an analysis or VV&A plan for using it and the data to justify an analytical hypothesis or establish credibility. (See Chap. 2 for more on using models in systems analysis, Chap. 11 on VV&A and App. C on basic statistical methods and experimental design.) These plans set up computational experiments by manipulating the data to show the argument is correct. Thus, we should structure input data to make defining and analyzing these computational experiments as simple and flexible as possible. From the point of view of developing model databases, this means second-guessing many of the applications for the model. It also means that model users must carefully avoid using inappropriate models or data. For more information on types of analysis plans, see Davis and Hillestad (1997), Bankes (1994), or Brooks, et. al. (1997).

When seen in this light, the modeler begins to get a more tangible feeling for the data-production challenges that lie ahead. Have I addressed too broad or too narrow a problem? What data do I need to produce? Where will I find it? Do I have a problem with phenomena that aren't well understood or are unknown? How much data am I expecting to assemble? For example, even with up-front planning, some model databases rapidly balloon to consume gigabytes (or even terabytes) of space—comparable to millions of printed pages. The sheer volume of this information is staggering, as is the intellectual effort required to collect and understand it.

9.2.2 Types of Output Data

You may have already exclaimed, "Don't forget the output—that's data, too!" We agree completely. The output data has many of the same characteristics as the input, particularly the important interactions with the model's structure. In many ways, the types of output data users want, its detail, and the need to explain it dictate that structure. We need tools to handle and understand the outputs' volume and complexity, but we'll focus on conceptually linking the output data and model structures. The first step is to define what kinds of output the model needs. Then, we can turn to five important things the output can do:

- Support the rationale that output values logically follow from the structure and methods of inputs and models
- Help determine cause-and-effect relationships
- Identify individual simulation runs
- Flow across replications and cases
- Flow to the input of another model

Classes of Output Data

Output data is often easy to regenerate from input data and a given model. Thus, you can store the model output or discard and regenerate it as needed. Also, single changes in input parameters can generate new and massive amounts of data to process. This "explosion" is why we must manage and classify output data.

Categories for output data depend on what purposes the output data must serve, not what we're trying to represent. Again, we'll give you a representative scheme from which you can tailor an appropriate structure. Let's consider six classes shown in Fig. 9.6 and summarized in Table 9.2: measures, intermediate measures, histories, repeated inputs, diagnostics, and graphics.

- **Measures.** This is the simulation's main output which captures the value of doing the mission. Measures typically evaluate how well a model meets objectives and are the main reason to create a simulation. We must make sure the measures directly address, or are suitable surrogates for, real-world mission outcomes. Often, study objectives are hard to quantify or require subjective and objective assessment. For example, in the fire-management study, we may want to know the adequacy of firefighting equipment and processes. "Adequacy" may be very difficult to quantify or be associated with several measures, such as aesthetic loss, number of fire deaths, loss of acreage, or time to contain a fire. Quantifying "aesthetic loss" is tough, although we may be able to use loss of acreage or other surrogate measures. Often, it's hard to "second guess" all useful measures for addressing objectives, particularly when the simulation applies to various mission studies. Thus, we want a simulation to be extendable in concept and size, so we can add measures as we learn more about, or discover new aspects of, the mission. For the fire-management

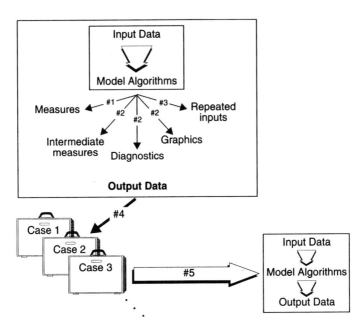

Fig. 9.6.   Relation Between Output Data and a Model's Structure. Modelers, analysts, and other users of a model need various forms of output data. Output processes must also take into account the need to archive cases, along with the model version and input data used to produce them. (Note: The numbers in this diagram refer to five important design considerations for output data discussed later in this section.)

study, these measures include lives lost; environmental damage; economic loss; time to detect, respond, and contain a fire; and the probability of a fire escaping.

- **Intermediate measures.** These more detailed measures help build confidence that we're correctly calculating the more general ones. Of course, some measures and intermediate measures may overlap. For example, the time to detect, respond to, and contain a fire may directly inform a decision maker and may also be an important intermediate measure of environmental damage. This class of data contains other, more detailed measures that are mainly valuable to the analyst or modeler. Intermediate data helps us better understand cause-and-effect relations in the simulation without getting lost in a "forest" of details. For the fire-management study, such intermediate measures could include detection, response, and containment time by system, forest type, and weather condition; time on the fire line by unit or equipment type; consumables expended; number of air drops; and density of units attacking parts of the fire.

Table 9.2.   Classes of Output Data. Defining classes of output data helps simulation designers make sure that the model provides a full range of information for diagnoses, verification and validation, and analysis.

Data Class	Definition	Examples
Measures	The simulation's main output used to determine if it meets objectives	• Lives lost • Environmental damage • Economic loss
Intermediate measures	More detailed outputs that help to determine if the measures are being calculated correctly	• Fire detection • Response to detection • Containment time • Consumables expended
Histories	Time-stamped chronicle of events	• Starting condition of all fire units • Status and disposition of fire units over time • Status and disposition of fire over time
Repeated inputs	Data that ties results to the input that created it	• Resource levels used • Type of fires occurring
Diagnostics	Information needed to determine and test how a simulation should run	• Warnings about inputs outside normal bounds • Abnormal algorithmic conditions • Inconsistencies
Graphics	Visual displays	• Map rendering • Animation • Summaries of dynamic measures

- **Histories.** This data provides a time-stamped chronicle of system conditions, events, and simulation states as they occurred in the simulation. The history essentially allows you to replay what occurred in a particular run of the model. Unfortunately, histories are usually very bulky, filled with excessive detail in some areas, and often likely to omit the one or two pieces of information needed to trace why a particular result occurred. Still, they enable analysts to study causes and effects more precisely. Few simulations produce enough information to determine the full range of causal linkages. Some languages have been designed to preserve causality [Rothenberg 1994]. Allowing users to select data for the history helps reduce bulkiness but may omit essential information. Yet, a disciplined use of this approach is a good idea. Otherwise, histories can be voluminous and difficult to interpret and digest. We must design them to get the information we need to understand outcomes without having to sift through a pile of less meaningful output. For the fire-management study, your history could include starting conditions for all firefighting units and equipment, when and where a fire breaks out, when and by whom it is detected, decisions made to deploy resources to attack it, departure and arrival times for each unit, significant events occurring during the fire, and the status of all units at containment.

- **Repeated inputs.** Most simulation outputs include some information about the inputs used because input and output files usually aren't well integrated and managed. Repeated inputs help analysts identify assumptions for a simulation run and trace a result backward through hundreds or thousands of runs. Of course, repeated inputs are usually only a fraction of the full database. That sometimes limits how well we can document and understand all run assumptions, particularly after some time has passed. For the fire-management study, you'd have to select carefully which inputs to repeat. For example, in runs dealing with firefighting forces, you'd probably want to repeat committed resource levels in the output but not necessarily all of the details associated with initial environmental conditions.

- **Diagnostics.** This data class provides analysts and modelers with information they need to determine if the simulation is working properly. During development, we must be able to reach into very technical parts of the code (such as the event queue, set handlers, or numeric algorithms) and observe data which reassures us that the code works properly. Diagnostics can also include messages that certain inputs conflict or are abnormal; normal algorithmic conditions have been exceeded; or some error, inconsistency, or other problem has occurred. Analysts who don't understand these warnings may not heed them, which could result in significant errors. We do recognize that many of the diagnostics modelers use are unnecessary for analysts. We highly recommend designing the model so diagnostics are selectable. In fact, the ability to turn specific diagnostics off and on easily is an important part of managing data.

- **Graphics.** Although usually not considered data, graphics definitions and commands have become intrinsic to some simulations. We may directly code them or place them in output for some post-processing or general-purpose software to render. In some cases, the output contains only definitional information—line types, colors, icon types, sizes, and positions. More recently, general-purpose software that renders maps and animation have linked to simulations through output files. This software includes special formats and embedded commands to time stamp key events. It also controls the appearance and disappearance of objects, scaling and zooming, and other display features.

It may seem artificial to separate measures and intermediate measures into two distinct categories. We do it to differentiate summary output data directed at informing decision makers from output data used by analysts to understand cause-and-effect relationships in the simulation. Histories, repeated inputs, and other diagnostics are mainly for analysts and modelers, but we discuss graphics last because decision makers and analysts can use them. Graphics can powerfully convey output information to build enthusiasm and advocacy. Pictures showing the difference in rate and direction of fire spread under alternative prevention approaches can more dramatically portray their relative value than a table of numbers. Graphics can also help analysts and modelers interpret the way a simulation works. For example, errors in geographical data, nearly impossible to see in a table, are often obvious on a map.

Five Things Output Data Must Do

In addition to the classes of data described above, five model-design considerations are important for output data. (Each is identified by a number in Fig. 9.6.) First, output measures must be realistic. There must be a firm rationale for how measures are calculated from input data and the model. We've often seen attempts to tie high-level measures to very detailed inputs, even though the connecting rationale, let alone the algorithms, may have been tenuous at best. For example, you may want to determine whether maintenance crews should change a fire engine's tires with one-quarter or one-eighth inch tread remaining. Why can't you put this detail in the same simulation that determines the "adequacy of firefighting equipment and processes?" To do so, you'd have to explain loss of life (output) in terms of tread depth (input) while allowing for vast uncertainties, specific conditions, and dominance of other factors. That seems impractical, and it is. You must select outputs (especially measures) and design the input and model structure with balance and a firm rationale. Overly extending these relationships can easily cause misguided conclusions. Begin by questioning what scientific theory, functional relationships, and data exist to calculate a particular output measure.

The second design requirement is to provide output data in forms and levels of detail that allow us to understand causes and effects in the model. For example, if a simulation predicts a fire will escape, is this due to deficiencies in a firefighting element, the firefighting tactics, the scenario's conditions, or a model artifact? You must carefully design and develop post-processors to answer this question, but you must also make detailed state and event data part of the model's output. Selectively examining intermediate outputs, historical data, diagnostics, and graphics is essential to focus rapidly on what is happening in the model. Furthermore, we don't know of any model that initially contained all the outputs we needed to determine causes and effects for a measure in any particular study. You should always expect to change the model to produce yet another output. This can be a painful experience if the model's structure isn't readily extendable. Too often, putting in another "print" statement has caused the model to malfunction. Some research has been done to develop modeling languages that allow users to more easily trace cause-and-effect relationships [Rothenberg 1994].

Design requirement three is to develop a system which identifies individual simulation runs unambiguously, even though some users won't think it's necessary. If the model has only a few inputs or does only a few things (in the tens), why bother to identify cases? Also, if a case gets "lost," just run it again. For larger simulations, identifying cases becomes much more important. Analysts commonly look at one case out of hundreds or thousands and say, "Hmm, which one is this?" Clever file naming or, as stated above, repeating inputs in the output may be enough to identify a case. Tools for managing data configurations (discussed later in this chapter) are essential, but they must be flexible enough to adapt to inevitable changes in data and models. Sometimes, modelers and tool developers don't work together closely enough or don't use the same version of the model. As a result, users become frustrated with data management tools and return to manual ways of handling data including simple, but inadequate, ways of identifying cases.

Because the outputs of one simulation run aren't enough to draw any conclusions, a fourth requirement is to design your simulation for easy correlation and accessibility across runs. Managing configurations can help a lot, but we're also interested in determining the logical relationships in defining and calculating measures. These relationships allow us to gain insights and build rational arguments. Conventional wisdom states that a simulation's absolute outputs shouldn't be expected to predict the real world precisely. Instead, we should use the differences between outcomes to select options. However, even the relative differences in output measures can be misleading without properly matching output to the model's structure. For example, if we represent a preferred output measure by inputs and algorithms that are biased against it, the model may evaluate this option as relatively worse, better, or about the same as a less preferred option. Without understanding the model's structure, especially the algorithms' biases and limits, we may misjudge even the relative outcomes across cases. It may also be difficult to understand how effectively the relative differences among options actually make them distinguishable.

Finally, simulation outputs are often the only source of information for another simulation. Defining outputs so information may credibly pass between simulations is a great challenge, particularly when the models aren't controlled by the same person or organization. We'll cover the data needs of multiple simulations in Sec. 9.3.

9.2.3   Contextual Interactions between the Data and the Model

While categorizing input and output data, we haven't yet asked a key question concerning data and the model: how much of the systems, processes, and other factors should you represent in the model and how much should you put in the data? This question lies at the heart of some of the thorniest design decisions modelers face. For example, you might ask if the model should explicitly represent how the fire-management dispatching system operates (with all of its detailed parameters) or whether to capture it in some set of simple data items such as system delays. In fact, there is a range of possibilities between these two extremes to represent the system with more or less of a data orientation (and correspondingly with less or more of a model orientation). The question is: where in this range should your simulation be positioned?* Although no exact answer exists, consider at least two perspectives. From an external perspective, how do the model's goals

---

* This chapter provides some criteria for this decision: whether data is available and accessible, how general and flexible the model is, what the model and data will cost, and how well we understand what we're modeling.

affect the relationship between the data and the model? From within the methods and algorithms in the model, how should the model and data balance?

Model Goals and Defining Model-Data Interactions

In answering the first question, you have to review why you're developing a simulation in the first place. If you omit too much breadth or depth from the model (making the representation more data-oriented), it will likely address fewer questions. But if you include too much breadth or depth (making the representation more model-oriented), the algorithms may be impossible to develop and the required data impractical to obtain. For example, if the fire-management study is to focus on humans in the dispatching system, you must include the essential factors in a way that permits their examination while omitting non-essential details, objects, or conditions. The context critically affects what to represent and how to capture it.

But determining what to include and what to drop isn't always easy, especially when the context is poorly established or the uses of a model expand too broadly. Designers usually make the model as "general purpose" as possible to justify the resources needed to develop it. Prudent designers recognize that a successful simulation will eventually apply beyond its original scope, often including factors initially considered to be outside the model. Even so, you should try to lay out clearly what the model does and doesn't include as a foundation for the initial design and enhancements.

You must also determine how outside conditions will affect the model and how the input data will reflect changes in these conditions. For example, if the simulation doesn't represent the locations of some firefighting equipment, how will changes in their real locations affect data items in the model? Sometimes, you'll want to omit such factors. For example, you may ignore weather conditions if you're only simulating how dispatch works. But if you want to model dispatching and deploying fire units, you may want to include weather, at least simplistically, for some of the simulated systems. By simplistically, we mean (for example) simulating the system with nominal travel rates and then resimulating with slower rates for bad weather. Weather may be outside the context of any particular run, but the data must implicitly include it across runs.

The kinds of data and modeling algorithms that are known and available also constrain what you'll include in a model. Many data items can't even be specified with certainty, and others may be unknowable, such as what a human might do under stress or how and when a fire may escape. Although you shouldn't merely place these very hard problems outside a model, you also can't just include them without careful thought. You must specify default values and overcome the potential pitfalls discussed in Sec. 9.3.2. Thus, differentiating between "known" and "uncertain" input data is significant to model development.

Balancing Representations between Models and Data

In the early days of modeling, data values often appeared within the model, but this approach was eventually deemed "bad coding." Now, we define much more of the structure, processes, and objects we wish to represent as data, at least partly because spreadsheets, object-oriented languages, and other devices allow it. The blurring of data and model code can, however, create some semantics problems. Are equations in a spreadsheet data or part of the model? To the spreadsheet, the contents of a cell are data, even though they may be interpreted as a function. If we decide to classify the function as part of the model, we may still have problems because all numeric values in the function (including coefficients, exponents, and variable values) can still be considered data. Despite these difficulties, using data to represent structure, processes, and objects can provide greater flexibility. The data just requires careful design and preparation, often by analysts who must skillfully match its content to the needs and quality of the analysis. In other words, it often requires greater skill, more time, and increased cost, but the value added may justify the expense.

Consider how you'd apply this balance to firefighting. You might represent it as

1.   A detailed model of how fire units, the terrain, and weather interact.
2.   A table that typifies a rate at which a fire is extinguished based on numbers and types of units, terrain, and weather.

In the first case, the model does extra calculations on more detailed input data, but the results are likely to be more straightforward. Because you've modeled firefighting as a function, you may more easily change input data within reasonable bounds. In the second case, the model's calculations are much simpler, relying only on a look-up table. But, it may be difficult to generate this table because more detailed off-line calculations are required. The data tables may contain many assumptions and may not be appropriate for a broader context. For example, if we're examining the effect of aircraft dropping water on rugged terrain, a table generated from open, flat-terrain conditions is likely to produce errors.

Notionally, model designers select a position along a continuum between model and data representations. In practice, this continuum may be difficult to define or visualize.* The choice of how much model and how much data depends on various factors, including what is known about how to represent the system or function, the desired level of aggregation, and the availability of data— particularly the availability of higher-resolution models to create the needed data. For example, firefighting may require complex algorithms, simulating how the fire

---

* In reality, the entire model is data in the form of coded statements compiled and stored in their binary, executable format. Although this "data" can be changed as well, we distinguish between the model code, which requires a programmer to manipulate, and the model data, which is more accessible to analysts. For some computer languages, such as LISP, this distinction is not as apparent as in others like Fortran or C.

consumes flammables, moves across variable terrain, and responds to retardants. A simple model may take out the algorithm for the flammables and replace it with a table of fire intensities. Another simplification would take out the detailed terrain and include only generic look-up tables for how fire moves across terrain. Which method should you choose? Detailed terrain data, for example, may be difficult to collect and may slow the model down a lot. Several types of "average" or generic terrain may be enough for some purposes. The way you resolve these issues depends on your analytic needs and a desire to achieve a reasonable balance between the model and the data.

By focusing on algorithmic representations, you don't eliminate data. In fact, models with more complex algorithms tend to include more detail, and hence more data—sometimes much more data. In these cases, each data element is likely to have a more precise and tangible meaning, embed fewer assumptions, and be more directly measurable. For example, a detailed model for firefighting may have actual measured values to represent terrain. Capturing the effects of terrain on firefighting in such data is likely to be easier than if the terrain was represented more generically.

In some cases, we'd like to vary the resolution of what we're representing—building in flexibility to change our emphasis on the model or data. Changes to either strongly affect the other. For example, if we add more detailed terrain to the firefighting model, we must produce more data to support this change. This added detail may affect other parts of the simulation which use or process it. Similarly, if we want to reduce the detail and quantity of the terrain data (maybe because we can't find a simple source for it), we'll need to modify the algorithms used in the simulation.

To summarize, you can't select a model's structure without considering the nature of the data and the challenges associated with creating and managing databases. Don't just select a convenient algorithm without considering its data needs. Compromises between the model and data are inevitable.

9.2.4 Data Architectures and Retrieval Systems

A third key to M&S design is the structure and method for storing and retrieving data. An effective combination of data-handling hardware and software must have three main characteristics. First, we need fast, reliable access to data for complex multi-tasking and multi-programming activities, especially in wide-area networks. Second, we must be able to update databases rapidly and accurately, with little dedicated effort. Finally, a data architecture (and its contents) must be able to help us verify, validate, and accredit a model. The data architecture enables database management and, thus, completes the system elements needed to make sure defined data items match model requirements.

The importance of these three factors for modern models and simulations is becoming increasingly clear in organizations such as Air Force Space Command at Peterson Air Force Base, Colorado. They're working on effective algorithms for correlating data and techniques for fusing near-real-time information in M&S projects such as FRONTIER ARENA. This community is recognizing that methods for storing, updating, and making data available to users are very important to understanding situations and assessing threats. In fact, the best predictive models and simulations seamlessly mesh these three essential ways of handling data with easily interpreted, user-friendly displays of results from combat situations.

Sizing the Storage Architecture

In building databases, we've learned that we usually end up with much more data than anticipated. Therefore, you should develop a virtual data structure that can allow real storage systems to grow many times larger than their original size without disruption or redesign. You'll also need to store and manipulate subsets of the master database tailored to users. Each master database spawns roughly ten customer-specific versions of itself, each requiring its own archives, analytical abilities, and "workspace." Plus, in frequently consulted databases, you must allow for continuous growth. Because storing data is cheap and growing steadily cheaper, you'll want to include as much excess space as you can afford immediately and secure the rest by providing for cost-effective growth. As a rule of thumb, you should size storage media at least 100 times larger than the initial data requires.

Trading Off Types of Storage Media

For data that must be immediately available, you have two main choices of storage media: CD-ROMs and hard disk drives. When such data is unlikely to change much, CD-ROMs may be most appropriate, but if you're storing dynamic data, the hard drive—typically arrayed in "stacks" or Redundant Arrays of Independent Disks (RAIDs)—is better. For archiving and backing up data, tape drives (especially automated or robotically controlled ones) are also useful. By archiving, we mean recording data configurations or user-defined data sets, or storing data before or after scheduled run times. Ideally, filing these archives for future reference should not require reformatting.

Media architecture must also allow for future technological advances, perhaps better combining data compression and accessibility. Again, you must design a virtual data architecture that's flexible (and independent of hardware) enough to include the technological advances which are sure to come. An example might be a high-speed server directly controlling a holographic optical memory, a CD-based read and write unit for intermediate storage, and a robotic tape library. With such an arrangement, the optical storage system could continuously update dynamic phenomena, such as weather or forest conditions; high capacity DVD-ROMs could store maps and terrain data, with writable CDs holding temporary or intermittent data that is cross-linked to the CD-ROM it modifies; and the robotic tape library could store scenario inputs, parameter lists, and streams of output data.

Correlating Data

Whenever possible, updates should be automatic and as safe from failure as possible. Thus, it's a good idea to index all data that describes dynamic phenomena so that, whenever possible, a change in one element automatically changes all related data in an internally consistent way. You'll also need to provide independent ways to systematically check the accuracy of these automated updates—particularly ones that can monitor and judge "write authorizations." This part of the design requires careful attention to detail, as discussed in Gray (1993).

Enabling Users to Interact with Data Architectures

Users of the products from each type of data repository (space, environmental, mapping, weather, logistics, intelligence, etc.) require authority to "read" the master database (based on security clearance and "need to know"). Rarely, if ever, do participating modelers and M&S users need "write" authority. Key repository services you'll provide to users will normally be tailored databases, residing in their own "data spaces" and completely at the disposal of the specifying (and paying!) user. Examples might be a synthetic environment for a wargame or exercise set five years in the future; a test bed to analyze candidate designs for a hardened communication system, complete with engineering-grade simulation of nuclear effects; or any other area of investigation impractical to pursue in the real world (such as possible responses to nuclear terrorism). In other words, keep intact all raw data from authoritative sources. If users want to manipulate this data for their own applications, they can make copies of it.

Analyzing and Manipulating Data

Ideally, simulations should be globally "aware" of the interrelationships among data elements and sets. In advanced simulation systems, a competent analytical engine—perhaps controlled by rule-based or logic-based artificial intelligence—should continuously prowl the data architecture for inconsistencies and alert human operators whenever it finds any. It's also helpful to incorporate various forms of defense (against hackers, viruses, equipment failures, etc.) into this monitoring system. Also include independent data spaces with fully equipped toolkits (analogous to workshops or laboratories), so you can develop data products users ask for.

Pre- and Post-processing. Preprocessors can interact with flat files to do more limit- and cross-checking before the model runs. They can read information in data dictionaries regarding the data type, upper and lower bounds for numerical data, allowable names for enumerated data, and source files to check for name data. When the preprocessor is asked to verify data, it goes through the model's current flat files and checks these aspects of the data. It also checks for missing data that a model needs to operate properly, as well as relationships such as whether a set of weights adds to 1.0 or whether all data is specified within a set of parameters. Rather than requiring users to interact with flat files through a text processor, you may present these files in formatted windows. Some of the flat files may come from interfaces tailored to management systems, rather than from a database.

Similarly, post-processors are an essential part of the data architecture. Many models produce voluminous output to trace cause-and-effect relationships. Dealing with it can be daunting unless you have tools to break it into manageable pieces or to focus on a specific object or a given sequence of events. Comparing data across runs is equally tedious. It may be easy to find all the differences between two or more runs, but it's much more difficult to find and categorize the essential differences. In both cases, post-processors can process and manage this information. They also help accumulate evidence from computational experiments. You can use them to create polished plots, charts, tables, and reports that may dramatically affect decision makers as you explain and justify conclusions drawn from these experiments. The same products can also help convince decision makers that the model is effective.

Graphical User Interfaces. Graphic display of the input data is also useful. Analysts may want to observe relative counts of objects in the inputs, compute aggregated values, and view abilities. These displays first help check anomalies in the data and later help explain them. Users also like to display positions of objects from other databases—places on the map or positions relative to one another. This graphical display can reveal data errors, such as inverted latitude and longitude or incorrect placement of objects with respect to those from the database.

Graphical user interfaces occur in various forms, some general purpose and some tailored to a model or application. They may be templates for data entry within interactive windows or allow people to use graphical mapping and drawing tools to enter and display spatial data. Accompanying programs may automatically check the consistency, scale, sign, and type of data.

Another use of these graphic interfaces is to globally change data values. For example, if information about aircraft types is organized as a set of objects presented to the user one aircraft type at a time, running through each object to change the same parameter may be cumbersome. Interfaces using scripts can ease such global changes.

The ability of graphical user interfaces to manipulate, manage, and visualize model data becomes even more important as the quantity of data or the model's complexity increases. These interfaces can help you understand more easily and thoroughly how input data converts to output data. They can also display large data arrays as three-dimensional landscapes, through which you can "navigate" (using simple point-and-click or menu-driven features) to "see" relationships between different parts of the data. Although they don't completely eliminate the need for filenames and complex naming conventions, properly designed graphical user interfaces can greatly reduce confusion and ease manipulation of complex data sets.

Documenting Data with "Metadata"

Descriptions of data, called metadata, are critical to the proper use and interpretation of data. This information might include the metrics associated with data items, formats, sources, assumptions, restrictions on distribution, reliability, usage limits, relation to other data, history of changes, application, and other useful comments. Metadata rarely feeds into the model's algorithms but does establish and helps preserve the data's accuracy and credibility.

Data always has a context. For example two models may call the same data item a movement rate, but they may have very different meanings or uses. One model may assume a particular kind of terrain, weather condition, or driver skill. The other may use an algorithm that requires more data. Metadata establishes this context, which may include such high-level questions as: What are the model's objectives? What does it measure? How does it link data inputs to these measures? How do algorithms manipulate the data? What are the model's assumptions and metrics? Documentation and metadata specified in the original design must answer all these questions.

Data also inherits meaning in particular studies. What assumptions does the study impose? What keeps data for a particular application from applying more generally? How does the study treat qualitative or subjective data and use work-arounds (with corresponding data) to represent some systems? You must document how your model will process data. What are the data's sources, classification, and sensitivity? When was the data last changed or examined for validity, and in what context? To answer these questions, data elements must have their own monitors of current status.

Too often, documentation is missing or excluded from the data. Traditionally, the metadata (when it exists) is in separate, printed, reference volumes. To decipher a model's database, users have to assemble a library of manuals, which typically describe parts of the model's database, such as terrain or effectiveness. If data-development efforts aren't tied closely to algorithm development, modelers are likely to produce overarching documentation that doesn't detail how the data is interrelated and manipulated before and during a simulation run. Advances in computer and data-management technology have opened the way for on-line documentation that provides simpler input of the metadata, faster access to the data dictionary, and more consistent descriptions.

A convenient way to keep track of metadata is to incorporate it in a model of its own—called a metadata model.[*] This type of model contains information about the database's structure, relationships among sets of data (particularly those whose values depend on each other), and the status of mechanisms for updating or cross-linking the data. Such models and their dictionaries precisely emulate the data repository's structure and operation. They're essential to successful, cost-effective planning of the repository's evolution and that of its supporting equipment. They can also help you answer "what if" questions about managing databases, reengineering software, designing migration systems, and so forth. Also, these models can help human operators and their automated servants "troubleshoot" the network and correct system failures or intrusions. Chapter 8 points out that we must have "meta-knowledge" for all model processes and must properly account for assumptions to get correct valid results. Similar knowledge and accounting are necessary for the data a model uses, so we need metadata. But

---

[*] A metadata model for command and control is described in "Command and Control (C2) Core Data Model, Version 2," 1 July 1994, DOD Information Systems Agency, Joint Interoperability Engineering Organization (JIEO), Center for Studies.

be careful not to develop metadata and models independently. Modelers and database developers should collaborate as closely as possible, agreeing **in advance** on the form and substance of the model's data sets and how they'll categorize, manage, access, and document these data sets. In other words, modelers and data managers ought to prepare data and metadata as a team so this information remains connected to the model it supports.

Metadata has many forms, which can and ought to serve various purposes. We've mentioned just some of them at the beginning of this section, but Rothenberg (1996) points out two other indispensable functions of metadata: to help ensure that data is appropriate and to enable the modeling team to update it. Properly designed metadata provides powerful tools for administering data, but you need to assemble and check it for completeness with the same care you devote to creating the model and selecting its supporting data. At the same time, integrate the metadata so it's internally consistent and, therefore, effective. Include in your unified approach the model, its data, and all of their collective interfaces, "metamodels," dependencies, references, and indexing. As Rothenberg (1996) correctly observes, M&S data **models reality**, and metadata comprises the charts and measurements that keep the modeling and data-management teams properly oriented and aware. To paraphrase a famous advertisement, you shouldn't leave the lab without it.

9.3   Sources, Availability, and Accessibility

Knowing what data you'd like to have doesn't always ensure you can get it. Model designers often represent systems very simply at first, intending to add detail later. If they're not careful, they can easily add algorithms (either simple or complex) for which data isn't available or accessible. In this section, you'll find out where to get data and, more importantly, where to look before finalizing too much of the model and data representation. Data sources, availability, and accessibility constrain simulation design.

9.3.1   Getting Data

Potential data sources include history, training or exercises, tests, experts, and other models, as briefly described in Table 9.3. Users of data are concerned about the scope, detail, accuracy, explanations, responsiveness, and credibility of these sources.

Historical Data

Historical data provides high-level, aggregate information useful for typifying the conditions, processes, and systems you'll investigate. Seeing the extremes of what has occurred in the past is valuable to make sure you don't overly simplify complexities, and it may even show a need to improve a piece of equipment or a system function. For example, you can find out when and where fires are likely to occur and how well equipment and tactics have worked. Historical data also helps

Table 9.3.   **Classes of Data Sources.** Simulation designers should remember that data can come from many sources. If you understand the benefits and limitations of these classes, you'll more likely use high-quality data and make multiple sources consistent early in development.

Source	Characteristics
Histories	• Useful for typifying conditions, systems, processes. • Show what has occurred • Include human decisions • May not capture enough detail • May contain plausible events that never occurred • May not apply to the future .
Training or Exercises	• Instrumented ranges provide a lot of quantitative data • Can examine specific conditions • Include human decisions but may contain biases • Emphasize training objectives and safety, so may introduce biases • Can't capture some events • Human learning prohibits consistently repeatable results
Tests	• Rigorously measures parts of the system • Control and classify experimental conditions • Capture characteristics and performance data • Have a limited scope • Use narrowly-defined conditions • Emphasize test objectives and safety, so may introduce biases
Experts	• Often necessary for extrapolating to the future • Good sources for strategies and tactics • May be the only sources for some information • Not rigorously measureable or standardized • Tend toward anecdotal information • May have organizational, institutional, or other biases
Other models	• Help reduce the overall context, breadth, or detail • Capture data from other sources above • May help automate data processing • Often difficult to join multiple models conceptually and physically • Difficult to aggregate and decompose

you check the validity of a model's results by placing bounds on what it can achieve. For example, if a simulation does command, control, and deployment faster than ever observed, its results are suspect even though it plausibly models the physics.

However, we often can't directly include historical data because many characteristics, such as system parameters, haven't been adequately measured, or scenario conditions haven't been detailed. We may want data on events that haven't occurred, such as careful tracking of fires. Unfortunately, historical data doesn't help us understand what might change with more accurate tracking or why tracking was poor in the first place. Histories don't capture system limitations, ineffective employment of resources, or slow reaction to warning in enough detail to show clear causes and effects for modeling.

Historical data often depends on perspective and interpretation. We even know of deliberate attempts to rewrite history, particularly in situations involving major successes or failures. Also if the simulation is supposed to analyze scenarios, systems, forces, or potential conditions beyond those observed, historical data is likely to be less useful. For example, we may want to estimate the effectiveness of a new technology for firefighting in a geographical area with characteristics our historical database doesn't contain.

Still, historical data helps us understand the system's nature and provides anecdotes of what has caused success or failure. In terms of our earlier categories, historical data includes contextual information and objectives within a similar context; recorded strategies, plans, and tactics; amount and type of resources and "targets" over time; environmental data; and costs.

Data from Training or Exercises

Training or exercise data can be collected more methodically and rigorously. For instrumented exercise ranges, such as the Air Force's RED FLAG training area and the Army's Fort Irwin National Training Center, we can often determine the specific conditions and shot-by-shot outcomes. Training data can provide insights, particularly into how human actions affect the simulation. In the firefighting example, information could include the reaction times of dispatchers and fire units under stressful conditions. Tests can set up critical conditions that have or are believed to have, an impact. By analyzing simulation parameters or other data, we may find it's critical to do some task—such as mobilizing airborne forces—within a particular time. Training can exercise the organization's response, measure its speed, and observe variations. Such an exercise generates data and reveals whether or not mobilization delay is a problem.

However, training data may be incomplete and significantly biased. First and foremost, training exercises intend to train, not collect data for other purposes. Exercises capture mistakes and help to correct them by developing lessons learned, giving rise to important questions such as: Should we carry these mistakes into the simulation data and use them to draw general conclusions? When failure does occur, how should we capture intent or the underlying value of the failed action? Catastrophic failure of an exercise usually isn't allowed because of the need to continue training. Some participants fear retribution for their mistakes, so they avoid risk; others consider training a good time to take risks they wouldn't take in the face of danger. Thus, it's hard even to identify the direction of biases in this data.

Because training exercises are typically costly and must operate within strict safety restrictions, they may not play out all scenarios. For example, one or two units may participate only in a "vignette" of fighting a real fire, avoiding tactics like setting fire breaks. Because we'd like to glean data from these "experiments," we want them to be repeatable and consistent. Unfortunately, cost typically limits the number of specific cases, and the human learning curve often limits repeatability and consistency.

Recently, technological advances in distributed interactive simulation (DIS) and advanced distributed simulation (ADS) have expanded training methods and captured data and information more thoroughly. ADS also has limits, but integrating it with traditional, constructive simulations should benefit both. We can use traditional approaches to make a simulation repeatable and consistent while narrowing the problem scope, for example, to areas in which ADS can uniquely examine human factors. Then, we can place the ADS results into the constructive simulations and improve that part of the representation.

Regardless of its limits, training data is a valuable, often unexploited source of information on human actions and effectiveness. In terms of our categories, it includes more of the detailed strategies, plans, and tactics; the amount and type of resources and "targets" used over time; and some limited information on a system's characteristics and performance.

Test Data

Test data usually gives a very clear picture of the assumptions and conditions under which the data was derived. Because tests are usually focused on a system's effectiveness, they often measure and instrument detailed interactions among parts of a system. For example, testing a new water-dropping aircraft can yield information on the carrying capacity; fill time; travel speed empty and full; release time, pattern, and accuracy; and "on-station" time. Thus, testing may be the most reliable source for effectiveness data and the system's significant relationships and interactions.

But test data often represents specific, narrow conditions. For example, data on the accuracy of the water-dropping aircraft will typically cover only a few conditions for approach, terrain, weather, and employment. Also, for practical reasons, some conditions (such as smoke obstruction in the target area) will be omitted or idealized. Suppose the model needs input on the firefighting ability of a group of heterogeneous systems, such as ground fire units, helicopters, and water-dropping aircraft. In this case, we'd have to specify unit configurations, firefighting tactics, resource allocations, and the like.

Like training, tests may not intend to develop data for a simulation. They're also expensive and may be restricted from sending out complete or thoroughly documented data (e.g., proprietary or military tests). Still, test data can be the most important available source of data on a system's characteristics and performance.

Information from Experts

Experts are a rich supply of information, even though the data they provide tends to be subjective, anecdotal, and mixed liberally with opinion or argument. Expert information may even include specifications for systems or parts of systems that don't exist. You may wonder how definitive, rigorous, or "measurable" this source is. Doesn't expert opinion often cause controversy? Perhaps. But it may be the only source of data, especially if it's more subjective or speculative than measurable. For example, if we'd like to know how much more effective a future type of firefighting equipment will be, we can't look at history, training, or tests. Experts would likely be our only source, possibly supported by theories plus calculations and methods for estimating and predicting outcomes. Experts can help us determine how to use a certain piece of equipment or provide other operational information. Finally they can examine outputs to make sure a model doesn't mislead or "lie." Our job as modelers is to use expert information appropriately.

Experts include technical specialists, operators, decision makers, analysts who will use the simulation, and—in the military—intelligence organizations. (Though based on observation, intelligence data usually includes interpretation and assumptions by regional or functional experts, particularly for future predictions.) You certainly must treat data from experts carefully because it may contain biases, particularly organizational ones. The experts' experiences can limit scope and detail. They also tend to give you ranges or increments (good, fair, poor) instead of precise numerical data. Interviews with them may also reveal anecdotes that are interesting but difficult to generalize or to fit into the simulation's database. For example, highly experienced firefighters may be an invaluable source of information about sensible ways of fighting fires. But if they focus too much on certain fires or conditions, you'll have a hard time applying this information broadly. Also, experts often can describe only symptoms and not the causes and effects you'd like in your simulation and database.

A few examples will show how experts sometimes focus too much on specific details. Firefighters may think air-dropping equipment is essential and exclude all other systems mainly because of their own personal experiences. Others may reject this equipment because they've experienced mechanical failures or poor results from improper use. Communication experts believe something like the R300 switch and its operation are key to firefighting and insist you model it as "realistically" as possible. Our experience shows that, even if you could accumulate all the detail on particular items, you probably wouldn't be able to generalize and determine causes and effects for overall firefighting. As an extreme example, a firefighter's sneezing at a critical time may have an impact, but is it rational to include a "firefighter-sneeze" model into a simulation used to determine firefighting outcomes? Probably not.

Yet, certain methods can partly compensate for the imprecision of data from experts. Various techniques—including Delphi, modified Delphi, and the Analytical hierarchical process—have helped extract expert advice and establish a remarkably strong consensus [Sackman 1974; Saaty 1986; Veit 1993]. This consensus (when it exists) makes the data consistently more reliable because the experts are saying, in effect, that only a few right ways exist to do certain tasks. They're also saying significantly different methods are likely to fail. Less consensus typically means more behaviors or methods can be successful.

Involving experts in data collection is very important. Without insights from people who have real experience, data collected for the simulation may be little more than an academic exercise, with limited relationships to the actual problem. The same can be said for the measures and intermediate measures such a simulation produces. Experts provide valuable data across our categories—particularly for strategies, plans, and tactics—and for checking the real-world accuracy of the simulation's whole range of output data.

Other Models

The remaining possibility for collecting data is to get it from other models. You can isolate data elements or whole classes of data that external models or calculations can generate. Other external models set the context, reduce the breadth, or reduce the level of detail of your simulation. For example, a simulation may rely on various external calculations to help analyze the combined efforts of air and ground equipment, units, and tactics. You could run externally a high-level deployment model that determines which units are available at which times, as well as what fire conditions your simulation will represent. Multiple runs of the same model could capture the effects of several fires, rather than capturing all of them in one model. Instead of modeling the specific equipment down to the last moving part, you can do more detailed calculations off line to capture the movement rate and other effectiveness information. All off-line calculations could contribute to the data your simulation needs. Note that your decision to use other models is part of the trade between data and models, which we discussed in Sec. 9.2.3.

Because this approach is so popular for supplying data, let's look more closely at how to link models and how to group and divide data across and between the models. We want to highlight only the data implications of linking models. See Chaps. 3, 8, and 10 for more detail on interoperability. We should also note that ideas in this area are changing rapidly because it's the focal point for a lot of current research.

Approaches to linking models. Linking means connecting one model's outputs to your simulation's inputs. Your approach will determine how much users must do to pass contextual data from the simulation to the external models and to get the data they want from the external models to populate the selected data items. The data may pass almost automatically or require manipulation or reformatting. Automation uses fewer resources for reprocessing, but future users may assume the values being passed need little or no examination. Also, the way you link the codes affects how the programs and links between them are maintained and developed. Let's examine some of these approaches, using a firefighting simulation that requires data for the effectiveness of aircraft. Another simulation, which details air-dropping operations, calculates this data. In what ways can we link these models so the more detailed simulation can supply what we need? Five general methods are embedded code, confederations, communication protocols, architectures, and traditional hierarchies. Table 9.4 lists these methods, which we'll discuss in increasing order of independence from each other and from linkage standards.

- **Embedded Code.** At one extreme, the code for the external model can merge into the simulation to form one larger simulation. This approach yields the most model-intensive representation, as discussed in Sec. 9.2.3,

Table 9.4.   Approaches to Linking Models. As you move down the "approach" column, you'll see the five general ways to link models, arranged in increasing order of independence from each other and from linkage standards.

Approach	Linkage Type	Characteristics
Embedded Code	Code from one model physically inserted into another model	• Dependent development of physical models • Dependent development of conceptual models • Automated transfer of data • No extra linkage software • Explicit linkage of conceptual models • No additional support tools
Confederations	Model code is physically separate, and functional links connect model to model	• Partially independent development physical models • Independent development of conceptual models • Automated transfer of data • Extra linkage software for specific models • Explicit linkage of conceptual models • No additional support tools
Communications Protocols	Model code is physically separate, and a general link connects the models	• Independent development of physical models • Independent development of conceptual models • Automated transfer of data • Extra, general-purpose software for linkage • Data passing links conceptual models • No additional support tools
Architectures	Model code is physically separate and "plugs" into an environment that provides services—communication between models, archiving and retrieval of models and data, case control, and results analysis	• Independent development of physical models • Independent development of conceptual models • Automated transfer of data • Extra, general-purpose software for linkage • Standards and data passing link conceptual models • Widely varying support tools
Traditional Hierarchies	Model code is physically separate, and conceptual links exist between the models	• Independent development of physical models • Independent development of conceptual models • Manual transfer of data • No extra linkage software • Data passing links conceptual models • No additional support tools

and it's how traditional models have been constructed. The model is actually a set of submodels embedded in the same overarching code. For example, our employment model is actually a series of submodels for, say, propagating the fire, operating fire engines, and mapping the fire-incident commander's decisions. Another submodel might describe how wheeled vehicles cross the terrain. Often, we may want to replace an existing submodel with a more detailed one. When this happens, we have to change the model and the new submodel to make sure they'll link conceptually and physically. For example, a detailed model of aircraft flight might be in the fire-employment model. But now, we may need to upgrade the employment model to supply enough information to the flight model and we must aggregate the flight model's outputs to use them in the employment model.

Embedded code gives us one significant advantage: models automatically interact, meaning that data flows back and forth between the simulation and the submodel. A key concern is making sure the linkage is conceptually and physically correct. In addition, high-resolution models tend to produce deterministic or "point" results, but low-resolution models often require an allowable range of outcomes with their relative frequencies. To overcome this problem, you can run the high-resolution model many times to produce an "output universe," and then include simple code in the low-resolution model to describe these results.

In some cases, embedding off-line models into the simulation may not be practical. First, separate groups typically develop, use, and maintain these models, so their management can be a problem. Expanding the simulation team with experts on these other models may solve the problem but drain resources. Second, the simulation as a whole requires a much larger set of potentially complex and unknown data values to meet the submodel's data requirements. Third, the combined model may require too much run time because of the added breadth or depth. Finally, and perhaps most importantly, models can become too complex. It's often easier to deal separately with two models rather than combining them into a giant, super-model. For example, suppose you have a supermodel and want to replace a submodel within it with a simpler representation. Removing the old embedded code may be very difficult, particularly if some shortcuts were taken in weaving the two codes together.

- **Confederations.** As an alternative to embedding code, we may keep the external model separate and start it only when the simulation requires it. Confederations, as defined here, keep some specifics of the models to simplify the linkage and maintain adequate contextual interaction between them. The advantage over embedded code is that we can develop the models separately while preserving their conceptual relationship. Also, we're more likely to be able to isolate the submodel's code and exchange it with another algorithm. One disadvantage of confederations: we must develop and maintain the code and data that connect the simulations in addition to the code and supporting data for the models themselves.

- **Communication Protocols.** This method takes confederations one step further by using a general-purpose mechanism that allows us to independently develop and operate the models. The protocols pass data among the models by linking with a matching code within the models. Aggregate Level Simulation Protocol (ALSP) and Distributed Interactive Simulation (DIS) are of this type, although their structures differ somewhat. General-purpose approaches can be reused, if truly general enough, with many submodels and simulations. The main challenge is the ability to develop and use protocols robust enough to apply across this range. Also, because the models are even more independent, the conceptual linkage is vital and the possibility of passing misleading or incorrect data increases.

- **Architectures.** A broader method of automating data communication between models is to build an architecture that provides many services to end users and enhances interoperability among models. Remember, an architecture is a combined hardware and software environment which contains, updates, and allows access to data and information. Some of these architectures mainly promote reuse of models; others offer additional services such as managing source data, generating model databases, and analyzing output. Typically, such architectures contain "libraries" of models we may "check out" from the repository and link on a "plug-and-play" basis. Two such architectures in development are the Joint Modeling, Analysis, and Simulation System (J-MASS) and the High Level Architecture (HLA).[*] Architectures require us to maintain standards in the models so they "comply," but the models can still be very independent. A disadvantage is that accurate conceptual linking is trickier to do.

- **Traditional Hierarchies.** A final way to create linkage is through a logical hierarchy or family of models. For example, in military modeling, the results from models of specific systems and physical effects provide inputs to models of engagements among platforms. These, in turn, provide effectiveness values to models of specific missions involving disparate types of platforms. The mission models provide measures such as mission success and resources expended to the models that represent an entire campaign or theater. Although more detailed models usually create data for broader, less detailed models, data doesn't move only in one direction. Higher-level models provide a context for focusing the more detailed models. For example, even though a physical-effects model shows a particular sensor is highly effective within a specific environment, data from higher-level models will show how often that environment occurs.

---

[*] This is an area of active research and thoroughly describing these two architectures is beyond this chapter's scope. For more information on J-MASS, consult J-MASS (1995) or visit the J-MASS web page at http://www.jmass.wpafb.af.mil. For more information on HLA, visit its web page at http://hla.dmso.mil.

This approach creates the most independence among the models—each designed, developed, and built without considering linkage with other models. But it also requires more careful attention to the format and content of information that passes between the models. Although post- and pre-processors help speed data from one model to the next, "sneaker nets" still transfer much of it from hand to hand. More importantly, the context from one model must be appropriate for the context of the next— especially for traditional hierarchies.[*]

For years, modelers have been fighting to achieve balance between two extremes: embedded code and traditional hierarchies. This struggle has a profound impact on M&S data and the architectures which contain and administer it. Independent design, development, and use are in tension with proper physical and conceptual linkages among models. But modelers have begun to examine alternatives and recently have developed possible structures such as confederations, communication protocols, and architectures. Many are still conceptual, so this is a very active area in current research.

Grouping and Separating Data. If your simulation depends on data from models of higher or lower resolution, it must appropriately process this data by adjusting for formats and metrics and by properly grouping (aggregating) and separating (disaggregating) the information. Often, you'll need to generate cases from these other models and, perhaps, fully analyze results before populating your simulation's database. To do so, you'll have to create a series of computational experiments with the high- and low-resolution models and use appropriate statistical methods to derive satisfactory inputs. This isn't easy. For example, our fire-employment model may need the detection range of a particular sensor. High-resolution models may be able to determine the sensor's footprint under various conditions (weather, terrain, operating modes, etc.), but how do we aggregate all of this detail and transform the outputs into something that makes sense to the algorithms in the employment model? In addition, we must trust the results of these other models and their data, as well as understand the models and their limits. The more models you use and the wider their span of control, the greater your challenge in preparing timely, appropriate data.

As you pull together and separate data, you'll affect certain simulation inputs—such as those describing time, geography, objects, and measures—which often depend on each other to some extent. For example, you may combine timing from separate models and find that the total time doesn't allow movement across the geography represented by available terrain data. In this case, you must adjust the algorithms that describe the relationships between time and geography. Let's look at this relationship more closely by considering our firefighting example.

---

[*] Even though we can diagram this hierarchy of models in some concise form (such as a pyramid), the extreme independence of this approach makes it virtually impossible to link the models so cleanly.

- **Time.** Although time occurs continuously and smoothly, simulations often represent only increments of it or treat it as a sequence of discrete events. For example, a detailed model of dropping water from aircraft may show time in very rapid, uneven increments totaling only a few minutes. A more widely scoped model of ground firefighting may simulate time over a few hours of operation. Simulation of all firefighting activities may represent days from the first detection to the final release of all units. Thus, if we simply extrapolate data from a detailed model to a lower-resolution model, the pace may be much too fast, and synchronization may not be possible. For example, a model that represents combined types of firefighting must adjust the rates for fast-moving aircraft to match the much slower pace of ground units. One of the most important aspects of modeling to consider for variable or selectable resolution is determining how to scale time and what this scaling depends on.

- **Geography.** Models with different resolution usually have different scales of geography. As with time, resolution for geography often depends on the movement rate of objects that traverse it. To represent geography, modelers have used elevation, terrain types, and terrain features in variously sized square cells, other regular geometric shapes, or generalized topographical relationships and networks. Registering the different sizes and shapes of geographic regions can be challenging. For example, suppose you represent ground forces with relatively high resolution and air units with far less detail. Because of its own lower resolution, an aircraft will "see" ground units less precisely, so a given unit may not appear in its precise location or elevation. This could present a problem. From the ground unit's point of view (at higher resolution) it may be next to the fire, whereas the aircraft sees it as in the fire! Thus, from its point of view, the aircraft can't drop water precisely on the fire without risk of hitting the ground unit. Furthermore, from the ground unit's perspective, a low-flying aircraft may actually appear to pass through hills even though it clears the terrain in its own frame of reference. Such unrealistic behavior would confuse simulation users and may impair a model's credibility. So you must carefully reconcile geographic perspectives among linked models.

- **Objects.** It's natural to think of objects at various resolutions—from parts to systems to platforms to units of various sizes. For example, a receiver is part of a sensor system that we can place into an airplane, which becomes part of a fleet of reconnaissance aircraft for firefighting, which in turn is part of the assets within firefighting companies and battalions. It's appealing to think of this kind of hierarchical building, but practice reveals it isn't a panacea. For example, once we group firefighting platforms into a company, where do we put the company? At the center of the platforms? In the same place as the company commander or headquarters? What about when we take units apart? If we know where the company is, how do we locate the platforms? Do we use some general template? While these problems may be solved, the solutions require careful attention to detail.

Another way to bring objects together is simply to group them into classes of similar systems or objects. For example, from the wide variety of aircraft types, you could create more specific classes that describe individual types of aircraft in the firefighting fleet. If necessary, individual airplanes could be modeled to reflect unique abilities. This approach allows you to use the advantages of "inheritance"—by which each successive subordinate class has all the attributes and characteristics of superior classes. Thus, a C-47 automatically possesses the attributes of "fixed-wing aircraft." Object inheritance provides flexibility and simplifies the process whenever you decide you must further specify an object (e.g., a "large-tank" C-47 versus a "small-tank" C-47). For example, you could define "large-tank C-47" and "small-tank C-47" as subclasses under "fixed-wing aircraft," or "large tank" and "small tank" as subclasses under "C-47," which is itself a subclass under "fixed wing aircraft." The difficulty here is to determine how the airplanes' attributes aggregate into their composite class and the boundary conditions for that class. When should you introduce a third class of aircraft?

- **Measures.** As we've discussed, linking models to the simulation to provide data requires grouping or separating the measures calculated from the external models. For example, we could use a simplified algorithm in the simulation that relies on putting together detailed performance measures from a higher-resolution model. Modelers have tried this approach by using combined scoring factors to describe the overall effectiveness of various kinds of units. A unit with better equipment and better trained firefighters receives a higher score and thus, performs better. But this aggregated method of scoring typically "hides" significant information (such as the effect of different kinds of equipment or training). To compensate, we could (for instance) add detail using scorecards that include these dimensions or statistical methods, such as response surfaces.

You may think we could test whether we've combined or separated data correctly by taking the results from the lower-resolution model and comparing them with the same case run in the higher-resolution model. This is not as straightforward as it seems. Most approaches appear to be logical but have limited scientific or mathematical basis. In these cases, we can't expect them to be more than loosely consistent across different levels of grouping. For example, we might want to calibrate scaling factors in the low-resolution model with specific cases in the more detailed model. Doing so would use less data from the higher-resolution models and works reasonably well as long as conditions in the less detailed model don't require extrapolations too far beyond the cases for which we've tuned the model. But it's tough to determine the "boundaries" of this type of calibration, and refining them can be time consuming.

Figure 9.7 illustrates the conceptual relationships between more and less detailed mappings and highlights some of the comparison problems. We can't just run the same case through both models and compare outputs. Each set of inputs to the low-resolution model represents a *range* of inputs to the detailed model because the less detailed model has fewer, typically more grouped, pieces of information. The detailed model's inputs for a model of air-to-air combat, for example, may describe many initial states of combatant geometry and speed, whereas the aggregate model's inputs may show only the number of aircraft engaging. Furthermore, if the detailed model provides stochastic outputs, the range of outputs becomes even broader because it expands by the possible distribution for each set of inputs. Still, as long as a low-resolution model's result falls somewhere in this range, it's consistent with the detailed model. If the low-resolution model is also stochastic, we have a tougher problem because we must compare the distribution of outputs from the low-resolution model to the distribution of the detailed model's outputs. All this means you must carefully consider and validate the connections between models and data. However, it can be done successfully, as evidenced by the Institute for Defense Analyses' recreation of the "Battle of 73 Easting" in Desert Storm.

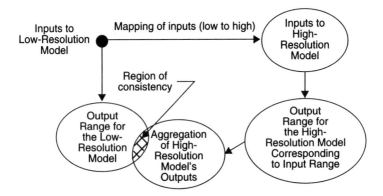

Fig. 9.7.   Getting Consistency from Models with Different Resolutions. To measure the consistency of two models, we must compare the models' input and output mappings. Low-resolution inputs are typically consistent with a range of high-resolution inputs because they combine or leave out inputs required at higher resolution. This range of detailed inputs leads to a range of detailed outputs which we must compare to the single output of the less detailed model (or a range of outputs if the low-resolution model is stochastic).

Although two low-resolution models (such as those intended to capture a fire's full dynamics) may tune similarly to the results of a more detailed model, they'll work differently. Thus, we'll need to use different forms of data and methods of combining them. For example, two high-level models for fighting fires may require rates at which fire units extinguish a fire. Although both models have commonly described data and need to get it from a more detailed model, they can't use the same aggregated data. Why? Each model has its own way of operating on the details, including how assumptions and further grouping affect time, geography, objects, or measures.

Finally, we can't always separate results from a less detailed model into the specific effects in a more detailed model—even for linear models.[*] If functions aren't linear—as in more complicated systems—satisfying consistency would be more difficult. Thus, most aggregations and disaggregations of data in such models are approximate, and it's hard to tell how approximate. Some fields, such as engineering and physics, understand the relationship between aggregate and detailed models, and modelers are researching them to increase their understanding.[†]

Authoritative Sources

First, you'll need to set up controls or standards to make sure agencies *are* authoritative and competent. Of course, particular data items may come from more than one legitimate source. But "more" may not be "better" if you have to reconcile differences in the data they supply. All too often, each organization has scrubbed the data in its own way—for its own model, way of thinking, or specific applications—and often without useful documentation. Even when they have the same rationale, results may differ because the data's meaning is uncertain, or best guesses (with implicit biases) have substituted for unavailable information. Your challenge becomes trying to establish consistency across these sources—almost like validating or certifying the data—which requires clear, authoritative policy.

Second, the sources you choose must be authoritative in the eyes of your users and subscribers. You'll need systematic, rigorous methods for resolving these disagreements—methods everyone considers valid. Your procedures for verifying, validating, and accrediting your models and simulations must cover data sources and ways to maintain currency. They must also consider the complex interdependence among the models and simulations themselves, their databases, and the data architectures they must interact with.

Finally, remember that information from authoritative sources isn't infallible or immutable. You must update it regularly and check it often for validity.

Verifying, Validating and Certifying Data

You may wonder why we discuss verification, validation and certification (VV&C) under "data sources, availability, and accessibility." Bringing several data sources together challenges us to ensure the information is valid, both in terms of

---

[*] See for example, *Cutting Some Trees to See the Forest: On Aggregation and Disaggregation in Combat Models.* Naval Research Logistics, Vol. 42, pp 183–209 (1995) by R. Hillestad and M. Juncosa.

[†] See *Aggregation in Model Ecosystems. Part I: Perfect Aggregation.* in Ecological Modeling, 37 (1987) pp 287–302, by Iwasa, et al.

individual data elements and in the aggregate. Even if some or all of the data comes from a single source, people will question whether it's accurate and precise enough for the represented system and its algorithms. By validating data, we mean ensuring that the data going into the model properly represents what the user intends and works well in the algorithms that manipulate it. By certification, we mean an authority designated by the user or customer must decide the data is valid.

Data must be credible and, eventually, approved for its intended use. How do we gain confidence in all those megabytes, much less impart it to others? We can validate data to some extent by clarifying how it appears to analysts and providing automatic checking. But this is only a beginning. Common efforts that encourage sharing data and critiquing approaches to data generation benefit us a lot and increase cost-effectiveness. In the defense area, we're now spending too much time developing databases and too little testing, reviewing, and documenting our approaches. The quality and timeliness of analysis suffer from organizational barriers and unscientific approaches to data development. In addition, there are few recognized standards, but this situation is steadily improving. Developing standards include the Defense Information Infrastructure (DII) [DISA 1997a], the Joint Technical Architecture (JTA) [DISA 1997b], the Technical Architecture Framework for Information Management (TAFIM) [DISA 1997c], and the Shared Data Environment (SHADE) [DISA 1997d]. And, verification, validation and certification may help remedy these deficiencies or, at least, make them apparent and explicit to future investigators.

For data and data architectures, certification is equivalent to accreditation in M&S, once the model and its databases are both validated.[*] The relationship is a close one at all levels, as discussed earlier. In fact, certifying and accrediting data are intimately connected with designing an architecture. All three will be more effective if they're part of a coherent process.

Be careful not to allow data validation and certification to become mere bureaucratic exercises. Organizations often hinder validation by designating one source as the only supplier of the "blessed" data. Certification authorities under various pressures may not ask hard questions. Thus, honest efforts to establish responsibility, reduce redundancy, and increase data quality too often become unsuccessful (or even counter-productive). The natural limits on availability and accessibility of data add to these problems. Avoiding these pitfalls takes organizational focus and effort, as we discuss below.

9.3.2   Relying on Available and Current Data

Designers may find it far too easy to create models which require data that can't be found or isn't updated often enough. For real-time simulations of firefighting, weather data is a good example of needing to keep data both available

---

[*] A good discussion of verifying, validating, and certifying data is in "Data Verification, Validation, and Certification to Ensure the Quality of Data Used in Modeling," Proceedings of 1994 Society of Computer Simulation (SCS) Summer Computer Conference, SCSSC '94, La Jolla, CA, July 18–20, 1994.

and current. Furthermore, it also exhibits the often complex relationships among data sources you must take into account. Because wind, temperature, humidity, and cloud cover are critical to successful firefighting, the latest forecasts (or accurate models from which you might simulate them) must be available. But your simulation must also get updated forecasts from observations, on-site measurements, recomputed model data, and the like to operate effectively.

Handling the "Unknown and Unknowable"

All too often, simulations require data that's simply unknown or unknowable. We recall the story of a colleague who developed a model but needed a certain data item to complete it. After much research and unsuccessful attempts to determine or derive the value from various sources, he made a best guess and put it in the model's database. Years later, he was happily surprised to find a paper that cited a government publication for the value of that data item, which was very close to what he had estimated. After tracing the data value through many articles and organizations, he discovered a reference to his original work as the authoritative source. You can always create a notional data value which it's impossible (at least for now) to populate.

By available, we mean existing. Data that doesn't exist may be unknown at the moment but discoverable through investigation or research. Or, it may be unknowable because of its subjective nature or great uncertainties associated with it. Most systems we wish to model are complex enough to contain unknown or unknowable objects or processes. You're probably wondering why we don't just avoid them. Unfortunately some are essential to complete analysis. For example, you can't ignore the effect of weather on firefighting. But you also can't know future weather precisely because weather prediction requires better instruments than are currently available to determine precise initial conditions. Also, some things aren't entirely unknown. How firefighting effectiveness declines with lack of sleep may be generally understood, but specific data may be hard to find. Yet, though quantitatively unknowable (with precision) or unknown, weather or fatigue data may be essential to your simulation. In any simulation, much of the scenario information and assumptions about behavior, as well as some physical phenomena, are uncertain and at least partly unknowable. Most simulations contain many so-called "soft factors," which define such aspects as the training, morale, and cohesion of forces; threshold levels at which, for example, fires are contained or escape; how the environment or other systems delay or disrupt actions such as movement; and how other systems work together.

To deal with data that may not exist, you should first ask, Is the data item necessary? If necessary, what can you know about it? Can you know enough to associate it with some thing or some outcome you care about in the real world? For example, the effectiveness of firefighters may depend strongly on how frustrated they are. You may want to design this into a simulation, perhaps by creating a frustration factor. The factor degrades overall performance, but exactly how? What functional form should you use? What values should the factor take on? What are the parameters for the function? And you might ask, does frustration have a linear or a non-linear effect on what firefighters do? Although you can't truly know this data, you may be able to determine which "soft factors" affect subjectively what is "good," "indifferent," or "bad." Don't fool yourself into thinking you can specify such data precisely, but also don't get discouraged and omit unknowables that affect the system. In other words, if you don't know a system's reliability, including five decimal places in your guess on its value does little good, but ignoring it also does little good. Believe it or not, we've seen many cases in which designers choose one of these two extremes.

Unknowns have many of the characteristics unknowables have, but we may eventually make them known through research, alternative analysis, testing, or some other means. For example, you may not know the speed of a particular kind of aircraft when you first build your input database. Yet, later on, tests of the aircraft will provide definitive values. Modelers typically put in data "hooks," hoping that the necessary data will eventually emerge. But you should be careful about using hooks. Make sure you don't assume default values and forget the need to derive a real value. Also, ask yourself, Is this data really necessary, or does it only increase the uncertainty in the overall model? Once you've decided to include a hook, document it carefully; don't leave it to be discovered by unsuspecting users of your model.

As you can see, simulation designers must distinguish and document unknowables from unknowns in the data and then use varying precision, algorithmic processing, and functional forms to match the data's uncertainty and availability. Efforts to analyze the unknowns may produce concrete solutions that eliminate future concerns, but efforts aimed at unknowables will yield only subjective interpretations. Still, both may be necessary to make important data available to a simulation.

Making Data Available

To make data available, you can identify ways to determine the data exactly or create an analytical process that appropriately applies to the simulation what you do know. As we've mentioned, you can make uncertain or unknown data more certain by testing and measuring, doing scientific research, further observing history, or running exercises. Unfortunately, none of these methods makes the unknowable data more rigorous. However, you can apply various analytical approaches to help a simulation use the data despite its deficiencies:

- **Best estimates.** Select various best estimates for values that an unavailable data item can take on. For example, estimate the rate at which a fire unit can put out a fire, which you can only know imprecisely. We don't recommend this approach because it suffers from far too little exploration of the possible values for an item. Still, it's by far the fastest way to come up with results, and we recognize it's often used because of time constraints.

- **Boundary analysis.** Instead of using one or a few best guesses, examine the likely maximum and minimum values to determine what the unavailable data item will do. For example, the firefighting rate is most likely between zero and some number, so run cases with each value to determine the system's extreme behavior and any differences between the values. But boundary analysis may not examine what's likely, and it increases the number of cases you must examine. If you face many such data items, you may have too many interactions for practical analysis. Even with statistical methods, such as experimental design, it's impractical to deal with hundreds of such variables.

- **One-sided arguments.** To reduce greatly the data values you must examine, create an argument with values that clearly exceed or underestimate the potential actual values and observe whether the results meet requirements. For example, select a poor rate for putting out a fire and see if it produces successful results. If it does, this value isn't likely to be critical because the actual rate will probably be better, so the results would be even more favorable. This approach is particularly valuable if the data is highly uncertain. It doesn't require highly accurate data and can reduce the number of cases you need to run. But such arguments are often difficult to frame and rely on creating an effect from extreme values of the data items.

- **Analyzing parameters or sensitivities and exploratory modeling.** Take discrete values across a data item's potential range to determine how one value affects another. Traditionally, we look at how inputs affect outputs, but exploratory analysis broadens this concept to include the effects of outputs on inputs [Brooks 1997]. Use statistical methods, such as experimental design and response-surface methods, along with exploratory modeling to determine the critical values and create a landscape of results. For example, use high, medium, and low firefighting rates. This method typically requires you to run many cases.

- **Distributional analysis.** Use a probability distribution to define the data and Monte Carlo methods to select the actual data values for particular cases. For example, define the firefighting rate as a Poisson distribution with a representative mean. Then, decide how to define the functional form of the distribution as well as the parameter's values. Because this data item is "unavailable," standard statistical methods aren't likely to work. Furthermore, you'll need to run many cases in order to establish statistical stability.

And what are the implications for you as a simulation designer? The preferred approaches for dealing with unavailable data often demand significant time and effort. They require more runs of the model and faster ways to analyze many results. Thus, you must include ways to speed up this kind of processing in order to make the data usable and accurate.

Making Data Current

To make data current, we must be sure it accurately depicts the state of things at an instant of simulated time and synchronizes with the operational models so they can properly calculate results. If model calculations change the data, the changes must propagate back through the data architecture in a synchronous and internally consistent way, so the models have timely new data for the next instant's calculations. It's critical to keep time-sensitive data intact through all these transactions, so it doesn't get corrupted—for example, by delayed or untimely updates that throw off the timeline or event sequence.

Simply put, data must always be as current as the users (and their models) require. The forms of the data, their precision, and the rates for updates must also satisfy users. At the same time, if the required update calculations take longer than the time-step interval in the simulation, we must slow the simulation's time sequence or place more powerful computing engines in the data architecture. We have some techniques for resolving conflicts that arise from these relationships. For example, we can calculate complicated, derived data off-line before or after a run. But these methods apply only to certain cases and have their own limits. More research is needed.

You can use at least two methods to keep data current: update master databases and update data products tailored to users. Of the two, the first is much more critical and requires the most care to avoid mistakes. We recommend backup data architectures that allow parallel computing, plus judiciously employing all the techniques discussed earlier.

Keeping data current mostly has to do with assessing its quality and matching update schemes to the requirements of the M&S structures that will use it. However, many other subtle considerations are necessary [Gray 1993]. For example, tracking and choosing from asynchronous update transactions, the dynamics of the composite metamodels describing the entire architecture, and other complex matters require much more applied research and documentation.

Our main point in discussing currency of data is that, if we document the source and latest update of any data element properly, everyone will likely agree on the validity of a particular model and its supporting database. Although consensus may still prove difficult to develop, it's much easier with well-defined data than without it. Also, the data architecture you design to support a model may well prove integral to verification, validation, and certification of the data (and of the model). Clearly, validity depends on matching the supporting data architecture (as well as the incorporated data itself) to the overarching concept and the specific requirements of the model and the application it serves.

A key to defining complex phenomena is keeping accurate records. How much data to keep, and how to keep it, are the perennial dilemmas confronting us. Generally, you should archive enough data to recall accurately any sequence of events deemed important enough to save. Whenever this rule would create overwhelming amounts of data (for example, in the case of data streams from the Defense Support Program), you should save anything a user asks for or receives, or anything a human operator contributed to.

9.3.3   Relying on Accessible Data

This brings us to a more institutional problem: designating agencies as authoritative sources of certain categories of data and accessing it. In some cases, it's easy to designate authoritative sources with high-quality data, but not always. Analyses are often hampered because we can't determine precisely who the authority is or because some organizations maintain only "raw" data that must be extensively scrubbed or manipulated to be useful. Thus, several user organizations may process data with parallel—and often redundant—efforts. They may waste resources, make different assumptions, and use different methods that may alter data content, which can lead to erroneous or irreconcilable results. For example, government agencies or contractors may manipulate raw trafficability data in various ways to derive very different travel rates. Which, if any, of these is "right" for a particular analysis is very hard to say. The key to preventing such unnecessary duplication of effort is coherent policy, based on sound standards and practices for producing data, as well as data architectures that make repositories useful and self-supporting. Just identifying sources often expends a lot of effort. The Defense Modeling and Simulation Office's M&S Resource Repository can help. Visit http://www.dmso.mil on the web for more information.

Dealing with sensitive, proprietary, or classified data automatically creates access problems. Some data may be highly classified and available only to military planners such as the Joint Staff. Data on the effectiveness of advanced systems may be accessible to only a few analysts. Clearly, sensitive data must be secure, but secure systems often impede analysis. This means data (hence, analysis) can't easily undergo broad peer reviews, and comparative analyses are more difficult across different analysis organizations and access approaches. Also, analyses are less responsive when they encounter delays in getting data or information on its context, assumptions, or limits.

Sometimes, organizations whose only product is data may impede access to it because they don't want a more open exchange. Their data becomes "organizational stock"—the substance that gives the organization its power and authority. Furthermore, organizations that are the "blessed" source of data may find what they've been asked to supply is simply unavailable (unknowable or unknown), imprecisely knowable, or not derived as well as they'd like or as advertised. The data may contain uncomfortable implications or known errors. For any of these "other" reasons, an organization may restrict access.

What should we learn from these problems with accessing data? Mainly that we can't simply create a program that requires data to be available. We must try early on to determine that it's also accessible.

Standardizing Data Formats

It's useful to standardize data, as long as standardizing doesn't interfere with collecting, combining, storing, maintaining, and retrieving it. In fact, data standards vary, and algorithms convert one form to another, depending on the intended use of the final product. The Defense Modeling and Simulation Office is creating standards to support common data representations across models, simulations, and command, control, communications, computers, and intelligence (C4I) systems as part of DOD's M&S Master Plan. Visit http://www.dmso.mil on the web for more information.

Primary users tend to define standards that match their requirements. A good example is the National Imagery and Mapping Agency (NIMA), formerly the Defense Mapping Agency, which uses and provides geographical and cartographical data. Because their work is exhaustive and impractical to alter, their methods of storing and retrieving this data have become fairly standard. (Several notable exceptions, such as cartographic data standards based on the Army's Hex-based models of battlefield encounters, have become increasingly dysfunctional.) Thus, data standards created by the maintainers of master databases often become de facto industry standards because their methods of deriving the data are unique. However, if other main users ask for the data in a different form to meet their needs and are willing to help defray the costs involved, they ought to be able to get it (or at least get data that can be easily modified into the right form).

Choosing an internal standard which suits those who maintain a master database makes good sense, but the maintainers must be careful not to set aside data or formats which potential users may want. If you operate a functional data repository, you must closely coordinate data standards with users and with other repositories that maintain related data, so the data will flow well throughout the network. We recognize, of course, that simulation requirements don't drive data repositories. In fact, simulation needs usually aren't part of their charter. Still, if you operate a data repository, you'll sometimes need to compromise by giving up internal standards for ones more suited to your customers.

Standardizing data formats has many advantages and disadvantages. Standard formats and procedures make storing and updating data much easier. Eventually, they will also allow us to convert data readily between standard formats. Still, whenever a standard keeps M&S structures from working right, we must redefine, reengineer, or even abandon the offending standard in favor of a better one.

Often, the repository architecture itself dictates what data standards will be, but again, if the repository structure doesn't work properly, we must redesign and rebuild it and any dysfunctional standards it may have caused. Carefully using repository metamodels may help anticipate structures that will misfire and suggest effective ways to migrate data and avoid such problems. However, controlling how repositories evolve and providing for orderly growth in abilities are never-ending tasks, which require careful definition, sound infrastructure design, and appropriate staffing.

Recent developments in M&S generally, and in the technology for graphical user interfaces in particular, strongly suggest a potentially advantageous way to store a lot of environmental data in readily retrievable forms. The technique would create highly detailed synthetic environments that can host complex situations and equally detailed actors. Situational and scenario-related data would flow into modular, interactive, environmental models which together would make up a virtual universe. The Joint Staff has already started such a program (see DoDD 5000.59, Modeling and Simulation Management, 4 January 1996), and the military services are all following DoDD 5000.59 policy guidance. Closer to home, other studies over the past several years by the NORAD/U.S. Space Command's Center for Aerospace Analysis suggest that such methods would help reuse complex code and greatly simplify verification, validation, and accreditation of models and verification, validation, and certification of data. Still, these methods are in their infancy, so much research remains to be done. Furthermore, they don't yet deal with the data's appropriateness for a particular application. If people do build a continent-wide network of interactive data repositories, they hope users will come—as paying customers.

Procedures for Subscriber Services

The National Imagery and Mapping Agency is a useful model for subscriber services because it has been providing comprehensive data subscriber services for years. However, this paradigm would only begin to answer the problem of easing access requirements for users. Data systems based on this paradigm will have to include many types of data (other than maps), as well as to define and develop widely varying services (some undreamed of, as described above). Simply stated, potential subscribers would have to establish accounts and then work with repository managers to define the services they want. Most of these services would be in tailored databases for various customers—entire databases or just access to data sets at the repository.

As the repository network develops abilities and sophistication, agencies will sometimes produce promotional material that caters to untapped markets. NIMA already offers such services and prospectuses. We must also watch for agencies who, for various reasons, try to remain anonymous or restrict their knowledge, as well as those who own specialized data.

Of course, these tailored services aren't free. If you manage a repository, one of your biggest challenges will be to decide how much to charge for its services. Another will be to keep paying customers happy by allowing them to influence new products or help customize established ones. Some commercial firms (especially Silicon Graphics Inc. and Autometric) have successfully addressed these issues, so they may be useful case studies.

This relationship between users and providers is embryonic (except perhaps in certain closed communities such as the National Security Agency). Thus, it's hard to forecast in detail. However, users tend to participate in managing repositories only because they think they must in order to get the data they need. Theater warfighters, for example, have already dictated many requirements for space-information systems—first in DESERT STORM and more recently in developing programs such as the Theater Support Operations Cell (TSOC). TSOC is an M&S-based, distributed system that can convey sophisticated but understandable information on battle situations to regional commanders and warfighters. See U.S. Space Command (1996) for a more detailed description of TSOC.

9.4   Data Structures and Distributed Architectures

Centralizing all types of M&S data usually isn't possible logistically and typically doesn't make economic sense. Thus, we build networks to connect authoritative sources, M&S centers, and users. In fact, the Defense Modeling and Simulation Office is already building a catalog of websites that offer an off-the-shelf architecture as a candidate solution. You'll need to understand the relationships among these communities if you're going to define networks that connect all M&S participants into a cost-effective, useful system of data repositories. Designing distributed data architectures is difficult and probably merits a volume of its own. Still, we can establish two clear principles: repositories of functional data should be near where the functions typically take place, and users should rank high among authoritative sources. We should also design connecting networks to support these basic relationships. The complexity of the desired architecture depends on the model, its application, and the required data. To help you make this decision, we'll look at the flow of data into the model, some alternative ways to structure the data, and some key issues in networking.

9.4.1   Data Flow Through the Model

Ways to Get Data into a Model

Figure 9.8 shows the way data typically flows into a model from temporary input files that come from a master database and from users. Data flows into the master database from controlled sources, including other organizations or groups, and many users may access it. Programs for accessing databases collect, group, and format data before creating a user's baseline subset of the original source databases. Actual model input files are drawn from the user's database and may include various excursions from the baseline. Users may also provide information, such as when they want to analyze outputs or what options they want. Users must not be allowed to change the master database directly. For any particular study, the baseline database should be "frozen" throughout the effort. Finally, the files a model uses typically remain in archives as documentation and sources for repeatable experiments.

How Data Flows Out from a Model

We also have to manage a model's output (see Fig. 9.9). It may contain one file or many files with the types of output discussed in Sec. 9.2.2. Often, these files appear as formatted text or numbers, but they may also be compressed into binary output to save disk space. Post-processing then reduces, groups, averages, and otherwise organizes this raw data into a form analysts can work with—a critically important part of analyzing and interpreting data. After post-processing, the organized data may flow into graphic animations, charts, or printed tables. At least some subset of the output data typically goes into archives for reference, along with the input data and run description. Post-processing often uses data from several model runs and compares or contrasts the results.

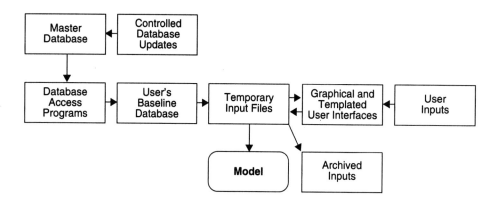

Fig. 9.8.   **How Data Flows into a Model.** Models get data from multiple sources, such as master databases and users. They also help analysts check the data for errors and may improve input through graphical user interfaces.

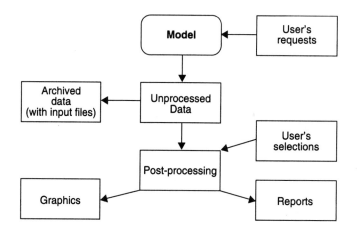

Fig. 9.9.   **How Data Flows out from a Model.** Output processes allow us to compare results, help archive cases, and extend the outputs through post-processing.

Physical Interactions between the Data and the Model

The physical structures of the data and model are also closely linked. More importantly, once you've defined the physical form of the input, changes to the model may drive new data or different groupings, which means the processes, files, and data structure may need to change. So may the interfaces used to manipulate the data. Unfortunately, this potential "ripple effect" often inhibits change and flexibility in modeling. To design a flexible model, you must also create flexible input tools and structures.

Outputs are also associated with the model's particular objects, attributes, processes, and structures. Changing any of these usually leads to new or modified outputs. The post-processors which operate on that data may also need to change. Furthermore, new outputs may make future model runs incompatible with and incomparable to previous ones. Thus, output data and its processes also strongly constrain changes to a model. You must consider the entire modeling process—from developing data to generating output—whenever you think about changing a model or developing a new one that can adapt to analysts' future needs.

Including the Data Dictionary with the Data

As we have discussed, data has context. To interpret numbers, we must know, among other things, how to read the numbers, what they measure, and how they relate to one another. The data dictionary gives us this interpretive information. Including the data dictionary in our data architecture permits us to check and manipulate the data more accurately and efficiently. It should contain enough information to define clearly the input and output variables, what they mean to the model, their allowable values, their units of measure (velocity in km/sec or mph for example), and whether they are required or optional.

9.4.2   Database Structure

So how do you structure the data to make sure the flow through the model is as smooth as possible? You have to consider various data characteristics—maintaining its overall simplicity, controlling its accuracy and appropriateness, and creating sufficiently powerful ways to manipulate and interpret it. One guideline for structuring data arrays is to follow real-world patterns whenever possible because, in a world growing more complex by the minute, no other reliable guide is available. Such structures also help you track cause-effect relationships. Therefore, organize your data structures to mimic patterns found in the real world in order to provide crucial insight into the types of transactions the described objects may undertake. For example, store topographical data as digitized maps but represent ballistics and orbital dynamics as observations, element sets, and the physics-based algorithms astrodynamicists use. At the same time, match your approach to the form of data you're aggregating. For example, don't store a sine wave in thousands of observations; instead, store it as an equation coupled with three parameters: a point, the amplitude, and the periodicity. Also, make sure you match the organizational structure for given sets of data to the requirements of subscribers who use them the most—or those likely to do so in the future. You should also consider creating a structure that provides easy access to the most refined form of the data, so you can better maintain the database, debug complex models, and verify, validate, and accredit your simulation. Potential structures include flat files, object-oriented data, and commercial off-the-shelf (COTS) and government off-the-shelf (GOTS) database-management systems.

Flat Files

One way to store data is in files that contain only data, with no embedded processing methods, explicit external linkages, or explicit internal structure—what developers call flat files or (if they're readable) text files. By using flat files as an interface, you can achieve efficient run times and control the configuration of a model's input data. Rather than using data management to search and organize the data model each time the model runs, you can do it once to create flat files for multiple runs. Furthermore, you can efficiently control configurations of the model cases by storing the flat files with the case output and description files, rather than pointing to an independent database-management system. If the model controls the format of the file, it may specify a fixed or stream format. Under a fixed format, it designates locations for each piece of data; stream format specifies only the order in which the data will appear. Fixed and stream formats may appear in the same flat file. You may also embed data-dictionary information usually as header lines describing the name, location, and domain of each piece of data in the file. But make sure the model or other processing software can interpret this information.

Object-oriented Data

Object-oriented models will most likely need object-oriented databases to work right. If we use newer techniques of data modeling and design the virtual data-storage architecture as a synthetic data environment, we can make interactions with the data structure very convenient. Such synthetic environments tend to need many transactions. But the speed, power, and low cost of new computers and data-storage media can readily overcome the potential for delay or asynchronous behavior. As discussed previously, graphical user interfaces can also make this kind of architecture intuitive and easy to understand. Also, many categories of data depend heavily on one another, such as those for fighting fires or managing a battle. In these cases, flat files and relational systems are unwieldy and impractical, so object orientation is an attractive alternative. Object-oriented databases are especially valuable for technical or engineering applications in which the data elements are less well-defined or are variable. That's because we need to develop the cross-linking rules governing an object or family of objects only once; then, we can reuse them in applications that follow object-oriented behavioral rules. Another advantage is the ability to represent object structure (particularly hierarchical structure) far more naturally, making it easier to verify correctness and eliminate redundancy. However, when object orientation and inheritance aren't useful (in geographic or atmospheric data, for example), flat-file representations can be combined with object-oriented structures by applying metadata relationships to the design of the interfaces between the two systems. For example, as an object (such as a bulldozer) modifies terrain, it operates in a virtual environment generated from the flat terrain files. The terrain changes produced are then converted to digital form and used to update the terrain files. Object-oriented structures tend to be highly modular, so we only have to reengineer the modules directly affected by the change and adjust the surrounding interfaces in order to create the new structure. In practice, this modular design greatly limits the amount of code (or data rules) that need rewriting whenever software evolves or migrates to new hardware.

Database Management System

A database management system (DBMS) controls how a repository manipulates and stores data. Good DBMS techniques lessen the space needed to store the data and the time to access it. The DBMS also delineates basic data management from the model's specialized needs. People who don't know the model can maintain the system, which may contain data for more than one model. Commercial systems for database management have tools that support entering, documenting, and changing data to maintain the database's accuracy and internal consistency. Proper archiving allows previous versions of the database to be reconstructed and protects the database from accidental loss.

The most mature commercial data systems are relational, meaning they're based on tables. Each column of the table represents an attribute on which data is collected. Each row of a table pertains to a specific entity. The entries in the columns of each row are that entity's attributes. For example, a table of airbase data would have a row for each airbase. The attributes of each airbase would be its name, number, lengths of its runways, etc. A relational database is a collection of tables. The relational management system provides procedures that operate on the tables, remaining consistent by adhering to "normal forms" and by enforcing "domains" for each attribute. Domain checking prevents operations on incompatible attributes and makes sure the entries for each attribute have the correct format and type. These relational systems also have techniques to reduce storage requirements and speed up access to the tables. Examples are compression, hashing, indexing, and sorting, which go on without the user seeing them.

The database-management system may contain all or some of the data a model uses and is most often organized as a relational database. Typically, users type control parameters and other data directly to the flat files, whose structure matches the model's. Users can edit these flat files with a word processor or with tools and graphic user interfaces the data-management system provides.

The relationship between the management system, data arrays, and model structure determines how easily you can use and modify a model. If the model's structure doesn't match the system's relational structure, extracting data to create the model's flat files can be complicated. For example, a squadron's attributes are stored in several relational tables for the airbase, aircraft type, deployment, and so on. In this case, a model that captures all of the squadron's data as a single object will need a data array consistent with that object. Creating such an array could be complicated and time consuming. In these cases, you might prefer an object-oriented data structure and database-management system.

9.4.3   Networking of Data Repositories

Because a single repository usually isn't practical for all types of data, you'll need to network your repositories to some degree. The key question will be: "How many repositories do I need to provide all potential users cost-effective services?" To answer this question, you'll need to consider how the repositories will work together physically, logically, and electronically.

Distributed vs. Centralized Architectures for Repositories

You'll need to centralize somewhat to get economies of scale and valid data maintenance, but only if an application requires it. Networking technologies blur the idea of centralization because physical or geographic centralization may be replaced by logical or virtual centralization. Examples of centralized architectures that make sense are those for space activities in Colorado Springs, Army wargaming at Huntsville, Alabama, and Fort Leavenworth, Kansas, and Navy wargaming at Newport, Rhode Island, and Dahlgren, Virginia. The rest of the network—users and smaller centers of knowledge such as universities—will almost certainly remain distributed. Thus, transmission speeds, bandwidths, and buffer capacities will become key to the best designs.

Within such a network structure, you can make M&S data much more useful by imposing conventions on inputs and outputs. One is to enter authoritative data only once. For example, don't separately enter the total number of aircraft when you can get it by counting the individual aircraft types of the entered squadrons. Often, designers enter data several times for simplicity, but keeping the repetitive data synchronized causes problems downstream. Graphical techniques, cross-correlating data efficiently, integrating data with data dictionaries, supplying database functions, and processing data output allow us to prepare data faster, manipulate it less, and facilitate verification and validation.

Designing and Creating a Network

Network design may become massive and complex, and design errors are very expensive to correct. The original success of the ARPANET (starting in 1969) set the stage for rapid enhancements to network technology. From these beginnings, we've seen recent innovations: the Defense Information Infrastructure (DII), the Global Command and Control System, the Defense Simulation Internet, and communications architectures/protocols such as the Synchronous Optical Network (SONET), which provides a medium for services such as bandwidth on demand and other features. These new approaches seem likely to make routine network operations truly cost-effective. (See DISA [1997] or JWID [1996] for more information)

The growth of M&S and of data repositories is beginning to resemble (maybe even clone) the Internet and the World Wide Web. Certainly recent trends in distributed modeling—especially in redesigns of the military services' architectures for communications and information management—strongly suggest encouraging growth won't be a problem. Instead, growth will be explosive well before the turn of the century, so we'll need to channel it into productive, cost-effective programs. As systems grow, so will the metadata and data metamodels needed to "feed" them.

9.5   Designing Information Storage and Archives

Because information will probably be more valuable and easier to store than the data it's derived from, you'll need to build extensive, capable information storage into your data architecture.

9.5.1   Information vs. Data

The balance between these two forms of knowledge has yet to develop fully, but several trends are evident. First, the older data becomes, the more likely it will be pared down to its essential information in order to save storage space and enable cross-referencing among archives. Second, messages usually convey information rather than data, and people will tend to save messages instead of data. Finally, data interpretation is usually intuitive, complex, highly dependent on human skill, or some combination of the three. In such cases, statistical simplifications (such as averages or correlations) or other methods are used to derive information from data that tends to supplant the data itself. Later, independent sources of information confirm (or deny) the appropriateness of these methods.

9.5.2   Information Models

War games, actual combat, and similar cases often contain non-linear effects, stochastic phenomena, or unpredictable circumstances. Thus, models may have to approximate certain transactions. Examples are combat outcomes in complex tank battles or many-on-many air engagements. In such cases, we typically use information models that don't predict outcomes precisely but are accurate in an actuarial sense. Such models use parameters that are generally accurate over ranges but are often derived empirically. These models depend on a lot of observed data and help us gain insight into complex, unpredictable phenomena which otherwise can't be studied. Their utility and the lack of workable alternatives usually offset their imprecision. In addition, iteration can correct many of their imperfections.

9.5.3   Analyzing and Validating Information

To validate information, we typically compare it with actual events, either after the fact, or by fusing data from several sources as events develop. A good example of the latter is using fragmentary missile-launch information from space to cue Patriot batteries during DESERT STORM. But data fusion may also fail, as in the abortive attempts to locate and destroy transporter-erector-launcher vehicles, also in DESERT STORM. Of course, better fusion methods currently under development may have solved this problem, or could solve similar problems in the future.

9.5.4   Enduring vs. Transient Information

To illustrate the difference between these two types of information, terrain models (and similar descriptors of slowly changing phenomena) tend to be enduring, whereas radar displays (and other dynamic interpretations) tend to be transient. However, many types of information (such as in-flight projections of ballistic-missile trajectories) don't fit consistently into either category. In such cases, whether we keep or discard information depends heavily on immediate needs. If we discard something and later find it useful, we may develop procedures for collecting similar information in analogous situations. With experience, it becomes easier to distinguish important information. But you'll usually want to collect too much information rather than too little, another reason for overdesigning the size and ability of your repository.

To manage information in a data repository, you'll need to start with what users want gathered and stored. This set of requirements should correspond to the metadata structure that allows you to fill in the actual data as it becomes available. But you must temper your approach by recognizing that, initially, no one knows for sure what information will prove essential. Again, in your prototypes, develop as much of the data and metadata as you can in concert with the user; then, gradually pare away the less useful data.

9.5.5   Evolutionary or Iterative Design for Data Repositories

All the above complexities virtually dictate iterative design, and the success of projects such as the Theater Support Operation Cell have shown how well it works. Of course, iterative design and refinement may seem never-ending, but they're powerful methods and often converge rapidly. If you don't introduce inadvertent errors or improper estimations, you can get acceptable accuracy in the type of data and the data itself in months, not years. Also, if you record accurate audit trails and document results at each stage, you can achieve greater accuracies in the future by simply picking up the iterative design where you left off.

9.5.6   What To Keep and for How Long?

These are also trial-and-error decisions, but you can follow one basic rule: keep what is operationally useful for as long as it's relevant to current or future operations. Work out this relevancy with users, but if you're in doubt, save it (at least temporarily). We're not suggesting here that you save everything. As you become familiar with the experimental regimes you're working with, you'll be able to determine more confidently what is useful and, therefore, significantly reduce storage requirements for historical data.

Also, do your best to overdesign your repository architectures to meet future needs. This will allow you to add newer, more efficient data-storage media to existing architectures without disrupting how they work, as well as to access older media without major changes. It's also becoming easier to edit and update databases of all types because of advances in powerful, low-cost computers, which can manipulate large blocks of data in near real time. The future appears bright, as well, because these trends appear to be well-established, are likely to sustain themselves, and may even accelerate in the future.

9.6   Summary

The difficult challenge in simulation is linking the conceptual interactions of reality, the problem under investigation, the model, and the data. More and more, data defines the representational structure, thus constraining people who use the model. The distinction between code and data blurs, and critical assumptions may lurk within the data. Models are sometimes designed for data that is unavailable or very difficult to get. Some models require a broad range and large amount of data. Others may require smaller data sets but a lot of detail. Producing data may be very time consuming. We've noted the extra effort needed for a simulation that will serve multiple purposes across a range of "realities" and problems. This kind of simulation demands more from its original designers and developers, as well as from later users and enhancers, to ensure that the data remains appropriate.

Traditional approaches to simulation often concentrate on designing and developing algorithms while neglecting or putting off how to handle data. Analyzing data before designing your model will help you decide what to simulate and how to represent it. You'll learn whether certain forms of data are critical to success or if you can get what you need from other sources. For example, you might gather data for how fast a fire moves based on undergrowth but find out (using sensitivity analysis) that undergrowth matters little compared to the wind speed or the density of trees. In this case, analyzing data first provides an important modeling insight that reduces the simulation's complexity. Furthermore, you learn something fundamental about fires even before using the model (although building the model may have motivated this learning). Thus, if you postpone or ignore data issues, you may have to tediously rework the simulation design or eventually be unable to apply the simulation.

Of course, short schedules and small budgets for analysis complicate these problems. Once you've worked hard to build a database, you'll be reluctant to change it, and people will use it for inappropriate situations. Users may not have time or money to develop a new database or seriously examine the existing one for needed changes. Rather, they judge it good enough and change only a few parameters of interest during a new analysis. In fact, experience shows that many users of model databases often don't know the many assumptions behind the data, settings for parameters, or how widely a database should apply. Obviously, this can lead to seriously flawed results and recommendations if you're unaware of the database's limits or choose to ignore some known limits under pressure from project deadlines. Analysts become the ultimate "repository" of how to interpret and apply the data, learned from years of experience. Managing databases is therefore a key to using such models in analysis.

Furthermore, you may need to do basic research in order to represent some features (such as command and control or the interactions among systems and the environment) and to decide how much of this representation should be in the model or the data. To capture the breadth of interactions in some models, you'll need to group details and show how and why you grouped them. At the same time, you must consider the sources of data to prevent the model from relying on unavailable or inaccessible information. As data accumulates, model users will need tools for managing and manipulating such wide varieties, styles, and formats of data. Other data-management challenges include developing data from other models, organizational barriers to data sharing, maintaining data currency, defining standards, and designing systems for storing and archiving.

Despite complexities and problems, we can be optimistic about creating or finding the data we need and then managing it effectively. Data-production techniques are better than ever, and high-density storage capacity is growing and becoming more cost-effective day by day. Models are also becoming increasingly sophisticated in their use of data. Organized efforts to standardize data are solving problems we presented in the case study that opens this chapter. High quality database architectures and maintenance tools are now available in commercial- or government-off-the-shelf packages. They're taking full advantage of these positive trends and offering analytical modelers many options for storing and retrieving data. As a result, national standards developers and oversight councils have been able to base standards for data architectures on the best archetypical systems and products. Of course, we must still make sure data is valid, accessible, accurate, and compatible across models using shared or distributed databases. But today we do have cost-effective tools and disciplined methods; tomorrow, they'll likely be even better.

References

The Analytic Sciences Corporation, Arthur Gelb (ed.). 1979. *Applied Optimal Estimation.* Cambridge, MA: The Massachusetts Institute of Technology Press.

AT&T Quality Steering Committee. 1992a. *Data Quality Functions.* Holmdel, NJ: AT&T Bell Labs.

AT&T Quality Steering Committee. 1992b. *Describing Information Processes: The FIP Technique.* Holmdel, NJ: AT&T Bell Labs.

AT&T Quality Steering Committee. 1992c. *Improving Data Accuracy: The Data Tracking Technique.* Holmdel, NJ: AT&T Bell Labs.

Bagby, CDR J.L., USN, Professor T.D. Burnett, et. al. 1977. *Naval Operational Analysis.* 2nd ed. Annapolis, MA: Naval Institute Press.

Bankes, Steven. 1994. "Computational Experiments and Exploratory Modeling." *CHANGE.* Vol. 7, No. 1.

Battilega, John A. and Judith K. Grange (eds.). 1978. *The Military Applications of Modeling.* Wright-Patterson Air Force Base, OH: Air Force Institute of Technology Press.

Bennett, Bart E. 1989. *A Conceptual Design for the Model Integration and Management System.* Santa Monica, CA: RAND N-2645-R6.

Blazek, Linda W. 1993. *Quality Databases for Informed Decision Making.* Pittsburgh, PA: Alcoa Technical Center.

Brooks, Arthur, Steven Bankes, and Bart E. Bennett. 1997. *Weapons Mix and Exploratory Analysis*. Santa Monica, CA: RAND DB-210/1-AF.

DISA. 1994. *Command and Control (C2) Core Data Model. Version 2*. DOD Information Systems Agency, Joint Interoperability Engineering Organization, Center for Standards.

DISA. 1997a. *The Defense Information Infrastructure Master Plan, Version 6.0*. DOD Information Systems Agency, Joint Interoperability Engineering Organization Center for Standards. http://www.disa.mil/diimp.

DISA. 1997b. *The Joint Technical Architecture, Version 2.0*. (Second Draft). DOD Information Systems Agency, Joint Interoperability Engineering Organization Center for Standards. http://www.itsi.disa.mil.

DISA. 1997c. *The Technical Architecture Framework for Information Management, Version 3.0*. DOD Information Systems Agency, Joint Interoperability Engineering Organization Center for Standards. http://www.itsi.disa.mil.

DISA. 1997d. *Shared Data Environment*. DOD Information Systems Agency, Joint Interoperability Engineering Organization Center for Standards. http://spider.osfl.disa.mil/dii/shade/shade_page.html.

DMSO. 1997. Data Verification, Validation, and Certification. Unpublished draft to be published by the Defense Modeling and Simulation Office.

DOD. 1995. *Modeling and Simulation (M&S) Master Plan*. Department of Defense, Undersecretary of Defense for Acquisition and Technology, CoD 5000.59-P. http://www.dmso.mil/docslib/mspolicy/msmp/.

Davis, Paul K. 1992. *Generalizing Concepts and Methods of Verification, Validation, and Accreditation (VV&A) for Military Simulations*. Santa Monica, CA: RAND R-4249-ACQ.

Davis, Paul K. 1993. "Guidance for Model Developers and Managers Regarding Verification, Validation, and Accreditation of Military Models." *Proceedings of the 1993 Multiconference on Simulation*, Society for Computer Simulation.

Davis, Paul K., and Richard Hillestad. 1993. "Families of Models That Cross Levels of Resolution: Issues for Design, Calibration and Management" in G.W. Evans, M. Mollaghasemi, E.C. Russell, and W.E. Biles, eds., *Proceedings of the 1993 Winter Simulation Conference*.

Davis, Paul K., Richard Hillestad, and Natalie Crawford. 1997. "Capabilities for Major Regional Conflicts" in *Strategic Appraisal 1997: Strategy and Defense Planning for the 21st Century*. Edited by Z. Khalilzad and D. Ochmanek. Santa Monica, CA: RAND MR-826-AF.

DIS Steering Committee. 1994. *The DIS Vision: A Map to the Future of Distributed Simulation, Version 1*.

Gad, Ariav, and J. Clifford, ed. 1986. *New Directions for Database Systems*. Norwood, NJ: Ablex Publishing Corporation.

Galway, Lionel and Christopher Hanks. 1996. *Data Quality Problems in Army Logistics: Classification, Examples, and Solutions*. Santa Monica, CA: The RAND Corporation, MR-721-A.

Gamble, Allan E., et. al., 1987. *Data Input and Methodology Manual*. Vector in Commander (VIC) Documentation, Ann Arbor, MI: Vector.

Gray, Jim and Andreas Reuter. 1993. *Transaction Processing: Concepts and Techniques*. San Francisco, CA: Morgan Kaufmann Publishers.

Harrington, Jan L. 1988. *Relational Database Management for Microcomputers*. New York, NY: Holt, Rinehart, and Winston, Inc.

Headquarters, Department of the Army. 1993. *Applications of Verification, Validation, and Accreditation on Army Models and Simulations*. DA Pamphlet 5-11

Hillestad, Richard J., and Mario L. Juncosa. 1995. "Cutting Some Trees to See the Forest: On Aggregation and Disaggregation in Combat Models." *Naval Research Logistics*, Vol. 49, pp. 183–208.

Hillestad, Richard J. and Louis Moore. 1996. *The Theater-Level Campaign Model: A Research Prototype for a new Generation of Combat Analysis Model*. Santa Monica, CA: RAND MR-388-AF/A.

Hillestad, Richard J., Bart E. Bennett, and Louis Moore. 1996. *Modeling for Campaign Analysis: Lessons for the Next Generation of Models*. Santa Monica, CA: RAND MR-710-AF.

Hughes, Wayne P. Jr., ed. 1984. *Military Modeling*. 2nd Ed., Military Operations Research Society.

J-MASS. 1995. *The Joint Modeling and Simulation System (J-MASS): A Technical Overview of the J-MASS Architecture*. Wright Patterson AFB, OH: J-MASS Program Office, ASC/XREM.

JWID. 1996. *Joint Warrior Interoperability Demonstration for 1996, Assessment Report*. http://www.army.mil/jwid96.htm.

Knepell, Peter and Deborah Arangro. 1993. *Simulation Validation: a Confidence Assessment Methodology*. Los Alamitos, CA: IEEE Society Press.

Law, Averill and D. Kelton. 1991. *Simulation Modeling and Analysis*. 2nd Ed. NY: McGraw Hill.

Loral Federal Systems Staff and SWSD/SMX. 1995. *Space Command and Control Architectural Infrastructure (SCAI), Air Force/STARS Demonstration Project, Experience Report*. Gaithersburg, MD and Peterson Air Force Base, CO.

Loudon, Kenneth C. 1986. "Data Quality and Due Process in Large Interorganizational Record Systems." *Comm of the ACM*. Vol. 29, No. 1, pp. 4–11.

Martin, Daniel.1986. *Advanced Data Management*. NY: John Wiley and Sons.

Meadow, Charles T. 1976. *Applied Data Management*. NY: John Wiley and Sons.

Parsaye, K., M. Chignell, S Khoshafian, and H. Wong. 1989. *Intelligent Databases*. NY: John Wiley and Sons, Inc.

Redman, Thomas C. 1992. *Data Quality*. New York, NY: Bantam Books.

Rothenberg, Jeff and S. Novain. 1994. *The RAND Advanced Simulation Language Project's Declarative Modeling Formalism (DMOD)*. Santa Monica, CA: RAND MR-376-ARPA.

Rothenberg, Jeff. 1996. "Metadata to Support Data Quality and Longevity." *Proceedings of the First IEEE Metadata Conference.* Silver Spring, MD.

Rothenberg, Jeff. 1997a. *A Discussion of Data Quality for Verification, Validation, and Certification (VV&C) of Data to be Used in Modeling.* Santa Monica, CA: RAND PM-709-DMSO.

Rothenberg, Jeff, Walter Stanley, George Hanna, and Mark Ralston. 1997b. *Data Verification, Validation, and Certification (VV&C): Guideline for Modeling and Simulation.* Santa Monica, CA: RAND PM-710-DMSO.

Saaty, Thomas L. 1986. "Axiomatic Foundations of the Analytic Hierarchy Process." *Management Science.* Vol. 32, No. 7.

Sackman, H. 1974. *Delphi Assessment: Expert Opinion, Forecasting, and Group Process.* Santa Monica, CA: RAND R-1283-PR.

Tichy, Walter F. 1985. "RCS: A System for Version Control," in *Software: Practice and Experience* 15,7.

U.S. Space Command. 1996. *Theater Support Operations Cell Program Management Plan.* Peterson Air Force Base, CO. (For copies, contact HQ United States Space Command, Peterson Air Force Base, CO 80916.)

Veit, C.T. and M. Callero. 1993. *Criteria for Validating Human Judgements and Developing Behavioral Representation Models.* Santa Monica, CA: RAND P-7823.

Wang, Richard and Henry Kon. 1992a. *Toured Total Data Quality Management (TDQM).* Cambridge, MA: TDQM Research Program, Sloan School of Management, MIT.

Wang, Richard, Henry Kon, and Stuart Madnick. 1992b. *Data Quality Requirements Analysis and Modeling.* Cambridge, MA: TDQM Research Program, Sloan School of Management, MIT.

Zdonik, Stanley and D. Maier, ed. 1990. *Readings in Object Oriented Database Systems.* San Mateo, CA: Morgan Kaufman Publishers, Inc.

CHAPTER 10

Implementing Models and Simulations in Hardware and Software

Tom Fall, *Lockheed Martin Western Development Laboratories*

Modeling and simulation (M&S) activities move from a vision to a concrete form. The model is the vision of what we want to capture of the system's behavior, which depends on the model's intended use (the experimental frame for the source system, as defined in Chap. 3). The simulation carries out this vision. In this chapter, we'll move beyond system characteristics and plans to creating a simulator that will express the appropriate behavior. The following chapters will address how to ensure the simulator works and the information gleaned is correct and usable.

If you're a manager or a person who must implement a model, you'll find out here how experienced modelers have coped with pitfalls and succeeded. You'll discover the most typical issues and sources of information concerning simulation tasks.

Trading Precision against Cost

In earlier chapters, we've been matching the modeling vision to the characteristics of the model we needed to capture. For the source system, we've developed an experimental frame (the conditions to be observed) and a model (the logical structure that captures the source system in the experimental frame). Now, we're ready to develop the simulation, which means we're matching our goals to our resources. To say we're **matching** implies that we have something to trade off. In simulation, we'll trade level of detail against amount of resources. Figure 10.1 shows that, as we increase the level of detail, we increase the number of simulation components—the software entities that we'll have to design, build, and exercise—at a much faster rate. This graphic shows how we break out the source system into components and functions. At the same time, we have to divide time or space into smaller units that match the more detailed components and tasks. For computation, we must consider the number of simulation objects and their interrelationships. Thus, increases in precision can lead to faster than exponential growth in the number of terms (or classes in object-oriented designs) the simulation must exercise. In other words, if lower precision is acceptable, it will save a lot of money. The better we can control the level of abstraction, the more efficiently we can carry out the simulation.

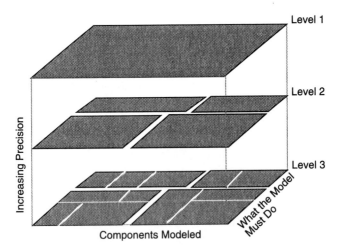

Fig. 10.1. **Precision Versus Number of Simulation Components.** Going to higher precision means handling more simulation components and the relations between them. Here, we break the single function and component in Level 1 into two functions with two components each in Level 2. Then, we decompose these functions and components further in Level 3.

What we've just described is the simplest scenario for implementing simulations. It's equivalent to a manufacturing company's "green-field" approach to a new factory—build it on an empty field without having to worry about how to fit the new operation into an existing factory. In practice, we have legacy systems or Commercial Off-the-Shelf (COTS) products that work in parts of the space displayed in Fig. 10.1. In these cases, we have to figure out where in that space they operate, how they fit together, and how we're going to build all the fragments needed to fill in the gaps that the legacy or COTS products don't cover.

Chapter 3 identifies the relationships between fidelity (or accuracy), validity, and level of detail (or precision). Fidelity doesn't just depend on a highly detailed simulation. It also relies on a model that correctly represents the source system. Typically, customers want as much fidelity as possible, but it's a lot easier to implement models with greater precision than with greater validity. Unfortunately, validity is often more important—as illustrated in Fig. 10.2, which shows that precision and fidelity aren't the same and that a more precise simulation may be less valuable (even though it costs more) than a less precise one. The figure illustrates the case in which the source system in the required experimental frame is strongly sensitive to initial or boundary conditions. If the user isn't aware of this sensitivity and does simulation runs with conditions that are just slightly different from the true initial conditions, the modeled source system's trajectory will be very different from the real system's trajectory. The appearance of precision could lead a user to conclude that the simulation had characterized the source system's behavior very accurately. But in fact, the coarser simulation better characterizes reality.

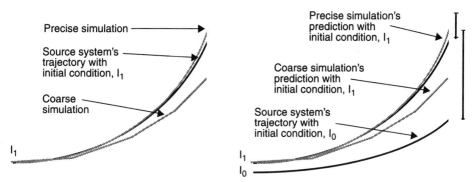

Fig. 10.2.   High Precision May Not Always Be Best. If the source system itself is extremely sensitive to changing conditions, precise models may accurately model trajectories that are far away from the true one.

High-resolution models are also more expensive to execute. Using the less precise simulation with the source system and experimental frame in this sensitive regime, the user could do several runs with several different sets of conditions. The results from these different conditions would demonstrate that the source system is in a sensitive region.

Implementing a simulation is like producing hardware from a design, so we can learn something by looking at a cutting-edge hardware project—the Rapid Prototyping of Application Specific Signal Processing (RASSP) program. This program is trying to reduce lifecycle costs four-fold on signal-processing assemblies. A cornerstone of the approach is to use low-resolution simulations in the early phases of design and development, then progress to higher resolution for identified high-risk components, so developers can explore more of the design space in the program's early stages. The RASSP lesson: "lower resolution equals more design space explored." This program is reducing cost, and the commercial world already uses a similar philosophy; the simulation community needs to benefit from it, too. Remember, only a short time ago, the rule of thumb for program managers was, "You'll never get fired for buying _____ (fill in the blank with the name of a big mainframe corporation)." For simulation program managers, the current wisdom is, "you'll never get fired for directing the highest fidelity." But economic demands urge us to look closely at requirements for precision and their implications.

Although level of precision is our major trade when carrying out a simulation, there are many other considerations we'll discuss as shown in Table 10.1.

Table 10.1.   Chapter Outline.

Step	Issues Addressed	Sections	Description
1	Characterize the Implementation Situation	10.1.1–10.1.3	To implement a model, you need to know what the model is expected to do as well as what is available to do it. Here we determine what we know and how to get what we don't know.
2	Assess & Evaluate Implementation Methods	10.1.4	Once you know the situation, you'll be able to understand the strengths and weaknesses of each approach, map them to the situation, and select the best method.
3	Evaluate & Select Software Structures	10.2	The software structures are the first architecture elements we need to determine because they underlay the rest.
4	Evaluate & Select Appropriate Languages	10.3	You can choose from many low- and high-level languages. Although higher levels can provide more productivity, they'll get in your way if they don't match your needs.
5	Select Appropriate Hardware	10.4	Choose hardware that satisfies any special needs or constraints identified in the first four steps.
6	Set up Activities that Maintain Integrity	10.5	Include how you'll manage configuration and verify the product (or parts of it).
7	Plan, Carry Out Plans, Assess, and Document Progress	10.6	Prior activities have broadly laid out the project. Now you fill in with finer detail and actually start building, testing, and eventually delivering the product.

10.1   Implementation Methods

Before starting to implement a product, we must first learn what people expect of it and what resources will be available. This knowledge helps us complete Step 1 in Table 10.1 and thus begins our journey toward an effective product.

10.1.1   What to Consider

To help assess expectations and resources, we start with questions about what we know concerning the source system, the likely size of the model, and what will constrain the model and our project. Although earlier chapters have discussed these issues, we'll now organize them to help us build the simulation.

Knowledge (K)

These are questions about expectations for the project or how it will interact with other parts of the analysis.

K1. "How ambiguous are the expectations for the project?" Particularly when the model and simulation are to support decision making in a fresh area, people may not know what the model is supposed to do. Here, finding and prototyping a nugget can help clarify the process by providing a clear need. (As Chap. 8 discusses, a nugget is a part of the expressed needs that seems particularly easy to prototype and which all players will understand.)

K2. "Is the system and system behavior similar to that of an already modeled system and system behavior?" ("Is there an analog?") If so, whatever drove that model's implementation would apply closely to this case (allowing for the progression of technology, an issue discussed in Chap. 14).

K3. "Does the model need to be extremely accurate?" But verifying accuracy depends on an accepted verification process, so this question often changes to "Does it need to be much more accurate or precise than an existing model?" Modeling is often used in situations, such as combat engagements for systems under design, that have no analog. In these cases, we must use analysis or another higher-resolution model.

K4. "How will the product be used and by whom?" Uses range from experimental proof of a concept for a special purpose and a narrow audience to very robust applications for a general audience. Users may know computers, modeling, or domains—or, if they satisfy the impossible dream, all three. But we'll discuss how to handle systems for more typical users, who know only some of what we do.

K5. "Will the product need to support more than one user at a time?" Multiple-player simulations require special attention to communication issues.

K6. "Do any interfaces between humans and computers require high output in the visual, auditory, or other senses?" For example, when the simulation is to be part of training.

Size (S)

We must also try to size the project as much as possible in terms of the model's breadth and fidelity.

S1. "How big is it?" That is, how many objects are there and how many interactions between these objects need to be tracked, at what degree of time resolution, over what time period. Section 6.2.2 discusses issues associated with sizing an effort.

S2. "How complex are these objects?" How many states do the objects have and how involved is the logic defining the state changes? Research in computer science shows there is a tradeoff between this and the previous issue—we could use more objects with simpler states and interactions or fewer objects with more involved states and interactions. (Li, 1990)

S3. "How many computations will be done?" Some simulations, such as those for computational fluid dynamics, include large numbers of simple objects that interact in the same way during each computation cycle. In these cases, it's possible to estimate accurately the number of computations that will be done. For other simulations involving branches that depend on dynamically-determined parameters, it's hard to determine beforehand how often each computational block will be run.

S4. "How big is the simulation's output file?" How many state vectors are interrogated and how often? This gives an idea of the output's size and complexity.

S5. "How many different ways will the results be analyzed?" So we'll know how much analytical capacity we'll need.

Constraints (C)

C1. "How much calendar time do we have?" We may have fixed milestones because this modeling project dovetails into another larger project, or a window of opportunity may drive the product toward an early release date.

C2. "What discretionary resources are available?" The most discretionary resource is, of course, cash. But we may also be able to use slack in the resources already in place, such as capturing unused CPU cycles on machines in a distributed network. This is particularly important in today's tight funding environment, because we must often show some kind of working model to persuade decision makers that the product is worth the cost and risk.

C3. "Will this model need to run across platforms?" Most projects aim at a single platform, or computing environment, because users have it or the project team provides it. But sometimes simulations must run across platforms. Because each platform has its own way of accessing files and interfacing with users, cross platforming stringently constrains the implementation. Typically, one handles this by having a shadow level— almost a virtual machine layer—that contains all the platform-specific language. Each platform would get a separate version of this layer, but we'd write the simulation on top of it in a language (such as C or C++) that can compile on all the platforms.

C4. "Is the product to be used in a high-risk situation?" The degree of risk strongly affects the level of fidelity and amount of verification—both potentially expensive issues.

The firefighting example illustrates this last point. For a reasonable amount of money, we may be able to produce a fire-propagation simulator for contingency planning. The firefighting planners use it to help determine possible fire-spread patterns, especially ones that could do a lot of damage. They also use it to determine whether they could do controlled burns or other tactics before the fire season to slow the spread or make the fire easier to deal with. They need a simulator that will provide insights into possibilities at a fairly coarse level. After all, at the time of this pre-planning activity, the actual conditions—hazard level, humidity, wind speed, temperature, etc.—that would prevail during the actual fire are largely unknown. Using a high-precision simulator would require precise guesses for these parameters, and the result could be very unlike the real fire (see Fig. 10.2).

The risks for using this simulator would be fairly low; it's a tool for exploration, not the sole tool for decisions. Further, the consequences of a bad decision would be that the actual fire, though less destructive than it would have been, is more destructive than with the best possible decision. On the other hand, a simulator that predicts how an actual fire propagates—so commanders can position people and equipment, would require much more accuracy because it would be central to decision making and wrong decisions would lead to loss of life and property. We'd have to carefully plan, build, verify, and validate this simulator. In fact, commercial companies probably wouldn't build a real-time simulator for fire propagation because of the legal consequences of failure.

10.1.2   Characterizing Available Resources

We may spend very little or a lot of time evaluating resources: hardware, software, and people. If we know we can build the simulator on an available platform (hardware and software) with available people, our evaluation is done. (Although better equipment is always good.) If performance requirements exceed the abilities of available hardware, software, and staff, we'll work longer and harder to evaluate resource issues.

To choose hardware and software, we must read the tea leaves to determine what will soon be available. With so much ground to cover, most project teams will concentrate on a part of the system that seems most critical and try to foresee what will happen with it. Hardware and software tend to evolve under various market pressures, but more than one type may influence the same component. For instance, the entertainment market drives development of operating systems, central processing units, dynamic-storage devices, and displays. The enterprise work-flow market, on the other hand, drives the development of distributed-processing software, permanent storage, database managers, and communication technologies, along with central processing units and dynamic-storage devices.

With technology pushing and market forces pulling, hardware and software change rapidly. Because we must stay current, it's worth highlighting important sources here—in addition to the printed materials, internet listings, colleagues, and conferences mentioned in Chap. 14:

Academic journals—many ideas, but you have to know an area well to understand them. Still, for difficult problems, this may be your only source.

Society journals—such as IEEE's "Spectrum" or "Computer," whose articles are "leading edge" but written to a wider audience—the society membership.

Practitioner magazines—such as "BYTE" or "PC World," which describe what (in the real world) you need to know. Keep in mind that, even in the early days, many significant developments came from the marketplace, not academia, and these magazines tend to emphasize what sells rather than what's interesting to researchers.

Although hardware and software issues may be tightly coupled to objective measures, human issues are more subjective—except for some general conclusions based on levels of training. We'll talk more about these shortly. In addition, we must also look carefully at people to ensure they have the skills required to handle the project.

Hardware

You'll need to consider central processing units, dynamic storage, permanent storage, displays (and other input/output devices), and communication links. However, some cases may be unusually demanding, as you'll discover when you characterize the implementation envelope based on the issues in Sec. 10.1.1.

Central Processing Units (CPUs). The major classes of CPUs are supercomputers, vector-processing machines (very appropriate for computational fluid dynamics), massively parallel processors, mainframes, workstations, and PCs. Because technology advances rapidly, you'll have to assess the current inventory and what you expect at rollout. Your concern here is, "How fast will my simulation run?" Of course, the simulation's programming—how much branching it does, whether calculations can be pipelined, and so on—strongly affects this speed. The metrics used are MIPS (millions of instructions per second). Test programs rate a computer's MIPS by exercising different facets of the computer's architecture, such as the arithmetic and logic unit, floating-point processor unit, cache memory, random-access-memory accesses, and disk accesses. Where resources would be shared, you need to know the peak, average, and guaranteed minimum available. Typically, with shared resources, allocating by priority guarantees each user a specified level of resources and distributes excess capacity by rank order. The average is typically available, so it doesn't fall under the scheme.

Dynamic Storage. Dynamic storage is what's available on a random-access-memory chip. You need to know how much each CPU can access—and with what speed—especially for large, object-oriented systems that demand a lot of memory.

Permanent Storage. Permanent storage can be disk or tape, though read/write optical disks and other newer technologies are coming on line. We now have gigabytes of storage available, which shortly will be terabytes and then petabytes. Again, if we're sharing with other users, we need to know the peak, average, and minimum amounts of space available.

Communications. Within a computer, the communications are handled by the bus, which moves data between the CPU, dynamic storage, permanent storage, the graphics processor, the keyboard, and connectors [modem or a local area network (LAN)]. The LAN carries traffic between neighboring machines and to peripheral devices such as printers; this is a subnetwork. Wide area networks (WANs) connect groups of subnetworks, perhaps over large distances. Here, we're concerned with not only how much traffic the bus, LAN, or WAN can carry but also how much your application will be able to use given the demands of other users. If you're the only user, the bus has the highest throughput (how much can be moved from one place to another) for three reasons: 1) buses typically connect through and use parallel connections that are 16, 32, or 64 bits wide, whereas LANs and WANs are typically serial, 2) buses go the shortest distance (it takes a nanosecond for light to travel a foot)—for a gigahertz machine, a bit of data would take one clock cycle to make a round trip between devices six inches apart, and 3) no-one else uses the bus, at least for your PC or workstation. LANs have less bandwidth, cover hundreds of feet, and have many users. If you could connect directly to a trunk of a major carrier, a WAN would offer massive bandwidth. But most subscribers can get to that trunk only through layers of switches and then must share it with a fair percentage of the world's users. Thus, the communications issues really come down to latency (how long it takes to get a bit from one point to another) and contention (how much bandwidth do you really have?).

Software

Available software falls into four categories: Commercial Off-the-Shelf (COTS), legacy, research, or dedicated. Typically, you can get pieces of what you need from each of the first three categories, but you'll have to fit them together and fill gaps to complete the effort.

Commercial Off-the-Shelf (COTS). You can buy, install, and use COTS immediately, but you have to consider its cost, applicability, support (near-term and long-term), and longevity. Installed base (the number of units in use) strongly determines cost, support, and longevity. If a company has a product with a large installed base, it will keep its cost within an envelope, ensure support, and try to migrate easily to new technologies as they arrive. Although a COTS product may apply to your simulation project, it will probably have more functions than you need because it's trying to satisfy many customers. As long as its cost is reasonable, you can accept this excess capacity. Finally, note that a large installed base means wider use and fuller testing than for a less-used application.

Legacy Simulations. You may have to use legacy (previously built) simulations for your modeling framework because the community has accepted them as valid. In fact, some may have been formally validated, so you can't lightly throw away this extensive investment. If it hasn't been validated, check its valid envelope of operation by talking with maintainers or original developers. Keep in mind that people less familiar with the simulation often believe it does much more than the developers intended, so consult people close to the product. Chapter 12 discusses the issues of integrating legacy simulations into enhanced environments.

Research Tools. The academic community develops these tools but makes them available to others. Consider them carefully. They may do more than COTS tools and may cost less. But they often lack support, which could cost you more trouble and money overall than other, less powerful tools.

People

People are hardest to evaluate because we have few universal guidelines. On one hand, we could divide the total project into milestoned tasks, pass the tasks to people, and then measure their performance against the milestones. But if we can get good results from people who work with only slight direction, our job is far easier. In particular, if they can respond quickly (and appropriately) to feedback without always consulting management, our project will go faster and smoother. In any case, we need to evaluate and use four main groups of people in an implementation project.

Systems Architects. These people must put together the overall design, plan for the project, and match the user's needs to an implementation scheme. Ideally, we want people with experience. Having been through the mill a couple of times, they see firsthand the typical pitfalls and their potential effects. Systems architects must know both hardware and software and, if they don't know the domain, they must at least be able to relate to people who do.

Programmers. Programmers work with the coding tools to write the software. To hire good programmers, you must assess their experience with

- Programming
- The particular software tools you expect to be using
- This type of software development

Alpha testers. Alpha-testers are people within your organization who want to use the tool your project is producing. They're important because they can exercise the tool realistically. They can also tell you early on what would make the product most valuable. They're "tight" with the developers. They identify the most obvious bugs, which go on the developer's to-do list and get fixed quickly. Developers are able to build new versions fairly quickly based on advice from this group.

Beta testers and early users. Beta testers are a select group of people outside a developer's organization who are computer savvy and need the product. They're willing to put up with bugs because they can work around them and because the program makes them more productive. They're closely involved with product development, but the releases they use are on a longer, more scheduled cycle than those for the alpha testers. Early users are the first paying customers for the product. They can tolerate some bugs if the software improves their productivity and their primary feedback is focused on possible enhancements in future releases.

10.1.3   Matching Characteristics of the Project and Inventory

We've just looked at the main characteristics we can use to categorize our inventory, but we won't apply all of them to a given project. Instead, we want to use our project's characteristics (questions K1–K6, S1–S5, and C1–C4) and our resource assessment to determine which inventory characteristics (and what levels of detail) we must consider.

The first questions concern whether the expectations are clear (K1), whether the system is similar to one already modeled (K2), and whether the model must be extremely precise (K3). Their answers help us decide how well we know what our implementation must do—in particular, how much precision it needs (see Fig. 10.1)—and whether existing tools address this (or a similar) problem. The rest of the questions talk to how that model interacts with the rest of the analysis effort or with sizing or constraint issues.

Assessing the Effect of Ambiguity

Figure 10.3 shows how we determine and clarify ambiguity. What we learn from this process largely determines what implementation method is appropriate.

The first question is whether the expectations are clear or ambiguous. One reason for ambiguity might be that the source system isn't clearly defined for M&S (see Chap. 3). As Chap. 3 discusses, we need to understand what we're studying about the source system, what performance criteria we need to estimate for that system, what information our model needs, and what the framework is for analysis. Ambiguity can also occur because customers haven't been able to form their objectives and requirements properly (see Chaps. 4 and 5).

If the expectations are ambiguous, we can't answer most of the project-knowledge (K2-K6) and project-sizing (S1-S5) questions, though the constraints (C1-C4) may be clear. In this case, we must take the time and resources to clarify expectations. A rapid, inexpensive prototype of one simple, end-to-end thread can often germinate into a full concept for the model.

Once we have a clear vision of the source system and what we're modeling we can proceed as shown in Fig. 10.3. Has a project accomplished a similar vision? If the answer is "yes, there is a similar project," it can guide us. In particular, we can use it to help us answer the sizing questions, S1-S5. Also, we would want similar types of hardware, although technological advances may have made it less expensive. If nothing similar exists, we must analyze the model and try to size its parts. Appendix A describes how to analyze work elements and estimate size. Here again, rapid prototyping can help by coarsely emulating candidate parts of the model and how they relate. Starting at the highest level and working downward, we ask whether these components have analogous simulations until we find a level at which they do. After all, at the very bottom, we can solve problems by applying first-principle physics. Of course, we typically don't have the resources to go all the way to this "last-chance" solution.

Searching for analogs contains one notable pitfall: if we find one, someone may pressure us to use it as is rather than as a guide. Management likes this solution because it appears to require fewer resources and seems less risky. But if the analog is a simulation of a different source system in a different experimental frame, it's not homomorphic. Thus, we have to change parts of it (kludges), and the "mix and match" system becomes harder to manage and requires more resources. When people finally recognize it won't work, they declare "technical victory," put the whole effort out of sight, and wait for a different group to start over.

If the model needs to be extremely accurate (the answer to question K3 is yes), we must next determine if we're modeling the source system for the first time or if we have a less accurate model of it. In both cases, we can implement at much lower risk if a closely analogous, successful effort exists. Because accuracy includes precision and validity, increasing accuracy means raising the level of precision, validation, or both. The strategy for implementing a more precise simulation is straightforward. As Sec. 3.5.1 points out, we do so by increasing the level of

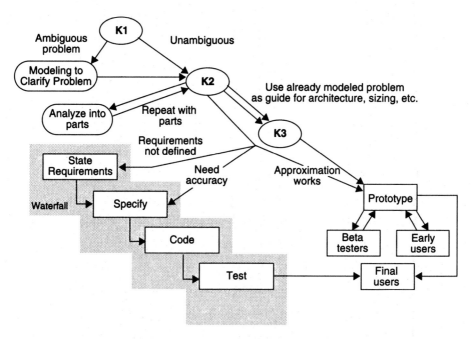

Fig. 10.3.   Flow to Characterize a Problem. Clarify ambiguity, analyze into components, determine level of detail, and then proceed to the implementation approach.

detail—the temporal resolution, the spatial resolution, or the number of types of objects being considered. On the other hand, increasing the level of validation isn't easy. Here, it's extremely valuable to have an analog—a simulator which has been accepted as valid for a source system—so we can use the same validation strategy. As pointed out in App. A, analogous efforts are also powerful tools for sizing a project and estimating productivity.

We determine an appropriate level of detail based on expectations for the simulation **and** on the scenarios under which it will run. Chapter 9 calls these scenarios contextual information while also discussing what behaviors should be simulated within the model and what should be part of those outside scenarios. If the contemplated range of scenarios can be addressed by running the simulation over the range of a few parameters, the level of detail is appropriate. However, if the set of runs is too large, we may need to aggregate many of the detailed parts into a few coarser components.

Relating Project Characteristics to Other Analysis

Now that we know the broad thrust of our effort, we need to map particular tasks into resources. First, let's characterize the intended user and what that user expects. Does this simulation go to a narrow audience or a general one? How much background does the anticipated user have in modeling, computers, or the domain? The less end users bring to the party, the more we have to supply. This means allocating more resources to the user interface, user tryouts, and documentation. Probably, we'll move toward software and hardware with very large installed bases because they're more "user friendly" (in fact, our intended users may already have them). If we're aiming at a general audience, beta testers and early users are vital to the development plan.

Another issue is whether more than one process will run at the same time (the K5 question), in which case we must synchronize them. As an example, say we're simulating a scenario in which an air-to-air missile is closing on an aircraft, and we're interested in how well the aircraft's electronic-warfare system will cope. During the closing part of the engagement, when they're separated by less than a kilometer, the pulse of the air-to-air radar will be transmitted, reflected, and received back in a few microseconds. The aircraft would monitor these pulses, and then the electronic-warfare system would compute what energy needs to be transmitted back to the missile to spoof it. This is the real world. Now, for the simulators. When the message from the air-to-air radar's simulator arrives, the aircraft's simulator must be at the point in its simulation that corresponds to the time the pulse would arrive. And similarly, when the message from the aircraft simulator conveying the echo and the additional energy arrives at the missile simulator, that simulator has to be at the correct time mark. If either gets ahead, it needs to be rolled back. This problem gets harder with live players because the total time of computing and transmitting a message has to happen within real time. This requirement constrains the simulators and the latencies, which drive the choice of communication links and protocols.

The requirements for an interface between humans and computers (the K6 question) can mean we must allocate resources to testing, perhaps even to a repetitive, tight feedback loop of development and test (preferably involving end users).

With the tasks delineated, we must now try to determine how big they are (the S questions). Part of the first phase was to find analogs for the simulation. As Sec. 6.2.2 points out, the soundest estimates derive from having done a similar effort before. Analogs not only guide our approach, but also help size the current effort. The final product may seem to be a massive beast, but if we can divide it into modules, we can build it in pieces, which often can stand alone to meet some users' needs.

The first three sizing questions—"How big is it?", "How complex are the objects?", and "How many computations will be done?"—all concern trading level of detail against resources. If the level calls for more objects than we have time to program or run, we must scale back the detail.

Determining the size of the output file (S4) relates to the resources needed for storage and communication. For instance, we could run large files if capacity were available during off hours so the communication system could transmit the data to available disk storage. But we'd have to complete the analysis (S5) before the demand for storage resources picks back up. Again, if we don't have the resources, we must work at a higher level of abstraction, have less detail in our output reports, and do less analysis (because there's less to analyze).

Let's turn to the constraints. "How much calendar time?" and "How many discretionary resources are available?" are really major issues because they size the box we must work in. The other two constraint questions—working across platforms and supporting risk-bearing decisions—tell us whether added tasks are going to require more resources.

Matching our project to these analytical results requires two steps. First, we match any specialized requirements against specialized resources. For instance, massive computing power for fluid dynamics may require a supercomputer. Second, we look at less specialized requirements, for which matching has more alternatives. For instance, if the simulation needs computations for fluid dynamics but there's no rush, we can use a supercomputer or, during slack time, a network of workstations.

For a multi-year project, rapidly changing technology complicates this matching process, as Fig. 10.4 shows. Thus, planning at year N may be somewhat of a dice toss. Digressing for a bit to the Rapid Prototyping of Application Specific Signal Processing (RASSP) project, mentioned earlier, can shed some light on this problem. DARPA supported the RASSP to demonstrate, through an example domain, that combining support tools and appropriate philosophies for design and development can dramatically reduce development and lifecycle costs. Two approaches from RASSP apply to matching needs and tasks to resources. The first, concerning the issue of technology and its affect on long-term projects, is the model-year approach. Instead of aiming at producing only one final product at some out year, they look to build intermediate products in the near term. For these near-term products, they use available technologies. If a new technology appears, they can incorporate it in the next model-year's version. The out-year delivery may be—in fact, probably **will** be—much different from that original vision, but it will include technology that hadn't been imagined and feedback from all users of the intermediate versions.

The second lesson is that the level of abstraction for the simulation needs to be very tightly controlled. Remember, RASSP is not a simulation project but rather uses simulation as a surrogate for rapid prototyping of candidate systems. As the investigators for RASSP have pointed out, simulating at higher levels of abstraction allows more of the decision space to be explored [Hein 1997; Rose 1997]. In other words, as I mentioned earlier in the chapter, more detail isn't better and can be worse.

Two groups typically must decide how to match resources to tasks: we, as implementers, who are trying to make workable plans for a usable tool, and the acquisition managers, who share our interest in providing the users with a usable tool. But each has a very different side agenda. We may have a technology we've

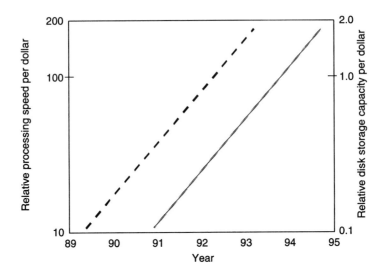

Fig. 10.4.   How Advancing Technology Improves the Ratio of Performance to Cost. Price to performance improves tenfold every three years. (Based on Fig. 1.1 of the National Resource Council's 1995 report: "Evolving the High Performance Computing and Communications Initiative to Support the Nation's Information Infrastructure.")

mastered, so we'd like to develop it further (the "if you have a hammer, every problem is a nail" syndrome). But some acquisition managers have gone round and round with studies that went nowhere; so they may believe they can finally leave their antacid at home if someone can come in and say "I'll give you what you want" (even somewhat plausibly).

To get synchronized, implementers and acquisition managers must both focus on users and involve them. As implementers, we can provide sample screens, day-in-the-life demos, or interim, standalone tools. This last idea can be most useful because it allows some users (what the commercial world would call early users) to get involved daily and give us detailed feedback. Further, if we use their feedback, they "own" the product, which firms and widens the support base. Acquisition managers should choose developers who will involve users and build in appropriate milestones to make sure they do.

However, when needs aren't clearly understood, this process must evolve with our developing understanding—as sizings become clearer, we'll better match needs to resources and constraints. Sometimes, it becomes apparent that the original goal was much too ambitious for the resources available within the prevailing constraints. Then, we have to downsize the project while keeping it useful enough to justify the costs.

10.1.4   How to Implement Models and Simulations

Once we know what we need to do and how much we have to do it, we must choose an approach to get there. Figure 10.5 shows that, although we have an iterative core process, different kinds of feedback vary the methods of iterating. From control theory, we know that we want tight feedback loops, but different kinds of simulation require different feedback at different times.

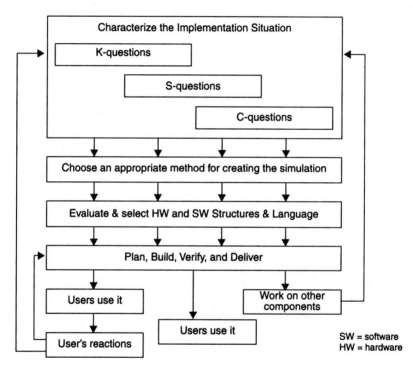

Fig. 10.5.   Implementation Process and Feedback. Implementation approaches differ mainly in how much they try to achieve in one pass, which means they have differing feedback loops.

We'll look at three approaches which show our main choices: waterfall, spiral, and evolutionary. Chapter 4 introduced them, but we'll discuss them as they apply to the seven implementation steps in Table 10.1. Remember Fig. 10.1 shows that greater precision means considering more components, functions, and relationships. The waterfall method tries to achieve the most precise layer in one pass, though that pass may be very extensive. The spiral method carries out one of the second level's components to level-three precision and then does another. The evolutionary approach starts by implementing all components at level-two precision, waits for feedback, and then takes the most useful features to level three.

Of course, we can combine approaches. For example, we could build a very precise user interface and keep processes less precise until someone asked for more—a mix of the spiral and evolutionary approaches. Choosing which one, or how much of each, depends mainly on what kinds of feedback loops we foresee. Perhaps we can see some intermediate products that would entice some beta users to use a potentially "buggy" program in order to improve their productivity or analysis. If so, we'd mix spiral and evolutionary approaches. Otherwise, we'd wait for written feedback after using the waterfall method to produce the best possible result with one long pass.

Waterfall

This is the classic flow from requirements to specifications to simulation. It's extremely valuable when tight, short feedback loops aren't possible. An example would be a model that must be very accurate even though we have no experience with the source system. The waterfall method organizes our analytical activity to produce a credible outcome, but it needs time, clear-cut goals, and well-identified end users. First, we assemble requirements that reflect what the simulation must do. Section 5.1.4 discusses several techniques the waterfall method traditionally uses to determine requirements for the simulation. Section 7.3 suggests building a virtual prototype to elicit requirements as part of the process for Promotional-Visual-Operational Requirements. Although virtual prototyping isn't part of the traditional waterfall approach, it can help identify dynamic features that produce better requirements than traditional static techniques do.

The waterfall method corresponds to the central path of Fig. 10.5, in which we go through the whole process before getting feedback. It doesn't have intermediate simulation models to show the users.

Spiral Development

With the spiral approach, we start with some of the model's functions or parts and build them at the finest level of detail to provide users with working simulations of those parts. Users can evaluate the simulations to help us improve them, and we can then move on to other functions or parts of the model. This approach requires us to understand the problem and how the model will address it. Spiral development corresponds to the right-hand loop of Fig. 10.5, in which we develop a component, then go back into the core loop to develop another.

Evolutionary Development

Evolutionary development (often called incremental prototyping) can be a powerful technique whenever requirements aren't clear. First, we define what parts of the model apply to each system function. We may have to divide these parts into different categories, such as the physical and functional components of a fighter aircraft. For example, a heads-up display does one thing but requires two widely separated physical boxes to do it: the display unit in the cockpit and the processing unit in the electronics bay. Discovering the right modules to capture a system's behavior may require us to build prototypes of behaviors under each choice. Users can then tell us which, if any, seem to act correctly. Sometimes, seeing this model will give users a further point of reference that will allow them to see the system more clearly and help us simulate it better. We hope they'll say, "No, that's not right, but with these changes, it'll be closer." But, even "No, that's not right at all" provides information and a chance to learn what would be right. This process corresponds to the left-hand loop of Fig. 10.5 and it requires careful selection of users who are tolerant and excited about what this tool will provide them on delivery.

Figure 10.6 shows that prototypes are the most flexible and least formal of the development stages. They are inexpensive because they model one, simple behavior all the way through a module with coarse resolution, yet they can still give us valuable information. With the cost low, we can afford to prototype functions that don't end up in the final product. Programmers keep most documentation in their heads and they use accessible hardware and software—a Rapid Application Developer such as Visual Basic or Delphi, or one of the modeling tools, such as Opnet, BONeS, or VisSim. People cost less too because junior programmers can use this kind of software under a senior modeler's guidance.

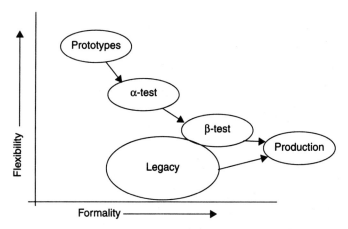

Fig. 10.6.   **Progression from Prototypes to Production.** We have the most flexibility early in developing new systems, whereas already implemented systems are inflexible.

When we've chosen modules for prototyping, we then determine which of their interactions we want to model and which modules seem most crucial. We do this by building emulators of the modules—look-up tables or simple code. It would be best if all were within the same process or could easily chain from one to the next (passing information through files or database entries). Until we better define these modules and their relationships, we should avoid bringing up the issues of communication across processes.

The next step is to divide the most important modules into their submodules. Even with simple models of these submodules, their behaviors and interactions will reveal that the module's behavior is much more complex. In fact, even at this stage, it may capture more of the source system than other tools in the inventory. If so, we can attract alpha testers in our organization, who give us several benefits:

- New uses that help us expand the model's operating envelope
- Awareness of "bugs" that make the system hard to use but that we didn't see because we knew how to work around them
- Feedback on the graphic user interface, which is vital to the program's effectiveness
- A very tight feedback loop, which allows us quickly to expand modules, submodules, or subsubmodules; introduce new interrelations and detail existing ones; and solve problems with interfaces

Thus, our model becomes richer, more complex, and more useful. With users involved, we can be more sure we're expanding in the right direction.

At some point, we must widen the audience, usually by asking the alpha testers if our program is useful enough to give to beta testers outside our organization. As I've mentioned, beta testers know how to use an imperfect tool and tell us how we can improve it. By folding their suggestions into our implementation plan, we can make later versions better represent the system's behavior and, therefore, more usable. Beta testers often focus on areas alpha testers don't consider, which makes the model more useful and us more confident in our modeling choices.

Because beta testers aren't in our organization, we'll probably be more formal in communicating with them, recording their suggestions, and tracking how their feedback changes our plan and the software. This wider experience may erode the confidence our alpha testers give us in the modules' high-level structure, in which case we must carefully reconsider that structure and, at least partly, return to alpha testing. Note, though, that the interfaces and some of the lower-level submodules may be relatively unaffected—they would just fit differently into the higher levels.

To make the program more usable, we may have to speed up certain processes or condense intermediate files or messages. This means breaking out some processes and writing them in another, lower-level language. Communication between processes also becomes an issue. At this point we'll need people with more technical depth on our team and will have to choose which changes to do within resource constraints. Users can help us with these choices, especially if we attach a phantom price (say, between $0 and $100) and tell them: "If you had $100, and each of these fixes costs the amount shown, how would you spend it?" This has reportedly worked quite well because users trade off wishes against cost instead of listing endless choices.

The three approaches we've discussed in this section differ in a development cycle's breadth and level of detail, as well as in the amount and kinds of feedback.

Users can review hardcopy illustrations, but feedback is much better if they interact with a "live" system. The chosen approach should include a tight feedback loop and a wide range of alpha and beta users. These two key characteristics allow us to change models while it's still cheap.

10.2   Software Structures

Computer simulation requires a software program from which we can extract how its objects change over time in response to the simulator's parameters. We use the software tool—written in Ada, C++, or another language—by itself or to build models for the simulation. In the latter case, the tool becomes a simulation language or toolbox that other organizations buy or acquire to simulate their domains (build models using one of the simulation languages). As developers, we would control the tool's (or language's) configuration, but the users must control the models. In other words, the tool and the model require validation. Many of these tools allow the modeler to "promote" parameters (set them at simulation time). Other analysts could take the models and do a series of runs while varying certain parameters to support their analyses, which also need management. Thus, simulation could involve two levels beyond those of a typical software enterprise, as shown in Fig. 10.7.

At the bottom of Fig. 10.7 is an imaginary language we'll call XamplScript, developed using a standard programming language. The left panel shows what the programmers actually code, and the right panel shows what users of XamplScript would see. The programmers have provided code for queues, traffic generators, branches, collectors, and the graphic interface. The next level is the modeler level. An organization has decided to acquire XamplScript and have a modeler build models with it. The modeler takes the coded functions, as represented by the icons, and pastes them into a work area. By connecting them, he tells XamplScript that he wants the packets to go from one to the next, undergoing the process indicated by the icon at that next location. In this case the modeler has two traffic generators—an exponential and a constant—feeding a first-in/first-out queue. The queue's output goes to a brancher, which routes the packets from the first generator to the first collector and from the second generator to the second collector. At the collectors, the delay time from creation to receipt is measured and written to a file. The modeler has promoted several parameters—the traffic rates, queue size, and queue service rate—so they can be set at run time. The top panel shows the level for the end users, who have built a script providing parameter values for several runs and have specified a number of probes that will be the data they want written to a file: the delay times for the two traffic streams. The results are the output files. Often, providers of a tool like XamplScript will condense these files and provide tools to help translate them back and analyze the results. They'll also include the ability to write an ASCII file that other analysis tools, such as spreadsheets, can read.

What happens if runs have traffic and service rates that fill up the queue? At the lowest level (as we can see from the code), the packet doesn't go in the queue

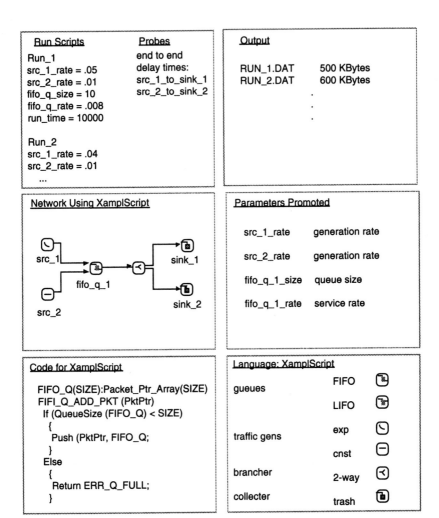

Fig. 10.7.　Levels of Software Structures. Using a simulation tool, you can program models at several levels—skilled programmers are needed at the lowest, but non-programmers could work at the highest.

and an error message is returned. The routine that called this should have code that does something with it—destroy it, route it to some default collector, or something else. But do modelers know what the developers have done? Are they even aware there could be a problem when the queue size gets too big? If not, they probably haven't used any of the provisions that would handle it. Or perhaps the modelers did provide a probe point for the dropped packets, but the users didn't recognize its significance and chose not to list it as a probe. The output reports anywhere in this chain could mislead by showing a very consistent delay time (namely the time it takes to serve a full queue). It does so because a new packet typically either sees a full queue and drops out or is pushed on the queue and fills it. If we don't know about the lost packets, this would be misleading.

As implementers, if we control the process from bottom to top, we can arrange to solve these subtle errors during verification and validation. By subtle I mean that the simulation outputs an apparently reasonable value instead of crashing. If we control only part of the stack, we must know about problems we could inherit from the developers lower in the stack or pass on to users higher in the stack. Then, we can help users by including a way of telling them they must do something with the queue overflow. I'll talk more about this issue under verification and validation.

10.2.1   Architectures

To build good models, we have to know how options for hardware (the CPU) and software (the operating system) affect our plans for the higher levels of a simulation.

Types of CPUs

The limitations of CPUs have forced us to write special code for simulations to work around these limitations and get required performance. Fortunately, this restriction is rapidly fading. We must now carefully match our choice of hardware architecture to the characteristics of our simulation to get the highest performance and most cost-effective solution. Some of the most common types of CPUs include:

Vector: You can pipeline operations in vector processors. If elements in a long array are going through the same sequence of operations, vector machines can achieve a very high throughput, which you'll need for simulations of computational fluid dynamics.

Scalar: Not as fast as other machines for redundant computations, but it's more appropriate if you expect to mix types of computation. Excellent for object-oriented approaches, which typically have a high level of dynamic branching.

Massively Parallel Processors: TMI's Connection Machine (a very large processor using a cellular control structure) was the early example, but IBM and others are the players now. Use them mainly to extract data from massive (more than 500GB) databases.

Symmetrical MultiProcessors (SMP): This architecture uses a smaller array of more powerful processors, typically high-end PC chips (P6s, P7s, alphas etc.). You can use SMPs equipped with microkernel operating systems (e.g., Windows NT) as net servers and for multiprocessor applications.

Mainframe: Though their CPUs may not be as powerful as supercomputers, mainframes have high input/output capacity and much tighter security. The term "mainframe" is becoming a "dirty word," so Lou Gerstner (CEO of IBM) refers to them as "large, scalable servers." This term probably sells better in the current "client/server" world. Use mainframes in multiprocessor applications whenever you need guaranteed transactions.

Remember, a particular CPU is not better for your simulation efforts just because it's more expensive. For example, using an expensive vector machine on a highly branched problem will not be as effective as a cheaper symmetrical multiprocessor because throughput will be lower. Carefully consider the abilities you need for your problem and then make your choice.

Types of Operating Systems

As hardware has become more powerful, operating systems (OS) have become more flexible. In fact, a major chip manufacturer and a major OS provider share costs of a research center so hardware and software can jointly move towards more powerful products. Even so, software changes more often and enters the market at a lower cost than hardware, so you may still have more than one software option for certain hardware. The types of operating systems you may encounter include:

Standalone: Runs by itself on a single CPU and is appropriate whenever the intended simulation would be used only on individual machines. It has the lowest entry costs because it's the most common OS and has more inexpensive support tools.

Distributed Microkernel: Here, the simulation application still doesn't interact with others on the same machine, but the processing is multi-threaded and may operate on more than one processor at a time. This approach is fairly new, but promises to become standard.

Client/Server: Here clients request processes residing on a server. The client/server approach is a proven technology for large applications, through such standards as the Distributed Computing Environment. This is the most mature of the technologies for distributed processing with multiple users.

Object-Request Broker: May be a great benefit to M&S because it allows knowledgeable organizations to establish and maintain distributed libraries of simulation objects, which others can call almost transparently. The downside for now is that we don't have complete standards for it. However, software is evolving to small, modular processes, so it will happen one way or another. The Object Management Group is developing standards for the Common Object Request Broker Architecture.

10.2.2   Control Structure

We must control the problem space and the interactions in a simulation. Do we carve the space into uniform temporal and spatial cells (and thus use machine cycles checking empty cells) or do we carve it into unequal pieces and focus computation on areas that tell us the most? We'd like to do the latter, but it's hard to know that we've selected the most important regions and included all critical areas.

We control interactions between the elements using random (non-deterministic) or set (deterministic) values. Random interactions fall under what's often called Monte Carlo simulation, which we use in two cases. First, we may not be able to predict the source system's behavior (e.g., because the Heisenberg Uncertainty Principle holds). Second, we may theoretically be able to predict the behavior, but we can't do it in practice because we don't know the experimental frame well enough.

For set values, we know how the source system behaves, but its behavior still ranges widely based on initial and boundary conditions we need to model. For example, suppose the source system is not linear but chaotic; that is, it's strongly sensitive to initial boundary conditions [Devaney 1986]. In this case, our model may have low or high fidelity, but to be accurate it must also exhibit this chaotic behavior. For example, one part of the firefighting scenario is the fire-propagation model. The source system itself could be very sensitive to slight variations. That is, at certain points as the fire spreads, a slight change in wind speed or wind direction or a slight difference of fuel level could strongly change how the fire propagates locally, but that local variation could quickly build to major variations. As modelers, we know that, when the model runs, we won't know these factors well enough to pinpoint which path the fire will take. No level of fidelity will allow us to fully characterize the experimental frame. Monte Carlo allows the model to explore several paths and, hopefully, to discover that the source system has either a stable or a chaotic trajectory. All control structures use one of the three formalisms described in Sec. 3.4.1: the differential-equation system specification (DESS), the discrete-time system specification (DTSS), or the discrete-event system specification (DEVS). Among the control structures are:

Cellular Automata: Cellular automata have uniform objects and a highly uniform topology and use the DTSS formalism. Control depends on assessing the state of each object at each time click. Generalizations of cellular automata, with more varied objects and less uniform topologies, have helped simulate the progression of diseases that compromise the body's chemical defenses, such as AIDS [Sieburg 1991].

Computational Fluid Dynamics: Computational fluid dynamics involves a volume of objects (the cells of fluid), which all obey the same physical laws and interact at their boundaries—though at a high level, similar to cellular automata. These techniques rely on a DESS formalism that uses a lot of mathematical modeling, in the form of partial differential equations, to accelerate the process and keep it accurate. Hydrodynamic flows (such as airflow over a fuselage) are typical examples of its use. If the objects are uniform and their behaviors are well described by partial differential equations describing the evolution, we'd choose this method. If the behavior is more discrete and general, cellular automata is better [Moin 1997].

Analog Emulators: Here, as in computational fluid dynamics, differential equations describe the behavior. So analog emulators are also DESS formalisms, except they handle different kinds of interacting objects—the class of time differential equations in Chap. 3. Much like cellular automata, control is on a time click, but with error correction to interpolate between clicks.

Discrete-Event Simulators: Here we place process interrupts in an event queue and invoke them when they pop off. As the name implies, this control method involves a DEVS formalism. We use it for models having different objects, especially whenever the objects tend to remain in the same state for some specified time unless an outside event changes them. Discrete-event simulators don't require computation if the object isn't changing state, which results in large efficiencies for certain classes of problems. Manufacturing shops, computer networks, and communication networks are key examples. They all involve piece parts, data files, or communication packets moving through a network of resources, not all on the same path, where the resources can serve only so many at a time. Commercially, they test control protocols for best use of resources; the larger the enterprise, the more likely we'll use them.

Petri Nets: Control here is on the objects and the communication links between them. Because control is based on events, the Petri Net structure is a DEVS formalism and is often used to model networks of computers.

These control structures differ in the types of simulation issues they address, the availability of prebuilt tools that support them, and the types of platforms we need. Analog emulators and discrete-event simulators probably have the broadest base of tools that support them and the widest choice of platforms to run on because they have the longest history. Computational fluid dynamics typically requires supercomputers and therefore limits the number of practitioners. Cellular automata are on various platforms but without a wide base of commercial support tools. Yet, they're easy to use and give us interesting results, so the internet (comp.CA newsgroup) carries a lot of information about them. The same things are true of Petri nets.

10.2.3 Structures for Visualizing Simulations

Limits on displays and graphics hardware and software determine how well we can visualize simulations. Each pixel (picture element) needs three color values, and we must compute, store, and transmit to the display a whole screen's worth of values. Thus, we have to work within a certain number of pixels and colors (typically 1024×768 pixels and 256 colors, which takes about one megabyte of memory). This is called "screen real estate."

Because screen real estate is limited, we want to display the most important information for the task at hand. Iterative prototyping helps us decide how. Although visual displays are more art than science, using common contexts (at least, common among the targeted community) will make them much more accessible. The three most common contexts for behavioral information are spatial (geographic), temporal (time line), and animation, but other contexts are more specific to certain domains (such as representing instrument panels for process-control simulations).

Geographic

Geographic displays require map backgrounds, which take up a lot of pixels from the screen real estate. In several projects in our shop, we developed maps because users thought this information was important. Unfortunately, much of the screen was empty (true, the map was there, but it was wallpaper—without real information) whereas other areas were so crowded that we couldn't display all of the information. Users didn't get much from these spatial presentations, so we stopped using them. However, in other domains, particularly combat simulation, the geographic context is vital.

Time Lines

Time-line displays, typically with time running from left to right, can show the activities of several objects and relations in behaviors that otherwise might not be apparent. Figure 10.8 shows the time-line display from the Planning and Analysis System tool we built in our shop. We had been working on tools to characterize the use of ground antennas belonging to the Air Force Satellite Control Network (AFSCN) and had developed several displays, but this one was an immediate winner. The figure shows this timeline in our current tool, but the original looked much the same. In fact, the satellite we looked at that first time was in the same program as the one seen in the figure. The display has a horizontal line for each day, which runs from 0–1440 minutes. In this figure, the contacts (including setup time) are seen as solid rectangles on the line for that day. The open boxes correspond to times the satellite can see the antenna, POGO-C (one of the antennas at Thule, Greenland). The original display didn't show when the antennas were in sight, but we saw that the satellite used POGO-C in the same time bands every day. At first we thought it was because of visibility constraints, but adding in the visibilities showed immediately they weren't the constraint. Our analysts then determined why this happened, which aroused interest beyond the original alpha testers. It reveals historical use of antennas and provides telling insights into the simulator's behavior.

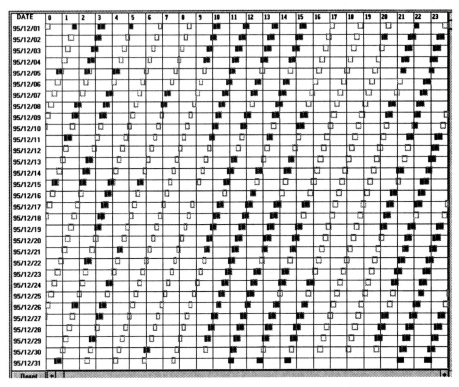

Fig. 10.8.   Timeline Chart for Using Ground Antennas. This chart shows when a satellite sees (open boxes) and uses (filled boxes) ground antennas.

Animations

Animation is a valuable tool for presenting a simulator's data to users. An animation is a dynamic graphic tied to a component's evolving state, such as where the component is (e.g., a packet moving through a telecommunications network) or how resources are being used (e.g., how full a reservoir is). It allows the user to see how components interact during a simulation run. This technique's power is that it directly connects simulations to the most powerful tool known for organizing data—the human visual system [Crawford 1990].

Figure 10.9 captures a display our shop developed to show AFSCN's Quality of Service metric, and Fig. 10.10 details its parts. This display can show data collected empirically or generated on a simulation run. It is a matrix of graphics representing use of visibilities, in which we show satellites (identified by Inter Range Operations Number [IRON]) vs. antennas. The summary for a satellite is at the right and for the antenna is at the bottom. The right bottom graphic summarizes everything. The size of the graphic reflects the relative weight of that element in the summary, which in this case identifies the satellite's use of that antenna. Each square contains a bar which displays how that satellite used its chances to see the antennas, as shown in Fig. 10.10. The black area at the top shows how much of the visibility was unavailable, either because another satellite was using the antenna or because the antenna was out of service. The bottom part (normally green, but dark gray here) shows how much visibility the satellite used and the middle part (normally light blue, but light gray here) shows how much was available but not used.

Notice this display conveys a lot of information. Finding the best way to present it has meant prototyping candidate displays, which we're still doing. By showing successive days at the rate of three displays per second, we help users clearly see how resources are used. They see what a normal day looks like and quickly perceive anything unusual that would merit deeper investigation.

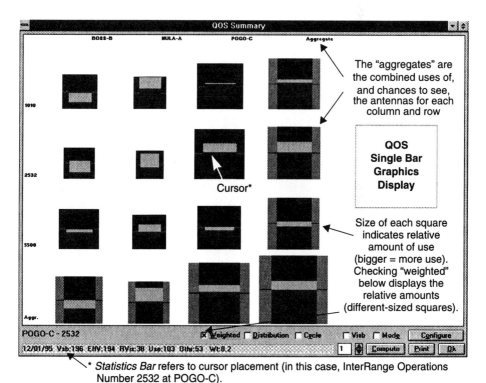

Fig. 10.9.   Display of Quality of Service for AFSCN. This is a matrix composed of graphical elements explained in Fig. 10.10.

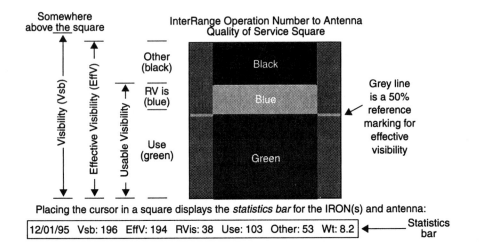

Fig. 10.10.   **Detail of Display for Quality of Service.** This is the individual graphical element for quality of service, which compresses a lot of information into a fairly concise graphic.

10.2.4   Data Structures

Choosing a data structure influences the speed of access, size of database, cost of tools and ease of programming. With these issues in mind, let's discuss the most common data structures: flat files, relational databases, and object-oriented databases.

Flat files are the simplest of the data structures because they're typically ASCII files. Line feeds supply their main structure. Secondary structure comes from tabs or commas (for files that will be somewhat like fixed-form record files) or from keywords (for files whose record structure is dynamic). The upside of flat files is that they are extremely flexible and can, at least initially, be cheap. The downside is that we have to code all the different types of accesses, so documentation and maintenance can become a problem. Also, let's suppose we build the files more compactly by using positional indicators instead of keywords. A minor hit to one indicator would cause the program to lose track of where things were.

Relational databases apply whenever we have a lot of relatively uniform data and queries typically access long, contiguous segments of it. For business applications, such as accounting data, the major vendors provide for distributed access and maintenance, offer easy methods for error checking and protect users from the consequences of common failures. But relational databases have higher up-front costs than compacted flat files. They're also slower and require more disk space.

Object-oriented databases (OODB) have had less push from business, but some technical areas have used them successfully; in an application for computer-aided engineering, an OODB was used to store all of the engineering data for a vehicle design. Particularly interesting was that the engineers' notes would connect to the appropriate points in the engineering drawings and still be text. In contrast, for a record containing a binary large object, the notes would be part of the graphic image and would require optical character recognition to retrieve the text. Another example is the ISLE/DOME environment developed by the RDT&E Division of the Naval Command, Control, and Ocean Surveillance Center (http://coke.nosc.mil/coaster) for combat simulation, which uses object-oriented databases to make the objects persistent—a great advantage for terrain. When a tank company crosses over a stretch of wet terrain, churning it up, the OODB records it as a side effect on the terrain part of the database participating in the program flow. When another unit later crosses that same stretch of terrain, the object from the OODB will show the earlier damage. On the one hand, OODBs are easy to work with because programmers don't have to write any separate access code. They refer to the object and, immediately, its data is there. On the other hand, without a separate query language, programming is the only access to the OODB.

Flat files, relational databases, and object-oriented databases are used to capture the input, dynamic state, and output data associated with a single simulation program. But data structures are also required to communicate with other simulators or computer tools during a run. A good example of this type of data structure is the protocol data units used in Distributed Interactive Simulation. This structure is a defined standard for formatting and timing messages between players in multi-player combat simulations, regardless of whether the participants are live, virtual, or constructive.

10.3   Choosing a Language for Programming and Simulation

In the previous section on software structure, we found that we can build a simulation at three different levels: the lowest involves using computer languages, the intermediate level uses simulation languages (which are themselves written in a computer language), and the highest relies on templates built with simulation languages. Choosing an appropriate implementation language involves many issues. First, you must consider what level language to use. Lower-level languages apply across a much broader range of applications but require more highly trained implementers and longer development times. Then, you must recognize that each language within a given level aims at a niche. Although most languages can address problems outside their niches, they'll cost more to develop than languages designed for those applications. The following sections describe the characteristics of standard languages and languages for rapid application development (which map to the lowest level) and simulation languages (which map to the middle level).

10.3.1   Standard Languages

Software languages are compiled or interpreted. In compiled languages, all source code converts to executable code, which you can run without reference to the language. In interpreted languages, source code converts as it runs, which means you must have available a reference to the language. Compiled code runs faster but is less flexible.

Fortran is the standard language for scientific programming, so it's used for computational fluid dynamics, but we also see it in many legacy simulations. Fortran is a compiled language.

C++ is the most common object-oriented language, with an increasingly large share of the installed base. It has more libraries of proven routines, programmers, and commercially available tools than the languages with smaller market shares, making it a good choice for spiral or waterfall development. It's a compiled language.

Ada is a compiled language for embedded systems (such as training simulators). Until recently, the DoD required it for these applications, so it focused on real-time issues. As a result, Ada addresses some real-time characteristics— such as concurrency—head on, whereas other languages (C, C++, Java) handle them only with add-ons.

Smalltalk, one of the earliest object-oriented languages, uses the paradigm of object-view-controller. Most of the object-based database managers use this or C++ as their host language. Compared to C++, it has a smaller installed base, but in certain arenas, such as the academic community, the ratio is different.

Lisp is a functionally oriented, interpreted language, though it has strong object orientation as well. Because it's interpreted, it has a run-time flexibility hard to achieve in a compiled language, but it also has a lot of dynamic requirements and processes more slowly. At one time, its flexibility made it the main choice for leading-edge development, but it was weak on graphics. Now, more platform-specific languages have taken the edge away from Lisp because they can access the platform's graphics abilities. If you were exploring internal structure and didn't need to worry about graphics, Lisp would still be a leading candidate.

Java is a product introduced by Sun Software that resembles C++ but also has some important differences. With Java, programmers don't have to worry about issues such as memory management. More importantly, we can run blocks of code (known as "applets") on any platform having a Java interpreter. Heterogeneous simulations should benefit from using applets across platforms, but because Java is interpreted, it's slower than a compiled language. No simulators have used Java so far, but as it gains more users, it will become a good candidate.

10.3.2   Languages for Rapid Application Development

Languages for rapid application development are fairly new because they've had to wait for appropriate foundation hardware and software. They have an associated, highly graphical environment that accelerates development. If you choose evolutionary development, these languages will work well for you.

Visual Basic is a Microsoft product that was the first widely available graphical programming language. It allows quick programming of some very powerful applications, but it doesn't support fully object-oriented concepts or pointers.

PowerBuilder, from PowerSoft, is a graphical programming language for object-oriented application development. It aims mainly at client-server applications.

Delphi, a Borland product, is a graphical programming language based on object Pascal. It gives programmers much more control than Visual Basic does, so they can write code that would be impossible in Visual Basic. Yet, it's almost as fast to produce.

10.3.3   Simulation Languages

Simulation languages, as mentioned earlier, are at the middle level for implementing simulations. Each language abstracts models in a certain way and provides prebuilt units for certain domains. For instance, languages aimed at modeling computer networks will provide prebuilt, validated entities for RAM storage, disk storage, LAN communication, the CPU, and so on. Although you could adapt many of them to your domain, each one has a learning curve. So, you should choose one to match your team's experience and the development's needs. If one of these languages applies to your domain, use it—you'll flatten the learning curve and keep your domain experts in familiar territory.

Simscript, supported by California Analysis Center Inc. (CACI), is one of the venerable programming languages for simulations. It uses discrete-event simulation and is quite generic.

ModSim, also supported by CACI, is an object-oriented programming language that allows you to model objects with methods specifying their behaviors. They can affect one another by sending messages and suspending the calling process until the called process responds, or by sending messages and proceeding.

BONeS, supported by the Alta Group of Cadence, is a powerful language for simulating communication networks. It works with Signal Processing Workbench to powerfully analyze communication-network hardware, from designing application-specific integrated circuits through network traffic flows.

Opnet is supported by Mil3, a commercial vendor of simulation tools. It's another powerful language for communication networks. It moves messages (packets) through a network that can be defined at several layers. At the bottom is the process layer, which has predefined elements such as queues, traffic generators, collectors, etc., but which you can augment with processes in C. Opnet allows you to create icons for the processes and connect them in the next higher layer—the node layer. It assigns icons to nodes, which you can then connect in subnetworks and networks. Using C, you can define almost anything as an output statistic and define different probe sets to collect these statistics. But don't collect too much data during a run; it can become overwhelming.

COMNET, another CACI tool, aims (as do BONeS and Opnet) at simulating communication networks. But it's at a higher level, having prebuilts for the prevalent bridges, routers, servers, etc., and for defining protocols to update the routing table.

VisSim, supported by Visual Solutions, is a PC-based tool that, by using error estimation, can emulate analog simulations on digital machines.

SLAM uses entities flowing through a network defined by activities whose starts and finishes are marked by nodes, as well as gates (which control transaction flow) and global network variables [Pritsker 1995].

GPSS, the General Purpose Simulation System, has been evolving for more than twenty years as a discrete-event tool. It consists of transactions (which could play the role of parts being assembled in a manufacturing scenario or packets in a communications scenario), facilities, storages, and logic switches [Schriber 1991].

10.3.4   Commercial Off-the-Shelf Tools

You must consider Commercial Off-the-Shelf (COTS) and Government Off-the-Shelf (GOTS) tools for modeling and simulation efforts, but only if many people in your community use them. Section 10.1.2 discussed why a large installed base is more important for software than whether it's commercial or off the shelf. Let's remind ourselves of the major pluses of an installed base:

- Likelihood of future support or easy migration to new versions
- Vested interest of the vendor in continuing to serve users
- Safer investment of your financial and intellectual capital
- Large pool of users, which gives you talent for development and testing
- Continual pressure to improve performance and lower cost, which enhances your project

Installed base also strongly influences whether an application will do what you need or if you have to develop certain abilities yourself. Still, you must work with a product to some extent to decide whether it applies to your project. Or you can rely on someone you trust who says it does. If no one has used the product and you can't evaluate it extensively, you need a senior architect who has had close experience with various tools, problem types, and solutions built to address those problems. This senior person can determine whether the central structures of the product and the problem will match.

"Templates" are pseudo-software built using COTS software. Referring to Fig. 10.7, you'll see they correspond to products at the middle layer of the structural hierarchy. So, even though you'll buy COTS tools for direct development, you may still have to develop and manage these templates.

10.4   Choosing Hardware

Figure 10.4 makes a point we can't ignore: the cost of computing hardware drops tenfold every three years. That is, a project officer in 1998 would expect to pay $20 thousand for the computational horsepower that a 1989 project officer would have bought for $20 million. This means we can do M&S for much less money, and the power will be available to many more people. This larger community can support the crafting of software-support tools, which can further decrease costs. For instance, the larger the number of platforms in place, the smaller the per-unit cost to develop a product. Thus, it may be cheaper and easier to produce a very professional display on a commodity platform than on a niche platform. To take advantage of this leverage, we need to look at the installed base as a main criterion for choosing equipment, just as we do for software and simulation languages.

But what if you have to model a special activity, for which time, space, weight, or other considerations drive you toward niche equipment? For instance, threat simulators in pods mounted onto training aircraft have to run on machines designed for that stressful environment. In these cases, you might need to design hardware to meet the need within the constraints. Of course, unlike software, hardware is inflexible, so you must know exactly what it is supposed to do before even thinking about buying it. If you must develop hardware, a software prototype can help delineate the requirements by at least emulating for users what they would expect to see from the hardware. As pointed out in Sec. 10.1.3, using low-resolution simulators in the early stages can allow you to explore more decision space than, say, brassboard mockups in hardware.

10.4.1   Choosing Processing Power for Special Areas

Real-time graphical simulators often support training by allowing trainees to learn by interacting with a virtual world. These simulators require very high resolution and very fast repaint times. Because the market for this type of equipment is relatively small, its high costs can't be spread over a large community.

Some simulations require large databases with random access. One example is terrain and environment databases for large-scale, high-resolution war games. Another is a simulator for designing high-density chips based on engineering drawings. Object-oriented databases have been successful in both cases.

As discussed earlier in the chapter, computational fluid dynamics was the first simulation area which demanded extremely powerful hardware. In fact, this area and crypto problems were for a long time the main customers for vector-type supercomputers.

Servers and mainframes require more processing power because they serve less powerful client machines. They also need to work continuously and to be secure.

10.4.2   Networked, Heterogeneous Simulations

Networked or heterogeneous simulations require special approaches to software and, especially, to the interface hardware. Chapters 15 and 16 discuss these issues. Most likely, as the rest of the world gets pulled into multimedia, the simulation world will also. Users will probably expect something close to what they see in games that run on PCs or over the internet. As one senior executive said: "I am tired of seeing my organization pay out millions of dollars over several years for something that can be bought for a couple of hundred dollars at Fry's [a local computer store] by the time it's delivered."

10.5   Maintaining Integrity

In the three previous sections, we discussed the third step of implementation (see Fig. 10.5)—in which we evaluate and select the software structure, software languages, and hardware. Now we're at the fourth step—planning, carrying out, verifying, and delivering the simulation. Before we start, we must make sure we can measure whether we're getting what we expected within the allotted resources. To do so, we must attend to specifications, standards, verification and validation procedures, and configuration management.

10.5.1   Specifications and Standards

Chapter 13 discusses specifications and standards, but I want to focus here on how they apply to implementation. We read specifications to understand what must be done and, in turn, use them to describe to our team what they must do. They also allow us to measure progress and focus on correcting discrepancies.

If the goals of the project aren't clear, the specifications won't be crisp, and our measurements won't be precise. The project could veer off course. In this situation, we must make sure feedback loops are tight and match our vision to the users' concept. As pointed out earlier, a working rapid prototype can get better responses than a hardcopy document. If the responses are positive, the prototype helps us meet specifications, check to see what's missing, and remove anything users see as "overkill."

Standards are essentially "general specifications" established for all simulations by the outside world. They help us make sure that the application will operate with others (when necessary) and that the outside world will accept it.

10.5.2   Verification and Validation

Chapter 11 fully details these two key tasks in M&S. We'll touch on them here because, as Chap. 11 says, they "must be an integral part of the simulation development and of the entire simulation life cycle to be effective and affordable." How can we ensure they are integral to our project? We know how many components we must deliver and what they must do. As we apportion tasks to the project team, we must define for them the specifications they need to meet. Then, we must make sure a feedback loop is in place and use the techniques in Chap. 11 to verify that the teams are meeting their objectives.

Multi-level efforts, in which different organizations are responsible for different levels of the structure, are becoming more prevalent and introducing issues of their own (as pointed out in Sec. 11.2). If commercial organizations provide the structure's lower levels, and if the installed base is significant, you can view adequate performance for other users as a vote of confidence for your application. In any case, implementers at a given level should develop tests that exercise the lower levels in the expected envelope for which they have alternate ways to predict results. For example, if we are at the network level of the example in Sec. 11.2, we could wire together a network and exercise it with Poisson traffic generators. The results of this test can be predicted analytically; so if we get agreement, we can be confident that the network part of the example will work correctly when we insert the actual traffic generators for the problem under study.

10.5.3   Configuration Management

To remember where we are, how we got there, and where we're going, we must set up guidance early on for recording bugs and other feedback, documenting how and when the team solves bugs, verifying modules, and releasing versions of the simulation. By managing these configuration items, we can see what remains undone, rank order open tasks, allocate them to revisions of modules, and combine module releases into a final release of the full system. Section 6.2.2 discusses the process of planning the development in detail.

10.6   Managing the Implementation

To manage a project, you must start with a plan for configuration management. It details what you must address at each release of each module. To this skeleton document, you add phasing, rank ordering, sequencing of tasks, feedback loops, and costing for each milestone. Management really means matching feedback to expectations. When they differ, you exert control to change outcomes. However, as control theory has taught us, these feedback loops need to be fairly short or the project will stray so much that you can't put it back on course with the controls available to you. Section 6.2.3 discusses the use of metrics to track and oversee development.

References

Crawford, S.L., and T. Fall. 1990. "Projection Pursuit Techniques for Visualizing High-Dimensional Data Sets." *Visualization in Scientific Computing*. Nielson, G.M. and Shriver, B., Editors. Los Alamitos, CA: IEEE Computer Society Press Tutorial. pp. 94–108.

Devaney, R. C. 1986. *An Introduction to Chaotic Dynamic Systems*. Menlo Park: Benjamin/Cummings Publishing Company.

Hein, C., J. Pridgen, and W. Kline. 1997. "RASSP Virtual Prototyping of DSP Systems." *Proceedings of the 34th Design Automation Conference (DAC)*, ACM, New York.

Li, W., N.H. Packard, and C. Langton. 1990. *Transition Phenomena in Cellular Automate Rule Space*. Santa Fe Technical Report. 90-008.

Moin, P. and J. Kim. "Tackling Turbulence with Supercomputers." *Scientific American*. Vol. 276, No. 1, January, 1997, pp. 62–68.

Pritsker, Alan B. 1995. *Introduction to Simulation and SLAM II*. New York, NY: John Wiley & Sons.

Rose, F. et. al. 1997. "Performance Modeling of System Architectures." *Journal of VLSI Signal Processing*. Vol. 15, The Netherlands: Kluwer Academic Publishers.

Schriber, T.J. 1991. *An Introduction to Simulation Using GPSS/H*. New York, NY: John Wiley & Sons.

Sieburg, H. B. and O. K. Clay. 1991. "A Cellular Device Machine Development System for Modeling Biology on the Computer." *Complex Systems*. Vol. V, pp. 575–601.

CHAPTER 11

Verification, Validation, and Accreditation

Dale K. Pace, *The Johns Hopkins University*
Applied Physics Laboratory

The value of a simulation lies only in the utility of its application. Whether used to describe and increase understanding of a subject or as a calculation process, the simulation must be accurate enough and precise enough to meet its intended uses and to develop confidence in its results. Verification, validation, and accreditation (VV&A) enhance the correctness and credibility of simulations and their results; thus, they ensure a simulation is acceptable for its intended purpose.

As Table 11.1 shows, the five sections of this chapter combine to address nine goals. Once you've completed all five sections, you'll thoroughly understand these goals, as well as the techniques and issues important to effective VV&A. Consult the list of references for current VV&A policies and more detailed treatments of correctness and credibility for simulation.

Table 11.1. **Goals for this Chapter.**

Goal	Description	Pertinent Chapter Sections
1	Help you determine when to apply techniques for verification and validation (V&V) in order to make simulations correct and credible	11.2.1 & 11.2.2
2	Help you appreciate the importance of validating the simulation concept (the requirements, conceptual model, and specifications that establish the "model" in the formalism of Chapter 3). Doing so will allow you to prevent or lessen simulation faults that arise from inadequate concepts.	11.2.1
3	Guide you in verifying that the simulation design, code, and hardware correctly represent the simulation concept	11.2.1, 11.3, 11.4, & 11.5.5
4	Help you understand what validation requires	11.2.1, 11.3, 11.4, 11.5.1, 11.5.5, & 11.5.6
5	Help you understand and appreciate the processes normally involved in accrediting simulations and provide a basis for estimating their effect on cost and schedule	11.2.1 & 11.5.3
6	Make you familiar with basic techniques for V&V and tell you about special V&V concerns for M&S: using artificial intelligence, requiring high fidelity, involving people or hardware	11.3 & 11.4
7	Show how validation depends on simulation data	11.2.1 & 11.5.2
8	Suggest ways of staffing and managing VV&A activities	11.5.4 & 11.5.5
9	Show how cost and time for V&V relate to the levels of validation and credibility you want. Also show how applying sound V&V principles can achieve a specified level of validation and credibility while reducing the effect of V&V on overall cost and schedule.	11.5.1 & 11.5.3

11.1　Definitions, Perspectives, and Limits

11.1.1　Definitions

The many varied definitions related to VV&A have created confusion. Some common definitions for verification and validation (V&V) are software oriented [Institute of Electrical and Electronic Engineers 1992] and differ from definitions of VV&A for models and simulations. In most of the latter, verification means the simulation satisfies its requirements and specifications ("the simulation was built right"), whereas validation means the simulation is correct ("the right simulation was built").

Since the mid-1990s, largely as a result of efforts by the Military Operations Research Society (MORS) and the Defense Modeling and Simulation Office (DMSO), the Defense community has used relatively consistent definitions for VV&A terms. This consistency is helping the entire modeling and simulation

(M&S) community develop a coherent vocabulary for VV&A. Here are some definitions [Department of Defense 1994]:

- *Verification:* Process of determining that a model implementation accurately represents the developer's conceptual description and specifications.

- *Validation:* Process of determining the degree to which a model is an accurate representation of the real world from the perspective of the model's intended uses.

- *Accreditation/Certification:* Official determination that a model, simulation, and/or data are acceptable for a specific purpose. Accreditation is used most often for models or simulations; certification is more frequently applied to data.

These general terms for VV&A are compatible with the more precise definitions in Chapter 3. In this chapter, I'll use the general terms, unless I need the more precise ones to clarify a concept.

V&V measure a simulation's correctness, abilities, faults, and limits. We don't have widely accepted metrics for measuring a simulation's correctness, but we do have useful metrics for estimating expected numbers of software faults [Jones 1996; Lyu 1996]. Other terms often used in VV&A include "fidelity," which addresses a simulation's accuracy and precision, and "testing," which determines a simulation's credibility. Sometimes, people use VV&A to describe all processes required to ensure that a simulation is correct, uses appropriate data, and produces confidence in its responses and results. Some people confuse quality assurance and VV&A. Quality assurance focuses on processes; VV&A concerns products (requirements, conceptual models, software code, simulation results, etc.).

Whereas V&V are technical activities, accreditation and certification are management functions that judge the suitability of input data, the simulation, and all its related elements for a particular purpose. The Defense community worked hard during the early 1990s to determine what kind of simulation use had to be accredited and who had accreditation and certification authority and responsibility. The references at the end of this chapter to directives and instructions from the military services and the DOD reflect this activity. "Warranties" and liability concerns related to simulation performance are civilian parallels to the DOD's focus on accreditation and certification. Sometimes the term "model qualification" is used in non-government circles for assessment of a simulation's credibility [Balci 1994].

11.1.2   Perspectives on Verification, Validation, and Accreditation (VV&A)

To give us a larger context for VV&A, we need to look at the complexity of contemporary simulation, the uses for simulations, and VV&A's relation to simulation development.

A modern simulation may involve people, hardware, and real systems as well as software. So V&V concepts for software alone won't work for all simulation

V&V—although applying the best software engineering to developing simulations will improve V&V for both. In this chapter, we'll discuss special V&V issues for simulations that involve people or hardware in single or distributed locations. We'll also look at the special challenges to VV&A posed by distributed simulations.

We can't discuss VV&A for simulation without considering the intended application (which can vary widely, as illustrated in Chap. 1), as well as the correctness of input data and appropriateness of software, hardware, systems, and people who are part of the simulation. We have to include the analytical process, training environment, objectives, and experimental design within which a simulation is to be used. Sometimes a simulation will have less accurate elements or limited data that we can overcome with adroit analysis. On the other hand, even correct and credible simulation results can be misused.

VV&A must be part of a simulation's total development lifecycle to be effective and affordable. A major problem with VV&A in the past has been starting V&V too late—leaving it to the testing phase. The later we detect a fault in a simulation development or application the more difficult and more expensive that fault will be to correct—up to one hundred times more expensive [Miller 1993]. Because upwards of 60% of software and simulation faults may result from inadequate initial requirements, conceptual models, and designs [Lewis 1992], we must start V&V early [Zelkowitz 1993]. Otherwise, we're doomed to address only late-detected faults. If we start early, we can prevent many faults by thoroughly (or at least extensively) verifying and validating simulation requirements and underlying conceptual models. As developers, we should try to decrease faults by applying rigorous V&V in all phases of a simulation's development.

11.1.3   Limits on Verification, Validation, and Accreditation (VV&A)

Some simulations, such as numerical models of natural systems, can't be "validated" absolutely because natural systems are never closed and simulation results don't apply to all possible outcomes [Oreskes 1994]. An example would be hydrological and geochemical simulations predicting the behavior of toxic and radioactive contaminants in proposed waste disposal sites. Other simulations represent subjects, such as battles, which can't be compared with the "real world" because we don't know enough about reality.

To understand the limits of VV&A more clearly, we need to distinguish between a given simulation's descriptive, structural, and predictive validity. For example, a simulation may represent all parts of a system and help us understand it but still not allow us to predict behavior because it doesn't have necessary parameter values and initial conditions. Such a simulation may be excellent for reconstructing events after they occur. Other simulations may not have the kind of internal structure we need to understand processes, but they may predict well. For example, statistical models based on history can help us estimate military losses in crises and low-intensity conflicts but reveal nothing about the way war works. Similarly, we can more accurately predict the cost of future weapon systems by modeling cost-per-pound than by doing more detailed, bottom-up engineering.

Of course, even the simulations we can't rigorously validate may still be useful because they enhance communication and understanding about the subjects they represent, including the relative importance of and interactions among the subject's parts [Hodges 1992]. Understanding the limits on validation allows us to apply VV&A appropriately by focusing resources on areas that will give us the best results and using sensitivity analyses to establish how less certain aspects will affect these results. VV&A also helps us choose appropriate applications for simulation (the experimental frame in Chap. 3).

Some people are more pessimistic about simulation validity, claiming that "no model can be validated in an absolute sense" [Quade 1985]. This perspective follows the belief of philosopher Sir Karl Popper [1959] that "falsification" is the central tenet of the modern scientific method. Falsification means we can only "prove" hypotheses, including models, wrong—never right. From this perspective, a simulation's credibility depends on how vigorously we try to prove a model is wrong. Thus, our plan for VV&A should include experiments designed for this purpose, so we can show that our simulation can't be proven wrong and is, therefore, credible.

We can't completely verify and validate a large simulation. It would take too long to check all possible paths through, and all possible operational combinations of elements in, a major simulation. As Jasper Welch said, "10^{31} is forever" [Hoeber 1981]. Even if we could check each possibility in a mere nanosecond, it would take longer than the age of the earth to check all 2^{100} (approximately 10^{31}) permutations of a simulation with just 100 two-state factors (branches or other significant alternatives). And large simulations, which may represent thousands or even hundreds of thousands of lines of code, have many more than 100 significant multi-state factors.

Because our resources are limited, we must order VV&A to give the more critical parts of a simulation our greatest attention. The more thoroughly we develop the conceptual model for a simulation, the easier it will be to identify those critical elements. We should also attend to the more common kinds of faults and the more detectable faults. Most software faults (in some cases 80–90%) fall into a handful of types: requirements incompletely describe how the simulation should operate, errors occur in logic and sequencing within the internal processing or coding of the simulation, data is incorrect or ambiguous, and so on [Lewis 1992; Miller 1993]. Not all V&V techniques are equally important; some can detect only a few kinds of faults, whereas others can detect more, and a few can detect many [Balci 1994; Miller 1993]. Some techniques require far more resources than others. Which techniques are most helpful depends on the phase of simulation development and the nature of the simulation, as well as the languages and environment the simulation uses. Consequently, knowledge and experience strongly affect the scope, effectiveness, efficiency, and cost of VV&A. Later in this chapter, we'll talk further about how to use V&V techniques.

Techniques to produce highly accurate (or "mathematically proven" correct) software for simulations, often called "formal" methods, have restricted applications [Bowen 1994a], although their use in safety-critical and security-critical applications appears to be growing [Larsen 1996]. Therefore, we should assume recent and future simulations will have faults. Simulation developers should consider fault-tolerant designs, especially for safety-critical systems. Large simulations should be able to tolerate infrequent "5,000-year" errors [Littlewood 1992], perhaps by using several redundant elements that employ different algorithms or approaches for the same function [McAllister 1996]. Fault-tolerant computing remains an important issue [Institute of Electrical and Electronic Engineers 1995].

Applying "formal" methods helps simulations, even when they can't mathematically prove all elements are correct. The benefits include improved correctness, enhanced communication between simulation users and developers, earlier error detection (which reduces effort for correcting errors), and easier maintenance, including a capability for documented links between simulation requirements, the conceptual model, specifications, and implementation [Lano 1995].

11.2   Basic Concepts for Verification, Validation, and Accreditation (VV&A)

11.2.1   Basic Stages of VV&A

Methods vary for simulation development, including the waterfall, incremental, spiral, and rapid prototyping methods discussed in Chap. 4. Figure 11.1 shows a VV&A paradigm that can apply to all of these methods. It's based on a scheme originally developed in the Navy's Interim Policy Guidance for VV&A [Pace 1993]. Of course, we must carefully determine when a simulation's requirements, conceptual model, specifications, and software parts are final enough for formal reviews. This is easiest for the waterfall approach, but the spiral and rapid-prototyping methods don't have simple rules. Thus, we need to maintain an audit trail for V&V from initial requirements to final use. Audit trails are especially important when elements of the simulation change repeatedly because accumulated information can help us judge a simulation's suitability through accreditation and certification.

Validating the Concept

Simulation development starts with defining the subject (the "source system" in Chap. 3) which the simulation is to represent and the intended uses for the simulation (the "experimental frame" in Chap. 3). Sometimes, users have trouble stating how they intend to use the simulation: What problems must it address? How will it support training? How will decision aids based on the simulation represent decision processes? But they must specify the subject and its intended uses before we can develop a concept (the "model" in Chap. 3). and express it in terms of *requirements*. Many software and simulation faults have resulted from inadequate (incomplete, ambiguous, or incorrect) requirements, so we must

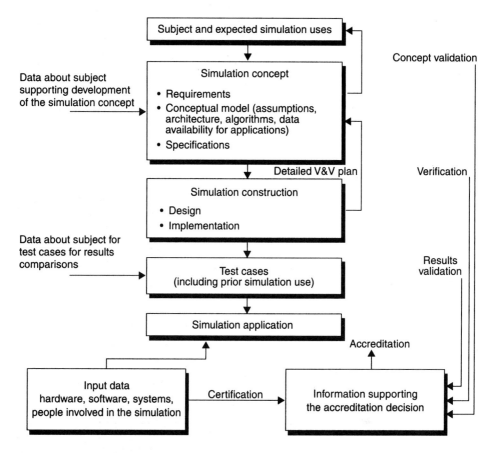

Fig. 11.1.   Basic Paradigm for Simulation VV&A. This figure shows the relationship of VV&A endeavors to simulation development and application. Note: Most feedback and iteration paths are not shown.

repeatedly and extensively review them before translating them into a *conceptual model*. The conceptual model

- Identifies assumptions for the model
- Specifies the architecture for relating one part of the simulation ("simulator" in Chap. 3) to another
- Suggests which algorithms to use
- Lists intended applications
- States what input data the simulation needs

Notice that this "conceptual model" combines Chap. 3's "model" with elements of its "experimental frame."

The conceptual model helps simulation developers, anticipated users of the simulation, and subject-matter experts (SMEs) evaluate the simulation's requirements and concept. (Here, "developers" include project developers, planners, and managers, plus the designers, integrators, and implementers of models and simulations—as described in Chap. 3.) The conceptual model allows everyone to communicate because it's stated in understandable language, which means the team can accurately specify what the simulation must do. Section 8.4.2 presents many ideas which are pertinent to validating the simulation concept. *The first step in V&V is to validate the simulation concept*, so

- The requirements state what the simulation must do

- The conceptual model completely embodies these requirements

- The specifications accurately depict the conceptual model

Algorithms in the conceptual model may be very general because they normally aren't fully defined until simulation design is well underway. Still, the better we can identify algorithms in the conceptual model, the more completely we'll know the simulation's abilities and limits. That, in turn, will allow us to respond to "requirements creep," which—for two-year projects— may increase requirements by up to 25% [Jones 1996]. Inadequately validating requirements and developing incomplete conceptual models (especially within the DOD) have hampered most legacy (existing) simulations. Despite the difficulties in defining a simulation's purpose and keeping up with changing requirements, we must make sure the requirements, conceptual model, and specifications still represent the subject and satisfy the simulation's intended uses. If we don't do this well, we may undermine confidence in the simulation's correctness.

Verifying the Design and Implementation

Once we've established the simulation's requirements, conceptual model, and specifications, we can finish its design. Verifying this final design is very important, even if we've already verified several preliminary designs to satisfy simulation requirements. In fact, we must formally verify each version of the simulation as it's finalized if we expect to use that version. This process is often called *"design verification"* or *"logical verification,"* which means the design satisfies specifications and fully represents its conceptual model.

Verifying that the simulation carries out its design is the most straightforward part of V&V and is most often addressed by the literature on software V&V. In fact, some software development environments provide automatic code production from specifications, which can improve fault detection and reduce personnel costs for V&V. This type of verification is often called *"implementation"* or *"code" verification.*

Validating Results

Chapter 3 discusses replicative, predictive, and structural validity, but this chapter focuses on the first two. Thus, validating a simulation means its results agree acceptably with observations about the subject (replicative) and its predictions agree acceptably with observations about the subject when it is in the same condition (predictive). Structural validity is not necessarily implied by validation as discussed here. To validate simulation results, we must collect, organize, and sometimes even generate accurate data. We need information about the subject a simulation represents to develop the simulation concept, as well as to form test cases that ensure the simulation works right. If this information isn't available, we can't completely validate the simulation. In some cases, we can only compare simulation results with the opinions of subject-matter experts—usually called *"face validation."*

Information (the system and process data described in Chap. 9) typically comes from historical data about the subject, experiments and tests (developmental and operational), or results from other simulations with validated ability to describe the subject's response. We may use a "standard" set of test data (see Chap. 9) as a "benchmark" to validate results, but an organization that develops a simulation often won't have the resources to generate this data. Instead, a higher authority or the community of users may need to produce it.

In some cases, expensive new tests and experiments may be necessary, but who pays for that kind of data collection? Should it be part of V&V costs? Most would say, "No." In fact, many would say paying to collect data shouldn't even be part of simulation development. Instead, developers are more likely to opt for validating pieces of the simulation where reliable data exists. We can do this "piecemeal" validation even when we don't have substantial, reliable data about the whole subject, but this limited approach makes thorough validation of the entire simulation unlikely.

Accrediting and Certifying the Simulation

Accrediting a simulation for a particular application requires us to certify that 1) the simulation's input data is appropriate, 2) people, software, hardware, or systems are appropriate, and 3) the application is within the domain in which the simulation appropriately represents the subject. We should base accreditation on this certification plus the accumulated information from concept validation, verification, and results validation.

Normally, we accredit and certify either a domain (general) or an application (specific). The former asserts that a simulation is useful for a kind or class of application. The latter addresses a specific use of the simulation. It has to consider

- The simulation's role in the application (for example, as part of an analysis or training exercise)
- The simulation's abilities and limits
- The appropriateness of input data and any software, hardware, systems, or people involved in the simulation

The same simulation may be accredited for one application but not for another. For example, a medium-fidelity simulation of an air-defense missile might be accredited for analyzing how many missile systems are needed but not for analyzing how effective the missile would be in an engagement, for which we'd need a high-fidelity simulation.

It's possible to abuse accreditation by inappropriately extending domain accreditation to particular applications or by using a previously accredited simulation for a similar or a different application, without fully analyzing it. We must be careful not to allow any of these abuses.

Developing a Detailed Plan for V&V

With validated requirements, conceptual model, and specifications in hand, we can develop a detailed V&V plan for the simulation. Note that we may have to validate a concept before contractual and administrative arrangements for development are complete. This can force our initial efforts to rely on inadequate simulation requirements and specifications, allowing many otherwise preventable simulation faults. That's why we must establish effective management and administration early enough to properly validate the simulation concept.

We can do a preliminary V&V plan before validating the simulation concept, but final (detailed) planning must come after this validation. The detailed plan

- Helps us verify that the simulation satisfies specifications
- Helps us validate results
- Identifies most (if not all) information about the simulation needed to accredit it
- May address certification processes for data, people, hardware, software, and systems that are part of the simulation

The detailed V&V plan should at least

1. Identify key V&V elements:
   - Subject-matter experts (SMEs) for face validation and other reviews (See Sec. 11.3.1 on using SMEs in reviews)
   - Specific computer aided software engineering (CASE) tools and other software packages to be used in V&V
   - V&V techniques for simulating and specifying any protocols or standards to which the simulation must conform
   - Data and data sources we'll use in validating simulation results (See Sec. 11.5.2 for more information)
   - Previous and other related V&V activities that may provide information
   - Documentation required for simulation V&V, including an audit trail from requirements through coding to demonstration of the simulation's correctness (See Sec. 11.5.5 for more information)

2. Specify where in simulation development V&V activities are to be done and by whom (the simulation developer's people, an independent agent, etc.). V&V should always be systematic [Sheng 1993]. Section 11.5.5 discusses how to manage VV&A.

3. Specify V&V criteria to be applied or which may affect accreditation. These criteria include identifying which elements of the simulation are most critical for V&V and their relative priority.

4. Specify documentation required for VV&A (what; who will prepare, review, and approve it; when; what format; where maintained; etc.). In addition, to establish a simulation's correctness and credibility, the Defense community often requires documented information about:

   • The model (description of the model and simulation, user's manual, analyst's manual, programmer's guide, etc.)
   • Configuration management (plan, reports, etc.)
   • The intended application
   • Data, people, and equipment that may be involved in applying the simulation

5. Estimate resources required for V&V activities and their effect on simulation-development and application schedules (Sec. 11.5.3 discusses how):

   • Staffing, including specific people
   • Special equipment or software packages
   • Collecting data
   • Coordinating with other organizations
   • Time to do tests or simulation runs
   • Costs

The detailed V&V plan may also identify V&V people or include administrative and contractual details on activities for V&V or independent V&V (IV&V). This plan may also suggest how the simulation will be used (beyond the criteria shown above), discuss relationships to existing or developing simulations, or describe the context for simulation development.

11.2.2   VV&A for Distributed Simulations

Distributed simulations connect several simulations for an exercise or application. These simulations may include real systems; software-, hardware-, or humans-in-the-loop; or traditional computer simulations. The Defense community uses the terms live, virtual, and constructive forces, respectively, to describe these three elements of distributed simulations.

VV&A of distributed simulations have to make sure individual and composite simulations are correct and credible. Figure 11.2 shows what is involved assuming we have information about the VV&A of individual simulations and each simulation is acceptable for a distributed environment. Now, in addition to basic correctness and credibility issues for individual simulations, VV&A are concerned with compliance and compatibility between elements as well as the composite simulation's correctness and credibility. Thus, we have to know about an individual simulation before we can start VV&A for the distributed simulation. Then, we can address

- *Compliance*, which means the individual simulations for a distributed simulation satisfy the protocols and requirements of the distributed simulation's environment. This check verifies that each simulation can work properly in that environment.

- *Compatibility*, which addresses (verifies) the simulations' ability to work together effectively. In the early days of distributed simulations, compatibility was a major problem. Incompatibilities in terrain representations for the Army's early distributed-simulation exercises caused some simulated tanks to float in the air, some simulated aircraft to fly underground, and so on. As indicated in Sec. 5.3.1, this can be a special problem for simulations with different formalisms.

- *Correctness*, which validates a distributed simulation's design and implementation. Can the design for this collection of individual simulations satisfy the application's objectives? Sometimes, we must experiment with the simulations to see if they can satisfy these objectives—and sometimes, we may need to replace individual simulations or change the distributed simulation in some other way to satisfy them. In distributed simulations involving live forces, we may not be able to test the entire composite simulation before using it because the live forces may not be available. In this case, we can't completely validate the distributed simulation before applying it.

- *Credibility*, which examines how confident we are in the experience or results of a distributed-simulation application. This step accredits a distributed simulation.

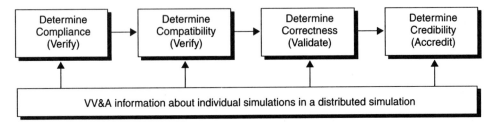

Fig. 11.2.   **Paradigm for VV&A of a Distributed Simulation.** For distributed simulations, we must add compliance and compatibility to the requirements for VV&A of each simulation.

Obviously, if we have to do VV&A on the individual simulations and on the composite simulation, we'll spend a lot of time and money. If we had a common format for all VV&A information, we could more easily ensure all simulations are compatible and verify that the composite simulation could do the job. No such accepted standards exist, but recommended VV&A practices developed for the Defense community in 1996—available from the Defense Modeling and Simulation Office's (DMSO) website (http://www.dmso.mil)—have at least identified some information items needed for a detailed plan. These items should be the core information available for individual simulations in a distributed simulation.

IEEE Standard 1278.4 defines a nine-step process for Distributed Interactive Simulation (DIS) exercises. These steps are the most thoroughly and formally defined process available for VV&A of distributed simulations:

1. Verify compliance standards
2. Plan for VV&A
3. Validate the conceptual model (of the DIS exercise, not of individual simulations)
4. Verify the architectural design (verifies that preliminary plans for the architecture of the DIS exercise will carry out the exercise's conceptual model)
5. Verify the detailed design
6. Verify compatibility (completes verification and ensures the composite distributed simulation will work right)
7. Validate the exercise (focuses on the exercise's operation to ensure entity behaviors are appropriate to satisfy exercise objectives)
8. Accredit the exercise
9. Prepare reports

These nine steps simply elaborate on the paradigm of Figure 11.2.

Though useful for DIS, this process doesn't apply fully to other distributed-simulation environments. Therefore, we must employ the VV&A protocols of our particular environment to check for compliance. For example, VV&A processes are being developed for distributed simulations using the High Level Architecture (HLA) environment. When complete, they'll be available from the DMSO website: http://www.dmso.mil. Still, the general ideas I've presented should apply to all distributed-simulation environments. Section 12.4 addresses some of the more practical aspects of V&V for distributed simulation.

11.3   Basic Techniques for V&V

Over a hundred techniques have been identified for V&V [Miller 1993], and a number of CASE tools have special features which help us verify code. Some techniques are easy to use; others require skilled people, such as subject-matter experts and statisticians, or specialized software or equipment [Halbwachs 1992;

McFarland 1993]. No single technique can detect all kinds of simulation faults, but some can detect more than others. And all faults can be detected by more than one technique. We can apply some techniques to validate concepts, verify simulations, and validate results; others are useful only for verification. To be effective, V&V must use techniques that can detect a broad range of faults for a particular kind of simulation. If experienced people do the detailed planning, we can use fewer V&V resources while remaining confident that a simulation is correct. We'll discuss many of these points in more detail later.

Table 11.2 shows how we can group more than forty techniques for V&V based on their characteristics. The Army's pamphlet on VV&A (1993) takes a different approach—describing V&V techniques for different phases of simulation development. We'll generalize these approaches in this section by examining five distinct classes of techniques: review, statistics, logic and structure, sensitivity analysis, and visualization. These classes aren't as complete as Table 11.2, but they give us a good starting point.

Table 11.2.   **Grouping Techniques for Validation, Verification, and Testing.** This table shows how we can categorize techniques for V&V, based on shared characteristics. Taken from Balci [1994].

Informal	Dynamic	Symbolic
Audit	Black-box testing	Cause-effect graphing
Desk checking	Bottom-up testing	Partition analysis
Face validation	Debugging	Path analysis
Inspections	Execution monitoring	Symbolic execution
Reviews	Execution profiling	
Turing test	Execution tracing	**Constraint**
Walkthroughs	Field testing	Assertion checking
	Graphical comparisons	Boundary analysis
Static	Predictive validation	Inductive assertion
Consistency checking	Regression testing	
Data flow analysis	Sensitivity analysis	**Formal**
Graph-based analysis	Statistical techniques	Induction
Semantic analysis	Stress testing	Inference
Structural analysis	Submodel testing	Lambda calculus
Syntax analysis	Symbolic debugging	Logical deduction
	Top-down testing	Predicate calculus
	Visualizing	Predicate transformation
	White-box testing	Proof of correctness

An important way to produce reliable software, which I haven't addressed, is using metrics to predict the number of faults expected in the software and then tracking fault detection and correction or removal [Jones 1996; Lyu 1996]. This approach suggests when we may need to use more resources to detect faults.

11.3.1   Review Techniques

Face validation: Face validation is the most common way to validate simulations and is extremely valuable to V&V. It simply means that at least one subject-matter expert has declared that the simulation's structure, processes, and results seem appropriate. At present, face validations have little guidance: some are structured and systematic; others aren't. Here are some ways to make face validation more valuable:

1. Before reviewing the simulation, subject-matter experts should specify what they'll consider and what criteria they'll use. They don't have to limit their reviews to these items, but writing them out in advance will make the review more comprehensive, systematic, and objective. This is particularly important when experts from organizations other than the one developing the simulation, possibly even competitors, are doing the validation.

2. Face validation should be limited to usual—not unusual or unexpected— situations. Other techniques should determine the simulation's statistical or mathematical stability and evaluate its responses in unusual situations.

3. Subject-matter experts must understand the subject's (and its parts') behavior and characteristics. They must be competent and articulate, so they can clearly communicate their perceptions to the simulation-development team. (Note: Sec. 9.3.1 addresses potential concerns about data from experts.)

4. The development team must describe the simulation's structure and processes so subject-matter experts, who may not know its language or notation, can quickly comprehend them. The team must fully share their understanding of known and potential simulation problems. Therefore, subject-matter experts and development teams have to trust each other and cooperate if face validation is to be effective.

5. Some experts need to be reasonably independent of the simulation development, so they can help ensure shared perspectives don't result in "blind spots" [Lewis 1992] or a loss of objectivity.

Peer reviews and walk-throughs: Peer reviews and walk-throughs are common in verification, and sometimes, in validation. In them, a group (often small, sometimes one person) examines the simulation's design (and sometimes its details, as in a walk-through of the code). These activities detect and document faults for correction. The more thorough and systematic a review or walk-through is, the more likely it will detect problems. Reviews or walk-throughs may cover one function or part of the simulation, or all of it. They normally cover model structure, consistency, adherence to standards, documentation, and methods (including the appropriateness of algorithms and their coding). Walk-throughs often employ some of the logical and structural techniques identified below. Peer reviews and walk-throughs are most productive whenever we specify in advance the examination's scope, methods, and coverage.

11.3.2   Statistical Techniques

Statistical techniques support validation of results better whenever simulations model well-known subjects because they compare and correlate the results of a simulation run with known data about the subject. We may have to use multivariate statistical techniques to correlate all of the simulation's output variables with observed data. Appropriate statistical techniques include regression analysis, time-series analysis, nonparametric tests for goodness-of-fit, analysis of variance and multivariate analysis of variance, factor analysis, and confidence intervals or regions [Balci 1994]. Appendix C discusses some of these techniques in more detail.

For models that include random processes, we must pay particular attention to the way we control seeds for generators of pseudo-random numbers, as well as the way the simulation generates these pseudo-random numbers. If we don't, "random" processes may actually be correlated and demonstrate predictable (not random) behavior. In general, it's good practice to have separate strings of pseudo-random numbers for each major stochastic process in the simulation. See App. C for more information.

Simulations with random processes typically replicate a process several times, using the same input data but different collections of pseudo-random numbers. We must have some measure of the statistical stability and dispersion of results as a function of the number of replications. Confidence intervals or other indications of results dispersion should be part of the simulation's standard outputs. Sometimes financial or time pressures limit replications of each case to only a few replications whenever the simulation is large or requires long processing times—without due regard for the statistical significance, stability, or dispersion of results for that number of replications. Besides consulting App. C, you may want to look at Dewar, et. al. [1995] to see how you can get meaningful results from simulations with many variables using fewer replications than some might suggest.

Unfortunately, even considering techniques to reduce replications, past analyses have often used too few replications for meaningful results. Traditionally, we'd detect the main effects with either comprehensive, full-factorial or low-resolution, fractional-factorial designs. But both approaches still require many more cases than we can normally consider, so we have to judge which variables are critical, which ones only slightly affect results, and which ones we may treat as "fixed." The number of critical variables will always drive the number of replications, but this approach allows us to use far fewer cases than we normally need for meaningful insights about main effects and their interactions.

11.3.3   Techniques Using Logic and Structure

Logical techniques include checking consistency, analyzing semantics, checking units, managing memory, tracing logic, and analyzing data flow to ensure we maintain consistent structures, parameter names, and definitions or units throughout the simulation (as part of verification). Analyzing boundaries and checking constraints apply to verification and validation. Typical techniques are ensuring probabilities remain in the 0–1 range and examining the simulation's performance for boundary conditions, such as when probabilities and velocities are set to zero. Structural techniques include examining a simulation's data-flow and control-flow, graphing, or analyzing paths. These techniques can help us assess the simulation's structural appropriateness and identify conditions under which it may not respond correctly.

Several CASE tools automate parts of logical and structural evaluations, and we should use these tools wherever appropriate. Some CASE tools apply only to limited phases of software development (such as detailed design and coding), whereas other tools apply more broadly (reaching from requirements, through preliminary and detailed design, to coding and testing). All CASE tools work with specific languages (Ada, C, LISP, etc.), software paradigms (Yourdon-DeMarco, Ward-Mellor, etc.), and applications (non-real-time or real-time) [Lewis 1992]. If we use CASE tools to develop software, verification activities should also use them. If the person who handles independent V&V can't access (or doesn't know) these CASE tools, the activities can suffer.

The object-oriented design (OOD) used by modern simulations allows us to evaluate the simulation's validity in parts, as long as each object in the model directly relates to a specific aspect or entity of the subject being modeled. This is sometimes called *piece-meal validation*, which allows us to assess the description and performance of each object and, in some cases, may help us validate structure. However, OOD brings its own special challenges to validation: interactions among objects, processes embedded within objects, and inherited characteristics for object interactions. For some time, developers have recognized the problems in applying data-flow and control-flow analyses to simulations using OOD [Smith 1990], particularly if objects interact through embedded processes and inherited characteristics. This is one of the reasons some people advocate applying more formal methods (mathematical proofs of correctness) to object-oriented development [Lano 1995].

We don't yet have a full spectrum of V&V techniques based on OOD to thoroughly evaluate simulations for appropriateness. Various graphical schemes and diagrams are used to describe simulations employing OOD. CASE tools generate some of these schemes, which can also allow some level of automated checking. The graphics common to OOD help us examine the simulation's structural relationship to the subject it represents, which allows us to appreciate the "big picture" and see detailed interactions. But in V&V, we must examine algorithms, assumptions, and processes embedded within objects as well as the relationships among objects.

11.3.4 Techniques Using Sensitivity Analysis

Sensitivity analysis systematically changes the value of a simulation's input variables and parameters over some range of interest and then observes the effect on its responses and results. The analysis can be for part or all of the simulation. It shows that simulation algorithms work right and identifies parameters to which simulation responses are very sensitive. *Mathematical stability testing* is a special sensitivity technique that uncovers potential chaotic behavior resulting either from the algorithms or from the way mathematical computations occur in the simulation and the computational hardware which runs it. Very large, even drastic consequences can result from tiny changes when a simulation is mathematically unstable or chaotic. Dewar, et al [1995] cite an example of switching a well respected land-combat model from a VAX to a CRAY-2. The new software operating system used different round-off computations. Thus, the original results of 597 enemy-tank kills and 835 own-tank losses changed to 477 enemy-tank kills and 445 own-tank losses. Without carefully analyzing a simulation's algorithms to ensure that they aren't vulnerable to such problems, it's hard to generate high levels of confidence in a simulation's results. Similar concerns exist for analyses which employ multiple simulations with different levels of fidelity [Pace 1992]. Different algorithms for similar processes in several simulations can cause highly varying responses to changes in an input parameter, thus creating discontinuities and inconsistencies in the analytical results.

As described above, sensitivity analysis used in concept validation can determine the bounds on acceptable behavior of the algorithms envisioned for the simulation. This approach to testing algorithms for conceptual models works the same way as precluding division by zero. Sensitivity analysis used in verification can determine if the hardware or software that embodies acceptable algorithms makes the simulation behave unacceptably. And we can use sensitivity analysis to validate results by identifying conditions which may need more evaluation— conditions for which responses don't fall within anticipated and acceptable bounds.

As discussed above, sensitivity analysis discovers the effect on a simulation's results if we vary a single parameter's values. But we can take a broader approach to sensitivity analysis—called "exploratory analysis"—in which we vary many parameters at the same time to examine interaction among them. Exploratory analysis is especially useful when we're uncertain about the importance of different elements [Bankes 1993].

11.3.5   Visualization Techniques

Advances in computing and display systems in the 1990s brought visualization techniques to the forefront in simulation. It's now common to display simulation outputs in two or three dimensions so we can rapidly understand and synthesize results. We use similar visual displays to more rapidly prepare and evaluate a simulation's inputs and even to allow effective operator control of a simulation during a run.

Human abilities to recognize visual patterns have proven very effective in problem solving whenever display systems are part of the simulation. As a technique for V&V, visualizing can apply to processing details [Palmore 1993] as well as to temporal or sequential events, kinematics, and spatial relationships among simulation elements. Unfortunately, we don't have objective guidelines for using visualization in V&V, so this kind of V&V depends strongly on the observer's expertise and judgment. This makes visualizing important to face validation and to convincing consumers of a simulation's credibility. The more flexibility observers have to visualize parameters in different ways, the more likely they will discover anomalies in the simulation. Thus, visualizing mainly identifies areas that need to be examined more carefully in V&V.

Visualizing a simulation's input parameters and results in static, two- and three-dimensional displays quickly reveals discontinuities and unexpected extremes. An example might be typing the wrong sign in an input parameter or in one of the simulation's algorithms. Dynamically representing the spatial relationships among simulation elements during a run provides an overall perspective for what is happening over time that is very difficult to get otherwise. This perspective can help us detect the simulation's faults and enhance its credibility.

Although visualizing has potential for V&V, it adds a human-machine interface to the simulation. We must verify this interface by showing how scales, icons, perspectives, colors, and so on affect the viewer's assessment. The simulation's developer and its user must attend to this issue. For humans in the loop, Knepell and Arangno [1993] identify as validation issues adequacy, timeliness, and completeness of information presented to the person, as well as what range of responses the person may have. The following section discusses this subject in more detail.

11.4   Special Techniques for V&V

Simulations which involve people, hardware or software, and artificial intelligence (AI) pose special challenges to V&V, as do safety-critical and other simulations which require high integrity.

11.4.1   M&S Involving People

Besides the normal role that people have in preparing a simulation for use, running the computing machinery and other systems, and analyzing results, people can

- Control a simulation, perhaps adjusting its parameters in the middle of a run to cause it to support its intended purpose—as might be needed in a simulation-supported war game or a training exercise for forest-fire management
- Serve as a surrogate for some process, particularly for decision making by a person or group
- Serve as human actors or players, represented by elements of the simulation

Each of these roles imposes different demands on V&V. We must integrate humans, hardware, and software in a simulation involving people if it is to be credible [Knepell 1993].

Using people to control simulations means we must verify the simulation's ability to record human changes, as well as verifying and validating the mechanism that ensures all affected elements change appropriately. For example, suppose we're running a manned-weapon simulator, war game, or training exercise for forest-fire management. If the human controller advances time so operators or players don't sit waiting for a long time, all parameters related to time have to change appropriately. These parameters would include the position and condition of objects, speeds of accelerating objects, time of night or day, and so on. Likewise, it may be necessary to generate artificial histories for some objects, such as track histories and associated reports that would have occurred during the skipped interval. As part of simulation V&V, it's good practice to 1) list items which human changes may affect, 2) identify how those items could and should change in response to the human changes, 3) verify that those items change properly, and 4) validate that these changes acceptably affect the overall simulation.

Using people as surrogates for processes imposes all of the validation issues of aggregate simulation—in which processes are represented implicitly instead of explicitly. For example, Lanchester's equations, which long have been used to calculate combat losses in models, implicitly represent military engagements. An explicit representation of the same battle would track weapons individually, attend to how individual targets are selected, and use the physics of each engagement to determine how lethal it is. There are no simple guidelines for V&V of aggregate simulations [Davis 1992b]. If the human is a surrogate for human decision making, representing that process well will require the human to understand it and its influences. At best, a human surrogate might pass a Turing Test—meaning judges can't distinguish between the real and surrogate responses. Objective measures of acceptable performance don't exist. Sometimes humans are surrogates for other processes, such as determining kills in a simulation-based war game or estimating a shift in wind direction and magnitude in a simulation-based training exercise for forest-fire management. In these cases, they may decide based on statistics, other factors such as range and weapon type, or reasons dictated by the exercise's training objectives. Different people give us different results, but even the same surrogate's performance will vary from one "replication" to the next, or under different scenarios. One surrogate's decisions may even vary within a single replication.

It is wise to treat human surrogates like algorithms—test their performance so we can expect certain behavior and variations. At least, we should collect information during simulation runs about the human surrogate's responses for that purpose. Such performance testing is like any process for collecting data. We must use the right people, good experimental designs, and effective controls. We also have to allow for the effect of learning on human performance. Unfortunately, unlike algorithms, past performance by a human surrogate doesn't always reliably predict future performance.

Whenever people are involved in simulations, we must consider three key elements of VV&A:

1. *Appropriateness.* Do we have the right people in the right functions? Using a junior person to represent the decisions of a senior decision maker, for example, is unlikely to provide good results. But determining appropriateness isn't simple. We must fully understand the characteristics a surrogate is to represent in order to judge how well he or she represents them. For example, a surrogate "operator" in a manned-weapon simulator must have the skills to use the system represented by the simulator.

2. *Timing and interfaces for human response.* Simulations that involve people must properly time information and display it effectively to be valid for use with human operators. Simulations for console or equipment-operator training (such as training for standardized proficiency) must be very accurate, whereas equipment can be less accurate in simulations supporting training for high-level decision makers (such as preparing people to cope with non-standardized situations) [Dewar 1995].

3. *Variation in human responses.* The uncertainty that stems from varied responses is similar to the uncertainty of stochastic processes—we must take both into account when validating a simulation. Some of the variation in human response is "random." People may perform faster (or slower) in some simulation runs than in others. They may misread information or speak incorrectly. We must measure this "random" variation so we can quantify this normal dispersion in the results. Measuring variations may require us to collect more data. For example, how often did a command or report have to be repeated in a crew simulator? Or how much does a variation in the time for an operator's response to a displayed stimulus depend on other things the operator is doing at the time? Other variations in human responses can result from differences in abilities. Some people do better than others. If we're examining how a system works with "average" people in it, we shouldn't use people who are "superstars" or "duds." In other words, choosing the *appropriate* people also helps us control variations. Although we can never eliminate variable responses, good V&V requires us to reduce uncertainty as much as we can and then to make intelligent, informed judgments about how they affect a simulation's results.

11.4.2   M&S Involving Hardware in the Loop

Hardware-in-the-loop (HWIL) simulations, and its subset of system-in-the-loop simulations, especially challenge V&V. Here, we'll consider software-in-the-loop as a subset of system-in-the-loop because it demands the same special handling that other in-the-loop simulations require. Information and phenomena (signals, currents, pressures) must flow appropriately to and from the hardware or system and other parts of the simulation—in time and in all other dimensions. Thus, time control is even more important in processing these kinds of simulations, and we must apply special techniques to all simulations that have to work in real time [Gerber 1992]. Most of these special techniques ensure that processing times for all elements of the simulation, including its interfaces, can occur within the time available for all possible conditions. Most static techniques for verification can't help in this area because they don't allow simulation time to change; instead, we must use dynamic techniques, which allow us to assess how delays in loading computations and passing information affect results. Often, we must use simplified algorithms in the simulation to satisfy processing times. But these simplified algorithms typically are less accurate than full algorithms, so they may cause problems for validation. During V&V for HWIL simulations, we must consider information and phenomena for all possible conditions and do thorough integration testing of all elements [Knepell 1993] because of possible interactions among these elements.

An important use of HWIL simulations has been to support flight tests for aerospace systems: rockets, missiles, aircraft, and spacecraft. HWIL simulations test integrated systems to identify potential problems before flight tests or to help evaluate the results of these tests. Data from each flight test further calibrates the simulation (and dictates appropriate changes)—a process known as *model-test-model*. Thus, with repeated use, this kind of HWIL simulation has its results validated by repeated correspondence with flight-test data. The validation occurs when the simulation is used to predict flight-test parameters and when it's exercised with varying parameters to replicate flight-test experience if we've encountered unexpected phenomena. Comparing the simulation's results to actual flight data allows us to quantify its accuracy, as long as we keep in mind that the actual flight data may be inaccurate because of limits in the test instruments. Remember nothing in testing is known or observed with absolute precision.

HWIL simulations have some basic limitations. Often, software must provide a substitute for the physical environment (pressure, shock, temperature) expected during actual operations because the in-the-loop hardware environment doesn't provide it. A simulation always simplifies its representation to some degree. Thus, the equipment's performance and response in the HWIL simulation won't identically match its response in the actual environment. The performance of particular equipment may vary because of production tolerances or other anomalies. Unless we use the actual operational equipment in an HWIL simulation, the simulation equipment's performance may differ slightly. To fully validate a simulation, we must be concerned with these kinds of issues.

Sometimes, an HWIL simulation will only intend to test system integration, not try to predict its performance. If so, we must not try to use its results to predict performance, as has sometimes been done. To validate a simulation properly, we have to understand its limits.

11.4.3   M&S Involving Artificial Intelligence (AI) or Similar Processes

More and more simulations are using artificial intelligence (AI) techniques, such as knowledge-based and rule-based "expert systems," neural networks, and genetic algorithms. They challenge V&V because verifying knowledge- or rule-based systems requires us to address technical issues about the rule set. These issues include identifying

- Inferred rules (rules we develop from other rules)
- Redundant rules (the same rule in a different form)
- Conflicting rules (rules which, for the same initial conditions, produce conflicting results)
- Subsumed rules (the same result for two rules, but one rule is more restrictive than the other)

- Circular rules
- Dead-end rules (resulting conditions halt progress)
- Dependencies among rules

Verification tries to ensure the "completeness" (no unreachable or undefined conclusions) and "correctness" (no conflicting or circular rules) of our knowledge. Redundant rules (identical or subsumed rules) mainly slow down runs of expert systems, but we should detect and eliminate them because they may ultimately cause inconsistencies or other difficulties with maintaining or changing a simulation [Department of the Army 1993].

Special programs can verify and test knowledge-based systems [Gupta 1993; O'Keefe 1993]. These special programs employ symbolic logic, set theory, and the ability of expert systems to draw inferences. Some of these programs have been developed by industrial and government consortia, such as ViVa in Europe, which offers tools for verifying, improving, and validating knowledge-based systems [Hollnagel 1993]. Unfortunately, these tools can address only the rules' completeness, correctness, and redundancy [Ayel 1991; Gupta 1991], not the fidelity of the knowledge-based system. We need a strategy to V&V expert systems if we're going to look at more than these technical aspects [Lee 1994]. Fortunately, we're defining frameworks for V&V of expert systems [French 1994; Zlatareva 1994], but none of these frameworks can yet completely ensure an expert system is appropriate.

Many of the conventional (non-AI) techniques for V&V also apply, with little or no change, to knowledge-based simulations, particularly to V&V of interfaces and tools or utilities [Miller 1993]. You can find descriptions of conventional techniques that apply to knowledge-based simulations in standard works on VV&A, such as Balci [1994], Youngblood and Pace [1994], Davis [1992a], the 1993 Army pamphlet on VV&A, or the guides that the Defense Modeling and Simulation Office and others are developing. Table 11.2 categorizes more than forty standard techniques.

The main way we measure rule-based and knowledge-based expert systems is by comparing their performance with that of human experts, but usually only over a very restricted domain and under normal conditions. This "face validation" isn't reliable in abnormal situations and it also doesn't account for systems that are superior to human experts.

Neural networks, genetic algorithms, and similar systems of adaptive control for AI techniques are very difficult to V&V because their processes are obscure and may even change as they evolve. Usually, the most we can say about them is that they produce acceptable results for a set of test cases. No theory allows us to extrapolate their performance to other conditions [Wildberger 1994b]. Some people doubt it's even proper to assume they interpolate reliably. To do so, the functions which guide their choices must be consistently well-behaved; in other words, there must be no discontinuities.

An implication of the above is that simulations, and their software, are likely to contain faults—sometimes, significant ones. Therefore, simulations should tolerate faults. The Electric Power Research Institute sponsors exploratory

Special Techniques for V&V

research that is trying to improve techniques for validating adaptive computing systems and for automatically verifying real-time, distributed software, but the work is still embryonic [Wildberger 1994a]. Most fault-tolerant designs depend on redundancy; they use multiple processes based on different algorithms to make faults less likely to affect all (or most) processes at any given time [Lyu 96].

The growing prevalence of AI techniques means simulations may respond unexpectedly if something unusual happens. For now, we don't have a theory for identifying all conditions in which simulation performance may be suspect. Some people have even suggested genetic algorithms and numerical Petri nets may be able to help identify problem areas in expert systems [Liu 1991; Roache 1995]. We do know that AI techniques are more credible if we can explain their results— whether the simulation is for computing, analysis, or decision making. Animation and other techniques for visualizing results have been very helpful as a way to identify anomalies in a simulation's data and response. Animating and visualizing responses make it easier for the observer to see how the simulation (with its AI and AI-like processes) acts, so the observer can determine whether or not the simulation's responses are appropriate. Thus, whenever the visual representations of its responses agree with expectations, the simulation becomes credible.

11.4.4   M&S Requiring High Integrity

Simulations that require high integrity must always work correctly because they directly affect system security or the safety of humans or systems. Standards guide development of high-integrity software [Ministry of Defense 1991; Wallace 1992], and we're able to produce mathematically proven software—software that will always perform as expected. Applications for these processes are limited [Bowen 1994b] but expanding rapidly [Larsen 1996]. Most applications to date have been for control processes of safety-critical systems, such as those in railway systems, aircraft systems, nuclear-power plants, medical systems, and automated systems for controlling ammunition. Also, we must remember that error-free software is only as good as the hardware it runs on, and hardware faults are also possible [Stavridou 1994].

The basic approach to V&V for high-integrity simulations is to use the best development processes, test the simulation very thoroughly over all operating conditions, provide redundancy by using different kinds of algorithms for all critical functions, and employ specialized, mathematically provable processes whenever they're appropriate. Except for mathematically provable processes, these approaches can only reduce the number and frequency of simulation faults, not eliminate them. Only the mathematically provable processes can eliminate simulation faults. But these "formal methods" require specially trained people, normally with advanced training in symbolic logic and set theory. They also demand specialized software environments and packages, such as theorem provers using higher order logic and a specification language such as Z.

A side benefit of using formal methods is more thorough documentation of the rationale for simulation-design decisions [Dahl 1992]. This documentation enhances V&V by making all assumptions and algorithmic implications more explicit. It also helps to clarify the potential effects of changes to simulations, including their V&V consequences, before their implementation begins. Similar formality in development, even when not at the mathematically provable level, is becoming a recommended characteristic of quality software [Rombach 1995]. Formal processes are now recommended for object-oriented developments, and specialized languages (such as VDM++ and Z++) help carry them out [Lano 1995].

11.5   Critical Issues in VV&A

To do effective VV&A, we must attend to certain critical issues: levels of simulation validation ("validation" has more than one connotation), simulation data, how VV&A affects cost and schedule, managing VV&A (people and documentation), and simulation fidelity.

11.5.1   Levels of Validation for M&S

The more explicitly a simulation represents the processes of the subject being modeled, the more accurate it is and the more computing resources it needs. For example, suppose we use a physics-based hydrocode simulation to represent the interactions of two bodies colliding. To simulate just a few milliseconds of collision takes a super computer scores, sometimes hundreds, of hours of processing. This kind of simulation most faithfully represents the physical processes involved. However, we can't do extensive sensitivity studies of collisions when we must consider hundreds (or even thousands) of cases. Therefore, we use less accurate simulations which retain high-fidelity representations of some processes and aggregate other processes using various algorithms. We can run these simulations rapidly enough to do sensitivity studies and acquire information about the subject. Sometimes, these simpler simulations may even allow us to better appreciate the significance of key simulation parameters. Normally, these lower-fidelity, aggregated simulations are calibrated by data from tests and by results from higher-fidelity simulations. Although we can validate the faster-running simulations based on how well they correspond to the data and results of the more accurate simulation, they're still not credible for other conditions.

The Defense community has wanted simulations to be seamlessly integrated across all applications ever since Defense leaders first stated that vision in the early 1990s. We can now meaningfully compare and integrate results from simulations at various levels of fidelity and from some applications, but we have a very long way to go before we can ensure results from many related applications will be compatible [Davis 1992b]. People outside the Defense community also want this coherence among related simulations because it can lead to simulation-based design that integrates financial, technical, design, production, marketing, and distribution information into the lifecycle for product development.

Unfortunately, having different levels of validation for simulations strongly hinders their integration. We don't have a widely accepted structure for validation levels, but it's still useful to distinguish among these levels. Otherwise, we might integrate simulations with different levels of validation and thus allow less reliable information to dominate more reliable information. Wisdom tells us we should integrate simulations with comparable levels of validation, or at least have processes in place to account for the differences.

The literature and experience with VV&A lead us to divide M&S validation into three basic levels: inspection, review, and demonstration. Unless we label and distinguish these levels of validation, we won't know how much merit a "validated" simulation really has.

Inspection-level validation. Merely another name for face validation in some cases, this common method is only as credible as the experts who say the simulation does what it's supposed to do. Important data about the subject may be lacking. Resources for more thorough VV&A may not be available. The expected application of the simulation may not justify more extensive VV&A. Whatever the cause, validity depends mainly on expert opinion. All "unvalidatable" simulations fall into this category because we lack adequate data about the subject. All theater and campaign level military models, as well as models of national economic and political behavior, are unvalidatable. We may be able to validate elements of these models at a higher level, but the total model remains at the inspection level.

Review-level validation. This is the level of validation given to most detailed simulations of physical processes, which are sometimes called "engineering-level" simulations. It usually establishes that the simulation structurally corresponds to the subject it represents and acceptably replicates and predicts the subject's behavior for the test cases considered. It often also establishes that a simulation behaves well enough from replication to replication so that it has mathematical stability. To support this level of validation, we must have adequate data about the subject being modeled and enough resources for extensive VV&A.

Demonstration-level validation. This level of validation applies to simulations which must work correctly all the time because safety is critical, such as those supporting medical diagnostic software and systems for controlling nuclear power plants or aircraft in flight. The simulation's performance and response can be predicted to perform correctly according to objective criteria so we can be confident in them. Normally, these simulations have structural validity.

The higher the level of validation, the more resources we need for VV&A. We can use inspection-level validation if the application requires only that results appear correct most of the time and incorrect responses won't be catastrophic. If the simulation must interact with real systems, we'll normally need review-level validation. Later on, I'll discuss the cost for each level.

11.5.2 Data Considerations

As highlighted in Sec. 9.1, people don't always understand how much data dominates a simulation's results—data about the subject a simulation represents and data used as inputs for simulation runs.

Data about the subject guides simulation development and supports validation test cases. For poorly understood subjects, we may have to generate or collect a lot of data to select the right algorithms for the simulation. For example, when the Defense community began seriously to consider hit-to-kill interceptors for defense against tactical ballistic missiles, they had to do a series of experiments and tests to generate data about intercept phenomena so they could develop credible simulations of competing missile systems. Besides guiding simulation development, data about the subject also allows us to validate results from the simulation. Whenever simulation results can replicate all known data about the subject, we can be very confident in the simulation.

The data we use as inputs into a simulation application must be not only the "best" available but also balanced—so all of its parts are of the same quality. In some situations, using balanced data may actually be more important than using the "best" data. For example, it's usually inappropriate to mix theoretical predictions for some parameters with test data results for other parameters in the input data for a simulation; likewise, it's inappropriate to mix data about some parameters' current abilities with data for other parameters' predicted abilities. Mixing data can cause some parts of the subject represented in the simulation to be described optimistically and other parts to be described more pessimistically—thus skewing results. Use "unbalanced" data only when objectives of the simulation application make it appropriate.

11.5.3   Effect of VV&A on Resources, Costs, and Schedule

Appreciation for all simulation-related costs can help put costs for VV&A into perspective [Pace 1995; Pace 1997; Poppiti 1994]. Too often, we consider only the cost of VV&A when we should also appreciate the value of a correct and credible simulation. This value is the return expected for the resources invested (including VV&A costs). Simulations have demonstrated their value in many application domains. Several Defense studies show that credible simulations saved a lot of money in the testing phase of system development because they decreased flight tests and exposed design problems which could be corrected before fielding the system. In fact, for a score of weapon systems, simulations saved 15 to 40 times their cost [Department of Defense 1995]. Thus, the potential savings in system development or lifecycle costs that a correct and credible simulation may allow dwarf even the most expensive VV&A. Unfortunately, these potential savings may not always persuade a simulation sponsor or developer to provide enough money, time, people, or other support for the desired level of VV&A.

Another way of looking at the cost of VV&A is to recognize what happens when it's inadequate. For example, some simulations were developed but never really used. Sometimes they were designed for the wrong problem (or were too late), but in other cases, no one trusted them enough to use them. Usually, this means the entire simulation-development cost is wasted (although sometimes the process may have been a valuable learning experience for people involved in the development). If a simulation produces incorrect answers or provides wrong training, it may lead to bad decisions that cost a lot of money. If a simulation contains undetected faults, those flaws may cause a catastrophe. For example, a fly-by-wire aircraft crashed because the software in its control processes was faulty. Another software fault caused an x-ray machine to use very high radiation, which harmed patients. And software problems in a new system cost a major bank millions of dollars [Lee 1991]. System failures because of simulation faults—especially in systems with second-generation, simulation-based artificial intelligence—can be very expensive, and they may also bring legal liabilities [Krause 1991]. Yet, discussions of VV&A cost often consider only the resources needed to carry them out, neglecting the return on investment from credible simulations or the potential costs of faulty simulations. Rational decisions on VV&A require a less myopic view.

Normal V&V activities are usually part of the simulation-development schedule, so they don't take up additional time. But we do have to plan for accreditation reviews, which might otherwise delay planned use of a simulation.

Cost of VV&A

The three main costs for VV&A are generating and preparing data, verification and validation, and the accreditation review (including certifying data, people, and hardware as appropriate).

Generating and Preparing Data. Three kinds of data are related to VV&A. First is the data about the subject to be modeled, which we use in developing a concept for the simulation. The cost of generating, collecting, and organizing this data isn't normally charged to VV&A; it may not even be considered part of the cost for developing a simulation. Still as indicated in the above example of hit-to-kill weapons, generating such data can be very expensive. The second kind of data is for comparison to, and validation of, simulation results. Sometimes generating, collecting, and organizing this data are charged to VV&A; sometimes, when other simulations are run as a standard against which to compare the new simulation's results, costs of running those other simulations aren't charged to VV&A. In any case, the V&V team usually collects and organizes this data, so their time contributes to VV&A cost. But usually this cost is small compared to other VV&A costs for a simulation. The third kind of data is the information we input to simulation applications. Collecting, organizing, and certifying this information may or may not be charged to VV&A.

Verification and Validation (V&V). There is a fuzzy line between V&V activities the simulation developer does simply as part of quality development and the reviews considered "V&V" for costing. IV&V contracts typically require about 10% of the costs for software development [Lewis 1992]. This percentage applies to the inspection and review levels of validation, not to the demonstration level. For VV&A of an exercise using distributed interactive simulation, costs are 5% to 15% of the overall development cost [Jordan 1995]. This amount doesn't include costs for VV&A of the individual simulations in the exercise. Obviously, the amount of V&V resources required will depend on the level of VV&A.

Fault detection and correction consume much of the cost for software development. The later a fault is detected, the more expensive it is to correct and remove—up to 100 times more [Miller 1993]. About 60% of faults corrected and removed in a number of software projects were the result of inadequate requirements and specifications [Lewis 1992]. Thorough concept validation will help reduce these costs. Likewise, standards for high-integrity software emphasize clear, unambiguous, and analyzable specifications so flaws can be found before the system is built [Wallace 1992]. Automation tools can help validate requirements [Burns 1991]. The more extensively and consistently V&V are applied, from the very beginning of simulation development, the cheaper simulation development will be. Early V&V will prevent or detect more faults when they can be corrected and removed most easily and cheaply.

When a simulation must have high integrity, V&V costs can be large. In fact, they may be more than half of the cost for simulation development whenever software undergoes formal specification and verification to prove a program's performance mathematically correct. Examples of this kind of program include those for railway-control systems, nuclear-power plants, spacecraft-control systems, medical-diagnosis systems, and ammunition-control processes [Bowen 1994b].

Accreditation Review. Accreditation review costs vary. Normally accreditation reviews start only after a simulation is complete and ready for a particular use. Thus, none of the V&V cost in simulation development is included in the accreditation review, which covers the cost of deciding whether the simulation's use is appropriate. The six examples from the Defense community summarized below represent about 100 accreditation reviews. They illustrate the time and effort needed to do accreditation reviews and can help us plan these reviews for other projects.

A simple summary of required resources for accreditation reviews includes 1) a couple person months for accreditation at inspection-level validation, 2) half a person year or more for accreditation at review-level validation, and 3) several person years for accreditation at demonstration-level validation. Obviously the resources required for a particular accreditation review will depend on the size and complexity of the simulation, the amount and quality of V&V information about the simulation, the importance of the simulation application, the level of credibility required for the simulation, and the availability of resources for the review.

Example 1. In 1993, fourteen Navy simulations underwent accreditation reviews at the inspection level. These simulations ranged in size and complexity from a spreadsheet model developed in about six person months to a large simulation with more than 100 person years invested in its development. A number of review teams were assembled, with 2–4 people assigned to review each simulation. The average cost for accreditation reviews of these fourteen simulations was 6–8 person weeks of review team time, at least 2–4 person weeks of developer time, plus additional time from the government sponsor of the accreditation reviews and travel costs related to the reviews.

Example 2. More than a half dozen simulations in the mid-1990s received "Level 1" of an accreditation review using "Analytic Tool Box," a process developed for the Ballistic Missile Defense Organization. Level 1 was between the inspection and review levels of simulation validation. Typically, a team of about ten people would assemble for a week to examine a particular simulation. The team also spent time before the meeting preparing materials and after the meeting reporting results. Thus, four or more person months from the review team per simulation, plus support from the simulation developer and associated travel expenses, were required for an accreditation review somewhat above the inspection level.

Example 3. The Center for Naval Analyses reviewed several dozen simulations in the late 1980s to early 1990s. These reviews averaged six person months per simulation and sometimes required more than a year to complete. The review, in general, was similar to review-level validation [Pace 1992].

Example 4. The TOMAHAWK Simulation Management Board has accredited or certified several dozen simulations of the TOMAHAWK missile and weapon systems. In general, these accreditations and certifications were at the review level of validation and required 6–12 person months for each simulation.

Example 5. For several years, the Army Materiel Systems Analysis Activity has been the accreditation-review agent for simulations to support the Army's decisions on acquiring major weapon systems. In these accreditation reviews, the Army reviewed information from previous VV&A of the simulation and ran, or had the simulation owner run, special tests on it. The level of validity for these accreditations was usually between review and demonstration. When the simulation represented a specific physical object, the result was closer to the demonstration level. For combat simulations representing a number of military units, the result was at the inspection level but closer to the review level than is often the case for combat models because of the Army's efforts to correlate simulation results with data about physical processes whenever possible. Normally, at least six person months of the agent's time was required for each simulation accreditation review, plus the efforts of the organization making the acquisition decision and its supporting contractors. Computing resources and travel costs added to the bill. Some of the accreditation reviews required several person years of effort from the Army Materiel Systems Analysis Activity's staff.

Example 6. The Joint Tactical Commanders Group for Aircraft Survivability began the Susceptibility Model Assessment and Range Test (SMART) Project in 1992 as a multi-year, multi-million-dollar program of VV&A for five legacy simulations (ESAMS, ALARM, RADGUNs, TRAP, and AASPEM). They intended to accredit these simulations near the demonstration level of validation and, along the way, developed VV&A methods they've shared with others in the Defense community.

Effect of VV&A on Development and Application Schedules

Six elements of VV&A can affect a simulation schedule: data certification, concept validation, design verification, implementation verification, results validation, and accreditation. Figure 11.3 schematically shows how.

Figure 11.3 shows question marks around "certify data" because its effect on schedule depends on whether we have adequate data for the test cases required to validate results. If we don't, accrediting the simulation will have to wait until we generate the data or will continue with limited confidence in the simulation's performance. If we do have the data for inputs to simulation runs, we can often certify it in parallel with other pre-run activities, so data certification may not affect when the simulation application occurs. Depending on the amount of data and the

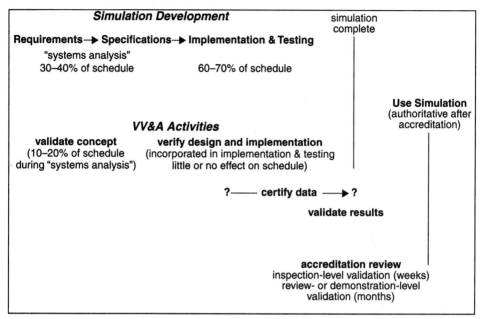

Fig. 11.3.   Effect of VV&A on Schedule. This figure outlines how each VV&A activity might affect the schedules for developing and applying a simulation.

amount of controversy about its appropriateness, data certification can be fast (days) or slow (weeks to months).

We often get little or no time in a simulation-development schedule to validate the concept. That's a shame because more thorough validation of the concept will speed up simulation development later by preventing faults. It should take 10–20% of the development schedule or about half the time allocated to systems analysis. It's common for systems analysis—moving from customer requirements to program specifications—to consume 30–40% of a software-development schedule.

Verifying the design and its implementation should be part of normal simulation development (which includes unit, integration, and system testing) and shouldn't cause delays. In fact, inadequate verification is likely to lengthen the schedule by allowing more faults, which will have to be detected and corrected during simulation testing.

We can validate results for elements of the simulation as they're completed and tested, then validate the rest of the results during final simulation testing. These efforts are usually part of the accreditation review and are accounted for in it, so they don't affect the development schedule.

The time needed for the final phase of simulation VV&A—accreditation reviews—depends on the level of validation: inspection level—a few weeks; review level—months; demonstration level—months or longer.

11.5.4   Allocating Responsibility for Tasks in VV&A

Sponsors, developers, and users share the main responsibilities for VV&A tasks. The sponsor of a simulation is the agent who pays for its development or who has the authority to set its requirements. The developer may include the system designer and project developer, planner, or manager, as well as the designer, integrator, and implementer of a model or simulation. If the simulation doesn't have a formal sponsor, the developer becomes the sponsor as well. Finally, the user includes the analyst and reporter from Chap. 3. In many cases, the developer is also the main user. Sometimes the developer operates and runs the simulation for a government agency, which uses its results. In that case, the government agency would be the user in the following discussion, even though it doesn't actually operate it. The simulation's "proponent" is the agency or organization that has primary responsibility for the simulation in its area of interest [Department of Defense 1996a]. That role can go to the sponsor, developer, or user.

Since 1992, the gist of the Defense community's published guidance on VV&A for simulations places the responsibility for accreditation mainly on the shoulders of the user, who must ensure the simulation is appropriate for—and can support—the application. This means the expected users should influence requirements for new simulations and upgrades of existing ones. The sponsor sets requirements and defines specifications. The simulation's proponent, which may be the sponsor, developer, or user, must ensure the simulation satisfies its intended purposes. The proponent must also provide the accumulated information from V&V to help accredit the simulation whenever that's appropriate [Department of Defense 1996a].

Responsibilities for VV&A of civilian simulations are not so precisely defined. Expectations and responsibilities vary from company to company, and within and across various industries. There have been too few court cases about simulation liabilities thus far to determine whether the principle of caveat emptor (buyer beware) will dominate future trials or whether simulations will carry implicit and explicit warranties about correct behaviors and responses.

11.5.5   Managing VV&A

This section addresses three management issues: the people who do VV&A and their organization, resulting documentation, and independence for V&V.

People in VV&A

Much of V&V is a normal and essential part of successful simulation development. In this section we'll focus on "formal" V&V, which provides the basis for validating the concept and requirements, verifying the design and its implementation, and validating results. Although practices vary, the following people usually carry out VV&A.

V&V Leader. The leader may be the same for all V&V activities, or different people may serve for different tasks. Often, the leader will be part of the simulation-development team, but sometimes a sponsor or user designates who is in charge of V&V. In any case, the leader coordinates activities of the V&V team so they properly apply details of the simulation plan.

V&V Team. The size and composition of the V&V team depend on the size of the simulation and the importance of its application, but they may also change as the team carries out different parts of the V&V plan. Some people may be part of the team throughout the simulation's lifecycle; others may do only certain tasks. The detailed V&V plan should address the size and composition of the team, as well as how it may change over time. The team should include people who:

- Understand the subject represented by the simulation
- Know the simulation (usually drawn from the simulation-development team)
- Have technical expertise in the software and hardware used in the simulation
- Have worked with similar simulations

Some people may satisfy more than one of these requirements. The simulation developer and the community with vested interests in the simulation must approve of the V&V team. Usually, this community includes the simulation's sponsor, its users, and people related to potentially competitive simulations. If the V&V team includes representatives from all of these groups—or at least reflects their interests—the simulation is likely to be given more thorough V&V and thereby have more credibility for its applications.

Attributes of the V&V Team. A V&V team requires several attributes to be effective. First, it must have enough independence for honest and probing assessments. This independence is important to software development [Lewis 1992] and to simulation V&V [Williams 1991]. Both real and apparent independence are important. Often, it's difficult to arrange for convenient funding of "independent" members of the V&V team—people who don't belong to the sponsor's, developer's, or user's organizations. Formal, independent V&V (IV&V) typically requires separate contractual arrangements. Creating appropriate arrangements for such "independents" is an important responsibility of simulation management.

Second, the V&V team must be recognized as competent, which means they have the necessary knowledge and expertise. Besides having the abilities listed earlier, the team must stay up to date through familiarity with the literature on V&V, such as that listed in Youngblood's [1993] bibliography. You can access this bibliography through the Defense Modeling and Simulation Office's home page http://www.dmso.mil/. Although basic concepts from the 1970s and 1980s are still valid, computers and software have advanced so much in the past few years that we must use newer techniques for V&V—especially visualization, CASE tools, and other kinds of automation. Newer techniques are particularly important for simulations that employ object-oriented design, artificial intelligence, and other advanced methods. Unfortunately, many people in modeling and simulation know no more about VV&A than is available in introductory articles such as Youngblood and Pace [1995] or in the Defense community's directives and instructions.

As mentioned earlier, the team should also have experience with simulations like the one being developed and with other simulations of similar subjects, so they know where to expect problems. The team should be able to select techniques and tools that can detect the most common kinds of simulation faults, as well as those which may cause the most damage. The team's experience should extend to the technical elements of the simulation's development, such as computer languages or human and system interfaces.

A third key attribute is trustworthiness in the developer's eyes. If a developer believes the V&V team has a hidden agenda which may harm the simulation development, the developer may not be candid about the simulation's weak spots and potential problems. Without knowing all the potential problems the developer knows, a V&V team can't thoroughly verify and validate a simulation.

Fourth, the V&V team must have good judgment so they can determine when they've examined the simulation enough; seldom will they be able to examine it completely.

Finally, the team must have the right objective—to determine a simulation's abilities and limits so it can be used appropriately.

Documenting VV&A

VV&A documentation should be a normal part of simulation documentation and should be wherever the simulation is. For example, some modern simulations include their documentation on-line with their code. If the on-line documentation stems directly from the software's development and configuration control, it will be current and represent the simulation in use. This situation is ideal, and fortunately, even long reports take up very little of a modern computer's storage capacity.

The documentation for VV&A should include

1. Requirements (what the simulation is expected to do)
2. Conceptual model (as described in Sec. 11.2.1)
3. Specifications
4. Detailed V&V plan (as described at the end of Sec. 11.2.1)
5. Reports validating the concept and requirements
6. Reports verifying the design and its implementation
7. Reports validating the results
8. Reports of the accreditation reviews

Reports should clearly show

- The names and affiliations of people who did the VV&A,
- The dates and results of their activities (including expected changes to the simulation),
- The extent of their activities (part of the simulation examined, input conditions considered, etc.),
- The criteria for judging the simulation (or any part of it),
- Data sources, including results from other simulations, compared with simulation results for validation reviews (include their pedigrees).

A common format for VV&A reports would be helpful because we could then automatically accumulate some of the information. For example, this common format would allow automatic synopsis of parts or objects in a simulation which have undergone particular kinds of V&V. We probably won't soon see a community standard for information items or formats, but a single organization or agency can establish its own standards and realize these benefits. (The Defense Department's Recommended Practice for VV&A in 1996 is a step in that direction, see http://www.dmso.mil).

A Special Note on Independent Reviewers for IV&V

Simulation developers will do most V&V. If they document well, others can focus on

- Checking the scope of their V&V
- Verifying that the developers have corrected or changed anything the V&V requires
- Doing selected tests, examinations, or reviews for confirmation

Still, as discussed above, some members of the V&V team should be relatively independent of the simulation developer, sponsor, and user for two reasons. First, vested interests must not compromise the candor of VV&A or even appear to do so. Second, for VV&A to be complete, someone must examine the simulation from a different perspective. If you're a sponsor, developer, or user who needs an experienced, independent person for V&V, you can get help from the Defense Modeling and Simulation Office (http://www.dmso.mil), the Society for Computer Simulation (http://www.scs.org), or the Military Operations Research Society (http://www.mors.org).

11.5.6   Simulation Resolution, Precision, and Fidelity

We know how precise scientific instruments are by reading their specifications: "This instrument can measure some parameter to within a specified amount." Unfortunately, we seldom know exactly a simulation's level of resolution or precision. For example, a time-step simulation has a time resolution dictated by the size of its smallest time step. A computation's resolution depends on the number of significant digits and the roundoff or truncation processes we use. Some kinematic simulations are described by the motion degrees of freedom they consider, such as simulations with three and six degrees of freedom. If a simulation has three degrees of freedom, it can't describe an item's orientation because it only addresses translational motion in the x, y, and z directions and doesn't compute or track the item's rotations. In most simulations, we can determine the precision of only the simulation's elements, not of the entire simulation. Non-linear interactions among simulation elements make it difficult, if not impossible, to determine the entire simulation's precision or level of resolution. Sometimes, one element will compensate for precision limits in another element; sometimes, it will compound those limits.

This inability to know a simulation's level of resolution can make it difficult to determine if a simulation is appropriate for a particular application, especially if the problem's solution depends on small differences in results. For example, a missile-engagement simulation with a precision (level of resolution) of a meter or two could successfully analyze intercepts for which miss distances of a few meters were common. But the same simulation couldn't represent intercepts acceptably whenever the missile must hit a small target (such as a part of a missile or aircraft that is smaller than a meter). To compound this problem, fidelity requirements (another way to describe simulation accuracy) have yet to be defined for most kinds of simulation applications. Efforts are under way, but the resolution, precision, and fidelity of simulations are important areas for continued research.

Of course, to quantitatively evaluate the precision and fidelity (accuracy) of a simulation, we must be able to validate it based on data about the subject. If we can't rigorously validate a simulation, the best we can do is to determine if it represents all relevant entities and processes. For these kinds of simulations, it's inappropriate to use terms like fidelity, precision, or accuracy.

11.6 Concluding Remarks

Without effective VV&A, even a significant simulation may not gain extensive credibility for the correctness of its responses. Current VV&A largely depends on human effort and judgment. More automation of verification techniques may allow us to reduce human effort and make V&V more affordable without decreasing their scope and effectiveness. Starting V&V early in simulation development and doing them right may reduce costs for simulation development and VV&A by preventing faults through effective concept validation and detecting other faults earlier. Simulation developers should organize and administer programs so they allow early, effective V&V. Knowledgeable people, appropriate techniques, and specialized equipment and software packages may be necessary for effective and affordable V&V. But even under the best circumstances, simulation validity is limited, so designs must tolerate faults. Techniques using artificial intelligence and object-oriented design pose special problems for V&V and require special attention early on to develop successful simulations on time.

Information in this chapter will help you determine when in a simulation's lifecycle to use V&V techniques that will enhance its correctness and credibility. I've emphasized the importance of validating the simulation concept (the requirements, conceptual model, and specifications) so you can prevent or reduce simulation faults arising from an inadequate concept. I've drawn your attention to the administrative and technical issues in concept validation, as well as how to verify that a simulation's design, coding, and hardware correctly represent this concept. We've also seen what's required to validate simulation results and reviewed accreditation procedures, their cost, and their effect on development schedules. With sound principles and effective techniques in hand for typical and unusually demanding simulations, you can staff, manage, and carry out VV&A that will make your simulations valid and credible.

References

In addition to the references listed below, you can find useful documents about VV&A and links concerning V&V at the Defense Modeling and Simulation Office's website (http://www.dmso.mil). These documents include an extensive bibliography on VV&A.

Ayel, M. and J.P. Laurent (eds.). 1991. *Validation, Verification, and Test of Knowledge-Based Systems*. New York, NY: John Wiley & Sons.

Balci, O. 1994. "Validation, Verification, and Testing Techniques Throughout the Life Cycle of a Simulation Study." *Annals of Operations Research* 53: 121–173.

Ballistic Missile Defense Organization. 1996. *Ballistic Missile Defense Organization (BMDO) Models and Simulations Verification, Validation, and Accreditation (VV&A) Policy*. BMDO Directive No. 5011.

Bankes, S. C. 1993. "Exploratory Modeling for Policy Analysis." *Operations Research*. Vol. 41, No. 3 (May–June).

Bowen, J. (ed.). 1994a. *Towards Verified Systems*. New York, NY: Elsevier Science B. V.

Bowen, J. P. And V. Stavridou. 1994b. "Safety-Critical Systems and Formal Methods." Chapter 1 in *Toward Verified Systems*, Bowen, J. (ed.). New York, NY: Elsevier Science B.V., pp. 3–33.

Burns, C. 1991. "PROTO—A Software Requirements Specification, Analysis, and Validation Tool." *Proceedings of the First IEEE International Workshop on Rapid System Prototyping RSP90*. IEEE Computer Society Press, pp. 196–203.

Dahl, O. 1992. *Verifiable Programming*. Englewood Cliffs, NJ: Prentice-Hall.

Davis, P. K. 1992a. *Generalizing Concepts and Methods of Verification, Validation, and Accreditation (VV&A) for Military Simulations*. Santa Monica, CA: Rand Corporation Report R-4249-ACQ.

Davis, P. K. and R. Hillestad (eds.). 1992b. *Proceedings of Conference on Variable-Resolution Modeling*. Washington, DC: 5–6 May 1992. Santa Monica, CA: Rand Corporation Report CF-103-DARPA.

Department of the Air Force. 1996. *Verification, Validation, and Accreditation Policies and Procedures*. Air Force Instruction 16–1001.

Department of the Army. 1993. *Verification, Validation, and Accreditation of Army Models and Simulations*. Department of the Army Pamphlet 5–11.

Department of Defense. 1994. *Modeling and Simulation (M&S) Management*. DOD Directive 5000.59.

Department of Defense. 1995. "DOD FY95 Master Plan for Target Interaction, Lethality and Vulnerability (TILV)." *Science and Technology (S&T) Programs. Volume I: Classical Ballistic Threats*. 4 May Revision.

Department of Defense. 1996a. *DOD Modeling and Simulation (M&S) Verification, Validation, and Accreditation*. DOD Instruction 5000.61.

Department of Defense. 1996b. *Verification, Validation, and Accreditation Recommended Practice Guide*.

Dewar, J., S. Bankes, J. Hodges, T. Lucas, D. Saunders-Newton, and P. Vye. 1995. *Credible Uses of the Distributed Interactive Simulation (DIS) System.* Santa Monica, CA: RAND Corporation Report MR-607-A.

French, S. H. and D. Hamilton. 1994. "A Comprehensive Framework for Knowledge-Based Verification and Validation." *International Journal of Intelligent Systems.* Vol. 9, No. 9 (1 September), pp. 809ff.

Gerber, R. and I. Lee. 1992. "A Layered Approach to Automating the Verification of Real-Time Systems." *IEEE Transactions on Software Engineering* 18 (9).

Gupta, U. G. 1991. *Validation and Verification of Knowledge-Based Systems.* Los Alamitos, CA: IEEE Computer Society Press.

Gupta, U. G. 1993. "Verification and Validation of Knowledge-Based Systems: A Survey." *Applied Intelligence.* Vol. 3, No. 4 (1 December), pp. 343ff.

Halbwachs, N., F. Lagnier, and C. Ratel. 1992. "Programming and Verifying Real-Time Systems by Means of the Synchronous Data-Flow Language LUSTRE." *IEEE Transactions on Software Engineering.* Vol. 18, No. 9, pp. 785–793.

Hodges, J. and J. Dewar. 1992. *Is It Your Model Talking? A Framework for Model Validation.* Santa Monica, CA: Rand Corporation Report R-4114-RC/AF.

Hoeber, F. P. 1981. *Military Applications of Modeling: Selected Case Studies.* Alexandria, VA: Military Operations Research Society.

Hollnagel, E. 1993. "ViVa: A Systematic Approach to Verification, Improvement and Validation of Knowledge-Based Systems." *Future Generations Computer Systems.* Vol. 9, No. 4., (1 December), pp. 371ff.

Institute of Electrical and Electronic Engineers. 1992. *An American National Standard Institute (ANSI)/IEEE Standard for Software Verification and Validation Plans.* IEEE Software Engineering Standards (Revised), ANSI/IEEE Standard 1012. Los Alamitos, CA: IEEE Computer Society Press.

Institute of Electrical and Electronic Engineers. 1995. *Twenty-fifth International Symposium on Fault-Tolerate Computing,* Digest of Papers, June 27–30, 1995, Pasadena, CA: IEEE Computer Society Press.

Institute of Electrical and Electronic Engineers. 1997. IEEE Standard 1278.4: *Standard for Distributed Interactive Simulation—Verification, Validation, and Accreditation (VV&A).* Piscateaway, NJ: Institute of Electrical and Electronic Engineers, Inc. (in final balloting).

Joint Chiefs of Staff. 1995. *Verification, Validation, and Accreditation of Joint Models and Simulations.* Joint Staff Instruction 8104.01.

Jones, C. 1996. *Patterns of Software Systems Failure and Success.* Boston, MA: International Thomson Computer Press.

Jordan, W., D. Charen, C. Cotten, and R. Lewis. 1995. "Planning, Optimizing, and Costing Verification, Validation, and Accreditation (VV&A) for Distributed Interactive Simulations (DIS)." *Proceedings of the 1995 Summer Computer Simulation Conference.* Ottawa, Canada, July 24–26. Society for Computer Simulation, pp. 597–602.

Knepell, P.L. and D.C. Arangno. 1993. *Simulation Validation.* Los Alamitos, CA: IEEE Computer Society Press Monograph.

Krause, P., M. O'Neil, and A. Glowinski. 1991. "Can We Formally Specify a Medical Decision Support System?" *EUROVAV 19: Proceedings of the European Workshop on the Verification and Validation of Knowledge Based System.* Cambridge, England, July 22–24. Logica UK Ltd (Cambridge, England).

Lano, K. 1995. *Formal Object-oriented Development.* Great Britain: Springer-Verlag London Limited.

Larsen, P. G., J. Fitzgerald, and T. Brookes. 1996. "Applying Formal Specification in Industry," *IEEE Software.* Vol. 13, No. 3 (May), pp. 48–56.

Lee, L. 1991. *The Day the Phones Stopped.* New York, NY: Donald I. Fine, Inc.

Lee, S. and R. M. O'Keefe. 1994. "Developing a Strategy for Expert System Verification and Validation." *IEEE Transactions on Systems, Man and Cybernetics.* Vol. 24, No. 4 (4 April), pp. 643–655.

Lewis, R.O. 1992. *Independent Verification and Validation: A Life Cycle Engineering Process for Quality Software.* New York, NY: John Wiley & Sons.

Littlewood, B. and L. Strigini. 1992. "The Risks of Software." *Scientific American.* (November), pp. 62–75.

Liu, N. K. and T. Dillon. 1991. "An Approach Towards the Verification of Expert Systems Using Numerical Petri Nets." *International Journal of Intelligent Systems.* Vol. 6, pp. 255–276.

Lyu, M. R. (ed.). 1996. *Handbook of Software Reliability Engineering.* Los Alamitos, CA: IEEE Computer Society Press.

McAllister, D. F. and M. A. Vouk. 1996. "Fault-Tolerant Software Reliability Engineering." Chapter 14 in *Handbook of Software Reliability Engineering,* Lyu, M. R. (ed.). Los Alamitos, CA: IEEE Computer Society Press.

McFarland, M. C. 1993. "Formal Verification of Correctness of Sequential Hardware: A Tutorial." *IEEE Transactions on Computer-Aided Design of Integrated Circuits and Systems.* Vol. 12, No. 5, pp. 633–654.

Miller, L.A., E. Groundwater, and S.M. Kirsky. 1993. *Survey and Assessment of Conventional Software Verification and Validation Methods.* Washington, D.C.: U.S. Nuclear Regulatory Commission Report NUREG/CR-6018.

Ministry of Defense. 1991. *Requirements for the Procurement of Safety Critical Software in Defence Equipment: Interim Defence Standard 00-55,* Interim Edition. Glasgow, United Kingdom: Directorate of Standardisation.

O'Keefe, R. M. and D. E. O'Leary. 1993. "Expert System Verification and Validation: A Survey and Tutorial." *Artificial Intelligence Review.* Vol. 7, No. 1, pp. 3–42.

Oreskes, N., K. Shrader-Frechette, and K. Belitz. 1994. "Verification, Validation, and Confirmation of Numerical models in the Earth Sciences." *Science.* Vol. 263 (4 February), pp. 641–646.

Pace, D.K. and D.P. Shea. 1992. "Validation of Analysis Which Employs Multiple Computer Simulations." *Proceedings of the 1992 Summer Computer Simulation Conference*. Reno, NV, July 27–30. Society for Computer Simulation, pp. 144–149.

Pace, D.K. 1993. "Naval VV&A Process." *Phalanx* 26 (3), pp. 27–29.

Pace, D.K. 1995. "Affordable and Effective Verification, Validation, and Accreditation of Computer Simulations." *Proceedings of the 1995 Summer Computer Simulation Conference*. Ottawa, Canada, 24–26 July. Society for Computer Simulation, pp. 182–187.

Pace, D.K. 1997. "An Aspect of Simulation Cost." *Phalanx* 30 (1), pp. 12–14.

Palmore, J. 1993. "Verification, Validation, and Visualization of Dynamical Processes in a Parallel Computing Environment." *Proceedings of the 1993 High Performance Computing Symposium*. Society for Computer Simulation. Society for Computer Simulation, pp. 197–202.

Popper, K. R. 1959. *The Logic of Scientific Discovery*. New York, NY: Basic Books.

Poppiti, J. 1994. "Managing V&V Costs." *Environmental Science and Technology*. Vol. 28, No. 6 (1 June), pp. 292ff.

Quade, E.S. 1985. "Predicting the Consequences: Models and Models." Chapter 7 in *Handbook of Systems Analysis*, Miser, H.J. And Quade, E.S. (eds.). New York, NY: Elsevier Science Publishing Company, pp.191–218.

Roache, E.A., K.A. Hickok, K.F. Loje, M.W. Hunt, and J.J. Grefenstette. 1995. *Mission Earth: Modeling and Simulation for a Sustainable Future*. Wildberger, A.M. (ed.). San Diego, CA: Society for Computer Simulation, pp. 45–50.

Rombach, H. D. and M. Verlage. 1995. "Directions in Software Process Research." *Advances in Computers*. Zelkowitz (ed.). San Diego, CA: Academic Press, Inc.

Secretary of the Navy. 1996. *Verification, Validation, and Accreditation (VV&A) of Models and Simulations*. SECNAV Instruction 5200.xx (Draft).

Sheng, G., M.S. Elzas, T.I. Oren, and B.T. Cronhjort. 1993. "Model Validation: A Systemic and Systematic Approach." *Reliability Engineering and System Safety* 42: 247–259.

Smith, M.D. and D.J. Robson. 1990. "Object-Oriented Programming—the Problem of Validation." *Proceedings of the IEEE Conference on Software Maintenance*. IEEE Computer Society Press, pp. 272–281.

Stavridou, V. 1994. "Formal Methods and VLSI Engineering Practice." *The Computer Journal*. Vol. 37, No. 2, pp. 96–113.

Wallace, D.R., L.M. Ippolito, and D.R. Kuhn. 1992. *High Integrity Software Standards and Guidelines*. Gaithersburg, MD: National Institute of Standards and Technology Special Publication 500–204.

Wildberger, A.M. 1994a. "Review of the Exploratory Research Program in Parallel and Adaptive computing at the Electric Power Research Institute." *Proceedings of the 1994 High Performance Computing Conference*. San Diego, CA: April 11–13. Society for Computer Simulation.

Wildberger, A.M. 1994b. "Assuring the Performance of Adaptive Control Systems." *Proceedings of the DOE Adaptive Control Systems Technology Symposium*. Pittsburgh, PA: October 24–25. Department of Energy.

Williams, M. 1991. "SIMVAL Mini-Symposium—A Report." *Phalanx*, (June) 24 (2): 1, 3–6.

Youngblood, S.M. 1993. "Literature Review and Commentary on the Verification, Validation, and Accreditation of Models and Simulations." *Proceedings of the 1993 Summer Computer Simulation Conference*. Boston, MA: July 19–21. Society for Computer Simulation, pp. 10–17.

Youngblood, S.M. and D.K. Pace. 1995. "An Overview of Model and Simulation Verification, Validation, and Accreditation." *Johns Hopkins APL Technical Digest*. 17 (2): 197–205.

Zelkowitz, M. V. 1993. "Role of Verification in the Software Specification Process." *Advances in Computers*. Yovits, M. C. (ed.), Vol. 36. Academic Press, New York, pp. 43–109.

Zlatareva, N.P. 1994. "A Framework for Verification, Validation, and Refinement of Knowledge-Bases: The VVR System." *International Journal of Intelligent Systems*. Vol. 9, No. 8, (1 August), pp. 703ff.

CHAPTER 12

Integrating and Executing Simulations

Brian Goldiez, *University of Central Florida*
Institute for Simulation & Training

Let's begin with definitions. Integrating a simulation means inserting it into another environment to create an enhanced system. Executing a simulation applies it within the context of its intended use (within an experimental frame). We execute a simulation to some extent while integrating it, but we don't integrate it while executing it. I'll explain further throughout this chapter.

Sometimes, we may question whether integration always precedes execution. In this chapter I'll assume we've gone through testing, verifying, validating, and accrediting an isolated simulation. Within its isolated environment, the simulation has been integrated and is operating. Now we'll begin integrating this simulation into a larger context for subsequent execution. The answer lies in knowing where the simulation is in its lifecycle; if you're interested only in execution, you should concentrate on Sections 12.2 through 12.4 and 12.6 through 12.8.

This chapter explains ways to integrate and execute simulations, examines the close relationships between these activities, and tells you when caution is necessary in carrying them out. After the simulation is on a computer, it's time to integrate and execute it. Development ends when integration is complete and users start exercising the simulation for its intended purpose. The simulation is verified and validated at this point. Accreditation occurs after the simulation enters execution. For a flow of this process and of the chapter, see Table 12.1.

Table 12.1.   Overview of Integration and Execution. To integrate and execute the simulation, we must assess and baseline it in advance and analyze results once the process is complete.

Step	Activity
Assess	Receive, inventory, and understand simulation
Baseline	Operate, dissect, and understand the simulation's basic operation
Integrate	Plan and carry out integration
Execute	Plan and carry out execution. Gather data.
Analyze Results	Assess whether goals have been achieved

I'll introduce the concept of operating the simulation, which is the same as "running the simulation through its paces" without regard to its ultimate operational context. During integration we operate the simulation many times, starting in isolation and progressively adding other components. During execution we also operate the simulation but always in an integrated environment.

If you're handling integration and execution, keep several cautions in mind. First, the developer of the simulation usually won't be available to you. Second, the simulation is emerging from development and hasn't been in an operational environment. Third, we don't live in a perfect world. Imperfection means you may not have all the information you need, and the simulation may differ from its description in the documentation. As we move through the chapter, you'll see how these cautions affect integration and execution. We can work within these limits, but they make our job more difficult.

Fortunately, we have various ways to integrate simulations, and properly designed simulations also tend to be flexible. Usually, flexibility is good because it allows different approaches, but it also leads to variable results. Finally, watch out for changes in algorithms that don't appear in the. documentation. These "beartraps" make integration and execution more difficult.

At the end of this chapter, you'll find all of the steps we discuss in a checklist that you and your team can use to guide your efforts and assess progress.

12.1 Basic Principles

Before we start integrating a simulation, we must understand its technical and programmatic characteristics and constraints. You'll find discussions of these principles throughout this book, but it's important to discuss some of them in the context of integration and execution. We also need to know when simulation is appropriate, where and what types of trade-offs are typically made during development, and the various types of simulators.

People use simulations for studies, decision making, measuring things not measurable in the physical world, planning, learning, prototyping, etc. We must understand a simulation's intended purpose before trying to integrate it. For example, it's not practical to create a large forest fire intentionally in order to study fire-extinguishing techniques or long-term effects on the environment. But simulations can help us study these areas. Likewise, simulations of operational systems or economic trends can support high-level decision making, such as Congressional decisions on the federal budget. How we integrate and execute a simulation depends on these and other early requirements.

Simulations are powerful because we can normally execute them at a lower cost ($, schedule, safety, etc.) than their operational counterparts and because they're flexible enough to use for many purposes. Of course, people can also misuse simulations by applying them inappropriately, thus arriving at incorrect decisions. Thus, developers must plan for simulations to be used for unintended purposes, but as we'll see later, we can sometimes extend a simulation's usefulness during execution by knowing its VV&A history. In fact, knowing the requirements and history for a simulation is vital to integration and execution. In a positive sense, if we know what the users want in a simulation, we can (in part) measure our success against these requirements. On the negative side, users may be disappointed in our integration and execution efforts because the resulting simulation doesn't exactly represent events in nature. Remember, Chaps. 2 and 8 imply that modeling requires focusing on some aspects of the real system and de-emphasizing or ignoring other features, which may produce disappointing robustness in the simulation and make integration and execution difficult physically and emotionally. Knowing the simulation's original requirements and history can help us assess our effort.

I've pointed out a simulator's power and diversity to explain their effect on integration and, ultimately, execution. Simulators are cost-effective ways of representing many situations which are tough to replicate in the real world. Whenever we integrate and execute a model or simulation, we must remain faithful to its design and to its valid range of operating conditions.

Decisions early in simulation development affect integration and execution. For example, systems engineering and quality function deployment (described respectively in Chaps. 2 and 5) define the environment the simulation addresses and begin to justify why simulations should be used to support system development instead of other techniques. This type of information becomes a baseline for integration and execution. Likewise, we can use measures of performance (described in Chap. 5) to assess our success.

We must know the type of simulation we're receiving (Chap. 3) and whether it is person to person, person to computer, or all computer. Computer simulations consist of algorithms and data, and are driven by data, algorithms, or more commonly, some combination of both. Knowing the mix of algorithms and data helps us integrate and execute simulations because it tells us how we can use the simulation and connect it to a larger set of objectives.

A simulation's type often depends on how real time and simulation time relate, as well as how the simulation uses time internally. For constructive simulations, our main emphasis is ensuring events occur in proper sequence. These types of simulations typically don't run in real time. For virtual simulations, our main purpose is to ensure that time advances at an agreed upon rate and that priority events occur in a given time period. These different uses of time affect human interaction with the simulation and the way we integrate and execute it. Figure 12.1 illustrates this concept for integrating a time-stepped virtual simulator with an event-stepped simulator. We must account for idle time in time-stepped simulations, whereas event simulations give events priority over time. To integrate and execute simulations successfully, we must maintain coherency of time, events, and space.

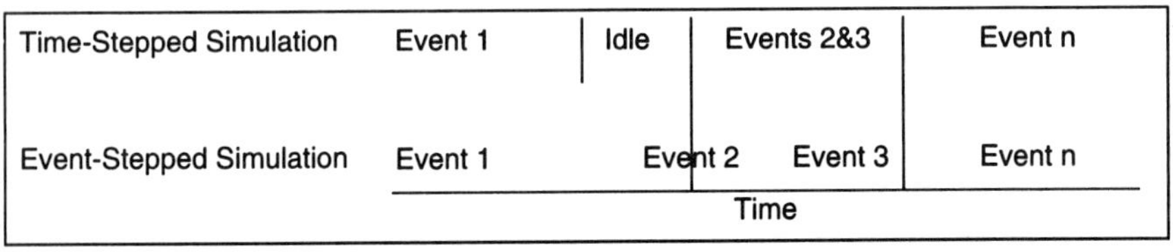

Time-Stepped Simulation	Event 1	Idle	Events 2&3	Event n
Event-Stepped Simulation	Event 1	Event 2	Event 3	Event n
		Time		

Fig. 12.1. **Keeping Time and Events Coherent in Integration and Execution.** When integrating simulations, we must properly sequence events.

Integration adds flexibility to a simulation and extends the range of application of an algorithm or simulation. Integrating multiple simulation models or a single simulation into a larger context provides dynamic interactions that are not always apparent beforehand. These interactions confirm the utility of simulation components and are more typical of the real world. If we integrate appropriately (as we'll see later in the chapter) the simulation's real power becomes available. Then, the execution process must harness this power.

As an example of our discussion above, consider the bounding cube for the fire- and land-management problem graphically depicted in Fig. 12.2. Select, for example, a simulation representing one of the smaller cubes, such as topography mitigation under engineering and manufacturing development. For this simulation to meet its objectives, it must be able to integrate and execute with adjacent small cubes. Interfaces must be specific, but designers may consider many options: common data or algorithmic interfaces, input/output interfaces between computer programs, input/output analyses between programs, or human analysis and assessment as the interface between programs. The option they select influences our strategy for integrating and executing the simulation, and it also could produce characteristics not evident in the simulation's singular state. It's easy to see, in a general way, how the flexibility of a simulation's design can dramatically affect integration and execution.

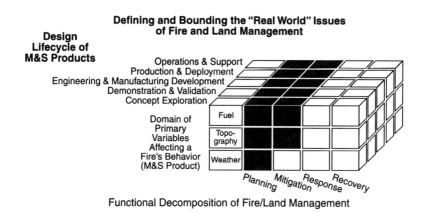

Functional Decomposition of Fire/Land Management

Fig. 12.2.　**How Issues Relate across the Domain of the Fire- and Land-Management Problem.** A simulation's functions and interfaces must be properly aligned for integration to be successful.

We need to know whether a simulation will be part of an operational system's development or will work with the delivered operational system. We can execute it to

- Analyze decisions and develop milestones for product development

- Test and evaluate new products without creating problems involving safety, environment, or release of sensitive information

- Train people to use new or existing products without running into safety and cost issues

Knowing the main use of a simulation determines how comprehensively we integrate or execute it. If errors in the simulation could harm people or cost a lot of money, we would integrate it more thoroughly and execute it under tighter constraints.

Finally, we must understand who the ultimate users and operators are and how well they know the subject and the simulation itself. Users can be trainees, product developers, testers, analysts, or decision makers, and their needs may drive how we integrate and execute a simulation. For example, if the user is an analyst, we should integrate the simulation with a strong mathematical basis to convince the analyst of its range of validity. If the user is a decision maker, we'd like to execute the simulation so its results are familiar to the decision maker. Likewise, if the operator doesn't have simulation skills, the simulation should self-check data values and start automatically. Knowing these basics helps speed and focus integration and execution.

12.2   Establish a Baseline

The baseline for integration and execution is the information needed to understand the simulation. We must be able to determine the origin of this information, and the simulation must either contain or generate it. Here, I don't mean word-of-mouth information, unless you can confirm it. Although we'll probably provide more information to later users by integrating and executing the simulation, we don't need this extra data before reviewing the baseline.

Integration and execution requires four classes of baseline information: mathematical descriptions of the simulation's algorithms, description of the data range for variables, users' manuals describing technical and programmatic information about the simulator, and configuration-control documents. Integration and execution will add information to these classes for subsequent users. We can never have too much information, unless it's disorganized.

Baseline information comes from two general sources: design and test. Design information is traceable back to the original simulation and operational requirement. The simulation's original requirements document, often stated as things the simulation must do, is useful. If the simulation is modeling an operational or conceptual system, we include or reference its functional and technical description in the design documentation. A document controlling configuration and data shows us how data is organized. Another useful design document is a requirements traceability matrix—a document tracing requirements from their origin into simulation hardware and software. As we integrate and execute the simulation, we often add important information to this matrix. All of this baseline information is useful for integration and execution because it reflects the simulation's history, requirements, and objectives.

The second source of baseline information is testing—exercising the simulation, its components, or its algorithms. Whether this test data comes with or is produced during integration or execution, we must strictly control its configuration. For all data, we state the date generated, the conditions under which it was generated, and who created it. We also include the version of the simulation, the module or algorithm used, our methods (e.g., number of runs and statistical process applied to the runs), and a description of any computer used to produce the data. The key to understandable and useful baselines is clear, documented organization, so others can get to the information they need. It's helpful to establish configuration-control tactics in advance.

Other information useful for execution and integration includes source code, test procedures, test data, post-test analyses, and sample runs of the simulation. The simulation could be executable software or a mixture of executable and source code for interfaces and other user-controlled functions. Source code gives us a way to see programming techniques and short cuts used to create the simulation. Sample runs tell us how the simulation works.

Table 12.2 lists the types of information we need to integrate and execute a simulation. See Chap. 9 for more details. Browse all information to get a sense of its organization and content. After browsing, study the details, keeping in mind the simulation's general objectives and your objectives for integration and execution.

Table 12.2. General Types of Information Necessary for Integration and Execution. This is a partial list of the wide variety of information that is necessary for integration and execution.

General Data Type	Information Type	Source
Simulation requirement documents	c	d
Operational system data	m, v, c	d
Configuration control	c	d
Data control	c	d
Requirements traceability matrix	c	d
Test data	m, v	t
Source code		
Test procedures	m, v	d
Sample runs	m, v, u	t
Definition terms	m, v, u, c	d
Development environment description	u, c	d

Information Type
m = math   v = data variable   u = user manuals   c = configuration management
Source
d = design baseline   t = testing

Knowledge of the environment for simulation development, evaluation, and operation is important baseline information. Here, environment means mainly the computer hardware and software. Manuals for users and design documents should contain this information. Whenever you execute or integrate the simulation, compare your current environment to one of the simulation environments noted above, so you can properly interpret the results.

As previously stated, we don't live in a perfect world and therefore don't always get the baseline information we think we need. One reason is the range of meanings for terms, depending on who is using them. Their explicit meaning may seem clear from a simple list of terms included as part of the baseline documentation. But implicit meanings are more subtle, so we have to figure out how to discover them. If we can talk to people who created the baseline information, we can usually just ask "Did you mean...?" or say "We assume this is what you wanted." If we can't talk to them, we must carefully document our assumptions during integration or execution. Or we can ask developers and users to view and interact with the simulation as it evolves, or independently verify and validate it as we integrate and execute it. Finally, communities who use modeling and simulation can include "dictionaries" with their requirements. But suppose clarifying terms still doesn't give us the baseline information we need? Then we have to couple results of having technical experts operate the simulation in isolation with observations from users of similar types of simulations. These sources can give us a "best-guess" baseline.

Another reason we don't get the data we need is that the simulation may represent a conceptual system without an operational counterpart. Inconsistencies arise because the simulation only approximates the real world or doesn't represent it all. For example, we recommend dividing a simulation into three basic components for integration: entities, environment, and behaviors. Simulations normally contain at least two of these three components, and many contain all three. But physical systems don't divide so neatly. Whenever we test and gather data on a new piece of fire-fighting equipment, we normally can't see how the operator's behavior or subtle changes in the environment will affect its performance. We try to use a "standard" operator, but standard skills and features are difficult to quantify. To solve this problem, we can try grouping operational characteristics into our three components and studying the supplied data to determine (or hypothesize) how each one affects the data. But if this grouping isn't practical, we need to study all components we're integrating with the simulation and find an alternate approach that will keep their interactions compatible. Finally, we must document all assumptions, so future users will learn something from our integration or execution.

Many simulations no longer operate in isolation. They're often integrated with other simulations or operational systems to create heterogeneous, synthetic environments, which are very useful because they make all simulations do more. However, creating a baseline for these environments is more difficult than for an isolated environment. As Fig. 12.3 shows, a single simulation operating in isolation has very limited points for input and output, which translate to better control. In a heterogeneous environment, potential inputs and outputs permutate rapidly and in greatly varying arrangements as the number of variables increases. These variations in number, order, and timing cause us to lose control of the interactions between simulations.

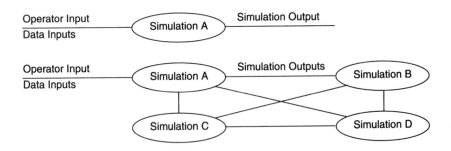

Fig. 12.3.   Complexity of Simulation Interactions Increases as the Number of Simulators Grow. Interactions among simulations arise from various sources. As the number of simulators operating together increases, the number of interactions grows dramatically, often making it difficult to identify the source of stimuli driving the system.

12.3   Collect Information and Document

To integrate and execute a simulation, as well as to assess our success, we must have input, output, and algorithmic data. See Chap. 9 for more discussion of types and uses of data. Simulations require data for operation, and some part of their derivation is rooted in data, which is either static or dynamic.

The data we use should cover all values the simulation could encounter. Dynamic data should include time histories and initial conditions. Because we're normally interested in the steady-state behavior of dynamic data, we should discard transients (unless we intend to study these effects). For static or boolean systems, such as a simulation of circuit breakers in an aircraft, we have to know the conditions for keeping the static state stable or for moving between states. In both cases, we present the data as lists of dependent and independent variables (more common) or as equations. We prefer data that comes from the operational system, followed by data from exercising the simulation's algorithms, and finally, data from previous versions of the simulation.

If data is simplified, we want documentation. For example, operational data normally contains noise and ancillary information, so mean values or filtering methods (e.g., Kalman filters) are typically used to process it for simulation. If we know the range of raw data, we can move away from the processed data to operate the simulation, perhaps for technical or programmatic reasons. Knowing the range of data also allows us to expand the simulation's uses without operating outside the data constraints and thereby invalidating the model, getting erroneous results, halting the simulation, or using too much computational time or memory.

To integrate and execute properly, we must know how to interpolate—to move between data values when a simulation uses discreet data sets or tables. Interpolation routines take a lot of computer time, especially for multivariable problems. Sometimes the interpolation routines use quadratic or higher-order equations. Multivariable data points can yield different values if the interpolation routines aren't linear and if the order of interpolation varies. We have to use consistent methods for interpolating data because we'll evaluate results against requirements or other baseline information—a critical point that's often forgotten. Also, although interpolation is acceptable for normal integration and execution, we should avoid extrapolating data values unless we're investigating how a simulation will operate outside its valid range. Extrapolation moves us outside this range because, by definition, it projects estimated values from known data.

Other information we need isn't typically in lists of numbers or symbols. Software tapes and listings in source and executable code are necessary for integration and execution because they help create a baseline for the simulation, serve as references for people who need to know more about how the simulator works, and back up the effort in case the computer fails. But software isn't very useful if written instructions (also data) don't come with it. These instructions tell us how to install, operate, and operationally load the software and are essential for effective integration and execution.

12.4   Assess the Delivered Simulation

Figure 12.4 shows that assessment drapes over the entire simulation: every time the simulation changes hands, we must assess it. Changing hands includes moving from one development stage to another, as well as changing the organization who maintains configuration control. Normally, integration and execution cause this kind of change because they require skills different from those of the developers.

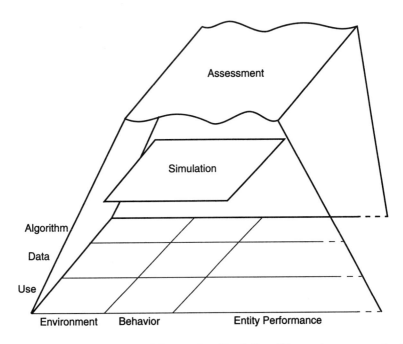

Fig. 12.4.   **Assessment Covers All Parts of a Simulation.** We must assess a simulation's algorithms, data, and intended uses in terms of its behavior and its components' performance, within all appropriate environments.

Whenever a simulation changes hands, it typically goes through some verification, validation, or accreditation, depending on the receiving organization's responsibility. For example, development tests, which are part of merging the simulation into a larger process or system, lead to verification and validation. Execution leads to accreditation.

How we assess the simulation depends on the information that comes with it and our access to its internal hardware and software. We should assess the simulation's data, algorithms, and uses, even though we may not have everything needed to baseline it. First, we must divide the simulation into its physical performance, its simulated environment, and its behavior or controls. Although these boundaries may not be clear, they'll help us analyze smaller parts of the simulation in typical operational contexts.

As an example for which boundaries may become blurry, consider the case of a firefighting vehicle operating in a field. The vehicle's speed (physical performance) depends on the condition of the terrain (environment). But it's not always clear where the mobility-based equations belong—in the environment or in the physical performance. What's worse, we may not be able to see the equations of performance or the terrain model. In this case, the integration group has to decide where to place mobility and then document this decision.

The assessment process begins when you receive the simulation, inventory it, review and understand its context, and operate the simulator to understand its basic features. Be sure to record what you receive. (See Sec. 12.3, for more on reviewing and understanding the simulation context).

Operating the simulation by running it establishes an operating baseline from which you can integrate or execute it. You must understand how the simulation software relates to the information you've received and how the simulation operates by itself first. This doesn't mean you're executing the simulation. Operating means "running the simulation through its paces" to understand basically how it works, without placing it in its eventual operating context. You should try to run the simulation on a computer, but you can also manually carry out the algorithms.

Operating the simulation or having someone operate the simulation for you is beneficial because you

- Learn how the simulation works and what its environment is
- Get, and often confirm, information about input and output formats for data
- Establish or confirm the simulation's range of data values and stable operating ranges
- Record this baseline information in the same form as for other data, so it will be consistent in future efforts

To determine the simulation's valid range, you'll need to analyze its algorithms, data, and operational uses. This means reviewing data and documentation or operating the simulation to determine the characteristics and limits of each of these three components. Analyzing algorithms requires you to look at the simulation's time step, hard limits to variables, and the order of execution. Analyzing data consists of investigating data ranges, data-point spacing, and techniques for moving between data points (e.g., discrete steps or interpolation techniques). Checking operational uses means understanding the context for which the simulation was built.

Assessing the simulation should include operating it through the complete range of inputs and outputs. This range includes data that is nominal, at the operating extremes, past the stated operating limit, and in error. We operate the simulation in this way to make sure its behavior generally corresponds to the data that came with it and it effectively handles adverse data (doesn't cause unrecoverable failures). By operating the simulation, we also start ensuring it will meet its intended purpose when integrated into the simulation strategy and executed as a system or part of a system.

Finally, assessment assures us at a systems level that the information received with the simulation, the analysis of the simulation through operation, and its range of values provide a complete picture of the simulation. At this point we should know the simulation's structure and what it will do.

Assessing the simulation consists of inspecting, analyzing, measuring, and operating each of its major parts, using the steps in Fig. 12.5. These efforts are also useful for verification, validation, and test and should take place before integration or execution begins. When we're finished, the assessment should cover all aspects of the simulation, as shown in Fig. 12.4. Although operating the simulation gives us the most complete results, it may not be practical—for example, whenever computers aren't available for a thorough run-through. In these cases, we must use inspection, analysis, or measurement. Inspection means examining a particular item, such as software code or computer hardware. Analyzing consists of separating the simulation into parts and determining whether each part does what it's supposed to. Measurement involves collecting relevant simulation parameters and ensuring they operate within range. Each of these methods has a different role in assessment—though the differences are sometimes subtle. Once we've used a method, we should document it.

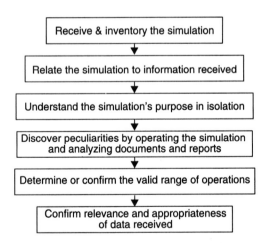

Fig. 12.5.   Steps in Assessing a Simulation. We assess first—before we start executing or integrating the simulation.

Next, we must verify and validate (V&V) the simulation, using inputs from its documentation. This V&V involves operating the simulation and checking to see if our results are the same (or nearly the same) as the test results in the documentation. It is much more limited in scope than the formal activities described in Chap. 11 and is used to qualitatively assure us that the simulation being integrated is the same as the one that is documented. Changes to the software, different operating environments, random errors, and other variations could cause differences. Remember, undocumented changes often occur when the simulation is operated by others. Of course, as mentioned above, we can't always operate a simulation as much as we'd like to during this first step in integration and execution. Schedule and cost constraints limit us, but so do large data packages and lengthy operating histories, which suggest a simulation needs little assessment. For example, we don't need to do much assessment if we're integrating a commercially available simulation package with other simulation components and executing the integrated system for a study because many users have established the simulation's operating characteristics. In fact, this approach is becoming more popular as simulations become more useful.

Determining model type (as discussed in Chap. 3) is part of assessment because integrating different types of simulation models may produce instabilities or anomalies. We should avoid these risks, if we can, by restricting attempts to integrate heterogeneous simulations which rely on different model types.

Executing the simulation also requires many steps. As with integration, we must assess the simulation before we try to execute it. That means determining or reaffirming the simulation's intended use and purpose, the completeness and appropriateness of documentation, and the appropriateness of configuration control. This assessment differs from what we do for integration—it includes many new items, as well as different approaches to existing items. For example, people who didn't develop the simulation will be operating it during execution. Therefore, we must assess its ease of use by operators, trainees, or analysts. They may also have limited computational hardware and software, a restriction not present during integration. So, we must evaluate how limited equipment affects the simulation's performance.

12.5 Integrate the Simulation

Many simulations are systems composed of systems. Simulation components represent systems, some of which can stand alone. The simulation also is a system, which we can integrate with other systems for various uses. The pieces are integrated iteratively to replicate an operational or conceptual system, with the type of simulation and degree of modeling defining the degree of replication. Integration isn't confined to components of a simulation; it extends to linking simulations with other simulations, as well as with other hardware components and, ultimately, with human users. We can extend the rules for integrating a simulation's components, which simulate a process or system, to integrating the simulation of a process or system with other processes or systems. The procedures are basically the same, although the specifics are more complex because we're now dealing with more complex components.

Integration is a long process because it covers a lot of a simulation's development cycle. Integration includes merging the simulation's components to create a self-sufficient system. It also includes merging this created system with other simulations or operational components to create an even larger system. Figure 12.6 describes the steps for integration. The previous section actually discussed the first step of the process—operating the simulation to become familiar with its characteristics in isolation, relating it to the received data, understanding its valid range of operation, and understanding its peculiarities, such as requiring a fixed time for results to stabilize.

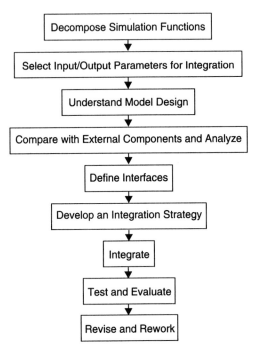

Fig. 12.6.   Diagram of the Integration Process. Integration should be an orderly sequence of steps.

Users' requirements influence integration; if they're broken out properly, we'll know what's important and what to spend less time on. Similarly, we must know how a simulation relates to its operational counterpart, so we can determine how much it's expected to do. An operational system under development could use results from incremental integrations as a design guide or to confirm design decisions. As we integrate the simulation, new results influence the operational system as well as how we continue to integrate the simulated system. Likewise, we may execute parts of simulations as we integrate them, so we can confirm that the simulation is on track to meeting its objectives. This approach is part of concurrent engineering or spiral development. Successive integrations during spiral development should quantitatively show we're converging on a solution by taking less time to integrate, producing fewer discrepancies, or otherwise improving performance.

We have to be sure simulations that model the same types of activity do so consistently. That means separating the simulation's tasks and investigating consistency between entities, environments, and behaviors in the heterogeneous simulations. For example, we may have problems trying to integrate a simulation that models a simple aircraft (such as a PC-based flight simulator) with a simulation that faithfully models an aircraft's detailed aerodynamic attributes and systems. Both simulations meet their individual baseline objectives, but the integrated system yields inconsistent and unreliable results if we're modeling air-to-air combat. It's easy to see how this problem quickly becomes very complicated as variations increase in the simulation and its operating requirements.

Integration should reduce a simulation's harmful effects on human operators. For example, we could integrate a flight simulator's visual display so it doesn't cause vertigo or nausea. Human operators are integral to—or control—the simulation's performance and immediately benefit from this performance. Because integration is the first chance for the operator or user to interact formally with the simulator, we must use this process to monitor human interaction with the simulation.

Integration is organized and methodical, as shown in Fig. 12.6. In this abstract form, it applies to isolated simulation components or to integrating a simulation into a larger context for execution. The key to integrating simulations is segmenting them whenever possible, so we can make sure processes, algorithms, data, input/output, and cross-system performance parameters all work together. If they do, our simulation will be compatible with other parts of the larger system. I previously suggested dividing the simulation into the environment, behavior, and physical performance of entities, then further separating each of these into data, algorithms, and use. But sometimes the delivered simulation is an integrated subsystem that you can't separate. If so, try to connect the simulation with other parts of the simulation strategy. Assess these connections while using consistent inputs between components and measuring outputs from the entities and elements suggested above. You may have to further split up complex physical systems, behavioral models, or environments. For example, fuel consumption (physical principle) versus driving habits (behavior) may be important variables to check for vehicles fighting remote fires, as long as the vehicle type and logistics are part of your simulation study. This approach allows you to check for consistency between similar characteristics. For example, if an environmental model doesn't include wind, and you integrate it with an environmental model that does, fire-spread rates in your example simulation won't be consistent between the integrated models.

Whenever you decompose (segment) a simulation, make sure cross-component dependencies don't disappear—especially at interfaces, where you must decide on which side to place a function. Consider our fire system from Fig. 12.2 (expanded in Fig. 12.7). If topography mitigation in Engineering and Manufacturing Development must interface with planning, response, or other neighboring components, you must divide it just as you do for those neighboring components.

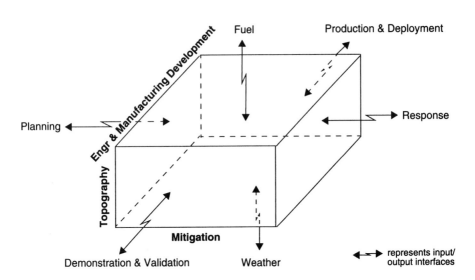

Fig. 12.7.   **Integrating a Simulation.** Integrating a simulation requires matching interfaces with adjacent components and maintaining cross-system dependencies.

Study the inputs to each part of the simulation and note where they come from—another part of the simulation, outside the simulation, etc. Usually, you can do this without knowing its internal algorithms. Use inputs that you can verify independently against an operational system or validated simulation. Outputs from the integrated simulation are then similar to those from the operational system, within defined tolerances. When integrating the simulation with other similar components, use inputs with the same range, upper and lower limits, and granularity; select the more conservative values whenever the simulation's parameters don't match those of the operational system; and document the values you select. Later on, you can decide whether you want to extend the simulation's range by experimenting with less conservative variables. Figure 12.8 graphically shows what I mean. Note how you must discard the lower range of the variable from Simulator A and the upper range of the variable for Simulator B to find a common range.

Successful integration critically depends on understanding the model design and ensuring the model designs between similar parts being integrated are compatible. Chapter 8 provides some excellent insights into designing models. If you're integrating part of a simulation with other parts, study their internal algorithms in terms of their enabling mechanisms (for software, enabling mechanisms are logic flow and semantics). This study may be difficult because enabling strategies vary and algorithm logic is elusive. As an alternative, use the input values noted above, stimulate similar parts of the simulation, and observe if the results are within some pre-established tolerance.

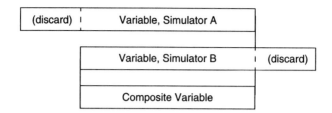

Fig. 12.8.   **Selecting the Range of a Composite Variable from Two Simulations.** Integrating the simulation with other components or simulations may require adjusting the range of selective variables.

We can assess compatibility between like components in several ways, including Z-transform analysis of dynamic components or using techniques from operations research to analyze the logic flow of discrete models. If data drives the simulation or component, we can analyze the range of data tables by comparing the number of break points, break-point spacing, or number of independent variables. We should also make sure similar interpolation algorithms are used. No one technique is best because simulations and integration strategies vary.

By now, you can see that linking simulations of different types is a complex business. Small differences in simulation types can balloon into significant integration problems. For example, integrating a simulation of a real-time, dynamic process (such as how a forest fire spreads) with a discrete-event model of equipment movement is difficult because of differences in simulation type (in this case, time scales and granularity). We have to create an interface to match up and integrate models while meeting the simulation's objectives. This is why successful integration demands careful decomposition and interfacing.

Integration also requires us to match hardware and software and to trade them off whenever they don't align. For example, if one computer uses Big Endian and another uses Little Endian (common between PCs and some Unix workstations), the simulation may have to do byte swapping for successful integration. The approach varies depending on the simulation strategy. One approach is to allow one part of a simulation to control a variable or function normally controlled by several components when they're not integrated. Or we can have something outside these components arbitrate the variable or function. Other approaches include forcing commonality by changing component software or hardware (not normally advised in virtual or live simulations), changing the simulation strategy, or developing software interfaces. Selecting an approach depends on how much computing capacity is available and whether we can access the software structure of the simulation being integrated with other systems.

Once we've decomposed each component, we can develop an integration strategy based on clear standards, which provide some structure and rules for connecting systems. (For more detail on standards, see Chaps. 13 and 15). Our strategy should include procedures for handling peculiar situations, such as when we're integrating human operators or hardware with the simulation. We must also consider how to handle interfaces and balance them against cost, schedule, technical requirements, and other simulation objectives. For example, we may have to use the simulation "as is" because many other systems use it. Finally, we must design experiments and tests to ensure the integration is progressing.

One basic decision involves top-down or bottom-up integration. Engineers often prefer top-down design and decomposition, but we believe in bottom-up integration. First, we check and integrate basic features before moving upward to integrate the simulator's functions. As an example, we have to look at word size and byte orientation. With basic features appropriately integrated, we next make sure the simulation's main parts match its external interfaces and then integrate more components into a progressively more complex, more complete system. A top-down approach works better whenever some of the systems being integrated with the simulation aren't available. In this case, we can "stub out" lower-level components and simulations until they become available.

Testing and experimenting are inherent to integration. Testing confirms the integration is proceeding as planned and helps identify problems early in simulation development. Include a test in every integration step and document all of them in an engineering log or other appropriate integration record. Develop tests before starting the integration and match them to the data available, the stage of integration, the information you have on the simulation's internal components, and the ever-present constraints on cost and schedule. Make sure your tests confirm the measures of performance (discussed in Chap. 5) established early in the simulation's development cycle.

You can improve integration by testing with the operators or those who execute the simulation, but you must have a complete set of simulation components so operators can judge them in an operational context. Use face validity or anecdotal tests (individual opinions or Delphi techniques) whenever the operators' opinions and observations are all you can get. You can also compare the simulation's operation to that of other similar simulations.

Quantitative tests are also available to us. For example, we can do simple, non-statistical tests before and after integrating parts of the simulation. First, we inject low, middle, and high values while holding other inputs constant, and then do pairwise tests. Later, we use groups of changing input variables, selecting them randomly unless our assessment suggests we should test particular variables or functions.

After integrating components, we should also test the simulation's operation with inputs at extreme values. This limit testing—using erroneous and out-of-range data—is appropriate after integrating components because we must be sure the simulation will respond well to varying conditions. Choosing the best non-statistical, quantitative tests will depend on your group's experience and rigorous assessment of the simulation.

Although non-statistical tests are useful, we prefer statistical tests to determine our progress. Sample size, random selection, and independence of data values are important considerations when testing under "real-world conditions" (App. C). Successful statistical testing depends on the size of the sample population. We prefer large, essentially infinite, populations over small sample sizes because we can use less conservative statistical approaches. We must carefully apply probability and statistics to the sample size and probability approach. It's critical to select samples randomly and to minimize any dependencies between data values. Of course, most sampling approaches include loose dependencies between samples. For example, traditional sampling of production-line products neglects the dependency that a finite set of machines produced the parts being sampled.

Population size and practicalities dictate the number of samples we can take from the population. Practicalities include trade offs between our statistical approach and the cost of acquiring a large sample. We often use binomial probability distributions because go/no-go criteria are easy to establish and maintain. Taking many samples allows more failures than taking a few, but it also requires more time and money.

Test outputs must be statistically relevant. For example, mean values and standard deviations commonly emerge from tests, but they're not statistically significant unless we include confidence intervals with them. Hypothesis tests and chi-squared tests are common ways to study outputs of integration tests. Student-T tests are useful for small sample populations. (See App. C for more information and some of the references at the end of this chapter for detailed treatments of probability and statistics.)

We also recommend Turing Tests because the simulations in this book are mostly computer programs. Turing tests determine how closely computer programs compare to human responses, so they're very useful for integrated simulations that mimic human behavior or involve human operators. An example, might be simulating how to fight forest fires. We might simulate the behavior of many firefighters to train an individual firefighter. Turing tests (and statistical analysis of their results) would show how closely the simulated firefighters resemble human firefighters in the trainee's eyes. Although Turing tests are somewhat controversial among computer scientists, no other approaches are reliable.

Finally, we arrive at the inevitable question, "How do you know you're finished integrating?" Usually, we can't make large simulations error free, so we allocate time for integration and assess how we're doing within this period by measuring the percentage of software and hardware integrated, tracking the number of errors, or tracking the number of discrepancies in expected outputs. It's important to establish completion criteria in advance and stick to them as much as possible. Here are some useful criteria for determining when you're done:

- No problems remain which affect the simulation's operation
- Small problems which do remain are documented
- The simulation operates within prescribed limits
- Statistical assessment shows operations meet requirements
- The simulation is consistent with the operational system, or with the integrated environment
- The simulation meets required objectives

12.6   Execute the Simulation

Executing the simulation means using it for its intended purpose: analysis, product development, training, testing, or concept development. Integration ends simulation development; during execution, operators, analysts, decision makers, support people, and others use the products of this development but don't change the simulation's internal structure. No longer are tools for managing data, compiling, debugging, or tracing requirements as important as they were during development. For execution, operating procedures, logs, and data analyzers are essential.

Operator skills and interfaces to the simulation become critical now, so we must answer these (and other) questions: Are many people going to operate the simulation? What skills or training do they need? Must the simulation support many different types of operators? Are users of the simulation different from operators? Analysts review and interpret the results from operating the simulation. Decision makers depend on the analysts' efforts or, sometimes, ask for more—or more specialized—executions to get the right information. Support people must be skilled in reconfiguring the simulation or correcting it if it fails. Trainees may also be involved. They should be able to learn from the simulation during execution without coming to any harm.

The simulation becomes public, so to speak, in its execution phase, so we have to start managing expectations—using the simulation for its intended purpose and not promoting its use for other purposes. In assessing the simulation for execution, we need to decide whether it can apply to a new problem by considering its users, where it fits into the strategy for the overall system, and how flexible it is. Flexibility is one of a simulation's greatest attributes and one of its greatest liabilities. Flexibility allows us to execute the simulation for its intended purpose and to extend its range, but it also allows us to use simulations for unintended purposes. If we do execute a simulation for a new purpose, we must again go through at least a short development process, including verification, validation, and accreditation.

We also must make sure we have enough hardware, software, and people to carry out the simulation. In your support plan, include hardware and software for troubleshooting, spare parts, and especially, regular upgrades of computer equipment. Match your support strategy to how critical the simulation is, including such choices as on-site versus on-call support. Operating the simulation during integration can provide valuable clues about its operational environment. Watch out for differences in hardware configurations and operating systems between the operating and execution environments. Specialists on computer systems are particularly useful here.

You should also pay close attention to the facilities where you plan to execute the simulation. You may need

- Separate space for operations and data analysis

- Special operating hardware such as high-speed printers and backup computers
- Security and communications consistent with your objectives
- Power filtering and conditioning
- Room for growth

Figure 12.9 shows the steps for executing a simulation. The first step is to review the goals of the project and ensure the simulation is consistent with them. As we previously discussed, we now emphasize using, not developing the simulation, so the success of execution will depend on how well we meet these goals. Chapters 2 – 5 show how to identify simulation goals by matching the project's objectives with the stated abilities of the simulation and noting variances. Variances may be present for several reasons, including variable data and gaps or differences in the simulated abilities, but we must identify and reduce them.

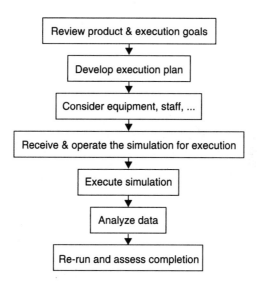

Fig. 12.9. **Steps for Executing a Simulation.** Execution should follow an ordered sequence.

The second step involves planning logistics and creating an execution plan. We have already discussed staffing and support, but you also must consider more esoteric logistics matters: how many simulation runs to meet objectives, sources of data and human subjects (as required), how to gather and analyze data, and special materials required. Knowing the ultimate user and goals of the simulation is critical to this step. Decide how much data you'll collect from the simulation execution based on your objectives. You'll normally generate too much information to keep everything, so document these decisions.

You especially have to consider how to handle advances in technology, which are very rapid for simulations. For example, computer performance is doubling every year and a half, so you must choose to sit tight, upgrade incrementally, or switch the entire computer system at some future (preferably pre-planned) time. These and other technology issues will affect your budgeting, development, integration activity, and down time. Chapter 14 provides detailed insight and methods for considering advances in technology.

The next step in execution is receiving and assessing the integrated simulation—following the steps in Sec. 12.4. You should go through all the steps if your group is different from the integration group or if a lot of undocumented time has passed between integration and execution.

You'll select and format input data during this step. Identify what you need, gather the raw data, and condition it for the simulation. Make sure you prepare the right data. To condition the data, convert it to units appropriate for the simulation, smooth it, check ranges, and align break points with the simulation's internal requirements. Bad data is always a possibility, and it causes errors or shuts down simulations. Be sure your conditioning techniques don't corrupt the data.

Data for execution falls into several types: experimental, intuitive (for heuristic simulations), analogous (to similar simulations or models), predictive, or probabilistic. Predictive data (which yields desired results) is useful in executions for reverse engineering or understanding of a simulation's internal structure or system concepts. Select probabilistic data based on standard sampling techniques, such as maximum likelihood parameters, goodness-of-fit distributions, and chi-squared techniques.

Be especially careful to review records of the simulation's VV&A. In particular, determine if the simulation is replicatively or predictively valid, which determines how you can expand the domain of simulation execution. Replicative validity tends to limit the simulation to its prescribed domain. Predictive validity means you can extend the simulation based on established evaluations of its range. In our example, simulation of fighting forest fires, a replicative model of fuel load might consider only trees, but a predictive model might have been evaluated using any fuel found in rural areas.

The fourth step in simulation execution is operating the simulation to learn about it, uncover problems, confirm that integration is complete, and informally cross check the simulation's execution against its objectives. During execution, you may encounter user-interface problems, software errors, and incompatibilities between development and operational hardware and software. Integration may not uncover these problems because the simulation doesn't run for long enough periods of time and scenarios don't change. If these problems aren't discovered early in execution, they can throw the simulation project off schedule.

The fifth step is executing the simulation, which breaks down into several smaller steps. The first is experimental design. Because we've created the simulation to meet certain requirements, a sound experimental design is necessary to produce data that meets these objectives. Decision makers sometimes depend on data with face validity, but we normally require more rigorous experimental runs to support our opinions. Thus, we need good data to get meaningful outputs. Don't invalidate the simulation by letting desired results drive the inputs.

Setting the simulation's parameters isn't easy. Most simulations have multiple initial states, which you must set for particular executions. Parameters could include selecting integration routines or threshold values. You must document these simulation states and do sample runs to ensure the simulation is using data correctly. Operate the simulation repetitively and scan the data after each operation to ensure it's not corrupt and the simulation is operating properly. Between runs, you can simply change data sets or do complex setups and analyses. Cost and schedule will often constrain how you operate the simulation during execution.

In the sixth step you'll accumulate and analyze results. This step seems simple at first glance, but it's difficult. What you get may not be what you wanted, and you may need special software and hardware to get good results. Accumulated data may be hard to access, distributed across several different computing platforms, and inconsistent because of variations in computer processing or random variables.

We analyze data in various ways depending on the simulation's objectives and user's needs. Often, we have to condition it first. Analyzing data to get answers from the simulation is the essence of execution, but it often discloses errors from the same kinds of sources as those noted in integration. Section 12.7 shows how to use analysis to detect errors.

You must review the analysis of execution outputs from several points of view. Outputs often vary, so you need to discover why and make sure they're within the limits of the simulation design or execution plan. If outliers skew the simulation data, discard them using standard statistical techniques. Analyze data only from steady-state operation unless the simulation objectives direct otherwise. For example, dynamic simulations often require a fixed time or number of cycles before reaching a steady state, but you should analyze the steady-state data, even if you've collected information from the entire operation. Make sure you consider whether the data is static or dynamic.

Use probability and statistics in analyzing execution data to produce more meaningful results. Probability and statistical techniques match the objectives of verification, validation, and accreditation. Sensitivity analyses are often necessary to determine which parameters most influence execution. Sensitivity analyses are also useful to determine that an execution is complete for particular circumstances because they show when results don't change much between executions. Appendix C provides more detail on a number of these techniques. If you need more information, Seigal [1996], Iman [1994], and Gibra [1973] are useful references.

Often, analysis shows we need to re-run a simulation to correct errors, answer other questions, change variables and investigate other issues, or confirm earlier results and firmly support decision making.

Execution goes on throughout the simulation's lifecycle, but a particular execution is complete when it meets the simulation's original objectives—or any derived or newly created objectives—for it.

Non-traditional executions warrant a brief discussion. Non-traditional means executing the simulation beyond its original design constraints and therefore confirming its expanded range. We may execute a simulation in this way whenever we don't know much about its development and integration. Doing so can confirm its proper uses or discover new or expanded applications.

12.7   Analyze Results and Assess Performance

The first step in analysis is reviewing simulation runs to find and reduce errors, then extracting data from the simulation and analyzing it. This process applies to integration and execution. We can then assess results against measures of effectiveness and performance established early in the simulation's lifecycle, which support decision making.

Although errors and problems always emerge when we integrate and execute a simulation, we try to reduce them through repeated use. These errors typically trace to problems from

- Design
- Programming
- Procedures for use
- Misinterpretation
- Misuse of the simulation

Design errors result from misinterpreting or being unable to meet requirements. Typically, these errors surface in hardware design (e.g., poor reliability) and algorithm development (e.g., using the wrong algorithm). Design errors aren't programming errors. Gross design errors usually become obvious during design, but unique operating conditions may expose other design flaws.

Programming errors include syntax and semantics. Syntax errors are easy to find because the simulation won't operate when they're present. Semantic errors are logical errors in, for example, transforming algorithms to software or branching to individual areas. These types of errors sometimes occur in execution because we're using new software paths and can't completely test the software during integration.

Procedural errors come from incorrectly setting the simulation's operating conditions. For example, the simulation's processes may need to follow a certain sequence, or we may improperly apply data.

Misinterpretation and misuse are largely self-explanatory. They're most common in execution. Interpretation errors typically arise when an analyst doesn't review all of the data or has too little experience to make valid judgments. Misuse means using the simulation for an unintended purpose. It is very common because simulation developments can be expensive, so we'd rather reuse them than pay for a new one. You can avoid or correct these errors by carefully reviewing the results of a simulation run and making sure you're executing the simulation within its operational boundaries.

Design and programming errors are beyond the users' control, so you'll have to go back to the developers or system maintainers to correct them. But before you do, you must make sure they weren't caused by poor procedures, misinterpretation of results, or misuse of the simulation. Review your activities for errors you may have caused, or ask a colleague to review your work. It may also be helpful to convene a group of developers and users to review the simulation's operation. This last approach is very common, but you have to make sure the frequency and scope of the meetings are consistent with the type of simulation you're using. For example, daily meetings to review the operation of a training simulation are probably too much; but daily meetings may be appropriate for simulations which affect peoples' lives.

To correct errors, you must trace them to their source. If you find them early, using techniques discussed previously, they're easier to correct. But once you operate the simulation during integration or execution, you have to test it and analyze output data to detect errors. Although you must choose tests based on how well they match the objectives, they fall into two basic types: quantitative and qualitative. Each has benefits and drawbacks. We prefer quantitative tests because they're based on scientific principles, but they usually consume more time, people, and money. Qualitative tests produce results that more people can understand. Users of the results often dictate the type of test you'll have to conduct, so it's worthwhile to touch on both types.

Quantitative tests serve various purposes. They're useful for exploring how well the simulation responds to variable parameters and to changing selected variables, how stable it is, and how effectively the simulation meets its stated purpose. Quantitative tests should cover the range of prescribed input or output variables and use statistics. Comparative quantitative tests are very helpful because they can use data from old simulation executions, operational systems, or analyses. Isolated quantitative tests can help you check errors in specific areas, but they're not useful for simulation execution because other tests can easily refute them. Tests that provide means and standard deviations are helpful, but hypothesis, regression, and other statistical tests can improve them. Hypothesis tests are extremely useful if you select the appropriate null hypothesis, independently choose values, and properly study Type I and II errors. Appendix C further discusses hypothesis testing and its associated errors.

Scientists malign qualitative tests, but they're very useful in integration and execution when time is short and we can't easily apply quantitative tests. They're also helpful to decision makers, especially if supplemented with some quantitative data. Qualitative tests include surveys, interviews, measures of effectiveness (meeting expectations), and written observations.

We can give qualitative data a quantitative "look" if we incorporate parameters in observations or surveys, develop heuristics, analyze results against other simulations or similar outputs, and properly apply statistics. As an example, a simulation of an election using opinion polls becomes quantitative if we add statistical uncertainty.

12.8   Special Considerations

I've described the typical and general conditions related to integration and execution, but other considerations and technologies constrain these general approaches. For example, tightly coupled simulations require extra care in integration and execution because they bind components and strategy to the operational environment. A typical example is a human-operated virtual simulator of flight. This type of simulation requires close coupling between the pilot's inputs, processing, and outputs. Speed and order of execution are the threads that bind the simulation. Time strongly influences its operation. For tightly bound simulations, we must keep the binding parameters during integration and execution within tolerances established during requirements definition and development.

Other considerations are more structural than operational. No integration should alter the simulation's structure, especially if it depends on object-oriented programming, because structural changes will "pollute" results. To avoid these structural variations, integrators have relied on constructs that have evolved or developed into three loose groups: centralized, hierarchial, or distributed. Centralized structures are useful for tightly bound, high-performance simulations. Hierarchial simulations have a central process and components connected to this process. Distributed architectures allow processes to move at their own rate under loose control but constrained by tight interfaces between simulation components. Whenever you integrate a simulation, you must preserve these architectures.

Several examples of each of these architectures are worthy of mention, in light of their affect on simulation integration and execution. Hardware-in-the loop simulations (in which the simulation is used to stimulate an operational system) normally have centralized structures for best performance. Hierarchial structures have been typical of flight simulators, in which a main computer interfaces with and controls visual systems and forced feedback systems. Distributed architectures are the simulations of today and tomorrow. Effective ones typically require strongly defined interfaces and basic operating rules. Distributed architectures are being used to create large synthetic environments, with the Department of Defense leading the way. The main examples are Distributed Interactive Simulation/Advanced Distributed Simulation (DIS/ADS) and the High Level Architecture (HLA). These architectures are compatible. DIS/ADS provides common message formats and a communication infrastructure for integrating many separate simulations [Institute for Simulation and Training 1995a, b, c; Seidenstecker 1994; and Simulator Networking Handbook 1993]. The HLA provides basic rules for capturing the interactions between simulations and separates interactions from the underlying strategy for passing messages. The HLA provides a distributed run-time infrastructure for connecting simulations. These architectures have been evolving, and will continue to evolve, to meet the needs of the modeling and simulation community.

Integrating simulations under distributed architectures requires close attention to the rules the architectures establish. Integration actually becomes easier with DIS/ADS and HLA because these architectures prescribe many of the rules for connections. Still, we must be careful because they're robust, flexible, and moderately general in their application. We can't simply use the rules and expect to integrate satisfactorily because we have many options, need to establish interaction rules between participants, and must describe interfaces not in the architecture. The evolution of architectures will certainly make integration of models and simulations easier in the future.

As simulations grow because of architectural advances, some integration techniques lag behind. Difficulties remain for integrating many simulations and for integrating live equipment and simulations. The issues include describing how simulated entities interact, getting consistent performance from like entities, building compatible environmental models, matching time sequences to reality, and improving data-transfer rates, connection mechanisms, and control mechanisms. The key to successful integration is deciding how much inconsistency we can tolerate, measuring inconsistencies during integration, and building interfaces that reduce them. A conservative rule of thumb for inconsistency (based on experience) is to limit the range of any simulated parameter to $\pm 10\%$. The integration's level of complexity will increase by the square of the number of simulations it must handle.

Integration with operational systems is the last type worth special mention. Operational systems operate continuously under, at best, limited control from another system or human operator. On the other hand, simulations exist in a computer, which is a discrete environment created by humans. In other words, simulations are limited representations of reality. Usually, the simulation can make up for these differences if it's flexible and if the simulation strategy develops from examining an unmodified operational system. During integration we must consider how often to update data, proper data formats, mechanical and electrical interfaces, etc. We also have to evaluate how to interface a simulation's unique (and usually troublesome) features—such as freeze, stop, restart, and playback—with the operational system.

Simulation integration and execution are closely related. They are next to each other in the simulation's life cycle, strongly rely on data and documentation, and need to operate the simulation in order to reach its established goals. Integration and execution both require baselining and assessment because integrators and executors are different from each other and from the people who created the simulation. Successful integration and execution rely heavily on mathematical principles, statistics, documentation, and configuration management. To help you track these techniques and the processes for integration and execution, I've consolidated them and given you cross references to other chapters in Table 12.3.

Integration is best when we do it from the bottom up—splitting the simulation into components and integrating like components with external parts of the simulation strategy. We evaluate during integration to make sure it's going well; and before and after integration, we ensure the simulation is operating within its designed range.

Whenever you execute a simulation, you'll design experiments that ensure it will work for its intended purpose. You'll run the simulation (often many times), gather data, analyze results, and assess the simulation against its original objectives.

By learning about the principles and techniques we've discussed in this chapter, you've begun preparing yourself for the challenges of integration and execution. As more people discover the usefulness of simulation, these tasks will become more complex and will demand even more of your ingenuity and attention.

Table 12.3. Checklist and Chapter Cross Reference for Simulation Integration and Execution.

Item	Process Description	Abbreviated Process Description	Related Chapter Material
1.	**Receive** and **inventory** the simulation Software, installation and build instructions, operating data	ASSESS	9 & 11
2.	**Understand** the context and purpose of a simulation received for integration and execution	ASSESS	1, 2, 3, 4, & 5
3.	**Maintain records** of activity	DOCUMENT	10
4.	**Operate** the simulation Develop the operating baseline, understand purpose, and learn about the simulation	ESTABLISH BASELINE	3, 6, & 9
5.	**Dissect** the simulation's components (software, hardware, and documentation) Processes, algorithms, data I/O, interfaces, internal interactions	ESTABLISH BASELINE	8, 10, 15, 16, & App. B
6.	**Analyze** the simulation's model design Documentation, algorithms, theoretical underpinnings	ESTABLISH BASELINE	8
7.	**Study** the external components you'll integrate with the simulation Identify processes, algorithms, data, I/O, interface compatibilities and interactions across systems	DEFINE INTERFACES	8, 10, 15, 16, & App. B
8.	**Assess** Compatibility Create interfaces wherever compatibility is a problem	DEFINE INTERFACES	8, 9, 10, & App. B
9.	**Create** an integration strategy and approach Assess benefit of using standards, consider top-down versus bottom-up (preferred) approach, evaluate progress incrementally	INTEGRATE	3, 4, 5, 8, 11, & 13
10.	**Integrate** according to your plan Integrate like components of the simulation and external system, test incrementally, assess cross-component interactions, statistically evaluate progress	INTEGRATE	5, 8, 9, 10, 13, 15, 16, App. B, & App. C
11.	**Complete** the integration (how do you know when you're done?) All problems affecting operations are resolved; small problems that remain don't affect operation within limits	INTEGRATE	2, 4, 5, 9, 10, & 11

Table 12.3. Checklist and Chapter Cross Reference for Simulation Integration and Execution.

Item	Process Description	Abbreviated Process Description	Related Chapter Material
12.	**Execute** the simulation (Operational phase) Observe similarities and differences with other phases of the simulation's lifecycle	PLAN EXECUTION	1, 2, 4, 5, & 11
13.	**Develop** an execution plan Staffing, facilities, equipment, support, planning for change (e.g., monitoring and inserting new technology)	PLAN EXECUTION	9, 13, 15, 16, 17, App. B, & App. C
14.	**Identify** and **ensure** requirements and skill mix of staff are clear and staff is available	PLAN EXECUTION	4 & 5
15.	**Identify** and **ensure** operational space and equipment are available and adequate	PLAN EXECUTION	4 & 5
16.	**Identify** and **ensure** equipment (e.g., computer hardware) is available to support execution	PLAN EXECUTION	4 & 5
17.	**Monitor** and **manage** pre-planned upgrades and insertion of new technology	PLAN EXECUTION	14
18.	**Receive** integrated simulation Review data from integration; review information from Steps 1 & 2; review VV&A	PLAN EXECUTION	9 & 11
19.	**Operate** the simulation and **assess and monitor** operation Note problems;` cross check objectives	ASSESS	2, 4, & 9
20.	Design experiments before executing the simulation	PLAN EXECUTION	4, 5, & App. C
21.	**Execute** and **gather** data Review initial runs and do repeated runs	EXECUTE	9 & 10
22.	**Analyze** data Cross check with the original and modified simulation's technical objectives	ANALYZE	4, 5, 9, 11, 13, 16, & App. C
23.	**Conduct** sensitivity analyses and **decide** whether to stop applying the simulation	ANALYZE	4 & 5
24.	**Assess** whether the simulation has met objectives	ANALYZE	4 & 5
25.	**Re-run** from step 20 on, as required	EXECUTE	--
26.	**Investigate** other application domains for the simulation	ASSESS	1, 2, 3, & 4

References

Gibra, Isaac N. 1973. *Probability and Statistical Inference for Scientists and Engineers*. Englewood Cliffs, NJ: Prentice-Hall.

Hawkins, Robert and Roy Crosbie, eds. 1988. *Tools for the Simulation Profession*. San Diego, CA: Simulation Councils, Inc.

Iman, Ronald. 1994. *A Data-Based Approach to Statistics*. Belmont, CA: Wadsworth Publishing Co.

Institute for Simulation and Training. 1995a. *DIS Networking Workshop Lecture Notes*. Orlando, FL: UCF/IST.

Institute for Simulation and Training. 1995b. *Standard for Distributed Interactive Simulation - Application Protocols (IEEE) Std. 1278.1*. Orlando, FL: UCF/IST.

Institute for Simulation and Training. 1995c. *Standard for Distributed Interactive Simulation - Communication Services and Profiles (IEEE) Std. 1278.2*. Orlando, FL: UCF/IST.

Maryanski, Fred. 1980. *Digital Computer Simulation*. Rochelle Park, NJ: Hayden Book Company, Inc.

Puigjaner, Ramon and Dominique Potier, eds. 1989. *Modeling Techniques and Tools for Computer Performance Evaluation*. New York, NY: Plenum Press.

Seidensticker, Steve, ed. 1994. *The DIS Vision: A Map to the Future*. Orlando, FL: UCF/IST.

Seigel, Andrew and Charles Morgan. 1996. *Statistics and Data Analysis an Introduction*. 2nd Edition. New York, NY: John Wiley & Sons.

Simulator Networking Handbook. 1993. IST-TR-93-08. Orlando, FL: UCF/IST.

Stallings, William. 1994. *Data and Computer Communications*. Fourth edition. New York, NY: Macmillan Publishing Company.

CHAPTER 13

Establishing Standards and Specifications

Emily B. Andrew, *Ballistic Missile Defense Organization*

So far, you've seen how to develop models and simulations: identify requirements, define a conceptual design, create the design in software and hardware, and integrate the elements into a final product. Effectively using standards and specifications is key to developing models and simulations [Department of Defense 1994]. Unfortunately, developers often view standards as one more obstacle they must overcome to complete a development within already tight constraints on schedule and budget. But judiciously applied standards and specifications can make developers' lives much simpler by helping them build a quality product that meets or exceeds a customer's expectations.

Standards and specifications are key to relieving development burdens because they provide a consistent way to achieve objectives and reduce the need for rework. This consistency covers everything in development, from managing the program, to satisfying customer requirements, to eventually carrying out and testing the conceptual design [Piplani 1994]. Imagine if each person on a project defines a requirement differently. Consolidating these requirements into an integrated document becomes more difficult, and programmers are likely to interpret differently how to code a function which must work with several other functions. Not using standards for the most basic development activities can cause costly errors and delay completion. In addition, today's simulations often require a complex mix of virtual, live, and constructive elements. Without standards to identify how these very different pieces interoperate, developing an effective product will be nearly impossible.

Standards help us reduce rework in every part of life. For example, just going to the hardware store to buy the right bulb for the light socket in your dining room hutch can be frustrating and time consuming if you don't know the size and wattage that match this kind of socket. You may eventually get the correct bulb, but life is simpler when you know the specifications or standards for the bulb—then, you'll get the right one in a single trip to the store.

13.1   Background Information

Before you can apply standards, you must understand the goals you're trying to reach for a development. Here, we'll assume you know these objectives and help you select appropriate standards based on them. First, though, we need to define some terms and describe the organizations who create standards and specifications.

13.1.1   Definitions

The American Heritage Dictionary defines a standard as an acknowledged measure or comparison for quantitative values or a norm and a specification as a detailed description of materials or something to be built. Organizations that develop and carry out standards define them as norms, and they say specifications are the detailed descriptions of standards and what needs to be done to meet them. Thus, standards define the normal way to do something and specifications provide the details or "recipe." For example, the standard might be to do formal inspections following each major development milestone, such as requirements definition. A specification would describe step by step how to do the formal inspection. In general, the rest of the chapter will refer to standards and specifications collectively as "standards," so we'll talk about the norm for developing models and simulations. Whenever a standard also describes how to meet its requirements or whenever we're truly talking about a particular specification, we'll use the term specification.

13.1.2   Standards Groups and Organizations

Any project offers us a lot of standards to choose from, and several will appear to address the same issues. For example, the Department of Defense's profile for standards identifies six different types that affect network security. Why six? How do they differ, especially when they all have similar titles? And, how can you figure out what a standard can do to support your development? Reading trade journals, weekly technical magazines, and World Wide Web (the web) sites involved in developing standards is a good way to stay aware of the latest ones. Another way is to join some of the groups and organizations involved in creating them. By doing so, you can learn about a standard and influence its direction as it moves from initial concept to formal recognition.

The three major types of organizations concerned with standards are international, national, and industry groups or consortia [ATCCIS 1994]. I'll briefly describe them, but you can find out more by searching the web for the organization you're interested in. One of the best web sites for M&S standards is that of the Defense Modeling and Simulation Office. This organization was established to promote the effective use and integration of models and simulations by the Department of Defense. Its web-site address is www.dmso.mil.

International groups develop standards that are open, based on consensus, and accepted internationally. Well known international groups include the International Electrotechnical Commission (IEC), the International Organization for Standardization (ISO), and the International Telecommunications Union-Telecommunications Standardization Sector. The IEC and ISO worked separately until overlapping interests led to the formation of the joint ISO/IEC Technical Committee in 1987. This committee creates standards for information technology—which includes most standards for M&S. Its members are volunteers, many of whom work with their countries' national standards organizations. The committee's main purpose is to promote the free exchange of goods and services. It's organized into several different subcommittees and various working groups that create and finalize standards. Some key subcommittees that work on standards for M&S include:

- Telecommunications and Information Exchange Between Systems Subcommittee, with working groups involved in developing standards for the Open System Interconnection mode
- Opens Systems Interconnection, Data Management, and Open Distributed Processing Subcommittee
- Programming Languages, Their Environments, and System Software Interfaces Subcommittee
- Common Security Techniques for Information Technology Applications Subcommittee

The Telecommunications Standardization Sector of the International Telecommunications Union works tariff issues to standardize telecommunications world wide. It's the former International Telephone and Telegraph Consultative and International Radio Consultative Committee. Of 15 study groups, three work modeling and simulation standards. They include data communications, telematic services, and integrated services digital networks (ISDNs).

National groups focus on developing similar standards for their own countries, usually with government backing. Examples of national standards groups within the United States which influence M&S development are the American National Standards Institute, Federal Information Processing Standards, Department of Defense, Tri-Service Group on Communications and Electronics, Standard Agreements, and Military Standards.

Industry groups develop standards for certain technologies. They include professional societies such as the Institute of Electrical and Electronic Engineers or trade associations such as the European Computer Manufacturer's Association.

Both of these organizations have working groups addressing related M&S standards and technology developments.

Consortia often include group members who are looking at international, national, and industry standards. An industry group may propose standards for national groups to adopt or go directly to an international group for adoption. Two consortia working on M&S standards are the Simulation Interoperability Standards Organization (SISO) and the Object Management Group. The SISO supports developing an M&S specification called the High Level Architecture, which developers can use to integrate simulations in a heterogeneous and distributed environment. The Object Management Group is working to develop a framework called the Common Object Request Broker Architecture, which will enable us to access simulation elements using a distributed client/server network architecture.

In addition to standards groups and bodies, many organizations are working on technology issues. For modeling and simulation, the Defense Modeling and Simulation Office, Defense Information Services Agency, National Institute of Standards and Technology, the Advanced Research Project Agency, and each military service are representative organizations which spend a lot of their resources on identifying supportive methods and standards.

13.2   Types of Standards for M&S

If applied properly, standards help prevent rework. To use them effectively, we must understand what work has to be done, when to do it, and how to do it. Let's examine the types of work we have to do during a typical development to better appreciate what this involves. As discussed in previous chapters, this work usually divides into defining a concept, analyzing and allocating requirements, designing, building, integrating, and testing. Other supportive processes, such as managing the project and its configuration or ensuring quality, are ways to administer the system's growth and operation. We must do more work if the model or simulation needs unique abilities, such as visual displays with three-dimensional graphics or interactions with another simulator. Once we develop the model or simulation, we have to apply another set of processes to make sure it meets requirements. To prevent reworking any of these functions or processes, we must usually follow standards or guidelines, unless we're handling a small project and routinely discussing our functions and roles. With open and frequent communication, we may suffer few consequences. But in larger projects, communication is usually limited, so standards are vital to success.

Table 13.1 lists the types of standards we need to ensure consistent work and limit rework: process, product, application interfaces, and interoperability. Except for interoperability, these standards support any typical software development. The interoperability standards were developed solely to help different simulations work together when connected by local or wide-area networks. The table also provides a representative standard or a standards model for each type. A standards model logically organizes standards so we can understand how to apply them. The table lists only standards that are publicly available and used for M&S developments.

Table 13.1. Types of Standards. We need standards to ensure consistent, organized work.

Types of Standards	Representative Standards or Model
Process a. Systems Engineering b. Software Engineering	a. MIL-STD 499A/B, IEEE P1220, ISO 9000 b. MIL-STD 498, SEI CMM, ISO 9000
Product	McCabe's Software Quality Metrics
Application Interfaces	Technical Architecture Framework for Information Management (TAFIM) Technical Reference Model (TRM)
Interoperability	Distributed Interactive Simulation (DIS) Common Technical Framework (CTF) Aggregate Level Simulation Protocol (ALSP)

13.2.1   Process Standards

We've discussed M&S development processes thoroughly in earlier chapters. Here, I'll relate them to standards. For M&S, these processes fall into those for systems engineering and those for software engineering. For systems engineering, we must identify system requirements, analyze these requirements to determine a conceptual design, and then allocate the requirements against this design. We also have to validate the requirements to ensure they meet the customer's needs and monitor system development to make sure it carries out these requirements. Some typical systems-engineering standards are MIL-STD 499B, Military Standard Systems Engineering; IEEE P1220, Standard for Application and Management of Systems Engineering Process; and ISO 9000, International Standards for Quality Assurance.

Under systems engineering are two major categories: hardware and software engineering. Hardware and software engineering follow similar processes, but we'll focus on the latter because simulations are typically software developments.

Software engineering involves using system requirements for software to derive separate software requirements, develop a supportive design, build source code modules, integrate these modules, and test the integrated source code as a system. Common standards for software engineering are MIL-STD 498, Software Development and Documentation; the Software Engineering Institute's Capability Maturity Model; and the ISO 9000 series. These standards document types of processes and products, but they don't dictate processes or how to use them in order to meet standards. For example, MIL-STD 498 (in Sec. 5, Detailed Requirements) specifies the need to plan, establish a software environment, analyze system requirements, design, manage configurations, and evaluate products for quality. Table 13.2 excerpts some of this section. The specified requirement (Col. 3) shows how the standard requires only a type of process. For example, it states the developer must develop and record plans, but it doesn't specify how. That's up to us as developers. Also, we can remove items from the standard if our development doesn't need them. Of course, if the contract requires a standard, we'll have to document this tailoring.

Table 13.2. MIL-STD 498, Process Requirements. Typical direction for developing processes which meet the standard. These guidelines identify what you must include in the process, not how to carry it out.

Detailed Requirements	Specific Process	Specified Requirement
5.1 Project Planning	5.1.1 Software Development Planning	The developer shall develop and record plans for conducting the activities required by this standard and other software related standards in this contract. This planning shall be consistent with system level planning and shall include all applicable items in the Software Development Plan (SDP) DID (see 6.2)
5.14 Software Configuration Management	5.14.1 Configuration Identification	The developer shall participate in selecting configuration items as performed under the architectural design in 5.4.2, shall identify the entities to be placed under configuration control, and shall assign a project unique identifier to each configuration item and each additional entity to be placed under configuration control.
5.15 Software Product Evaluation	5.15.1 In-process and final software product evaluations	The developer shall perform in-process evaluations of the software products generated in carrying out the requirements of this standard.

　　Like MIL-STD 498, the ISO 9000 standards address processes. But they differ from MIL-STD 498 by focusing on processes for effective quality management and quality assurance. This series includes five generic standards that aren't tied to any product (such as simulations). ISO 9000 provides four guidelines for quality management and assurance, with the third one focusing on developing, supplying, installing, and maintaining software. ISO 9001, 9002, and 9003 provide models of quality systems for external quality assurance. They support contractual obligations for quality assurance between the developer and customer. Of the three, ISO 9001 is the most comprehensive and covers design, manufacturing, installation, and system services. ISO 9002 covers only production and installation, and ISO 9003 covers final product inspections and testing. The fifth standard, ISO 9004, provides guidelines organizations can use to create an effective quality system that will meet specified goals. Deciding to use the ISO 9000 standards depends on what your company or organization does. The United States has adopted them through the American National Standards Institute, and you can get more information by visiting the American Society for Quality (ASQ) website at www.asq.org.

　　So how do process standards prevent rework? If used correctly, they'll identify the types of processes we must use to meet the standard, and clearly define and document what each process requires us to do. This, in turn, will help us understand what has to be done and when it has to be done—a key step in eliminating rework. If we follow them—and occasionally check our work against them—they'll also ensure consistency and help us communicate how we plan to meet our objectives.

13.2.2 Product Standards

Product standards (see Table 13.1) are often called the "ility" or quality standards. We use them to be sure the developing product meets specifications. Examples of products include a Software Development Plan, Requirements Specification, Quality Assurance Plan, and code. Table 13.3 uses MIL-STD 498 to show the type of product required.

Table 13.3. Product Requirements under MIL-STD 498. This standard describes what to address for each product and requires developers to provide sufficient details.

Product	Requirement	Contents
Interface Requirements Specification (IRS)	The IRS specifies the requirements imposed on one or more systems, subsystems, hardware configuration items, computer software configuration items, manual operations, or other system components to achieve one or more interfaces among these entities. An IRS can cover any number of interfaces.	1. Scope 2. Referenced Documents 3. Requirements 3.1 Interface identification and diagrams 3.x Project unique identifier of interfaces 3.y Precedence and criticality of requirements 4. Qualification provisions 5. Requirements traceability 6. Notes A. Appendices

Products are usually measured in terms of their "goodness." Goodness means meeting the requirements satisfactorily, consistently, and relatively free from error. Metrics are quantified measurements used to determine a product's goodness and described using quality factors and criteria [McCabe 1980]. Quality factors are attributes that contribute to a product's goodness or quality. They're based on three distinct activities that a product undergoes once it's developed: operation, revision or maintenance, and transition or migration. As Table 13.4 shows, these quality factors have corresponding questions that we should ask about a product's ability to be used or modified during the three activities.

Table 13.5 identifies when you should measure these quality factors and when people will notice how poor quality affects a program. It shows you should measure quality when you're developing a product. Once it's developed, people will notice the effect of poor quality whenever the product is

- Operated
- Modified for maintenance
- Transitioned for use on another platform, with another simulator, or as a part of a new development

Performance criteria further define the quality factors and show their relationships (see Table 13.6). These criteria also help us define metrics, as Table 13.7 shows for traceability and completeness. Note how the metrics are quantifiable measurements taken at specified times during the product's lifecycle to determine how well it's meeting criteria.

Table 13.4. How a Product's Activities Relate to Quality Factors [McCabe 1980]. Objective questions about product development translate into quality factors that address the effectiveness and consistency of a product's activities.

Product Activity	Questions Asked	Quality Factor	Definition
Operation	Does it do what I want?	Correctness	How well a program satisfies its specification and fulfills the user's mission objectives.
	Does it do so accurately?	Reliability (Validity)	How well we can expect a program to do what we want with required precision.
	Will it run on my hardware?	Efficiency	The amount of computing resources and code a program needs to do something.
	Is it secure?	Integrity (Security)	How well we can control access to software or data by unauthorized people.
	Can I run it?	Usability	Effort needed to learn, operate, prepare input for, and interpret output from a program.
Revision or Maintenance	Can I fix it?	Maintainability	Effort required to find and fix an error in an operational program.
	Can I change it?	Flexibility	Effort needed to modify an operational program.
	Can I test it?	Testability	Effort required to test a program to ensure it does what it's supposed to do.
Transition	Will I be able to use it on another machine?	Portability	Effort needed to transfer a program from one hardware configuration or software environment to another.
	Will I be able to reuse some of the software?	Reusability	How well we can use a program in other applications, based on how these programs package and handle certain functions.
	Will I be able to use it with another system?	Interoperability	Effort required to couple one system to another.

So how can product standards help reduce rework? They can quantify whether your program will meet an expected level of "goodness." To use product standards, you must first identify what development traits make up this goodness, such as making all documented requirements traceable to the operational code, having no errors in the operational code, or delivering a product on time and within budget. Once identified, these "goodness" traits become the quality standards. Then, you'd develop metrics to measure the product's goodness. Identify them early and collect them throughout your development because they truly indicate a product's impending quality.

For example, suppose your standards include tracing all requirements to the operational code. Now suppose you can trace only 70% of the requirements to your design. This situation often occurs because requirements evolve throughout the development. Suddenly, many more requirements exist than when the development started. If requirements are not closely tracked as they're added, changed, or deleted (another good example of the need for standardization), tracing

Table 13.5.   When to Apply Quality Factors to Your Program [McCabe 1980]. Measure quality factors during product development; people will notice poor quality only when they use the product.

Factors	Require-ments Analysis	Design	Code & Test	System Test	Opera-tion	Mainte-nance	Transi-tion
Correctness	Δ	Δ	Δ	*	*	*	
Reliability	Δ	Δ	Δ	*	*	*	
Efficiency		Δ	Δ		*		
Integrity	Δ	Δ	Δ		*		
Usability	Δ	Δ		*	*	*	
Maintainability		Δ	Δ			*	*
Testability		Δ	Δ	*		*	*
Flexibility		Δ	Δ			*	*
Portability		Δ	Δ				*
Reusability		Δ	Δ				*
Interoperability		Δ			*		*

Δ = where you should measure quality factors
* = where people see the effect of poor quality

these requirements through the development can be quite difficult. Under these conditions, you must correct the problem; otherwise, your product isn't going to meet your product standard. If you wait until you're integrating and testing the code, you'll have to work much harder to correct this lack of traceability. If you don't use product standards and associated metrics, your product's development won't be as clear, so rework will be more extensive, and your schedule may suffer.

13.2.3   Application Interfaces

Application-interface standards will allow you to use external applications that you need to develop or operate your model or simulation. Examples include displays, database managers, tools for distributed processing on a network, and software-development tools known as engineering environments. Effective interfaces allow applications to exchange information easily with the developed simulation. Standards detail the information that must be exchanged and its format. The DOD's Technical Reference Model (Fig. 13.1) covers the types of applications that might need to exchange information with a simulation.

Although the Technical Reference Model was developed for use by the DOD, commercial organizations can also apply it because it provides a framework for developing simulations regardless of the type of application. As I will show shortly, tailoring this framework to military or commercial applications depends largely on the types of standards selected to support the framework's functional areas.

Table 13.6.   Relating Criteria to Quality Factors [McCabe 1980]. Criteria help us further define quality factors and show their relationships.

Criterion	Definition	Related Factors
Traceability	Provides a thread from the requirements to the finished program	Correctness
Completeness	Shows we've fully carried out requirements	Correctness
Consistency	Provides uniform techniques for designing and building a program	Correctness Reliability Maintainability
Accuracy	Provides required precision in calculations and outputs	Reliability
Error Tolerance	Provides continuity of operation whenever errors occur	Reliability
Simplicity	Makes it easy to understand how a program works	Reliability Maintainability Testability
Modularity	Allows us to build a program from highly independent modules	Maintainability Flexibility Testability Portability Reusability Interoperability
Generality	Gives functions greater breadth	Flexibility Reusability
Expandability	Allows us to expand requirements for storing data or computing	Flexibility
Instrumentation	Allows us to measure uses or identify errors	Testability
Self-Descriptiveness	Explains how a function works	Flexibility Maintainability Testability Portability Reusability
Execution Efficiency	Provides for minimum processing time	Efficiency
Storage Efficiency	Requires minimum storage during operation	Efficiency
Access Control	Controls access to software and data	Integrity
Access Audit	Allows us to audit access to software and data	Integrity
Operability	Allows us to operate and to define operating procedures for software	Usability
Training	Allows people to learn a program and to transition to new applications	Usability
Communicative-ness	Provides inputs and outputs the program can use	Usability
Software System Independence	Shows how much a program depends on its environment (operating systems, utilities, input/output routines)	Portability Reusability
Machine Independence	Shows how software links to particular hardware	Portability Reusability
Communication Commonality	Allows us to use standard protocols and interface routines	Interoperability
Data Commonality	Allows us to represent data in standard forms	Interoperability
Conciseness	Allows us to use minimum code for any function	Maintainability

Table 13.7.   Examples of Metrics for Traceability and Completeness [McCabe 1980]. Metrics should be objective, quantifiable measurements taken at specified times during the product's lifecycle to determine the degree to which criteria are being met.

Criterion	Metric	Value	When Measured
Traceability	$\dfrac{\text{\# of Itemized Requirements Traced}}{\text{Total \# of Requirements}}$		Design Implementation
Completeness	Completeness Checklist: 1. Unambiguous references 2. All data references defined 3. All defined functions used 4. All referenced functions defined 5. All conditions and processing defined for each decision point 6. All defined and referenced parameters for calling sequences agree 7. All problem reports resolved 8. Design agrees with requirements 9. Code agrees with design System Metric Value = Number of Checklist Items Met		Requirements Design Implementation

The Technical Reference Model is documented in the DOD's Technical Architecture Framework for Information Management [Defense Information Systems Agency 1994c]. The top part of the model, called the mission application, represents the particular product being developed. This product must interface with the services (support applications) shown in the top box of the diagram, which include multimedia, communication, business processing, etc.

The middle part of the diagram is the Application Platform, where the actual applications or services logically reside. An Application Program Interface couples the developing product and the servicing application. Developing this interface requires a standard if it is to operate with different products. This standard describes what information the applications will exchange. Table 13.8 lists the types of services these applications can provide and representative standards you can use to allow the developed product to interface with these applications [Defense Information Systems Agency 1994b]. The DOD believes these listed interface standards are "open"—matching many types of commercially available applications.

The bottom part of the Technical Reference Model in Fig. 13.1 represents the external environment and the interfacing applications to it. The external environment includes all elements outside the developing product—users, communications, and information interchange. The external interfaces allow direct access to the product, so they ultimately dictate what types of applications the product must work with and how you must specify these interactions using appropriate interface standards.

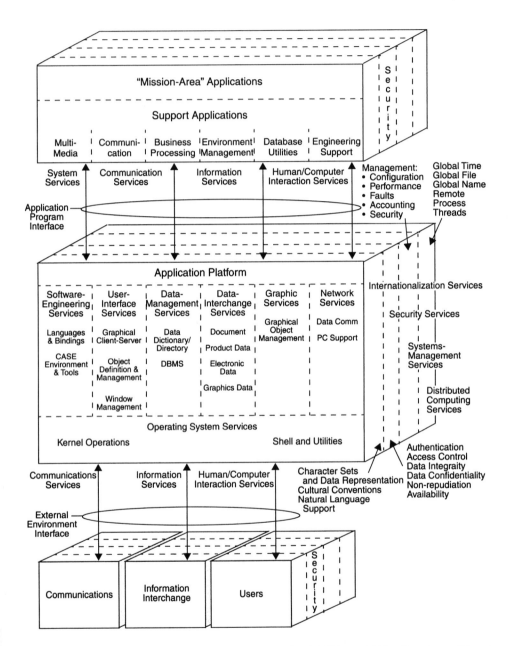

Fig. 13.1.   The DOD's Detailed Technical Reference Model. This model identifies eleven different types of application services and defines their interfaces to the mission and to the external environment [Defense Information Systems Agency 1994a].

Table 13.8. Representative Standards and Profiles of Services from the DOD's Technical Reference Model. Many standards are available to define the interfaces between developed products and the applications required to operate these products.

Service Areas	Services	Representative Standards
Operating System	Kernel Shell and Utilities Real-time Extension	FIPS Pub 151-1 (POSIX.1) IEEE P1003.2 IEEE P1003.4
Software Engineering	Programming Language Case Tools and Environment	FIPS PUB 119 (Ada) ECMA Portable Common Tool
User Interface	Client/Server Operations Object Management Window Management Dialogue Support	FIPS PUB 158 (X Windows) DOD Human Interface Style Guide FIPS PUB 158 (X Windows) Future Standard IEEE P120.X
Data Management	Data Dictionary-Directory Data Management	FIPS PUB 156 (IRDS) FIPS PUB 127-1 SQL
Data Interchange	Document Interchange Vector Graphics Display Raster Display Product Data Interchange Electronic Data Interchange	FIPS PUB 152 (SGML) FIPS PUB 128 (CGM) FIPS PUB 150 (Type 1) Planned FIPS PUB (IGES) FIBS PUB 161 (EDI)
Graphics	Graphics	FIPS PUB 153 (PHIGS)
Network	Data Communications Telecommunications	FIPS PUB 146-1 (GOSIP) MIL-STD-187-700 IEEE 1278
Security	Compartmented Workstations Digital Signature Operating System Data Management Network Services	DRS-2600-6243-91, Version 1 Draft FIPS PUB (DSS) Draft FIPS PUB IEEE P1003.6 NCSC- TG-005 (TNI) ISO 7498-2
Distributed Computing	Distributed Data Transparent File Access Distributed Computing	ISO 9579-1, 2 (RDA) Draft IEEE Standard P1003.8 Draft OSF Specification (NCS/RPC)
System Management	System Management	FIPS PUB 179 (GNMP)
Internationalization	None identified	None identified

The Technical Architecture Framework details (in several volumes) what you must consider to ensure your product can work with different applications and external elements:

- Volume 1, Overview
- Volume 2, Technical Reference Model and Standards Profile Summary
- Volume 3, Architecture Concepts and Guidance
- Volume 4, DOD Standards Based Architecture Planning Guide
- Volume 5, Support Plan
- Volume 6, DOD Goal Security Architecture
- Volume 7, Information Technology Standards Guidance
- Volume 8, DOD Human Computer Interface

You can get these documents directly from the Defense Information Systems Agency or download them from the agency's home page (www.itsi.disa.mil).

Application-interface standards are important to M&S because they specify how to interface with various applications. Thus, we don't have to re-code the interface to use these applications, which makes models or simulations more useful. Examples include three-dimensional visual displays, access to networked databases, and word processors. Because these applications are complex and widely used, developing them on our own wouldn't be cost effective. Application-interface standards make such development unnecessary.

13.2.4   Interoperability

Interoperability standards allow different simulations to work together almost as though they are a single simulation. These standards include almost any aspect of development that addresses the ability of one simulation to function with another. We can easily see the need for interoperability standards by examining a simple example. Let's say two simulations are being integrated and must process and share information about a single person walking across the Earth's surface. If the two simulations don't share a common approach for modeling this activity, one simulation could receive information from the other that would cause it to portray the person's position several hundred miles above the Earth's surface and measure each step in miles instead of feet.

Determining the type of interoperability standards needed depends on what information is processed and shared between the simulations that must operate together. In the simple example above, the two simulations must have a common approach for modeling the person walking and the Earth's surface. In this section, I address some basic concepts and representative standards for interoperability that you should consider in almost any development that includes integrating simulations. I'll also describe three prominent interoperability standards supported by the DOD: Distributed Interactive Simulation, the Aggregate Level Simulation Protocol, and the Common Technical Framework. Each of these standards takes a different approach to defining methods which help integrated simulations work together. Although developed for the DOD, they also apply to commercial simulations.

Basic Concepts for Interoperability

For simulations to interoperate, we must make sure everyone on the development team uses the same model to describe common aspects (such as terrain), represents parameters in the same way, and chooses common formats for mathematical units and data. Most of these concepts are common sense. For example, if a project doesn't represent commonly used elements in the same way, the elements will vary among the simulations. Another good example is using different coordinate systems to identify locations. If we identify one entity's location using rectangular coordinates and another's using polar coordinates, they won't be able to interact unless we employ a costly conversion mechanism.

Thus, following these concepts not only enables a simulation to operate with other simulations but also allows the simulation to operate within itself. Because they're not part of any formal standard, your team must determine which of these concepts apply to your development, document them, and follow them throughout the development. Table 13.9 lists concepts you should consider to create standards for a project, or even for your organization, to ensure a simulation works alone and with other simulations.

Table 13.9.   Basic Concepts Used to Develop Standards for Interoperability. Every development should use some basic concepts to create standards for interoperability to ensure a simulation will work well on its own and with other simulations.

Basic Concept	Example of a Standard
Models and Algorithms	Modeling all terrain elevation from the Earth's core versus the Earth's surface.
Parameters	Using 3.14 for π, not 3.1416.
Units	Using metric versus English measurements.
Coordinate system	Using polar versus rectangular coordinates especially when trying to interface live elements with virtual or constructive simulations.
Data Formats	Requiring the use of Protocol Data Units (PDUs) from Version 1.4 of the Distributed Interactive Simulation standard and implementing other types of PDUs when this standard does not support your data requirements.
Conversions	Requiring metric measurements and using a standard method to convert other measurements to kilometers, liters, grams, etc.
Mathematical Approaches	Rounding all mathematical data to the second decimal point.
Languages	Using a standard language, such as Ada 95.
Analysis Approach and Tools	Requiring Excel™ version 7.0 for all spreadsheet calculations.
Scenarios	Requiring the following steps to analyze fuel burn rates for a Cessna 152 aircraft: engine startup, taxi, engine check, takeoff, climb, level flight, descent, landing, taxi, and engine shutdown.
Timing	Requiring all participating simulations to synchronize their clocks in a specified way.

Models and Algorithms. Models and algorithms represent elements or entities within a simulation. They're usually detailed, including long descriptions about what the entity is and how it works. Using these descriptions, we generate source code to build the model or algorithm. Examples include models or algorithms that describe the Earth, terrain, weather, or oceans. Whenever models and algorithms are complex and you use them often, be sure to establish and use common descriptions (or standard lexicons, if available) for them throughout your development. Doing so will keep you from having to re-invent these elaborate descriptions and will give your models and algorithms consistent, "tried and true," characteristics and functions.

Parameters. Parameters include variables and constants in mathematical expressions. An example is π equaling 3.14. π could also equal 3.1416 and still be correct. However, depending on the sensitivity of the calculation, using different values for π in a simulation may produce conflicting results. To avoid this type of error, your team should agree on what parameters to standardize and their values before starting. Once you decide, document the parameters and require all developers to use them throughout the development.

Units. Units are any elements used to express quantities. For example, the metric system uses grams and the English system uses ounces as a basic unit of weight. Using different units may cause errors that can be difficult and time consuming to locate. To prevent this problem, determine what units to include in the simulation, agree on the type of measurement that most effectively supports these units, and measure everything by this standard.

Coordinate Systems. Coordinate systems allow us to locate elements or entities of a simulation in three-dimensional space. Examples include using x-y-z measurements from a common origin (rectangular coordinates) or two angles and distance from a common set of axes and origin (polar coordinates). Errors result when entities receive coordinates that differ from what they're designed to support. Because the different coordinates can't be interpreted correctly, entities move to the wrong locations, or system faults occur that can stop the simulation. Typically, if the need for conversions isn't closely examined, simulation elements that should be moving along the Earth's surface are either floating above it or burrowing below it. The results can be humorous—tanks floating over trees or airplanes traveling unencumbered under mountain ranges. However, fixing these problems isn't funny and often requires a lot of time. To prevent this type of error, agree on a coordinate system that most effectively supports the simulation's goals and objectives and apply it throughout your development.

Data Formats. Data formats define the scheme or layout of the data shared within a simulation's modules and between simulations. An example of a data format might be five bytes of information for a header, one byte for a trailer, and ten bytes for the information within the data structure. Modules using this data are designed to recognize this structure and know that after the fifth byte, they'll receive usable information that must be processed. A Protocol Data Unit (PDU) for a specified version of the Distributed Interactive Simulation (DIS) standard is another example. PDUs are elements used by distributed interactive simulations to transmit information from one simulation to another. If the version you're using doesn't support your requirements, such as passing information about the intensity of the heat caused by a forest fire, your development team may have to develop a unique PDU to transmit this information. Different data formats can cause problems because the wrong parts will be processed. To avoid these errors, decide what types of data formats you need and use them consistently.

Conversions. Conversions are required when the same element has different values or formats in various simulations. I've covered several of these conversions already: for data formats, units, and parameters. To ensure consistency, determine what conversions you'll need and standardize them for your project. If you don't, you'll waste resources by developing duplicate methods and may introduce more errors into your simulation.

Mathematical Approaches. I'm talking here about simple operations, such as dividing and multiplying, as well as more complex calculations for particular simulations. Depending on sensitivity, the variations in even the most basic calculations can cause significant differences and catastrophic errors. For example, subtle errors, such as different approaches to truncation or rounding, can produce enormous differences when the simulation performs a routine many times. To prevent these errors, be aware of how mathematical functions will work, determine your calculation precision, standardize your calculations on this value, and identify any differences which will affect the overall calculations. Once you've identified functions that can cause problems, adopt one method for carrying them out and use it as the standard for your development. You must factor these issues into your development standards if you want your simulation to perform consistently.

Languages. Languages are intelligible words and formats used to capture a simulation requirement, model, or algorithm in source code. Examples include Fortran, C, C++, Ada, and Java. Several commonly used languages, such as C++ and Java (at the time of this writing), aren't standardized. In some cases, this lack of standards can cause inconsistencies, especially among different simulations. For example, if different languages handle basic mathematical calculations differently, errors can occur. In other cases, nonstandardized languages can provide greater flexibility and increase overall productivity. To prevent errors, use a standard language—or one mature enough so you can control minor inconsistencies by adopting more standards and guidelines when using it. If you've determined that a nonstandardized language provides greater benefits, explore the errors it may introduce. Then, document those potential problems as a way to develop standard approaches for using it.

Analysis Approaches and Tools. Analysis approaches and tools enable us to review the results of a simulation. For example, an analysis approach might use a procedure with a specified set of parameters to calculate a particular function, such as the amount of fuel an aircraft consumes. To do this analysis consistently, you should repeat the same steps in the same sequence, using the same parameters, and capture the analysis information in a spreadsheet. Finally, you should use standardized methods for porting data to make sure captured data from an analysis can export to other storage formats or tools without special conversion mechanisms. In general, you can make these approaches and tools consistent by specifying them as standards or by guiding analysts to use them consistently. Including these mechanisms in your simulation will reduce rework and keep you from having to justify why the simulation doesn't provide consistent results.

Scenarios. Scenarios capture steps or stages in a system's operation. For example, suppose a model must analyze how much fuel a Cessna 152 aircraft burns while flying from one airfield to another. The steps in this operation should be consistent: starting the engine, taxiing to the takeoff point, checking the engine, taking off, climbing, flying level, descending, landing, taxiing, and shutting down the engine. Minor differences in this scenario from one simulation to another are likely to produce varying results. To ensure consistency, provide ways to capture a scenario's steps so future analyses can reuse them or have your analysts document these steps and ensure they're followed for a given scenario.

Timing. Timing determines how the clock is set and incremented while a simulation runs. When several simulations with various timing mechanisms participate in an integrated simulation, you must standardize timing to ensure all participating simulations are in step. Timing is also a consideration when a simulation integrates live elements into it. Live elements can't support time delays or jumps forward and backward in time. They are tied to "hard" real time, unlike most "real-time" constructive simulations, which can vary time and get away with it. Thus, integrating live elements into simulations requires a special set of timing standards to ensure the simulation properly accounts for the passage of time.

Distributed Interactive Simulation

Distributed Interactive Simulation (DIS) is an evolving standard for models and simulations [Fischer 1996]. Its main purpose is to help link simulations that are physically separated from each other. Once linked, the simulators create a realistic virtual world—simulators acting separately in real time within a distributed scenario or exercise plus environmental representations, such as those for terrain, weather, and nuclear phenomena.

To link the simulators connected to local or wide-area networks, we pass messages between them. The messages are packaged as standardized protocol data units (PDUs) and broadcast on the network by participating simulators, which behave as autonomous network nodes or entities. Thus, each simulator operates independently, using its own models, database, and unique equipment.

The broadcast data units provide various information about the participating simulator. Although many types of information are available, the key information most often transmitted describes

- Each distinguishable entity, such as a ship or aircraft
- Its location and movement
- Engagements with it
- Whether it is still operational
- Any entity emissions, such as radio frequencies, that might allow other entities to identify its location

This information allows the participating simulator to interact with the other simulators if required and helps live elements in the simulation distinguish between ground truth (what really happened) and perceived truth (what an entity or user of the simulation thinks happened).

The main data units include start/resume, entity state, fire, and detonate. Start/resume manages starting, stopping, and resuming a scenario, as well as timing for each operation. Ideally, a simulation-control manager—on the network as an autonomous node—transmits this data unit to the simulation. The data unit for entity state describes the entity, its location, and its movement. It provides dead reckoning information for one simulator to forecast an entity's static appearance, information on articulated parts, and location in another simulator until another data unit with an updated entity state is issued for that simulator. A simulator issues the fire data unit whenever it physically engages another simulator's entity. This unit contains the type of engagement and its characteristics, as well as the identity of the engaged entity. The fourth main protocol data unit is detonate. It communicates information about the status of the fire data unit and whether the engaged entity stopped operating. The engaged entity also assesses its own situation to determine the damage caused by the engagement.

Distributed Interactive Simulation (DIS) uses a standard User Datagram Protocol/Internet Protocol (UDP/IP) approach to transmit data units across local-area or commercial wide-area networks. The UDP/IP is the same protocol used for file transmissions via FTP (file transfer protocol) on the internet. A special network called the Defense Simulation Internet is also available just for simulators participating in a distributed scenario. Each transmitted data unit contains a header and body. The header includes the protocol version, scenario identifier, type of data unit, time stamp, and length of the data unit. The body contains information about the data unit. For example, the body of a data unit for the entity state describes the entity, the entity's location, velocity, orientation, dead reckoning used, and appearance. It also details the entity's features and abilities, if required.

Figure 13.2 shows the basic operations for two DIS-compliant simulations. The simulators operate together by responding to the information transmitted on the network using distributed data units. A simulation-control manager issues a start/resume data unit (1) to all participating simulators. The participating simulators respond by broadcasting data units for entity states (2) on the network. Then, Simulator A (located at node A on the network) determines an entity is close by that poses a threat. Simulator B, at node B, owns this entity. In response to this threat, the simulator at node A issues a fire data unit (3) at node B. Node B receives the "fire" and calculates whether it resulted in an engagement—defined here as a hit or miss. The results of this calculation return to the simulator at node A. If the calculation shows the fire data unit produced a hit, the simulator at node B issues a kill response (4) and stops moving the now inoperable entity.

For time management, the standard uses a set time when the simulation begins. As a new simulation enters the overall simulation's run, it must offset the time it began participating from the time when the overall simulation started. For example, if the overall simulation started running at noon, and simulation B enters it at 12:05 P.M., simulation B should set its internal clock to indicate it's five minutes into the run. This type of time synchronizing may be fine for most virtual simulations, but not all participants may want to adhere to it. For example, the military test and evaluation community uses what is called absolute time and synchronizes their participant clocks to another standard medium such as the Global Positioning System. Using an offset timing method is not suitable for this group of participants. In fact, different timing mechanisms may be necessary for any type of interoperating situation that includes diverse simulations. To prevent

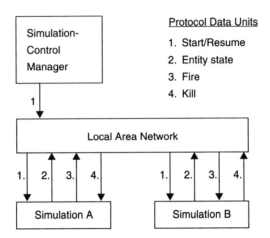

Fig. 13.2.   Operation of a Distributed Interactive Simulation. Different simulations interoperate in a distributed environment by transmitting important information across a network using protocol data units [Goldiez 1995].

timing complications, you shouldn't assume all participants will want to adhere to the same mechanisms. Instead, develop standards and guidelines that match various timing requirements.

The Distributed Interactive Simulation standard also comes with a variety of tools. Some examples include data-logger formats, so data can be automatically collected, and a terrain format called the Standard Interface Format, which allows distributed interactive simulations to interface easily with other simulations that include terrain. Thus, you won't have to develop much software to collect or process data.

Although the standard for distributed interactive simulation is evolving, the IEEE has standardized it and updated it with more abilities by working with special-interest groups in its standards organization. These groups address issues such as effectively applying dead reckoning, training and testing, data standards, and mobile-communication technologies. The main standards are IEEE 1278.1 for application protocols, IEEE 1278.2 for communication services and profiles requirements, and IEEE 1278.3 for managing exercises and recommending practices.

This standard for interoperability is valuable because it allows simulations to operate together without large individual changes. They need only a network to connect them and several protocol data units to communicate. Additionally, the distributed standard enables simulators to use functions that would otherwise have to be developed for a particular simulation. Thus, using this standard makes participating simulations work better and prevents rework by allowing resource sharing.

Aggregate Level Simulation Protocol

This protocol supports integrating physically separated simulations. A standard network protocol, such as Transmission Control Protocol/Internet Protocol (TCP/IP) transmits information between them. The largest application of this aggregate protocol is the Joint Training Confederation—a group of simulations used to train operational military forces. One of the main users of the Confederation is the Joint Training, Analysis, and Simulation Center in Suffolk, Virginia [JTASC 1996]. The United States Atlantic Command manages this center to train US-based military forces, using a confederation of simulations mainly to train senior military leaders and their close support staff on how to manage a military operation. Each military service provides participating simulations, which represent essential assets that might be involved in a military operation—tanks, fighter aircraft, infantry forces, and aircraft carriers.

The confederation has several strict design features which must be carefully negotiated and programmed in with additional software before the simulations can work together:

- Simulations may join or depart the confederation only after notifying other participants
- Physical separation
- A message-based protocol to transfer information between the simulations
- Time management to coordinate simulation times
- Data management
- Ownership of attributes by the participating simulations
- Identified functions, entities, and other simulations that each simulation will control

As a participant in a confederation of simulations, each simulation must broadcast attributes of its own objects to the confederation, broadcast interactions with the other simulations, respond to interactions with the objects it owns, and coordinate time. Also, a simulation's object that needs to interact with another simulation transmits attributes to give the impression that a copy of the object resides within the non-owning simulator. We call this technique "ghosting" the object.

The aggregate-level protocol has three main parts (Fig. 13.3):

- The infrastructure software, which supports distributed runtime simulations
- The translation segment, which provides reusable interfaces that incorporate rules for exchanging generic message protocols between the infrastructure software and the participating simulations
- Participating simulations adapted for use with the aggregate-level protocol

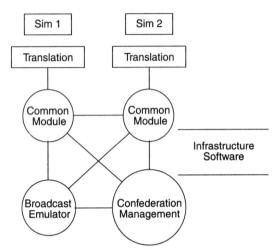

Fig. 13.3.   The Three Main Parts of an Aggregate-Level Simulation Protocol (ALSP). ALSP includes the infrastructure software, a translation segment, and the participating simulations. The infrastructure software provides distributed runtime support to integrate participating nodes.

The infrastructure software is central to integrating the participating nodes. It includes common modules, a broadcast emulator, and confederation management. The common modules provide data and time management to all participating simulations through direct connections that use standard network-communications protocols, such as TCP/IP. The common module also coordinates simulations joining and leaving the federation, as well as the simulation's local time. It filters messages so only information of interest to a simulation is received by that simulation and coordinates the simulations' enforcement of attribute ownership. The broadcast emulator distributes messages to other simulations based on their unique requirements. The third part of the infrastructure is confederation management, which controls the federation of simulations from a single point. It monitors each simulation through direct links and controls the federation's overall activities.

This software and protocol, developed by MITRE, are still evolving, as are most M&S technologies for linking diverse simulations. Although it is an Advanced Research Projects Agency program, the U.S. Army Simulation, Training, and Instrumentation Command acts as the executive agent for the program. You can get more information by accessing the home page for the aggregate-level simulation protocol at http://alsp.ie.org/alsp/.

The aggregate-level protocol differs from distributed interactive simulation in that it combines simulations, uses TCP/IP to transmit messages, and has a much more robust way to manage time standards for the participating simulations. However, it requires extensive negotiation with other participating simulations and probably additional coding to support the agreed-on functions. To choose between these standards, carefully examine both and select the one which best meets your goals for interoperability.

Common Technical Framework

The Common Technical Framework is the most recent standard recommended by the Department of Defense for integrating simulations [McGarry 1995]. It contains a High Level Architecture, which integrates its other two pieces: the Conceptual Model of the Mission Space and data standards. Table 13.1 lists the Common Technical Framework under interoperability standards. As you learn more about it, you may ask why it isn't under application interfaces. After all, a major part of the standard's specification—the High Level Architecture and its runtime infrastructure—interfaces simulations in a standard way. I've placed it here because it's being developed and used mainly to promote the interoperability of many existing simulations.

High Level Architecture (HLA). The HLA requires participating simulations to behave as objects that interact with each other through a central framework called a runtime infrastructure. This infrastructure allows participating simulations to exchange object attributes.

The main parts of the HLA are the participating simulations, the infrastructure, and the interface between the simulations and the infrastructure. The group of simulators participating in an HLA simulation is termed a federation. The federated simulations have object models, which interact within the HLA and are described using standardized templates. The templates help characterize each object so all participating objects clearly understand what it can do. Each template includes such items as data-dictionary formats, graphical representations, and matrix structures. Although the HLA standard doesn't dictate what information participating object models must process, it does require certain features in the object models so they can interact—object attributes, associations, interactions, and the ability to import and export attributes, transfer ownership of attributes, and manage time locally to support the overall simulation.

The Run-Time Infrastructure manages the federation, declarations, instances, ownership, and time. It manages the federation—creating it, dynamically controlling it, handling needed changes to it, and deleting it when the run is over. Declarations are the simulations' declared need for data, which means each simulation may have to export and receive information. The infrastructure manages these exchanges. It also creates, changes, and deletes instance objects generated by the simulations to execute for defined periods of time. And it makes sure only one simulation owns a unique object during any given time. Finally, the infrastructure manages time, ensuring all federation events are synchronized.

The third main part of the HLA standard is the interface between the runtime infrastructure and the federated simulations. This interface uses an application-program interface to transmit formatted information on object attributes between the infrastructure and the participating simulations. Figure 13.4 shows how it works. First, the simulation affiliates itself with the federation. In so doing, the simulation must establish initial requirements for data by stating what it has and what it needs to operate. Then, the simulation electronically publishes its object states and receives any needed objects from the federation. Next, the simulation runs normally—advancing time, updating object states, creating and deleting new objects, and receiving and transmitting updated information. When the simulation's role in the execution ends, it leaves the federation, and the run ends or proceeds without it. Because the HLA is an evolving standard and still maturing, you must carefully define its interface to the federated simulations if you want them to work together. This is a good example of where defining additional guidelines or even specifications for an existing standard, such as the HLA interface, will greatly reduce rework by helping the development team complete their effort.

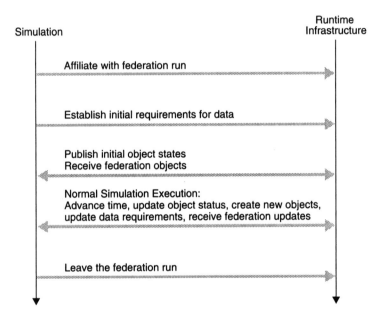

Fig. 13.4.   Overview of the Relationship between the Simulation and the Runtime Infrastructure. The interface between the runtime infrastructure and a participating simulation manages the simulation.

The Advanced Research Project Agency started developing the HLA standard as a program for advanced distributed simulation. The Defense Modeling and Simulation Office (DMSO) now manages and develops the HLA through the DOD's Architecture Management Group, but management responsibility is being transferred to the Simulation Interoperability Standards Organization. You can get baselined versions of the runtime infrastructure and its interfaces by contacting DMSO.

Conceptual Model of the Mission Space (CMMS). The Conceptual Model of the Mission Space fosters consistent and authoritative representations of simulation models. Once authorities develop and approve them for use, they're available to simulation developers. The models depict entities, actions, and interactions between real objects developed from accepted definitions of those objects (e.g., the Joint Mission Essential Task List for military objects). Using these definitions, different teams can develop simulation objects with the same functions and abilities. You can then integrate these models into the HLA and use standardized data. This program keeps you from starting over whenever you develop models for common mission areas. These mission areas are broad and can include combat operations, other military operations, training, acquisition, and analysis.

The Conceptual Model of the Mission Space intends to

- Develop a common technology framework, within which representations are consistent and data is accessible, to bridge the gap between developers and end users

- Develop the model semantics and syntax needed to help integrate the simulations

This program also identifies authoritative sources for these conceptual models, which essentially "blesses" them as accurate depictions of their program elements. These authoritative sources also validate the models and support broad access to them.

The Conceptual Model of the Mission Space uses a technical-framework document to guide development of its resources and tools, ensures its products fit well with the HLA, and provides data standards needed to support its own activities and the HLA. This program is in its initial stages, but it will involve three distinct phases to determine whether its systems will work: developing the first prototype, testing actual elements for usability, and building an operational system.

Standardizing Data. This part of the DOD's Technical Framework standardizes and validates data in a common format that various models and simulations can easily access. The DMSO-sponsored data program has four parts: data engineering, authoritative data sources, data quality, and data security. Data engineering technically supports the data-interchange format, which is the common format for data across various models and simulations. The authoritative data source provides a way to identify the sources of data and describes what these sources are. Data quality provides tools and processes to verify, validate, and certify data, so we can access, review, and assess it. Data security is self-explanatory; it applies to data transmission and use and ensures sensitive data is not compromised.

The Common Technical Framework differs from distributed interactive simulation and the aggregate-level simulation protocol by providing a comprehensive architecture that includes an integrating framework, a way to capture information about elements and reuse this information for other simulations, and common data formats and quality standards. To use this standard, you'll need to do a lot of development because it's still evolving. When trying to interface your framework with live systems, such as command and control elements for military applications, you'll run across several other issues people are still working.

13.3   Applying Standards to Models and Simulations

To apply standards to your development, you must define what you need to choose the right ones, determine what you must do to identify them, and decide what you'll get from applying them. I'll also cover areas that can cause problems when you use standards and some guidelines on tailoring them.

13.3.1   What Do You Need to Choose the Right Standards?

Of course, you must consider your development goals, customers' requirements for standards, project constraints, company-mandated standards, and your conceptual architecture. Earlier chapters covered these common considerations, so I won't discuss them. Key concerns here are your knowledge about a standard, your experience in using it, its availability, and your users' needs.

Knowledge of Existing Standards. You can't select a standard unless you know which ones exist and their value to your project. Your team must stay in touch with standards organizations and consortia working on new or emerging standards. Join these groups or attend conferences whenever possible.

Expertise Using Standards. Knowing about a standard isn't enough; you have to know how it works. That means experience from team members, or at least the ability to evaluate new or emerging standards based on experience with similar ones. Thus, before you decide to use a standard, make sure you have this expertise or can get it from within your company or through new hirings, training, or consultation.

Available Standards. Once you've selected a standard, make it available to your development team. You can get documented standards at a reasonable cost from standards organizations. To find current information on emerging or evolving standards, check the world wide web to locate information and sources.

What Users Need. Considering your users' needs may drive your program toward additional standards. Analyze how—and on what platforms—your users will operate the simulation. Don't assume they want more complex, futuristic abilities. For example, if people are working at home with a simulation, they're more likely to be using personal computers than high-powered workstations. In this case, you should set standards to build the simulation on a PC, not on a workstation.

13.3.2   What Must You Do to Select the Right Standards?

I recommend 12 steps to select and maintain effective standards for your project. If you prepare well for your selection (see Sec. 13.3.1) and follow these steps carefully, you should reduce rework, delays, and budget overruns on your project.

Review Goals and Objectives. Start by reviewing your development's goals, your customers' requirements, program constraints, and your company's requirements for standards and specifications. This review will help you understand where to apply standards during the development.

Examine Notional Architectures. By understanding how the model or simulation will be developed, its major parts, and how these parts will operate or integrate with each other, you can better decide which standards you need to meet stated development goals, requirements, and constraints. This is particularly true when you attempt to reuse parts of existing simulations. You may have to modify the architecture according to specified guidelines or standards unique to your development in order to include specific reused modules in the overall architecture.

Select a Set of Standards. After you've considered goals, objectives, and the notional architecture, review standards that appear to support them and select standards based on their usefulness, your team's experience with using them, and their maturity. You may also revise the list of candidate standards to accommodate software targeted for reuse. Remember you may need to re-evaluate standards after you've tailored them and analyzed their benefits.

Review for Tailoring. Next, determine whether you need all or part of your defined standards. This tailoring can save you a lot of money and time.

Examine the Need for Unique Standards. Check to see if your development needs unique standards beyond the tailored ones you've established. If so, you may have to create them.

Identify Needed Expertise. Determine what your team must know to use the selected standards—especially for rapidly emerging technologies and their standards and specifications. You may be faced with using a standard for the first time during an actual project, but that's risky. Be sure an unfamiliar standard's value warrants its use, and don't forget to get support—either internal or hired— for your staff until they become familiar with it.

Determine Associated Risks. Some risks are obvious: lack of expertise, increased costs, and schedule delays. But other risks may be lurking. For example, you may choose to apply a standard that looks helpful but doesn't benefit the development. Or, you may choose to apply a standard which, when implemented, yields counterproductive results (e.g., selecting a standard to improve bandwidth use in a networked simulation, only to find it consumes more bandwidth when applied). To avoid these problems, thoroughly investigate all risks before deciding to use your selected standards. You can use an aggressive prototyping activity that implements different aspects of the standard to explore these risks before development begins.

Analyze Effects on Cost and Schedule. Compare the costs of extra work to use the standard against the risk of rework if you don't adhere to it. Also consider the fees for buying and using the standard. In other words, thoroughly compare costs with benefits to confirm that your standard adds value to your development.

Develop a Process for Applying Your Standards. Write a comprehensive plan that

- Convinces your development team of the standards' usefulness
- Describes where and how you'll apply them
- Estimates the cost, schedule, and risks associated with using them

Use the Standards. Your standards will often apply throughout the development lifecycle, beginning with initial specifications and ending with final testing of your model or simulation.

Monitor for Correct Use. Despite your development team's best efforts, incorrectly using standards may harm your development. Thus, you must continuously monitor their use to ensure they're properly incorporated and don't generate errors.

Review for Alternates. As you're using a standard, you can judge its usefulness. If you determine it's not meeting goals, requirements, or constraints, consider alternative standards. If you can use an alternative without adding greatly to schedule, cost, or risk, change your development plan to allow for it. Of course, your earlier risk analysis should identify these potential alternatives.

13.3.3   What Will Result from Examining and Selecting Standards?

Your selection activities should result in a set of specific standards; an approach for using them; an understanding of the risks in terms of cost, schedule, and operations; an understanding of the types of expertise needed; and assurance that the standards will allow you to meet goals, requirements, and expectations.

Set of Standards. The most important result is the set of standards for your project. If done correctly, they should allow everyone to see their value, where to apply them, and how to tailor them.

Plans for Using Standards. Once you've selected standards, you must plan how to use them. If interoperability is a standard, you have to map out when to apply the HLA, for example—as well as who will do it.

Risks to Cost, Schedule, and Operation. Each standard comes with risks—a possibility of longer schedules, higher costs, and special measures needed to meet this standard. Be sure to understand these risks and figure out how to reduce them.

Requirements for Special Expertise. Standards may require special knowledge or skills, so you'll need to determine what is available, what you need to hire, and what you may be able to develop through training. Trade off the costs for new hires versus training, keeping in mind cost-effectiveness and risk to your project.

13.4   Applying Standards to Developing Models and Simulations for National Fire Management

To apply standards to this problem, we'd determine which inputs, functions, and outputs (standards) are needed. Let's step through this process to recommend standards for developing these models and simulations.

13.4.1   Inputs

I've listed in Table 13.10 typical inputs for selecting a set of standards and how they apply to National Fire Management. Notice, the development requires simulations to operate with other simulations and to meet the usual project constraints on budget and schedule. From this list, you can start analyzing potential standards. For example, given a distributed development, you'll probably need to use Distributed Interactive Simulation and eventually migrate to High Level Architecture. If so, you should specify key capabilities required for migration to ease the transition. Also, you'll need a mature team that can create a reusable new development, which is required for SEI Level 3 as discussed in Chap. 6 [Paulk 1993]. Minimum errors in the delivered product and other implications for standards are clear from Table 13.10.

Table 13.10. Generic and Possible Inputs for National Fire Management. Identifying appropriate standards to develop models and simulations that support National Fire Management relies on sound inputs, such as those identified here.

Generic Inputs	Inputs for National Fire Management
1. Goals	a. Must operate with specific fire management models and simulations b. Must have minimum errors
2. Customer requirements	a. Must address fire-management directives
3. Project constraints	a. Must be within schedule and cost b. Must be reusable for other projects c. Must be portable to other types of platforms
4. Organizational requirements	a. Must follow company policy for software developments b. Must adhere to processes under SEI level 3
5. Notional architecture	a. Must use DIS and be prepared to migrate soon to an HLA standard
6. Knowledge about standards	a. Team knows about standards groups but not those for DIS and HLA
7. Expertise with use of standards	a. Several members have experience with DIS b. None of the members have experience with HLA or are involved in developing the HLA standard
8. Availability of standards	a. Most of the documentation regarding key protocol data units (management and entity state) is widely available and understandable
9. Targeted user	a. Most users will use personal computers b. Most users will use the Internet to reach tools available at other fire-management centers

HLA = High Level Architecture
DIS = Distributed Interactive Simulation
SEI = Software Engineering Institute

13.4.2   Results

Once we've gleaned the right inputs from Table 13.10, we can apply our selection process (Sec. 13.3.2) to identify the standards we'll use, possible risks, and anything else that affects using standards while developing models and simulations for National Fire Management. In so doing, you can see how applying what I've covered in this chapter will help you make smart decisions when selecting an appropriate set of standards and specifications. Table 13.11 displays these results.

Table 13.11. Generic and Possible Results for National Fire Management. Potential outputs from identifying standards for M&S development to support National Fire Management fall into six categories.

Generic Results	Results for National Fire Management
1. Set of selected standards and specifications	a. Interoperability b. DIS with migration to HLA c. SEI's Level 3 processes
2. Approach for using standards and specifications to meet requirements and constraints	a. Get smart on standards b. Develop plan to use c. Start using from the start
3. Understanding risks	a. Good experience using DIS b. Little to no experience using HLA; get training, attend conferences, and become involved in groups working on standards for the HLA; hire expertise to assist early development until the team becomes familiar with HLA c. Conduct a small pilot project and prototype using HLA
4. Effects on cost and schedule	a. All standards identified except HLA have reduced overall projected costs and schedules b. Don't know the effect of HLA; must analyze after learning more about the standard (see item b under result 3)
5. An understanding of the types of expertise needed	a. Complete experience with DIS b. Need more experience with HLA; might try the technique on a pilot project that can fail without affecting the development c. Extensive experience in using processes under SEI level 3—very low risk
6. Expected results of using selected standards and specifications.	a. Expect development to go very smoothly using DIS and processes under SEI Level 3 b. Don't know results whenever development must migrate to HLA

HLA = High Level Architecture
DIS = Distributed Interactive Simulation
SEI = Software Engineering Institute

References

ATCCIS—Army Tactical Command and Control Information System. 1994. "Technical Standards for Command and Control Information Systems (CCISs) and Information Technology." Working Paper, Edition 4. Alexandria, VA: Institute of Defense Analysis.

Defense Information Systems Agency. 1994a. DOD Technical Architecture Framework for Information Management, Vol. 1. *Overview*. Washington, DC.

Defense Information Systems Agency. 1994b. DOD Technical Architecture Framework for Information Management, Vol. 2 *Technical Reference Model and Standards Profile*. Washington, DC.

Defense Information Systems Agency. 1994c. DOD Technical Architecture Framework for Information Management, Vol. 3. *Architecture and Design Guidance*. Washington, DC.

Department of Defense. 1994. *Information Technology Standard Guidance, Part 1*. Washington, DC.

Fischer, Mary. 1996. "Advanced Distributed Simulation Protocol through Aggregate Level Simulation Protocol." Proceedings of the 29th International Conference on System Sciences. Vol. 1.

Goldiez, Brian. 1995. "Educational Tutorial." 13th DIS Workshop. Institute for Simulation and Training. Orlando, FL.

JTASC—Joint Training, Analysis, and Simulation Center. 1996. "Modeling & Simulation Handbook." Ver. 1. Suffolk, VA.

McCabe, Thomas. 1980. *Software Quality Assurance, A Survey*. Thomas J. McCabe Associates, Inc. Columbia, MD

McGarry, Stephen, Richard Weatherly, and Annette Wilson. 1995. "The DOD High Level Architecture (HLA) Run-Time Infrastructure (RTI) and Its Relationship to Distributed Simulation." 13th DIS Workshop. Institute for Simulation and Training. Orlando, FL.

Paulk, Mark C., Bill Curtis, Mary Beth Crissis, and Charles Weber. 1993. *Capability Maturity Model for Software, Version 1.1*. Pittsburgh, PA: Research Access, Inc.

Piplani, L.K., J.G. Mercer, and R.O. Roop. 1994. *Systems Acquisition Managers Guide for the Use of Models and Simulations*. Fort Belvoir, VA: Defense Systems Management College Press.

CHAPTER 14

Adapting to Changing Technology

David Eccles, *The Aerospace Corporation*

Sometimes rapid changes in technology seem to be more of a curse than a blessing. For example, are you frustrated by dealing with email and voicemail in addition to a pile of regular mail each day? (And heaven help you if you subscribe to several usenet news groups on the internet!) What about that feeling in the pit of your stomach each time you read an article in a trade journal about a new technology that someone has used to beat out their competition and open a whole new market? Do you feel you have to spend four hours a night reading books or surfing the net just to keep up?

In 1957, the editor in charge of business books for Prentice Hall said, "I have traveled the length and breadth of this country and talked with the best people, and I can assure you that data processing is a fad that won't last out the year!" How do we avoid drawing similar conclusions about technologies available to us today while not chasing wildly after technology that won't last? We'll answer this question by establishing a way to evaluate new technology and apply it to modeling and simulation (M&S). This chapter will lay out phases, steps, and background information so you (as a manager or developer) can prudently select new technology. It identifies several general principles which can help you "eat the elephant" of new technology in small, reasonably sized chunks. Figure 14.1 highlights the three steps you'll repeat until you've developed a plan for using technology in your models and simulations. The same steps also apply when transferring technology from one application to another.

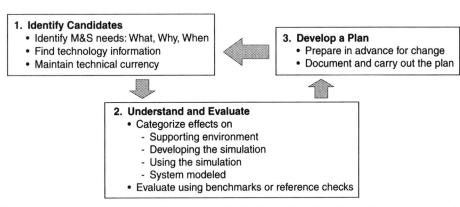

Fig. 14.1.   Steps for Using or Transferring Technology. You should follow these three steps to plan effectively for using technology in your models and simulations, or transferring it from one application to another.

14.1   Identifying Candidate Technologies

Why is it we're so reluctant to adopt new technologies? Here are some common excuses for avoiding change and maintaining the "status quo":

- If it ain't broke, don't fix it!
- We'll have to retrain the staff!
- It will cost too much money.
- It wasn't invented here!
- The current technology is fine.

In general, sticking with old, "safe" technology limits innovation—there may be a totally unexpected, beneficial application for a new technology, or your competitor may realize benefits from a new technology before you do. Still, new technologies can cause trouble if we get carried away and believe

- ALL useful tools have point & click interfaces and use fancy computer graphics
- Object-oriented development is the solution to ALL software problems
- COTS (Commercial Off-the-Shelf) products are the solution to ALL problems
- We can easily hook together ALL simulations, COTS products, and models

As you can see, these beliefs follow a pattern: "<fill-in-the-blank> new technology will solve ALL problems." Difficulties arise when we try to apply a given technology too broadly. The fact is that well-chosen new technologies can strongly improve models and simulations by allowing us to

- Build and use quality simulation tools faster and easier
- Build tools that better support long-term maintenance
- Generate simulation input data and scenarios more easily, with fewer errors
- Execute simulation studies more rapidly, permitting us to explore more tradeoffs
- Interpret simulation results more easily and present them to decision makers so they understand them and can make better decisions

Once we understand that technological change is a natural part of modeling, simulation, and analysis, we must embrace it and work with it, as outlined in Table 14.1.

> **Table 14.1. Phase One: Identifying Candidate Technologies.** Changing technology is a natural part of modeling and simulation. You should consider the following guidelines for identifying potentially useful technologies as a first step in developing an effective plan to use technology in your modeling and simulation project.

> 1. **Identify Technology Needs:** Outline operational and technical requirements of new and existing simulations and list technologies for carrying them out. (See Chap. 5, Chap. 10) Take a first cut at what new technologies you might use to improve M&S, why they're necessary, and when you should use them. Rank order these technologies.

> 2. **Find Technology Information:** Systematically gather information until you can evaluate one or more targeted technologies. Sources include printed publications, the internet (world-wide web, usenet), conferences, colleagues, and vendors. Allow time for accidental discoveries and look for new applications of technologies you find. Refine and expand the entries in the matrix as necessary to include new discoveries.

> 3. **Maintain Technical Currency:** Take advantage of continuing education, special training, and mentoring. Habitually participate in professional societies, use the internet, and explore other sources of information.

14.1.1   Identifying Technology Needs: What, Why, When

Identifying technology needs builds directly on what you've seen in Chaps. 5 and 10. Chapter 5 covered how to develop simulation objectives and derive alternative approaches for creating a new simulation. We move in an orderly way from Operational Requirements for the overall system to more specific Technical Requirements—some of which we find appropriate for simulation. At this point, we drop down to individual simulations and check their Operational Requirements (what must or can the simulation do?) and Technical Requirements (how can we provide or improve its abilities?). Each operational requirement typically leads to multiple technical requirements, which directly drive technology needs. Chapter 10 covered how we build simulations, beginning with characterizing the situation, selecting appropriate methods, and then evaluating and selecting the hardware and software to do the job.

The process here is similar except that we can apply it to existing and new simulations, as well as to a range of simulation activities at the same time. Imagine a small group doing M&S for a fictitious National Fire-Suppression Agency. Table 14.2 lists what the simulations can or must do and the technologies in place to meet each technical requirement. This is just an example, so the list isn't comprehensive. As you can see, some of our agency's tools need updating. To the left of these elements are three columns labeled "What?," "Why?," and "When?" plus "Risk?" Let's look at how to answer these questions.

Table 14.2.   Matrix of Abilities for Fire-Suppression Simulations. This table provides an example of relating available technologies to the requirements of several simulation projects for fire suppression.

Needs	Technology Used Now	What?	Why?	When? (Risk?)
Rural Fire Simulator:				
1. Accurately predict a fire's progression, given weather, terrain, fuel, firefighting, etc.	Continuous simulation, mainframe, FORTRAN 77	Workstations, personal computers, C++	Improved speed, maintainability, software reuse	Next 6 months (Medium)
2. Provide quality graphics output for interpretation of results	2D map plots, color contours	3D graphics, geographic information systems	Better interpretation of results	Next 6 months (Medium)
3. Provide user-interface for local fire departments to use tool (NEW)	Batch input through file editing	graphical user interface	Easy use by local firefighters	Next 6 months (Low)
Urban Fire Simulator:				
1. Provide modern graphical user interface	X/Motif graphical user interface	Cross-platform graphical user interfaces	Easiest access to software	Next 12 months (High)
2. Run on personal computers (NEW)	GL on Silicon Graphics workstations	Open GL	Puts high-end graphics on personal computers	Next 12 months (High)
3. Analyze fire department's communication network (NEW)	None	COTS network simulation	Saves a lot of software development	Next 6 months (Medium)
National Urban/Rural Historical Fire Database:				
1. Extract fire data to support legal inquiries	Relational database	Object-oriented database	Latest database technology	Next 2 years (High)
2. Provide fire scenarios to other simulators	Text files	Interprocess communication	For distributed simulation	Next 6 months (Medium)

What? Finding Possible Technologies

To fill in the matrix, begin by asking the question, "What technologies will best satisfy this requirement?" Don't worry too much about whether or not you've selected the "right" answer—the important thing is to get something down as a starting point. You can probably rely on your experience and knowledge of current trends to provide candidate technologies at this stage. As you ask this question for each technical requirement (and capability, if it exists), record the first time a particular technology comes to mind. The same technology will probably appear next to more than one technical requirement. You should end up with a fairly comprehensive list. Table 14.2 also shows the "What?" column of our agency's matrix of technical requirements filled in with initial alternatives.

At this point, we could get excited about a particular technology and start using it, but we have to refine the list before we create a final plan. What follows is an example of the negative effects that can occur from trying to move to a technology that doesn't match the needs of a particular development project.

A particularly successful trajectory-simulation tool had inhabited a large mainframe computer for many years. The software faithfully produced results that customers relied on to predict the performance of launch vehicles. The group who maintained the software decided to rehost it on a new supercomputer. To port the software, they completely rewrote it over two years. But by the time the work was done, distributed workstations had become the platform of choice for engineering computation, so they had to start over and rehost the software again. Their initial effort turned out to be completely unnecessary.

How can we avoid this type of error? Section 10.1.1 offers some valuable questions to ask about technology:

- How much do we know about particular requirements? (the knowledge questions)
- How large is the project we've undertaken? (the size questions)
- What constrains the operation? (the constraint questions)

Knowledge questions apply most to new requirements, but we should apply size and constraint questions to any new technology. In the rehosting example above, the scale of the rehosting task and the time constraint (because a new technology arrived) made the technology inappropriate for the application.

Why? List the Possible Benefits

Before adopting a new technology, you must see a clear benefit in doing so. For example, if you're confident that computer software for animated 3D graphics will significantly improve your ability to interpret the results of analyses, you should use it. But if you get this program because "everyone else is using it," you may be wasting your money. As you've seen several times in this book, if you can't say why you need a certain ability (or technology), chances are you don't need it. Here are some possible benefits of new technology with examples:

1. Applying modern user interfaces to legacy simulations can improve productivity. For many years, the Aerospace Corporation had maintained 13 legacy simulations to analyze load cycles. This analysis is a standard part of launch certification, which requires very detailed modeling of the spacecraft, upper stages, and boosters, so we can simulate the dynamic loading conditions spacecraft encounter during launch and deployment. Each of the 13 simulation tools represented a particular element, and analysis for a typical spacecraft required two person-years of effort. An executive program was developed to encapsulate the 13 tools in a common X/Motif interface and provide common rules for using them. A relational-database system was added to keep track of projects, input parameters, cases, runs and outputs. Productivity quintupled, costly errors went down, and training someone to use the system became much easier. The team used Commercial Off-the-Shelf software to automate building the user interface.

2. Rapid prototyping or "visual-programming" languages can speed development of simulations. For example, the Jet Propulsion Laboratory's Automated Testing Laboratory successfully developed an end-to-end simulation of the Pluto Flyby Spacecraft. In just four months, they used visual programming to model the spacecraft's subsystems and verified that the system worked as designed. Developers used schematic entry (interactively connecting predefined elements of the simulation on the screen with "wires" representing inputs and outputs) to create the simulation, retaining the flexibility to test and refine the model over time.

3. Using 3D computer graphics to display a simulation's outputs is an example of a strategy that pays off in marketing strength as well as technical value. Understanding how a complex space system works is often difficult. Figure 14.2 shows 3D displays of requirements for a constellation of military communication satellites; these displays allow operators to understand and improve loading and overcome jamming environments. An analyst can manipulate the display in three dimensions, turning communication networks on and off to understand quickly which requirements are being missed and why.

To summarize, you may want to use a particular technology to improve productivity, flexibility, and understanding. Grouping tools under a single interface (mentioned above) improved productivity for analysis and simulation development—a main driver for adopting new technology because it directly reduces cost. The Pluto Flyby example showed the benefit of flexibility—the ability to model a system and adapt quickly to the customer's changing needs. The improved understanding gained by using 3D graphics is somewhat less tangible but still apparent to anyone who must interpret and present complex results. Other possible "whys" include improved training, fewer errors, maintainability,

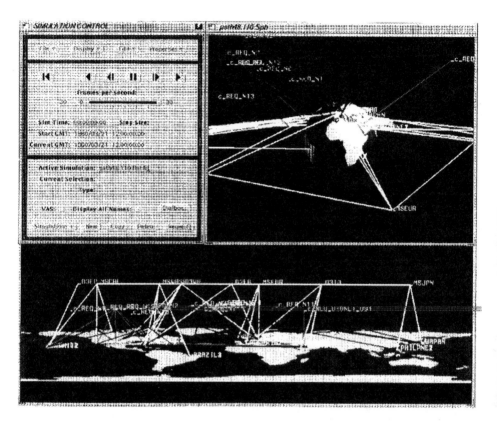

Fig. 14.2.   3D Graphics Display Showing that a Simulation Satisfies Communication Requirements. Using 3D graphics to present simulation outputs can dramatically improve understanding and enhance users' abilities to interpret results.

responsiveness, and easier marketing. Synergism—magnifying a technology's benefit by combining it with another technology—is another consideration.

Returning to Table 14.2, look at how I've stated each "why" as a benefit we can derive from adopting a technology. Now look at the "why" entry for using an object-oriented database to track historical fires (second from last). I had trouble coming up with a reason I needed an object-oriented database and finally settled on "latest database technology." This is clearly a weak benefit, which suggests we may not need it. By the way, list as many benefits as you can for each "what" item.

When? The Timing Has to Be Right

In the earlier example of rehosting a trajectory simulation, late adoption of a supercomputing technology led to difficulties. But adopting a new technology too early can be just as troublesome. Here's an example:

The developers of an object-oriented tool for a large simulation decided to develop an object-oriented database (OODB) to handle much of the required internal bookkeeping for the tool. The idea was to provide persistent storage for simulation objects and permit simulation runs to stop and restart at will. Unfortunately, interfacing the simulation to the OODB greatly increased the software's complexity, introducing a vast amount of new code. At the time of this development, OODB technology was immature. This immediately complicated the effort because each new version of the OODB software (a COTS product) required many changes to the simulation code. The project would have been better served using a simple text file or relational database until OODBs were stable enough.

Now let's look at an example of getting the timing right:

For several years a development team had been working on a DOS application, with a fairly primitive graphical user interface (GUI), and simple, but effective, 2D graphics. They had a reputation for being very responsive to their customer's analytical needs and could change rapidly because they knew the tools and systems so well. They were careful to develop the software in ANSI C, so it would be portable. Recently, they decided to develop a more advanced GUI and make the tool available on multiple platforms. But they waited until development tools became available that permitted them to build the interface once, on a particular platform, and have the framework automatically reproduce it on other platforms. So far, the results have been very positive.

Are there some general principles for deciding *when* to adopt particular technologies? Well, it's a little bit like investing in the stock market—it depends on the level of risk you're willing to accept. You can decide to be on the "bleeding edge," in which case you're researching, inventing new technology, or adopting new technology just as soon as someone else invents it (high risk/high payoff). You can adopt technology once a few organizations have successfully used it (medium risk/moderate payoff). Finally, you can wait until the technology is widely accepted or you are driven to accept it because your competitors are using it (not necessarily low risk). I favor medium risk and moderate payoff for new technologies, with occasional forays into high risk. (See managing risk in Sec. 14.3.1.) The keys to good decisions are to *understand* the technology and to envision *practical applications* that strongly benefit your applications.

Once you've determined the risk you can accept, record preliminary "when" answers for the technology candidates you've identified. Estimate the penetration of each technology into modeling and simulation, think about your risk threshold, say when you think you'd like to use it, and categorize its risk. Table 14.2 shows the results. At this point, you may not be able to determine a "when" for everything on your list, but you can fill in the blanks later.

Up to this point, we've populated our capabilities matrix based purely on knowledge and experience and created just the skeleton of a technology plan. The real work begins as we try to understand each technology more completely, thereby increasing the plan's accuracy. Also, we'll find only the technologies we know something about—not allowing for new technologies or for unusual applications of known technologies. Target a few of these technologies as starting points for the search. Ask yourself if a particular one is a "must have" or a "nice to have."

14.1.2   Finding Technology Information

While researching the targeted technologies, you may also discover previously unfamiliar technologies and uncover new applications for them. So, you should allow some extra time for accidental discoveries. Learn about some of the topics that interest you, even if they don't seem to apply directly to the technology you're researching. Genius could be defined as the ability to transplant ideas.

Where do you find the detailed technology information you want? How can you find it efficiently? Consider the following:

Printed Publications: Read about what others in the field are doing! Managers should encourage staff to spend time reading periodicals and books. One approach is to circulate interesting publications. I recommend starting a reference center to gather interesting material and including a terminal to access the world wide web. Put a table and chairs in the room, maybe even a coffee machine—make it a friendly, comfortable meeting place. You can get many trade publications free once the publisher knows you may become a customer. But it's easy to get carried away and subscribe to far more publications than you can ever read. Generally, avoid vendors' publications unless you're heavily involved with their products—as you might expect, they present a very one-sided view. Table 14.12 (at the end of the chapter) lists some of the most highly-regarded books, journals, and other periodicals in modeling and simulation, as well as publications which extend to other technical areas: graphics, software development, computer hardware, etc.

The Internet: The Internet has certainly received more than its fair share of hype in recent years. Amazingly enough, some of the hype is justified. For example, much of the research for this chapter came from the internet. Begun in the late 1960s, it was created by the U.S. government to allow researchers to share information electronically. Over the last three decades, it's gradually added many abilities, including web technology (a common document format and standardized server software to read and display documents) in 1989. CERN (Conseil European pour la Recherche Nucleaire), the European Laboratory for

Particle Physics, started the web with this technology, but its phenomenal growth really began in 1993 with the introduction of HyperText Markup Language (HTML) and MOSAIC (the National Supercomputer Center's browser for HTML documents). These tools permitted world wide web (WWW) users to easily create and view "pages" containing text and graphics. Beginning with only about 50 web servers in January of 1993, the WWW had more than 10,000 servers only one year later and millions by 1997. It continues to grow exponentially.

The world wide web is only part of what is available on the internet. Other services include e-mail, file-transfer protocol (ftp) for downloading files, telnet for remote system logins, and news (more on this later). The internet is a marvelous source for product information, databases, software (often including source code), algorithms, etc. You can find databases of maps and ship and air traffic, algorithms for computer graphics, plus information (and honest opinions) about commercial simulations and hardware or software in general. Need a weather database to do clutter calculations for space-borne IR sensors? You can find it on the internet and incorporate it into your tools. Other experts may even volunteer to help you.

Figure 14.3 shows the WWW "home" page for the Defense Modeling and Simulation Office (DMSO) displayed with "net-browser" software from NetScape Communications, Inc. Browsers allow you to jump from site to site, sampling information along the way. You can save pointers or "bookmarks" to interesting sites so you can quickly access them during future hunting expeditions. Table 14.10 (at the end of the chapter) lists some of the many web sites with information on modeling and simulation.

Critical to using the web effectively is proper searching for the type of information you want. Recently, so-called "search engines" have multiplied. They go out and gather data based on search criteria you specify. Some web sites index the vast amount of information on the web, which grows daily. Table 14.9 (at the end of the chapter) lists popular index sites and search engines for the web.

Usenet is another part of the internet, perhaps even more valuable to simulation developers than the WWW. It consists of targeted news groups which center on particular topics. Most internet service providers now offer access to Usenet, and web-browsing software usually includes utilities for reading and posting to newsgroups. One newsgroup (comp.simulation) shares information about the latest developments in M&S. Table 14.8 (at the end of the chapter) lists and describes other interesting newsgroups. These newsgroups can be sounding boards for people with problems related to particular areas of interest. People "post" problems to the newsgroup, so others will suggest solutions. Be careful, though. Your words appear before a large audience, and questions that are naive or often seen will attract unpleasant attention. For proper use of the internet, consult "Zen and the Art of Internet," by Brendan Kehoe [1996]. Most newsgroups have a Frequently Asked Questions (FAQ) posting which can save a lot of time and embarrassment for new users. Just as with print publications, it's very easy to overwhelm yourself with information by subscribing to too many newsgroups. At first, limit yourself to a handful of groups to avoid getting swamped.

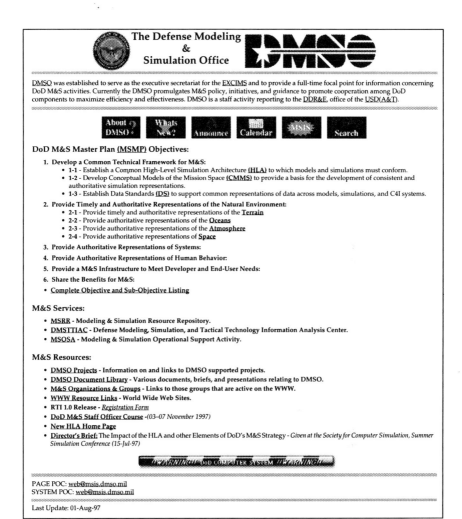

Fig. 14.3. **Home Page for the Defense Modeling and Simulation Office (DMSO) on the World Wide Web.** Many web sites contain information on modeling and simulation. The home page for the Defense Modeling and Simulation Office, shown here, is a good starting point for finding this information.

Colleagues, Conferences, and Vendors: Technical conferences regularly occur on many subjects. They're usually organized by a professional organization. Table 14.11 (at the end of the chapter) lists technical conferences for simulation developers and analysts, along with a description, time of year they're usually held, and the sponsoring organization. Conferences are good places to hear the latest breakthroughs in the field, and even more importantly, to network with colleagues who are trying to solve problems similar to yours. Many conferences also contain exhibits for vendors' products; there, you can ask questions and see demonstrations. It's important to cultivate good relationships with vendors of hardware and software, but don't try to substitute a conference demonstration for a thorough evaluation at work and on your own problem (see Benchmarking in Sec. 14.2.2). Products always look better at a trade show than they really are. To get information at a technical conference or trade show, you can't be bashful; you must talk to people around you.

Join a few carefully selected professional societies and participate in local chapters—attending activities, serving on committees, etc. Professional societies provide more chances to network. Management should support conferences, training seminars, and professional societies because of the benefits to staff and to the organization.

Encourage information sharing within your group by organizing informal (lunchtime?) gatherings to talk "shop" with colleagues. Take advantage of your staff's expertise. Invite your resident "guru" on UNIX, windows, graphics, internet, and so on to talk about them. These sessions can generate new interests for staff specialists, thus cross-training them and increasing their flexibility.

Invite vendors to your offices to discuss their products and expertise. You'll get a sales pitch, but you may also glean a lot of useful information about new technologies. Many vendors will provide non-disclosure briefings to their best customers to keep them aware of their upcoming products. Direct meetings with vendors give you the time to ask questions and explore alternatives with much less stress than during a major technical conference.

14.1.3   Maintaining Technical Currency

Perhaps the biggest obstacle to successfully adapting advancing technology is simple obsolescence. We get comfortable with the technology we're familiar with and wake up one day far behind. Instead, we should emphasize "long-term maintenance"—maintaining technical currency. In the same way you might change your diet now to enjoy continuing good health, you must change your work process to remain technically current. Tasks such as combing the internet, reading technical publications, and reviewing the information sources already discussed in this chapter must become a regular part of your work schedule. I know of one simulation expert who makes a point of reading one new technical book a week and is a "knowledge storehouse." (But don't worry. The rest of us "mortals" can probably get by reading a few books per year.) Other activities include continuing education, training, and mentoring.

Go back to school yourself and make it easy for others to do so. Management should encourage staff to continue their education by providing any technical book they request and by reimbursing tuition for college courses or other specialized training. Obvious choices would be courses in areas appropriate to your group's simulation applications and development activities. Does your group simulate the weather? Meteorology might be a good choice. Software engineering is important, including methods, programming languages, and project management. As of this writing, object-oriented and internet technologies seem to be gaining momentum in M&S. Many product vendors and private consultants also offer training in new technologies, but beware of the short course that tries to jam everything you need to know about a particular topic into three or five days. In my experience, absorbing a difficult subject over time and applying it really stick with you.

Most people know about mentoring—pairing experienced and junior staff to train the junior person, increase corporate memory, and encourage teamwork. But junior staff (particularly those just out of college) also have something to offer: exposure to new technologies and the ability to apply them to your organization's projects. Successful mentoring usually depends on active promotion rather than just "letting it happen." I recommend assigning mentors to new employees as soon as they arrive. Make sure the mentor isn't a direct supervisor, so the new person will find it easier to ask for help.

14.2 Understanding and Evaluating New Technologies

Phase two of planning to use technologies involves understanding and evaluating them carefully so we can gauge their potential effects on our M&S activities. In other words, we must gather information and evaluate it.

We'll begin by defining categories into which we can place candidate technologies for detailed study. We'll also look at ways to evaluate technologies, including basic research, reference checks, and benchmarking. Sections 14.2.2 through 14.2.4 discuss in more detail many of the technologies that fit in each of the defined categories. These sections are more than just a "laundry list" of technologies related to M&S; they emphasize how these technologies affect developers, users, and customers of M&S. I'll present historical trends in each technology area, along with current trends and possible future directions. We'll also discuss common consequences and implications, which we'll be able to deal with using some of the strategies discussed later (in phase three). Table 14.3 outlines the steps for understanding and evaluating new technologies.

Table 14.3.   Phase Two: Understanding and Evaluating Technologies. The second step in developing an effective plan to use changing technology relies on the three elements shown here. By completing these tasks, we should be able to gauge the effects of these technologies on our M&S activities.

1. **Categorize and Target Technologies:** Re-examine the expanded technology list ("What" column) from the matrix previously generated and categorize each entry as affecting: the supporting environment for M&S, simulation development, or simulation use. Again target the most promising technologies for examination using the "why" and "when" columns to help choose.
2. **Understand Technology Effects on Modeling and Simulation:** Seek to understand the possible effects of the targeted technologies on your models and simulations. Use the information sources previously discussed to gather much more detailed information about the technologies you have targeted. Document the data.
3. **Evaluate Targeted Technologies:** As you examine each technology in more detail, use basic research, reference checks and benchmarking to evaluate how the targeted technologies apply to your project.
NOTE: Steps two and three form a "loop" within this phase, repeated for each targeted technology. As the process continues, look for new entries to the matrix in the "What" and "Why" columns.

14.2.1   Categories for Technology

The sheer number and variety of new technologies require us to categorize them, so we can organize our searches and evaluations. My categories aren't sacred, and you can certainly come up with equally workable ones (the "formal structures" in Chap. 10, for example). I've chosen this breakdown because it roughly aligns with the groups I consider major stakeholders in any M&S effort: customers, users, and developers. Customers, of course, are the sponsors of the effort—the ones who pay the bills, usually ask the questions, and expect results. Users employ M&S tools to analyze something. Developers build the tools. Of course, any person may belong to one, two, or even all three groups.

Supporting Technology

Modeling and simulation, more than most fields, relies on supporting technologies (operating systems, CPUs, peripherals, graphics boards, computer memory, even office furniture). Some changes in technology, such as a faster computer platform or a new operating system, can essentially "pull the rug out" from under the way we may have been doing business. Uncertainty about whose computer hardware will dominate the market, for example, could force us to consider making the software portable, which can limit the quality of computer graphics. These changes often come from an external source, such as a hardware or software vendor with a revolutionary new product, a government regulation, or a national laboratory with a breakthrough. They're usually beyond the simulation developer's control, and they introduce changes we must deal with. I'll discuss a few of these "rug-pullers" in Sec. 14.2.3.

Technology for Developing Simulations

Software development is key to the success of any M&S project. Simulation software must respond flexibly to continually changing questions. Naturally, a lot of programs have popped up to make software professionals and development more productive: evolving programming languages and paradigms, CASE (Computer Aided Software Engineering) tools, simulation environments and languages, and other COTS and GOTS (Government Off-the-Shelf) tools. Developers must respond to these changes. The migration in recent years from procedural languages (FORTRAN, C) to object-oriented languages (C++, Ada, Java) is a good example, which we'll treat further in Sec. 14.2.4.

Technology for Using Simulations

New technologies may also help us use M&S tools more efficiently. If we need to run a simulation more often and more quickly, we may need to buy a high-performance computer. We may also need to adopt a graphical user interface if we have to make a tool accessible to more users or improve training efficiency. Section 14.2.5 says more about using new technology to enhance productivity in these ways.

14.2.2   Evaluating Technologies

We must evaluate the quality of any technology before applying it to real problems. One workable approach is simply to gather information and decide (basic research). We can also check references and benchmark. Checking references is better if you can do it, because it saves time and effort (as long as you trust the references!). As we work our way through candidate technologies and add newly discovered ones, we can apply these evaluating techniques and adjust the risks and benefits recorded in our capabilities matrix.

Checking References

Often, we can simply ask someone else who has been there what they found—let others go to the "bleeding edge" and learn from their mistakes. Of course, if no one were willing to risk trying new technology, the rest of us couldn't follow. Fortunately, a lot of brave souls are out there hacking away, willing to share what they've experienced. You'll get opinions on what's good and what's not, but you'll have to judge these opinions yourself.

Benchmarking

Benchmarking is the more formal process of systematically rating options against pre-determined sample problems or scenarios. You can use it to evaluate anything, not just new technologies. The criteria are the basic things you—as a simulation sponsor, developer, or user—need to do to be successful in your current application. The basic steps are

- Define common terms
- Establish selection criteria
- Weight the criteria
- Define sample problems and scenarios
- Run each technology and rate it against selected criteria
- Document results

Table 14.4 shows sample criteria and ratings for a fictitious comparison of simulation tools with generic features. This approach is similar to the matrices for ranking choices that are part of Quality Functional Deployment [Brassard 1989], discussed in Chap. 5. Chapter 5 also mentions the Analytical Hierarchical Process, which is useful for nested criteria. Here, you can probably use any scheme you know for ranking choices.

In this example, the last two alternatives were fairly close—alternative C won because its high and low scores tended to trend with the weights we assigned (high score with high weight, low score with low weight). The trickiest part of evaluation is defining the criteria and weights and specifying the sample problems used for the evaluation—they need to fit your application. Defining criteria is particularly tough—does "performance" in the above example mean execution speed or flexibility? Define your criteria in a separate document and use more

Table 14.4.   Benchmarking Matrix for Three Similar Commercial-Off-the-Shelf Programs. Benchmarking is a systematic approach to compare functions, weight evaluation criteria, and rate options against pre-determined scenarios. This table shows an example comparison of three different tools with generic features.

Key Feature	Weight	A	B	C
Modeling flexibility	15%	75	60	70
Functionality	10%	60	60	70
Data import/export	5%	50	60	40
Computer platforms (availability)	15%	30	50	70
Cost (initial and annual)	10%	45	80	40
Performance	15%	60	70	65
User interface	10%	50	60	80
Use of 3D graphics	10%	20	25	40
Interfaces to other tools	5%	20	70	55
Plotting and reporting	5%	50	70	50
Total Weighted Scores	100%	48.25	59.50	61.00

words to make them clear. Also, set criteria and weights using a small group that represents users, customers, and developers so you'll get diverse opinions. Keep the group small to avoid long, confusing lists of criteria and extensive disagreement on weighting. Finally, pick the sample problem yourself. Vendors often play "tricks"—selecting sample cases that seem difficult but just happen to align perfectly with their software's (or hardware's) features.

14.2.3   Effects on the Supporting Environment

The supporting environment consists of operating systems, processing hardware, and graphics hardware. In addition to describing the effects of technology on each, we'll also talk about consequences that cut across these areas.

Operating Systems

The operating system (OS) is the underlying software that makes a computer work. It manages memory, runs programs, interacts with users, handles inputs and outputs, controls system peripherals, and generally puts its stamp on every other piece of software that runs on it. Chapter 10 includes a good description of the types of systems you may encounter. What follows are historical, current, and potential trends in the OS and what they mean to M&S.

Rise, Fall, and Consolidation of the OS. Figure 14.4 shows how operating systems tend to become popular, hold their position for a while, and then gradually decline—the clear message is that sooner or later you have to switch! Over the years, operating systems also periodically disappear and leave fewer available.

One OS tends to dominate until a better one appears on the scene. The one exception to this trend has been UNIX, which has been around nearly 30 years, but it now has much less market share than Windows™ or Windows NT™.

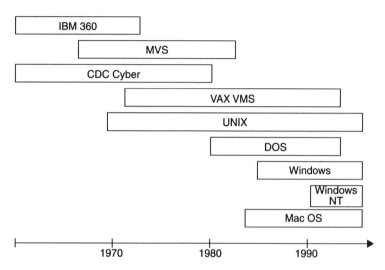

Fig. 14.4.   How Operating Systems Rise, Fall, and Consolidate. As this timeline suggests, every operating system becomes obsolete eventually.

The main results of a consolidation or decline of operating systems is that your software could be "orphaned" unless you're developing for an OS that survives the shakeout. Follow how much "market share" a particular OS has—it could help you choose what OS to use because better supporting tools may be available to you. A declining market share for your application's OS can signal a need to investigate porting to another. If you give your tools to other users, you'll want to concentrate your efforts on the OS they're using.

More Built-in Services. Modern operating systems are expanding what they can do (libraries of 3D graphics software, graphical user interfaces, and internet browsers are recent examples). Built-in services allow applications to do more for little extra cost, but they may shut out of the market third-party developers who have better products for this service (a net browser, for example).

Multi-tasking, Multi-processing. UNIX introduced an OS's ability to support several processes at the same time on one or many CPUs, but this multi-tasking is now common. It helps simulations run faster and improves support for distributed simulation.

Increased Address Space. OS developers are mirroring the trend among hardware manufacturers towards ever more address space, with 32- and 64-bit operating systems now widely available. Increased word-size enables larger simulations with greater accuracy and promises to make simulations more robust and capable.

Improved Object Orientation. Several operating systems have undergone re-writes to make them more object-oriented so we can access OS services as "objects" from within applications. Naturally, object-oriented applications are in the best position to take advantage of this trend. Some operating systems also permit users to add their own objects.

Improved Network Support. Operating systems now make services available to applications over the network, which means they match the entire local area network rather than individual platforms. This improves support for client-server applications and distributed simulations.

Internet as an OS? By extending the idea of local networks, we can imagine the internet itself mutating into a new type of "operating system." Under this scenario users access and run applications without knowing what computer is supporting them. The entire network becomes one massive, time-shared computer with many processing units available. The web browser would become the OS's interface. If this happens, distributed simulations could be easier to use, but it's unclear how fast things would run. Network traffic, rather than a particular CPU's performance, would likely be the bottleneck. A common environment for software development would also help. Java is trying to fill this role. It's a common, object-oriented, development language for internet applications.

Processing Hardware

In discussing processing hardware, we first deal with the basic elements—mainframes, workstations, microcomputers—and then move on to parallel computing and network computers. *Mainframes* simultaneously support many users and require special facilities and staff. *Workstations* support a handful of users and tend to be dispersed into individual workgroups. *Microcomputers* or *personal computers* (PCs) are desktop machines usually used by one person. *Parallel-processing* technologies support using multiple CPUs at the same time to achieve a computing task. *Network computers* are just appearing in the marketplace; they interface inexpensively with the network and leave number crunching to other machines. See Chap. 10 for more detailed descriptions of computing hardware.

Hardware is critical because it constrains your software development. This is why, when you start a new development from scratch, it's best to determine the software requirements *before* deciding on the hardware. When you try to apply new technology, always consider what new hardware to buy (if you can afford it) rather than trying to "force fit" new applications into existing hardware. Chapter 10 contains an excellent discussion of hardware appropriate for various applications. Here are some hardware trends and consequences:

Limited Life for Architectures. Remember the trajectory-simulation example earlier in this chapter? It was originally hosted on a large mainframe. The scheduled disappearance of this mainframe forced migration to a supercomputer. Hardware architectures, like operating systems, don't live long (usually less than ten years for a particular microprocessor family). Most manufacturers stay with a hardware architecture as long as they can, but sooner or later they must redesign the low-level hardware to continue improving speed. That usually means rewriting applications. Although this rewrite is painful, the eventual benefits (much better performance) usually outweigh the cost. We must develop simulations knowing that, sooner or later, processing hardware will change drastically and probably require significant changes to our software. This is the time to think about moving to another architecture because the re-hosting effort may be similar either way.

Improved Performance at Lower Prices. CPU power continues to increase geometrically (by a factor of two every three years since 1960) while its cost decreases. Some applications genuinely require the very high performance of their hosting hardware (mainframe/workstation/microcomputer), but many would run just as well on lower, much less expensive, equipment. Right now, high-end microcomputers have roughly the same ability as low-end or even mid-range workstations. Thus, rehosting simulations to new hardware may greatly decrease total cost, even considering its own expense. Look at price versus performance rather than just raw speed and consider mainframes, workstations, and microcomputers. Microcomputers are cheap and have tremendous abilities for most M&S applications.

With the continual increase in CPU performance, why is simulation performance still an issue? Modern CPUs do a lot more—graphical user interfaces, 3D graphics, finer time-steps, increased network interaction. But analysts also naturally increase the resolution of their analysis (whether they need to or not)— for example, generating more discrete events or more simulation objects. A better way to apply increased CPU speed is to explore more trade spaces by trying more cases and therefore developing a better understanding of the problem.

Migration from Centralized to Distributed, Desktop Computing. Over the last two decades, computing has moved from large, centralized machines toward workstations and PCs. Workstations are convenient for simulation development by small teams of analysts and developers because the team has complete control over its computing environment. PCs have traditionally been relegated to activities such as word-processing or spreadsheets but are quickly becoming important for simulation development. In fact, it's very convenient to have word-processing, presentation, and simulation tools together on the PC. Additionally, software-development tools for PCs are very robust and are much less expensive than those found on workstations. PCs are also most numerous, with unit sales in the millions, whereas workstations sell in hundreds of thousands.

The increasing ability and accessibility of microcomputers again increase the pressure to move simulation tools to them. Consider that microcomputers can be or go anywhere—it's quite reasonable to put your simulation tools and results on a disk and demonstrate or present results right in your customer's office.

Improved Parallel Processing. Using multiple CPUs simultaneously to run complex simulations is becoming easier. This parallel processing can use specially built hardware or harness the built-in parallelism of a computer network. We need special software to make parallel processing work efficiently because we have to balance the amount of processing (the "load") on each CPU so processors don't sit idle. This requires either special operating systems (on special-purpose hardware) or tailored software that controls the applications. Computational fluid dynamics, weather prediction, and other special requirements can justify unusual equipment or software, so don't be afraid to use it if you need it.

Unfortunately, software for parallel processing needs to be written differently from software for traditional, serial processing. We must decide if the faster execution is worth the extra time and effort. Parallel-processing applications are also difficult to debug, but improved compilers are now able to take existing code and partially automate changes needed to make it suitable for parallel processing.

Network Computers. These computers are just appearing. Their only purpose now is to interface with the internet and run programs available over the network. But they bear watching because they might become the hardware front-end to the internet-based "operating system" mentioned in the previous section. In the future, you might interact with a simulation running on a remote computer server by means of a web browser running on a network computer in your office.

Graphics Hardware

Computer-graphics technology is expanding rapidly, and hardware has evolved to keep pace. The main trends in graphics are moving capability from software to hardware and giving users better access through improved accelerator boards and special terminals.

Moving Graphics from Software to Hardware. Moving graphics to hardware has an obvious motivation—speed. Special-purpose hardware operates graphics well enough to speed up results by several orders of magnitude. Workstations on the market now often have three-dimensional (3D) shaded graphics as standard equipment for "real-time" manipulation of geometric objects. One positive consequence for M&S is that we no longer have to write software for these tasks (which can be as much as 50% of the code in some applications). Of course, placing graphics abilities in hardware can also restrict your simulation to a particular platform. Thus, when the graphics hardware changes, so must your software. Adopting graphics standards, such as X or OpenGL, is beginning to combat this problem (see Chap. 13).

Increasing Graphics Abilities. Recently, graphics accelerator boards have begun to bring high-end, 3D graphics to workstations and PCs. These products are relatively inexpensive and are already forcing vendors of graphics software and hardware to reduce prices and re-host applications. Another trend is the creation of graphics "terminals" that support popular graphics standards like X (2D) or OpenGL (3D). So-called X or OpenGL terminals have just enough computing power to handle the graphics for user-interfaces or basic 3D displays, leaving most of the application on a central mainframe or workstation. This increased access means everyone (users, customers) will want it for M&S. Network computers continue this trend by interpreting HyperText Markup Language (HTML) and Virtual Reality Markup Language (VRML) in the same way.

How to Handle Changes in Graphics Technology. The application and the number and type of users determine which way to go on graphics hardware. If you must have 3D, shaded graphics that animate dynamically, you have to invest in the hardware and accept the expense and narrow options. If you must distribute your simulation to many users, who may own a wide range of hardware, you'll probably want to offer simpler displays for those with simpler equipment. Hopefully, cheap 3D-graphics boards for microcomputers will begin to solve this problem.

Common Consequences of Changes in Technology

As you may have noticed, whenever the OS, CPU, or graphics hardware changes, the application software must change. As a result, we must

- *Rewrite source code.* Certain elements, such as input/output features and graphics, may be different, which forces major changes. Variations in memory structure, word size, and so on, also cause rewriting. And developers often improve performance by using some feature that depends on the OS or the hardware—a feature that may disappear from new versions of the OS or hardware.

- *Recompile source code,* even the part you didn't have to re-write. Typically, we discover something that doesn't compile successfully, usually for an obscure reason (sometimes because of bugs in the compiler itself!). That's why you must know where all the source code is.

- *Make sure supporting software works with the new OS*—compilers, editors, integrated COTS products, etc. You're in trouble if the vendor for a product you must have takes months to upgrade its product to support the new OS. Worse, the vendor may decide not to support the OS or hardware you're using, leaving you high and dry.

- *Watch out for problems with emulation.* Emulation promises that the new OS or hardware will mimic behavior so your old code will still run without being recompiled. But applications usually run much slower under emulation because every instruction your program generates must be parsed, interpreted, restructured, and sent to the new system.

Given these headaches, why would anyone want to change the supporting environment? First, because the new technology really is worth the effort. I remember the first time I saw texture mapping and thought immediately about overlaying satellite images on terrain and on the entire earth for orbital simulations. Modifying the code to handle images and convert them to textures seemed like a small price to pay. Second, you typically have no choice! As time marches on, you may not be able to maintain your old system. For example, all the commercial products you're using change to support a new architecture, so you can't use the latest versions. Third, and perhaps more subtly, you have to stay current in order to attract top talent and cutting-edge assignments to your group! We'll discuss strategies for dealing with software changes in Sec. 14.3.1.

14.2.4   How New Technologies Affect Simulation Construction

Chapter 10 discusses many technologies that affect how we build a simulation, but here we'll focus on understanding their trends and benefits. Will the technology or tool help us develop simulations faster? Will long-term maintenance be easier? If basic programming paradigms are changing, how will these changes affect current and developing simulations? One common thread is proper software engineering. In Chap. 6, we discuss the Software Engineering Institute's maturity rating. Knowing how your organization rates can help you evaluate technology— new technology won't help if your basic practices are flawed. Let's discuss some technology trends.

Changing Programming Paradigms and Languages have always strongly influenced simulation development. Chapter 10 details some of the choices available in languages and environments. Two trends dominate. First, we're moving away from structured programming towards object-oriented development. (We'll talk more about this move to object-oriented languages below.) Second, programming is more abstract because we're moving from third generation (FORTRAN, C) and object-oriented (C++, Smalltalk) languages to fourth generation integrators of databases, user interfaces, and statistical-analysis functions. Examples include Visual C++, Visual Basic, Powerbuilder, Delphi, or even Mathematica. This second trend means more non-programmers can develop software for M&S. These remarkable changes make it important to closely monitor software engineering.

Proliferation of Computer Aided Software Engineering (CASE) Tools. Many tools, supporting many different development methods, help us create software products. These range from diagramming tools for specific methods to reverse-engineering software for particular languages. Vendors are rushing new tools to market as fast as they can to support every new language or development fad. How do we sort through the avalanche of tools to determine which ones might be helpful? Some tools are "no-brainers": Chap. 10 points out the importance of configuration management, even on small projects (my own favorites are memory-leak detectors for C and C++ programs). But if you have a hard time stating how you'll use a tool, don't get it. Also consider the scale of the work you're doing. You may need expensive diagramming or planning tools for a 500,000-line simulation, but they probably don't make sense for developing a "quick and dirty" simulation to answer a question by next week.

Increasing Acceptance of Object-Oriented Techniques. Object-oriented programming models real-world objects (airplanes, tanks, power-plants, conveyor belts) as software objects. The idea is to encapsulate an object's attributes, functions, and data within a single software unit. (For more details, see *Object Oriented Analysis and Design with Applications* [Booch 1991]). The difficulty seems to be that object-oriented languages take some getting used to. C++, the most well-known example, requires months of effort to learn and much longer to master. In addition to learning the syntax of a new language, developers must take a new approach to analysis and design. You must train or hire competent object-oriented developers. Afterall, you can write spaghetti code in any language.

In many ways, object-oriented languages are a natural fit for M&S. The purpose of simulation, after all, is to model real-world elements in the computer. Developing this software may take a bit longer, but the payoff comes whenever we have to change or reuse it. We can change small parts of the code with fewer "side effects," and easily reuse objects in other applications. Many vendors are now selling libraries of objects that you can "plug in" to your object-oriented simulations.

When should you adopt this technology? Good indicators are the appearance of standards from the American National Standards Institute and of supporting software for the given technology. We're seeing both now, and new technologies in many areas have an "OO flavor." Using an investment analogy, object-oriented languages are a definite "buy" for new applications.

Expanding Compilers. Compilers, the basic tools for building software applications, are rapidly adding features. These are the Rapid Application Development Languages discussed in Sec. 10.3.2. They're "going visual"—loops, case statements, variable assignments, and data structures appear as icons or menu items that you can "drag and drop" into a schematic representation of your program. Other features include built-in support for graphical user interfaces, databases, and printing. Most come with a "template project" that you can copy and use as a starting point for new applications. Although these expanded compilers take up a lot more disk space on your workstation or PC, they ease development of new applications.

Improving Simulation Languages and Environments. Programming languages tailored for simulation have existed since the early 1960s (see Sec. 10.3.3). Some advertise the ability to build simulations "without coding" because you don't have to type in text. Instead, you select icons that abstractly represent pre-defined, useful functions for particular applications. Figure 14.5 shows a display from COMNET III, commercial software developed by CACI, Inc. of LaJolla, California, to simulate communications equipment and networks. Icons on the display represent objects such as wide-area or local-area networks, routers, or data sources.

Using these displays, analysts and customers can see immediate progress and can more quickly zero in on what they really want from a simulation. They can rapidly try new ideas and approaches and discard poor options, thus responding quickly to customers' needs. Contrary to stereotype, these tools are more than toys—they generate real work and real results, even for complex systems.But they're not a universal "cure" because their pre-defined objects don't match every part of the real world. For these special cases, you'll need to program (using a built-in interface) new objects that become part of your simulation's environment.

More Automated Development of Graphical User Interfaces (GUI). GUIs began to appear in the early 1980s and really took off when the Macintosh computer appeared in 1984. Although easier for users, GUIs require much more development. Fortunately, software now helps us design them graphically. We can lay out buttons, windows, sliders, etc. in two dimensions and then push a button to generate code that runs the interface.

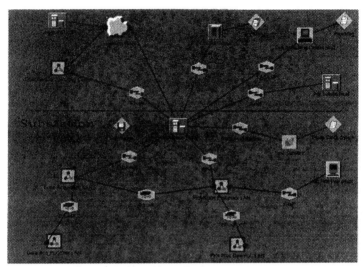

Fig. 14.5.   Using COMNET III to Rapidly Develop Simulations. New simulation environments, such as COMNET III for network simulations, provide graphical representations to represent pre-defined functions. Although not a universal "cure," these environments can help analysts and customers see immediate progress and more quickly zero in on what the simulation must do.

Should you apply this technology? If few people will use your application, you can get by without a GUI or automated development software. But GUIs make learning easier and can reduce operator errors when designed properly. If you need to make a tool work across operating systems (say UNIX and Windows), you can find software that will allow you to create the interface once and then translate it to other platforms. Of course, you'll have to generate new code whenever you change the interface.

Increasing Integration of Databases. As discussed in Chap. 9, modern simulations often rely on databases to manage scenarios, parameters, simulation events, objects, and results. Database design is different from software design, although the two are closely related. Today, databases are typically relational or object-oriented (see Sec. 10.2.4), and you'll choose the type that's better for your application. You can find various software that will help you lay out and create the databases you need. In deciding which one to use, check to see how they match up with your language compilers and programming environments.

14.2.5   How New Technologies Affect the Way We Use Simulations

Graphics, visualizing techniques, user interfaces, and changes in communications equipment and networking are greatly affecting modeling and simulation.

Graphics and Visualizing Techniques

The tremendous growth in computer-graphics applications reflects their power to communicate and inspire. Over the last twenty years, we've come ever closer to making computer-generated images mirror reality. Although still a long way from perfect, high-quality graphics are now more available than ever, and the cost of producing good graphics continues to decrease. In this section we'll discuss how technology has affected data display, three-dimensional viewing, geometric modeling, photo-realism, and animation.

Improving How We See Data. The most familiar form of data display for simulation users is the venerable XY plot. Today, a lot of commercial and public-domain software can produce virtually any type of 2D or 3D plot. For example, Commercial Off-the-Shelf (COTS) software can produce charts, contour plots in color, and animated strip charts. Map displays are also readily available from public-domain databases and COTS tools. Unless you have special needs, use COTS software for these tasks.

Moving toward 3D Views. The same commercial and public-domain packages have tackled 3D surface plots, 3D bar graphs, and realistic system geometries—including shaded, 3D displays. The same display often combines 2D and 3D graphics. Figure 14.6 shows a performance parameter for a satellite constellation. One window shows the coverage contours in color on a rectangular projection of the earth's surface; the other depicts them in three dimensions.

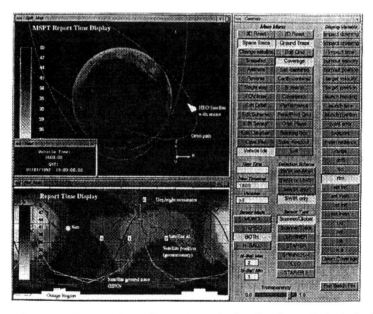

Fig. 14.6.   Display in Two and Three Dimensions of a Satellite Constellation's Performance.
3D graphics displays and strong graphical user interfaces help users interpret data and make decisions.

Improved Geometric Modeling. Geometric modeling is critical to viewing and analyzing data. Computer-aided design software has improved so much during the last ten years that we can model sophisticated shapes on PCs. To apply these technologies to your simulation, decide what models you need for graphics displays and animations. Do the geometries include unusual curved surfaces? Complex part assemblies? Intersections? Standards also play a role here. Standards for exchanging models allow us to import them into other applications. Examples are output formats under Interactive Graphics Exchange Specification (IGES), Autocad (DXF), or Wavefront (.obj).

Increasing Photo-realism. Once only appearing in high-priced films, very high-end graphics are now becoming more widely available and somewhat less expensive. Hardware and software can produce images like photographs—with textures, realistic lighting, reflections, and shadows. But do you need them? Sometimes, people deride them as "pretty pictures." Yet, photo-realistic graphics can convert stacks of unintelligible numbers into easily understood results. They can also help people make good decisions by providing a new way to understand complex results without having to delve into the technical details. Don't underestimate the importance of this "technical marketing." The danger, of course, is that people tend to trust realistically rendered results just because they look right!

Increasing Use of Animation. Static images can communicate, but animation can often bring out more detail and generate more insight. Consider data from a weather radar—a static image of the results tells you where it's raining at a particular instant, but an animation shows you how the storm cells are moving and allows you to predict where it will rain next. Software for workstations and PCs can produce movie-quality animations. Videotapes and "movie clips" are replacing traditional viewgraphs or plots in briefings. Animations are commonly shared over the internet, and most hardware platforms support "movie" displays.

User Interfaces

User interfaces obviously affect how we use simulations. As tools become easier to use, more people will use them more often, eliminating the need for a "priesthood" who, through painstaking toil, have learned their idiosyncrasies. We'll still need trained analysts who understand the way internal models operate, but visual interfaces can reduce input errors and help operators run a simulation more efficiently. That's why user interfaces have moved from text-based systems to virtual reality.

Moving from Text Input to Graphical User Interfaces (GUI). Traditional user interfaces are based on text. They either read data from a file ("batch" input) or prompt input from the user's console (interactive). (I've described GUIs in Sec. 14.2.4). In adopting GUI technology, remember that it's often more efficient to use an editor and quickly change a batch file than to laboriously point and click your way through a GUI to the parameter that needs changing. Batch input is also ideal for setting up parametric or monte-carlo studies, in which you must slightly change multiple parameters over many runs. Likewise, interactive input is robust and requires no special hardware. Thus, you should probably apply GUI technology only to parts of your user interface. New research areas for GUIs are three-dimensional "handles" attached to geometry or objects in the simulation, so we can manipulate them more intuitively, and 3D cursors we can move throughout the display.

Increasing Virtual Reality (VR). Virtual reality divides into augmented reality, which simulates only part of the user's surroundings, and immersive reality, which envelops users in a virtual world. Most systems employ sight and sound, but some are also using touch for feedback (see Chap. 16 for more detail).

Applications of VR to modeling and simulation include such things as virtual wind tunnels; analysts explore data by "flying" through it (e.g., the fluid flow within a jet engine). Figure 14.7 shows the Cave project in the Electronic Visualization Laboratory at the University of Illinois-Chicago (a room reminiscent of the fictitious "holodeck" on Star Trek's Starship Enterprise—at least with respect to audio-visual feedback). VR could likewise provide a powerful way to understand complex simulation scenarios and results. One can imagine "flying" through a scenario (in a battle simulator, for example), to check the position and composition of units before starting a run.

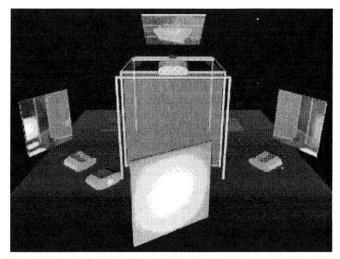

Fig. 14.7.   Configuration of Cave. Facilities such as the Electronic Visualization Laboratory's Cave at the University of Illinois-Chicago provide powerful ways to investigate and understand complex simulation scenarios and results by immersing users in a virtual reality environment that allows them to "fly" through a given scenario. The user sits in the center room above and views displays projected on the walls.

Using VR technology requires a lot of money for hardware and software, but these costs will go down over time. Software frameworks for virtual reality are also available; they contain virtual "objects," from which we can construct VR systems. The logical extension of user-interface technology is controlling a simulation through virtual reality, as is essentially the case for military and commercial flight simulators.

Communication and Networking

With the tremendous growth of the internet and increased availability of communication technology, it becomes possible to share character, voice, images, and video across great distances. Thus, groups around the world can more easily share results of simulations or work together on complex, distributed simulations. For details on network terms and communication issues, see Chap. 15. This section discusses trends in distributed simulation and data sharing.

Increased Use of Distributed Simulation. Perhaps the most significant trend in modeling and simulation is the accelerating use of several simulators through serial or parallel connections. File interfaces connect serial simulations, from which we combine detailed individual results to represent a phenomenon efficiently at a higher level. Parallel (distributed) simulations run "federations" of simulations at the same time. Simulation developers used to write a single, monolithic program that tried to do everything. Now that we're reusing software more and developing with advanced tools, it's becoming easier to piece simulations together.

Protocols for distributed simulations consist of the Aggregate Level Simulation Protocol (ALSP), Distributed Interactive Simulation (DIS), and High Level Architecture/Run-Time Infrastructure (HLA/RTI). The ALSP has a central executive that rigidly controls time progression for each actor in the simulation. It also maintains a central database of objects and messages the actors share. DIS follows a real-time clock, without central control of time, so participating actors must conform to real time. HLA is the emerging architecture for distributed simulation [DMSO 1996], which the DOD must move to when it's fully developed. It tries to combine the features of ALSP [MITRE 1996] and DIS [IEEE 1993]. Chapter 13 discusses these protocols in much more detail and covers other technologies, such as common object request broker architecture (CORBA), which help run networked applications [OMG 1991].

Why do distributed simulation? Not necessarily to make simulations run faster—they'll often run more slowly unless we code especially for parallel processing. Rather, we want to take advantage of the best models available at different locations and to have these models affect one another as they run (so we can model "collective" behaviors). Distributed simulation also supports human-in-the-loop testing, and improves development because we can reuse some simulations. Of course, an offsetting issue is the need to change each simulation to pass messages to the confederation. It's easier now than it used to be, but it's still a pain in the neck!

Increasing Use of the Internet. When I discussed the internet earlier, I concentrated on using it as a source of information about new technologies. It's also a warehouse of information which can help us use simulations—of data (scenarios, models, algorithms), of code fragments, and of free software tools we can use in developing simulations. The internet is also an excellent way to send simulation results to customers and colleagues for review and collaboration, using browsers, web-page editors, and other web-development software to make it easier.

Increasing Telecommunication in Video Formats. Most workstations and many PCs now support formats for accepting and displaying video. Some have video cameras to record video e-mail or hold video "conversations" across networks. Users share on their local screens image data and sketch illustrations that appear immediately on receivers' screens. Image compression now makes this possible over ordinary phone lines. How can these techniques affect M&S? Imagine using video-teleconferencing to share data and accelerate analysis. Or sharing 3D animations of computer graphics to explain complex results. Or having your colleagues redline presentations and collaborative reports in real time and feed off one another's ideas. There are many possibilities.

14.3   Developing a Plan to Employ New Technology

How do we apply new technologies to our models and simulations? What strategies can relieve some of the negative consequences our research and evaluation uncover? How do we resolve the risks of using a particular technology? We're now ready for phase three—developing a concrete plan for employing new technology. First, we must use methods and develop strategies that prepare us in advance for change:

- Adopt flexible development methods
- Practice good software engineering
- Make software portable
- Soundly manage risk

Second, we have to write and then execute the plan:

- Using identified risks, refine the "when" column in the original capabilities matrix for each technology we'll adopt
- Schedule tasks needed to integrate new technologies on time
- Document the capabilities matrix, the risk, and the task breakdown
- Start carrying out the plan, updating as necessary by iterating through the entire process outlined in this chapter

14.3.1   Prepare in Advance for Change

It may be oversimplifying to say that "an ounce of prevention equals a pound of cure," but you can take definite steps to anticipate technological change. By doing so, you can soften many of the negative consequences discovered earlier from research and evaluation. Assume change will occur sooner, not later.

Adopt Flexible Methods for Development

The methods you use to develop models and simulations strongly affect your ability to adopt new technology. For example, if you rigidly define the entire system from the beginning, you'll naturally want to avoid any action that might change or expand these requirements. In addition, building simulations and adapting new technology are iterative rather than linear. Thus, if your methods don't support iteration, they'll also inhibit innovation simply by limiting the number of chances to apply new technology. The key is flexible methods that support change and allow for new technologies while minimizing risks.

Chapter 10 already talked about methods for developing software. They all share a common thread of tasks from defining requirements to designing, building, testing, and using the software. The differences concern how often and how quickly you follow the thread. Here we'll briefly review the main approaches and evaluate how well they meet our criteria.

Waterfall. The traditional, sequential model of project development travels once through the sequence. It fixes requirements at the beginning and proceeds linearly until it satisfies those requirements. This approach doesn't handle changes easily and thus discourages using new technology. Also, it tends to provide only one chance to consider new technologies: the initial design phase. If you're already past this phase, you may still be able to apply new technology to the development process itself, such as inserting a new system to manage configurations.

Incremental. This method also fixes requirements but identifies interim stages or "builds," each of which is a complete, working simulation for the subset of requirements it represents. We go through the development phases for each build. This method suffers from fixed requirements but does allow us to introduce new technologies for each new build.

Evolutionary. In this method, we don't know the final requirements at first. Instead, we "discover" them along the way. Each build is a working simulation for the requirements we know at the time. This method supports change and gives us many chances to use new technology. Feedback from software users helps us set new priorities after each build. The Rapid Development Method is closely related to this approach [Spuck 1993].

Spiral. The spiral approach, popularized by Barry Boehm [1988], also supports variable requirements and gives us chances to use new software techniques. Our simulation does more as the development spirals (iterates) outward. But it adds risk assessment to user feedback before starting each iteration. Designers estimate the technical risk for each new requirement—a natural step when evaluating whether to use a new simulation technology.

Rapid Prototyping. This is a variant of the spiral method in which we quickly develop a prototype to try out a concept—usually something considered risky. Once we test the concept, we usually discard "quick and dirty" code, which is unsuitable for long-term production. This approach can be ideal for trying out a new technology if you can afford it.

I recommend the evolutionary or spiral approaches to take advantage of new technology, because they support change and iteration. I believe the spiral method may have a slight advantage because it assesses risk before each iteration. For especially risky technologies, I recommend rapid prototyping to try something out without affecting actual development—as long as you can stick to discarding the resulting code and keeping only the knowledge gained.

Once you've selected appropriate methods, document them for your group so they become official policy and an important part of your technology employment plan. The other strategies mentioned in this section can fit into the basic framework you've selected.

Practice Good Software Engineering

Good software design and engineering can make it much easier to adopt new technologies. Simulation software thrown together to meet a short-term need can be painful to change when technology forces you to do so. Documentation describing models and software usually doesn't exist, and a simulation often withers away when the specialists who developed it retire or move on because no one else can figure out what they did. Many chapters in this text outline good software-engineering practices, but here are a few I believe are particularly important to adapting new technology:

Document. This may seem obvious, but it's most often neglected. I'm referring not only to comments in the code but also to separate records describing where the source code files are, how the application can be compiled, and what code formatting conventions, naming schemes, and so on you used during development. In addition to a developer's reference which describes the software design, you should also provide a technical reference which describes the physics, math, and algorithms behind the software. As an example of how this applies to new technology, consider the dilemma faced by a simulation developer who wishes to apply object-oriented techniques to new software that replaces an older simulation. Without good documentation, the developer might have to reverse-engineer the application by deciphering the source code.

Manage the Configuration. To adopt new technology, you should know what you have. Configuration management keeps track of versions of source code, documentation, data files, and similar information so you can retrieve any previous version. This reduces the risk of adding new technologies because you can go back to what you had before if you mess up.

Review. Some kind of peer or supervisory review can allow you to insert new technology as a solution to problems the review discovers. Reviews also improve the software's quality, which makes it easier to adopt new technology later on.

Consider the Software Lifecycle. The software lifecycle encompasses not only developing but also using, enhancing, and maintaining software over the long term. Most simulation tools of consequence are modified continually during their lifetimes as new uses and new technologies arise. When budgeting for simulation development, you must consider long-term maintenance, which usually takes the biggest bite out of your budget. For example, at some point, you'll almost certainly have to re-host your application or interface it with a distributed simulation. Eventually, a tool may die from disuse, but it often makes sense to plan for possible "reincarnation" (documentation is essential for this). It's a good idea to have a transition plan that will take the lessons learned, algorithms developed, and in some cases even source code on to future simulations.

Make Your Software Portable

Perhaps the most annoying consequence of changing technology is the need to update and upgrade your simulation software. If you don't, your application will probably die. The good news is that it's never too late to start making your simulation tools easy to transfer from one development or execution environment to another. This portability means your software will need fewer changes whenever you must move it to a new environment. For more details, see Kevin Jameson's *Multi-Platform Code Management* [1994]. Here, we'll discuss separating functions and adopting standards as ways to make your applications portable.

Separate Functions. Think about the functions that are most likely to change during the tool's lifetime and code them separately, so new technologies for that function will require changes only in certain places, rather than in hundreds of locations throughout the code. This principle applies to more than just the obvious elements, such as the user interface or the graphics displays. It includes functions that depend on operating systems, non-standard compiler features, distributed simulation protocols, network interfaces, interfaces to commercial or government off-the-shelf tools, and much more. You should consider for separation anything that isn't part of the application's core. Ask yourself, "Does this part of the code interface with anything outside the simulation?" If the answer is yes, separate it if you can. If you were using procedural techniques for software development, you could, for example, collect all user-interface or graphics-display functions in separate, named modules. An object-oriented approach might require burying technology-specific code in abstract base classes or "helper" classes to reduce places that will need changes.

Adopt Standards. Standards offer one of the best hopes for making simulations portable. We can broadly define "standard" as any method, format, technology, interface, language, or tool that is widely accepted and used by the computing industry or the modeling and simulation community. Adopting a widespread standard usually assures us the application will run even if the execution environment (hardware/software) changes. Writing your core simulation software in one of the American National Standards Institute's (ANSI) standard languages, for example, ensures that many compilers can compile the application on many different platforms.

The key to picking the right standards is market share. You must track new and existing standards to see how users are adopting them. Standards typically come about, not through committees (although that happens eventually!) but because the marketplace adopts someone's very popular approach to solving a problem. One vendor gets an advantage whenever many customers adopt their "standard." Then, other vendors come up with their own competing "standards" (even pooling their resources if the first outfit gets enough of a headstart), and a "standards war" begins. Eventually the marketplace sorts it out and all of the vendors come together behind the winner. Sometimes the best technical solution doesn't win out (remember Beta versus VHS?). Unfortunately, it's usually not practical to wait until a standards war settles out before adopting a new technology. You must watch the market and be ready to change if necessary. Chapter 13 provides a very complete discussion of standards and their effect on M&S, and Table 13.8 categorizes and lists some official standards. The DOD's standards in the Technical Architecture Framework for Information Management are even more comprehensive [DISA 1996] (See Fig. 13.1).

Manage Risk

Understanding the risks in adopting a new technology is critical to deciding whether to go forward with it. Here's a simple approach to risk management, patterned roughly after that used for the Cassini project at the Jet Propulsion Laboratory [Surber 1995]:

1. Identify and characterize all significant risks by severity (consequence × likelihood of occurrence). Select risks you'll manage.

2. Analyze risks quantitatively or qualitatively. Compare risks against system requirements or benchmark projects.

3. Manage and track risks. Develop ways to combat risks and periodically report their status.

Identify and Characterize Risks. Start by listing the risks associated with a particular technology from the capabilities matrix. To do this, you can draw on your engineering or project-management experience, plus your knowledge of the money and people available to get the job done, lessons learned, interviews with other experts, and so on. Be sure to consider the risks of **not** adopting the candidate technology as well as those of using it.

Tables 14.5 through 14.7 show how you can characterize risks by defining the likelihood of a negative event occurring as well as its consequence. Rate both on a 0–10 scale, as shown, ranging from "very low" to "high." You define the percentages of likelihood and describe the consequence—I've included some examples. Then, you multiply likelihood by consequence to compute a "risk class" and list risks you'll consider for management.

Table 14.5.   Characterizing Risks Based on Likelihood.
One way to quantify risk is to define the likelihood of a negative event occurring.

Rating	Adjective	Description
8–10	High	>10%
5–7	Medium	5–10%
3–4	Low	1–5%
0–2	Very Low	<1%

Table 14.6.   Characterizing Risks Based on Consequences. Another way to quantify risk is to assess the consequences of a negative event.

Rating	Adjective	Description
8–10	High	Loss of project—new technology is total failure OR tool becomes useless because no new technology introduced
5–7	Medium	Moderate harm to capability
3–4	Low	Small harm to project
0–2	Very Low	Minor inconvenience

Table 14.7.   Characterizing Overall Risk. You can calculate total risk as the product of likelihood and consequence. Using this approach, you can quantify the risks associated with different approaches, rank them, and decide which ones you'll manage.

Product*	Risk Class	Adjective	Management and Reporting
>50	A	Significant	Managed by project lead, reported weekly
20–50	B	Moderate	Managed by team member, reported monthly
10–19	C	Minor	Not managed
5–9	D	Slight	Not managed
<5	E	Insignificant	Not managed

* Product = Likelihood × Consequences

Analyze Risks. You can evaluate risks quantitatively in terms of cost, schedule, manpower, etc. or qualitatively with respect to some benchmark project (the "Reference Check" mentioned in Sec. 14.2.2). If a project similar to yours used a technology successfully, you might lower the risk in your matrix. At this point, you should be able to decide whether to use a given technology.

Reduce and Track Risks. I've already discussed strategies for reducing risks of adopting new technologies. One other way to reduce risk is to start by biting off something you can chew. Don't try to build the "mother of all simulations" using a new technology that your analysts and developers don't know. Pick a project (or a piece of one) with clearly defined goals that fits well with the technology you're considering. If you fail, you haven't bet the farm on the outcome. If you're successful, you look like a genius and set yourself up to try something more ambitious next time. Tracking risks involves setting a regular schedule for reporting their status and making someone responsible for each one. Regular reporting will allow you to see trends—is a risk increasing, decreasing, or remaining constant?

14.3.2   Writing and Carrying Out the Plan

Now write your plan for using new technology; it records the decisions you've made and the tasks you've generated (using quality functional deployment or some other method). Include the capabilities matrix and your associated plan for managing risk. Document precisely how various technologies will apply to specific elements of your selected simulation project. As you consider each candidate technology write down your decisions and tasks before moving to the next one. Notice that developing a simulation is iterative, so your plan will grow and develop along with it.

14.4   Summary and Conclusions

Throughout your modeling and simulation project, you should repeat the three-phase process I've presented because it pays to be continually on the prowl for new technologies that can benefit your work. To take advantage of new technology, you need to remember first, that the technology must be appropriate for your application; second, that the timing for insertion must be right; and third, that the payoff can be tremendous. Burgeoning new technology for modeling and simulation is fun and exciting, not ominous or threatening. Fear only sets in when we try to keep up with everything instead of targeting specific technologies that apply to our M&S activities. Managers should especially support continuing education for staff members and encourage technical currency at every opportunity.

14.5   Special Sources on Adopting New Technologies

The following tables capture some sources of information on new technologies for modeling and simulation, which you can use to keep your team up to date. These lists are current as of 1997 and provide a good indication of the type of resources you can expect to be available.

Table 14.8.   Usenet News Groups. This table presents some of the news groups that should be interesting to simulation developers and users.

comp.benchmarks	Hardware/software performance data, comparisons
comp.client-server	Client-server architectures, hardware and software
comp.compilers	General group regarding compiler technology
comp.databases	19 subgroups associated with specific database vendors, technologies
comp.graphics	30 subgroups: algorithms, animation, OpenGL, visualization, application-program interfaces
comp.internet	Internet technologies, applications
comp.lang	Many subgroups for programming languages: C, C++, Java, Perl, Fortran, you name it!
comp.newprod	General announcements on new products
comp.object	Object-oriented technologies
comp.org	Computer organizations: ACM, IEEE, etc.
comp.parallel	Parallel-processing hardware, applications
comp.simulation	General discussions on simulation
comp.soft-sys	15+ subgroups including .khoros, .math, .mathematica, .powerbuilder, .matlab
comp.software-eng	Discussion group for software engineering
comp.software.config-mgmt	Configuration-management approaches, software
comp.sys	Individual hardware vendors, 200+ subgroups, place to go for latest announcements, bug fixes, etc.
comp.unix	50+ subgroups: many Unix topics
comp.windows	15 subgroups: various topics on the Windows™ operating system
comp.windows.x	Discussion group for X-windows

Table 14.9.   Internet Search Engines, Indexes. This table lists some of the most commonly visited sites on the world wide web, which you can use to search for information.

Netscape Search	http://www.netscape.com/escapes/search/ntsrchmd-1.html
Yahoo Index	http://www.yahoo.com/
Open Text	http://index.opentext.com/
Alta Vista	http://www.altavista.digital.com/
Lycos	http://www.lycos.com/
DejaNews	http://www.dejanews.com/
WebCrawler	http://www.webcrawler.com/

Table 14.10.   Internet Sites. This table identifies several useful web sites devoted to modeling and simulation technology.

Modeling & Simulation Resource Repository (MSRR)	http://www.msrr.dmso.mil
Defense Modeling, Simulation and Tactical Technology Analysis Center (DMSTTIAC) Home Page	http://dmsttiac.hq.iitri.com/
Joint C4I at Naval Postgraduate School	http://www.stl.nps.navy.mil/c4i/
Defense Modeling and Simulation Office	http://www.dmso.mil/
DMSO links to other modeling & simulation URLs for DoD, Academia, Industry	http://www.dmso.mil/urls.html
Master Lists of Standards sites	http://www.cmpcmm.com/cc/standards.html

Table 14.11.   Conferences and Symposia. This table lists some of the regularly scheduled meetings and conferences that could be interesting to simulation developers and users.

Society for Computer Simulation Spring Multi-Conference	Combined conferences for the power industry, manufacturing, the military, and parallel computing (April)
ACM SIGGRAPH	Premier showcase of hardware and software for computer graphics (Late July or early August)
Military Operations Research Conference	War-gamer's paradise (June)
IEEE Visualization Conference	Graphics visualization and super-computing (October)
Simulation Interoperability Workshops	Distributed simulation (Spring/Fall)
AIAA Modeling & Simulation Technical Conference	Meeting on aerospace modeling and simulation (August)
SPIE Simulation Technology Conference	(March)

Table 14.12.   Printed Publications. This table identifies several important publications of interest to simulation developers and users.

Simulation Digest	ACM, P.O. Box 12115, Church Street Station, NY, NY 10249
ACM Transactions on Modeling and Computer Simulation	ACM, Inc., 1515 Broadway, NY, NY 10036
International Journal of Approximate Reasoning	Elsevier Science, Inc., P.O. Box 882, Madison Square Station, NY, NY 10159
Journal of Algorithms	Academic Press, Inc., 6277 Sea Harbor Drive, Orlando, FL 32887
Applied Mathematical Modeling	Elsevier Science, Inc., P.O. Box 882, Madison Square Station, NY, NY 10159
Computer Simulation, Modeling and Analysis—an electronic journal	See web page
European Journal of Operations Research	
ACM Transactions on Mathematical Software	ACM, Inc., 1515 Broadway, NY, NY 10036
Mathematics and Computer Simulation	Elsevier Science B. V., P.O. Box 211, 1000 AE Amsterdam, Netherlands
Transactions of the Society for Computer Simulation	The Society for Computer Simulation, P.O. Box 17900, San Diego, CA 92177
Simulation	Hilde Lynn, Managing Editor, Simulation, 4838 Ronson Court, Suite L, San Diego, CA 92111 Phone: (619) 277-3888
IIE Transactions on IE Research	David Goldsman, Simulation Area Co-Editor. School of Industrial and Systems Engineering, Georgia Institute of Technology, Atlanta, GA 30332-0205
IEEE Journal of Systems, Man and Cybernetics	Andrew P. Sage, School of Information Technology and Engineering, George Mason University, Fairfax, VA, 22030-4444
International Journal in Computer Simulation	George W. Zobrist, editor-in-chief, Department of Computer Science, University of Missouri-Rolla, Rolla, MO 65401 Phone: 573-341-4492
Operations Research	Barry Nelson, Department of Industrial Engineering and Management Sciences, McCormick School of Engineering and Applied Science, 2225 N. Campus Drive, Northwestern University, Evanston, IL 60208-3119
ORSA Journal on Computing	David Kelton, Simulation Area Editor, Department of Quantitative Analysis and Operations Management

References

Boehm, Barry W. "A Spiral Model of Software Development and Enhancement." *IEEE Computer Journal*. May, 1988.

Booch, Grady. 1991. *Object-Oriented Analysis and Design with Applications*. 2nd Edition. Menlo Park, CA: Benjamin Cummings.

Brassard, Michael. 1989. *The Memory Jogger Plus+ (TM)*. Metheun, MA: GOAL/QPC.

DISA. 1994. *DoD Technical Architecture Framework for Information Management. Volume 1, Overview*. Washington D.C.: Defense Information Systems Agency.

DMSO. 1996. *High Level Architecture Interface Specification. Version 1.0*. Washington, D.C.: Department of Defense.

IEEE. 1993. *IEEE Standard for Information Technology—Protocol for Distributed Interactive Simulation Applications: Entity Information and Interaction*. IEEE Standard 1278–1993. New York, NY: IEEE Computer Society.

Jameson, Kevin. 1994. *Multi-Platform Code Management*. Sebastopol, CA: O'Reilly & Associates, Inc.

Kehoe, Brendan P. 1992. *Zen and the Art of the Internet, A Beginner's Guide to the Internet*. Chester, PA: Widener University Computer Science Department.

MITRE Corporation. 1996. *Aggregate Level Simulation Protocol-Technical Specifications*. MITRE Informal Report. Contact Dave Prochnow at prochnow@mitre.org or go to http://ms.ie.org/alsp on the World Wide Web.

OMG. 1997. *The Common Object Request Broker: Architecture & Specification*. Revision 2.1, OMG Document Number 97-09-01. Digital Equipment Corp., Hewlett-Packard Co., HyperDesk Corp., NCR Corp., Object Design Inc., SunSoft Inc. (http://www.omg.org/corba/c2indx.htm)

Spuck, William H. 1993. *The Rapid Development Method (RDM)*. Pasadena, CA: Jet Propulsion Laboratory, California Institute of Technology (JPL D-9679).

Surber, F. T. February 28, 1995. *Cassini Project Risk Management Plan*. Pasadena, CA: Jet Propulsion Laboratory, California Institute of Technology (JPL D-11934).

CHAPTER 15

Network Issues in Distributed Simulation

Mark Pullen, *Department of Computer Science and C³I Center, George Mason University*

By definition distributed simulation involves multiple computers connected by a network, whose performance is critical to an effective simulation. The network often accounts for much of the simulation's cost and usually is on a critical development path because getting and configuring its elements take so long. Thus, we must understand the critical aspects of networking for distributed simulation.

Distributed simulation can be one of the most demanding networking applications known, depending on the simulations used, scope of the problem being simulated, and degree of distribution. Networking itself is an emerging discipline which brings together communications, computing, and protocol standards in a systems-engineering domain. Elements interact in complex ways that can be hard to understand. We'll thread our way through this complexity by focusing on real-time networks that incorporate people.

15.1   Overview

The main challenges in networking for distributed simulation are the need to

*   Transfer information in *real time*
*   *Multicast* (deliver the same transmission to multiple destinations)
*   Develop strong *network security*
*   Solve difficulties in *network management*
*   Develop adequate *standards* in each of these areas

In this chapter I use "simulator" to mean mock-up systems for virtual simulation; computers hosting simulations for individual, human-operated systems (*automated agents* or *automated forces*); or real weapons systems used to put data into other distributed simulations. Distributed interactive simulation (DIS) describes an architecture and standards for simulation within which simulators exchange state information over a network at frequent intervals. As a result, the entire simulation is able virtually to depict the simulated environment in real time to human participants. High-level architecture (HLA) refers to the U.S. Department of Defense's technical-management structure, which defines the role of distributed interactive and other networked simulations [U.S. Department of Defense 1996]. See Chap. 13 for a more detailed discussion of HLA.

15.1.1   Transferring Information in Real Time

Real-time information must be provided quickly enough to support decisions without delay. If we have an interactive system with humans in the information loop, it usually means the information is presented so it's understandable to humans. The most definitive guideline for real-time operation in distributed systems is IEEE Standard 1278.2, which quantifies how long a simulator has to display a result to users. Acceptable delays are defined in terms of *tightly coupled* or *loosely coupled* applications. The former have objects interacting with each other, such as high-performance aircraft engaging targets. The latter sense objects but don't have them interacting directly, such as spotting widely separated ground vehicles. The recommended maximum delay is 100 milliseconds in tightly coupled simulations and 300 milliseconds for loosely coupled simulations. Actual exercise experience shows that somewhat longer delays may be acceptable; in the 1994 exercise, Synthetic Theater of War Europe, delays up to 600 milliseconds occurred without complaints from human users.

Distributed simulation is supported by *packet-switched* networks, in which information is broken down into units (packets) containing everything needed to deliver them to another destination in the network. The real-time requirement is a serious design constraint in packet networks. The key advantage of packet networking is that packet switching doesn't require communication links of fixed capacity between each sender-receiver pair in the network. Instead, the network has enough connectivity among the participating computers (*nodes*) to allow them to support each other by forwarding blocks of information (*packets*) through intermediate nodes from the source to the intended receiver. A network so constructed costs much less and, if well designed, can provide superior communications, but predicting how many packets will flow through each processing node will be difficult or impossible. Whenever one of the links between nodes is already occupied transmitting a packet, any new arriving packets must go into a queue and await transmission. Cumulative delays in these queues, plus the time to actually transmit the packets through the links, must not exceed the time specified for transmission between sender and receiver. Modern networks adapt to presented traffic load by dynamically routing the packets so all data flows effectively share the network's resources. But for real-time traffic this may not be enough; today the most advanced networks provide ways for data flows to reserve transmission resources (data circuits and routers) in a path from sender to receiver, which will meet the real-time requirement.

A basic difference between typical data applications of networks and real-time applications, such as distributed simulation, is how they treat lost or corrupted data. Typical networks place a premium on *reliable transmission* for accuracy and completeness. They use *transport protocols* which automatically account for correct transmissions between sender and receiver, as well as retransmissions of missing or incorrect data. An example is the *transmission control protocol* (TCP) of the internet protocol suite. In real-time applications we must check data to confirm its validity, but data must arrive on time to be useful. Therefore, we may use a simpler transport protocol that doesn't try to retransmit packets with errors. Instead it simply drops the data, expecting the next transmission to update the value. The *user datagram protocol* (UDP) of the internet protocol suite can be used this way. The transmission control protocol is said to be reliable, whereas the user datagram protocol is a best-effort protocol.

15.1.2   Multicasting

In distributed simulation each simulator must be able to reach all other simulators that simulated sensors (vision, infrared, radar) can detect in the virtual space. Except for the most trivial configurations, each simulator can't send individually to every other simulator because the number of packets grows as the square of the number of simulators and overwhelms a network's capacity. Instead, we do multicasting—making the network deliver copies of each packet to all simulators that need it.

In multicast communication, senders can reach an established collection of receivers with a single transmission. A more correct name is *multipeer* because the collection of senders and receivers can all reach each other with a single transmission. (The difference is one-to-many vs. many-to-many, but we'll use multicast in both cases.) A less specific case is the broadcast network, in which a sender reaches all connected receivers with a single transmission. A local-area network is a simple broadcast network. More complex distributed simulations, particularly those involving wide-area networks, may have several multicast/multipeer groups to reduce the amount of information that must transfer throughout the network. In this case, each group consists of simulators with access to the same sensor inputs. Very large distributed simulations may also use multicast to reduce the amount of information that flows to individual simulators, thereby limiting their processing requirements and cost.

An important characteristic of multicast is that it can't effectively use ordinary reliable protocols, such as the transmission control protocol. These protocols rely on regular acknowledgments from receiver to sender that would greatly increase network traffic to the sender if done by each simulator in the distributed simulation. Instead, it uses the user datagram protocol, which doesn't need acknowledgments because it doesn't guarantee reliable delivery.

15.1.3   Building Strong Network Security

Some uses of distributed simulation require the network to secure the data it's carrying. Chapter 17 treats security for simulation broadly; here, we'll look only at network-related issues. Network security protects against

- Changing transmitted information before it's received (integrity)
- Misrepresenting the source of the information (authenticity)
- Revealing transmitted information to unauthorized people (confidentiality)
- Losing information availability (accessibility)

In addition, we must consider the cost of providing security in light of its value. If we don't, the effort and costs for security can easily dominate all networking efforts, or even the whole distributed simulation. The tradeoff between the value and cost of securing information is easiest for unclassified but sensitive data. It becomes much harder with classified military systems, but commanders can still accept reasonable risks.

Military use of distributed simulation requires commanders to determine which elements of information must have integrity, authenticity, confidentiality, and accessibility. In some cases industrial users of distributed simulations may consider their data proprietary and therefore require similar security.

We must balance these four security requirements. A system which protects information so well that it's not accessible when required doesn't have adequate security; neither does a system that isn't reliably available. In other words, we must provide adequate, cost-effective security on the network while still allowing people to use the data.

An important issue in security is *labeling*, which is necessary whenever the system must partition access to information among system users and maintain this partitioning. An example is classified military data which requires different levels of protection (CONFIDENTIAL, SECRET, TOP SECRET) and different release characteristics, such as SECRET RELEASABLE TO NATO. One of the most difficult problems today is multilevel security: creating integrated systems we can trust to contain information with mixed labels while restricting information flows among categories according to predetermined security rules. An example would be "users cleared for SECRET access may access CONFIDENTIAL information, but not vice-versa."

In a military simulation the labeling usually is already determined for any element of information, and the need to use this information will depend on what that part of the distributed simulation must do. Different commanders commonly control elements of information with different levels of classification, so military networks need various levels of security (see Sec. 15.4.2 for more detail).

15.1.4   Managing Networks

We manage networks at two levels. Network planning and development results in requirements for engineering, installing, testing, and ultimately removing a network. Managers of communications and computing resources within the organization requiring the network usually do these tasks, which are part of planning the distributed simulation application. Usually, this planning must take place very early because networks are so complex, require long lead times to acquire some of their parts, and strongly affect operations if some of their functions turn out to be too difficult or expensive.

A second level of management applies to operational networks dispersed over a wide area. These are extremely complex systems, with many parts operated by different organizations. They require continuous monitoring to ensure they're operating as required, as well as action to restore service in case of failures. Distributed-simulation operations critically need acceptable network performance to be successful. This management of operational networks is usually most effective if coupled closely with the operation center that coordinates the application.

15.1.5   Developing Standards

Chapter 13 addresses the general role of standards in simulation. Here I'll talk about networking standards, which are formally agreed-to specifications for system architecture and components. The architecture defines possible system building blocks and how they may relate. Without workable standards, we can't get network components that work together to do what we need. The components are typically electronic hardware and computer software that do, in standard ways, what the architecture defines. Interface standards and protocols are critical. Interface standards define how hardware and software fit together at their boundaries. Protocols define how each part works so sending and receiving processes match and allow information to transfer.

Standards exist at all levels so components and subsystems can work together. IEEE Standard 1278.2 for distributed interactive simulations defines a complete set of protocols for interoperable communications architectures. It specifies protocols selected from the internet protocol suite maintained by the Internet Engineering Task Force.

In addition the working group for distributed interactive simulations has drafted standards for command, control, and communications, as well as intelligence and exercise management. In general, standards aren't mature for architectures or network functions unique to simulation applications. Thus, much network development depends on specialized knowledge growing from exercise to exercise. As standards and experience mature, it will become practical to buy parts "off the shelf" and straightforwardly assemble a distributed simulation network. Ultimately, the High Level Architecture (HLA) can be expected to include these standards.

15.1.6   Steps in Developing a Network

To build a working network it's critical to select:

A Strategy for Developing and Operating a Network. Simply stated, this means deciding whether to create your own networking group or let someone else develop it for you. The pros and cons are very similar to those for any technology project, but remember that networking is still very much a specialty (in part, an art). Considering the network probably won't be a large part of the simulation effort, you may want to pay an experienced company to put the network in place and operate it, particularly for short-term use. If you out-source the network, a contractor will do the rest of the development as your organization oversees it.

Overall Protocol Standards. Following the published standard for distributed interactive simulation, IEEE 1278.2, this will be the Internet Protocol Suite. Other options exist, such as the Open Systems Interconnect standards, but we have very little experience using them with distributed simulation. For wide-area, distributed, simulation networks on a large scale, the protocol family selected must support multicast packet networking in real time.

Technology for the LAN's Protocols and Components. Commonly, developers select IEEE 802.3 (such as Ethernet) operating at ten megabits per second, but several other choices exist. Here, performance determines which technology to choose. Typical high-performance systems use the Fiber Distributed Data Interface (FDDI). A recent arrival is an Ethernet running at 100 megabits per second.

Technology to Connect Wide-Area Networks (WAN). Networks for distributed simulation typically use leased terrestrial circuits in the WAN. See the discussion on Circuits, Propagation, and Errors below to see why satellite circuits have drawbacks in real-time systems.

Router Model. A router is the key element in a WAN that "routes" or "switches" packets among LANs and the interconnecting communications paths (links). Your router must support required protocols and performance in the WAN. See the section below on Switching for details.

Technology for Network Security. Determine the security architecture for the network and select the technology you'll use to create it.

Technology for Managing the Network. Determine how you'll manage the network and select the technology to do so.

These selections usually occur in the above order, but the process may be iterative. Also, special considerations may drive you to select out of order—for example, when someone has directed one of the decisions in advance. In addition, you'll have to consider real-time support and multicasting, as noted earlier. For a good general description of network design see Stallings [1994] or Tanenbaum [1995]; for more details on the Internet Protocol Suite see Comer [1995] or Stevens [1995]; for a more technical description of network technologies in distributed simulation see Pullen [1995b].

We've summarized the problems in networking distributed simulations and how to do it successfully. If you're going to create a network, you'll also need to understand the technology issues of real-time operation, multicasting, and secure networks, including a general knowledge of network management and security. Read on for more about these issues.

15.2   Issues in Packet Networking to Support Real-time Applications

Critical issues include switching (moving the packet along appropriate communication links); controlling delays due to the communication links and switching; and selecting appropriate circuits (links) to keep errors and delays within acceptable limits.

15.2.1   Switching

Distributed simulation networks are *packet-switched*, which means collecting information into packets and sending it from computer to computer through digital communications media. The computers serving end users are called *hosts*; the ones routing traffic around the network are called *switches*, or more commonly, *routers*. A host can also be a router, but recently we've begun using separate routers for better performance—a host supporting other tasks is likely to handle arriving packets more slowly. The computers connect so each has at least one path to all others. The paths may be direct (A connects to B) or indirect (packets from A can reach B because A and B both connect to C). Today most computers connect to local-area networks (LANs), which behave as links that send packets to all attached hosts at the same time. Typically, a LAN supports high data rates (10 million bits per second or higher) and is within a single building. A LAN often appears in network diagrams as a wire with multiple hosts attached, as shown in Fig. 15.1.

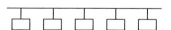

Fig. 15.1.   **Local-Area Network.** A local-area network is a simple configuration that reliably provides low-cost, high-capacity interconnection among hosts within a relatively small area (one building or, at most, a campus).

A wide-area network (WAN) usually links separated LANs into an internetwork (see Fig. 15.2). Leased communications links and routers combine to form most WANs. Each LAN that is part of a WAN has at least one router providing a path to other LANs. More complex internetworking occurs when routers couple two or more networks (sometimes known as *gateways*). The "Internet" consists of tens of thousands of WANs and LANs linked in this way.

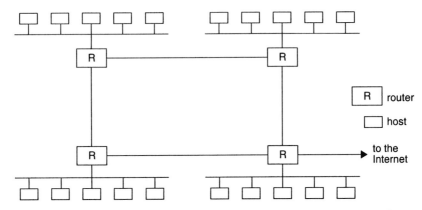

Fig. 15.2.   A Wide-Area Network Composed of Interneted Local-Area Networks. Routers pass packets over the wide-area links (thin lines). A host doesn't know whether a packet comes to it on its own LAN or from a remote LAN.

With packet networking, we're able to share expensive resources (such as wide-area communications) with great ease and to build networks that can route packets from source to destination despite component failures, so long as a path exists. Unfortunately, these same characteristics become a problem in real-time communications. Packet networks usually can't limit the amount of traffic individual hosts place on the LAN and WAN. Thus, we can't predict how much of the system's capacity will be used. Performance in packet networks depends heavily on the quantity of traffic (*loading*). At forty percent of the LAN's capacity and 80 percent of the WAN's capacity, the system's host-to-host delay (*latency*) increases dramatically. A network that achieved 100 millisecond latency between its most distant hosts when lightly loaded might increase to 500 milliseconds at high loading, thereby failing to meet requirements for distributed simulation. Similarly, if a major wide-area link fails, the network may keep working by dynamically routing packets. But delays may be unacceptable because paths lengthen or more packets passing through some of the routers create congestion. Let's look further at how delays and communications errors occur and then see how to control delays and support real-time requirements.

15.2.2   Delay Because of Limited Capacity

The main source of delay in packet-switched networks is congestion that arises whenever too many packets go through a single link. Although packet-routing procedures try to lessen such congestion by spreading traffic evenly across available paths, the load may still exceed link capacity, at least for short periods. Whenever a router has a packet going across a link and another arrives that needs to take the same path, it holds the new packet in memory and forms a *queue*. In extreme cases, this queue can grow so long that no more memory is available, in which case packets find the queue full on arrival and are dropped. This discarding of packets may lead to even worse congestion in networks that require reliable delivery of data. In such networks, the receiving host's transport protocol recognizes that data has been lost and requests retransmission, adding to the already great load. In networks supporting only distributed simulation, retransmission doesn't create extra loading because distributed simulation, like other real-time applications, doesn't attempt reliable delivery of packets. A real-time packet that doesn't arrive when needed is useless and shouldn't be delivered late. However, networks that mix distributed simulation and reliable data traffic can experience runaway congestion from transmissions to replace dropped packets. If they do, parts of the network may fail completely for seconds to minutes.

A common misconception is expecting data links on wide-area networks to operate continuously at full capacity. It seems logical that 32 packets per second can be transmitted if a communications link is rated at 64 kilobits per second and the packets average 2,000 bits in length. But the network uses control packets and distributes routing information that must also pass through the links. Also, routers take a little time to determine how to process each packet. Most importantly, a certain fraction of the packets will drop out due to communications errors on the link and may require retransmission. Considering all these delays and loading, we typically have only up to 70 percent of a link's capacity to carry data. Thus, we must provision links so they can handle at least 1.5 times the expected traffic to avoid dropping packets because of congestion.

Local-area networks usually allow even less use of link capacity. The most common LAN protocol, IEEE 802.3 (often called "Ethernet"), operates in *carrier sense multiple access with collision detection*. In other words, the LAN has no central control. Instead, all stations continuously monitor whether the link is in use (carrier sense). If they have data to send, they wait until the link is free. But if several of them are waiting to send, at least two are very likely to start sending at the same time, thus causing a "collision." The sending stations sense such collisions and stop transmitting. To avoid repeating the collision, they then wait a random length of time before trying again. Although this procedure is effective, an 802.3 LAN with several active stations still can carry only up to forty percent of the rated link capacity. This means a circuit rated for 10 megabits per second would have an effective transmission rate of 4 megabits per second, which all connected stations must share. To support real-time traffic, you must select a LAN technology with this limit in mind.

15.2.3   Delay Because of Propagation and Errors in Communications Links

Another major source of delay in WANs is electromagnetic propagation over long distances. In a wire or fiber-optic cable, signals travel at 2×10^8 meters per second. Thus, a leased circuit using optical fiber requires about 30 milliseconds to propagate data from the eastern to the western United States. The propagation delay for satellite transmission typically is about 250 milliseconds because communications satellites occupy orbits 22,300 miles above the Earth. Satellite transmission is also unattractive because of its relatively high error rate, which may be as much as 10,000 times more than that of fiber-optic transmission. As a result, many more packets must be retransmitted or dropped, so satellite transmission is usually unacceptable for distributed simulation.

For this reason, WANs in distributed simulations use leased ground circuits, mostly on fiber-optic cables that have very low error rates for communications. Unfortunately, leased lines have limited capacity options; they're usually available in North America at data rates of 56 kilobits per second, 1.5 megabits per second (T1), and 45 megabits per second (T3). Thus, if you need more than 56 kilobits per second, you'll have to lease a T1 circuit. Similar circuits are available in Europe with data rates of 64 kilobits per second, 2.0 megabits per second (E1), and 34 megabits per second (E3). Circuits on fiber-optic cable under the Atlantic and Pacific Oceans are available in multiples of 64 kilobits per second up to 2.0 megabits per second. The "last mile" from the telecommunication carrier's building to the point of use typically employs twisted-pair wire for speeds up to E1. T3 and E3 require special installations, often with long lead times.

Leased circuits with the highest capacities use fiber-optic cable end-to-end and the synchronous-optical-network format. They're available in data rates of roughly 150 (OC3), 600 (OC12), 1200 (OC24), and 2400 (OC48) megabits per second. Such circuits aren't widely available. To date, distributed simulations have considered only the slowest (OC3). They're used mainly to pass huge numbers of telephone and data circuits by *multiplexing*—aggregating many smaller circuits into one large-capacity circuit.

15.2.4   Reserving Resources

Because delays are unpredictable in packet networks, developers of distributed simulations and other real-time applications—such as video conferencing—have shied away from them. As a result, the technical community for networking is working hard on protocols that allow reserving of network resources. In concept, users of such systems specify capacities (say, 100 packets per second with no more than 1000 bits per packet); latencies; and whether the requirement is for guaranteed delivery or statistical reliability (such as 99% of packets delivered within the required latency). Such sophistication exists only in experimental systems for now, but some are operating, and at least one is moving to commercial use. If you create a network as part of a distributed simulation in a demanding application, consider reserving resources.

Reserving resources means setting aside enough capacity in each router to meet the network application's stated needs or *quality of service* requirement. In other words, you reserve some of the router's processing capacity, some of the buffers for queuing, and (most important) a fraction of the average data rate available on the circuits. Allocation can get complex, particularly for multicasting, in which different end systems want to share the same stream of packets but don't necessarily have the same capacity requirements.

You can consider the following protocols and techniques to allocate resources in a distributed simulation.

The *Internet Stream (ST2)* experimental protocol has been part of the Defense Simulation Internet and its predecessors since 1990. It's a protocol for multicasting and reserving resources that uses a *connection-oriented* networking model. This means resources are reserved for the life of a packet stream at each router along a fixed path. Several commercial vendors have versions of ST2 which don't fully interoperate. (ST2+ is specified for versions that will work together fully, but no-one has built a commercial system.) The ST2 specification for quality of service is a flowspec that defines the number of packets per second the application is likely to present to the network.

The *Resource reSerVation Protocol (RSVP)* is intended for use with Internet Protocol—multicast (IPmc). Under development since 1992, it's available in an experimental version that uses Sun workstations as routers. Because this protocol will support real-time applications on the Internet, at least two vendors have committed to providing commercial versions by 1998. It's distinct from ST2 because it tries only to convey setup information to routers, not to support data forwarding. Also, it doesn't set up a lasting connection. Instead it uses *soft state*, in which the reserved path can change during the life of a packet stream and stays active only if a minimum number of packets are flowing. Soft state is more flexible than ST2's rigid setup procedure. This RSVP flowspec may also contain a data rate in bits per second or packets per second, an end-to-end delay, and an acceptable rate for packet loss.

Frame Relay is commercially available and frequently offered with Internet services. This transmission model links multiple sites as if they were all on one extended local network. Frames from any site destined for another site get a header and move toward the next router. The routers form a logical chain—each one simply forwards any received frame not intended for its attached local network. Frame relay reserves resources by specifying a committed information rate: the number of bits per second the network intends to support across the relay chain.

Networks using *Asynchronous Transfer Mode (ATM)* over fiber-optic links on a synchronous optical network inherently reserve capacity, because data flows through a virtual circuit require us to state the needed capacity at setup. But in practice it's available only for permanent virtual circuits which require manual setup. Dynamic switched virtual circuits are available in some systems but don't offer resource reservation. The switched unit in asynchronous transfer is a 53-byte cell (5 bytes of control information and 48 bytes of data). This protocol specifies quality of service as a data rate in bits per second and an acceptable rate for cell loss. We can determine the data rate by multiplying the average packet size by the average packet rate. Unfortunately, the relationship between the loss rates for cells and packets isn't so straightforward. That's because each packet typically divides into many cells and losing one cell also means losing a whole packet. A reasonable approximation for low loss rates is the acceptable rate for packet loss multiplied by the ratio of average packet length to the 48-byte payload of the asynchronous-transfer cell.

The final technique you must consider isn't a protocol. It's a form of "insurance" that is the most common way to deal with the demands of real-time networking on distributed simulations—provisioning more link capacity than the distributed simulation is likely to need. You can do so only if the network is dedicated to an application and has no competing requirements. Estimate the highest capacity any part of the network might need and acquire at least twice this capacity in every element. It's crude and uneconomical, but it may be your only alternative and at least it requires relatively little sophistication in designing and assembling the network.

15.3   Issues in Multicasting

As explained in Sec. 15.1.2, a distributed-simulation network that exceeds a LAN's broadcast capacity must use multicasting.

15.3.1   Multicasting on a Wide-Area Networks (WAN)

Multicast networks can deliver packets to group addresses representing multiple host computers. Efficiency is the best reason to provide this service in a WAN. If a host must reach all the other hosts in a group of n by sending a separate packet to each one, the amount of data transmitted will grow at a rate of almost n^2. Even for moderate group sizes, this approach wastes network resources by transmitting many copies of each packet. Therefore, some routers have protocols that flow the data across tree-like branches (a *multicast tree*—see Fig. 15.3, below). Routers at forks in the flow must replicate packets as they arrive, thus distributing communications over the network so duplicate copies of any packet need not cross any link. Whenever you need a wide-area network, the savings in circuit and router costs usually will more than offset the extra cost of installing multicast protocols.

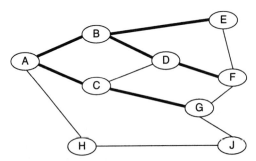

Fig. 15.3.   Network with Multicast Tree. Routers A, E, F, and G connect local-area networks with group members. Routers B, C, and D pass packets through. Since B is at a fork in the tree, it must replicate each packet, sending one to D and one to E. Routers H and J aren't participants in the group.

To route packets in networks, we have two general approaches. *Connection-oriented* networks establish a sequence of routers called a *virtual circuit*, through which any given data flow always passes. Although forwarding packets becomes simpler, these networks require complex setup and lose the ability to work automatically around link and node failures. *Connectionless* networks independently route each packet through the network, removing the need to set up a virtual circuit and allowing the network to route packets around failed network elements.

Heavy use in any part of the virtual circuit's path will degrade a connection-oriented network's performance. In such cases, we can only disconnect the virtual circuit and repeat the connection sequence because connection information (state) must be present in each node. For this reason, connectionless protocols (such as the Internet Protocol) have been adopted widely. Under these protocols, each packet moves forward separately according to the router's routing table. The table may change dynamically to account for failed network elements or to adapt to changing traffic loads. The state information is in the routing table. It's a "soft" state, in that the router deletes it if neighboring routers don't refresh it.

Unfortunately, the connectionless approach has proved difficult to adapt to resource-reserved, multicast networks. The only commercially available protocols for such networks are the Internet Stream and Frame Relay protocols (see Sec. 15.2.4), both connection-oriented. The *Internet Protocol multicast* (IPmc)— a protocol which dynamically creates the multicast tree—appears likely to be much more successful commercially. But IPmc won't be able to reserve resources until the Resource reSerVation Protocol (see Sec. 15.2.4) is commercially available. In principle the latter's soft-state model should improve resource-reserved multicasting, but the complexity of the resulting protocol appears to be slowing its availability. As resource reservation matures, we can expect to get resource-reserving networks off the shelf for distributed simulation (perhaps as early as 1998).

15.3.2   Multicasting on Local-Area Networks (LAN)

LANs lend themselves to multicasting because they typically use broadcast architectures. Computers connect to the LAN through adapters that can compare the address of each incoming packet to the one assigned to the adapter. Because each packet goes to every LAN adapter, the adapter can also check the address to see if it matches a multicast group. But we need a way to form multicast groups. Because coordination in a LAN is distributed among its adapters, no central controlling computer establishes group addresses and membership. But we may be able to form groups at an application gateway (a network interface that processes data for an application rather than for a standard network protocol). Or we can use distributed algorithms that allow simulators to coordinate group addresses among themselves. Typically, the distributed simulation pre-selects a block of unused multicast addresses and then assigns them to groups based on data elements it contains, such as location on a map grid.

We have two methods to compare the addresses in arriving packets with the multicast groups to which the simulator subscribes. First, the adapter may simply accept all packets, leaving the simulator's software to determine which ones have group addresses of interest. But this method directly contradicts the goal of using multicast to reduce simulator input because the simulator host must process every packet. The alternative is for the LAN's adapter to hold a list of multicast addresses for comparison. This method effectively supports multicasting but is limited because most LAN adapters can handle only sixteen multicast groups, and the largest compares addresses for 64 groups. This limitation requires a system element, marked "application multicast gateway" in Fig. 15.4, to organize traffic so each simulator needs to monitor only a small number of multicast groups.

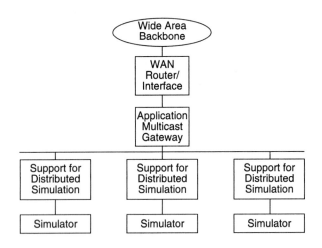

Fig. 15.4. **Simplified Architecture for Multicast Networking in a Distributed Interactive Simulation.** The router participates in the wide-area network, exchanging packets with other routers and passing those needed locally toward the LAN. The application gateway provides services unique to distributed simulation, such as assigning packets to multicast groups based on the geographic area in which the event in the packet occurs. All simulation hosts are connected to the Application Gateway by a local-area network.

15.3.3   Multicasting for Distributed Interactive Simulation and Wide-Area Networks (WAN)

Distributed Interactive Simulation especially needs the economy of transmission that multicasting brings to interconnected groups. Each protocol data unit (packet) contains enough data to describe the complete state of a single virtual-space entity. Therefore, the network need not deliver every packet reliably. Combined with broadcast, this permits all simulators to be able to display sensor inputs (in particular, vision) from all others. When only a few objects are in the virtual space, this is a very effective way to distribute the problem of determining which objects can sense which others. Each simulator receives all packets, checks to determine whether it can sense the emitting object, and discards or uses the packet as appropriate. For up to hundreds of virtual objects, low-cost microprocessors can do this broadcasting.

Unfortunately, in medium- to large-sized distributed simulations, broadcasting becomes ineffective because the number of packets increases beyond a low-cost computer's capacity. For WANs, several sites may be involved but may not need every packet at every site. Thus, using several multicast groups may reduce the total amount of data crossing the network's links. At this point, we can organize the simulators and simulations into areas in the virtual space, based on shared data from sensors, and use one multicast group for each area. As a result, data should enter the simulation computers at a lower rate, and the network should see lower traffic and therefore cost less. Again, the application's multicast gateway (Fig. 15.4) will carry out this function.

In principle, creating as many multicast groups as shared sensor spaces is highly appealing. In practice, it's hard to organize the groups across a dynamic virtual engagement featuring many sites. One successful approach, which I call *dual-mode multicast*, simply collects all data into a single multicast group within the wide-area network and delegates to an application gateway the task of organizing groups needed to reduce simulator input. Another approach, *bilevel multicast*, coordinates multiple groups on the WAN, again allowing application gateways to organize them. Dual-mode multicast trades off somewhat greater WAN traffic to gain a simpler architecture; bilevel multicast does the opposite. In both cases multicasting in the WAN must be connection-oriented until connectionless protocols that reserve resources are commercially available. Figure 15.4 shows a WAN/LAN architecture in its simplest form.

15.3.4   Compressing Data for Transmission

Many distributed simulations, including those created under the current version of Distributed Interactive Simulation, don't try to economize in using network capacity. This approach keeps the transmission protocol simple. For example, it doesn't need to be reliable because any error is corrected as the next protocol data unit arrives. Each unit contains the entire state of the emitting object, no matter how infrequently it may change (a favorite example is the Country of Design which can't change). Entities stopped or even dead on the battlefield still send data units at a reduced rate (one every two seconds).

In a medium to large distributed simulation, particularly one involving a WAN, sending the full state in every data unit takes a lot of network capacity and is therefore very expensive. *Static compression* (recoding the data more densely) is possible, but that doesn't avoid sending the same information over and over, often needlessly. We can do *dynamic compression* by sending some of this information less often than the actively changing entity states—if we deal with two issues. First, a late joiner (simulator connecting after startup) must be able to obtain the full state for all entities within its sensor range. Second, we must make sure the infrequent information gets transmitted reliably, so all simulators that need it receive it.

Methods for reliable transmission generally fall into two categories: (1) sending the information enough times so it's highly likely to be received, and (2) sending some unique code in the unreliable protocol data units, showing what the last reliable unit should have been, so the system can request retransmission of any reliable data unit not received. Distributed simulations have used both methods—for example, in protocol-independent compression from Lincoln Laboratory [Calvin 1995]. But we must avoid sending frequent acknowledgments (positive or negative) to the source; in multicasting they would overwhelm the originator of the data with a volume far greater than the original protocol data unit. Stanford University has proposed using a local cache on each LAN [Holbrook 1995]. I have suggested combining proven methods into a selectively reliable transport protocol [Pullen 1995a] and standardizing it for distributed simulation. This protocol would work within unreliable multicast and thus not need a separate reliable protocol to deal with lost data.

15.4   Network Security for Distributed Simulation

Security is one of the thornier problems in networking today. It is a system-level concern because system designs must incorporate it cost-effectively. Security measures must balance in all parts of the system; otherwise, one "weak link" can compromise the system. Managers must also balance costs—in dollars and in restrictions to the operation—against the system's overall goals and the need to protect information. Chapter 17 deals with these system concerns; here, we'll consider issues of network security.

Some aspects of networked systems create particular problems. In general a secure system which interacts with a less secure system requires special attention—for example, at wide-area communications links in a WAN. A less evident, but important, boundary is the one between multiple levels of security within a secure system. We'll focus here on problems unique to networked systems because we can deal with more common problems using customary methods, such as maintaining effective physical security.

15.4.1   Network Security Architecture and Devices

To secure a distributed simulation, we must encrypt or "scramble" all information passing over communications links outside the boundaries of a site's physical security so outside parties can't decipher it. Figure 15.5 shows a general architecture for this purpose.

A secure system has certain parts in common with an unsecure system (Fig. 15.4): a wide-area backbone, WAN router/interface, multicast application gateway, distributed simulation support, and simulator. But it adds other elements:

Security overlay: This approach encrypts the binary data stream passing through it according to a key that the receiving end must know, so a matching device and key can decrypt and reproduce the original data. If we use the right encryption method, anyone not holding a copy of the key can't understand the data.

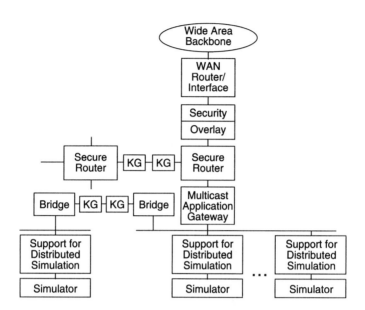

Fig. 15.5.   **Reference Architecture for Secure Multicast Networking in Distributed Interactive Simulations [Pullen 1995a].** This architecture provides an element of every type that a secure, multicast network for distributed simulations might use.

Used with packet networks, the security overlay takes the form of an *end-to-end encryptor* for the Ethernet LAN protocol, the Internet Protocol, or for Asynchronous Transfer Mode (ATM) cells. In each case it encrypts the data in the packet and leaves the address "in the clear," so the backbone network can treat the secured packet like any other. (I'm using "packet" loosely here to refer to the transmitted unit of Ethernet, frame relay, Internet Protocol, or ATM, each of which properly uses a different term.) End-to-end encryption, also known as E^3, allows sharing of a backbone network among many different secure and non-secure communities. NSA-certified E^3 is available for Ethernet and the Internet protocol, with data rates up to 1.5 megabits per second. The developmental version of E^3 for asynchronous transfer mode will handle data rates up to 150 megabits per second.

E^3 has one security weakness. It allows people outside the secure system to determine which sites are communicating, and how much, by analyzing traffic using in-the-clear sources and destinations of packets seen in the backbone network. This "traffic analysis" is usually not considered to be a problem.

Secure router: The security overlay box in the diagram has a line across its center, which represents the boundary between the system's unsecure side (traditionally called "black") and its secure side (called "red"). The routers shown below this box are processing unencrypted packets, so they must be in a physically secure area with all other links and devices on the secure side. Secure routers may connect through E^3 systems (on a network) or through link encryptors (on links).

KG: This box represents a *link encryptor* that "scrambles" all data passing through it, leaving no information which could be used to deliver a packet. Such encryptors can be used only in pairs, at opposite ends of a communication link. Units are available to support virtually any data rate you may need. The encrypted data is as secure as with E^3 and also immune to traffic analysis, but the data can go only to one other secure system. In this way, you can use link encryptors on the links between routers or pairs of bridges to create networks in which all components except the links between encyptors are "red." This means any data could appear at any red section of the network, so all data must be in the same secure community.

Bridge: This box represents a unit that takes packets off the LAN and passes them over a link to another LAN an arbitrary distance away. The other half of the bridge interfaces with that LAN. Thus, the two LANs can behave as one extended LAN, even though they're not in the same local area. A KG may secure the link used with the bridge, or it may be within a physically secure area.

These added system elements increase the cost of the distributed-simulation network to two or more times that of an unsecure network, but they ensure outside parties won't access information in the simulation. Commanders or other managers must decide whether to spend this money. Fortunately, well defined, "off-the-shelf" solutions are possible, so managers can accurately estimate costs.

15.4.2   Network Security beyond Encryption

For many, network security stops with confidentiality, but you may need authentication, multilevel security, and key management to keep distributed simulations secure.

Authentication: If information itself isn't sensitive but the system must be reliable, you may want to use authentication. A system using E^3 or KGs won't accept altered or fabricated packets because they'll fail in decryption. But people with bad intentions can manipulate data on an "in the clear" network used for non-sensitive data. How do you foil them? Authenticate—send in the packet a code, computed from the data according to some key they can't know. Normally, authentication doesn't occur in a separate "box"; rather, the computer that generates the original data packet also authenticates it. In turn, the receiving computer validates the authentication. Commercial packages, such as Kerberos [Kohl 1989], offer this ability.

Multilevel security: Military operations require collections of systems operating at different levels of classification. To protect classified data in simulations, these levels must be strictly separate. We can store and manipulate multiple security levels within a single computer, but under security doctrine that computer must be *trusted* (certified by a competent authority) to maintain the separation. Evaluating trusted systems has been slow, so only a few, limited systems are available. Market demand hasn't been strong enough to motivate developers to complete the extended, detailed process required for government approval. Trusted Mach (developed by Trusted Information Systems, Inc.) is close. A multilevel secure system is of great interest in secure networking because it could be a gateway or router on the red side of a single common network for all classified and unclassified levels. We could do the same thing using several separate E^3 systems that share a network, but only with a lot of redundancy.

Key management: Encryption requires keys to be changed periodically, often daily, because the chance that supercomputers will "crack" the key increases with the amount of data it has been used to encrypt. The keys must themselves be distributed securely and accounted for, which means manual or automated key management. Procedures for distributing keys over the network help a lot—as in Motorola's Network Encryption System [Motorola 1995]. If you don't have these procedures, include external key management in your security plan. For example, you can distribute keys by trusted means, such as registered mail, and maintain backup keys for each encryptor in case the primary keys are compromised.

15.5   Network Management

Most networks need management to ensure they work as designed, so they must be able to monitor their own performance and report it to a network operations center. Typically, each major part of the network with a computer maintains its current state and recent performance in a management information base. This information can flow—automatically or in response to a query—into a network management workstation for display and analysis. Logically, we could then send directions to routers and other system elements from the management workstation. However, in an open network, you'll need to authenticate control information to prevent anyone with bad intentions from causing a denial of service by changing key network parameters.

Organize your network so at least one management site graphically displays the status of every network element that is critical to the distributed simulation. This display should show the status of every LAN, including all simulation hosts, and all routers and communication links on the WAN. Status information should at least include the network element's up or down condition and the recent information-transfer rate in packets per second and bits per second. Helpful additions are a display that uses color to distinguish between normal operation and elements with problems and software to sound an alarm when a problem occurs. In large networks you may need to arrange this information hierarchically, so the top-level display shows whole-site characteristics, with details available on demand.

Collecting this information and bringing it to a central site would be a major effort in itself, were it not for standard management systems for network information, which most vendors support in their network software. Using a standard protocol, a network-management station can query every element through the network and receive a response showing the element's status. Two protocols exist for network management. The *Common Management Information Protocol* (CMIP) was developed as part of the networking standards for Open Systems Interconnect and still has some adherents despite what many consider to be unnecessary complexity. However, the *Simple Network Management Protocol* that is part of the Internet Protocol suite has won widespread and increasing use. Off-the-shelf software is available for either of these protocols to display network status graphically, log and track problems, and control network devices. An example is Hewlett-Packard's *Open View* [Hewlett-Packard 1993]. Using such network-management software, combined with network elements that support the Simple Network Management Protocol, you can manage your network by collecting accurate descriptions of all network elements into a database for the display software.

15.6   Network Standards

As described in Chap. 13 and in Sec. 15.1.5 above, standards are essential to networking because they allow hardware and software from many sources to work together on a "plug-and-play" basis.

15.6.1   Networking Profiles for Distributed Interactive Simulation (DIS)

IEEE Standard 1278.2 [IEEE 1995], developed by the DIS Working Group's Communications and Security Subgroup, defines in profiles the network and transport protocols appropriate for distributed simulations. A profile is a collection of compatible standards intended to meet a particular need. All participants in a particular application should adopt the same profile to guarantee interoperation. The current standard specifies one profile for simple broadcast, usable on a LAN or bridged LAN, and another for Internet Protocol multicast, usable on a WAN.

15.6.2   Internet Stream Protocol

The Internet Engineering Task Force calls its standards documents "Request for Comments" (RFC). RFC 1190 specifies the experimental internet stream (ST2) protocol as a multicast started by one sender to multiple receivers with a common level of resource reservation for each stream. Multipeer operation is possible because each participating data source creates a stream with all other participants as targets. Bolt, Baranek, and Newman, Inc., BayNetworks, and Syzygy, Inc. sell commercial versions. IBM uses Syzygy's software in the RS-6000 family of workstations but doesn't sell the protocol directly. These products can operate together somewhat, but none of them uses all of the ST2 specification's abilities. RFC 1819 provides a refined, still experimental, specification called ST2+. It's supposed to have fewer, but more interoperable, abilities; however, many believe this sender-started, connection-oriented model doesn't scale well. I've observed that moderately large configurations (20 nodes) are possible when carefully managed.

15.6.3   Internet Protocol—Multicast

This protocol is based on RFC 1112, the Internet Group Management Protocol. It defines simple extensions to the basic Internet architecture that permit large multipeer groups to multicast and receivers to start join procedures. Resource reservation won't be available until we get the Resource reSerVation Protocol (see Sec. 15.2.4). The basic version is a multicast router daemon (mrouted) in UNIX workstations from Silicon Graphics Inc. and Sun Microsystems. Recently BayNetworks and Cisco Systems have put features into their routers to support this protocol. An open issue is what routing protocol to use: *Distance Vector Multicast Routing Protocol, Multicast Open Shortest Path First,* or *Protocol Independent Multicast.* The last of these is most attractive because it provides for pruning routes that don't have active participants and tries more effectively to manage tunnels through parts of the network that can't multicast.

15.6.4   Frame Relay

Frame relay, a standard of the American National Standards Institute, uses a connection-oriented model. It links multiple LANs into private networks with up to 255 nodes using a common, router-based backbone. It offers resource reservation and limited forms of multipeer multicast. Internet operation is possible through at least one of the LANs with an Internet gateway router. Frame relay is compatible with networks that use asynchronous transfer. This protocol will work well for small- to medium-sized configurations but won't do well with larger networks because of its connection-oriented model.

15.6.5   Asynchronous Transfer Mode (ATM)

The International Telecommunication Union—Telecommunications Sector originally defined this protocol, but the *ATM Forum* has developed it rapidly and become its most important standards body. The User-Network Interface 3.1 is the most important current standard for using asynchronous transfer mode because it specifies how end systems connect to ATM systems. Until the Network-Network Interface is mature, the User-Network Interface will also connect ATM switches from different vendors. Asynchronous transfer mode is connection-oriented and requires resource reservation. It's still in its infancy, with most practical applications yet to come. But LAN switches for asynchronous transfer mode are available from several sources, such as Fore Systems' ASX-100 (16 ports), and much larger switches are under development, such as Nippon Electric Corporation's switch with 2048 ports. The major carriers for long-distance communication (AT&T, MCI, Sprint) have begun trial offerings of ATM in major communications markets using limited switches under restricted conditions.

15.6.6   Simple Network Management Protocol

RFC 1157 defines this protocol as a simple management model based on a management information base that can be queried remotely. These information bases are standardized by device type and typically have an open part, available to any query, and a closed part, available only to authenticated queries from privileged sources. It also allows control of network devices under authentication. We may be able to use this protocol to manage exercises if we can create a standard information base for distributed simulation. If so, we can use off-the-shelf tools for network management that display and log status and allow remote control of key network resources. In other words, we could integrate exercise and network management for distributed simulations.

15.7   Summary

Distributed simulation can be one of the most demanding networking applications known because it requires high performance in real time. In turn, networking is a challenging, emerging discipline. It brings together communications, computing, and protocol standards, with elements interacting in complex ways that can be hard to understand. The main challenges in networking for distributed simulation are transferring information in real time, multicasting, maintaining strong network security, managing the network, and developing adequate standards. We've seen that creating a network for distributed simulation is complex but manageable. With enough time and resources, a qualified technical staff, and careful attention to the key issues highlighted in this chapter, you can confidently create the network needed to support your distributed simulation.

References

Calvin, J., J. Seeger, G. Troxel, and D. Van Hook. 1995. "STOW Realtime Information Transfer and Networking Architecture." *12th DIS Workshop on Standards for the Interoperability of Distributed Simulations.*

Comer, Douglas E. 1995. *Internetworking with TCP/IP.* Vol. I, 3rd edition. Englewood Cliffs, NJ: Prentice-Hall, Inc.

Hewlett-Packard Corporation. 1993. *HP OpenView SNMP Management Platform 3.0 Administrator's Reference.* Camas, WA: Hewlett-Packard Corp.

Holbrook, H., S. Singhal, and D. Cheriton. 1995. "Log-Based Receiver-reliable Multicast for Distributed Interaction Simulation." *Proceedings of SIG-COMM '95.*

IEEE. 1995. *Standard for Distributed Interactive Simulation—Communication Services and Profiles.* Piscataway, NJ: Institute of Electrical and Electronics Engineers, Inc.

Kohl, J. 1989. "The Use of Encryption in Kerberos for Network Authentication." *Proceedings of Crypto '89.* Berlin, Germany: Springer-Verlag.

Motorola Inc. *Network Encryption System (NES) Technical Manual,* 5th edition. Scottsdale, AZ.

Pullen, J. and V. Laviano. 1995a. "A Selectively Reliable Transport Protocol for Distributed Interactive Simulation." *13th DIS Workshop on Standards for the Interoperability of Distributed Simulations.*

Pullen, J. and D. Wood. 1995b. "Networking Technology and DIS." *Proceedings of the IEEE, Special Issue on Distributed Simulation.*

Stallings, W. 1994. *Data and Computer Communications.* 4th edition. Englewood Cliffs, NJ: Macmillan Publishing Company.

Stevens, W.R. 1995. *TCP/IP Illustrated.* Reading, MA: Addison-Wesley Publishing Company.

Tanenbaum, A.S. 1996. *Computer Networks.* 3rd edition. Englewood Cliffs, NJ: Prentice-Hall PTR.

U.S. Department of Defense. 1996. *High Level Architecture for Modeling and Simulation.* Washington DC: Defense Modeling and Simulation Office.

CHAPTER 16

Interactive Simulation: Inserting Humans into Distributed Virtual Environments

Martin R. Stytz, *Air Force Institute of Technology*

The problems encountered when inserting humans into distributed virtual environments (DVEs) are formidable, and many issues remain unresolved. But the M&S community envisions a time when DVEs will regularly help people evaluate systems and subsystems, develop tactics, plan missions, validate system requirements, and train for large-scale operations. DVEs now exist mainly for training but are slowly moving into other areas of M&S (see Chap. 1). As DVE technology becomes more cost effective and efficient, we can expect to see it move from military uses into entertainment, education, business, manufacturing, and medicine.

The technologies for inserting humans into distributed simulations can be called distributed virtual environment (DVE) technology, distributed interactive simulation, or advanced distributed simulation. In this chapter, I'll use the term DVE to refer to the generic ability to insert humans into a simulation environment and reserve the term distributed interactive simulation (DIS) for discussions of the IEEE suite of protocols (IEEE 1278–1993 and revisions). The technology of distributed virtual environments permits real-time human interaction with complex, computer-generated environments. By necessity, these environments contain 3D graphical descriptions of human- and computer-controlled entities and mathematical models that interact and move according to real-world constraints. Most distributed virtual environments allow a human user to control 3D icons (or avatars) that represent real objects. These icons are present and interact with other human- and computer-controlled icons, as well as non-iconic representations of events. All users perceive the same world from different viewpoints and, usually, at different levels of fidelity.

The impetus for DVEs came from the insight that the best training occurs from doing and not from watching. Modern DVEs trace their beginnings to Air Force Colonel Jack Thorpe, who worked at the Defense Advanced Research Projects Agency and started the Simulator Networking (SIMNET) project at Fort Knox, Kentucky. This project showed that networked, low-cost simulators could effectively train armored-vehicle crews for combat at lower cost than routine field exercises. The training was also safer and more repeatable, comprehensive, and scaleable than traditional techniques.

Table 16.1. Framework for Analyzing the Technologies of Distributed Virtual Environments. We can effectively describe these technologies by their characteristics, components, and underlying technologies. The framework presented here is a starting point for characterizing them.

Topical Area	Significant Players and Characteristics
Characteristics	1. Purposeful 2. Complex 3. Active
Components	1. Virtual participants 2. Computer-generated forces and semi-autonomous forces participants 3. Network communication protocols 4. Constructive participants 5. Phenomenology participants 6. Live-(instrumented) range participants
Technologies	1. Software architecture 2. Networking 3. Virtual environments 4. Computational models 5. Artificial intelligence

Based on my experience with DVEs, I've developed a framework for analyzing and discussing these technologies (shown in Table 16.1) that will help you follow the discussions below. The distributed virtual environments I'm discussing go far beyond current gaming technology. They are purposeful, complex, and active. In a purposeful virtual environment, actors have goals and act to achieve them. Based on the actor's objectives and alliances, these goals may be mutually supporting, antagonistic, or individual. A complex environment has many actors and numerous goals being pursued at any time. Finally, an active environment changes from moment to moment and is unpredictable at the actor level and globally.

Distributed virtual environments have six main parts:

1. Virtual participants (human-controlled entities that operate within the DVE)
2. Computer-generated forces or semi-autonomous forces
3. Network communication protocols
4. Constructive participants
5. Phenomenology participants
6. Live-range participants

As we move through the chapter, I'll discuss each one in varying depth.

Of course, neither traditional nor interactive simulation is a panacea for all problems. To determine which to use, we must compare a problem's characteristics with the strengths and weaknesses of each type of simulation. Traditional simulations and DVEs differ in the origins of their technologies, how humans are involved in the environment, and whether they resolve outcomes entity by entity or in combination. Table 16.2 summarizes these differences. DVE technology arose from the need to train humans to operate as a team even though dispersed at separate locations, whereas traditional simulation began by simulating large-scale engagements to support planning and acquisition. Because DVEs directly involve humans, they lack the statistical power of traditional simulations, making their runs unrepeatable but more suitable for training. As a result, we can generalize the outcomes from DVEs and apply them broadly to real-world situations. On the other hand, we can use the statistical power of traditional simulations to reach conclusions about a specific set of circumstances, but we can't generalize these conclusions as readily to other situations. Using distributed computing with a DVE allows it to scale up to larger simulation environments. On the other hand, single computers typically host traditional simulations, thus limiting their ability to compute detailed information about individual participants within the units of large-scale simulations.

16.1   Terms and Concepts

Before discussing DVEs in depth, let's introduce some terms and concepts that you may not know. We'll use these terms in this chapter, and you'll also find them in much of the technical literature on distributed virtual environments. These

Table 16.2.   Differences between Traditional Simulation and Distributed Virtual Environments. Traditional simulations and Distributed Virtual Environments have distinctive characteristics.

Traditional Modeling & Simulation	Distributed Virtual Environments
Point statements—hard to generalize	Generalizable statements about outcomes
Statistically meaningful & "repeatable"	Weaker statistical basis; due to human interaction, repeatability is difficult to achieve
Little or no human input or interaction	Human input and interaction are paramount
Ignores many real-world conditions—the real world isn't random	Incorporates as many real-world conditions as the system can compute
Can't train in it	The evaluation world is the same as the training world
Limited scaleability because host computer has limited power	Scaleable, up to the network's bandwidth limit

definitions allow us to discuss how to design and build DVEs because they help us describe how DVEs interact, where they reside within the networked computer system, the types of DVE participants, and the level of fidelity we can achieve.

The terms entity and actor represent the dynamic parts of a DVE. An *entity* can change its state or cause events to occur. One example is terrain that can be changed by plowing, explosions, or traffic. Clouds, weather, radar emissions, aircraft, and armored vehicles are also entities. Terrain or other things that don't change are not. An *actor* is an entity that moves with apparent intelligent purpose. Actors can be virtual (human-controlled); constructive (traditional, simulation-controlled); live (derived from instrumented range data); or computer-generated (controlled by a computer program using artificial intelligence). So piloted aircraft, aircraft under computer control (semi-autonomous forces) or crewed armored vehicles are actors, but a cloud isn't. In some of the literature, actors are called *players*.

A *host* is a computer system within a DVE that inserts entities into the DVE or allows its human or computer users to control actors within the DVE. It also allows observations of actions by other actors in the virtual environment, whether they are machine- or human-controlled. An *observatory host* allows its users to observe actors and entities and to position themselves anywhere within the virtual environment. But users in an observatory don't directly control actors or entities. Local and remote hosts are important whenever we discuss *dead reckoning* (extrapolating position based on known velocity and elapsed time) or other network-based issues. The *local host* for an entity is the host that controls it. The *remote hosts* for an entity are all the other hosts participating in the DVE.

Virtual environments that have investigated distributing computations locally and among multiple hosts in the DVE are forerunners to realistic DVEs. *Computation distribution* typically partitions the computing workload among several cooperating machines that appear to the rest of the DVE as a single host. These machines use a single shared model of the virtual environment (as in

[Appino 1992; Codella 1992; Hill 1992]). The shared model need not reside in a single shared memory but may be divided among several machines. In the latter case, each machine holds only the part of the model relevant to its tasks in achieving the virtual environment. The cooperating machines typically pass messages through shared memory to update the parts of the distributed model in other machines. Computing bottlenecks arise out of the need to update the model's shared description in memory before computing the model's new state and rendering the environment.

Environment distribution uses several networked computers (wide-area or local-area) to form a single virtual environment in which each node has its own local model of the environment and there are no clients or servers [Bess 1992; Blau 1992; Falby 1993]. This is essentially a DVE approach. The challenge here arises from the need to keep the environment consistent among the distributed systems. Dead-reckoning only partly solves this problem. The environment must also be visually consistent [Ferguson 1992]. Commonly, several central processing units at a single host are set aside to manage the user interface, handle communication tasks, check consistency, create displays, and compute audio outputs. These processes maintain an acceptable frame-rate and portray the virtual world as accurately as possible. Thus, distributed-environment systems build on the work of distributed-computation systems.

Phenomenology participants include all entities that aren't actors. This term encompasses all aspects of weather (clouds, fog, snow, rain, total rainfall, air pressure, humidity, etc.); radar, radio, and sonar emissions; the time of day; the moon's location; and the Sun's location. Modeling (Chap. 8) is crucial to effectively building and inserting these components into a DVE.

Constructive simulation applications can insert many actors into a DVE; they're usually traditional simulations modified to participate in a DVE. They use models of processes (see Chap. 8) to determine simulation outcomes, and human interaction at run time is very limited or impossible. Because they've typically been built for other purposes, they pose several difficulties when they interact with human- and computer-generated actors. The difficulties stem from the differences in time scales for activities, aggregation of actors in a traditional simulation, and ways to resolve interactions. We'll discuss these issues further in Sec. 16.5.1.

All distributed simulations build on the technologies of networks and protocols. The *networks* can be local-area (LAN) or wide-area (WAN). The *protocols* define the types of data that must be exchanged, the data formats, the exchange frequency, and ways to identify participants. Simulation standards don't specify a type of network protocol, so Asynchronous Transfer Mode (ATM [Vetter 1995]), Ethernet, and Transport Control Protocol/Internet Protocol (TCP/IP) are all acceptable ways to transfer data. Every entity commonly broadcasts its information to all other entities, but concepts such as multicast and bundling of protocol data units are part of the standard for distributed interactive simulation, even though designers rarely use them. As Pullen notes in Chap. 15, these techniques are central to using DVE technologies in all applications.

The term *distributed interactive simulation* (DIS) refers to the protocols defined in IEEE standard 1278-1993. This standard specifies how to transfer data within large distributed virtual environments (DVEs) by employing standard communication protocols to exchange data between heterogeneous databases and computer systems over wide-area and local-area networks. The protocols provide a way to compose a single, seamless DVE from a number of live, constructive, computer-generated, and virtual simulation applications. Using these protocols, we can insert humans into a simulation environment and allow them to interact with its entities in real time at reasonable cost. Each computer host of an application in a DVE based on distributed interactive simulation typically supports one or more entities (or actors) that participate in the distributed virtual environment. Communication protocols allow each participating host to inform all other hosts of the position, velocity, acceleration, weapons employment (launch and impact), and visual characteristics of each of its actors and entities. Hosts that comply with the DIS protocols can also use them to transmit and receive weather conditions, electronic emissions, and data from space-based sensors. Using these protocols, they also can manage the DVE and communications between actors, as well as transmit information on the position, orientation, and posture of actors and entities using these protocols. In a distributed interactive simulation, every host must maintain a complete description of the DVE's state at all times. This type of simulation environment is transitioning from its roots as a small-scale system for unit training to a simulation base that can handle small to large virtual environments. The scale depends on the number of participants, how much time and real-world activity a simulation represents, or a combination of these factors.

Advanced distributed simulations (ADS) are DVEs that conform to the requirements of distributed interactive simulation. But they extend the DIS protocols to more accurately represent the environment and more easily meet the needs of live actors. They also support traditional computer wargames better than distributed interactive simulations by providing a standard way to reconcile differences in time, aggregation, and terrain among constructive, computer-generated, and virtual entities.

For a DVE application with virtual participants, users can operate *immersively* or *non-immersively*, depending on the type of interaction and degree of presence they need (see Slater [1993] and Schloerb [1995] for a discussion of presence). Non-immersive operation gives users a portal, or viewport, on the DVE they can move about. It usually relies on a monitor, mouse, and keyboard but has also used true three-dimensional displays [Stytz 1995]. In general, non-immersive operation gives observers a sense of psychological "distance" from the activity rather than a sense of presence (or being in the "middle of the action"). It seems best suited for analysis and possibly for commander's workstations, but definitive studies in this area haven't been done.

Immersive operation, on the other hand, tends to invoke a sense of presence, so users feel they're intimately involved with the environment and the activities taking place in it. It gives users the impression of being surrounded by the environment no matter where they look. Immersion can be achieved using a head- or helmet-mounted display, a dome, or a cave [Cruz-Neira 1992]. In a dome the display surrounds the user and projects on a spherical surface. In a cave, the display appears on the inside of a cube that surrounds the user. Of course, immersion is only one way to invoke presence. Touch and hearing can also be used effectively, but they usually only augment the sense of presence created by sight. As you might expect, immersive operation tends to be more expensive than non-immersive operation.

16.2   Overview of Technologies that Enable Distributed Virtual Environments

Five enabling technologies allow us to insert humans into a distributed virtual environment (DVE) and present them with realistic situations in real time: software architectures, networking, virtual environments, computational models, and artificial intelligence. We'll discuss these technologies here and identify the relationships between them and the six parts of a DVE in the rest of this chapter.

16.2.1   Software Architectures

The software architecture for the host of a DVE application is one of the most complex software systems constructed. Its performance must be reliable and validated, and we must be able to modify and extend almost all of its parts. It affects all aspects of a DVE—especially the virtual-environment participants, computer-generated actors (or forces), and constructive participants. How we address software architecture issues determines how much a system can change to meet new requirements or adapt to new technology and how much that change will cost. If a system doesn't adapt well, it quickly becomes obsolete and costs more to change. To be able to modify and extend a system, we must

- Isolate components and maintain a loosely-coupled application, so changes to any part of it won't overwhelm the overall architecture[*] and it will remain coherent
- Carefully manage how we move data within the architecture and constrain programmers to stay within the architecture as they build and maintain the system
- Make the control flow a visible and separate part of the architecture (which makes the architecture more complex)
- Balance scaleability and reusability with performance by partitioning computations, using object-oriented design and programming, and separating graphical computations from those needed to maintain the world state

---

[*] Usually, the original architectural design tightly encapsulates objects or functions, but implementing and maintaining the software cause this tight structure to crumble as developers try to boost performance, make quick fixes, or add features—a concept commonly referred to as "architectural entropy." Eventually, the original design gets lost within a maze of software patches and departures from the specified approach.

Software architectures are still evolving. So far, no single architecture has emerged as the best one, but object-oriented technology seems to be a key to developing systems that can expand and adapt to new requirements and advances (see App. B). Common methods for decomposing software designs include one centered on users and another centered on functions. The former makes the parts of the system a user deals with the main objects and defines the rest in relation to them. The latter identifies objects based on what the system must do. Overall, though, successful architectures are taking on common characteristics: object-oriented technology, objects based on functions and sub-functions, and precisely specified communication between modules. Table 16.3 describes some proposed architectures that have focused on making systems modifiable and improving performance by distributing computations.

One of the earliest architectures is Robertson's Cognitive Coprocessor architecture [Robertson 1989]. This architecture addresses the problem of allowing multiple, autonomous agents[*] to interact while maintaining the required frame rate for the virtual environment. The Cognitive Coprocessor separates computations needed for user interaction and rendering from those required to update the virtual environment's state. Its key feature is this division and a governor that ensures it meets the required frame rate. The task machine computes updates to the virtual environment's state. The user-discourse machine computes user interactions and rendering. The user-discourse machine's heart is the animation loop, which contains pending computing tasks requested by the user, another part of the architecture, pending displays, or the governor. The governor ensures display updates are timely.

The University of Alberta's MR toolkit [Shaw 1992] represents the virtual environment in four parts: computation, presentation, interaction, and geometric models. The computation component includes the simulation software; it runs independently from, and communicates asynchronously with, the other parts. The presentation component computes the audio and visual output for users. The interaction component accepts users' inputs from body tracking, hand tracking, gloves, and voice devices. The geometric models represent the visual parts of the virtual environment.

Blau [1992] developed the VERN architecture around customized C++ class hierarchies that support distributing virtual environments over local and wide-area networks. VERN supports distributed virtual objects, computing loads, and users among simulation platforms. The main classes are the router, state, player, and ghost. Each entity in the simulation is represented on its host system as a player and on other systems in the virtual environment as a ghost. Locally, a player process communicates with the ghost processes of the other players to acquire information about the status of the remote player that the local ghost is mimicking. Each player process ensures that its remote ghosts' status is correct by sending updates to the remote ghost process when dead reckoning doesn't correctly portray the player's position or state.

---

* In this context, an agent is a process that carries out a task.

Table 16.3.   **Representative Architectures for Virtual Environments.** These six architectures differ based on approach, major components, and design philosophy. (See the discussions in the text for references.)

Architecture	Characteristics and Approach	Components
Cognitive Coprocessor	Computations for the user interface are separate from those for maintaining the virtual environment's state. The virtual environment is on only one machine and one CPU. Designed to distribute computations.	Rendering—controlled by *governor* computations for the virtual environment's state—*task machine* Rendering & user interface—*user discourse machine*
MR Toolkit	Divides what the virtual environment does into: 1) user output, 2) environment's state and user input, 3) 3-D models, 4) system computations. Components communicate through shared memory and update independently. The virtual environment is on only one machine. Designed to distribute computations.	Virtual environment's state and user input—*interaction* Maintain virtual environment's state—*computation* User output—*presentation* Visual parts of the environment—*geometric models*
VERN	Distribute virtual objects, computing load, and users among multiple simulation platforms. Transport all state information using local and wide-area networks. Use dead-reckoning to maintain the approximate state of remote actors. Designed to distribute computations and the environment.	Uses C++ hierarchies Major components are: 1) *router class*; 2) *state class*; 3) *player class*; and 4) *ghost class*. The local actor is the player; remote actors are ghosts.
Veridical User Environment	Use asynchronous message passing between autonomous processes. Distinctly split the user interface from the application process that generates the virtual world. Eliminate the need for a central animation loop. Manage dialogue in several stages. Designed to distribute computations.	Communicate with input and output devices—*device servers.* Maintain and render the virtual environment—*application processes* Manage communication between processes—*dialogue manager*
NPSNET	Capitalize on the parallelism in multiprocessor systems by placing different application threads on different processors. Decompose the application into objects that run within the simulation thread. Use Performer™ to manage multiprocessor rendering. Place all network communication within a network thread to increase throughput at the host. Use shared memory to communicate between threads on a single host. Use dead-reckoning to maintain the approximate state of remote actors. Designed to distribute computations and the environment.	Render the virtual environment— *Performer™ cull and draw threads* Communicate on the network— *network thread* Maintain the virtual environment's state and vehicle dynamics; communicate with input/output devices, sensors—integrated into the *simulation thread*

Table 16.3.   Representative Architectures for Virtual Environments. (Continued) These six architectures differ based on approach, major components, and design philosophy. (See the discussions in the text for references.)

Architecture	Characteristics and Approach	Components
Common-Object Database (CODB)	Decompose the application into large objects, which are themselves built from objects. Build the application around a common set of objects, the world-state manager, common-object database, and environment database. Reduce coupling by using containers to asynchronously send an object's public state to a central data repository, called the common-object database. Asynchronously forward information the common-object database receives to the intended recipient objects. Within large objects, use more containers and a new common-object database to communicate information between the object's parts. Use dead-reckoning to maintain the approximate state of remote actors. Designed to distribute computations and the environment.	Data repository to hold public data moving between parts of the system—*Common-Object Database* Fixed size and format data structures to asynchronously move data between the common-object database and parts of the system—*containers* Single object that interfaces to other parts of the distributed virtual environment and communicates across the network—*World State Manager* Object to hold description of the environment—*Environment Database* Other objects for particular applications, such as agents, input/output devices, dynamics, and sensors

The Veridical User Environment (described in [Appino 1992; Codella 1992; Lewis 1991]), has three main parts: device servers, application processes, and a dialogue manager. These parts communicate asynchronously using "message passing"—moving data between components by placing it in shared memory or sending it across a network using a data-transmission protocol. This approach clearly separates the user interface from the virtual environment (the application processes) or, equivalently, the virtual environment's style from its content. Device servers manage communication with the input and output devices. The application processes simulate the virtual environment and render it. The dialogue manager manages the "dialogue" that allows the input servers to communicate with the processes that need their information and captures output from image generators the servers need to display results.

NPSNET [Falby 1993; Macedonia 1994; Zyda 1993], has been developed at the Naval Postgraduate School as they investigate computing and network issues for distributed virtual environments. It uses a network thread to handle incoming and outgoing message traffic, thereby allowing several processes on a single host to communicate effectively through a single Ethernet port. This approach describes the network services to the host program using an interface based on shared memory. NPSNET has also investigated using multicast as a middleware layer between the application and network within a DVE based on distributed interactive simulation (DIS). Multicasting allows it to partition the DVE, thereby reducing the network bandwidth and host computations required to maintain the DVE's state.

The Common-Object Database architecture [Stytz 1997] was designed to rapidly evolve and explore systems using prototypes. As a result, it can be used to develop and create software while discovering and refining system requirements. This approach uses containers—data structures that move a lot of data between system components—to manage and control communication between these components. The container's size and format remain the same while the application runs. The Common-Object Database architecture further accentuates decoupling of the system's components by routing and storing all data that moves between them. As part of its routing function, it can repackage information from incoming containers into a single container that takes tailored information to each component.

The main parts of this architecture are objects, consisting of system-specific components, the Common-Object Database, the World State Manager, and the Environment Database. These hierarchically-defined objects employ containers to communicate with other parts of the architecture through the Common-Object Database. The World State Manager completely holds the distributed virtual environment's communicated state using DIS-formatted protocol data units. The Environment Database describes the environment's static elements, such as terrain, for all wavelengths for which sensors are available.

Based on these systems, we can draw several useful conclusions about software architectures for DVE applications. An architecture should divide a system into its major components based on what the host must do. It should isolate the inputs, outputs, and network from the rest of the system, so we can insert new devices and change network protocols without affecting the code for most of the application. A governor to ensure desired frame rates is attractive but complex. Thus, many designers have chosen to build systems without governors; instead, they let the systems render complete scenes as fast as possible. As a final observation, trying to build larger virtual environments inevitably leads to larger terrain models. Terrain paging looks like a sound approach to managing these larger datasets, but we don't yet have ways to combine terrain paging with multiple levels of detailed representations for terrain.

16.2.2   Network Technology

Creating useful distributed virtual environments depends on network technology because a single CPU or a set of CPUs communicating in shared memory can't support them. Network technology is the glue that binds the geographically separate hosts into a seamless environment that appears to reside on each user's computer. It supplies the communication bandwidth and protocols needed to pass data between hosts, and it's the only way to provide the realism, accuracy, and large numbers of actors these applications demand. (See Chap. 15 for more detail.)

The key challenges for network technology are bandwidth, bandwidth allocation, and protocols. In general, as bandwidth increases, more entities can participate in the DVE. But this relationship won't hold forever (even though advances in telecommunications hardware will make more bandwidth available) because each host's central processing unit can devote only a limited number of cycles to processing entity data. Therefore, bandwidth allocation is a second important concern. It allows us to partition the battlespace and build large, complex DVEs because hosts aren't burdened with processing extra information. Of course, the hosts must be able to get from these partitions all information relevant to entities they support, so partitioning is complicated. The schemes investigated to date use a mosaic of the battlespace geography plus an entity's function or motion (or other criterion) to partition the battlespace.

Network protocols are important because they can conserve bandwidth and they determine what type of information remote hosts get about each entity. Besides allocating bandwidth, network protocols also determine how efficiently data moves through the network. Basic network protocols are relatively straightforward to craft, but supporting the wide variety of interactions, entities, and conflicting requirements in a DVE makes these protocols complex, as witnessed by the semi-annual *Workshop on Standards for the Interoperability of Distributed Simulations*. You'll find developments on DVEs in the workshop's proceedings. For news on general networking and protocols, see the IEEE's *Communications Magazine*, *Networks Magazine*, *Transactions on Communications*, and *International Conference on Communications*.

16.2.3   Technology for Virtual Environments

In virtual environments, humans use displays, sensors, and effectors to perceive and interact with a computer-generated synthetic environment as if it were real. When properly constructed, a virtual environment induces a sense of presence in the user. This concept of humans and computers interacting and cooperating to complete a task originated in the 1960s [Sutherland 1965]. Figure 16.1 illustrates what we must consider to create a complex virtual environment. For training, a system should have a high degree of presence; portray a realistic, physically correct environment; and have an interface that replicates the layout and functions of the corresponding real-world systems.

Virtual-environment technology differs from multimedia in several respects. The first and most pronounced difference is that conventional multimedia depicts the system's users within physical space, such as an office or conference room. In a virtual environment, the depicted space and elements within it need not have a physical counterpart. Second, conventional multimedia constrains time and space, possibly with some system lag being apparent to users. In virtual reality, individuals can manipulate space and time to suit their needs. In the extreme, they can interact with an environment whose components are separated in time but next to each other physically or that are adjacent in time but not in the virtual space. This flexibility allows users to structure the environment so they can extract data from it as they prefer. You can read more about developments in virtual-environment technology in *Presence: Teleoperators and Virtual Environments* by MIT Press, *IEEE Computer Graphics and Applications*, and the *Society for Computer Simulation* conference series, especially the series on *Military, Government, and Aerospace Simulation*.

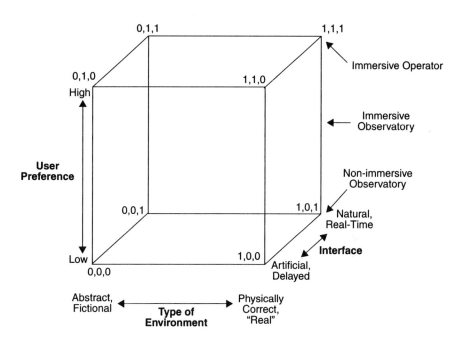

Fig. 16.1. **The Dimensions of Technology for Virtual Environments (after [Zeltzer 1992]).** Virtual environments vary according to three characteristics: how much user presence they try to induce, the fidelity of the environment (its type), and the user interface. The more technologically challenging virtual environments fall at the top, right, rear of the cube; the more traditional virtual environments, which rely on human imagination, fall at the front, lower, left.

The most important improvements in virtual environments are those related to human-computer interaction and 3D computer graphics. These technologies allow users to control actors and to observe activities within the DVE. They're critical because they provide the portal through which humans enter the DVE and determine whether users accept it as real. But they also require a lot of computing. The human-computer interface enables users to communicate commands to the system, gathers these commands, presents them to the simulation, and displays the system's response. Three-dimensional graphics determine how images appear.

The *human-computer interaction* aspect addresses the "look and feel" of interactions with virtual environments. Laurel [1990] and Schneiderman [1992] present good introductions to this area. The look and feel consist of user-interface devices, software that ties the components together, and the form of the user's interaction with the application. The form is what we commonly refer to as the interface. It's the presentation or display, as well as operations and aids the software offers to help users do things. For our purposes, it consists of how the information appears to users and how the system supports interactions with the presentation. The interface is important because users construct models for a system's operation based on the presentation's form and content and how it interacts with the underlying system. For developments in this field, see *IEEE Interactions*; the annual conference proceedings on *Human Factors in Computing Systems* by the Association for Computer Machinery's Special Interest Group on Computer-Human Interaction (ACM SIGCHI); the ACM's *Transactions on Human-Computer Interaction*; the annual conference on *Human-Computer Interaction*, the ACM's annual *Symposium on User Interface Software and Technology*; and the journal, *Presence: Teleoperators and Virtual Environments*, by MIT Press.

Virtual reality also depends on 3D computer graphics because they render, or portray, the virtual environment realistically. Issues in 3D computer graphics include rendering, managing scene databases, and modeling terrain. I won't review the foundations of this technology here, but you can find excellent introductions in Foley [1992] and Hearn [1994].

Rendering means converting a mathematical description of an object into a visible image. The mathematical description can consist of equations, polygon vertices, voxels, or some other format that describes the object. Given this description, a graphics program will then position and orient the object correctly, illuminate it with simulated light sources, shade or color it, and place it on a display device—commonly a cathode ray tube or liquid crystal display screen. All 3D graphical models used to describe a virtual environment make up the scene database.

Important rendering issues in 3D computer graphics are antialiasing, removing hidden surfaces, geometric transformation, the illumination model used to model how light interacts with objects, and the shading algorithm. Antialiasing removes high-frequency signals from the display so rough edges (like "stairsteps") aren't present. Aliasing is very noticeable and detracts from the realism of the display. Removing hidden surfaces involves examining each element of the scene database and removing all surfaces that users can't see. Geometric transformation uses matrix multiplication to place each object in the display in its correct position relative to the viewpoint and to all other parts of the rendered scene. The illumination model is an algorithmic description of the interaction between light and the image's surfaces. The shading algorithm determines how each surface's color is computed from its orientation, base color, and the illumination model.

Other significant issues for rendering are mapping textures, detecting collisions, and using multiple levels of detail to represent an object. Texture mapping increases the image's visual complexity by placing a highly detailed image over an underlying 3D graphical definition of an object, much as one might hang wallpaper on a wall. Detecting collisions involves determining whether two objects have intersected, or touched, each other. To do this properly for a single rendered image, we must examine each pair of objects in the scene database to determine if they have collided. Using multiple levels of detail means generating several 3D graphical models of objects. Each model represents the object at a different level of fidelity. Close-ups use the most detailed model; distant views use the least detailed one.

These basic components of computer graphics allow us to render an image from any position within the virtual world accurately enough so it appears to be real, at least at first glance. All require many computations but they're necessary to make a rendered image look realistic. Research is focusing on reducing the cost of these operations while improving their quality. For more information on computer graphics, see the ACM's *Transactions on Computer Graphics,* the IEEE's *Transactions on Visualization and Computer Graphics,* the proceedings of the annual conference on *Computer Graphics* sponsored by ACM's SIGGRAPH, and the proceedings of the bi-annual *IMAGE Society* conference.

The second main issue for 3D computer graphics is managing the scene database, which allows a simulation to efficiently retrieve terrain and 3D graphical models for rendering while it's running. Scene databases for most virtual-environment applications are very large (tens to hundreds of megabytes). Efficiently managing these large amounts of data at runtime is essential to realistic portrayals of DVEs that operate at interactive frame rates. Managing graphical databases now requires moving polygon-based terrain and entity models from flat files or hierarchically organized databases into memory for rendering. The databases normally stay in memory as a tree, with the root of the tree placed at the origin for the virtual environment. The databases are typically organized based on the virtual environment's coordinate system. A poor database or database-management scheme hurts the host computer's runtime performance and increases the cost of the virtual environment.

A final aspect of 3D computer graphics that relates to DVEs is terrain modeling. Terrain modeling requires combining elevation points and corresponding terrain photographs to depict the area in the photographs. This depiction must appear real, have 3D characteristics on a computer display, and have enough detail to satisfy users. The terrain model should be accurate, with multiple levels of detail and photo-quality realism, as in SIMCORE and its world reference model [Brockway 1995]. But much remains to be done to make these models more accurate, to get them to work together, to move them rapidly from secondary storage to main memory, and to render them quickly. Terrain-elevation data provided by the National Imagery and Mapping Agency (formerly the Defense Mapping Agency) is the basis for most terrain modeling, but at times we need higher resolution for interactions within a realistic environment that imposes constraints like those in the real world.

A further issue is correlating terrain representations and coordinate systems between hosts. Because users of the hosts must operate within the same DVE, the location and accuracy of terrain features are important. They determine tactics for any given situation. A coordinate system determines where the entities are in each host's representation of the DVE. For example, let's assume two hosts are operating within the same DVE, but their terrain depictions and coordinate systems aren't identical. As a result, the entities, hills, valleys, roads, and buildings are in slightly different locations in each system. The standard for distributed interactive simulation only partly solves this problem. It specifies a coordinate system for communication (WGS84 with 64-bit accuracy in each dimension), but it doesn't specify a coordinate system for the host. Therefore, the hosts must transform coordinates between their internal and external representations (which degrades precision) and resolve discrepancies during operation in a way users won't notice.

16.2.4   Computational Models

We must have computational models to provide levels of fidelity that portray the motion of aircraft, ground vehicles, weather systems, sensors, and weapons in flight. They're crucial to

- Realistically portraying human- and computer-controlled entities
- Developing constructive participants in a DVE
- Computing sensor performance (air and ground) and system avionics
- Representing vehicle movement accurately under different terrain, weather, and atmospheric conditions
- Properly reporting sensor information that a real-world counterpart would sense within the same field of view and range
- Computing accurate times of flight and target damage for various weapons

Although we have acceptable computational models in all of these areas, they're not complete or scaleable. Yet, they're vital to the DVE experience because they determine if the training, preparation, and analysis from a DVE will transfer to the real world. Assembling these models is difficult because it requires us to minimize the number of computations while also making them scaleable and accurate. If we ignore or downplay this part for a DVE, the environment may produce invalid or irrelevant results. Ignoring or downplaying it for an entity may make that entity ineffective or misleading. But a model that is 100% accurate isn't practical. Therefore, when developing an entity, we must determine whether the entity's dynamics, sensors, or avionics model needs the greatest fidelity. Doing so requires us to examine the entity's objectives and review the DVE's purpose and intended experience. Then, we can allocate the proper amount of computing power to meet this demand and distribute the remaining computing power in priority order to the rest of the entity's components.

16.2.5   Artificial Intelligence

A final technology to enable DVEs uses low-cost, computer-controlled (computer-generated) actors to place more actors into the DVE without adding humans. Because human-controlled actors are expensive, computer-generated actors are critical to low-cost, realistic, usable, complex DVEs.

Computer-generated actors (CGAs) require artificial intelligence, human behavior models, and models for their vehicle's dynamics (as discussed in the previous section). Recent advances in artificial intelligence have made possible reasonably accurate CGAs. These advances include large, complex reasoning systems, improved behavior modeling, and more extensive knowledge bases for decision making. But most systems don't use all of these advances, and much remains to be done in order to achieve

- More accurate performance—meaning closer to that of a human-controlled actor
- Multiple skill levels (such as rookie, skilled, and ace) within a given class of computer-generated actors
- Workable approaches to rapid prototyping for designing and assembling knowledge bases
- Computer-generated commanders
- Replanning of missions in real time
- A generic, broadly applicable architecture to enhance decision making by CGAs
- Accurate management of sensors

This technology depends on advances in software architecture for its success because of the systems' complexity and the need to modify and maintain them. For developments in artificial intelligence, see the journals *Expert Systems with Applications*, *IEEE Expert*, and *Knowledge Engineering Review*. Also, consult proceedings for the *Conference on Artificial Intelligence Applications* and the *International Conference on Tools with AI*. For more on computer-generated forces and actors, see proceedings for the *Conference on Computer Generated Forces and Behavior Representation* (operated by the Institute for Simulation and Training) and the *Interservice/Industry Training Systems and Education Conference*.

16.3   The Virtual Participants

Virtual participants allow humans to enter the DVE and control virtual actors as they interact with the terrain, other actors, and DVE phenomena. They create the impression of "being there" and entice users to react to the DVE's changing states as though they were real. The technology for virtual environments allows humans to interact in real time with complex environments composed of 3D graphical descriptions that interact and move according to the real world's physical constraints.

To use virtual participants, users must have

- Visual and audio queues that are accurate enough to entice them to suspend disbelief
- Sensors to determine their position, posture, and orientation and to map them from the real to the synthetic world
- Devices that allow them to control appropriate parts of the environment, their actors, and displays of the environment

To meet these needs, researchers have investigated many rendering techniques, image-display devices, input and output devices, sensors, 3D graphical models of the environment, and user interfaces. The key to creating a realistic virtual environment is the proper blending of technologies for human-computer interaction, simulation, 3D computer graphics, graphical databases, rapid software prototyping, software architecture, and object-oriented design.

16.3.1   Visual, Audio, and Haptic Devices

To display virtual environments, developers have typically used a cathode ray tube, a liquid crystal display, a head- (or helmet-) mounted display, a free-standing display, a surround dome, or a device for true 3D viewing. True 3D is a "total-volume" display that exploits the human perceptual system's physiological cues—such as movement parallax, motion perspective, and binocular parallax (stereo vision)—when viewing the actual depth of different parts of an image in the display. Some forms of true 3D display (using varifocal mirrors or holographic images) further enhance the depth illusion by allowing users to see structures superimposed in the volume and to segment and separate the structures by moving their heads. Developers have used varifocal mirrors, several types of shutters on cathode-ray tubes, rotating helical displays illuminated by lasers, and a rotating plane filled with light-emitting diodes in three colors to generate true 3D displays. McKenna [1992] reviews the major display types that capture 3D techniques, and Lipscomb [1989] compares human interaction with various devices, paying particular attention to 3D displays. Despite all the apparent advantages of true 3D, head- (or helmet-) mounted displays have been the technology of choice for displaying immersive virtual environments since Sutherland [1968] first described a virtual environment. Computing and hardware costs are lower than for true 3D, and these displays can provide a generally equivalent experience because they allow the user's head to move freely.

Developers must create inexpensive helmet-mounted displays which provide a wide field of view and high resolution (up to 2 arc-seconds to eliminate small, but visually noticeable defects in a displayed image). The displays also must offer stereo viewing, full color, high image quality, low weight, and customizable fit. Challenges arise because of the need to build a heavier or more expensive display to meet these requirements. Increasing the field of view requires a larger surface to display images and optical systems that can present the image to users with little or no distortion. Stereo can drive up the weight and cost because it requires two optical systems to bring the image from the display to the user's eyes. High resolution conflicts with the need for a wide field of view because it calls for many pixels per unit area whereas a wide field of view increases the display area. Together, resolution and field of view increase the computing load on the host dramatically. In general, we trade off resolution and field of view, keeping the field of view as large as possible while allowing the host computer to compute pixel values at a real-time rate. Adding color to the display imposes two penalties: increased computing cost at the host and increased weight, which again conflicts with other requirements. But users expect color displays and usually prefer them even at the cost of reduced field of view or increased weight. The image quality of a helmet-mounted display usually depends on the quality of the optics and of the image-display device. Improvements in either add cost or weight. To date, no single device has satisfied all these needs, but many have been proposed or developed, and commercial research is active.

The typical design for a helmet-mounted display consists of one or two devices that use combinations of optics and mirrors to project, focus, and display an image in front of the user's eyes. To reduce the weight of the helmet-mounted display, liquid crystal displays have replaced cathode ray tubes, but they usually have poorer resolution and brightness. Fiber optics have also been explored for helmet-mounted displays. In this approach, the image sources aren't on a viewer's head. Instead, they're belt mounted, placed elsewhere on the user's body, or detached from the user. Fiber-optic bundles bring the light from the image source's display faceplate to the optics used to project the image before the user's eyes. This technique provides high resolution, color, and a wider field of view than cathode ray tubes or liquid crystal displays. Fiber optics also cost much more and suffer from noticeable drop-outs in the image when fiber bundles break.

Engineers of virtual environments typically convey most information to users through their sense of sight, but audio can also reduce workload by providing cues to the location of significant activity [Gaver 1991; Cohen 1992] and increase the sense of presence in the environment through realistic sounds [Burgess 1992; Takala 1992; Wenzel 1991]. For the latter, systems try to compute audio cues that simulate sound as we'd perceive it within an enclosed space. They match the characteristics for location, spatial extent, reverberation, and echo that would occur in the real world.

Haptic devices add to the information from video and audio whenever touch is important to a user. Examples might be handling delicate materials or positioning an object. Haptic devices have indicated the force of interaction between parts of a virtual environment [Brooks 1990; Iwata 1993; Minsky 1990] and simulated the way an object's surface feels [Hirota 1995; Rosenberg 1993]. Research has also addressed using gestures to control the virtual environment, as in Sturman [1994]. For example, people can use their hands as a 3D mouse to point and select or to input commands that control a system. In these ways, touch and gestures add to the user's natural control of a virtual environment.

16.3.2 Interaction between Humans and Computers

Human-computer interaction is critical to DVE applications with virtual participants because users must employ physical devices and displays to assess situations and issue commands to the system. If users are immersed, they must be able to access controls for the environment displayed on their helmet-mounted displays. If the interaction must simulate an existing system, the positioning, color, and shape of the interaction devices are already defined. The interface must model these characteristics as well as possible within limits on time and funding. If the simulator doesn't model an existing system, the human-computer interface must be easy to use, icons and symbols must be easy to read and comprehensible, and controls must be accessible.

When developing an immersive system, the type of manipulation an interface device offers is important. Thus, it's useful to consider Card, MacKinlay, and Robertson's [1990] method of categorizing technologies for interaction with a virtual environment. They categorize input devices according to the manipulations performed by the interface. Operators include linear and rotational motion, absolute and relative measurement of the input, and whether the input is based on the input device's position or the force applied to it. Table 16.4 illustrates these relationships.

Table 16.4. Physical Properties Sensed by an Input Device (from [Card 1990]). This table shows how force sensing, position measurement, and linear and rotary motion can combine to form an input device.

	Linear	Rotary
Position Absolute Relative	Position **P** Movement Δ**P**	Rotation **R** delta Rotation Δ**R**
Force Absolute Relative	Force **F** delta Force Δ**F**	Torque **T** delta Torque Δ**T**

Composition operators take these six degrees of freedom and create devices that map physical actions in the real world into meaningful values for applications. The composition operators are merge, layout, and connect. Merge composition combines input properties of the underlying components that make up a device. Layout composition places controls for the underlying components on the device. Connect composition maps the output of one of the underlying devices into the input of a device connected to it.

Besides the interface, we must consider three other important aspects of human-computer interactions: the system's interactivity, the workload a system imposes, and how well it captures reality. Interactivity is important because the system must render and display images of the virtual environment to users at an interactive frame rate—at least 15 frames per second—so they don't perceive a lag between inputs and responses. The workload a system imposes determines a human's ability to keep pace with a DVE's changing state.

A system's realism and fidelity depend on its visual portrayal of objects and the underlying computational models used to propagate objects through the environment. Fidelity and realism determine a DVE's accuracy and, therefore, our willingness to accept it and act accordingly. Realism doesn't mean an image must always be of photographic quality, nor must motion always be computed using highly accurate models; rather, images and motion must be real enough to convince the user. Yet, fidelity is important because it determines how well the system portrays the real world, as well as how useful the training, analysis, or planning based on it will be. For example, a system with low fidelity may incorrectly depict vehicle dynamics. As a result, users will expect unrealistic motion from real vehicles.

16.3.3   Requirements for DVE Applications

Virtual actors in DVEs must have a modifiable software architecture, high fidelity and realism, support for human-computer interaction, and support for situation awareness. How well they satisfy these requirements determines

- The cost of building and maintaining the system
- How well users accept the system as real
- The degree of presence the system induces in users
- How easily users can operate within the DVE
- How much useful work users can do
- How much the DVE will help users complete a task

Poor performance in any of these requirements can lead to unacceptable costs, low acceptance from users, or overloading users with things to do and information to absorb.

A modifiable architecture allows the application to support change, to enhance abilities, and to respond to newly discovered requirements. It ensures the application can readily adapt to meet new performance and communication protocol requirements during development, as well as to support maintenance of the fielded system through occasional upgrades. The architecture should force us to encapsulate an application's components so we can change one or more of them with limited effect on the rest of the system. Designing for flexibility will increase the cost of design. But it should make the system easier to modify because programmers can consider parts of it in small, tightly encapsulated units with precisely defined functions rather than in large, intertwined globs of code that do many things. Until now, modifiable architectures haven't been able to perform in real time, but increased computing power and better compilers are eliminating this limitation.

High-fidelity virtual environments and realistic virtual actors require accurate representations of the real world; computational models for vehicle dynamics, sensors and weapons; and 3D graphical models for entities other than terrain and for static objects. Representing the world means creating a terrain model for the virtual actor that we can change during execution in response to the actions of other entities in a DVE. However, because virtual actors don't operate in isolation, their world representation must have a counterpart in other human-controlled systems as well as in systems for computer-generated forces. In the virtual environment, vehicles, weapons, and sensors must operate no better or faster than they do in the real world. The 3D graphical models that represent entities in a DVE must be able to portray different types of damage, weapons loads, and entity states. To meet this goal, several graphical models at different levels of detail are often needed. Because the virtual-environment application has to interact with other applications, these models must also coordinate with—and be calibrated to—the representations other applications use in the DVE. Achieving high fidelity makes the system more complex and demands more from the architecture because high-fidelity code tends to be more complicated than low-fidelity code. Higher fidelity also makes real-time performance more difficult to achieve.

The virtual-environment application also must effectively use the principles of human-computer interaction. Outputs must incorporate high-quality, accurate images. When an application is emulating a real-world system, the rendering should closely match the real system or, at least, get users to accept and respond to the resulting images as though they were real, not computer-generated. Issues related to output are color, frame rate, field of view, illumination model, shading model, and type of display. Although users prefer color, don't use it if the real-world counterpart doesn't. The frame rate should be as high as possible—from 15 to 72 frames per second. The field of view should match that of human sight. The illumination model should accurately represent the propagation of light, its interaction with materials in the environment, and shadows. The shading model should consider surface normal and distance, as well as angles to the observer and sources of light, when computing surface colors. Your choices of color, frame rate, field of view, illumination model, and shading model will largely determine the users' sense of realism and presence in the DVE. To choose a type of display, consider whether users must be able to look rapidly in any direction. If so, you'll probably want to use an immersive display.

For input, consider whether or not you're modeling a real-world system. If you are, copy its input devices as closely as possible and support its forms of interaction using switches, toggles, mice, or throttles. If you aren't, just make sure the devices and forms of interaction are usable by developing prototypes and having users evaluate them before finishing your design [Nielsen 1993].

The need for human-computer interaction affects the system's complexity, architecture, performance, and scaleability. It tends to increase complexity because it requires a lot of code, typically up to half of the application's total. The architecture becomes more complex because it must transmit users' inputs to parts of the system and display information for users to view. Also, real-time performance may suffer because so much code has to run in one-fifteenth of a second or less; yet, effective human-computer interaction requires real-time performance.

To be effective for some types of training and analysis or mission planning, a system must address situation awareness because people need information to make a decision. In fact, the typical problem in a DVE application is limiting the data available to users so the information they receive is only what they would get in the real world.

The four requirements I've outlined above are hard to satisfy because we have to use large software systems that must work in real time, render high-quality 3D graphics, and support advanced interaction between people and computers. The interplay between these requirements complicates the design and architecture of the system. Table 16.5 summarizes how each requirement affects the application's complexity, software architecture, ability to perform in real time, and scaleability.

Table 16.5.   How Actor Requirements Affect Some Software Metrics in a Virtual Environment. This table examines how the requirements for modifiable software, high fidelity, natural human-computer interaction, and situational awareness affect the complexity, performance, and maintainability of application software.

Actor Requirements	Effect on Software Metrics			
	System Complexity	Software Architecture	Real-time Performance	Scaleable
Modifiable	Reduces	Control flow must be visible and traceable	Tends to compete, but not as much of a problem as CPU power and compiler performance improve	Complementary
High Fidelity	Increases	Must be able to manage multiple levels of fidelity models	Competes because high fidelity increases the computing load	No effect
Human-Computer Interaction	Increases	More complex, increases entropy	Competes because it requires more computing, but human-computer interactions demand real-time performance to be effective	No effect if components for human-computer interaction are properly isolated
Situational Awareness	Increases	More complex	Competes because of additional computing costs	No effect

16.4   Computer-Generated Actor Participants

Computer-generated actors (CGAs) [also known as computer-generated forces (CGFs)] are useful in a DVE because they can increase the complexity and realism of the DVE without using many (more costly) people. To be effective, computer-generated actors must behave as though people are controlling them, which calls for artificial-intelligence techniques and models of human behavior. Computer-generated actors differ from a constructive simulation because they

- Operate in real time, not in time steps

- Interact with other entities individually, not as aggregates

- Reason about the environment

- Determine outcomes based on actions by, and interactions between, individual entities instead of probability tables or other probability-based methods

We can use CGA technology to control aircraft, armored vehicles, ground vehicles, naval vehicles, command and control centers, and spacecraft in a DVE to meet the simulation's objectives.

Modeling human behavior makes computer-generated actors "behave" realistically. It focuses on the output of human decision making, not on the decision process (or human cognition) itself. These behavior models key on three important parts of decision making:

- Acquiring knowledge—getting the information needed to effectively model human behavior
- Structuring knowledge—arranging the knowledge base so a CGA can rapidly access information and use it to analyze situations and make decisions
- Building the apparatus to make decisions

Knowledge acquisition and structuring should determine the key static and dynamic information needed to model human decisions. The decision-making apparatus supports near-term, reactive decision making and long-term planning. For either type, we can use case-based reasoning, frames, fuzzy logic, or other techniques for artificial intelligence. We must continue to refine all three parts of these behavior models until we get the realistic results we want. Of course, we also need software to manage DVE communication and vehicle dynamics, as well as to respond to human voice commands (in some cases).

To create intelligent entities for distributed interactive and advanced distributed simulations, developers must consider knowledge engineering, information structuring, decision making, and scaleability. Most systems have addressed these problems piecemeal because they've had to meet program schedules and demands for realism and real-time performance. Typically, these ad hoc solutions aren't scaleable. As a result, it's difficult to add knowledge or decision making to computer-generated actors, and the systems are expensive to modify and maintain.

16.4.1   Application Requirements for Computer-Generated Actors

Artificially intelligent CGAs must operate in real time and support realistic training and analysis at a reasonable cost. Real-time performance, coupled with realistic training and analysis, demands multiple skill levels for classes of entities, a gradual reduction in reasoning ability under stress, a modular knowledge structure that expands easily, and adaptive mission planning. For example, an application can provide rookie, expert, and ace levels of behaviors for aircraft actors within the same battlespace; this broad mix of combatant skills should enable better training and analysis. The computer-generated actor should have a complete set of behaviors for the types of missions it must do, but not all behaviors require the same quality. Users in the field should be able to customize the actor's performance and skill level, and general-purpose programmers should be able to adapt it to new weapon systems, vehicles, and tactics. The actor's vehicle dynamics should be accurate, meaning they should correctly respond to changes in the environment and be based on an accurate mathematical model of the vehicle's motion. The actor should also respond acceptably to unforeseen circumstances and uncertain information. Finally, it should exhibit complex, realistic behavior within the battlespace and adapt its mission parameters to changes during the mission.

A computer-generated actor must be modifiable, highly accurate, adaptable in its decisions and behaviors, and able to incorporate the results of past reasoning automatically into the decision process. These requirements derive from the need to support various training scenarios at the lowest possible cost while also credibly representing the modeled entity's behavior. Table 16.6 summarizes how each requirement affects the computer-generated actor's software in terms of its complexity, architecture, ability to operate in real time, difficulty in knowledge engineering, and scaleability.

A modifiable actor requires rapidly expandable knowledge for particular domains and a flexible software architecture. Expandable knowledge is necessary because the actor must be able to incorporate new strategies, tactics, and maneuvers that reflect the current concepts from allies and opponents. Otherwise, it will stagnate and require expensive maintenance to remain useful for training. A flexible software architecture likewise ensures a computer-generated actor can readily adapt to new requirements for performance and communication protocols. The architecture should support developing and fielding systems. It won't change often for a fielded system, but it must incorporate upgrades with limited effect on the rest of the system.

For high fidelity, a computer-generated actor must use accurate world representations, dynamic models for vehicle motion, models for sensors and weapons, and models for human behavior. The world representation should come from the National Imagery and Mapping Agency's digital terrain and elevation data or data from the U.S. Geological Survey. However, because actors don't operate in isolation, their world representation must have a highly accurate counterpart for use by manned systems as well as other computer-generated actors. Vehicles, weapons, and sensors must operate no better than their real-world counterparts. In addition, we must faithfully capture such characteristics as an operator's eyesight or the systems for radar and infrared sensing.

Modeling human behavior is the biggest challenge to fidelity. To be useful for training, the model must correctly compute the outputs of human decision making as quickly as people make decisions, and it must be unpredictable and certifiable. The actor's decisions must also appear human. That is, the actor shouldn't make decisions that are disjointed, disregard the world state, or disregard the mission's success or its own preservation.

The second characteristic of human behavior—unpredictability—requires computer-generated actors to behave in an unpatterned way, so human opponents can't detect and use patterns to defeat it. Unpredictability forces an opponent (human or computer-generated) to rely on training and knowledge to defeat it. By unpatterned behavior, I don't mean random; rather, the actor's behavior must be as rich and varied as a human's behavior.

Table 16.6.   How Computer-Generated Actors Affect Some Software Metrics. This table examines how requiring modifiable software, high fidelity, adaptive decision making, and learning affects software for computer-generated actors.

| Actor Requirements | Software Metric | | | | |
	Complexity	Architecture	Real-time Performance	Knowledge Engineering	Scaleability
Modifiable	Increases complexity because it requires more knowledge and a more flexible decision structure	Increases architectural entropy: requires control flow to be visible and traceable within the architecture	No effect	Increases amount of development work	Complements
Highly Accurate	No effect	Must manage models at multiple levels of fidelity	Competes	Increases amount of development work for the knowledge base and decision mechanism	No effect
Adapts Decisions to Environment	Increases complexity because it requires mechanisms for adaptive decisions and decision control	No global effect	Supports	Increases amount of work to elicit and represent principles for adaptability	Complements
Automatically Incorporates Experiences	Increases complexity because it complicates decision making and requires an evaluation engine to determine how to score and incorporate results of decisions.	Requires an evaluation engine to determine how to score and incorporate results of decisions	Competes	Increases amount of work to design a learning mechanism and capture experience	Complements knowledge representation part of decision making

Finally, an actor's behavior must be certifiable—measurable against and comparable to a human's exhibited behaviors in a similar situation. However, this doesn't mean that the system is provably correct or that it responds credibly in all situations.

To make adaptable decisions—the third major requirement for computer-generated actors—the actor must flexibly respond to situations in the virtual environment. It must adapt to varying amounts of information and varying levels of required performance in the battlespace. Adaptable decision mechanisms permit the system to maintain an actor's robust, credible behavior at run time under various external circumstances and for operators with different skill levels. Robust, credible behavior is necessary so the actor will act and react even when confronted by conflicting or incomplete information and under system stress. Multiple skill levels increase the realism of the DVE and provide more realistic training.

The requirements I've outlined above are difficult to satisfy because we have to use large software systems with extensive knowledge bases. The interplay between the knowledge bases and decision mechanisms further complicates the system. Thus, we must eventually build ways to learn into architectures of computer-generated actors, so they'll improve their decision making as they operate in distributed virtual environments.

16.5 Constructive, Live, and Phenomenology Participants

Constructive, live, and phenomenology participants round out the types of entities in a distributed virtual environment (DVE). Constructive participants are the aggregate actors we insert into the DVE using traditional simulation systems. Live participants come from real-world activity within an instrumented area. Instruments capture the motion and orientation of these real-world participants and convert them into protocol data units for the DVE. Phenomenology participants include anything that isn't an actor, such as weather, radar, and communications. Because these three types of participants increase complexity and realism in a DVE with virtual and computer-generated actors, let's look briefly at each one.

16.5.1 Constructive Participants

Constructive participants are essential if we want to create DVEs with many entities but reduce the number of protocol data units that a network and host computers must handle. But using constructive participants in a DVE increases the computing load for the constructive application and the other applications in the DVE. Constructive participants differ from virtual and computer-generated actors in several ways. Traditional simulations that generate these constructive participants operate with fixed intervals of minutes, or even hours, between successive states; virtual and computer-controlled actors operate in real time.

Also, traditional simulations don't make decisions. Instead, they use probability tables to determine results at each decision point for each part or unit. Constructive participants typically insert multiple actors into the DVE as groups (aggregates) that are handled statistically.

This statistical handling of groups of entities forces us to consider two key issues. First, we must correlate environmental representations from constructive simulations with those from live and virtual actors. Constructive simulations typically portray terrain at a low resolution and statistically represent the rest of the environment; human- and computer-controlled actors use non-statistical representations at a higher resolution. Second, whenever these two main types of simulations interact, we must reconcile differences in the ways they represent entities and time.

As a result, we must take special precautions when constructive participants interact with live, virtual, or computer-generated actors. Anytime they come in contact, we must de-aggregate the constructive actor into a set of individuals, determine the outcome for these individuals, and then re-aggregate the group back into a single constructive actor. For example, we would divide a tank platoon into tanks, infantry, and supply vehicles, and then insert them into the DVE as new actors. The new actors must be at a location in the battlespace that correlates with the location of the original constructive actor and at a correlated time. This partitioning can occur whenever actors intrude upon each other's area of influence, an aggregated unit enters a designated area of the battlespace, or certain other events take place. We have to clearly define criteria for breaking up constructive participants so those at the margins of the criteria don't cycle continuously between aggregated and individual representations. Otherwise, this oscillation will eat up the computing power of the constructive participant's host computer and waste network bandwidth. We also must contain the de-aggregation, so it doesn't ripple across other aggregated participants and make their host computers waste computing resources. Once we've introduced new actors into the simulation, we must control them either by modifying the main simulation or by using technology for computer-generated actors. Then, we resolve the interaction using the time scale and environmental representation of the live, virtual, and computer-generated actors. Finally, the system re-aggregates the constructive participants using the constructive simulation's version of it— usually, a statistical representation of its abilities. The cost to integrate constructive simulations with virtual, live, and computer-generated actors is minimal for the latter; the constructive simulation bears almost all the cost because it does the computing to divide and recombine the constructive participants.

16.5.2   Live Participants

Integrating live participants into a DVE is difficult because we have to use instruments to capture their movement and engagements, convert this information into data units, and then transmit these units to other participants in the DVE. These other participants must convert the information into a virtual portrayal of the activity, as they must for every entity. But getting data on live players is just the beginning. To use live participants, we must make sure we have enough data from them and correlate live and DVE activity to a common, safe representation of the world state. The situation becomes even more complicated when the DVE contains live, virtual, and computer-generated actors. For example, voice communication between live and virtual actors can be a problem because live actors typically use standard field equipment whereas human operators of virtual actors use whatever is at hand (usually an office telephone). When live and computer-generated actors must communicate, speech synthesis and voice recognition with text generation must occur in real time. Also, range instruments typically aren't extensive enough to portray precisely the orientation and posture of live actors in the DVE. As a result, the DVE represents actors at different accuracies, which may reduce its usefulness for training, planning, and acquisition. Because most of these issues are related to a DVE's infrastructure, modifying actors and entities to operate with live participants doesn't cost much. All of these issues are open research topics, which you can review in the *Workshop on Standards for the Interoperability of Distributed Simulations* and the *Interservice/ Industry Training Systems and Education Conference*.

16.5.3　Phenomenology Participants

These participants can improve the realism, visual appearance, and fidelity of the environment by making conditions more accurate. For example, if rain and snow are part of a DVE, ground vehicles can more accurately simulate operation for changing traction as rain or snow accumulates. To use this extra information, the vehicles in the DVE need an appropriate dynamics model, and the DVE must provide a protocol for distributing information to the vehicles. Inserting phenomena into a DVE creates three challenges: calculating their distribution throughout the DVE, modifying actors to respond to their effects, and developing a protocol to inform other entities of their presence and concentration. The first challenge arises because most phenomena—such as weather, radio, and radar emissions—aren't distributed uniformly throughout a volume, which means increased computing to determine their distribution and concentration. The second challenge is to retrofit actor applications that were developed without the ability to respond to phenomena. This may mean a simple change in vehicle dynamics or something more complicated, such as modifying the knowledge base and mechanisms which allow computer-generated actors to make decisions. To meet the third challenge—informing all entities of the phenomena and their concentration—we typically divide the DVE's volume into sub-volumes and broadcast the phenomena's concentration for a volume only when an entity needs it. We may need to use different sized sub-volumes to calculate the phenomena's distribution. Another problem is having to change computer-generated actors and traditional simulations so they'll include phenomena forecasts in their plans and actions. Most DVEs don't have protocol data units for phenomena forecasts, such as weather forecasts, but developers are working on this ability. Once it's available, systems that must plan autonomously will have to change so they can use these forecasts in planning.

Inserting phenomena into a DVE increases requirements for computing and network bandwidth, and other entity applications may need costly software changes to respond to a particular phenomenon. For example, if you're putting weather into the DVE, you'll need a dedicated server to calculate it. Because of computing cost, servers typically calculate weather only at gridpoints (grid crossings) on a 3D grid throughout the DVE. With a server in place, you'll still need protocols that distribute the weather information by determining broadcast frequency, the weather behavior between broadcasts, and algorithms to interpolate weather between grid points—before the system can operate in the DVE. At that point, your job is still less than half done, because you must change application software for the actors.

You'll need to change the human-controlled actors to account for weather in their dynamics calculations, to interpolate weather between grid points, and to respond to these conditions in their motion. Computer-generated actors require the same changes, plus you must augment their reasoning ability to permit decision making when weather changes. Probability tables in traditional simulations must change to consider different types of weather. Finally, because weather (or any other phenomenon) may affect other phenomena in the DVE, the servers for these other phenomena must change as well. Using phenomena in a DVE is costly, so it has moved slowly while developers have addressed other, more pressing, issues. But research is likely to continue because it can increase the realism of DVEs.

16.6   Communication and Networking

To transmit data effectively between host computers in a DVE, we must have enough bandwidth and efficient data formats (protocols). Pullen discusses this topic fully in Chap. 15, so I'll talk here only about how networking and protocols affect inserting users into DVEs. The two major approaches available now are the IEEE's protocols for distributed interactive simulation and the DIVE system.

The IEEE protocols for distributed interactive simulation (see [Harvey 1991; McDonald 1991], and IEEE 1278–1993) use any hardware layer for communication and can support distributed simulations involving many actors. Using these protocols, each host must maintain a complete description of the virtual environment, plus the actors and their motion in this environment. Every entity can access complete information about the state of all other entities because data is broadcast at infrequent, but fixed, time intervals. Each entity application uses dead reckoning to estimate other entities' position, velocity, and orientation between broadcasts. It extrapolates the position of an entity (or a part of an entity) based on the latest position and velocity information from the entity and the elapsed time since the last broadcast was received. Each entity application runs its own entity's dead-reckoning algorithm and broadcasts updated position and velocity information whenever the position computed by its dynamics unit differs significantly from the dead-reckoned position or at the end of a time-out period. As Singhai [1995] notes, dead reckoning in DVEs reduces bandwidth but can create errors in the entities' position and orientation. This is acceptable in distributed interactive simulations because real-time performance is more important than reliability or accuracy. That is, packet drop-outs and dead-reckoned entity states cause some data loss, but we accept the loss to move data rapidly through the network. We assume people won't notice these minor effects and will accept the results because they help keep the system interactive.

A different approach prevails in DIVE [Benford 1995; Carlsson 1993; Fahlen 1993; Hagsand 1996]. This system enables high-bandwidth communication between people collaborating on a work project, so it transfers audio and video as well as text and entity state. It uses a central server in a client-server approach. DIVE conserves bandwidth by permitting communication only between entities that express an interest in communicating, but once engaged, each entity can exchange data at high bandwidth. On the other hand, distributed interactive simulations limit the amount of data entities can transmit, but each entity knows the state of all other entities. In DIVE, entities don't communicate when they're outside an entity's zone of interest (horizon), so we must carefully choose these horizons. Participating hosts share descriptions of the virtual environment and dynamically update the DVE's state using a shared-memory paradigm. Network communication uses a reliable multicast protocol, and dead-reckoning is based on linear and angular velocity. As a result of these characteristics, DIVE supports only a few entities interacting within a relatively small area. It may not suit large-scale simulations, but many of its concepts may apply to situations needing high bandwidth communication between entities to get accurate interactions.

16.7   Preparing to Use Technology for Distributed Virtual Environments

Whenever you assemble a DVE, clearly establish the goals and objectives for human involvement in the environment—assuming you've established the simulation's overall objectives (Chap. 5). End users of the system play a key role here. Make sure the resulting loss of statistical power in the DVE is acceptable in light of these goals. If not, traditional simulation technology is probably better than DVE technology. Table 16.2 gives you some idea how to choose, but you'll need to consider other factors, too. If the simulation doesn't need to interact with people while it runs, you may not need humans in the simulation. As an example, a DVE may not be a wise choice if it's important to statistically analyze a simulation's results. But you may need a DVE if the simulation must help you examine the usability of a real-world system, adequacy of training in using the system, team tactics, or the human aspects of a mission plan. Unfortunately, you don't have much empirical data to help you decide when to use DVE technology. But typically, you'd benefit from it if

- You don't need the simulation to be repeatable (people don't repeat actions precisely)
- Humans must be in the environment

- Training is necessary for individual actors
- Many individual entities must interact
- You must train and evaluate many people on real-world tasks

If humans must be involved, you'll need interactions in real time. In general, this increases the required computing power and drives up costs for equipment and development. You also have to consider the time grain for the simulation environment. If it must be very fine (under a millisecond), distributed interactive simulation may not work because network and processing lags can easily consume 100 milliseconds. You can partly make up for these lags by using absolute timestamps [Katz 1994], but no-one has shown that timestamping can reduce effective lag to under 1 millisecond.

If you don't need the simulation to interact with people, you may still want to use DVE technology if a single platform can't support the needed scale and complexity, or if virtual, live, and constructive simulations might have to interact. In these cases, you may need DVE technology to link components together.

If you decide to try a DVE solution, you'll need to construct the environment by establishing the

- Terrain model
- Numbers and types of participants
- Coordinate systems
- Network component
- Virtual-environment technology for virtual participants
- Number and type of computer-generated actors
- Number and type of constructive participants
- Design and execution of experiments to validate the DVE

First, select a terrain model. For new systems, base it on the National Imagery and Mapping Agency's Digital Terrain and Elevation Data or other standard data in a high-resolution format so you can place features as accurately as possible. Put photographic textures on the terrain, so it appears as realistic as possible. The standard for resolution isn't authoritatively established, so the National Imagery and Mapping Agency's data may not be good enough in some cases. You'll also need to reconcile terrain features from legacy systems with the Agency's data. This may be as simple as transforming coordinate systems but may involve determining systems that have the highest resolution available and using them to resolve discrepancies. Trott [1995] examines several terrain standards, compares them, and describes the desirable features for a DVE. Spuhl [1994] discusses general considerations for correlating DVEs. If possible, you should upgrade the terrain descriptions for legacy systems to the highest resolution used by any participating system to eliminate inconsistencies that can result in poor training or analysis. For example, suppose one system is using the National Imagery and Mapping Agency's standard data with photographic textures, and a second system is using a coarse approximation with no texturing.

In the high-resolution system, a tank hiding in a forest wouldn't be visible from the air, whereas the coarser system wouldn't even show a forest to hide in. To resolve these discrepancies during a real-time simulation, the actors must exchange visibility data to determine the true visibility [Purdy 1995]. But the DVE's objectives may not be compatible with the time or bandwidth this exchange requires.

After selecting the terrain, establish the coordinate system for individual host computers and for the complete DVE. Usually, you'll choose between the coordinate system defined by the IEEE standard for distributed interactive simulation and the terrain's (topocentric) system. The former is a geocentric Cartesian coordinate system, which means its origin is at the center of the Earth and it uses Cartesian coordinates with 64-bit precision. The X-axis passes through the equator at the Prime Meridian, the Y-axis passes through the equator at 90° east, and the Z-axis passes through the North Pole. This system preserves the shape of real-world lines, is the same coordinate system used by protocols in distributed interactive simulation, and can readily represent large-scale DVEs. However, the 64-bit representation is unwieldy and doesn't transform readily into other systems, such as a topocentric or Universal Transverse Mercatur (Army) system. Topocentric coordinates, on the other hand, depend on a planar representation of a DVE's terrain rather than of the entire world. As a result, 32-bit accuracy is plenty, but scaling up to larger DVEs is difficult. A further complication arises when the DVE includes constructive simulations, because they normally use yet another coordinate system based on geographic coordinates (latitude, longitude, and altitude relative to a standard geodetic spheroid referenced to the Earth).

Whichever coordinate system you choose for the host computer's application and the DVE, you'll need to have a way to convert between it and the coordinate systems other hosts use. (See Evans [1995] or Toms [1995] for more on this issue.) You'll also need to convert coordinates for

- Inputs from tracking devices for live-range or immersive systems
- Information from dynamics and sensor models
- Outputs of head-mounted displays (if used)

Network design is another key issue. You must make sure the network provides enough bandwidth to meet the DVE's objectives, define all required data transmission protocols, specify the network topology, and ensure participating hosts can be properly identified. Specify the bandwidth for the wide-area network's connections and acquire it from a telecommunications provider. Also, consider multicasting. It may reduce the computing load for host computers and increase the number of entities within the DVE. Selecting protocols is somewhat simpler than specifying bandwidth because most DVEs use the ones established for distributed interactive simulation—they are prevalent and available. But examine these protocols carefully to determine if you need to change them in order to support the DVE's objectives.

You'll also need to log data and manage the DVE. In theory, you can manage the DVE using the protocol data units defined for this purpose by the IEEE standard for distributed interactive simulation. However, many systems don't recognize or respond to these data units, and their content is poorly defined. Equipping applications to respond to them and defining their content are difficult because no-one wants to spend money on modifying legacy products. Activity logging, or data logging, means recording all data units broadcast in an experiment for later analysis. It usually requires a dedicated host to capture the data. In a multicast environment, data logging is even more expensive because it must take place—and may require a dedicated system—for each multicast group.

Other choices for your design of network components include a set of dead-reckoning algorithms and time stamping. For a DVE based on DIS protocols, use the dead-reckoning algorithms defined in the standard, with minor changes to account for unique circumstances or error criteria. Use time stamping of protocol data units whenever you want position or velocity data to be highly accurate (see [Foster 1994; Katz 1994; Katz 1995; Saunders 1995; Swaine 1995]). Absolute time stamping based on the global positioning system is very precise but also expensive. If you're short of money, relative time stamping is better than none at all. It allows participating systems to account for some of the time the data spends in transit from the issuing host to the receiving host. That, in turn, improves the position estimate for an entity from the data in its protocol data unit.

An issue you must address for newly developed, human-controlled applications is the quality of virtual-environment technology and whether you need to immerse users in the environment. Funding will limit what you can do, but at least use high-resolution polygonal models that are Gouraud shaded and antialiased (see Sec. 16.3.3). Use texture mapping if possible. These approaches seem to provide the minimum rendering quality needed to achieve a sense of presence. Immersion is beneficial if users must have a heightened sense of being within the DVE, such as when piloting an aircraft or driving an armored vehicle. The currently popular display choices for immersion are helmet-mounted displays and small dome (or mini-DART) devices. Whichever you choose, make the device usable by providing the best affordable resolution, field of view, and weight (for helmet-mounted displays). For training and rehearsing missions, immersion is almost always a given, even though no-one has proved its benefits.

To build a large, complex DVE, you'll probably need to use computer-generated actors and constructive simulations, but you need to ask, "how many?" and "what type?" The best choices for constructive simulations are those that comply with the protocols of your chosen network. You'll probably need to change the constructive simulation (and the protocols it uses) so it can participate in the DVE. In this case, trade the cost of the changes against the benefit of making other compliant simulations more capable. Having selected the constructive simulations, make sure you establish criteria for determining when to aggregate and de-aggregate entities. Researchers are still trying to decide on these criteria.

Using computer-generated actors poses different problems:

- Number and type
- Required skills for each type
- Mission plans, objectives, and (possibly) tactics needed for applications, so their behavior and activity supports the DVE's objectives

Banks [1996] and Stytz [1996] discuss these techniques, but they're an active topic for research.

The final step in developing your DVE is to conduct experiments that satisfy the simulation's objectives or to evaluate the DVE (as discussed in Chap. 11 and 12) so you can ensure it meets these objectives. For current DVEs, this step is difficult and time consuming. You need to do a lot of planning and coordination to establish the environment and to verify that all component models operate correctly. You'll also need to detect and resolve inconsistencies between system portrayals of the DVE and determine whether they arise from terrain models, coordinate systems, differences in using protocols of distributed interactive simulation, object models, dynamics models for actors, different dead-reckoning systems, insufficient network bandwidth, or something as simple as different resolutions in cathode-ray tubes. These problems are simple in the abstract, but they're difficult to detect and resolve in a DVE because the participants are geographically separated. Tools for DVEs don't help with debugging for specific experiments, but Gustavson [1995] shows that researchers have recognized this need and begun working on it. As of this writing, though, expect planning and coordination to be time consuming.

16.8   Open Issues for Research

Table 16.7 summarizes the many open issues in DVE technology. Research is under way on each area, as well as on integrating them into a single architecture. I've discussed most of these issues throughout this chapter, so I'll just comment briefly on some of the more significant ones here.

To raise limits on the number of actors, we'll probably need to increase network bandwidth, improve dead-reckoning algorithms, apply data-compression techniques, and use Asynchronous Transfer Mode (ATM) with multicast groups [Chirielson 1995; Pullen 1995]. Eventually, though, we may have to use separate physical networks to handle different entities' requirements, plus intelligent gateways to move data between networks in the virtual environment.

Efforts are under way to increase the fidelity of phenomenology participants in the DVE by introducing weather and atmospheric effects. Among several treatments of this subject, the most complete are Berg [1995], Fiori [1995], Lamar [1995], Lasarus [1995], Mayes [1995], and Neff [1995]. Researchers are also addressing issues in radar and tactical communications [Severinghouse 1995; Flanagan 1995]. Others are just beginning to examine how we can manage the interplay between several types of these environmental effects [Grigsby 1995]. Usually, effects of phenomena enter a DVE through servers that either broadcast environmental states for selected large areas or respond to queries about states at the requester's location. For now, the demands of interactivity and computation limit fidelity.

Table 16.7.   Research Issues in Distributed Virtual Environments (DVE). The drive toward more complex DVEs fuels many open research issues for nine crucial technologies.

Topic	Research Issues
Terrain modeling	1. Portray terrain with high resolution 2. Model transformable terrain in real time 3. Support multiple levels of detail in the terrain
Weather phenomena	1. Calculate weather in real time 2. Display and portray weather (clouds, wind, rain, snow, etc.) [deJonckheere 1995; Haque 1995; Herbst 1995; Johnson 1995; Levy 1995; Smith 1995a]
Electronic emissions	1. Simulate transmission and reception of radar and radio signals
Communication protocols	1. Develop new protocols to address and support the open research issues listed in this table 2. Create protocols that use less bandwidth but still provide the same quality of information
Computer-generated actors	1. Improve fidelity of their behavior through better modeling of human behaviors 2. Make them able to learn 3. Develop advanced, open software and knowledge-base architectures 4. Make actors able to compute an acceptable response to unforeseen circumstances and to deal with uncertainty in its data
DVE actors	1. Increase the number of actors 2. Improve dynamics and sensor models for actors, including weather and other phenomena 3. Increase frame rate, improve rendered images, and improve interaction between humans and computers 4. Increase detail in the actor's 3D graphical models and support multiple levels of detail
DVE fidelity	1. Depict the DVE accurately and consistently and make sure that heterogeneous hosts—which use different terrain databases, display devices, actors, graphical models, and sensor models—can work together
DVE system architecture	1. Make parts of a simulation reusable 2. Provide a standard network interface to the DVE for each application 3. Establish common abilities that each application must provide 4. Reduce bandwidth required to maintain accurate state information on entities 5. Support attribute filtering, multicast, and run-time ability to enter and leave multicast groups 6. Define common simulation-management commands that each application must respond to 7. Promote reliability and stability
General technology for virtual environments	1. Build display devices—especially helmet-mounted displays—that have higher resolution, a larger field of view, and lower cost 2. Improve haptic interface devices 3. Portray virtual environments under various weather conditions at different times of day 4. Improve rendering algorithms so displays appear more realistic

If a person must use a virtual-environment application that emulates an existing system, we must determine how accurate the human-computer interface should be. Normally, we don't need the simulator and the real-world system to correspond perfectly, but an appropriate level of fidelity has yet to be established and no heuristics are available. Human-factors studies are necessary to determine when the interaction has enough fidelity to meet goals for using the system in evaluation, training, and mission planning. For work in this area, see Smith, Waltensperger, and Marshak [1995b]. If the application doesn't have a real-world counterpart, human factors and usability evaluations of the user interface are critical to developing a usable system.

The last basic issue I'll touch on is the architecture for system software. Trying to reuse software for simulation applications has been difficult. Thus, the Department of Defense (DOD) has developed the High Level Architecture for applications in distributed virtual environments. This architecture departs from protocols for distributed interactive simulation in that it mandates transmitting only the attributes that have changed in an entity's state space; it also efficiently supports filtering data by attributes as well as by entity type and geographical location. The DOD expects applications to consist of modules connected by a general-purpose infrastructure, much as in the Common-Object Database architecture (see Sec. 16.2.1). This architecture promises to relieve builders of DVE applications from many common tasks by providing a standard interface to the networking part of the DVE.

The High Level Architecture is designed to support all objectives of simulation: training, analysis, planning, and acquisition. One of its main goals is to establish an architectural framework that helps simulations work together. To achieve this goal, it separates application functions from communication functions. The host application's software manages all of its functions, whereas the runtime infrastructure (RTI) manages all communication functions. This infrastructure manages communication between running applications and makes sure each application gets the data it has subscribed to and publishes the data other applications request. The infrastructure has a publish-and-subscribe mechanism which limits transmitted data to only what the applications need. Because of the standard framework, different types of simulation exercises (known as federations) can customize the data protocols to suit their needs, typically without having to coordinate these changes among the other types of simulation applications. For developments on the high level architecture, consult the *Workshop on Standards for the Interoperability of Distributed Simulations* proceedings and the Defense Modeling and Simulation Office's website—http://www.dmso.mil. The essential papers are in the *15th Workshop on Standards for the Interoperability of Distributed Simulations* [Calvin 1996; Dahman 1996; Fujimoto 1996; Miller 1996; Stark 1996].

Distributed virtual environments are dramatically improving their ability to insert humans into the action in a DVE because hardware and software are improving, network bandwidth is increasing, protocols for communication between hosts are improving, and an overall architecture for DVEs is developing.

Computer-generated actors are being developed that better portray human behaviors using realistically moving vehicles. Helmet-mounted displays, haptic devices, and voice recognition are improving rapidly. Together, these developments are expanding the ability of DVE applications to immerse the user in a realistic environment. To end users' isolation and decrease their workloads, researchers are developing agents that support human decision making and the ability to collaborate within a DVE. A major challenge for now is networking. Broadcasting in distributed interactive simulations (DIS) for local and wide-area parts of the network overwhelms hosts with protocol data units that aren't relevant to entities at the host. Thus, a DIS-based DVE can't support enough entities to replicate the real world. Multicast may solve this problem, but the community is still debating how to partition DVEs to use it. Finally, we'll soon see a modest ability to insert various environmental phenomena and thus improve a DVE's realism for human and computer-generated participants.

References

Appino, Perry A., J. Bryan Lewis, Daniel T. Ling, David A. Rabenhorst, and Christopher F. Codella. 1992. "An Architecture for Virtual Worlds." *Presence: Teleoperators and Virtual Environments*. Vol. 1, No. 1, pp. 1–17.

Banks, Sheila B., Eugene Santos, and Martin R. Stytz. 1996. "The Automated Wingman: An Intelligent Entity for Distributed Virtual Environments." *Proceedings of the Sixth Conference on Computer Generated Forces and Behavioral Representation*. Orlando, FL: pp. 101–111, July 23–25.

Benford, S., J. Bowers, L.E. Fahlen, C. Greenhalgh, J. Mariani, and T. Rodden. 1995. "Networked Virtual Reality and Cooperative Work." *Presence: Teleoperators and Virtual Environments*. Vol. 4, No. 4, pp. 364–386.

Berg, S.L., S.H. Grigsby, H. Heckathorn, J.C. Herbst, J.H. Kirkland, and D. Anding. 1995. "Improving the Fidelity of Distributed Simulations Through Environmental Effects." *13th DIS Workshop on Standards for the Interoperability of Distributed Simulations*. Orlando, FL: pp. 683–692, September 18–22.

Bess, Rick D. 1992. "Image Generation Implications for Networked Tactical Training Systems." *Proceedings of the IMAGE VI Conference*. Phoenix, AZ: pp. 77–86, July 14–17.

Blau, B., C.E. Hughes, J.M. Moshell, and C. Lisle. 1992. "Networked Virtual Environments." *Proceedings of the 1992 Symposium on Interactive 3D Graphics*. Cambridge, MA: pp. 157–160, March 29–April 1.

Brooks, F.P, Ming Ouh-Young, and J. Batter. 1990. "Project GROPE—Haptic Displays for Scientific Visualization." *Computer Graphics*. Vol. 24, No. 4, pp. 177–185. August, Addison-Wesley/ACM Press.

Brockway, Dan E. and Michael E. Weiblen. 1995. "World Reference Model." *12th DIS Workshop on Standards for the Interoperability of Distributed Simulations*. Orlando, FL: pp. 239–245, March 13–17.

Burgess, David A. 1992. "Techniques for Low Cost Spatial Audio." *Proceedings of the ACM Symposium on User Interface Software and Technology.* Monterey, CA: pp. 53–59, November 15–18.

Calvin, James O. and Richard Weatherly. 1996. "An Introduction to the High Level Architecture (HLA) Runtime Infrastructure (RTI)." *15th Workshop on Standards for the Interoperability of Distributed Simulations.* Orlando, FL: pp. 705–715, March 11–15.

Card, Stuart K., Jock D. MacKinlay, and George G. Robertson. 1990. "The Design Space of Input Devices." *Human Factors in Computing Systems. SIGCHI '90 Conference Proceedings.* Seattle, WA: pp. 117–124, April 1–5.

Carlsson, C. and O. Hagsand. 1993. "DIVE - A Platform for Multi-user Virtual Environments." *Computers and Graphics.* Vol. 17, No. 6, pp. 663–669.

Chirielson, Don, Laura Cunningham, Dallas Scott, and Sally Tarquino. 1995. "DIS Communications Service Interface to ATM." *12th DIS Workshop on Standards for the Interoperability of Distributed Simulations.* Orlando, FL: pp. 691–704, March 13–17.

Codella, Christopher, Reza Jalili, Lawrence Koved, J. Bryan Lewis, Daniel T. Ling, James S. Lipscomb, David A. Rabenhorst, Chu P. Wang, Alan Norton, Paula Sweeney, and Greg Turk. 1992. "Interactive Simulation in a Multi-Person Virtual World." *Human Factors in Computing Systems. SIGCHI '92 Conference Proceedings.* Monterey, CA: pp. 329–334, May 3–7.

Cohen, Michael. 1992. "Integrating Graphic and Audio Windows." *Presence: Teleoperators and Virtual Environments.* Vol. 1, No. 4, pp. 468–481, Fall.

Cruz-Neira, Carolina, Daniel J. Sandin, Thomas A. DeFanti, Robert V. Kenyon, and John C. Hart. 1992. "The CAVE: Audio Visual Experience Automatic Virtual Environment." *Communications of the ACM.* Vol. 35, No. 6, pp. 65–72, June.

Dahman, Judith, Donald R. Ponikvar, and Robert Lutz. 1996. "HLA Federation Development and Execution Process." *15th Workshop on Standards for the Interoperability of Distributed Simulations.* Orlando, FL: pp. 327–335, March 11–15.

deJonckheere, Richard, Mark Tollefson, Terri Franklin, David Wilson, Bob Graves, Louis Henbree, Richard Siquig, and Mark Kilby. 1995. "Prototyping and Experimentation of a Distributed Synthetic Environment for E2DIS." *12th DIS Workshop on Standards for the Interoperability of Distributed Simulations.* Orlando, FL: pp. 389–404, March 13–17.

Evans, A. and T. Stanzione. 1995. "Coordinate Representations for CGF Systems." *13th DIS Workshop on Standards for the Interoperability of Distributed Simulations.* Orlando, FL: pp. 415–421, September 18–22.

Fahlen, Lennart E., Charles. Grant Brown, Olov Stahl, and Christer Carlsson. 1993. "A Space Based Model for User Interaction in Shared Synthetic Environments." *Conference on Human Factors in Computing Systems.* Amsterdam, The Netherlands: pp. 43–50, April 24–29.

Falby, John S., Michael J. Zyda, David R. Pratt, and Randy L. Mackey. 1993. "NPSNET: Hierarchical Data Structures for Real-Time Three-Dimensional Visual Simulation." *Computers & Graphics.* Vol. 17, No. 1, pp. 65–69. January.

Ferguson, Robert L.; Randy Brasch, Curtis R. Lisle, and Brian Goldiez. 1992. "Interoperability of Visual Simulation Systems." *Proceedings of the IMAGE VI Conference*. Phoenix, AZ: pp. 517–526, July 14–17.

Fiori, J., R. Davis, G. Koenig, J. Henson, and R. Bates. 1995. "Cold Regions Environmental Modeling for Distributed Interactive Simulation." *13th DIS Workshop on Standards for the Interoperability of Distributed Simulations*. Orlando, FL: pp. 79–84, September 18–22.

Flanagan, Mark J. 1995. "A Modeling and Simulation Communications Taxonomy." *13th DIS Workshop on Standards for the Interoperability of Distributed Simulations*. Orlando, FL: pp. 31–42, September 18–22.

Foley, James D., Andries van Dam, Steven K. Feiner, and John F. Hughes. 1992. *Computer Graphics: Principles and Practice*. 2nd edition. Reading, MA: Addison-Wesley.

Foster, Lester and Paul Maassel. 1994. "The Characterization of Entity State Error and Update Rate for Distributed Interactive Simulation." *11th DIS Workshop on Standards for the Interoperability of Distributed Simulations*. Orlando, FL: pp. 61–73, September 26–30.

Fujimoto, Richard M. and Richard M. Weatherly. 1996. "HLA Time Management and DIS." *15th Workshop on Standards for the Interoperability of Distributed Simulations*. Orlando, FL: pp. 615–628, March 11–15.

Gaver, William W., Randall B. Smith, and Tim O'Shea. 1991. "Effective Sounds in Complex Systems: The Arkola Simulation." *Human Factors in Computing Systems. CHI '91 Conference Proceedings*. New Orleans, LA: pp. 85–90, April 27 – May 2.

Grigsby, S.H., J.C. Herbst, J.P. Kirkland, S.L. Berg, H. Hackathorn, and D. Anding. 1995. "The E2DIS Environmental Manager." *13th DIS Workshop on Standards for the Interoperability of Distributed Simulations*. Orlando, FL: pp. 567–574, September 18–22.

Gustavson, Paul. 1995. "White Board PDU for Exercise Management and Feedback." *13th DIS Workshop on Standards for the Interoperability of Distributed Simulations*. Orlando, FL: pp. 475–481, September 18–22.

Hagsand, O. 1996. "Interactive Multiuser VEs in the DIVE System." *IEEE Multimedia*. Vol. 3, No. 1, pp. 30–39, March.

Haque, Suraiya, Richard Schaffer, Limberly Neff, Gregory Weidman, Anthony Beverina, and Christopher Dobosz. 1995. "Dynamic Environment Simulation Protocol." *12th DIS Workshop on Standards for the Interoperability of Distributed Simulations*. Orlando, FL: pp. 293–300, March 13–17.

Harvey, Edward P. and Richard L. Schaffer. 1991. "The Capability of the Distributed Interactive Simulation Network Standard to Support High Fidelity Aircraft Simulation." *Proceedings of the Thirteenth Interservice/Industry Training Systems Conference*. Orlando, FL: pp. 127–135.

Hearn, Donald and M. Pauline Baker. 1994. *Computer Graphics*. 2nd edition. Englewood Cliffs, NJ: Prentice Hall.

Herbst, Judith C., Steve L. Berg, James H. Kirkland, David Anding, Harry Heckathorn, Stanley H. Grigsby, and Robert Graves. 1995. "The Robust Approach for Providing Environmental Effects to DIS." *12th DIS Workshop on Standards for the Interoperability of Distributed Simulations.* Orlando, FL: pp. 591–600, March 13–17.

Hill, Ralph D. 1992. "The Abstraction-Link-View Paradigm: Using Constraints to Connect User Interfaces to Applications." *Human Factors in Computing Systems. SIGCHI '92 Conference Proceedings.* Monterey, CA: pp. 335–342, May 3–7.

Hirota, Koichi and Michitaka Hirose. 1995. "Providing Force Feedback in Virtual Environments." *IEEE Computer Graphics & Applications.* Vol. 15, No. 5, pp. 22–30. Sept.

Iwata, Hiroo and Haruo Noma. 1993. "Volume Haptization." *Proceedings of the IEEE 1993 Symposium on Research Frontiers in Virtual Reality.* San Jose, CA: pp. 16–23, Oct. 25–26.

Johnson, David J. and Roy E. Bates. 1995. "Winter in Distributed Interactive Systems." *12th DIS Workshop on Standards for the Interoperability of Distributed Simulations.* Orlando, FL: pp.119–128, March 13–17.

Katz, Amnon. 1994. "Synchronization of Networked Simulators." *11th DIS Workshop on Standards for the Interoperability of Distributed Simulations.* Orlando, FL: pp. 81–88, September 26–30.

Katz, Amnon. 1995. "Precision Under DIS." *12th DIS Workshop on Standards for the Interoperability of Distributed Simulations.* Orlando, FL: pp. 531–535, March 13–17.

Lamar, C.; A. Boehm, D. Bodnar, W. Gebhart, and W. Cook. 1995. "A Methodology for Defining Atmospheric Environmental Simulation Requirements." *13th DIS Workshop on Standards for the Interoperability of Distributed Simulations.* Orlando, FL: pp. 381–386, September 18–22.

Lasarus, Earl; Al Gordon, Chuck Lamar, Welman Gebhart, and Chris Rule. 1995. "A DIS Architecture for the FASTPROP Atmospheric Environment Server." *13th DIS Workshop on Standards for the Interoperability of Distributed Simulations.* Orlando, FL: pp. 247–258, September 18–22.

Laurel, Brenda (ed.). 1990. *The Art of Human-Computer Interface Design.* Reading, MA: Addison-Wesley.

Levy, Stephen; John R. Mostow, Mark R. Lambert, Arvids Vigants. 1995. "Developing Climate Factors for Application to Distributed Interactive Simulation." *12th DIS Workshop on Standards for the Interoperability of Distributed Simulations.* Orlando, FL: pp. 671–674, March 13–17.

Lewis, J. Bryan; Lawrence Koved, and Daniel T. Ling. 1991. "Dialogue Structures for Virtual Worlds." *Human Factors in Computing Systems. CHI '91 Conference Proceedings.* New Orleans, LA: pp. 131–136, April 27 – May 2.

Lipscomb, James S. 1989. "Experience with Stereoscopic Display Devices and Output Algorithms." *Three-Dimensional Visualization and Display Technologies.* SPIE Vol. 1083, Los Angeles, CA: pp. 28–34, January 18–20.

Macedonia, M. R.; M.J. Zyda, D.R. Pratt, P.T. Barham, and S. Zeswitz. 1994. "NPSNET: A Network Software Architecture for Large-Scale Virtual Environments." *Presence: Teleoperators and Virtual Environments.* Vol. 3, No. 4, pp. 265–287, Fall.

Mayes, W.; E. Pollak, and M. Bustos. 1995. "An Enhanced Prototype DIS Environment Manager." *13th DIS Workshop on Standards for the Interoperability of Distributed Simulations.* Orlando, FL: pp. 561–566, September 18–22.

McDonald, L. Bruce; Christina P. Bouwens, Ronald Hofer, Gene Wiehagen, Karen Danisas, and James Shiflett. 1991. "Standard Protocol Data Units for Entity Information and Interaction in a Distributed Interactive Simulation." *Proceedings of the Thirteenth Interservice/Industry Training Systems Conference.* Orlando, FL: pp. 119–126.

McKenna, Michael and David Zeltzer. 1992. "Three Dimensional Visual Display Systems for Virtual Environments." *Presence: Teleoperators and Virtual Environments.* Vol. 1, No. 4, pp. 421–458, Fall.

Miller, Duncan C. 1996. "The DOD High Level Architecture and the Next Generation of DIS." *15th Workshop on Standards for the Interoperability of Distributed Simulations.* Orlando, FL: pp. 799–806, March 11–15.

Minsky, Margaret, Ming Ouh-young, Oliver Steele, Frederick P. Brooks, Jr., and Max Behensky. 1990. "Feeling and Seeing: Issues in Force Display." *Proceedings of the 1990 Symposium on Interactive 3D Graphics.* Snowbird, UT: pp. 235–243, March 25–28.

Neff, Kimberly. 1995. "Chemical and Biological Environments Described via a Subscription Service." *13th DIS Workshop on Standards for the Interoperability of Distributed Simulations.* Orlando, FL: pp. 267–270, September 18–22.

Nielsen, Jakob. 1993. *Usability Engineering.* Boston, MA: Academic Press Professional.

Pullen, Mark J. and Elizabeth L. White. 1995. "Analysis of Dual-Mode Multicast for Large Scale DIS Exercises." *13th DIS Workshop on Standards for the Interoperability of Distributed Simulations.* Orlando, FL: pp. 613–622, March 13–17.

Purdy, Richard. 1995. "A PDU Solution to the Inter-Visibility Problem in Distributed Interactive Simulations Due to Mis-Correlated Terrain." *12th DIS Workshop on Standards for the Interoperability of Distributed Simulations.* Orlando, FL: pp. 101–117, March 13–17.

Robertson, George G., Stuart K. Card, and Jock D. Mackinlay. 1989. "The Cognitive Coprocessor Architecture for Interactive User Interfaces." *Proceedings of UIST '89. The Second Annual ACM SIGGRAPH Symposium on User Interface Software and Technology.* Williamsburg, VA: pp. 10–18, November 13–15.

Rosenberg, Louis B. and Bernard D. Adelstein. 1993. "Perceptual Decomposition of Virtual Haptic Surfaces." *Proceedings of the IEEE 1993 Symposium on Research Frontiers in Virtual Reality.* San Jose, CA: pp. 46–53, October 25–26.

Saunders, Randy. 1995. "Its About Time, Its About Space - Time and Space in DIS." *13th DIS Workshop on Standards for the Interoperability of Distributed Simulations.* Orlando, FL: pp. 63–66, March 13–17.

Schneiderman, Ben. 1992. *Designing the User Interface: Strategies for Effective Human-Computer Interaction.* 2nd Edition. Reading MA: Addison-Wesley.

Schloerb, David W. 1995. "A Quantitative Measure of Telepresence." *Presence: Teleoperators and Virtual Environments*. Vol. 4, No. 1, pp. 64–80, Winter.

Severinghaus, Richard J. 1995. "Tactical Voice Communications in DIS Exercises." *13th DIS Workshop on Standards for the Interoperability of Distributed Simulations*. Orlando, FL: pp.195–200, September 18–22.

Shaw, Chris, Jiandong Liang, Mark Green, and Yunqi Sun. 1992. "The Decoupled Simulation Model for Virtual Reality Systems." *Human Factors in Computing Systems. SIGCHI '92 Conference Proceedings*. Monterey, CA: pp. 321–328, May 3–7.

Singhai, Sandeep K. and David R. Cheriton. 1995. "Exploiting Position History for Efficient Remote Rendering in Networked Virtual Reality." *Presence: Teleoperators and Virtual Environments*. Vol. 4, No. 2, pp. 169–193, Spring.

Slater, Mel and Martin Usoh. 1993. "Representations Systems, Perceptual Position and Presence in Immersive Virtual Environments." *Presence: Teleoperators and Virtual Environments*. Vol. 2, No. 3, pp. 221–233, Summer.

Smith, W. Garth, Eric Schmidt, Maureen Cianciolo, Robert Reynolds, Patricia Doren, and Greg Mealy. 1995. "A Weather Server to Support Distributed Interactive Simulations." *12th DIS Workshop on Standards for the Interoperability of Distributed Simulations*. Orlando, FL: pp. 369–372, March 13–17.

Smith, Scott, Mark Waltensperger, and William Marshak. 1995. "Human Factors Engineering in the DIS/ADS Environment." *13th DIS Workshop on Standards for the Interoperability of Distributed Simulations*. Orlando, FL: pp. 735–740, March 13–17.

Spuhl, Karl A. and David A. Findley. 1994. "Correlation Considerations in the Simulation Environment." *11th DIS Workshop on Standards for the Interoperability of Distributed Simulations*. Orlando, FL: pp. 55–60, September 26–30.

Stark, Thomas S., Richard Weatherly, and Annette Wilson. 1996. "The High Level Architecture (HLA) Interface Specification and Applications Programmer's Interface." *15th Workshop on Standards for the Interoperability of Distributed Simulations*. Orlando, FL: pp. 851–860, March 11–15.

Sturman, David J. and David Zeltzer. 1994. "A Survey of Glove-based Input." *IEEE Computer Graphics & Applications*. Vol. 14, No. 1, pp. 30–39, January.

Stytz, Martin R.; Bruce Hobbs, Andrea Kunz, Brian Soltz, and Kirk Wilson. 1995. "Portraying and Understanding Large-Scale Distributed Virtual Environments: Experience and Tentative Conclusions." *Presence: Teleoperators and Virtual Environments*. Vol. 4, No. 2, pp. 146–168, Spring.

Stytz, Martin R., Sheila B. Banks, and Eugene Santos. 1996. "Requirements for Intelligent Aircraft Entities in Distributed Environments." *18th Interservice/Industry Training Systems and Education Conference*. Orlando, FL: December 3–5. Publication on CD-ROM.

Stytz, Martin R., Terry Adams, Brian Garcia, Steve Sheasby, and Brian Zurita. 1997. "Rapid Prototyping for Distributed Virtual Environments." *IEEE Software*. Vol. 14, No. 5.

Sutherland, Ivan E. 1965. "The Ultimate Display." *1965 Proceedings of the IFIPS Congress*. Vol. 2, pp. 506–508.

Sutherland, Ivan E. 1968. "A Head-Mounted Three Dimensional Display." *Proceedings of the Fall Joint Computer Conference*. Vol. 33, San Francisco, CA: pp. 757–764, December 9–11.

Swaine, Steven D. and Theodore F. Marz. 1995. "DIS at Nine Gs." *13th DIS Workshop on Standards for the Interoperability of Distributed Simulations*. Orlando, FL: pp. 259–265, September 18–22.

Takala, Tapio and James Hahn. 1992. "Sound Rendering." *Computer Graphics. Proceedings of SIGGRAPH '92*. Chicago, IL: Vol. 26, No. 2, pp. 211–220, July 26–31.

Toms, Ralph M. 1995. "An Efficient Algorithm for Geocentric to Geodetic Coordinate Conversion." *13th DIS Workshop on Standards for the Interoperability of Distributed Simulations*. Orlando, FL: pp. 635–642, September 18–22.

Trott, Kevin C. and Tim Langevin. 1995. "DIS Terrain Database Exchange Format Analysis." *12th DIS Workshop on Standards for the Interoperability of Distributed Simulations*. Orlando, FL: pp. 105–117, March 13–17.

Vetter, R.J. 1995. "ATM Concepts, Architectures and Protocols." *Communications of the ACM*. Vol. 38, No. 2, pp. 31–44, February.

Wenzel, Elizabeth, Frederic L. Wightman, and Doris J. Kistler. 1991. "Localization with Non-Individualized Virtual Acoustic Display Cues." *Human Factors in Computing Systems, CHI '91 Conference Proceedings*. New Orleans, LA: pp. 351–359, April 27 – May 2.

Zeltzer, David. 1992. "Autonomy, Interaction, and Presence." *Presence: Teleoperators and Virtual Environments*. Vol. 1, No. 1, pp. 127–132, Winter. MIT Press.

Zyda, M.J., D.R. Pratt, J.S. Falby, C. Lombardo, and K.M. Kelleher. 1993. "The Software Required for the Computer Generation of Virtual Environments." *Presence: Teleoperators and Virtual Environments*. Vol. 2, No. 2, pp. 130–140, Spring. MIT Press.

CHAPTER 17

Information Security in Simulator Design and Operation

David E. Gobuty, *Lockheed Martin Western Development Laboratories*

A simulation computer is a specialized automated information system (AIS). Modern simulators, like other AISs, may be interconnected much the same way office workstations are networked, so users may share data and system resources. Security becomes especially important when managers of simulation systems lose some of their ability to control critical aspects of stored, processed, or protected data. Security is also important when the nature of the simulation itself, or the characteristics and behavior of simulation elements, in some way need protection from disclosure outside a limited, privileged community.

In this chapter we'll discuss *data integrity* and *compromise control*, which are important to engineers and managers. Both are key to protecting investments in a simulator and, in some cases, to preserving technical and proprietary advantage. They may also affect criminal blame and civil liability, so people who design, use, or administer AISs are keenly interested in security.

17.1   Security Policy

A computer security policy is a document which presents the security rules that specific hardware, software, and firmware elements enforce while users operate an AIS within a known environment. A sound, approved security policy is the cornerstone to secure simulation. It lays the foundation for making the security-related architectural and operational decisions that enforce it. The policy allows us to identify needed components and regulates data flow. It's characterized by assumptions, statements, and words-of-art. Policy assumptions describe characteristics of the operational environment that are relevant to security. Similarly, real and virtual perimeters are important if we are to visualize where to put security mechanisms. Finally, access-control models help us understand what we may need to build in if we are to create and maintain a secure state. Everything depends on clearly understanding stated rules within the security policy. We'll see that policy enforcement can be procedural, mechanical, or automated, or can combine all three. Ultimately, the approved policy forms the basis for answering all questions regarding secure, correct operation of the system.

By way of example, let's suppose a file cabinet contains sensitive information, which we want only certain people to access. Our policy must unambiguously identify these people. As a control mechanism, we could say we rely on all members of the organization to enforce these rules. Or we could describe another control mechanism, such as a uniformed guard, to provide the needed amount of enforcement.

Similarly, we may need to restrict access to the data within a simulator or operation of the simulator's controls, if only to keep people from corrupting preset parameters. If so, we can define a policy of controlled access to the simulator's AIS resources at the beginning of design and therefore meet security objectives at the lowest cost in schedule and dollars.

The policy should use positive, unambiguous language to convey information in three main areas. First, it needs to state assumptions about the simulator's environment: expected user trustworthiness and behavior, permitted external connections, and expected physical protections. Here are two different examples of policy assumptions:

- Simulator users may access any data in the AIS
- Simulator users may only access data in the AIS that relates to their jobs

Next, policy statements cover security rules the AIS needs to enforce if it is to become and remain security accredited. Ultimately, AIS design and written procedures enforce these rules. Thus, we must carefully craft a policy so we can clearly trace all of a system's security requirements to at least one policy statement. Here are two examples of policy statements:

- Simulator users identify themselves, and the AIS authenticates their claimed identity before doing anything on their behalf
- The AIS audits user actions to enforce accountability

Finally, we need to define words-of-art so our rules and assumptions are as unequivocal as possible, including terms whose definition depends on context. For example, we might define "user" as "a person with a login account to the simulator AIS within its physical security perimeter." According to this definition, only people may have login accounts. The simulator must have identified and authenticated them. And they may try to log in only while they are within the simulator's physical security perimeter. Remote or dial-up logins aren't specifically permitted, so they're prohibited.

To ensure buy-in by all necessary parties, the policy needs approval from at least the customer and the data owner. Customers must approve the security rules because they have to develop and deliver the simulator, as well as establish and control the system's cost and schedule. Owners of data are even more important because they decide whether to accredit the system. They're often referred to as the Designated Approval Authority (DAA). At the start of simulator design, they must agree that the simulator's security framework presents an acceptable risk.

The policy, therefore, provides designers with architectural guidance to ensure policy rules are enforceable. People who build a system can trace all security requirements to the policy and make sure they create only what's needed. Test and evaluation staff can devise tests and analyses to prove the design properly represents policy-related requirements. The DAA can rely on the policy, plus test results, to gauge the effectiveness of the system's security and decide whether or not to accept any remaining security risk. Therefore, the security policy is the cornerstone of a secure modeling and simulation environment.

17.1.1   The Security Environment

Our security policy must describe important variables in a simulator's environment, so we can create and maintain a secure state. These variables relate to users, data sources, and intended data destinations. Designers must understand details about the environment to ensure related policy rules are enforceable.

Typically, simulator users are people with approved access and some job-related need to use the simulator. Security engineers must describe these attributes to specify an accreditable system. For example, if a simulator is locked within a controlled space, with access restricted to authorized users, we probably wouldn't need access controls within the simulator itself. In other cases, we may need to grant access to authorized users only if the data relates to the users' jobs. For example, we may grant certain users access to parametric values in a mathematical model but not allow them to read or change the file of user passwords. Simulator designers must prescribe rules in the policy, so we can later provide the right controls for need-to-know access.

Data sources and destinations can present security-related environmental challenges. For example, if a simulator operates with data at one level of sensitivity, trying to put in more sensitive data could compromise security, especially if its sensitivity exceeded authorizations. The same would be true if the simulator tried to send sensitive data to a destination authorized at a lower sensitivity.

17.1.2   Security Perimeters

It's useful to envision an information system existing and operating within physical and logical boundaries, so we can generalize about the system's behavior and security. Security perimeters important to us are the physical, signal isolation, and information security perimeters (see Fig. 17.1).

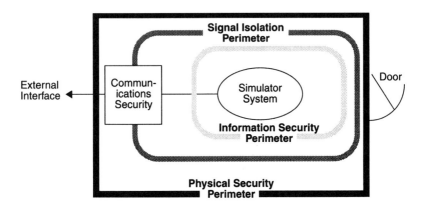

Fig. 17.1.   Three Main Security Perimeters. The information security perimeter bounds where we can enforce security policy. The signal isolation perimeter describes the area where clear-text data may reside. The physical security perimeter locates controls on physical access.

The physical security perimeter bounds the simulator's "home"—by a room's walls or a fence around a compound. If we must control physical or touch access, we have to provide controlled entry and exit points such as doors or gates on the door, as well as automated or procedural checks (or both). Examples are a cipher lock (automated) and a sign-in sheet (procedural).

The signal isolation perimeter defines a logical zone inside the physical security perimeter, within which *red* data may exist and outside of which you'll find *black* data. Red and black are words-of-art in the security community. Red refers to sensitive or classified information in a form which people can read directly and comprehend. Black refers to data that is, or has become, unsensitive or unclassified. We can usually read directly and comprehend data that is intrinsically black. But whenever red data is converted to black, it's systematically modified into a format that protects its true sensitivity against compromise. The cipher-text version of an encrypted document is a good example of this kind of data because, if properly enciphered, only the intended recipient can decipher and read it.

A signal isolation perimeter is critical if we need an electronic interface between simulators processing sensitive or classified data. We must control information against compromise from the signal isolation perimeter of the sending system to the signal isolation perimeter of the intended receiver.

Physical protection and encryption are the two main ways to control against compromise. With physical protection, we extend the physical security perimeter to enclose the source automated information system (AIS) and the intended receiving AIS (see Fig. 17.2). In this case, the physical and information security perimeters are congruent, so data never crosses either and compromise control is ensured. Figure 17.2 presents an example of two systems in different rooms or buildings for which interface cabling is protected within approved, guarded conduit.

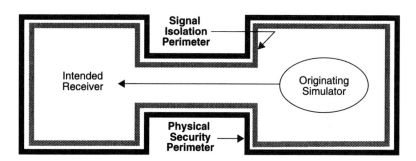

Fig. 17.2.   Protecting Against Compromise by Extending the Physical Security Perimeter.
Sensitive or classified information that doesn't cross the signal isolation perimeter needs no special protection as long as the physical security perimeter remains intact.

When information is destined to cross the signal isolation perimeter, we must protect it in transit. As Fig. 17.3 shows, the transferring data converts from red to black through encryption at the originator's signal isolation perimeter and then moves to the intended recipient. At the receive end, the data is deciphered into comprehensible red data as it crosses the signal isolation perimeter of the intended recipient. We won't discuss symmetrical (single key) and asymmetrical (public key) cryptography and cipher systems, key management, or issues regarding the international transfer of such technology. You can consult the references if you'd like to know more about them.

The information security perimeter is inside the signal-isolation and physical security perimeters. Within it, we must enforce rules for computer security. These rules, as described in the system's security policy, cover mechanisms within the simulator's AIS itself. For example, a communications-security device outside the simulator can protect from compromise any red data placed on an external interface by converting it to black data. Of course, a cipher-locked door at the physical security perimeter can control unauthorized people from touching communications-security devices and the simulator. But suppose otherwise authorized users try (in error or maliciously) to access the password file, which they don't need to know. In this case, the simulator's AIS itself must contain a way to protect against the unauthorized access.

We need to construct a block diagram of the system's architecture and understand the actual and logical locations of each security perimeter. Locating

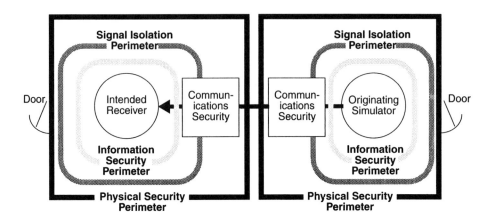

Fig. 17.3. Protecting Against Compromise by Encrypting Data at the Signal Isolation Perimeter. Sensitive or classified information that must exit a physical security perimeter needs encryption at the point where it crosses outside one signal isolation perimeter and decryption where it crosses inside another.

the physical security perimeter will focus our attention on needed administrative controls. Identifying the parts of the AIS that must enforce rules in the security policy will define the information security perimeter, within which policy is enforced by design. Defining the interface between interconnected systems will locate the signal isolation perimeter so we can identify and deal with issues of separating red and black data. Therefore, our policy must clearly identify rules for computer security, communications security, and physical security.

17.1.3 Characteristics of Data Flow

Typically, simulators need inputs or generate outputs that must flow electronically across one or more of the identified security perimeters. For this reason, a secure system needs ways to enforce appropriate security rules while data is flowing. A standard flow-control model and our policy rules help us control these data transfers.

Perhaps the most widely used model for describing information flow in secure systems was developed by David Bell and Leonard LaPadula in 1971 at MITRE Corporation. This model, adopted by the United States' Department of Defense, distinguishes:

- Active and passive elements in a system (its subjects and objects)
- The sensitivity (high, equal, or low) of data accessed by or contained within subjects and objects
- The type of information flow which can occur between systems, or between components within the same system, while still maintaining a secure state

In the Bell and LaPadula model, whenever two pieces of information have the same sensitivity, they are said to be equal. Flow of equal data between parts of a system within the same physical security perimeter usually doesn't affect the secure state. We also don't violate the secure state with data flowing from a region of low sensitivity to one of high sensitivity because the low data will be adequately protected in the high environment. We call this flow *write up* when looking from the low domain or *read down* when viewing it from the high domain. But we must manage flow in the opposite direction—from a region of high sensitivity to one of low sensitivity—because it can lead to compromise. We term this flow *write down* when viewing it from the high domain or *read up* when viewing it from the low domain.

When sensitive or classified information is to be stored, processed, and protected within a simulator, we have to be aware of these issues. Controlling write-down and read-up flows seems obvious, but our security policy needs to state permitted access so the design will contain the required controls. If a simulator must maintain data at multiple sensitivities, the policy should say something like this:

- **Reading.** A subject may read data from an object only if the subject's sensitivity *dominates* the object's sensitivity.

- **Writing.** A subject may write data to an object only if the object's sensitivity *dominates* the subject's sensitivity.

Here, dominate is a word-of-art, defined as a sensitivity that is equal to or greater than another sensitivity. Policy writers must account for the security characteristics of all possible information flows, intended or otherwise.

17.1.4   Access Controls

Access rules needed to create and maintain a secure state can be *rule-based* or *identity-based*, and we may need to use either or both in the policy. Rule-based or mandatory access controls depend on the dictates of laws, regulations, or written permissions that unequivocally state how information may flow. For example, the law doesn't allow people without security clearances to access classified information. Therefore, if the simulator must store, process, or protect such data, we must have a policy rule that prohibits write-down to uncleared users.

Identity-based or discretionary access controls relate to information flow between equals, where access decisions depend on role or job function. Virtually all policies for secure AISs contain identity-based rules that permit users to share information with equally cleared peers. The first user is allowed discretion to grant access to the peer, based on the first user's knowing the peer's identity and role (or job-related need). As security engineers, we must determine whether or not the simulator contains information some otherwise cleared users don't need to access. If so, our policy must call for identity-based access controls.

17.2   Some Architectural Considerations

A security architecture describes all parts of a trusted AIS, highlighting its security perimeters. Typically, it's a block diagram like the one in Fig. 17.4. Secure simulators rely on several components working together to enforce the system's security policy. These components (hardware, software, firmware, and operating procedures) comprise the trusted computing base, whose mechanisms enforce policy rules.

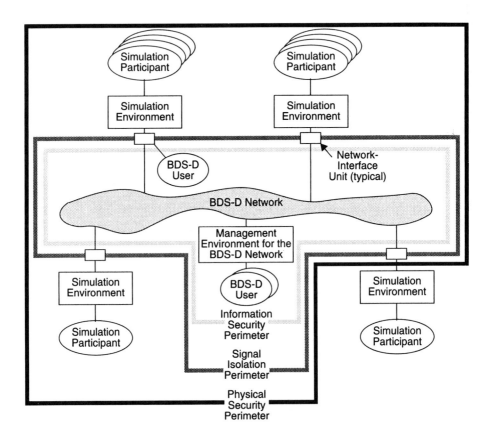

Fig. 17.4.   Typical Security Architecture. A security architecture for the Battlefield Distributed Simulation—Demonstration (BDS-D) system shows how all three security perimeters interact. Policy enforcement is centered within the information security perimeter. Communications-security devices are at the points where sensitive or classified information will cross outside the signal isolation perimeter. And controls on physical access are at the physical security perimeter.

17.2.1   Identifying and Authenticating Users

All rule-based and identity-based access controls depend on special knowledge about users, so they can regulate the users' access according to policy. Users must identify themselves to the AIS, which must be able to authenticate claimed identities before doing anything else for them. Standard login schemes involving username and password are common to identification and authentication, but we sometimes need greater assurance. For example, if the policy allows login from outside the physical security perimeter, we may need to prevent unauthorized login attempts, or spoofing, by people posing as users. Here, the challenge is to construct and maintain a trusted path between the user and the simulator.

Depending on the sensitivity of the data to be protected, we can use several trusted-path mechanisms. We can control spoofing by changing the password more often—even requiring a new password for each login attempt. We can also use authentication tokens. For example, we can get more assurance by requiring the use of PIN-ignited cards that generate a pseudorandom number users must enter as part of the login. In this case, the host must receive a correct number to permit access. Some methods involve having users respond to a host-generated challenge number by entering another, which is a function of the challenge, as part of the login. Only correct responses allow access. Other techniques range from biometric authenticators, such as fingerprint readers or retina scanners, to session-level encryption. We match the trusted-path technique to the sensitivity or value of the data we're protecting. As the cost of unauthorized access increases, so should the complexity of identifying and authenticating methods.

17.2.2   Observing Users' Roles

Modeling and simulation users range from researchers running a model on desktop PCs to students in a laboratory manipulating a simulator's controls, reading its instruments, feeling its motion, and hearing its sounds. Security-related behavior of the former may be more predictable than that of the latter. We have to match access controls to what users must do in authorized roles if we are to keep a system useful, but secure.

17.2.3   Accounting for Users' Actions

The U.S. government requires individual accountability for systems that process data which is classified, or sensitive but unclassified. Other data owners may also require this accountability. To provide it, we can record the security-related actions of users in a protected database, often called the audit file. The audit file records users' actions, plus other relevant data, such as the event's date, time, and success or failure. When users know about this recording, they tend to behave according to their duties and responsibilities. The audit trail also tracks system errors. Auditing can provide data for intrusion-detection and reporting systems, which our security policy may require. In any case, we must capture relevant events, protect them from change or destruction, and let only people with need-to-know see the audit records.

17.2.4   Maintaining Data Integrity

Integrity means protecting data against loss or alteration. It's similar to nonrepudiation, in which mechanisms assuredly preserve the identity of someone who starts, or receives the outcome of, a transaction. To ensure integrity, we use check sums, encryption, and careful inspection of the executable software while building and testing it. Uncertainty about the integrity of data in an AIS that processes sensitive or classified data can undermine its ability to protect that data against compromise. Therefore, the Designated Approval Authority or security accreditor will want assurance that appropriate mechanisms are provided to protect data integrity.

17.3   Security Architecture and Policy Enforcement

We've seen that generating and gaining approval of a security policy is the first step toward developing a simulator that can be trusted to store, process, and protect sensitive data and resources. We've also discussed some key ideas about architecture. Now let's focus on how the security policy shapes a system's architecture and design. A system architecture describes all of an AIS's components and interfaces, so developers can build it efficiently. Effective security measures need to be a cornerstone of the architecture, not an add-on. To make them so, we can develop trusted systems using an integrated product team, whose members represent several engineering specialties. In this way, the security engineer, architect, and others work toward a system that can meet performance and cost requirements, while enforcing all rules in the approved security policy.

17.3.1   Simulators Processing Sensitive or Classified Data

The security-engineering community has created standard ways to highlight the security mechanisms required for successful security accreditation. In other words, the AIS must meet or exceed these standards to become security accredited. We must keep in mind that security accreditation is our ultimate goal when we build systems which store, process, and protect sensitive or classified data. The best simulator is worthless if data owners won't allow it to use that data because of security shortcomings.

Before describing operating modes for AIS security, let's revisit some policy concepts related to flow control. The policy stipulates flow-control rules, so we need to know whether or not the data in the simulator is classified and, if so, whether or not it is required to be associated with a sensitivity label. Since sensitivity labels indicate security sensitivity, they must be bound with assurance to whatever they label. For example, *CONFIDENTIAL* is a label for certain data in a defined context. In the same way, Confidential Clearance is a label associated with a user whose background has been checked and verified according to a standard. All of these security labels help designers and security accreditors determine the required security operating mode for the simulator.

For security accreditation, security mechanisms in AISs fall into two categories. Some enforce policy rules on recognizing and processing security labels on data and users. Others don't. AISs that process security labels do so to carry out rule-based access controls.

Rule-based Access Controls

We know from earlier discussions that access controls support flow-control policy aimed at preventing compromise. Where read-up or write-down flow is possible, rule-based controls must prevent unauthorized disclosure by limiting access only to those authorized according to a published code. No-one can deviate from the rules without risking civil or criminal sanctions. For a simulator AIS, we may need to keep people without specific authority from accessing the system. For example, we could lock the door to the simulator room to prevent them from crossing the physical security perimeter. If more complex policies are involved, the AIS may have built-in mechanisms for rule-based access control, such as requiring users to log in by name, password, and security level. After authenticating the user's claimed identity, the simulator AIS compares the user's desired level for the session with the user's authorized level and grants or denies access. Remember that these rule-based mechanisms usually control access based on policy rules that allow read access in read-equal and read-down instances and permit write access in write-equal and write-up cases only. Systems without rule-based mechanisms don't control access in this way.

Identity-based Access Controls

We may also regulate access to AIS resources based only on a claimed and authenticated identity. The grantor allows access only to requesters with a need-to-know, usually depending on the requester's job. The grantor has latitude, or discretion, in allowing access so identity-based control is also known as *discretionary access control*. Access control list mechanisms in many operating systems allow users to control access to file space and specify the type of access (read, write, execute). Since 1992, the Department of Defense has required AISs (including simulators) developed for them to use identity-based access controls as a minimum if the AIS will handle sensitive but unclassified, or classified, data. Other government agencies in the United States and elsewhere have similar minimum requirements.

Security Operating Modes

To determine whether or not a secure AIS should be allowed to operate, the Designated Approval Authority identifies a security operating mode and then measures the system against that mode's requirements. Security operating modes are a way of outlining which security mechanisms must be in place for safe operation. They're based mainly on the data's security characteristics and the users' trustworthiness. If both are similar, the risk of compromise is low, so we need only simple security mechanisms. If we have very sensitive data and very trustworthy users, the risk may still be low enough to allow a simple solution. But if we combine the potential for access to highly sensitive data with users whose trustworthiness is unknown, we'll need a more complex solution. Therefore, operating modes describe the

- Expected clearances for users (trustworthiness)
- Range of users' need-to-know for the data in the AIS
- Sensitivity of data the AIS delivers
- Trust we place in the AIS's ability to provide its own mechanisms for downgrade

We categorize systems based on their operating modes. In ascending order, from least to most complex, these modes are Dedicated, System High, Compartmented (also known as Partitioned), and Multilevel. See Table 17.1 for the basics on each mode.

Table 17.1. **Security Operating Modes for Automated Information Systems (AIS).** Security-accreditation requirements for an AIS increase (from few in Dedicated Mode to many in Multilevel Mode) as the users' trustworthiness decreases (from high to unknown).

Operating Mode	User's Clearance	Need-To-Know	Output Level	Downgrade
Dedicated	Cleared (and indoctrinated, if required) for access to all data	Established for all data	At AIS-accredited sensitivity level	Mechanism outside the AIS
System High	Cleared (and indoctrinated, if required) for access to all data	Established for some data	At AIS-accredited sensitivity level	Mechanism outside the AIS
Compartmented (or Partitioned)	Cleared for all data (and indoctrinated, if required, for some data)	Established for some data	At correct sensitivity level (which may be lower than the AIS-accredited sensitivity level)	Mechanisms within AIS
Multilevel	Varies	Established for some data	At correct sensitivity level (which may be lower than the AIS-accredited sensitivity level)	Mechanisms within AIS

Systems with One Sensitivity Level

Systems in Dedicated Mode enforce the simplest of security policies. They don't need built-in security mechanisms. If they must process sensitive or classified data, something external to the AIS must control access, such as a lock on the door to the room housing the simulator. Anyone granted physical access to the machine may access all the data within it, in terms of clearance and need-to-know.

Early personal computers, without password mechanisms to control access, are good examples of systems operating in Dedicated Mode. We can select Dedicated Mode whenever a statute or the Designated Approval Authority doesn't impose rules for the AIS to control access and we can show all users have necessary clearances and need-to-know.

We must associate Dedicated Mode with its accredited sensitivity level, a label that represents the highest sensitivity of data a system can legally store or process. The Dedicated Mode system may legally process data whose sensitivity is no greater than that of its accreditedaccredited sensitivity level. All data exported from the Dedicated Mode system must be protected at this level until a classification authority outside the system reviews it. This authority may determine its correct sensitivity, which may be lower than the accredited sensitivity level. For example, a Dedicated Mode simulator accredited to operate at the accredited sensitivity level of SECRET may contain SECRET, CONFIDENTIAL, or UNCLASSIFIED data, but all users must have at least a SECRET clearance. In addition, all output must be protected at the accredited level (SECRET), and no data more sensitive than SECRET can touch the AIS.

An AIS operating in System High Mode is almost like one in Dedicated Mode, except it uses identity-based access controls. This mode is still single-level because it identifies a single accredited sensitivity level. Again, all data entering the system must be at a sensitivity no greater than the accredited sensitivity level, and all data that leaves the system needs to be protected at this level until reviewed for possible downgrade by a classification authority outside the system. But System High Mode uses identity-based access controls to enforce policy rules that base users' access to information on their roles or job requirements, or some other user's discretion. It enforces rules the Department of Defense specifies for systems built after 1992. Systems using this mode have the built-in controls necessary to keep unauthorized users from accessing and trying to change important information, such as password files and audit trails. Of course, identity-based mechanisms for access control make systems harder to build and test, which could drive up a project's cost and lengthen its schedule.

Systems which Distinguish between Sensitivity Levels

Systems operating in Compartmented Mode have identity-based and rule-based access controls, as well as complex mechanisms to segregate all data, storage, and user access based on their sensitivity label or clearance. To accredit these systems, we must still specify an accredited sensitivity level, but users' security credentials differ from those of the single-level systems described above. All users are cleared to the same standard, but some are authorized access to certain data, and others aren't. For example, SECRET may be the correct classification of data for Project A and Project B. But access to either requires not only a SECRET clearance but also specific authorization for Project A, Project B, or both; user discretion isn't allowed. An authority assigns access to Project A or Project B, and the AIS, operating in Compartmented Mode, must grant access strictly according to the access-control rules. Also, users may have different needs to know. Data inputs must still be no greater than the accredited sensitivity level, but because systems in Compartmented Mode are label-based, output can be at any level equal to or less than its accredited level. A classification authority within the system can vouch for downgrades.

A system in Multilevel Mode is just like one in Compartmented Mode, except that users may be cleared at different levels. Therefore, systems in Multilevel Mode must enforce the most complex security policies. To do so, they must have robust enough mechanisms for maximum control over data access. Typically, the modeling and simulation community doesn't use them because of their high cost, lengthy programs for development and security accreditation, and specialized applications.

17.3.2   Distributed Systems Operating at Different Levels

Let's turn for a moment to our most challenging situation: two or more simulators, each security accredited to run in a different operating mode at a different accredited sensitivity level, and both required to pass data to one another. The major security challenge in this situation is to identify at least one security label common to all simulators. If one isn't obvious, we have to find a way to generate data with a common label. In all cases, ultimately we must meet operational objectives and gain acceptance from the Designed Approval Authority (DAA). Data with the same sensitivity can be safely exchanged, but the DAA will want assurance that it's correctly labeled and that write-down or read-up errors are unlikely before approving it.

When no common security label is apparent, we may be able to downgrade data to a lower sensitivity level, but nearly all data owners view downgrading as risky. The DAA would require strong evidence that the downgrading mechanism is foolproof to avoid compromises.

Developing and accrediting trusted systems is a complex process. In the United States, the Department of Defense and the National Institute of Standards and Technology have defined how to determine the level of assurance a trusted AIS needs and how to develop AISs according to acceptable performance criteria. Briefly, the approach is first to analyze risk using a method that considers

- The AIS's security operating mode (Dedicated, System High, Compartmented, Multilevel)
- The sensitivity of the data to be protected
- The trustworthiness (clearance) of the people who would operate the AIS

Essentially, high sensitivity and low clearances mean security accreditation will depend on greater assurances and more stringent operating modes. At the present time, you can find details on the philosophy and criteria for developing trusted systems in the US Defense Department's *Trusted Computer System Evaluation Criteria*, commonly known as the Orange Book. To develop a high-assurance system, we must

- Design, build, and test the system to meet the Orange Book's criteria
- Document the design and users' operating procedures according to the Orange Book's requirements
- Develop enough evidence that the system operates properly to convince the DAA that the remaining security risk is acceptable.

Be aware, these tasks are difficult and time consuming. Security accreditation can delay your project if not diligently planned, scheduled, and coordinated.

The international security engineering community is also working to standardize assurance criteria for the development of secure systems. There are currently three main nation- or region-specific criteria—the *Trusted Computer System Evaluation Criteria* (TCSEC) for the United States, the *Canadian Trusted Computer Product Evaluation Criteria* (CTCPEC) for Canada, and the *Information Technology Security Evaluation Criteria* (ITSEC) for Europe and other regions. Recently, an international Common Criteria development project gained recognition with its efforts to develop trusted systems assurance standards for use in the emerging global economy by the year 2000. Although these criteria will be designed to supersede existing standards, legacy systems built to Orange Book or other existing criteria will not have to be redesigned. In the United States, the National Security Agency and the National Institute of Standards and Technology actively support this project, and a first draft of these criteria was published in 1996. You can find out more about the Common Criteria project by visiting the National Institute of Standards and Technology's Computer Security Resource Clearinghouse website at http://csrc.ncsl.nist.gov/.

17.4   Certifying and Accrediting a Secure System

When the simulator is finally built, we must demonstrate its ability to enforce the rules in its security policy and operate within its defined environment. At this point, we have to assure the DAA that our system is secure—that it will protect data against compromise or breaches of integrity. Certifying a system requires a technical judgment about the security design following formal review, test, and evaluation. Accrediting the security of a system includes technical and management reviews, as well as the Designated Approval Authority's judgment that it will meet prescribed security objectives.

17.4.1   Process for Security Certification

Systems built to satisfy performance specifications negotiated with buyers typically go through a formal certification review, which allows customers to make sure they're getting what they agreed to buy. Building a simulator's AIS is no different from building any other system, so certification depends on demonstrating that requirements levied on us when the AIS was conceived are implemented and operational when delivered.

Requirements may have changed during the project, but we need a final set of agreed-on abilities and features when it's done. Certification involves a due-diligence inspection by the buyer that proves the system meets requirements. For a secure system, certification also means data owners—represented by the DAA—must agree the risk of allowing the AIS to process sensitive or classified information is acceptably low.

Buyers and the DAA may delegate certification tasks to experts, who may be separate contractors experienced in evaluating results of system-level testing. Everyone must be part of the design review. This means inviting the certifier and DAA. Keeping everyone aware of issues concerning design, certification, and security accreditation encourages team building.

During certification testing, developers exercise the system and show it can work as required. Usually, we submit plans and procedures for these tests to the certifier for approval. As security engineers, we must contribute test cases and planning to the system's test-plan document, and develop all test procedures needed to show the system meets security requirements. Then, we have to review the test plan and security-testing procedures with the certifier to make sure everyone agrees. During the certification test itself, we should get the certifier to acknowledge in writing all successful tests and make sure the certifier's test report is accurate before it becomes final. The certification process results in the certifier's statement about how well the AIS meets requirements. Certification that the security mechanisms within a secure simulator work as specified is key to security accreditation from the DAA.

17.4.2   Process for Security Accreditation

When a simulator is to store, process, and protect sensitive or classified information, getting security accreditation is arguably the activity most important to its success. Without security accreditation, the AIS can't access or process data. Although the security-accreditation decision comes after the system is developed, designers and developers must focus on it from the very beginning.

Security accreditation is a statement of permission the DAA issues to the AIS's owner. It grants authority to operate with data under the DAA's control. A typical accreditation document describes the

- Prescribed security operating mode
- Accredited sensitivity level at which the AIS may operate
- Data allowed to be stored, processed, and protected
- Specified physical environment
- Specified internal and external connections
- Approved operating procedures
- Users and operators
- Times and dates during which the AIS may operate
- Mission the AIS may complete
- Residual security risk which the Designated Approval Authority agrees to assume

Because the DAA accepts responsibility for specific security risks, we must not only meet stated requirements but also identify and describe uncontrolled vulnerabilities. We have to know the data owners' needs almost from the start, so rules in the security policy can cover criteria for security accreditation, the built system can enforce these rules, and testing can eventually show the AIS satisfies security requirements.

As security engineers, we have to recognize the strong personal commitment the DAA must make to grant authority to operate. To get operating authority, we must develop a close working relationship with this person and build trust as early as possible. Building trust is crucial because everyone must understand the AIS's security strengths and shortcomings before the DAA can determine whether to accept any residual security risk. If he or she is surprised about a security-related detail following security accreditation, our system may be unceremoniously shut down.

17.5   Summary

Security accreditation is the ultimate goal when a simulator's automated information system is intended to store, process and protect sensitive or classified information. The first step is to consider security engineering and accreditation issues from the very start by defining a security policy and identifying the Designated Approval Authority who will grant authority to operate. The policy focuses engineering, design, implementation, and test and evaluation energy on security rules that must be enforced to create and maintain a secure state. Informing the Designated Approval Authority of all security-related decisions and issues will keep surprises out of security accreditation and increase your chance of getting authority to operate. Security and integrity are complementary. If you don't provide adequate safeguards, your development may suffer from lost time, corrupted data, unreliable results, sanctions, and liability. Because securing automated information systems is a broad subject, we've identified several references. You should read more about secure systems and talk to your Designated Approval Authority to more fully appreciate the challenges of getting approval to operate.

References

Abrams, M.D. and H. J. Podell. 1987. *Tutorial: Computer & Network Security*. Los Angeles, CA: IEEE Computer Society Press, Order No. DX756.

Department of Defense. 1985. *Trusted Computer System Evaluation Criteria, DOD 5200.28-STD*. Washington, D.C.: United States Department of Defense (U.S. Government Printing Office number 008-000-00461-7.)

Ford, Warwick. 1994. *Computer Communications Security—Principles, Standard Protocols and Techniques*. Englewood Cliffs, NJ: Prentice Hall.

Gasser, Morrie. 1988. *Building a Secure Computer System*. New York: Van Nostrand Reinhold.

National Computer Security Center. 1987. *Trusted Network Interpretation*. NCSC-TG-005. Washington, D.C.: United States Department of Defense, National Computer Security Center. (Available on the World Wide Web at www.radium.ncsc.mil/tpep/library/ rainbow/NCSC-TG-005.html.)

Pfleeger, Charles P. 1989. *Security in Computing*. Englewood Cliffs, NJ: Prentice Hall.

Estimating Cost and Schedule

Jerry W. Lawson, *The Peak Technologies Group, Inc.*

To build models and simulations, we must plan using realistic work estimates. A successful project satisfies requirements within expectations for cost and schedule. Established requirements often change as a project proceeds, which can wreak havoc on the outcome. But procuring agencies and developing contractors can actively manage these changes and adjust cost and schedule to cover them.

Estimating cost and schedule can be difficult, so estimates often vary, but certain tools and methods can make estimating easier and less variable. First, we must develop a baseline schedule—a measuring stick that allows us to monitor cost and schedule—by

1. Determining the size of the work effort required
2. Determining the productivity of the engineers who will do it
3. Determining the cost of the workers
4. Creating a work schedule based on the productivity of the available workers

Once we've established a baseline schedule, we use the same four steps (see Fig. A.1) to adjust it whenever new or changing requirements are added to the contract. If a requirement is out of scope, we must estimate its size and predict productivity and cost, so the modified schedule can reflect it. Thus, a good plan is based on a realistic estimate of the proposed work and a detailed schedule of that work. Then, we can use management reviews (see Chap. 6) to monitor and adjust the schedule as required.

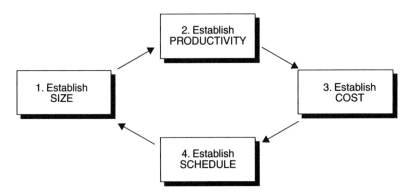

Fig. A.1.   **Estimating Cost and Schedule.** An effective plan for M&S development requires accurate estimates of cost and schedule. The process shown here produces a sound baseline and can be used iteratively to adapt the estimates to new or changing requirements.

A.1   Estimating Software Size

First, let's determine the size of the proposed work. Just as a housing contractor needs to know the basic square footage (or size) of a proposed home in order to begin an estimate, we need to know the basic size of the models and simulations to be developed. Knowing the basic size allows you to adjust the estimate to account for variations. Among the many units of measurement that can quantify software size, the most common are source lines of code [Conte 1986], token counts [Conte 1986], function points [Dreger 1989], modules, and screens. Regardless of the units chosen, you must eventually translate software size into the number of engineering hours it will take to create, test, and build the system.

To estimate size, you must

1. Divide the work into smaller, more manageable units (tasks) and then describe each one.
2. Establish an estimate and justify it (form a "basis of estimate"). The basis of estimate and task descriptions are the foundation of a solid size estimate.
3. Review ("scrub") the estimates.

A.1.1   Describing Tasks

Task descriptions tell us what a given task does. For example, a task description for a requirements document may state that it must adhere to a certain standard or meet other conditions specified by the procuring agency—if you want to save all output reports, you could say: *provide the ability for all reports to be saved to disk, so people may view or print them later.*

Next, you need to map each task description to units of work, so all units of work will relate to at least one task description. This mapping results in a thorough estimate. Table A.1 depicts some common mappings that may apply to different parts of the overall effort. For example, some elements of work may map directly to specific requirements, whereas others map to a particular design approach. Still others may map to a similar model or simulation built under a different development effort—maybe by a different contractor.

Table A.1. **Mapping Task Descriptions to Sources of Work.** Task descriptions should map to various sources of work to completely describe the elements we must estimate.

For	Each task description maps to
Requirements	a contractual requirement
Design units	part of a completed design
Work breakdown structure	one element of the work breakdown structure
Related model or similar unit of work	a completed development similar to the required work

Task descriptions are a way to account fully for all elements you need to estimate. Otherwise, you could overlook some required work. Fortunately, many contracts contain a built-in mapping mechanism—the work breakdown structure. This document details software efforts, hardware efforts, and services developing contractors will carry out to fulfill their contractual obligations to the procuring agency. It tries formally to identify all work you must do, so it's an excellent place to begin writing task descriptions. But you'll usually have to break the work into smaller units in order to estimate its total size. Figure A.2 shows a partially expanded work breakdown structure.

Using the work breakdown structure as your main approach to mapping doesn't keep you from using the other methods in Table A.1. For example, the first element in the work breakdown structure—Detection—may map task descriptions directly to each sub-element, as shown in Table A.2. On the other hand, Element 2—Attack—may map some task descriptions to each requirement allocated to the Attack element, rather than to the individual sub-elements. The task description for Element 3—Fuels Management (not shown in Fig. A.2)—may draw from a fuels-management model for a trucking company that has requirements very similar to those for the U.S. Forest Service. The type of mapping you use with any task description depends closely on the most accurate basis of estimate available.

A.1.2   Forming the Basis of Estimate

Whereas the task description describes what is to be estimated, the basis of estimate establishes how much work the job needs and why. It's the foundation for a cost estimate and thus gives the process validity. A sound basis leads to more accurate estimates of work size, which makes the tools and methods for estimating cost more effective.

Fire-Management Mission
1 Detection
1.1 Requirements
1.1.1 Definition
1.1.2 Requirements Document
1.1.3 Requirements Review
1.2 Design
1.2.1 Top Level Design
1.2.1.1 Top Level Design
1.2.1.2 Design Document
1.2.1.3 Preliminary Design Review
1.2.2 Detailed Design
1.3 Implementation
1.4 Testing
2 Attack
2.1 Requirements
2.2 Design
2.3 Implementation

Fig. A.2.   **Sample Work Breakdown Structure.** This document is often the first formal description of all work needed.

Table A.2.   **Task Descriptions May Map Directly to Subelements of a Work Breakdown Structure.** Some line elements of the structure won't have a task description or basis of estimate because they're summary lines or not broken out.

Work Breakdown Element	Associated Task Description
1. Detection	None, Summary Task Line
1.1 Requirements	None, Summary Task Line
1.1.1 Definition	Yes
1.1.2 Requirements Document	Yes
1.1.3 Requirements Review	Yes
1.2 Design	None, Summary Task Line
1.2.1 Top Level Design	Yes
1.2.1.1 Top Level Design	Yes
1.2.1.2 Design Document	Yes
1.2.1.3 Preliminary Design Review	Yes
1.2.2 Detailed Design	None, summary task not exploded in Fig. A.2
1.3 Implementation	None, summary task not exploded in Fig. A.2
1.4 Testing	None, summary task not exploded in Fig. A.2

Of the several ways to establish a basis of estimate, three main methods have emerged:

- Engineering judgment, or asking those who will do the work—the most common method
- Referencing a similar work effort—one of the simplest and most accurate methods
- Analyzing the various work elements—a method that eliminates or reduces most guesswork

Regardless of the method you use, you should analyze smaller elements of work, apply the best basis of estimate to each element, and build the best possible size estimate for the overall work effort.

Using Engineering Judgment to Estimate Work Size

Although using engineering judgment for estimates is common, it's also the least accurate method because it's a "best guess" for a job the engineer hasn't done before. For example, if a job requires screens for a graphical user interface, a more accurate estimate will likely come from engineers who have built them, rather than from engineers who write communications protocols and drivers. The former will base their estimate on similar work; the latter would be making an engineering judgment based on their overall knowledge of programming.

One real-life example of using engineering judgment comes from a bid to write a simulation that replaced and upgraded a real-time detection system. This judgment determined the simulation would take 4,500 source lines of code. With a contract awarded, the program manager began planning and determined the original system contained more than 40,000 source lines of code. Even with newer hardware and software languages, the program manager faced a huge challenge to replace those 40,000 lines of code with only 4,500. A little research would have revealed a very similar effort from which to estimate accurately the size of the job. The lesson learned? Never use engineering judgment unless neither of the following methods is available. It always increases the risk of inaccurate bids.

Referencing a Similar Work Effort to Estimate Work Size

Comparing the current work to similar completed work will give you a more accurate estimate. For example, if an existing simulation required 40,000 lines of code, any developer is likely to write nearly 40,000 lines of code to develop a similar simulation. If special considerations reduce or increase this estimate, you can adjust accordingly.

You can use similar work to estimate the work on your entire project or any part of it. The more elements of proposed work you can relate to similar work efforts, the more accurate your overall estimate. The fewer engineering judgments you use and the more sound reasons you give for as many elements of the effort as possible, the more accurate your overall estimate will be.

Analyzing Work Elements to Estimate Work Size

Most size estimates won't map exactly to similar or related work efforts because no two simulations are exactly alike. As a result, you must analyze the work by breaking it into smaller, more definable, elements. In some cases, smaller work units may relate well to elements of previous efforts which will allow you to develop accurate estimates. For example, the timing drivers for dividing cycles and frames may be similar to previous timing drivers. Then, even though the remaining, smaller elements don't map perfectly, your overall estimate will still be reasonably accurate.

To illustrate the value of analyzing smaller units of work, suppose a project is bid at 7,500 lines of code. As a reviewer, you could easily argue the work will actually take 10,000 lines of code or 5,000 lines of code. If you don't have a unit of similar work to compare, the basis for estimate is weak, and you should question it. Now suppose someone has divided the same unit of work into several smaller units. One unit is estimated at 1,000 lines of code because it covers 20 time-frame modules, and each module should require 50 lines of code. At this point any disagreement is over just 50 lines of code for the single module. Once you've established a sound basis of estimate for this module, the overall estimate will be more believable. Even though a new simulation may work differently, if it uses a time-frame module that requires 50 lines of code in another simulation, you'll have a sound basis of estimate. At worst, someone could argue that it could be written in 45 lines instead of 50—a much smaller margin of error. Thus, even though you may not find a similar work effort overall, decomposing the effort can give you a better chance to establish a sound basis of estimate.

A.1.3   Reviewing Size Estimates

To establish a sound size estimate, you'll need a manager, preferably with a strong technical background, to review the task descriptions and basis of estimate. The manager must determine the estimate's validity by taking three main actions:

1. Examine the task description to determine the work is identified and proper.

2. Evaluate the basis of estimate for validity. Look for similar work efforts and evaluate analyses.

3. Review all questionable estimates (including all based on engineering judgment) with the engineer. Try to uncover any areas the engineer hasn't considered.

Often, engineers believe management reviews try to reduce estimates so the bid will be more competitive. That's not so. They simply make sure the estimate is accurate. A good review may increase or decrease an estimate.

A.2   Estimating Productivity

Once you've established the work size, you must apply a productivity rating to the work. Productivity is defined as the rate of work for any given work element. For example, housing developers can build, on average, four houses per year. Thus, if they must build six houses, they'll need 1.5 years of effort. In this case, the developers' productivity is four houses per year. For modeling and simulation, productivity tells you how many engineering hours you need to do the job. You can estimate productivity using past or projected performance.

A.2.1   Using Experience to Establish Productivity

The best insight into how long a job will take comes from having done that job (or a similar one) before. Let's suppose another project required 10 screens for the graphical user interface, taking five days per screen. It follows that 25 similar screens for a new model or simulation would take about 125 days (25 screens at five days per screen). Of course, you'll need to adjust for variations and differences before calculating the productivity. For example, user-interface screens on the prior job may have presented only database information, whereas the new screens must also process complex algorithms before presenting the data. In this case, you'd have to factor into your estimate the extra work for these algorithms, so your final estimate may be seven days per screen, instead of five.

You can see that similar work performance is the best metric for productivity, just as it is for a basis of estimate. Collecting metrics on each development is important for any company; yet, many companies still don't do it consistently. You can also use parametric models to double check estimates from similar work, but real work always more accurately predicts productivity.

A.2.2   Using Parametric Models to Determine Productivity

If you don't have prior performance to calculate productivity, you'll tend to rely on engineering judgment. But you can improve this judgment by using parametric models developed over the past 25 years [Conte 1986] to predict metrics for software development. For example:

- COCOMO [Boehm 1981; Boehm 1984] and COCOMO II[*]
- The Putnam Resource Allocation Model [Putnam 1984]
- The Jensen Model [Jensen 1984]
- SoftCost [Tausworthe 1981]
- Before You Leap by the Gordon Group
- CA-Estimates by Computer Associates

---

[*] Information on COCOMO II can be found on the World Wide Web at http://sunset.usc.edu/COCOMOII/Cocomo.html.

By taking in descriptions of the complexity of the work and development factors, parametric models try to predict productivity and other information, such as scheduling and staffing. These results are for typical development, so they won't necessarily reflect what a particular developer may achieve. Still, they're the best alternative when you don't have productivity metrics from actual work.

As an example, let's use the Jensen Model to calculate productivity for a sample work element (Detection) of a fire-management simulation at the forest level. This model (and most other parametric models) uses parameters for size, complexity, technology, and the environment.

As mentioned previously, various measurement units exist to quantify software size. For this example, we'll use a size estimate of 15,000 lines of code, so the Jensen Model's input screen (Table A.3) shows an estimated standard size of 15k source lines of code ±3K (to allow for minimum and maximum ranges).

Table A.3.   **Input Screen for the Jensen Model.** Sample input parameters required for parametric models.

Schedule Constraint:		12.0 months	
SIZE BOE	MIN	ML	MAX
Estimated Size (KLOC)	12.00	15.00	18.00
COMPLEXITY BOE	MIN	ML	MAX
Estimated Complexity	11.00	8.00	5.00
TECHNOLOGY BOE	MIN	ML	MAX
Analyst Capability	1.20	1.00	0.90
Application Experience	1.10	1.00	0.90
Modern Development Practices	1.05	1.00	0.95
Programmer's Ability	1.10	1.00	0.95
Automated Tools	1.00	0.90	0.85
Turnaround	0.87	0.90	0.93
ENVIRONMENT BOE	MIN	ML	MAX
Special Display	1.00	1.00	1.05
Re-hosting	1.00	1.00	1.15
Language Experience	1.06	1.00	1.00
Required Reliability	1.00	1.00	1.00
Memory Constraint	1.00	1.00	1.00
Multiple Site	1.07	1.13	1.20
Requirements Volatility	1.05	1.00	0.95
Resource Dedication	1.21	1.11	1.00
Resource Location	1.00	1.00	1.00
Real-Time Operation	1.00	1.00	1.00
Development System Experience	1.26	1.08	1.00
CPU Time Constraint	1.00	1.00	1.00
Development System Volatility	1.00	1.00	1.00

BOE = Basis of Estimate
KLOC = thousand Lines of Code

We also have to describe the application's complexity. Table A.4 shows a sample guide to complexity ratings for parametric models (each model will have its own rating scale). For this example, I've selected a complexity rating of 8, as shown in Table A.3. You can see from Table A.4 that an 8 rating reflects a fairly complex application, which contains re-entrant code, interrupts, differential equations, etc.

Table A.4.   **Complexity Rating for Parametric Models.** These complexity ratings describe a system's sophistication or difficulty.[*]

Rating	Control Operations	Computational Operations	Device-Dependent Operations	Data-Management Operations
28	Straight code with a few non-tested operators: DOs, CASEs, IFTHENs. Simple predicates.	Evaluates simple expressions: for example, A = B+C*(D-E)	Simple read/write statements with simple formats	Simple arrays in main memory
21	Straightforward nesting of operators. Mostly simple predicates.	Evaluate moderate level expressions, for example, D=SQRT (B**2-4 *A*C)	Doesn't have to recognize a particular processor or I/O device characteristics. I/O done at Get/Put level. No cognizance of overlap.	Single file subsetting with no data structure changes, no edits, no intermediate files.
15	Mostly simple nesting. Some intermodule control. Decision tables.	Uses standard math and statistical routines. Basic matrix and vector operations.	I/O processing includes device selection, status checking and error processing.	Multifile input and single file output. Simple structural changes, simple edits.
11	Highly nested operators with many compound predicates. Queue and stack control. Considerable control between modules.	Basic numerical analysis: multivariate interpolation ordinary differential equations. Basic truncation, roundoff concerns.	Operations at physical I/O level (physical storage address translations: seeks, reads, etc.) Optimized I/O overlap.	Special purpose subroutines activated by contents of data stream. Complex data restructuring in records.
8	Re-entrant and recursive coding. Handles interrupts on fixed priorities.	Difficult but structured numerical analysis: near singular matrix equations, partial differential equations.	Routines for interrupt diagnosis, servicing, masking. Handles communication lines.	A generalized routine for file structuring, driven by parameters. Builds files, processes commands, optimizes searches.
4	Multiple resource scheduling with dynamically changing priorities. Microcode level control.	Difficult and unstructured numerical analysis: highly accurate analysis of noisy, stochastic data.	Coding depends on device timing, microprogrammed operations.	Highly coupled, dynamic relational structures. Manages data in natural language.

[*] Adapted from B.W. Boehm. *Software Engineering Economics*. 1981. p. 391.

Next, let's look at technology parameters (see Table A.5). Table A.3 shows there is one input for each of the six technology parameters in Table A.5. But we need an acceptable range for each parameter. For example, Table A.6 gives the acceptable range for the 4th parameter, Programmer Ability. In Table A.3, you'll notice we selected a "nominal" 1.00 for the programmer's ability, which "translates" to average or the 55th percentile in Table A.6.

Finally, let's consider environment parameters (see Table A.7). Table A.8 shows the ratings you could use to describe the environment parameter, "Reliability Requirement" (how software failure affects your mission).

Some of the values the Jensen model will calculate are described in Fig. A.3, which shows the "development cost" will be 42.9 engineering months. That's what we mainly wanted to know, but the Jensen model also gives us the minimum development time and effort, along with staffing levels and major schedule milestones. Table A.3 shows that we needed an expected, a minimum, and a maximum value for all input parameters. These parameters allow the model to produce a confidence chart, which depicts an estimated development effort (see Fig. A.4).

Whenever you use any parametric model, you have to know its limits and restrictions, such as:

- The model may not account for system engineering, computer time, documentation, program management, line management, or other similar efforts
- The model may have limits on size, duration, and peak staff
- Most models use lines of code to measure size
- The model may be tied to some classes of language and independent of others (e.g., third-generation, but not fourth-generation languages)

A.2.3   Calculating Engineering Hours

If you use a parametric model, it will automatically produce the estimate of engineering hours for the job element. If you use productivity metrics, multiply the size of an element by the productivity for that element to get the engineering hours needed to build it. Table A.9 shows some examples.

A.2.4   Adding Overhead Hours

Engineering hours are only one part of the cost estimate for developing models or simulations. You must also consider project management, administration support, configuration management, quality assurance, and other support functions. Because developing organizations have different structures, the cost and ratios of these disciplines will vary.

All development efforts require some form of management, such as project managers, line managers, and contract managers. Depending on the size of the development and the structure of the developing firm, management can take from 5% to 25% of the engineering hours. Usually, you should examine any bid in which management takes more than 15% of the engineering hours.

Table A.5.   **Technology Parameters for Parametric Models.** These parameters describe the development staff's sophistication.

Type	Description
Designer's Ability	The average ability of the software designers assigned to the project
Application Experience	The average experience of the software developers assigned to the project in the related technical field
Development Practices	How much has the software developer used modern methods for software engineering
Programmer Ability	The average ability of the software programmers assigned to the project
Automated Tools	How automated are the software practices
Turnaround	The average compile time

Table A.6.   **Programmer Capability Ratings.** Programmer capability is one of six technology parameters.

	Very Low	Low	Nominal	High	Very High
Rating	1.46	1.17	1.00	0.86	0.70
Description	15th percentile of software programmers	35th percentile of software programmers	55th percentile of software programmers	75th percentile of software programmers	90th percentile of software programmers

Table A.7.   **Environment Parameters for Parametric Models.** These parameters describe the development technology's sophistication.

Type	Description
Display Requirements	Level of human interaction with the interface
Rehosting	Effort required to transition from development site to operational site
Language Experience	Average programming experience with targeted development language
Reliability Requirement	How software failure affects the mission
Memory Constraint	Effort required to meet memory requirements
Multi-Site Development	Site diversity of application development
Requirements Volatility	Expected changes to requirements baseline
Resource Dedication	Programmers' access to development equipment
Resource and Support Location	Degree of access to development resources
Real-Time Operation	Percent of real-time operations
Development System Experience	Average team experience with development environment
CPU Time Constraint	Percentage of special timing code required for performance
Development System Volatility	Instability of software-development environment

Table A.8.   **Reliability Requirement—One of 12 Environment Parameters.** All environment
parameters, including reliability, equate difficulty to a numerical scale.

	Very Low	**Low**	**Nominal**	**High**	**Very High**
Rating	1.00	1.16	1.31	1.48	1.77
Description	Inconvenience	Recover easily	Moderate loss; recover without extreme penalty	Major financial loss	Loss of human life

SCHEDULE AND STAFFING PROJECTIONS

BASIC RESULTS	STAFFING

MINIMUM DEVELOPMENT TIME	**Maximum Staffing Rate** **8.3** persons/year
SRR → FQT Schedule (months) **12.5**	**Peak Staff Level** **5.3** persons
Development Cost (person-months) **42.9**	**Peak Programmer Staff** **2.8** persons
MINIMUM DEVELOPMENT EFFORT	SCHEDULE (Months from SRR
SRR → FQT Schedule (months) **12.0**	PDR 2.4
Development Cost (person-months) **#N/A**	CDR 5.4
	Peak Staffing 6.6
	FQT 12.5

SRR = System Requirements Review
PDR = Preliminary Design Review
CDR = Critical Design Review
FQT = Functional Qualification Tests

Fig. A.3.   **Calculations from the Jensen Model.** A sample output of the Jensen parametric model.

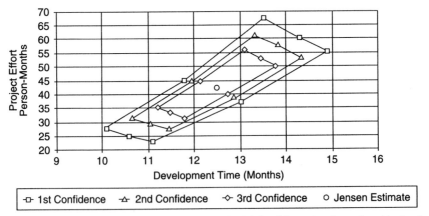

Fig. A.4.   **Estimates of Effort from the Jensen Model.** Confidence levels produced by the Jensen parametric model.

Table A.9.   Calculating Engineering Hours. To get engineering hours, multiply size by productivity.

Size	Productivity	Engineering Hours
25 interface screens	40 hours per screen	1000
3 element interface modules at 2000 lines of code per module	3 lines of code per hour	2000
15 reports at 300 lines of code per report	10 lines of code per hour	450

Secretaries, technical writers, and administrative assistants are just some of the support staff who will absorb 5% to 10% of the engineering hours.

The development contractor should have an independent staff for quality assurance—one that reports not to the development manager but to a separate manager within the contractor's organization. Smaller development firms find this independence harder to maintain, but they can ensure quality with some straightforward practices—for example, having engineers test each other's written code. Depending on the amount of testing, quality-assurance hours can range from 3% to 25% of total engineering hours.

Various versions of software, hardware, and documentation call for careful configuration management. Sometimes, you'll have to reload previous versions of software to correct a new bug caused by recent changes. Documentation must be current—an old user's manual can't help much if the system doesn't work as documented. Three percent of the engineering hours is typical for proper configuration management.

A.2.5   Allowing for Labor Categories

To determine productivity accurately, you must take into account a development company's mix of labor categories. One company may have many junior engineers, another may have a lot of senior engineers, and yet another may have an equal split. The company with more senior engineers should have a higher productivity rate than the one that uses a lot of junior engineers, so it will work faster. (Of course, it could still cost you the same number of dollars: faster work at higher hourly pay may equal slower work at lower pay.) Table A.10 shows an example of the different types of labor categories and the labor mix that a company may use in developing an application.

Table A.10.   Example Mix of Labor Categories for Development Companies.

Program Manager	6%
Senior Analyst	20%
Analyst	28%
Junior Analyst	36%
Clerical	10%

A.2.6   The Final Product—Task Description and Basis of Estimate

To document results, we commonly complete a two-part form that covers the task description and the basis of estimate.

The first section describes the work to be done and the basis of estimate for the particular work element being quoted. (Fig. A.5 illustrates the first part of this form.) Using this form allows us to map all work and analyze it, as well as to complete a size estimate and clearly justify it.

Task Description/Basis of Estimate **Part 1 of 2**	
Estimated By: _____	Reviewed By: _____
Task Description: (State requirement or element of work being estimated) Ability to Save Output Report (Requirements 3.2.1.1.3): Provide the ability for all reports to be saved so they may be viewed / or printed later.	
Implementation Analysis and Basis of Estimate: Many report tools don't allow printing to file or handle encapsulated postscript. That means we must save the report data to a flat file or a database so the data can be re-read to reproduce the report. In addition, each screen will require a pull-down or hot-key menu to give operators the ability to save or load a screen. Based on providing a similar ability on the Integrated Electronic and Radar Weapons (IERW) project, the save code will be 100 lines of code per screen whereas pull downs were around 25 lines of code per screen. Load and redisplay software, though not included in the IERW project, are estimated to be similar to the save code at 100 lines of code per screen. 15 screens * (100 + 25 + 100) = 3375 lines of code	
Page 1 of 2 Date:	

Fig. A.5.   Task Description and Basis of Estimate—Part 1. Task Descriptions and Basis of Estimates describe the work to be done and justify the estimate of work.

In the form's second section, we calculate engineering and overhead hours, as shown in Fig. A.6. Here, we associate productivity with the size of the effort (from section one of the form), so we can derive a total number of engineering hours, automatically compute a company's overhead, and distribute the total hours among the company's labor categories.

Task Description/Basis of Estimate Part 2 of 2		
Estimated By: _____	Reviewed By: _____	
SIZE: 3375 sloc	**PRODUCTIVITY:** 4 SLOC / HOUR	
ENGINEERING HOURS:		
Software Engineering Hours = Total SLOC / SLOC per hour		844
System Engineering Hours = 15% of software hours		127
System Integration & Test Hours = 18.5% of software hours		156
Total Engineering Hours		1127
NON-ENGINEERING HOURS:		
Configuration Management Hours = 3% of engineering hours		34
Quality Assurance Hours = 3% of engineering hours		34
Clerical Hours = 10% of engineering hours		113
Project Management Hours = 6% of engineering hours		68
Line Management Hours = 5% of engineering hours		56
Network Administration Hours = 5% of engineering hours		56
Security Hours = 3% of engineering hours		34
TOTAL NON-ENGINEERING HOURS		395
Total Hours		1522
LABOR BREAKOUT		Project Manager	91
Senior Analyst	304	Junior Analyst	548
Analyst	426	Clerical	152
Page 2 of 2		Date:

Fig. A.6.   **Task Description/Basis of Estimate—Part 2.** These documents can automatically add non-engineering hours and distribute hours among labor categories.

A.3   Establishing Cost

Each developing contractor will have hourly costs associated with each labor category. By applying these costs to the total estimated hours, you can estimate cost.

In addition to labor hours, other costs will depend on the structure of a developer's non-labor costs. Because each company has its own model for these non-labor costs, we can't establish firm guidelines. But some examples would be costs for telephone, travel, reproduction, and computer services. Other non-labor costs can be directly mapped to a particular labor activity. Examples would be a site survey to determine locations of RF equipment being installed or costs of procured off-the-shelf software, such as operating systems and network communications. We include these costs in Part 1 of the Task Description/Basis of Estimate form under "Implementation Analysis and Basis of Estimate" (Fig. A.5). Ultimately, we'll identify a final total cost which will be compared to cost proposals by other companies.

A.4   Establishing a Schedule

Once you know the size and cost of the development effort, create a schedule that shows the detailed tasks, their durations, the dependencies among these tasks, and finally, the people assigned to do them. Many development firms still take a casual or "ad hoc" approach to planning and tracking tasks, which too commonly results in "reactive" or "crisis" management. Yet, the extra cost for tools and time to actively schedule and track tasks is a small investment that returns huge savings.

Companies sometimes have a person or group trained in project planning and tracking, which makes the effort more efficient. The larger the development effort, the more critically you need a dedicated business manager (full-time or part-time). Otherwise, program managers and engineering line managers must collect data and prepare reports for project tracking. In either case, the program manager and engineering line managers must help create a schedule (with or without the help of a business manager).

A.4.1   Using Four Steps to Create a Schedule

Although every schedule has unique problems and people who develop the schedule have different approaches, creating a repeatable process will make this job easier.

The four steps outlined below are widely used in modeling and simulation, as well as in many fields that develop applications. Also, if you use automated scheduling tools, you'll find many of them contain a tutorial demonstrating these basic steps.

Step one is to identify all tasks needed to do the work—many of which you can get from the task descriptions and basis of estimates or the work breakdown structure used during the bidding process. With these sources as starting points, several approaches are possible; the traditional top-down or bottom-up approaches are most popular. In the top-down approach, you first define the major activities and then break each one into smaller, more manageable sub-tasks until you've covered all tasks needed to do the work. A bottom-up approach is just the reverse. You might brainstorm to list as many likely sub-tasks as possible. Next, sort and organize activities into groups, which become the major tasks. Then, re-evaluate each major task to determine if you need sub-tasks not identified during brainstorming. A bottom-up approach may develop major tasks that don't map to the original work breakdown structure. Hybrid approaches are also very common.

For example, the major elements of the work breakdown structure may help you define the major activities. Then, you could do a bottom-up approach for each major activity to identify sub-tasks. Variations are numerous, but it's important to find an approach that works well for those who will develop the schedule. Depending on the development's size, that could involve many people.

Step two consists of establishing the dependencies between the various tasks and sub-tasks. In any schedule, some tasks must be completed before others and some can be done in parallel. Sometimes, we need to schedule so they finish at the same time; sometimes, a task can't finish until another starts. Table A.11 illustrates these relationships.

Table A.11.　　Types of Task Dependencies. The four basic task dependencies establish relationships between start and finish times for coordinated tasks.

Type of Dependency	Description
Finish-to-start	One task must finish before another task may start
Start-to-start	One task must start before another task may start
Finish-to-finish	One task must finish before another task may finish
Start-to-finish	One task must start before another task may finish

Finish-to-start relationships are most common. For example, the design task must finish before the assembly task can start in creating a prototype hardware board. Or a critical design-review task must finish before the coding task can start. Start-to-start relationships are those in which one task may not start until another task starts. This relationship is useful whenever we identify two tasks that can occur at the same time. Finish-to-finish and start-to-finish relationships cover other dependencies that occur less often.

Step three is to establish the size and length of each sub-task. Sometimes, you can directly map the size of summary tasks and sub-tasks to the task descriptions and basis of estimates. Summary tasks break into sub-tasks, so you'll need to distribute the size of a summary task among those sub-tasks. By taking the overall size of sub-tasks, you can allocate resources (engineers) to them and then increase or decrease resources to complete the sub-tasks faster or slower, respectively.

In step four, you'll refine resource assignments and task durations to achieve the schedule you want. This step will identify potential risks and establish profiles for required staffing. Two of the most common problems are that the schedule is too long and that assigned resources are overworked at certain times and underworked at other times. Thus, you must reassign resources and shorten or lengthen tasks to meet delivery dates and keep work loads reasonable. Finally, this four-step process will establish staffing requirements and hiring dates (if needed)—which may or may not present risks. It will also identify sub-tasks that are critical to the project's success. For example, if the sensor tower assembly isn't built before winter, the entire installation must be postponed until the following spring. Once you've finished all four steps, you'll have a baseline schedule that you can use to measure how well the work is done (see Chap. 6 for details on project tracking and oversight).

A.4.2 Using Common Tools to Create a Schedule

Creating a schedule is a dress rehearsal for the actual development. If you can replicate what the engineers must do, they probably will be able to do it; if you can't, they probably won't. To improve scheduling, we often use Gantt or PERT charts.

Gantt Charts

Gantt charts, invented by Henry Gantt [Rakos 1990], provide a timeline of the tasks that must be done and, often, the interdependencies or relationships between them. If you're using an automated scheduling tool, it will typically calculate critical paths for your project—paths that, if not completed on schedule, will retard delivery dates. Figure A.7 shows a partially completed Gantt chart for developing the fire-management mission.

Forest Level Fire-Management Mission	% Complete
1 Detection	**36%**
1.1 Requirements	**100%**
1.1.1 Definition	100%
1.1.2 Requirements Document	100%
1.1.3 Requirements Review	100%
1.2 Design	**22%**
1.2.1 Top-Level Design	**50%**
1.2.1.1 Top Level Design	70%
1.2.1.2 Design Document	25%
1.2.1.3 Design Review	0%
1.2.2 Detailed Design	**0%**
1.2.2.1 Detailed Design	0%
1.2.2.2 Design Document	0%
1.2.2.3 Design Review	0%

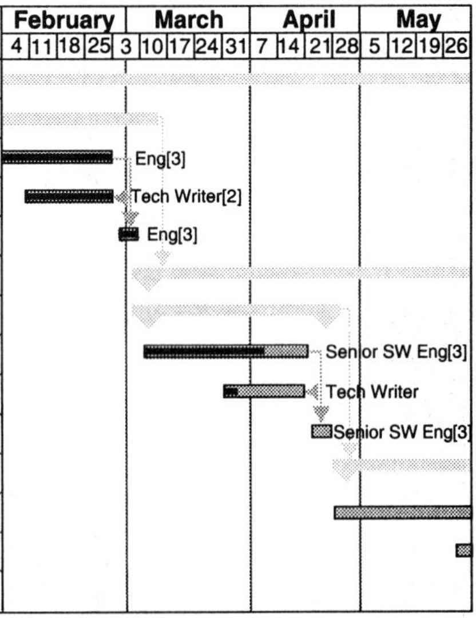
February
March
April
May
4 11 18 25 3 10 17 24 31 7 14 21 28 5 12 19 26
Eng[3]
Tech Writer[2]
Eng[3]
Senior SW Eng[3]
Tech Writer
Senior SW Eng[3]

Fig. A.7. Gantt Chart for Building a Fire-Management System at the Forest Level. The Gantt chart is the most commonly used scheduling view.

Gantt charts are popular because they visually represent needed work and its status. By quickly examining the Gantt chart, managers can see critical paths or tasks that are behind or ahead of schedule or over or under budget. Then, they can reassign resources to solve these problems. Automated tools can present various information in the table and timeline sections of a Gantt chart. For example, in Fig. A.7, "cost or schedule variance" could replace "% Complete" in the table section.

Then, you could place "% Complete" in the timeline section at the beginning of each sub-task or at the end of each sub-task (where resources are now).

PERT Charts

Program Evaluation and Review Technique (PERT) charts [Rakos 1990] also focus on tasks and their interdependencies. Figure A.8 shows a partially completed PERT chart for developing the fire-management mission. PERT charts differ from Gantt charts mainly in the way they present information. For example, in Fig. A.8, boxes represent tasks, and arrows show the relationships between them. A limited amount of information can appear in each box. In this example, each box displays the task name and four items of data (Percent Complete, Duration, Start Date, and Finish Date). If you use an automated scheduling tool, you can display any four types of data. Again, managers can quickly examine the PERT chart for critical paths or tasks that are behind or ahead of schedule or over or under budget—allowing them to reassign resources or create alternative solutions.

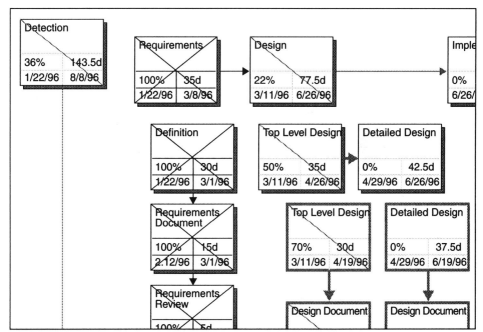

Fig. A.8. **PERT Chart for Fire-Management System at the Forest Level.** The PERT chart can display various types of vital project information, which managers use to reassign resources or devise solutions to problems.

Automated Tools

The example Gantt and PERT charts I've presented come from Microsoft Project©, a popular scheduling tool for personal computers. Several similar tools [Rakos 1990] offer the features you'll need (see Table A.12). These tools enable you to develop a schedule and track the engineers' progress, so planning and tracking become much simpler.

Table A.12.   Automated Scheduling Tools that Use Gantt Charts. Automated scheduling tools are available to simplify scheduling and tracking.

Tool	Platform	Vendor
Project Scheduler [Higgs 1995]	PC	Scitor Corporation
Timeline [Higgs 1995]	PC	Symantec Corporation
Super Project [Higgs 1995]	PC	Computer Associates
MS Project [Higgs 1995]	PC	Microsoft
Harvard Project Manager [Rakos 1990]	PC	Software Publishing
Artemis [Rakos 1990]	Mini/Mainframe	Metier Management Systems
DECSPM [Rakos 1990]	Mini/Mainframe	Digital Equipment Corporation
Project / 2 [Rakos 1990]	Mini/Mainframe	Project Software & Development, Inc.
Primavera [Rakos 1990]	Mini/Mainframe	Primavera Systems
PAC I, II, III [Rakos 1990]	Mini/Mainframe	AGS Management Systems

Most scheduling tools allow you to configure a Gantt or PERT chart so it will display different data. They'll also produce reports on many items you can use with the Gantt or PERT charts. Table A.13 lists some of the task data available from Microsoft's Project©. Other scheduling tools will present similar information.

A.5   Summary

The four basic steps in estimating cost and schedule consist of establishing the project's size, productivity, cost, and baseline schedule. The task description/basis of estimate is the foundation for calculating the project's size. The best task descriptions/basis of estimates are those based on actual similar work. Actual work will always provide a more solid foundation than pure engineering judgment. Similarly, actual productivity metrics are more sound than productivity estimates from parametric models. Parametric models provide good backup data, and whenever no productivity data exists, the parametric model is much more accurate than engineering judgment. Although parametric models provide data on how the average company may perform, the actual performance of most companies will be below or above average performance. That's why you should use a company's actual productivity data if available.

Once you've established size and productivity, you can add estimates for support functions and, using the various labor categories and associated salaries, establish a final cost estimate. With sound cost and size estimates in hand, you can use any number of automated scheduling tools to establish the baseline schedule against which to track progress on cost and schedule. The baseline schedule is the backbone for successfully tracking and overseeing a development activity.

Table A.13. **Supplemental Data from Scheduling Tools.** Scheduling tools provide many types of information to help us plan, schedule, and track projects.

Actual Cost	Actual Duration	Actual Finish	Actual Start
Actual Work	Baseline Cost	Baseline Duration	Baseline Finish
Baseline Start	Baseline Work	Budgeted Cost of Work Performed	Budgeted Cost of Work Scheduled
Confirmed	Constraint Date	Constraint Type	Cost
Cost Variance	Created	Critical	Delay
Duration	Duration Variance	Early Finish	Early Start
Finish	Finish Variance	Fixed	Fixed Cost
Free Slack	ID	Late Start	Linked Fields
Marked	Milestone	Name	Notes
Objects	Outline Level	Outline Number	Percent Complete
Percent Work Complete	Predecessors	Priority	Project
Remaining Cost	Remaining Duration	Remaining Work	Resource Group
Resource Initials	Resource Names	Resume	Resume No Earlier Than
Rollup	Start	Start Variance	Stop
Subproject File	Successors	Summary	Schedule Variance
Total Slack	Unique ID	Unique ID Predecessors	Unique ID Successors
Update Needed	Work Breakdown Structure	Work	Work Variance

References

Boehm, B.W. 1981. *Software Engineering Economics*. Englewood Cliffs, N.J.: Prentice Hall.

Developing and executing realistic schedules for building models and simulations requires a sound understanding of software costs. This book established the basis for software costing models with the introduction of the COCOMO model.

Boehm, B.W. January 1984. "Software Engineering Economics." *IEEE Tranactions on Software Engineering.* SE-10, pp. 4–21.

This paper provides more information on software costing based on real-world implementations of the COCOMO model. Additional information can be found on the World Wide Web at http://sunset.usc.edu/COCOMO II/Cocomo.html.

Conte, S.D., H.E. Dunsmore, and V.Y. Shen. 1986. *Software Engineering Metrics and Models.* Menlo Park, CA: Benjamin/Cummings Publishing Company, Inc.

To accurately estimate the size, productivity, and cost of modeling and simulation development efforts, you must define and collect metrics. This book describes how metrics can be applied in software engineering to improve the overall software engineering process from bidding to maintenance.

Dreger, B. 1989. *Function Point Analysis.* Englewood Cliffs, NJ: Prentice Hall.

Accurate software size estimates play a crucial role in developing accurate cost and schedule estimates. Dreger's Function Point Analysis method is commonly used in the industry to determine the size of a model or simulation.

Higgs, Scott. April 1995. "Project Management for Windows." *Byte Magazine,* v. 20, n. 4, pp. 185(5).

This article reviews some of the more popular PC-based project management, schedule, and tracking tools that can automate and enhance your ability to plan and track modeling and simulation development activities.

Jensen, R.W. 1984. "A Comparison of the Jensen and COCOMO Schedule and Cost Estimation Models." *Proceeding of International Society of Parametric Analysis,* pp. 96–106.

The Jensen and COCOMO software costing models are two of the most popular parametric models used to estimate productivity. This paper analyzes and compares these two models.

Putnam, L.H., D.T. Putnam, and L.P. Thayer. January 1984. "A Tool for Planning Software Projects." *The Journal of Systems & Software.* pp. 147–154.

This article describes the Putman Resource Allocation tool—another parametric modeling tool for estimating productivity and schedules.

Rakos, John J. 1990. *Software Project Management.* Englewood Cliffs, N.J.: Prentice Hall.

This is a comprehensive book on software development management. It covers all phases of planning, development, implementation and maintenance and provides more detailed information on many of the topics presented in this chapter.

Tausworthe, R.C. 1981. *Deep Space Network Software Cost Estimation Model.* Publication 81-7. Pasadena, CA: Jet Propulsion Laboratory.

This paper describes the SoftCost Estimation Model—another parametric modeling tool for estimating productivity and schedules.

Software Design

Christopher Landauer and Kirstie L. Bellman,
Aerospace Integration Sciences,
The Aerospace Corporation

In this chapter we consider how to make good software that reflects our models and helps answer our questions about their subject phenomena. We're assuming the models for which we'll organize and design software are already written because it's usually a mistake to start designing software before good models are in place.

Design means selecting appropriate constraints and identifying the main drivers (constraints that most affect the system's important properties, such as cost, schedule, or performance). Only then do we determine a solution space for those constraints and describe the boundaries. We can use these descriptions to identify easy changes, hard changes, and, sometimes, even the most helpful technological improvements to remove or ease the constraints.

Design doesn't merely mean solving constraints and then demonstrating solutions. This approach usually leaves no record of how constraints and solutions relate, so we have no way of tracing the design to requirements or identifying pathways for change. Unfortunately, most large simulations and simulation systems are in this state. To retain relationships, we must maintain the meta-knowledge produced during design, including information about the models and their roles, assumptions, limits, and provenance or pedigree (i.e., where the models come from, who created them, and what technical authorities were used.) This information is as important for software as it is for models.

For little problems, an individual designer can usually track all relevant details if they're focused on one design problem; in this case, design choices have at least an intuitive rationale. But we must write down rationales if we have more than one problem or if the problem becomes large, diverse, or involves several people. That's the only way to record agreements on the design constraints and their significance. Even for a smaller project, writing out the design rationale strongly helps us determine if it's coherent and addresses all important questions.

Remember, large problems lead to large software systems that have many components, complex interactions, and often very subtle relationships between structure and performance. We must construct models or simulation prototypes (as discussed in Chap. 7) of the large simulation software system itself. (Nobody would let us build such a big system of any other kind without prototypes or scaled-down test models; yet, people and organizations have repeatedly tried to build very large simulations without them.)

Once we've agreed on what software design requires, we still must try to describe a "design process." No one method can cover the entire range of complexity from individual programs for personal computers to large developments on mainframes. In fact, a single simulation can scale up or down depending on how we describe its models: superficially, because they're not the focus of the simulation, or in great detail. But you can follow one important principle: be careful. Having a method (systematic procedures) is much more important than which one you use—as long as you try to minimize unnecessary structure. On the other hand, methods can't prevent bad design; the best can only encourage good practices.

In this chapter, we'll concentrate on the high end of the problem (large systems) because they have the most difficulties and the most expensive failures. Many of the steps we recommend aren't necessary for small problems, but you should probably follow them anyway because most simulations are picked up and used elsewhere. If so, the meta-knowledge about their architecture and design decisions is very important. When you record meta-knowledge, write down answers to design questions **and** the questions themselves. For large simulations (or any complex software) these questions explain the design choices.

B.1   Divide Your Design Into Phases

The only general way to simplify complex processes is decomposition—breaking them into parts called "phases" and providing criteria to determine what these phases should contain and when they begin and end. Almost every description of software design includes four variously named phases:

- Establish requirements
- Develop a reference architecture
- Design a detailed architecture
- Program the software code

Establishing requirements means identifying the system's important performance and surface features—aspects that affect, and are affected by, users or the external environment. Consider them design criteria and constraints. Next, you must gradually build architectures to describe system components and relationships. Nearly every developer has a different notion of what an architecture is, but we emphasize two kinds. The reference architecture allocates requirements as problems or specifications which can be satisfied by any software program that meets the specifications. It breaks the simulation into parts that correspond to pieces of the original problem, describes software modules that match these parts, and apportions constraints and criteria to these modules. The detailed architecture explicitly decomposes the modules into programmable units. Then, the last phase converts these units into code. The boundaries between these phases are sometimes difficult to find and certainly aren't fixed, but the information from each phase has important differences from the rest.

Here, we'll assume we have decided what the program is for: implementing models that we've developed and at least partly examined. But developing software is parallel to developing models, so you can read our description as a way to design software, or as a way to design models and the software that carries them out. In either case, be sure to relate the software's structure as clearly and closely as possible to the detailed model's structure, so anyone who analyzes your software can refer to these models. This similarity also allows people to study many interactions in the models and potential performance of the software before programs are written.

B.1.1 Establishing Requirements

During the requirements phase you'll collect and organize information about the external environment for your software and how the program should behave in that environment. This information includes many kinds of constraints, which limit the possible designs. Constraints derive from choices of, or mandates on, the operating system and languages, available or expected hardware platforms, expected operating conditions, and many other sources. You should make some of these constraints into models, so you can study them and their effects before writing the software. For example, geostationary orbits usually best serve a space system that requires continuous coverage of one location on the Earth's surface, and your orbit models should reflect this fact. Models of orbits and many other physical phenomena can be more accurate, and more easily and safely used, when they incorporate real-world assumptions. This practice also reduces the need to rely on an expert who knows how to use the program.

At this point, we need to ask two important questions about context:

- What do we know about the problem domain?
- What is the execution environment?

What we need to know about the problem should be in the domain models used in developing the model, so they should be available to software designers and programmers. For our Debris Analysis Workstation (DAW), Integration Concept Evaluator (ICE), and Firewatcher examples, we have domain models from Chap. 8, so we have enough information to write reasonable programs.

The execution environment also affects how models become programs. Programs always need to run on existing software, operating systems, and hardware; they may also need to interact with other programs, possibly running on other machines or even in other places. You can represent these conditions as constraints on designs, but these constraints differ from the others because they're not in the problem models.

For our DAW and ICE examples, we started with a few programs (see Chap. 8), so almost all we had to write was infrastructure code that connected the programs to each other and presented the combination to the user. Actually, that made some programming for ICE difficult because the programs weren't written to run together. For the Firewatcher example, we want the simulation to work as much as possible across operating systems and hardware. Choosing these support systems in advance is a bad idea because it locks constraints on the execution environment into model designs, which makes them much harder to change.

B.1.2   Developing a Reference Architecture

The reference architecture models your software's functions or requirements. It's where you first break the problem into sub-problems you can consider separately and integrate all requirements (and corresponding constraints) into computational processes that can address the sub-problems.

Every process has certain entities that either act on others or are acted on. Therefore, every process has at least three parts: the actor or subject (the entity that causes or performs the action), the "actee" or object (the entity acted on or with), and the action. To describe a process, you'll adopt a style that corresponds to its center of attention. For example, a data-driven description focuses on data structures that are transformed at stages into others, whereas a process-driven description steps through the transformation, with each step gathering data, doing something to it or with it, and putting out transformed data.

By modeling first, you can develop a general structure for programs to address the identified problem and sub-problems without choosing which style of process description to use for the problem at hand. Instead of naming the entities involved, you explain the role they are to take, when they must compute or inform, and any specifications for these roles and actions. Separating roles from the entities that can fill them is just like separating roles from models (see Chap. 8). It makes your architecture much more flexible and keeps you from losing many design decisions or making them too soon.

To clarify how reference architectures work, compare Figs. 8.1 and 8.2 in Chap. 8. Figure 8.2 shows the developer's viewpoint for ICE, which is part of a reference architecture for the software. Figure 8.1 shows the user's viewpoint for DAW, which is part of a reference architecture for the models. What's the difference? Users focus mainly on services and interfaces, whereas developers concentrate on computing resources to provide services and present interfaces. We had to augment both pictures with information about the kind of data each component requires and produces. The picture for ICE shows parts of the infrastructure that we needed to combine existing programs, but a complete reference architecture would define what each one assumed, expected, and produced. The VEHICLES system provided the infrastructure for DAW, so we wrote extra code only for some data-conversion programs. Most of our integration effort was writing the descriptive models of information (meta-knowledge) which VEHICLES used to interact with models.

B.1.3   Designing a Detailed Architecture

The detailed architecture models the software's structure. It organizes the reference architecture and models of the execution environment for computations and data descriptions that you'll implement in the next phase. During this phase you must convert the reference architecture's generic modules and models (for many different environments) into programmable modules that reflect the execution environment and the constraints on interfaces and performance developed in the requirements phase.

Widely varying architecture styles and viewpoints of systems have one thing in common—pictures, usually in the form of annotated boxes and lines. They're common partly because they can be the most useful artifacts of design. For example, architecture diagrams are models of decomposition, describing roles for more detailed models, as well as all expected or desired transfers of information within and among models. But pictures have many possible interpretations, so we need much more information. For example, meta-knowledge about the components provides detail about the roles and constraints on the models that might fill them. You must supply this information with the pictures, but don't try to replace the pictures because they are a very natural way to describe entities and relationships.

Among the many ways to describe architectures with pictures, our view of software design emphasizes at least three:

- System components
- Control flows—which component invokes, calls, interrupts, or ends which other component
- Data flows among components—which data elements travel among components, how they're transformed, and what paths they follow

For object-oriented systems, these pictures correspond respectively to the hierarchy for object inheritance, the message-sending graph (which objects send what messages to which other objects), and the message graph (the trajectory each message follows).

Your detailed architecture must account for the execution environment—the computing and hardware resources available to run your software. Resources such as space and time drive software design. But developers often don't consider them in the original modeling because they overly constrain the architecture up front.

For many resource-critical applications, carefully modeling how you'll use and allocate resources will help you write programs that interact properly with them and determine design changes needed when available resources increase or requirements decrease. Your reference architecture should model these resources but not constrain your program's structure until you develop a detailed architecture.

B.1.4 Programming the Software

Now we know what the system's components are, what they do, what other components they talk to, what they say, and how much time they have to do and say it. It's time to start writing a program.

It may seem strange that, in a chapter on software design, we've left software for last—almost a footnote. That impression is nearly right, and we do it deliberately. Many software projects founder on misguided notions of efficiency: "let's not fool around; let's just start coding." These projects often start well, with certain parts of the application ready quickly, but then the progress dries up and disappears, as hard architectural problems emerge and the designers' neglect of them becomes more disastrous. That's why we so strongly advocate explicit, detailed models and "end-to-end" prototypes. The former help you think of many questions about the system design; the latter force you to answer enough questions to build software that will run. Only then is it time to "just start coding."

In programming the software, you translate detailed models into functions and subroutines, object classes and objects, clause groups and clauses, or commands, depending on which programming language you've chosen. If you've modeled properly and completed previous phases, this phase should be easy. Eventually, it will be automatic because we'll better understand modeling languages and have robust language translators. Then, your detailed architecture will be a "program," and this phase will disappear.

B.2 Choose Your Design Strategies

A design strategy is a collection of choices about where and when to place boundaries between design processes. Perhaps the most important strategy is to avoid deciding on just one. Just as no one model can describe a large system, no single strategy can produce any but very small programs [Plauger 1993].

The first major design strategy was "structured" programming, which means using hierarchies to break out and organize programs. Basically, it encapsulates functions into modules to hide irrelevant details and build the program. This strategy has been standard for imperative programming, including languages such as Fortran, PL/I, Algol, C, and Ada. As a contrast to what had come before — "spaghetti code"—it was very successful. In fact, it has become part of the background of all trained programmers. But as the single "right" way to do things, it's deficient. Plauger [1993] describes these deficiencies and discusses a dozen other important ways to structure problems. Still, all modern design strategies include this kind of structuring.

We won't write much on particular strategies because their differences aren't important, except for the object-oriented strategies. Many new and old books are adequate references, once you've developed detailed models according to Chap. 8. Perhaps the most popular current fad in computing is "object-oriented" design, analysis, or methodology, which can mean anything from writing designs in C++ (in the worst case) to explicitly modeling a system's important aspects before coding (in the best case). But as we've mentioned before, no method can prevent bad designs. So, you may want to use object-oriented design, as long as you don't take it too seriously [Plauger 1993] and don't allow it to impose too much unnecessary structure. Just make sure you record the models and other entities as objects and capture their interactions as events and data transfers.

The main thing to watch out for in object-oriented strategies is not to confuse objects in the design strategy with actual objects in the application domain. They're very different. The objects in your strategy should be the models in and of the domain. Some of them model actual objects in the domain, but others model processes, requirements, constraints, and other phenomena. If you don't confuse these two kinds of "objects," most object-oriented strategies apply well to model-based development.

Recently, developers have extended object-oriented strategies to "Design Patterns" [Coplien 1995; Gamma 1995], which are partially structured descriptions of a software component, a model, or a process. In our context, these are collections of partial model templates that you can use to organize models in your detailed design architecture. For some applications, especially in designing communication protocols, these design patterns have already simplified building efficient programs. Software developers are just beginning to understand how organizational and other managerial decisions affect design and are finding ways to abstract decisions, so we can record these processes in the design rationale (and use them directly in design). Over the next few years, we expect to see many more books on this subject. It's important because it makes us think about design as one of many organizational processes.

B.3 Identify Adequate Computer System Support

B.3.1 Manage Configurations

Our approach to designing software through models and meta-knowledge means we must develop and coordinate many models and other artifacts, plus a lot of information about those models and artifacts. We need computer support to keep the development flexible as long as possible, so we don't decide on a design too soon. Programming languages must help support computations, and the operating system for development must also allow certain connections and interactions.

In one sense, computer support is mainly clerical: it must help track all development artifacts and their relationships, note inconsistencies or gaps, and show how changes to part of a system affect other artifacts.

Computer-Aided Software Engineering (CASE) tools usually take on the clerical function by organizing all artifacts in a big system. Without them, it's very hard to track the many varied artifacts in a large system, though models help because they separate problems from the programs that address them.

Many CASE tools are commercially available. A good CASE tool should

- Display the various architecture diagrams, including those of component structures, data, and control flows.
- Connect the models to the software so it can relate model changes to program changes, and vice versa.
- Know all the programming languages well enough to display structures as defined by their own mechanisms for encapsulation and reference (such as nested blocks, function calls, and data references).

But nearly all CASE tools impose too much extra structure and are therefore cumbersome and awkward. Most require just one modeling language or approach, and some even assume a particular programming language. Almost all ignore (make it impossible to specify) a system's important aspects outside of its structure. Almost none can interpret the semantics of the other artifacts, such as meta-knowledge, or check their consistency over all the artifacts. Few can interface to other systems that support design.

Despite these deficiencies, CASE tools are essential, not just worthwhile, for "big-enough" projects—and they're improving. Even medium-sized development projects require an enormous amount of information, much more than any one person can remember or use effectively. The difficulty of maintaining this information and relating it to project goals is one reason for the inconsistencies we find in most large simulations.

B.3.2   Choose Appropriate Languages

An important question about software is the programming languages you choose because they determine what the programs will look like. Don't choose programming languages until you know the detailed architecture. If you choose them earlier, you'll have a tougher time matching them to the models you're translating into programs. Detailed models allow you to choose programming languages late enough in development to benefit from having much more knowledge about what the programs will be expected to do, and in what context.

You don't need to choose just one language. In fact, doing so often causes trouble. If the operating system supports communication between languages, write parts of the system in languages suited to their own needs. For example you should probably write a model that describes a process essentially as conditions and actions in Prolog or some kind of rule-driven, expert-system shell. On the other hand, use an imperative language for models that use many step-wise descriptions of behavior. One of the worst things a developer can do, from the point of view of the person who has to maintain the code, is to be "clever"— writing a "style X" software problem in a "style Y" language. Doing so makes the code difficult to write correctly in the first place, and very difficult to understand and change later on. If your system is distributed or otherwise large enough, direct connections, shared files, or even message-passing will support interactions—not function calls—so you don't need to use the same programming language for all components, as long as they support the interactions.

Developing models that show what the system does and how its parts interact also allows you to study performance issues in advance. Large simulations call for large programs, so they deserve the same kind of preliminary correctness and performance modeling as any other large software system. If you have performance models from the modeling process or the detailed architecture, you can use them to predict performance before completing the project. The lack of predictive performance models for large simulation projects is a common source of expense, difficulty, and sometimes, outright failure.

The bottom line here is that the programming language usually doesn't matter, but it should have at least four abilities:

- Conditional compilation
- Invocation parameters
- Interrupt monitors
- Model-based debugging

(Some of these also require support from the operating system.) Although you can develop correct programs without them, it's much harder.

Conditional compilation is a way of inserting code fragments at particular points in a program and choosing whether or not to include them before compiling. These code fragments are very useful for instrumenting a program and are often used to customize a program to different operating environments. They allow you to display, or record for analysis, debugging information and other measurements, as well as to check certain safety conditions while developing your program. Configuration-building programs such as the "make" utility in UNIX can set the appropriate flags, so you can choose how to customize for a particular construction. If you don't have conditional compilation, you must manually insert and remove the software, which is prone to errors.

Allowing a program to get invocation parameters (specifying some operating parameters at run time) is important for flexibility. It means you can specify some parameters when the program starts, without requiring an interactive dialog. It also separates parameters for run-time experiments from those for defining scenarios. (Don't put experiment-control parameters in a scenario definition; describe the problem being simulated, not the program doing the simulation). This feature depends on the operating system to provide parameters that start a program. If you don't have it, you must put all of the program's parameters, including those for the scenario, into files. That's an extra step you shouldn't need for simple experiments or something users must specify through an interactive dialog, which is clumsy. Of course, you can go too far—the speed of light and other physical or engineering constants shouldn't be defined as invocation parameters.

Interrupt monitors allow users to examine the system's state at certain points in its execution. You can bring them up for requested or asynchronous interrupts, so you can arrange to examine particularly difficult places in the architecture or execution and respond to unexpected behavior. This feature depends on the operating system to provide an interrupt mechanism, so the language can use it. If you don't have it, you must allow users to interactively state whether to continue and provide criteria for monitoring the system's behavior. Or you can use a run-time debugger to provide some of these features, which usually means paying the cost of running with the debugger on.

Because programs (especially new ones) often don't work, you must be able to examine the program's state at run time to determine what happened. Many operating systems have run-time debuggers for this purpose. Most provide only the actual program code in symbolic machine language, though some can also link the machine language's location to the part of the source code that generated it. Very few can relate the program's state to the models you've used to generate the program, but that's what users want. Thus, we expect model-based debuggers will allow this explicit connection in the future.

B.3.3   Develop on a Robust Operating System

After the language compilers, you probably most need basic text and picture editors. Text editors allow you to write down the extra information about models so other programs can read it. We aren't talking about word processors. Word processors support a text's appearance and document structure, so they typically write very structured files, from which it's hard to extract (and sometimes even hard to identify) the text. We recommend **not** using these advanced word processors because they make it almost impossible for programs to extract information from their files. Most editors allow multiple windows into the same file and multiple files to appear at the same time (to compare consistency and move text). Most can read in only part of the files when they start (for efficiency), and most allow you to position the cursor using text commands or pointing devices. A good editor must also allow you to match it to your programming languages (matching indentation, checking for balanced parentheses and such delimiters, and even detecting some syntax errors).

Picture editors allow you to build pictures in your models. Again, we insist these editors represent pictures as ASCII text, so other programs can read and analyze them. That's hard for images, but we're talking about simpler, labeled boxes and lines. These "pictures" are so ubiquitous in computer-system descriptions because they clearly illustrate complex structures. Text forms for the pictures help others verify the architecture, such as checking for consistency and completeness or identifying anomalies, whether it's done by humans or computer programs.

Any system with more than one developer needs ways of coordinating to prevent interference. Even as we've learned to partition problems into smaller ones, we need a way to manage their scopes and boundaries. It allows us to group closely related parts and separate those that differ. Most major operating systems now handle directories in hierarchies and nested folders, which helps developers of large programs keep local contexts clear and avoid interference.

Many operating systems now allow us to collect groups of files in multiple directories or folders and move them around as a unit, so we can track complex artifacts while developing software. Notice that we're building a structured list of artifacts produced during development and showing their relationships. In other words, this is a model of the complete software system, so it deserves all the considerations we described for other models in Chap. 8—attention to the components (development artifacts) and their relationships.

Another important support program is one for configuration construction, such as the "make" program and "make files" in UNIX. A make file for a program describes all the files that contain program components which aren't part of the default libraries, how they depend on other components, and how to build them when their source files change. It's invaluable for large programs—and helpful for small ones—to track artifacts and the processes used to build them.

For larger problems, you also need multiprocessing (allowing many concurrent processes on one machine) and networking (allowing programs on many different machines to interact). You need multiprocessing because very few programs use the machine they run on efficiently. Networking is necessary because large programs (especially large simulations) often can't cost effectively meet performance requirements on a single machine. The speeds of small computers today make distribution a very cost-effective approach compared to buying a single computer fast and large enough for the entire program.

Although you want to develop your software on a robust operating system, some features are unnecessary or even "dangerous." For example, "integrated tools" (as opposed to the desirable "toolchest") usually mean only one way to do things. Designers of these programs have already integrated them—making many choices for you. That's helpful if you're doing exactly what they expected, but it's almost always too limiting for experimental systems, which many simulation programs are. Another danger is the tool that "supports the Brand-X design method," which you then must use, whether it's appropriate or not. When developers with very different criteria and viewpoints from yours build supporting software, it's often not flexible enough to match your requirements.

Commercial Off-the-Shelf software may also be too rigid for your program. Commercial software aims at sales, but simulation programs—especially large ones—try to capture appropriate models of complex phenomena. Simulations often need so many custom features that no commercial product will work. If you think one will, check its models and the other artifacts it provides to support simulation development. Verify that it allows many kinds of constructions and provides a lot of supporting information for those constructions. Several commercial simulation languages with supporting environments are becoming increasingly helpful.

B.4   Deliver a Complete Package

In writing a program, you must bring together several kinds of information, from the models' design structure to the constraints imposed by the language, software, operating system, and hardware on which you're writing the program. The design process we've described recommends four phases: establish requirements, develop a reference architecture, design a detailed architecture, and program the software. All through this process, you build design artifacts and relate them to others, in a complex network of related information and software called a simulation system. Thus, you must deliver more than the software to users. You must include the other development artifacts you've produced: models; meta-knowledge; requirements; limitations; assumptions; expected environment; descriptions of how to construct, install, and use the programs; and the code. When you've brought all of the artifacts together, you'll be able to give your customer a complete package.

References

Budde, R., K. Kautz, K. Kuhlenkamp, and H. Zullighoven. 1991. *Prototyping: An Approach to Evolutionary System Development*. Springer.

This book is a good description of design processes, including organization and users, with some notes on programming languages for prototyping and process description.

Budgen, David. 1994. *Software Design*. Addison-Wesley.

This book emphasizes the importance of modeling, describes some of the more popular methods, and points out how design processes have important organizational aspects in addition to the technical aspects. It is nicely done and easily readable.

Coplien, James O., Douglas C. Schmidt (eds.). 1995. *Pattern Languages of Program Design*. Addison-Wesley.

This book is a collection of articles containing many descriptions of designs and design patterns, both within programs and organizations. It mentions the important point of reification: making objects for system entities or aspects that are not "things."

Freeman, Peter, Anthony I. Wasserman (eds.). 1983. *Tutorial on Software Design Techniques*. 4th ed., IEEE Computer Society Press.

This book is a collection of articles reprinted from software engineering and other journals and magazines from 1971 through 1983. It has many classic articles, and some overviews of different methods. We recommend it as a source of different kinds of methods.

Gamma, Erich, Richard Helm, Ralph Johnson, and John Vlissides. 1995. *Design Patterns: Elements of Reusable Object Oriented Software*. Addison-Wesley.

This book is a collection of designs for object classes and their interactions, unnecessarily restricted to object-oriented design (i.e., the design patterns apply much more generally). It is a nice coherent collection, but it suffers from a lack of models: the examples are all in code, so they cannot be automatically used for anything else (or even for any applications either without rewriting).

Lowry, Michael R., Robert D. McCartney (eds.). 1991. *Automating Software Design*. American Association for Artificial Intelligence.

This book has many articles on knowledge-based software design, both principles and particular systems.

Plauger, P. J. 1993. *Programming on Purpose: Essays on Software Design*. P T R Prentice Hall.

This book is a collection of magazine columns on philosophical principles, anecdotes, horror stories, and lots of practical advice for writing programs rather than system design, but the lessons and principles apply much more generally. This is an important book to read. If you only read one of these books, or only one book on software design, this book should be the one.

Statistical Analysis and Experimental Design

Stephen R. Schmidt, Mark J. Kiemele, and Ronald J. Berdine,
Air Academy Associates

C.1   Basic Statistics

"Statistical thinking will one day be as necessary for efficient citizenship as the ability to read and write."

H.G. Wells

Although most of us are well aware of the illiteracy our society faces, few understand the problem of "innumeracy" which Wells alluded to almost 100 years ago. Misadventures with numbers are increasingly common. Witness the Simpson trial, the Challenger disaster, and the Iranian hostage rescue mission. Learning how to collect, analyze, and interpret data *correctly* is a survival skill, and statistics address these issues. Because modeling and simulation studies often generate many inputs and outputs, you must know how to use statistical techniques and terms. This section will get you started. If you want or need more information, we recommend Kiemele, Schmidt, and Berdine [1997].

C.1.1   Random Variables

Variation is a major reason we need statistical analyses. It's part of all processes, products, people, and organizations. Service times for customers at a bank vary. Arrival rates vary for packets at a particular node in a network. Not every MAVERICK missile will disintegrate the same way when detonating. Simulation models are only as good as the statistics that describe their varying processes. The basic building block for describing variation in processes is the "random variable."

Definition

Let's begin by intuitively defining a **random variable** as a quantity that can take on different values, depending on chance. Traditionally, uppercase letters from the end of the alphabet represent them. As examples:

X = number of speeding tickets issued per day on a particular section of highway

Y = resistivity of a piece of stealth material

Z = time to failure for a receiver or transmitter

Random variables are classified according to the number of values they can assume. Discrete random variables take on only a finite number of values or possibly a countably infinite number of values. Countably infinite means the possible values can correspond one-to-one with the positive integers. X, above, is a discrete random variable. Continuous random variables take on an uncountably infinite number of values. That is, they're measured on a continuous scale or can take on any value in a given interval. Examples are time, distance, or weight (such as Y and Z above).

Expected Value and Variance

Two of the most important descriptors of any data set or distribution are the mean or average, which describes where its center is, and the variance, which describes its dispersion characteristics. Because we model distributions using random variables, let's examine these two features, which "depend on chance." If a discrete random variable, X, takes on the values $x_1, x_2, x_3, \ldots, x_k$ with the associated probabilities $P(x_1), P(x_2), P(x_3), \ldots P(x_k)$, its *expected value* (denoted by $E(X)$ or μ_x), is

$$E(X) = \mu_x = \sum_i (x_i)P(x_i)$$

The set of probabilities, $P(x_i)$, associated with the values x_i that X can assume is called the **probability distribution** for X. From the definition, clearly μ_x measures the "weighted" average of all the values X can take on, where the "weighting" for the value x_i is the probability, $P(x_i)$, that X will assume the value x_i. The expected value is also known as the **mean of the random variable** or the **mean of its probability distribution**.

A second important feature of a random variable is a measure of its variability, or how dispersed the distribution is. Typically, we express this measure as the *variance of the random variable* or the *variance of its probability distribution*:

$$V(X) = \sigma_x^2 = \sum_i (x_i - \mu_x)^2 P(x_i)$$

This equation shows that variance is essentially a weighted average of the squared deviations of each of the possible values (x_i) from the mean (μ_x). The square root of the variance is called the *standard deviation*, denoted by σ_x. Note that σ_x is in the same units as the original unit of measure for X, whereas σ_x^2 is in squared units.

The definitions of expected value and variance given above use summation (Σ) notation because the variable is discrete. In defining the expected value and variance for a continuous random variable, Y, this summation notation changes to integral notation because the random variable is continuous:

$$E(Y) = \mu_Y = \int_{-\infty}^{\infty} y f(y) dy$$

$$V(Y) = \sigma_Y^2 = \int_{-\infty}^{\infty} (y - \mu_Y)^2 f(y) dy$$

where $f(y)$ = the (continuous) probability density function for Y.

C.1.2　Probability Distributions

We mentioned probability distributions above in the context of a random variable's expected value and variance. In fact, "distribution" and "random variable" are often used interchangeably. To visualize distributions, consider the real or simulated data from some process, such as manufacturing stealth material. Suppose we're measuring the product's resistivity, Y, in ohms as a critical characteristic. Figure C.1(a) shows how multiple products may vary in resistivity. The graphic on the left of Fig. C.1(b) depicts many product measurements stacked on top of each other, which forms a pattern called a histogram (a bar chart for numerical intervals). Placing a smooth curve over the histogram gives us a picture of the probability distribution, as shown in the right graphic of Fig. C.1(b). Note from Fig. C.1(c) that distributions can differ in location, spread, and shape.

Certain distributions occur often in nature and, therefore, in modeling and simulation. Let's look at three: the normal, exponential, and Poisson distributions. The normal and exponential distributions are continuous; the Poisson distribution is discrete.

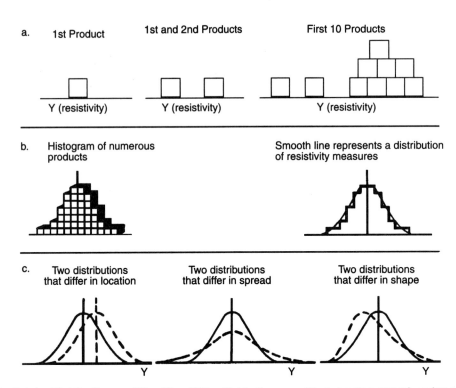

Fig. C.1.   Distributions and How They Differ. Distributions can differ in location, spread, or shape.

Normal Distribution

This important and common distribution can help us model many phenomena. It's also known as the Gaussian distribution. The probability density function, f(x), for the normal distribution is

$$f(x) = \frac{1}{\sqrt{2\pi}\sigma}e^{-\frac{1}{2}\left(\frac{x-\mu}{\sigma}\right)^2} \quad \text{for} \quad -\infty < x < \infty$$

In general, the probability density function is used to describe the weighting function for a continuous random variable. For a normal random variable, it's the famous bell-shaped curve. It has two parameters—μ (the mean) and σ (the standard deviation)—which uniquely determine the distribution's location and spread (see Fig. C.2). As shown in Fig. C.3, the standard deviation (σ) gives us a graphical way to determine the percentage of measurements we would expect to fall inside a band centered at μ. For example, 99.73% of the measurements fall between $\pm 3\sigma$ of the mean. Table C.1 summarizes the key attributes of the normal distribution.

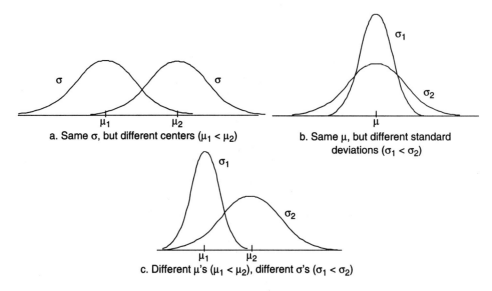

a. Same σ, but different centers ($\mu_1 < \mu_2$)

b. Same μ, but different standard deviations ($\sigma_1 < \sigma_2$)

c. Different μ's ($\mu_1 < \mu_2$), different σ's ($\sigma_1 < \sigma_2$)

Fig. C.2.   The Effect of μ (the Mean) and σ (the Standard Deviation) on the Normal Curve.

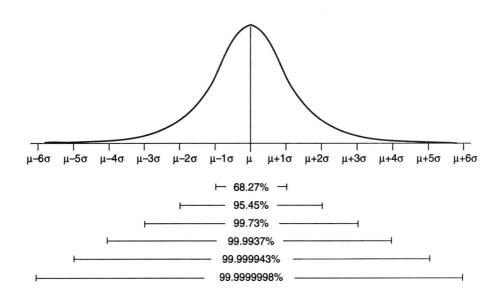

Fig. C.3.   Graphical Meaning of a Standard Deviation, σ.

Table C.1. Summary of the Normal Distribution.

Parameter or Characteristic	Description
X	normally distributed (Gaussian, bell-shaped) random variable
Parameters: $\mu = E(x)$ $\sigma = \sqrt{V(X)}$	mean (where center of distribution is) standard deviation (determines how narrow or flattened the distribution is)
Probability Density Function f(x)	$f(x) = \dfrac{1}{\sqrt{2\pi}\,\sigma}\, e^{-\frac{1}{2}\left(\frac{x-\mu}{\sigma}\right)^2}$ for $-\infty < x < \infty$
Cumulative Distribution Function	No closed-form function. Must use tables in a textbook or computer software to find areas under f(x). Probabilities associated with any continuous random variable, such as the normal one, are equivalent to areas under the probability density function.
X	$N(\mu, \sigma^2)$
Shape	symmetrical about μ

Exponential Distribution

This continuous distribution also applies to many problems and is very useful in modeling such variables as "service times" and "time or space between occurrences." Some examples are a bank teller's service time, time between calls to an emergency dispatcher, time until failure of a receiver or transmitter, or the survival time for patients diagnosed with a certain disease. The probability density function for the exponential distribution is:

$$f(x) = \lambda e^{-\lambda x} \text{for } x \geq 0 \text{ and } \lambda > 0$$

It has one parameter, λ, which represents the *average* number of occurrences per interval.

Figure C.4 shows the effect of λ on the shape of the exponential distribution. If λ represents the average number of occurrences per interval, $1/\lambda$ represents the average time (or space) between occurrences. For example, suppose a simulated process produces a time between failures that follows an exponential distribution. If we calculate the mean time between failures (MTBF), $\lambda = 1/\text{MTBF}$. The cumulative distribution function, F(x), for the exponential distribution is

$$F(x) = \int_0^x f(t)dt = \int_0^x \lambda e^{-\lambda t}dt = 1 - e^{-\lambda x}$$

which is the area under the curve between 0 and x (the shaded area in Fig. C.4 for $\lambda = 0.5$). Table C.2 summarizes the key aspects of the exponential distribution.

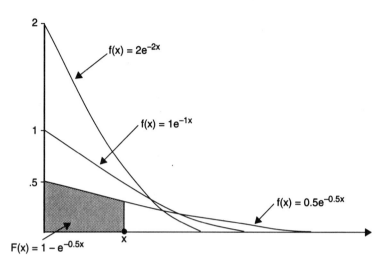

Fig. C.4.   Three Exponential Probability Density Functions. This figure shows the probability density functions for three different exponential distributions ($\lambda = 2$, $\lambda = 1$, and $\lambda = 0.5$). The shaded area is the cumulative probability at x when $\lambda = 0.5$.

Table C.2.   Summary of Exponential Distribution.

Parameter or Characteristic	Description
X	random variable representing the time or space between occurrences (could also be time until failure)
Parameter: λ	average number of occurrences per unit interval (the same parameter as in the Poisson distribution) Note: the unit interval used here must match the time or spatial unit used in the definition of the random variable X.
$\mu = E(X)$ $\sigma^2 = V(X)$	$1/\lambda$ $1/\lambda^2$
Probability Density Function	$f(x) = \lambda e^{-\lambda x}$ for $x \geq 0$ and $\lambda > 0$
Cumulative Distribution Function	$F(x) = 1 - e^{-\lambda x}$ for $x \geq 0$
Shape	skewed right

Poisson Distribution

Unlike the normal and exponential distributions, which are continuous, the Poisson distribution is discrete. We can apply it to many randomly occurring phenomena, such as the number of speeding tickets issued per day, disk-drive failures per month, calls arriving at an emergency-dispatch station per hour, or defects per circuit board. Each of these scenarios has something in common—the "number of occurrences per unit interval." An occurrence can be a defect, an arrival, a failure, etc., where the interval is a unit of time or space. The Poisson distribution has one parameter, λ, which denotes "the *average* number of occurrences per unit interval." To find the probabilities for discrete random variables following a Poisson distribution, X, we use the probability mass function, $P(X = x)$:

$$P(X = x) = \frac{\lambda^x e^{-\lambda}}{x!} \text{ for } x = 0, 1, 2, \ldots \text{and } \lambda > 0$$

This mass function describes the weighting function for a discrete random variable. It isn't continuous like the probability density function (described earlier).

The parameter λ is the same as in the exponential distribution; it's the unique link between these two distributions. For example, suppose X is a Poisson random variable denoting the number of occurrences per time (or space) interval with, on average, λ occurrences per time (or space) interval. Then Y, the random variable denoting the time (or space) between occurrences, is exponentially distributed with parameter λ and has an average value of $1/\lambda$. Table C.3 summarizes key characteristics of the Poisson distribution.

Table C.3.   Summary of Poisson Distribution.

Parameter or Characteristic	Description
X	random variable representing the number of occurrences per unit interval (time or space); X = {0, 1, 2, . . .}
Parameter: λ	average number of occurrences per unit interval (Note: this unit interval must match the unit interval given in the definition of the random variable)
$\mu = E(X)$	λ
$\sigma^2 = V(X)$	λ
Probability Mass Function	$P(X = x) = \frac{\lambda^x e^{-\lambda}}{x!}$ for x = 0, 1, 2, . . . and $\lambda > 0$
Shape	skewed right

C.1.3   Estimating and Computing Confidence Intervals

One of the most common problems in statistical analysis is to estimate the mean, μ, of an unknown population. Suppose, for example, that the Food and Drug Administration wanted to estimate the average nicotine content (in milligrams) for a particular brand of cigarettes. Analyzing every cigarette that comes off the production line would be too expensive, so they decide to sample a small number of cigarettes. They measure the nicotine content of each cigarette in the sample and find the average nicotine content is $\bar{x} = 15.6$ mg. Although 15.6

mg is an estimate of μ, it doesn't equal μ because averages for other samples would be different. That leads to the question, how close is 15.6 to μ? To answer this question, we'll begin by looking at the central limit theorem, which allows us to bound the error for our estimate of μ.

Central Limit Theorem

This theorem is a powerful result that says a sample mean ($\bar{x}$) belongs to (or is extracted from) a normal distribution, regardless of the shape of the distribution being sampled. Fig. C.5 illustrates this concept. The bimodal (twin-peaked) probability density function represents the distribution for which we want to estimate the expected value, μ. Although μ appears on the sketch, it's actually unknown, and we want to estimate it. Suppose we sample five elements from the population of X. We show those elements using the symbol "$\bigcirc$." The average (or balance point) of these five "$\bigcirc$"s is "$\bar{\bigcirc}$." Now, suppose we take a different sample, again of size five, and label these points with a "$\triangle$." $\bar{\triangle}$ represents the average of the five "$\triangle$"s. If we were to repeat this sampling (of size five) indefinitely, each time plotting the average of the five, we would create a new distribution of averages which carries a special name—the *sampling distribution of the mean*. It's the distribution of all possible averages that can arise from all possible samples taken from X, when the samples are of a given fixed size (like sample size = n = 5). Figure C.5 shows only two of the infinitely possible number of averages. The central limit theorem *guarantees* that the shape of the $\bar{X}$ distribution is approximately normal. That is, if we were to build a histogram (see Fig. C.1) of all possible averages and place a blanket over it, the blanket would take the shape of a normal distribution, as shown in Fig. C.5. Thus, if we choose a sample from X and find the sample mean, $\bar{x}$, we know this $\bar{x}$ is from a normal distribution. It isn't the same as the unknown μ we must estimate. But because $\bar{x}$ comes from a normal distribution, we can build an interval estimate for the unknown μ and have some confidence in it.

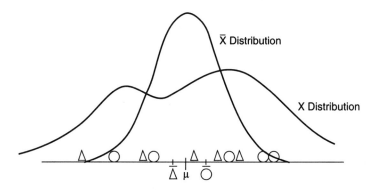

Fig. C.5.   Illustration of the Central Limit Theorem. The distribution of the average values ($\bar{X}$) computed by taking samples from the unknown X distribution is normal.

Computing a Confidence Interval on the Mean

Confidence intervals arise from the percentages attached to the standard deviations to the left and right of a center point (μ) on a normal curve (Fig. C.3). For example, approximately 95% of the elements in a normal distribution will fall within two standard deviations of the center, and about 99% will fall within three standard deviations. These percentages represent a certain level of confidence. To illustrate what we mean, let's compute a confidence interval for our example of nicotine in cigarettes.

Example: Calculating a Confidence Interval for Nicotine in Cigarettes

Suppose a test on a random sample of nine cigarettes yields an average nicotine content ($\bar{x}$) of 15.6 milligrams and a standard deviation of 2.1 milligrams: n = 9, $\bar{x}$ = 15.6, and s = 2.1. Although $\bar{x}$ = 15.6 is the sample average, μ—the average nicotine content of the true population (all cigarettes from this process)—is not 15.6. The computing template in Fig. C.6 shows how we can add sampling error to, and subtract it from, the point estimate ($\bar{x}$ = 15.6) to get a confidence interval. The quantity $s/\sqrt{n}$ is sometimes called the "standard error of the mean." It is an estimate of the standard deviation of the sampling distribution of the mean (see the $\bar{x}$ distribution in Fig. C.5).

$$\binom{U}{L} = \bar{x} \pm Z\left(\frac{s}{\sqrt{n}}\right)$$

where   U = upper confidence limit
            L = lower confidence limit
            $\bar{x}$ = sample average
            Z = 2 (for 95% confidence) or 3 (for 99% confidence)[*]
            s = sample standard deviation
            n = sample size

[*] This is a Rule of Thumb. Specify the level of confidence you want; then, use the appropriate Z-value. 95% and 99% are the two most common levels of confidence. (See Kiemele (1997) for more precise values.)

Fig. C.6.   Computing Template for Confidence Limits.

Using this template, and supposing we want a 99% confidence interval, we find

$$U = \bar{x} + Z\left(\frac{s}{\sqrt{n}}\right) = 15.6 + 3\left(\frac{2.1}{\sqrt{9}}\right) = 17.7 \text{ mg}$$

$$L = \bar{x} - Z\left(\frac{s}{\sqrt{n}}\right) = 15.6 - 3\left(\frac{2.1}{\sqrt{9}}\right) = 13.5 \text{ mg}$$

Note that the bounds are determined by multiplying a number of standard deviations (or Z-value) by the value of a standard deviation in the $\bar{x}$ distribution. Thus, we can be 99% confident that the unknown μ is between 13.5 mg and 17.7 mg.

C.1.4   Testing Hypotheses

To test hypotheses, we gather and use evidence from one or more samples of data to conclude which of two complementary hypotheses expresses the true state of nature. A very common hypothesis test in our society is a trial by jury. The hypotheses are

$$H_0: \text{The defendant is not guilty.}$$

$$H_1: \text{The defendant is guilty.}$$

H_0 is called the null hypothesis and H_1 is the alternative hypothesis. Because we seldom know the true state of nature with 100% certainty, each conclusion carries a probability of error, which we divide into two main types. Table C.4 describes these errors. Very simply, a Type I error is convicting an innocent person and a Type II error is letting a guilty person go free. Typically, the Type I error is considered more serious.

Table C.4.   Meaning of Type I and Type II Errors.

		True State of Nature	
		H_0	H_1
Conclusion Drawn	H_0	Conclusion is Correct	Conclusion results in a Type II error
	H_1	Conclusion results in a Type I error	Conclusion is Correct

To illustrate hypothesis testing, let's consider a process for putting an oxide coating on silicon wafers. We want to test whether the population's average thickness (μ) differs from the required 200 angstroms. The producer says the most critical error would be to conclude that μ doesn't equal 200 angstroms when it really does. Thus, we set up the hypothesis test with $H_0: \mu = 200$ and $H_1: \mu \neq 200$. As in a court of law, we'll assume H_0 is true until proved otherwise. Because it's too expensive to measure every wafer thickness, we sample the population and find

$$\bar{y} = 196 \quad \text{(sample mean)}$$

$$s = 20 \quad \text{(sample standard deviation)}$$

$$n = 100 \quad \text{(sample size)}$$

Based on this evidence, let's investigate the difference between $\bar{y} = 196$ and $\mu = 200$ (which we assume to be true), so we can determine if it's large enough to be at least 95% confident that H_1 is true. To do so, we calculate the test statistic

$$Z = \frac{\bar{y} - \mu}{s/\sqrt{n}} = \frac{196 - 200}{20/\sqrt{100}} = -\frac{4}{2} = -2$$

Figure C.7 below shows the strength of the magnitude of $Z = -2$.

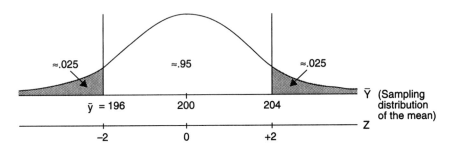

Fig. C.7. **Test Statistic of Z = –2 and Its Probability.** The shaded area represents the probability of obtaining a Z -value greater than +2 or less than –2.

The test statistic $Z = -2$ shows that, if H_0 is true, the probability is only about 0.05 that we'll obtain a sample mean by chance which is at least as extreme (in either direction) as the one $\bar{y}$ we observed ($\bar{y} = 196$). This small probability means we can be about 95% confident in concluding H_1—that we're producing an average wafer thickness other than 200 angstroms. Conversely, if we conclude H_1, the probability of making a Type I error is about 0.05. This example illustrates the nature of a hypothesis test: set up the hypothesis, collect sample data, and then determine if the sample data provides enough evidence to "convict" (to conclude H_1 with a fairly high level of confidence).

C.1.5   Regression Analysis

Regression analysis is a statistical technique for determining the mathematical relation between a measured dependent (or response) variable and one or more independent (or predictor) variables. It's often used to predict the response variable from knowledge of the predictor variable(s). Regression analysis can also be thought of as model building or curve fitting, in which we try to fit the "best" curve or model through the data. The most common regression models are simple linear, polynomial, and multiple regression.

Simple Linear Regression

Consider the scenario of measuring yield as the response variable of a certain process, for which we've measured three yields at each of four levels of temperature (the predictor variable), as shown in Table C.5.

Simple linear regression is the technique of fitting the "best" line through this data. The word "simple" refers to having only one predictor variable. Figure C.8 shows the scatter plot of the data along with the "best" line that fits the data, represented by $y = 0.0317x + 0.1$. To determine this line, we commonly use the "least-squares" criterion: the least-squares regression line is the one that minimizes the sum of squared deviations of the points about the regression line.

Table C.5.   Three Yields at Each of Four Temperatures.

Temperature			
70°	80°	90°	100°
2.3	2.5	3.0	3.3
2.6	2.9	3.1	3.5
2.1	2.4	2.8	3.0

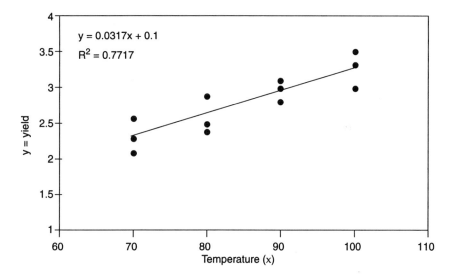

Fig. C.8.   Simple Linear Regression Line for Three Yields at Each of Four Temperatures. This line is the "best" line in the sense that it minimizes the sum of squared deviations of the points about the line.

This sum of squared deviations is shown as $\sum e_i^2$ in Fig. C.9, a simpler example of only three points to illustrate the concept. The "best" line is the line that minimizes $e_1^2 + e_2^2 + e_3^2$. You can use equations to determine the slope and intercept of the "best" line, but we encourage you to use software instead. See Kiemele [1997] and Schmidt [1994] for formulas to calculate the regression coefficients.

Once we have a regression model, such as $y = 0.0317x + 0.1$, it's natural to ask how good the model is. In other words, how well does the curve fit the data? A measure most software packages use and print out is R^2, formally referred to as the coefficient of determination (or the square of the correlation coefficient). R^2 represents the proportion of variability in the response variable (y) that the model accounts for. Figure C.9 shows how to calculate R^2 and depicts its meaning as the reduction in variability of the points about the horizontal line ($\bar{y}$) to the variability of the points about the regression line. Clearly, if we have a perfect fit (all points precisely on the regression line), $\sum e_i^2 = 0$ and $R^2 = 1$. But if the constant $y = \bar{y}$ line fits the data as well as any other line, $R^2 = 0$. If the regression model accounts for

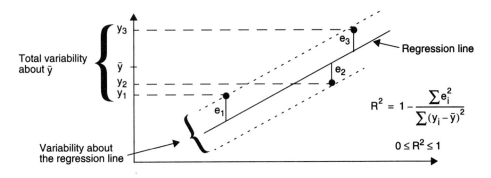

Fig. C.9.   Calculating a Least-Squares Regression Line. R^2 = strength of the relationship represented by the model.

at least 70% of the variability in the y values ($R^2 > 0.7$), it's "strong." The model for our silicon-wafer example (Sec. C.1.4) illustrates an R^2 of 0.7717, meaning the model accounts for about 77% of the variability in y. $1 - R^2 = 0.2283$, which means 23% of the variability remains unaccounted for.

Polynomial and Multiple Regression

Suppose we take three more observations of yield at 50 degrees, resulting in the 15 data points shown in Table C.6. As you can see from the scatter diagram of this data (Fig. C.10), a curved (quadratic or polynomial) model based on the least-squares criterion obviously fits the data better than any straight line would. As $R^2 = 0.6732$ indicates, the model accounts for more than 67% of the variability in the response variable and is thus a fairly strong model.

Table C.6.   Three Yields at Each of Five Temperatures.

Temperature				
50°	70°	80°	90°	100°
3.3	2.3	2.5	3.0	3.3
2.8	2.6	2.9	3.1	3.5
2.9	2.1	2.4	2.8	3.0

If we include a second predictor variable, such as pressure, in the model, this multivariable problem would lead to a multiple-regression model, and we'd use multiple-regression analysis to produce it. (Details on this method are beyond the scope of this chapter.) We highly encourage using software for any kind of regression analysis. But least-squares techniques and R^2, as shown above for simple linear regression, apply equally well to polynomial and multiple regression.

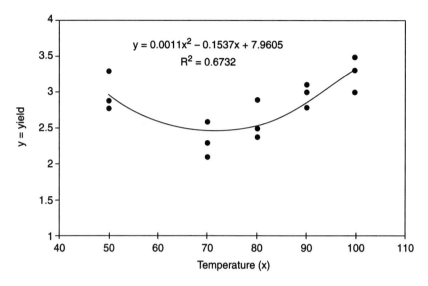

Fig. C.10.   Polynomial Regression for Three Yields at Each of Five Temperatures. This is the best fit to the data provided by a second order (quadratic) polynomial.

C.2   Analyzing Inputs and Outputs

Because variation is present in almost all processes, we can seldom assume a situation in real life is completely determined. To account for variability, we should model natural variation in our simulations by generating random variates wherever it occurs.

Random-variate generators are themselves very simple simulators. They need inputs and provide outputs as any simulator would. The inputs are the probability distribution that defines the random variate, a "seed" or number that starts the generation (may also be random), and parameter estimates related to the distribution. The simplest type of generator is a uniform random-number generator (see Fig. C.11). In this case, the user or a time clock usually provides the seed. The output is a random variate with equal probability of occurrence on the interval from 0 to 1. Other generators, which provide random variates that follow other distributions (normal, Poisson, or exponential), use the uniform output as their input.

Our goal here is to develop simple generators. We'll look at ways to generate uniform random variables; how to transform them into normal, exponential or Poisson random variables; and how to analyze and compare these generators. For more complex distributions and types of analysis, please see the references.

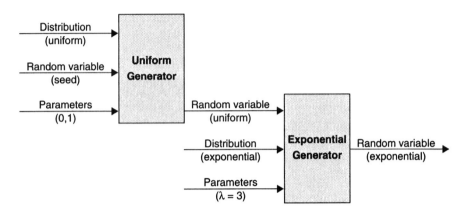

Fig. C.11.   Uniform and Exponential Random-Number Generators.

C.2.1   Designing Inputs

To design inputs, you must know what type of distribution the variability or "noise" in the process follows. This is not always as difficult as it might appear. For example, mechanical processes often vary based on the combined effects of many variations in components. If so, you can use the normal distribution to model their overall variability. If you want to model independent, random, discrete events that have a constant probability of occurrence, use the Poisson distribution. The time between these events would be exponential (see Sec. C.1.2). Table C.7 gives some examples of process variation that would follow these distributions.

Table C.7.   Typical Distributions in Real Processes.

Distribution	Example Processes
Normal	• Machining variations in a mechanical process • Deviations in spacecraft tracking • Deviations in packing weight in a food-processing plant
Poisson	• Telephone-call arrivals per minute (hour, day) • Flaws per square yard of fabric • Mechanical malfunctions per day for an airline
Exponential	• Time to failure for electrical or mechanical processes • Time between atomic-particle bombardments • Time between accidents at a busy intersection

C.2.2   Generating Uniform Random Variables

The term "random" numbers is actually misleading because we can't generate truly random numbers. We can only provide a way to generate numbers that appear to be random and recognize that some methods are better than others. Because we'll derive all random numbers from uniform random numbers, we will begin by looking at methods for generating uniform random numbers on the interval 0 to 1. Then, we can transform these U(0,1) random variables into random variables from other distributions.

The most common method for generating U(0,1) random numbers is called the linear congruential method. In this method, the i-th uniform random number is

$$U_i = (\alpha\, U_{i-1} + c)\ (\mathrm{mod}\ m)$$

where α is the multiplier, c is the increment, m is the modulus, and U_0 is the seed. This equation has several interesting features:

1. Although each U_i depends on the previous value (U_{i-1}), each random number should appear to be independent of the others.

2. The sequence $U_0, U_1, U_2, \ldots$ eventually will repeat itself. If you choose α, c, and m poorly, the period of the sequence is very short. If you choose correctly, you'll get a very long sequence of random numbers that doesn't repeat.

3. To choose the seed, U_0, you can take any number "out of the air," or you can make the choice automatic if the system looks at clock values or some other number that varies with time.

4. Many "canned" generators use c = 0. However, if $U_i = 0$ in this case, the sequence degenerates. Avoiding zero as a seed will prevent this problem.

Generators of this type are designed for computers, so the choices of α, c, and m depend on how the computer works. If it uses 32-bit words, the longest sequence of numbers you can generate is 2^{31} (theoretically). But a theoretically long sequence may not give you a "random" sequence. In fact, generators need to satisfy many statistical properties for their output to appear random. Thus, a generator that provides a long period may not be best. For example, the following generator has a long period, but each value is not "independent" of the previous value:

$$U_i = (1\, U_{i-1} + 1)\ (\mathrm{mod}\ 2^{31} - 1)$$

Notice that, with a seed of $U_0 = 117$, the generated sequence is (118, 119, 120, 121, ...) which doesn't appear random.

One generator that has been used and tested extensively is

$$U_i = (16807\, U_{i-1})\ (\mathrm{mod}\ 2^{31} - 1)$$

This generator is called a pure congruential generator because c = 0 [Shed 1980].

Choosing α, c and m isn't easy. If you want to build your own generator, refer to Knuth [1981] for more discussion. Other ways to generate series of U(0,1) random variates include tables and "built-in" or "canned" generators. The CRC Handbook of Tables for Probability and Statistics lists 14,000 uniform random numbers. Many programming packages or language compilers offer canned generators. Although some generators have had problems, most people agree that modern canned generators from reputable software companies are "safe." That is, they provide relatively long sequences and pass tests for randomness.

C.2.3   Generating Non-Uniform Random Numbers

Now that we have a U(0,1) random number, we need to transform it to fit our desired distribution. Below we present some of the most common transformations (algorithms) that are easy to implement. You may find faster algorithms, but improved computers probably make ease of use more important than speed.

An Algorithm for Normal Random Numbers

The algorithm below actually produces normal random numbers in pairs. But because the variables are independent, you get two random numbers in each pass.

     Step 1.   Generate $U_1 \sim U(0,1)$ and $U_2 \sim U(0,1)$

     Step 2.   Set $V_1 = 2U_1 - 1$ and $V_2 = 2U_2 - 1$

     Step 3.   Set $W = V_1^2 + V_2^2$

     Step 4.   If $W \geq 1$ then reject and go to step 1

     Step 5.   Otherwise, calculate $Y = \sqrt{-2(\ln(W))/W}$

     Step 6.   Return $Z_1 = V_1 Y$ and $Z_2 = V_2 Y$

This algorithm yields two random variables with mean 0 and variance 1. To get a normally distributed random variable X with mean μ and variance σ^2, use $X = \mu + Z\sigma$ for each Z value.

An Algorithm for Exponential Random Numbers

The exponential distribution is easiest to model because its form results in an extremely simple algorithm:

     Step 1.   Generate $U \sim U(0,1)$

     Step 2.   Set $X = (-\ln U) / \lambda$, where X is exponential with parameter λ

An Algorithm for Poisson Random Numbers

To generate a random number N with a Poisson distribution having parameter λ, use this simple algorithm:

     Step 1.   Set $N = 0$ and $k = 1$

     Step 2.   Generate $U \sim U(0,1)$

     Step 3.   Set $k = kU$

     Step 4.   If $k > e^{-\lambda}$ then set $N = N + 1$ and return to step 2

     Step 5.   Otherwise return N

This algorithm is very fast as long as λ is small, so you may want to use a scale that provides a small λ. For example, instead of using accidents per year (say, $\lambda = 200$), use accidents per week ($\lambda = 3.846$).

Many other algorithms exist for these and other distributions. See Kennedy [1980] and Shedler [1980] for more information.

C.2.4   Analyzing Output Data for a Single System

There are, of course, many ways to analyze output data from a random variate generator. For example, a run test detects non-random sequences of numbers in a set of generated random variates. A gap test compares successive "gaps" between each pair of numbers in a sequence, looking for non-random situations. As tests for non-randomness become more powerful, they usually become more complex. The spectral test [Knuth 1981], for example, identifies subsets of random variates that tend to lie in planes in higher dimensions. For more information on these types of tests see Kennedy [1980] and Knuth [1981].

One of the most common tests is the chi-square goodness-of-fit test. It tests how well the data fits an hypothesized distribution (uniform, normal, exponential, or Poisson). You can use it to validate your model by testing the simulation's output. You can also use it to test real-life data and validate a hypothesized distribution in a given situation—for example, testing historical data on failure times for a mechanical process to see if the exponential distribution is a good fit. Look at Table C.9 to see how this test works.

Let's apply these steps for a chi-square test to the data in Table C.8. First, you'll want to answer the question—"Is the input data really U(0,1)?"—by stepping through the chi-square goodness-of-fit test [Kiemele 1997]:

Table C.8.   Uniform and Exponential Outputs from a Random-Number Generator.

Output: Uniform Random Numbers			Output: Exponential ($\lambda = 3$) Numbers		
0.085	0.503	0.891	0.820	0.229	0.038
0.053	0.813	0.515	0.980	0.069	0.221
0.269	0.163	0.262	0.438	0.606	0.446
0.277	0.587	0.725	0.428	0.178	0.107
0.909	0.289	0.031	0.032	0.414	1.158
0.174	0.216	0.432	0.581	0.510	0.280
0.177	0.182	0.563	0.576	0.568	0.191
0.560	0.109	0.740	0.193	0.739	0.101
0.157	0.889	0.571	0.618	0.039	0.187
0.211	0.466	0.393	0.519	0.254	0.312
0.484	0.383	0.231	0.242	0.320	0.489
0.082	0.762	0.754	0.834	0.090	0.094
0.686	0.978	0.765	0.126	0.007	0.089
0.841	0.638	0.903	0.058	0.150	0.034
0.249	0.064	0.805	0.464	0.916	0.072
0.030	0.902	0.895	1.171	0.034	0.037
0.868	0.759		0.047	0.092	

Step 1:   The null and alternative hypotheses are

H_0: The population distribution is U(0,1)

H_1: The population distribution is not U(0,1)

Step 2:   Let $\alpha = 0.10$. This gives you a 10% risk of error if you conclude H_1 and H_0 is virtually true.

Table C.9.   Steps for a Chi-Square Goodness-of-Fit Test [Kiemele 1997] .

Step 1: Establish the null and alternative hypotheses:

H_0: The population distribution is <u> <fill in the blank> </u> .
H_1: The population distribution is not <u> <fill in the blank> </u> .

(Note: The null hypothesis specifies the distribution to use in calculating the **expected** frequencies. For example, if the hypotheses are

H_0: The population distribution is Poisson with $\lambda = 2.0$
H_1: The population distribution is not Poisson with $\lambda = 2.0$,

use the Poisson distribution with $\lambda = 2.0$ to find the expected frequencies. However, if the hypotheses are

H_0: The population distribution is Poisson
H_1: The population distribution is not Poisson,

estimate λ with $\bar{X} \approx E(X) = \lambda$ and calculate the expected frequencies from a Poisson distribution based on $\lambda \approx \bar{X}$).

Step 2: Determine a planning value for α. As before, your choice will depend on your risk of a Type I error.

Step 3: Calculate the test statistic given by

$$\chi_0^2 = \sum_{i=1}^{k} \frac{(f_i - F_i)^2}{F_i}$$

where k = the number of classes (after pooling)
          f_i = observed frequency for cell i
          F_i = expected frequency for cell i, calculated under the assumption that the null hypothesis is true

Step 4: Using the $\chi^2(v)$ distribution, compute the area in the tail beyond χ_0^2. To use the tables, first determine the appropriate degrees of freedom, v:

$$v = k - m - 1,$$

where k = the number of classes (cells) after pooling
         m = the number of parameters estimated from the data

Determine the number of parameters estimated from the data by the distribution being tested and by the hypothesis. For example, if the hypotheses are

H_0: The distribution is normal
H_1: The distribution is not normal

estimate the two parameters of the normal distribution, μ and σ, by $\bar{x}$ and s, respectively; then, calculate the expected frequencies. In this case, m = 2. However, if the hypotheses specify the parameters, don't estimate the parameters μ and σ from the data to calculate the expected frequencies. For example, if

H_0: The distribution is normal with $\mu = 5$, $\sigma = 1$
H_1: The distribution is not normal with $\mu = 5$, $\sigma = 1$

use the values for μ and σ given in the hypotheses to calculate the expected frequencies. In this case, m = 0.

Step 5: Check to see if the area in Step 4 is equal to P.

Step 6: If $P \geq \alpha$ then conclude H_0.
           If $P < \alpha$ then conclude H_1.

Step 3: Calculate the test statistic, χ_0^2, based on the data in the following table

Interval	f_i (actual frequency)	p_i (Probability)	$F_i = p_i \times N$ (expected frequency)	$\dfrac{(f_i - F_i)^2}{F_i}$
0 to < 0.1	6	1/10	5	0.2
0.1 to < 0.2	6	1/10	5	0.2
0.2 to < 0.3	8	1/10	5	1.8
0.3 to < 0.4	2	1/10	5	1.8
0.4 to < 0.5	3	1/10	5	0.8
0.5 to < 0.6	6	1/10	5	0.2
0.6 to < 0.7	2	1/10	5	1.8
0.7 to < 0.8	6	1/10	5	0.2
0.8 to < 0.9	7	1/10	5	0.8
0.9 to 1.0	4	1/10	5	0.2
Total	N = 50	1.0	50	8.0

The intervals were designed to meet two requirements:

- All expected cell frequencies (F_i) are greater than or equal to 2
- At least half the expected cell frequencies (F_i) are greater than or equal to 5.

If either of these conditions isn't satisfied, you must combine intervals. Also notice that the probabilities (p_i) are the probabilities that any one value falls inside the corresponding interval if H_0 is true. The expected frequency is then $F_i = p_i \times N$. In this example, the final chi-square test statistic turns out to be:

$$\chi_0^2 = 8.0$$

Step 4: Determine the degrees of freedom, v, remembering that $m = 0$ because you didn't estimate any parameters in calculating each probability, p_i (the interval, 0 to 1, was given). Therefore, $v = k - m - 1 = 10 - 0 - 1 = 9$

Step 5: Using software or tables, determine the area to the right of $\chi_0^2 = 8.0$ to be 0.5341, as shown in the diagram below:

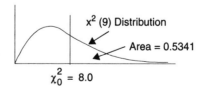

$$\chi_0^2 = 8.0$$

Step 6: Because 0.5341 > 0.10, conclude H_0: The distribution is U(0,1).

Because of the nature of statistical tests, you can't conclude H_0 with any statistical significance. Statistical significance or confidence is associated only with concluding H_1. In this case a more precise conclusion would be: Evidence is insufficient to suggest that the data doesn't come from the U(0,1) distribution.

You may also want to test the output shown in Table C.8 to see if it follows an exponential distribution. Use the same procedure:

Step 1: H_0: The population distribution is exponential

H_1: The population distribution is not exponential

Step 2: Let $\alpha = 0.10$.

Step 3: Note: $\hat{\lambda} = \dfrac{1}{\bar{X}} = \dfrac{1}{0.34396} = 2.91$, and calculate p_i for the following data:

Interval	f_i	p_i	F_i	$\dfrac{(f_i - F_i)^2}{F_i}$
0 to < 0.1	15	0.2525	12.62	0.449
0.1 to < 0.2	8	0.1887	9.44	0.220
0.2 to < 0.3	5	0.1411	7.06	0.601
0.3 to < 0.4	2	0.1055	5.27	2.029
0.4 to < 0.5	6	0.0788	3.94	1.077
0.5 to < 0.6	5	0.0589	2.95	1.425
0.6 to < ∞	9	0.1745	8.72	0.009
Total	N = 50	1.0	50	5.81

As an example,

$$P(0.1 \le X < 0.2) = P(X < 0.2) - P(X \le 0.1)$$
$$= (1 - e^{-\lambda(0.2)}) - (1 - e^{-\lambda(0.1)}) = 0.4412 - 0.2525 = 0.1887$$

$$\text{So: } \chi_0^2 = 5.81$$

Step 4: $v = k - m - 1 = 7 - 1 - 1 = 5$, ($m = 1$ because you estimated λ by $\hat{\lambda} = \dfrac{1}{\bar{X}}$)

Step 5: Using software or tables, determine the area to the right of $\chi_0^2 = 5.81$ to be 0.3251, as shown in the diagram below:

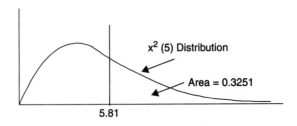

Step 6: Because $0.3251 > 0.10$, conclude H_0: The distribution is exponential.

Interpreting the conclusion is the most common source of mistakes in using the chi-square test. Remember, you can't conclude H_0 with statistical confidence. The test detects data that deviates from the hypothesized distribution with statistical levels of confidence. But no test can prove the data comes from a specified distribution. If the test results in H_0, an accurate conclusion would be "the exponential distribution adequately fits the data."

C.2.5   Comparing Systems

If you want to compare simulations, you'll consider many statistical aspects of the systems. If you want to evaluate the distributional forms of the data, you might use a chi-square test or a Kolmogorov-Smirnov test [Daniel 1978]. To compare variances, you'd use an F-test [Kiemele 1997]. Another common comparison is a test of means. Consider the following two systems:

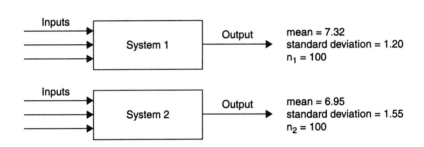

If you want to know whether the two systems generate the same mean, you can use the two sample t-test:

Step 1: H_0: $\mu_1 = \mu_2$

          H_1: $\mu_1 \neq \mu_2$

Step 2: $\alpha = 0.05$

Step 3: $\bar{y}_1 = 7.32$ $\bar{y}_2 = 6.95$

          $s_1 = 1.20$ $s_2 = 1.55$

          $s_1^2 = 1.44$ $s_2^2 = 2.4025$

          $n_1 = 100$ $n_2 = 100$

$$s_p = \sqrt{\frac{(n_1-1)s_1^2 + (n_2-1)s_2^2}{(n_1+n_2-2)}} = \sqrt{\frac{99(1.44) + 99(2.24025)}{198}} = 1.386$$

$$t_0 = \frac{\bar{y}_1 - \bar{y}_2}{s_P\sqrt{\frac{1}{n_1} + \frac{1}{n_2}}} = \frac{7.32 - 6.95}{1.386\sqrt{\frac{1}{100} + \frac{1}{100}}} = 1.888$$

Step 4:

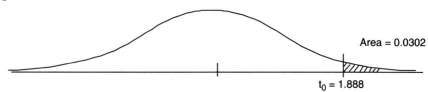

Area = 0.0302

$t_0 = 1.888$

Step 5: Based on the graphic in Step 4, P = 2(area) = 2(0.0302) = 0.0604.

Step 6: Because P > α (0.0604 > 0.05), conclude $H_0 : \mu_1 = \mu_2$

That is, the evidence doesn't show a significant difference at the 0.05 level, but it's useful to look at the p-value of 0.06. Recall that the p-value is the probability of concluding H_1 (the means are different) when H_0 is actually true. We interpret this as the probability (risk) of making a false conclusion if the means are actually the same. How much risk is acceptable? We can't say. Statisticians often arbitrarily select 0.05 or 0.10 as an acceptable level of risk, but users must decide what is acceptable.

C.3 Introduction to Design of Experiments

C.3.1 Introduction

For any simulation that processes inputs (referred to as x's) to produce outputs (referred to as y's), we can use design-of-experiment techniques to represent the simulation's algorithm by a simple mathematical model. These models depict the output as a polynomial function of the inputs. The degree of the polynomial fit (linear, linear plus interactions, or quadratic) depends on the type of designed experiment and the experimenter's needs.

Thus, designed experiments can reduce very complex simulations to mathematical models that are simple and easy to understand. These models feed one or more of the following:

1. Low-fidelity simulations (reduce the simulation's algorithm to a single mathematical approximation relating outputs to inputs)
2. Sensitivity analysis (identify how sensitive the outputs are to slight changes in the inputs)
3. Optimizing analysis (determine precise settings for the inputs to achieve desired objectives for the outputs)
4. Tolerance analysis on the x's (determine how much the inputs can vary around their ideal value while keeping the output within a desired range)

Using the definition of a simulation as a process with inputs (parameters) and outputs (responses), three examples that demonstrate the breadth of possible applications are aircraft-system design, computer-network performance, and electrical-circuit design (see Fig. C.12).

a. Designing an Aircraft System.

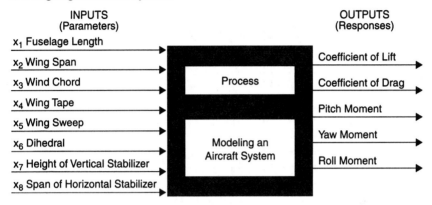

b. Analyzing a Computer Network's Performance.

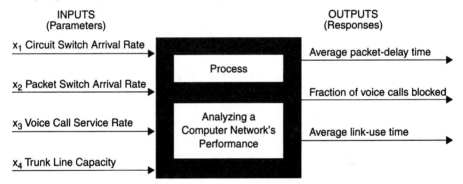

c. Designing an Electrical Circuit.

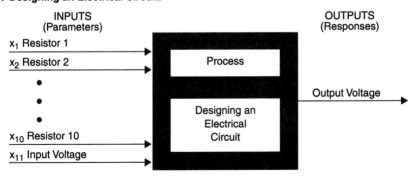

Fig. C.12. **Example Applications for Designed Experiments.** Designed experiments can reduce very complex simulations to mathematical models that are easy to understand. The input-output processes shown here demonstrate the breadth of possible applications for this technique.

A simulation, like any other process, has different types of variables. To gain process knowledge while avoiding ambiguity, we should understand all types of variables and their roles in an experiment. The four types are

1. Response (output) variables—variables measured to evaluate performance of a process or product
2. Controlled variables to be held constant—a standard operating procedure typically ensures their consistency
3. Uncontrolled (noise) variables—variables that can't be held constant during the experiment or while producing or using the product. We'd like the process or product to be robust (insensitive) to these variables
4. Key process or experimental variables—key parameters we intend to vary during an experiment (x's)

Using all four categories of variables, experimenters can graphically represent a process more completely, as shown in Fig. C.13. This type of graph simply depicts and clearly communicates the roles of all variables during the experiment.

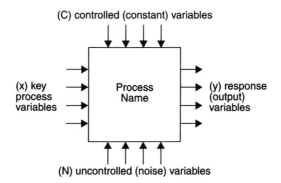

Fig. C.13.   Complete Process Diagram with Four Categories of Variables.

Using design of experiments can help you determine which parameters shift the response average, its variability, its average and variability, or neither the average nor the variability (see Fig. C.14). These parameters are the x's—designated as $x_1, x_2, x_3, x_4, \ldots$ or A, B, C, D, $\ldots$ Knowing the process in this way allows you to choose the proper input (x) settings to achieve desired output targets with minimum variability.

C.3.2   Most Common Types of Designed Experiments

Full Factorial Designs (each factor at two levels)

Typically used for five or fewer x's, a *full factorial* designed experiment consists of all possible combinations of testing levels for all parameters. The total number of different combinations for k parameters at two testing levels is $n = 2^k$. For example, if you intend to experiment with two factors at two testing levels

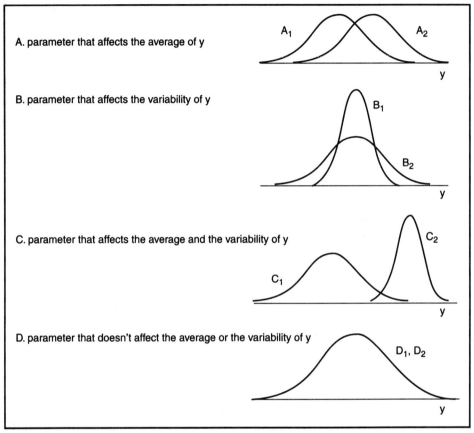

Fig. C.14.   Graphical Description of Different Types of Parameters. The subscripts 1 and 2 represent the parameter's low and high settings, respectively.

each, you'll have $n = 2^2$ or four combinations. The combinations to be tested are often displayed in a test matrix as runs (see Table C.10). By testing the full factorial at two levels, you'll get information on the linear effects of all parameters, plus all interactions. Unfortunately, it requires many experimental runs whenever you have more than four parameters.

As an example, consider a simulation for designing circuits with two parameters designated A and B. Table C.10 contains the experimental runs of all possible combinations for parameters A and B, each at two testing levels. For the sake of discussion, assume A is the resistance for resistor 1, B is the resistance for resistor 2, and y is the output voltage. Then, the first run sets A at 4 Ohms and B at 16 Ohms to collect a response value on output voltage, and the remaining three complete the experiment. The objective is to determine quickly where to set resistance values for A and B, so we can achieve an output (y) value equal to 120 units with minimum variability.

Table C.10. Experimental Runs for a Simulation Process.

	Parameters		Response
Run	Resistor 1 A	Resistor 2 B	Output Voltage (y)
1	4 Ω	16 Ω	
2	4 Ω	32 Ω	
3	12 Ω	16 Ω	
4	12 Ω	32 Ω	

In Table C.11 we've displayed 20 observations taken by replicating each experimental run five times. In other words, we conducted five non-deterministic simulations for each run. The columns labeled $\bar{y}$ and s represent the average and standard deviation, respectively, for each run.

Table C.11. Results of Experiment Using Two Parameters.

	Parameters		Replicated Response Values Using Monte Carlo Simulation for Each Run						
Run	A	B	y_1	y_2	y_3	y_4	y_5	$\bar{y}$	s
1	4	16	116.1	116.9	112.6	118.7	114.9	115.8	2.278
2	4	32	106.7	107.5	105.9	107.1	106.5	106.7	0.607
3	12	16	116.5	115.5	119.2	114.7	118.3	116.8	1.884
4	12	32	123.2	125.1	124.5	124.0	124.7	124.3	0.731

$$\bar{\bar{y}} = 115.93$$

Although you need the actual parameter settings shown in Table C.10 to run the experiment, you'd use **coded values** of –1 for the low setting and +1 for the high setting to set up and do the analysis. Coding the x's standardizes the units and scales all input parameters. To transform coded settings to actual settings, and vice versa, you can use the formula or graph in Fig. C.15.

For a simple example, consider parameter B (resistor 2) = 32 in Table C.10. The actual value is 32, but you'd determine the resulting coded value using the following expression:

$$\text{Actual}_B = \left(\frac{32+16}{2}\right) + \left(\frac{32-16}{2}\right)(\text{Coded}_B)$$

$$32 = 24 + 8\,(\text{Coded}_B)$$

$$\text{Coded}_B = 1.0$$

Converting all the actual parameter settings in Table C.10 to coded values produces the coded experimental matrix in Table C.12. Basically the high actual values are coded as (1) and the low actual values are coded as (–1). However, the previous figure and equation will also allow you to transform intermediate values, as we'll show later while optimizing.

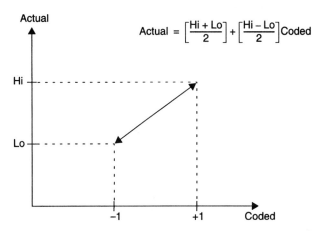

$$\text{Actual} = \left[\frac{\text{Hi} + \text{Lo}}{2}\right] + \left[\frac{\text{Hi} - \text{Lo}}{2}\right]\text{Coded}$$

Fig. C.15.   **Transformation from Actual Parameter Settings to Coded Setting (and Vice Versa).**

Notice we've added an AB column in Table C.12. We use this column to evaluate the A×B or Resistor 1 × Resistor 2 interaction. To get the (−1) and (1) values in the AB column, we multiply the coded values in the A and B columns, respectively. Interaction effects represent a coupling (or combined effect) between the A and B parameters. The true interaction effect appears in the mathematical model as a coefficient times the product of the respective parameters.

Table C.12. Coded Experimental Matrix.

Run	Parameters & Interactions			Replicated Response Values					$\bar{y}$	s
	A	B	AB	y_1	y_2	y_3	y_4	y_5		
1	-1	-1	1	116.1	116.9	112.6	118.7	114.9	115.8	2.278
2	-1	1	-1	106.7	107.5	105.9	107.1	106.5	106.7	0.607
3	1	-1	-1	116.5	115.5	119.2	114.7	118.3	116.8	1.884
4	1	1	1	123.2	125.1	124.5	124.0	124.7	124.3	0.731

Ultimately, you'll want to find the settings of A and B that will generate an average y value at its desired target (120 units) with minimum variation. To determine which terms in the test matrix (A, B, AB) shift the average of the response, first evaluate each column or term by computing the average response at the low setting (−1) and the average response at the high setting (1). For example, parameter A is at its low setting during runs one and two. The average of the ten response values for these two runs is 111.3 (see Table C.13). The Δ row in Table C.13 shows the difference between the response average at the highs (1) and the response average at the lows (−1). The absolute size of these differences measures the relative importance of the terms in the columns.

Table C.13. Summary of Analysis for the Simulation Example.

Run	A	B	AB	y_1	y_2	y_3	y_4	y_5	$\bar{y}$	s
	Parameters & Interactions			Replicated Response Values						
1	-1	-1	+1	116.1	116.9	112.6	118.7	114.9	115.8	2.278
2	-1	+1	-1	106.7	107.5	105.9	107.1	106.5	106.7	0.607
3	+1	-1	-1	116.5	115.5	119.2	114.7	118.3	116.8	1.884
4	+1	+1	+1	123.2	125.1	124.5	124.0	124.7	124.3	0.731

	Parameters & Interactions			
	A	B	AB	
Avg y@ − 1	111.3	116.3	111.8	
Avg y@ + 1	120.6	115.5'	120.1	Grand Mean: $\bar{\bar{y}}$ = 115.93
Δ	9.3	−0.8	8.3	

To manually generate the mathematical model relating the output to the inputs, you can use this general equation:

$$\hat{y} = \bar{\bar{y}} + \frac{\Delta_A}{2}A + \frac{\Delta_B}{2}B + \frac{\Delta_{AB}}{2}AB$$

where $\hat{y}$ represents the predicted average response. For our example, the model will be

$$\hat{y} = 115.93 + \frac{9.3}{2}A - \frac{0.8}{2}B + \frac{8.3}{2}AB$$

This model describes how the output relates to A, B, and the interaction of A and B. The value of 9.3/2 = 4.65 represents the magnitude of A's linear effect. Similarly, −0.8/2 = −0.4 is the magnitude of B's linear effect, and 8.2/2 = 4.15 is the magnitude of the interaction effect. Use statistical software to automatically build the model and do statistical analysis. Table C.14 depicts the statistical results from a package called DOE KISS [1997] in a format typical of most packages.

To keep the model as simple as possible, use the following rule of thumb on P(2-tail):

P(2-tail) < 0.05 implies the term is significant; place it in the $\hat{y}$ model.

P(2-tail) > 0.10 implies the term is insignificant; leave it out of the $\hat{y}$ model.

0.05 ≤ P(2-tail) ≤ 0.10 is a gray zone where most experimenters will typically decide to place the term in the $\hat{y}$ model.

Note: (1 − P (2-tail)) *100% is your confidence that a given term belongs in the model.

Table C.14. Computer Output from DOE KISS for the Experimental Example in Table C.13.

Dep Var: y N: 20 Squared Multiple R: 0.953 Adjusted Squared R: 0.944 Std Err Est: 1.552		
Variable	**Coeff**	**P(2 Tail)**
constant	115.930	0.000
A	4.650	0.000
B	−0.400	0.255
AB	4.150	0.000

where

Dep Var: y reminds us that our output or dependent variable is y

N: 20 indicates that the total number of output values is 20

Squared Multiple R, also referred to as R^2, represents the model's strength. (The range of R^2 is 0 to 1.0, where $R^2 = 0$ implies the model is insignificant and $R^2 = 1.0$ implies the model is perfect. The value $(1 - R^2)$ represents the proportion of noise in the data that the model doesn't explain.)

Adjusted Squared R adjusts the value of R^2 down whenever the model has many terms compared to the number of observations. [Kiemele 1997; Schmidt 1994].

P(2-tail) quantitatively measures the statistical significance for each term in the model. (In other words, not all terms or effects have a magnitude that is significantly different from zero.)

Again, if you have any doubt, it's better to place a term in the model rather than to leave it out. Therefore, use $P < 0.10$ as a rule of thumb. Rules of thumb aren't as precise as decision criteria. Neither rules of thumb nor rigorous statistical tests should ever replace common sense, size of effects, and prior knowledge when you're trying to find the best model to fit the data.

The software will produce the same results (within rounding) as a manual analysis. Using only the significant terms based on P(2-tail), the software model will be

$$\hat{y} = 115.93 + 4.65A + 4.15AB$$

However, the hierarchal rule of modeling dictates that associated linear terms (significant or not) must accompany the significant interaction or quadratic term in the model. Therefore, the final prediction model for the average will be

$$\hat{y} = 115.93 + 4.65A - 0.40B + 4.15AB$$

The prediction equation has now given us information on parameters that shift the average. But we still need information on parameters that shift the variability. To find it, let's use the data in Table C.12 with the values in the s (standard deviation) column as our response values. The calculations in Table C.15 are similar to those in Table C.13. Note that in Table C.15, δ is defined to be (Avg s @ 1) minus (Avg s @ −1). In general, a model for predicting a response's standard deviation for two-level parameters is

$$\hat{s} = \bar{s} + \frac{\delta_A}{2}A + \frac{\delta_B}{2}B + \frac{\delta_{AB}}{2}AB$$

where $\hat{s}$ = predicted standard deviation. Therefore, the full model for $\hat{s}$ is

$$\hat{s} = 1.375 - \frac{0.135}{2}A - \frac{1.42}{2}B + \frac{0.259}{2}AB$$

Table C.15. Summary of Variance Analysis for the Simulation Example.

Run	A	B	AB	s
1	−1	−1	1	2.278
2	−1	1	−1	0.607
3	1	−1	−1	1.884
4	1	1	1	0.731
Avg s @ -1	1.4425	2.081	1.2455	grand s
Avg s @ 1	1.3075	0.669	1.5045	average is $\bar{s} = 1.375$
δ	−0.1350	−1.42	0.2590	

We can test columns for significance using the following simple rule of thumb for two-level designs: $|\delta| \geq \bar{s}$ indicates that the corresponding term is significant at approximately $\alpha = 0.05$, so we should place it in the $\hat{s}$ model. But remember, a rule of thumb is just a guideline, so you must use common sense to evaluate values close to its boundary. Using this rule of thumb for $\hat{s}$ models, a prediction equation for $\hat{s}$ including only significant terms is

$$\hat{s} = 1.375 - \frac{1.42}{2}B$$

Remember that the $\hat{s}$ equation is for coded values. Therefore, to minimize $\hat{s}$, set parameter B at the coded value of 1 (the high coded setting), which results in a predicted standard deviation for the response of $\hat{s} = 0.665$.

Having found the parameter settings that will minimize the response's standard deviation, you must return to the prediction equation to determine the remaining parameter settings that will achieve a target value for the average output voltage—120 units. To do so, follow these steps:

1. Set the prediction equation for $\hat{y}$ equal to the desired target value.

   $$120 = 115.93 + 4.65A - 0.40B + 4.15AB$$

2. Insert the parameter settings previously determined from minimizing variances. For this example, set B = 1.

   $$120 = 115.93 + 4.65A - 0.40(1) + 4.15A(1)$$

3. Set all but one of the remaining parameters at coded values that correspond to low cost, convenience, etc. (Because only A remains in this case, there are no extra parameters to set).

4. Solve the remaining equation for the one remaining parameter.

$$(4.65 + 4.15) A = 120 - 115.93 + 0.400$$

$$A = \frac{4.47}{8.80} = 0.508$$

5. Decode the coded value in step 4, using Figure C.15 and its associated equation:

$$\text{Actual}_A = \left(\frac{12 + 4}{2}\right) + \left(\frac{12 - 4}{2}\right)\text{Coded}_A$$

$$= 8 + 4(0.508) = 10.03$$

Obviously, selecting parameter settings to minimize variance, achieve target response values, and minimize cost means you must use prediction equations for ŝ and ŷ plus a lot of process knowledge and common sense. Often, you must trade off objectives based on what you know from the two prediction equations.

For circuit design, the best parameter settings appear to be A = 10.03 ohms and B = 32 ohms. Now, we need some confirmation runs to verify our conclusions. In this test for confirmation you want response values to fall within ŷ ± 3ŝ. For our example, all confirmation runs should have output voltages between 120 ± 3(0.665) or (118.005, 121.995).

Designing Three-Level Models

If you expect the relationship of the output to the inputs to be non-linear, you'll need a three-level design. Assume you have four factors (A, B, C, D) to test and your objective is to build a non-linear model for the average response ($\bar{y}$) and the standard deviation (s). In addition, you want a target average y greater than or equal to 0.3, with a minimum standard deviation. You could use a Box-Behnken design of 27 runs or a central-composite design (which will also have 27 runs), assuming you choose three center points. Both designs will produce a similar non-linear model. To choose the better design, you could build them both and see which one has desirable combinations. You could also review the advantages and disadvantages of each type in Schmidt [1994]. If you decide to do the central-composite design, the software package DOE KISS will build the design matrix shown in Table C.16. The –1 in the design represents the low setting for the parameters, 1 represents the high setting, and 0 represents the midpoint between them.

Assume you run the experiment and do two replicates per experimental run as shown in Table C.16. Analyzing the ŝ model results in the values shown in Table C.17. Using the rule of thumb on P(2-Tail) shows the only significant terms in the ŝ model are A, D, and D^2. The three-dimensional response surface (Fig. C.16) and contour plots (Fig. C.17) indicate that a minimum ŝ of 0.024 occurs for coded values of A = +1.000 and D = –0.333.

Table C.16. Data from a Central Composite (Face) Design.

	A	B	C	D	y_1	y_2	$\bar{y}$	s
1	1	1	1	1	1.904	1.711	1.807	0.136
2	1	1	1	-1	1.256	1.310	1.283	0.038
3	1	1	-1	1	1.146	1.189	1.167	0.030
4	1	1	-1	-1	0.702	0.673	0.687	0.021
5	1	-1	1	1	1.658	1.723	1.690	0.046
6	1	-1	1	-1	0.892	0.885	0.888	0.005
7	1	-1	-1	1	0.043	0.078	0.060	0.025
8	1	-1	-1	-1	0.847	0.799	0.823	0.034
9	-1	1	1	1	0.409	0.255	0.332	0.109
10	-1	1	1	-1	0.321	0.211	0.266	0.078
11	-1	1	-1	1	0.324	0.529	0.426	0.145
12	-1	1	-1	-1	0.179	0.312	0.245	0.094
13	-1	-1	1	1	0.453	0.306	0.379	0.104
14	-1	-1	1	-1	0.255	0.399	0.327	0.102
15	-1	-1	-1	1	0.257	0.118	0.187	0.098
16	-1	-1	-1	-1	0.191	0.266	0.228	0.053
17	0	0	0	0	0.328	0.488	0.408	0.113
18	0	0	0	0	0.434	0.512	0.473	0.055
19	0	0	0	0	0.341	0.438	0.389	0.069
20	-1	0	0	0	0.247	0.311	0.279	0.045
21	1	0	0	0	0.986	0.943	0.964	0.030
22	0	-1	0	0	0.436	0.428	0.432	0.006
23	0	1	0	0	0.412	0.465	0.438	0.037
24	0	0	-1	0	0.391	0.385	0.388	0.004
25	0	0	1	0	0.526	0.611	0.568	0.060
26	0	0	0	-1	0.362	0.426	0.394	0.045
27	0	0	0	1	0.589	0.433	0.511	0.110

Table C.17. Results of Analyzing the $\hat{s}$ Model.

Regression Output for Std Dev, $R^2 = 0.677022$		
Effect	**Coeff**	**P (2 Tail)**
Constant	0.05182	0.00143
A	-0.0257	0.00774
B	0.01202	0.16110
C	0.00967	0.25302
D	0.01858	0.03957
A^2	-0.0004	0.98462
B^2	-0.0167	0.44855
C^2	-0.0061	0.78025
D^2	0.03953	0.08808
AB	0.00296	0.73470
AC	0.00712	0.42083
AD	0.00066	0.93938
BC	0.00155	0.85923
BD	0.00694	0.43216
CD	0.00473	0.58978

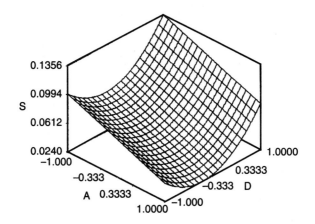

Fig. C.16.   Plot of Response Surface for the ŝ Model.

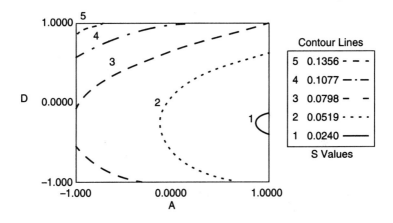

Fig. C.17.   Contours of Constant Values for Standard Deviation.

The next step is to model $\hat{y}$, which has a target objective for the response of greater than 0.3. The analysis in Table C.18 shows that several terms have P(2-tail) values less than 0.100 and thus should be in the model. The three-dimensional plot of response surfaces, the interaction plot, and the contour plot for A and D are in Figs. C.18, C.19, and C.20, respectively. We've held factors B and C constant at −1. Because the objective for $\hat{y}$ is greater than or equal to 0.3, the settings of A and D that minimize ŝ will also satisfy $\hat{y}$.

Combining the analyses of $\hat{y}$ and ŝ shows that the coded settings of A = 1.000, B = −1.000, C = −1.000 and D = −0.333 will produce $\hat{y}$ = 0.493 and ŝ = 0.024. If these values aren't what you want, set B and C to other values and recompute.

Table C.18. Results of Analyzing the ŷ Model.

Effect	Coeff	t	Tolerance	P(2 Tail)
	Regression Output for Y_i, Coded $R^2 = 0.881912$ F = 20.80447			
Constant	0.43184	9.34283	1.00000	0.00000
A	0.37228	12.5925	1.00000	0.00000
B	0.09094	3.07626	1.00000	0.00454
C	0.18489	6.25399	1.00000	0.00000
D	0.07886	2.66753	1.00000	0.01237
A^2	0.18574	2.37468	0.42857	0.02440
B^2	−0.0007	−0.0097	0.42857	0.99232
C^2	0.04224	0.54004	0.42857	0.59329
D^2	0.01649	0.21083	0.42857	0.83449
AB	0.08347	2.66191	1.00000	0.01254
AC	0.16966	5.41053	1.00000	0.00001
AD	0.04909	1.56566	1.00000	0.12828
BC	−0.0515	−1.6433	1.00000	0.11110
BD	0.07503	2.39283	1.00000	0.02342
CD	0.09922	3.16420	1.00000	0.00364

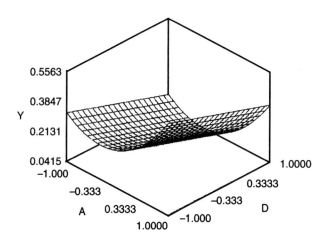

Fig. C.18.   Plot of Response Surface Plot for the ŷ Model (B = −1, C = −1).

Screening Designs

Whenever we have many inputs to vary in an experiment, we can't do a modeling design because of the large number of runs. Typically, having more than five inputs calls for a screening design to identify which are most important. These designs require complex mathematics. Their purpose is to identify the fewest runs that still allow an independent analysis of input variables. The L_{12} design matrix shown in Table C.19 contains 11 columns that are tested over 12 combinations (runs). So this screening experiment can test up to 11 input variables (factors).

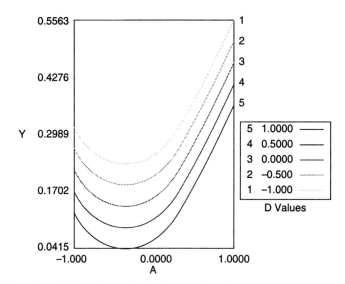

Fig. C.19.   Interaction Plot for the ŷ Model (B = –1, C = –1).

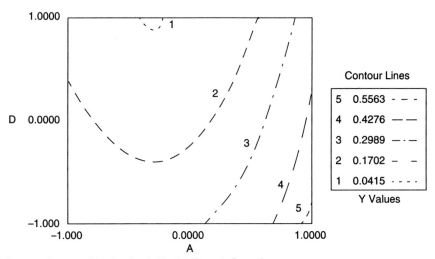

Fig. C.20.   Contour Plot for the ŷ Model (B = –1, C = –1).

Use this L_{12} design to test 11 factors by choosing the low and high settings for each factor and making the 12 runs. Table C.20 shows four replicates of data for this screening experiment.

Table C.21 shows the result of finding the average response and the average standard deviation at the low (–1) and the high (+1) settings.

Table C.19. Taguchi L_{12} Design Matrix.

Run	Factors														
	x_1	x_2	x_3	x_4	x_5	x_6	x_7	x_8	x_9	x_{10}	x_{11}	y_1	y_2	y_3	y_4
1	-1	-1	-1	-1	-1	-1	-1	-1	-1	-1	-1				
2	-1	-1	-1	-1	-1	+1	+1	+1	+1	+1	+1				
3	-1	-1	+1	+1	+1	-1	-1	-1	+1	+1	+1				
4	-1	+1	-1	+1	+1	-1	+1	+1	-1	-1	+1				
5	-1	+1	+1	-1	+1	+1	-1	+1	-1	+1	-1				
6	-1	+1	+1	+1	-1	+1	+1	-1	+1	-1	-1				
7	+1	-1	+1	+1	-1	-1	+1	+1	-1	+1	-1				
8	+1	-1	+1	-1	+1	+1	+1	-1	-1	-1	+1				
9	+1	-1	-1	+1	+1	+1	-1	+1	+1	-1	-1				
10	+1	+1	+1	-1	-1	-1	-1	+1	+1	-1	+1				
11	+1	+1	-1	+1	-1	+1	-1	-1	-1	+1	+1				
12	+1	+1	-1	-1	+1	-1	+1	-1	+1	+1	-1				

Table C.20. Data From a Taguchi L_{12} Screening Design.

Run	y_1	y_2	y_3	y_4	$\bar{y}$	s
1	532.412	460.059	646.676	500.971	535.094	80.11
2	647.412	435.147	624.000	493.706	550.066	102.18
3	1270.882	1356.265	1198.647	1248.000	1268.449	65.85
4	895.471	966.794	837.853	1043.265	935.846	88.94
5	1572.118	1699.882	1693.059	1518.882	1620.985	88.87
6	1584.706	1395.088	1334.059	1388.677	1425.632	109.53
7	1092.835	1100.765	1049.576	1072.729	1078.976	22.88
8	1205.729	1235.765	1224.047	1253.153	1229.674	19.94
9	694.459	681.506	748.741	643.518	692.056	43.54
10	1423.235	1461.318	1411.247	1416.706	1428.126	22.66
11	806.859	849.635	779.353	773.212	802.265	34.80
12	950.706	966.518	923.259	957.388	949.468	18.64

Table C.21. Analysis of Effects (Δ) for Taguchi L_{12} Design.

	x_1	x_2	x_3	x_4	x_5	x_6	x_7	x_8	x_9	x_{10}	x_{11}
Avg $\bar{Y}$ @ -1	1056.012	892.386	744.132	1052.235	970.026	1032.660	1057.829	1035.097	1033.807	1041.071	1050.368
Avg $\bar{Y}$ @ +1	1030.094	1193.720	1341.974	1033.871	1116.080	1053.446	1028.277	1051.009	1052.299	1045.035	1035.738
Δ	-25.918	*301.334*	*597.842*	-18.364	*146.054*	20.786	-29.552	15.912	18.492	3.964	-14.630

	x_1	x_2	x_3	x_4	x_5	x_6	x_7	x_8	x_9	x_{10}	x_{11}
Avg S @ -1	89.41	55.75	61.37	55.57	62.03	49.85	56.14	54.81	56.09	60.79	60.76
Avg S @ +1	27.08	60.74	55.12	60.92	54.46	66.64	60.35	61.68	60.40	55.70	55.73
Δ	*-62.33*	4.99	-6.25	5.35	-7.57	16.79	4.21	6.87	4.31	-5.09	-5.03

To determine the critical factors that shift the average and the standard deviation, look at a display (the Pareto diagram) of the average and standard deviation effects (Δs), sorted by order of magnitude (Figs. C.21 and C.22). Closely examining these figures reveals that factor X_1 may reduce variance, and factors X_3, X_2, and X_5 will shift the average. From Table C.21 you can see that, at the high setting, factor X_1 has roughly one-third the variation as at the low setting. Therefore, you can reduce variation by setting X_1 high. And you might consider X_2, X_3, and X_5 for a later modeling experiment, in which you hold the remaining factors constant at low cost, high throughput, etc.

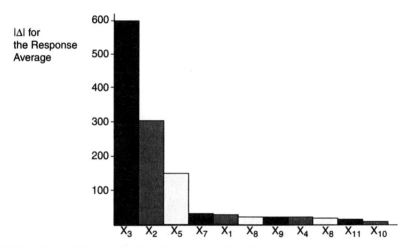

Fig. C.21.   Pareto Diagram for How Responses Affect the Average.

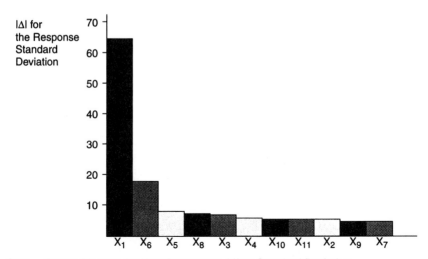

Fig. C.22.   Pareto Diagram for How Responses Affect Standard Deviation.

C.4   Introduction to Statistical Process Control

We control processes to make economically sound decisions. This means balancing the risk of adjusting a process when action isn't necessary against the risk of not adjusting it when action is necessary. A process is operating in **statistical control** when common causes are the only source of variation and special causes of variation are eliminated. (Common causes produce only background noise in the data, whereas special causes produce abnormal events.) But statistical control isn't a natural state for most processes. We achieve it by eliminating each special cause of excessive variation. Thus, a process-control system must first provide statistical signals whenever special causes of variation are present and avoid giving false signals when they aren't. We can act on these signals to remove special causes and prevent their reappearance (see Fig. C.23).

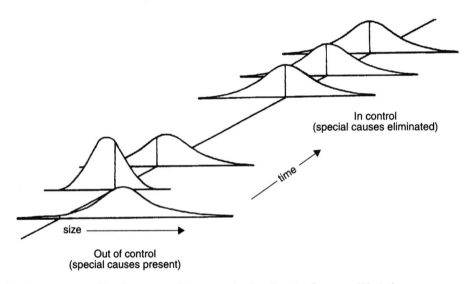

Fig. C.23.   Controlling Processes Means Eliminating Special Causes of Variation.

Process control must also estimate how well the process can perform by measuring "process capability"—how well the process is behaving with respect to the output specifications. To measure process capability, we assess the total variation that comes from common causes, which is the minimum variation we can get after removing all special causes. In other words, process capability describes the performance of a process when it operates under statistical control, and a good way of viewing it is to see how much of the process's output meets product specifications. Because a process in statistical control is stable, we can describe it with a predictable distribution and estimate the constant proportion of out-of-specification parts from this distribution. To improve the process's consistency in meeting specifications, management must reduce variations from common causes (see Fig. C.24).

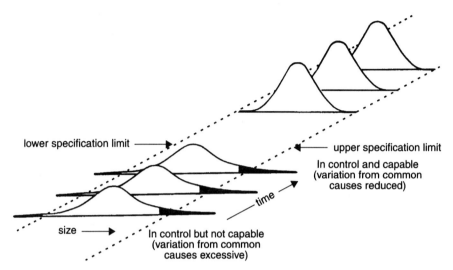

lower specification limit

upper specification limit

In control and capable
(variation from common
causes reduced)

size

time

In control but not capable
(variation from common
causes excessive)

Fig. C.24.   **Process Capability.** Process capability measures how well a process is behaving. We determine it by assessing the total variation that comes from common causes.

In short, you must first bring the process into statistical control by detecting and eliminating special causes of variation. When its performance is predictable, you can assess its ability to meet a customer's expectations, which allows for continuous improvement. (See Fig. C.24.)

C.4.1   Using Control Charts to Assess a Process

A control chart is simply a chart of data plotted over time. It includes statistically generated control limits that provide us with upper and lower bounds on the common-cause (natural) variations in the process's output. Dr. Shewhart of Bell Laboratories developed the first control charts in the 1920s to separate common causes from special causes of variation. Since then, the United States and other countries (notably, Japan) have used them for many processes. Although we can use them to analyze variations, attributes, and counts, Shewhart pointed out they all have the same basic purpose: *to show whether a process has been operating in a state of statistical control and to signal the presence of special causes of variation so someone can correct them.*

Process improvement using control charts is iterative. It repeats three basic phases: carefully collecting data, using the data to calculate control limits, and assessing the process's ability to meet customers' needs. To control a process,

1. **Collect Data:** Run the process, gather data for the characteristic you're studying, and convert it to a form you can plot on a graph. Examples are the measured values of a machined piece's dimensions, the number of flaws in a bolt of vinyl, a rail car's transit times, or the number of errors in bookkeeping.

2. **Control the Process:** First, calculate control limits based on data from the process's output by determining how much variation you can expect if all variation were from common causes. Draw these limits on the chart to guide analysis. Remember, control limits aren't specification limits or objectives; they reflect the process's natural variability. Then, compare the data with the control limits to see whether the variation is stable and appears to come only from common causes. If special causes of variation are evident, study the process to determine what is affecting it. After management has tried to correct problems, collect more data, recalculate the control limits (if necessary), and study and correct any other special causes.

3. **Assess the Process:** After all special causes have been corrected and the process is running in statistical control, assess its ability to meet the customers' needs. If common causes produce too much variation, investigate the process and help management improve the system.

To continue process improvement, repeat these three phases. Gather more data as appropriate, work to reduce the process's variation by operating it in statistical control, and continually improve its capability.

Applying Statistical Control to a Gas-Mileage Example

As a simple example of generating control charts and assessing process capability, consider a vehicle's gas mileage, which varies weekly. You want to know whether this variability is natural or due to specific causes. Let's step through the process for statistical control to find out.

Phase 1: Collect Data

Step 1:   Build a run chart (see Fig. C.25). Normally, you'll need 20–25 points to get good estimates of the average and the standard deviation and construct control limits.

Step 2:   Determine the average gas mileage and its variability. Computing the average gas mileage over the 20 weeks will give you a feel for the vehicle's expected gas mileage. To find this average, use

$$\bar{y} = \frac{\sum_{i=1}^{20} y_i}{20} = \frac{[21 + 19 + 20 + \ldots + 22]}{20} = \frac{400}{20} = 20$$

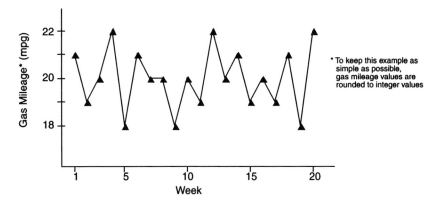

Fig. C.25.   Run Chart of 20 Weeks of Gas Mileage Data for a Single Vehicle.

and plot it as the centerline of your control chart. Then, determine variability by calculating the estimated variance, s^2, of the 20 mileage measurements using the equation

$$s^2 = \frac{\sum\limits_{i=1}^{n} (y_i - \bar{y})^2}{n - 1}$$

which can be described as the sum of the squared deviations from the mean, all divided by $(n - 1)$. Figure C.26 shows the deviations of the measurements from the mean and the variance calculation for this problem.

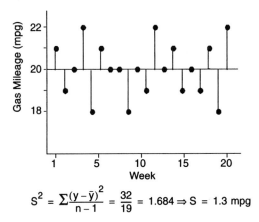

$$s^2 = \frac{\sum (y - \bar{y})^2}{n - 1} = \frac{32}{19} = 1.684 \Rightarrow S = 1.3 \text{ mpg}$$

Fig. C.26.   Average Gas Mileage and Variability in the Gas-Mileage Data.

Step 3: Depict the data's distribution in a histogram—a graph that displays how often a given outcome occurs (see Fig. C.27). If you superimpose a smooth line on the histogram, it appears to be symmetrical and bell shaped, much the same as a normal curve. Assume that it is normal and, if you like, validate this assumption by doing a Chi-square goodness-of-fit test (described in Table C.9).

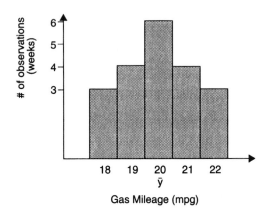

Fig. C.27.   Histogram of Gas-Mileage Data.

Phase 2: Control the Process

Step 1: Based on your assumption that the gas-mileage data follows a normal curve, use the empirical rule shown again in Fig. C.28 to help develop control limits. Most control charts establish the upper and lower control limits at ±3 standard deviations from the centerline. As a result, according to the empirical rule, approximately 99.73% of all gas mileage values for this vehicle should fall within these limits. For this example, $\bar{y} \pm 3s = 20 \pm 3(1.3)$ results in a lower control limit of 16.1 and an upper control limit of 23.9.

Step 2: Use these limits in a control chart to evaluate the vehicle's current and future performance (see Fig. C.29). For instance, if week 21 produced a gas mileage of 23, chances are that nothing specific has caused this value; however, a value of 16 is outside our control limits (outside the natural variability) and indicates a 99.73% chance that a specific change in the vehicle caused this value. Other rules for statistical process control exist to detect out-of-control conditions due to trends or increases in variability [Kiemele 1997]. But Fig. C.29 doesn't exhibit any of these conditions, so you should extend the control limits out in time and watch the process to detect any special causes of variation.

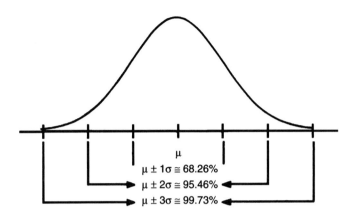

Fig. C.28.   **Percent of Areas Under a Normal Curve.**

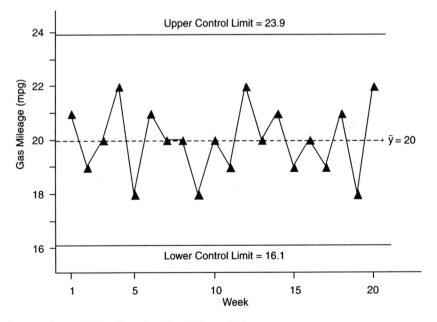

Fig. C.29.   **Control Chart Based on Gas-Mileage Data.**

Step 3: If you detect an out-of-control condition, such as a gas-mileage reading of 16, determine its cause. To do so, brainstorm with management and try to concentrate on inputs that are most likely to affect the gas mileage. The result will be a set of inputs you can investigate each time the control chart detects a change in gas mileage. Display these inputs in a cause-effect diagram like Fig. C.30.

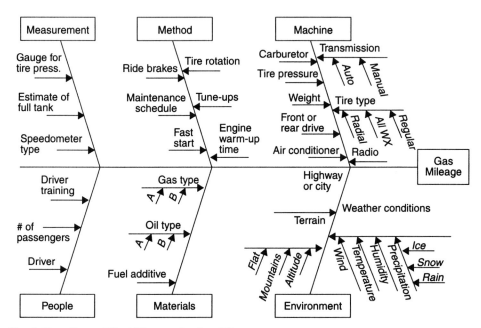

Fig. C.30.   Cause-Effect Diagram for Gas Mileage.

Step 4: Correct and control special causes. For example, suppose your investigation reveals an extremely low tire pressure that you determine to be causing the out-of-control value for gas mileage. You would obviously correct the low tire pressure and possibly begin to chart tire pressures weekly. In this way, you're now controlling a critical input to the process instead of waiting for a substantial change in the output. Thus, you're preventing problems instead of merely detecting poor quality in outputs.

Phase 3: Assess the Process

If your control chart shows a stable or predictable process, that doesn't mean it's necessarily a good process. The process could be predictably bad, so you still need to measure its ability to meet a customer's requirements or specifications. You don't need to know anything about these specifications to determine if a process is in control, but you must compare the current, stable process with specifications to determine its overall ability to meet them.

Step 1: Use ȳ (the centerline of the "in-control" control chart) to estimate the process's center, and s to estimate the standard deviation of the overall process. You may use the symbol, ô (in this case, ô = s), to denote a predicted or estimated value for the unknown σ.

Step 2: Apply the specifications and sketch how the process relates to them. For the gas mileage data, ȳ = 20 and ô = 1.3. For this make and model vehicle, suppose you're given a lower specification limit (LSL) of 17 mpg and an upper specification limit (USL) of 25 mpg. Although this USL isn't entirely realistic, we'll use it here to illustrate two-sided bounds. Superimposing the specs (or goalposts) onto the process curve will give you

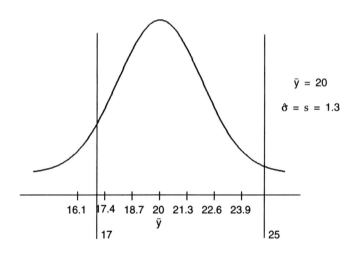

Step 3: Calculate the σ level, which is the number of ô's you can fit between the center of the process and the *nearest* spec. In general,

$$\sigma \text{ level } = \min\left[\frac{\bar{y} - \text{LSL}}{\hat{\sigma}}, \frac{\text{USL} - \bar{y}}{\hat{\sigma}}\right]$$

You can see from the sketch that the process isn't centered at the midpoint between the specs. ȳ = 20 is closer to the LSL = 17 than it is to the USL = 25. Hence,

$$\sigma \text{ level } = \frac{\bar{y} - \text{LSL}}{\hat{\sigma}} = \frac{20 - 17}{1.3} = 2.31$$

Step 4: Find the process capability, C_{pk}, directly from the σ level by

$$C_{pk} = \frac{\sigma \text{ level}}{3} = \frac{2.31}{3} = 0.77$$

The C_{pk} index tells us what proportion of the process's natural tolerances falls within spec. Natural tolerances of a process are considered to be ± 3 sigma. That's why we divide σ level by 3 to get $C_{pk} = 0.77 < 1$. A σ level of 3 corresponds to a C_{pk} of 1, a σ level of 6 corresponds to a C_{pk} of 2, and so on.

Obviously, the bigger that σ level or C_{pk} is, the more likely all of your data is falling within the specifications. Current benchmarks for acceptable capability measures are a σ level of at least 4 or a C_{pk} of at least 1.33. But increasing σ level or C_{pk} is much more important than being able to compute them. Assuming that customers fix the specs (goalposts), the previous sketch clearly shows you must reduce a process's variations to increase its capability and continuously improve it.

If you're interested in more detail, consult Kiemele [1997] for answers to questions such as "Which control chart should I use?" "How do I construct it?" "How do I interpret it for process control?" and "How do I use the information in a control chart to determine process capability?"

References

Daniel, Wayne W. 1978. *Applied Nonparametric Statistics*. Boston, MA: Houghton Mifflin Company.

An excellent reference for applying non-parametric statistics. It explains each tool, lists assumptions, and includes at least one example. In many cases, it gives normal approximations for large sample sizes. It's an excellent reference for people with limited background in statistics.

DOE KISS Software. 1997. Colorado Springs, CO: Air Academy Associates.

State-of-the-art software for design of experiments. It runs with Microsoft Excel 5.0 or later, providing graphical and statistical analysis. It follows the Keep-It-Simple-Statistically (KISS) approach, so it's very easy to use.

Draper, Norman and Harry Smith. 1981. *Applied Regression Analysis*. New York, NY: John Wiley & Sons.

Often considered the "Bible" of regression analysis, this text comprehensively covers its mathematics and applications.

Kennedy, William J. Jr. and James E. Gentle. 1980. *Statistical Computing*. New York, NY: Marcel Dekker, Inc.

Provides computation methods for estimating parameters from many distributions including the normal, exponential, and Weibull. It also covers random-number generation, but in less detail.

Kiemele, Mark J., Stephen R. Schmidt, and Ronald J. Berdine. 1997. *Basic Statistics: Tools for Continuous Improvement*. 4th ed., Colorado Springs, CO: Air Academy Press.

This applied-statistics text should be on every user's shelf. It is an excellent reference for statistical hypothesis testing, parameter estimation, reliability, statistical process control, regression, design of experiments, and probability, among other topics. It's easy to read and includes exercises and applications throughout.

Knuth, Donald E. 1981. *The Art of Computer Programming*. Vol. 2, 2nd ed., Reading, VA: Addison-Wesley Publishing Company.

The definitive text on random-number generation. It provides the theory and algorithms for generating general, uniform random numbers; several procedures for testing sequences of random numbers; and references and exercises with answers.

Schmidt, Stephen R. and Robert G. Launsby. 1994. *Understanding Industrial Designed Experiments*. 4th ed., Colorado Springs, CO: Air Academy Press.

Presents designed experiments so they're easy to understand and apply. Its intended audience is engineers and scientists rather than statisticians. Offers many case studies.

Shedler, G.S. 1980. Unpublished IBM Research Report RJ2789(35455).

This paper provides many algorithms for random-number generation and explains their advantages and disadvantages. The first section discusses common generators of uniform random numbers. Later sections list generators for distributions including the normal, exponential, and Poisson. The algorithms vary with complexity and computing time. The paper is brief with mostly short discussions. You may ask for copies from IBM, Thomas J. Watson Research Center Distribution Services, P.O. Box 218, Yorktown Heights, NY 10598.

SPC KISS Software. 1997. Colorado Springs, CO: Air Academy Press.

This software runs with Microsoft Excel 5.0 or later and provides a comprehensive statistical package using the Keep-It-Simple-Statistically (KISS) approach. It enables users to do Pareto charts, histograms, scatter diagrams with regression analysis, process-control charts and capability measures, probability distributions, failure mode and effect analysis, and measurement system analysis.

Glossary

Abstraction: [noun] *model*

[verb] (informal) Creating a *model* by abstracting features of the *system* it is to represent. Used in the same sense that a work of art is said to be an abstract representation. As the *model* moves farther from the counterpart *system*, the *level of abstraction* increases.

Acceptor: The part of an *experimental frame* that checks whether a *model* or *system* experiment remains within the conditions of interest.

Accommodates:

1. Link between a *model* and the *experimental frame*. The converse of *applies to*: A *model* accommodates an *experimental frame* just in case the *experimental frame applies to* the *model*.
2. Relation between a *system* and the *experimental frame*. The converse of *applies to*: A *system* accommodates an *experimental frame* just in case the *experimental frame applies to* the *system*.

Accreditation: Gaining approval for using models. Usually depends on prior *verification* and *validation*.

Other meaning: The official certification that a *model* or *simulation* is acceptable for a specific purpose.

Aggregate Model: Target *model* in an *aggregation* or other *simplification procedure*. Synonym: *lumped model*.

Aggregation: Mapping a source model, called a *base model*, into a target model, called a *lumped model* or *aggregate model*. This process involves grouping *base model elements* and combining each group into a single *lumped model element*. Grouped elements thus become indistinguishable in the target model. Aggregation is a *simplification procedure* and a form of *abstraction*, usually done to create a *homomorphic model* representation within an *experimental frame*.

Other meanings: [verb] Collecting data elements without losing their identities (in database literature).

Algorithm: Well defined set of steps for carrying out a computational task. A *simulator* of a *model* may be such an algorithm.

Amount of Detail: (informal) The degree to which *details* are included in a *model* description. The amount of detail is a product of the *model's scope* and *resolution*.

Applicability: Relation containing pairs of *experimental frames* and *models*, in which the *experimental frame* is *applicable (applies) to* the *model*.

The relation is many-to-many. Many *models* may *accommodate* the same *experimental frame*; likewise, many *experimental frames* may be *applicable to* the same *model*.

Applicable to (also "applies to"): Association between *experimental frame* and a *model*.

(informal) Answers whether it's possible to do the experiments on the *model* characterized by the *experimental frame*.

(formal) This association holds just in case the *experimental frame* is *derivable* from the *scope frame* of the *model*.

Attribute (of *model*): Same as *variable* (of *model*)—a named slot that can take on a value from its associated range set.

Autonomous Model: *Model* that no *input* affects.

Base Model:
1. Source *model* in an *aggregation* or other *simplification procedure*.
2. Conceptually complete representation of all aspects of interest in a modeling study, hence having the widest *scope frame* of interest.

Behavior: Collection of *trajectories*. Specific form of *data* observable in a *system* or generated by a *simulator* over time within an *experimental frame*.

Calibration: Fitting a *model's behavior* to match a corresponding part of an observed *system's* behavior by adjusting model *parameters*.

Certification: Same as *Accreditation*—gaining approval for using models, usually after *verification* and *validation*.

Complexity (of a *model*): Intrinsic difficulty in simulating a model. Determines the minimal resources (time, space, etc.) required by any *simulator* for *correct simulation*. Typically, complexity increases with the *amount of detail*. Thus, simulating a model that has many *components* and *interactions*, each described with high *resolution*, is likely to consume a lot of resources for any *simulator*. Under this assumption, if you have fixed resources, you must trade between *scope* and *resolution* in a *simulated* model.

Component (of *model*): Identifiable part of a *model*. The *model* consists of its components.

Constructive Simulation: *Simulation* in which humans only observe its *execution*. Contrasts with *interactive simulation*.

Correct Simulation: (Association between a *simulator* and a *model*.) A *simulator* correctly simulates a *model* if it is guaranteed to faithfully generate the *model*'s *behavior* in every *simulation run*.

Cross-Model Validity: The consistency of a *model behavior* or *structure* with another *model*'s *behavior* or *structure*. Usually can't establish it by direct comparison, but may be possible by proving *homomorphism*.

Data: Raw information. Behaviors of a *system* or *model* are collections of time-indexed data.

Derivability: Relation containing pairs of *experimental frames* such that the first is *derivable* from the second.

Derivable: Association between a pair of *experimental frames*.

(informal) Answers whether an experiment that runs within the first *experimental frame* can also run within the second.

(formal) See Zeigler, B.P. 1984. *Multifaceted Modelling and Discrete Event Simulation*. Orlando, FL: Academic Press.

Detail: (informal) The particulars of a *model*'s description including its *components*, *variables*, and *interactions*.

Deterministic Model: A *model* in which the *input* and *state* determine the next *state* and *output*. If the model is *autonomous* (not affected by inputs), the current *state* uniquely determines the next *state* and *output*.

Distributed Simulator: *Simulator* whose operation distributes over distinct processing nodes (may be geographically remote). The *model* being simulated may also be distributed among the nodes. Related to *parallel simulator*.

Dynamic Modeling Formalism: *Modeling formalism* that can express *models* which generate *trajectories* exhibiting *state*-dependent changes in the values its *variables* assume over time.

Efficiency: Measure of how sparingly a *simulator* uses resources when executing a model. A simulator can be no more efficient than the level allowed by the *model*'s *complexity*, which establishes the minimum resources for *correct simulation*.

Element: Generic term for a *variable, component*, or *interaction*.

Execution (by a *simulator* of a *model*): Generating *model behavior* in a *simulator* that obeys the *model* instructions, rules, or constraints.

Experiment Design: Systematic plan for executing a set of *simulation runs* with varied initial *states* and *parameters* to efficiently explore *model behavior* within an *experimental frame*.

Experimental Frame:

(informal) The conditions under which we observe, or experiment with, a *system* or *model*.

(formal) The *data* space into which we'll place the behavior of an *accommodating model* or *system*.

Clarification: The experimental frame makes an M&S project's *objectives* operational. It contains elements of the "conceptual *model*," as used in the literature for verification, validation, and accreditation.

Generator: The part of an *experimental frame* which generates the input trajectories to a *model* or *system*.

History: A *trajectory* of *system behavior* or *model behavior*.

Homomorphic Model: See *homomorphism*.

Homomorphism: (informal) A correspondence of the *states* of two *models* such that the *models* exhibit the same *behavior* when started in corresponding *states*. Homomorphism makes it possible to test for *valid simplification*. We can demonstrate homomorphism if we can show that corresponding *states* always 1) transition to corresponding *states* under the same *input*, and 2) yield the same *output*.

Input: *Variable* whose values are determined outside a *model*. The *model* receives this input through an external interface or *input port* and responds to it.

Input Port: See *port*. This term emphasizes how inputs must interface to a *model* or real-world *system*.

Interaction: *Static* or *dynamic* constraint between *elements* of a *model*.

Interactive Simulation: *Simulation* in which humans interact strongly with the *model* while it *executes* through its *experimental frame*. *Virtual simulations* use *models* that humans should perceive as real. In *live simulation*, real actors or objects may play the roles of some *model components*.

Isomorphic Model: *Homomorphic model* with an underlying one-to-one correspondence in its *states*.

Level of Abstraction:

(informal) The degree to which a *model* has been abstracted from the *system* it's supposed to represent. A higher level means greater *abstraction*.

(formal) Level of abstraction is a relational concept. It refers to the relative position of the *scope frames* of *models* in the *derivability* partial ordering. That is, if one *model's scope frame* is *derivable* from a second *model's* frame, then the first *model* is at a higher level of abstraction.

Level of Resolution: A *model's* level of resolution correlates strongly to its *level of detail*. High resolution implies a great *amount of detail*.

Live Simulation: *Interactive simulation* in which real elements may become *model components* (e.g., a battle simulation may include real tanks firing blank rounds).

Lumped Model: Target *model* in an *aggregation* or other *simplification procedure*. Same as *aggregate model*.

Measures of Effectiveness: *Outcome measures* that rate a modeled system for the effectiveness with which it carries out its mission.

Measures of Performance: *Output variables* or *metrics* that measure how well part of a modeled system works.

Metric: Mathematical measure for computing distance between two entities (points, curves, sets). Choice of metric and *tolerance* can be critical in judging a *model's validity*.

Model:

(informal) Instructions, rules, equations, or constraints that help us generate results that resemble a *system's behavior*.

(formal) Specification of *behavior* in a *dynamic modeling formalism*.

Other meaning: Physical, mathematical, or logical representation of a *system*, entity, phenomenon, or process.

Modeling Formalism: Mathematical language for expressing *models*.

Modularity (modular): *Systems* in the framework are modular: they have input and output ports that channel all interaction with the outside.

Nondeterministic Model: *Model* in which the *input* and *state* alone don't determine the next *state* and *output*. In a *probabilistic model* (stochastic model), probability distributions constrain the possible next *states* and *outputs*.

Objectives: An M&S effort's objectives are the questions it intends to answer.

Outcome Measures: *Metrics* specified in an *experimental frame's transducer* that reduce the *trajectories* of a *model's output variables* to easily comparable quantities related to the modeling *objectives*.

Output: *Variable* whose value is determined by a *model*. Think of the *model* generating this output through an external interface's *output port*.

Output Port: See *port*. Term that emphasizes how an *output* must interface to a *model* or real-world *system*.

Parallel Simulator: *Distributed simulator* whose goal is to speed up the *simulation* of a *model* that a *serial simulator* could run. Concurrent processing of tasks on individual units results in parallelism.

Parameter: *Model variable* that is set before a *simulation run* and doesn't change during the run. Its value may influence the *model behavior* a run generates.

Port: Ability to interface with the external world and to couple in order to compose larger systems. For example, the pins on a transistor chip are ports.

Predictive Validity: *Validity* of a *model* with respect to a *system* within an *experimental frame*. We can affirm it if we can initialize the *model* to a *state* such that, for the same *input trajectory*, the *model*'s *output trajectory* predicts the *system*'s *output trajectory* within an acceptable *tolerance*. Predictive validity is a stronger criterion than *replicative validity*.

Replicative Validity: *Validity* of a *model* with respect to a *system* within an *experimental frame*. We can affirm it if, for all the experiments possible within the *experimental frame*, the *trajectories* of the *model* and *system* agree within acceptable *tolerance*.

Resolution: Refers to the degree of *detail*, usually in space or time, a *model* includes. The greater the included *detail*, the higher the *level of resolution*.

Scope (of a *model*): (informal) The part of a *system* the *model* represents independent of its *level of resolution*. Also called breadth. The greater a *model*'s *scope*, the higher its *scope frame* will be in the *derivability* partial ordering (i.e., the more frames it can *accommodate*).

Scope Frame (of a *model*): (informal) The most extensive *experimental frame* that *applies to* the *model*.

Every frame that is *applicable* to a *model* is *derivable* from its scope frame.

Simplification Procedure: Method or algorithm applied to a *model* to reduce its *complexity* while preserving its *validity* in an *experimental frame* (to achieve *valid simplification*).

Simulation: Execution of a *model* by a *simulator*.

Clarification: The Distributed Interactive Simulation (DIS) glossary defines a simulation as a *model* (see DIS: simulation). In contrast, we sharply distinguish between the two concepts in any context in which a computer is essential. We consider computer simulation to be the process of generating a *model's behavior* using a *simulator*.

This term is often ambiguous, but we'll list common meanings and suggest how to add phrases that remove the ambiguity.

(noun) The M&S product—replace with "simulator," "model," or "model/ experimental frame pair" depending on what you're referring to. Example: replace "you must validate the simulation" with "you must validate the model." Another example: replace "running the simulation will produce outputs" with "launching the simulator will produce outputs."

(noun) The overall enterprise of M&S—for example, replace "simulation is a broad field" with "modeling and simulation is a broad field."

(noun) Simulation experiments—for example, replace "the firespread simulation revealed that," with "the modeling and simulation study revealed that."

(verb) Executing a model with a simulator—for example, replace "simulating the firespread" with "executing the firespread model."

Simulation Run: Executing a *model* with a *simulator* by starting from an initial *model state* and generating a *model trajectory*.

Simulator: Computer system (*algorithm*, single processor, or processor network) that can execute a *model* to generate its *behavior*.

Clarification: This concept refers to the device that executes a model. It could be software, hardware, or both. In current practice the term "simulator" often refers to a particular hardware device, such as a flight simulator, whose underlying model may not be explicit. A simulation program is a software example of the "simulator" concept. "Simulation engine" is a term that emphasizes the specialized hardware or software ("engine," as in "graphics engine") necessary to execute models. The simulator concept defined here includes all these connotations and gets to the core issue: ability to execute a model in order to generate its behavior.

State: Characterizing the knowledge of a *model's* past *behavior*, which we need to uniquely compute its future *behavior*. Often considered (erroneously) to be the current values assigned to all *variables*.

Static Modeling Formalism: *Modeling formalism* only able to express *models* that generate *trajectories* which don't depend on *state* (or *memory*).

Structural Validity: (informal) A *model* is structurally valid when its internal *structure* represents that of the *system*. Structural *validity* implies *predictive validity*, which implies *replicative validity*.

Structure (of a *model*): Refers to a *model's elements* rather than the *behavior* it generates. Think of the structure as what makes the *model* behave as it does.

Subsystem (of a *system*): A subset of the elements of a system specification that itself constitutes a system at the same level. For example, a subsystem at the state level contains a subset of the original states that is closed under transitions. A subsystem is different from a component system (which is a projection, rather than a subset, of the original).

Synthetic Environment: A *simulator* capable of *live, constructive,* and *virtual simulation.*

System (or source system): Real or virtual environment viewed as a source of observational *data* (*behavior*). This data is viewed or acquired through *experimental frames* of interest to the modeler. We construct *models* of the system to generate *behavior* that is identical to the system's *behavior* within one, or more, *experimental frames*.

Tolerance (on *trajectory* comparison): (informal) Criterion for determining when two *trajectories* are close enough to each other to be accepted as equal.

The tolerance is given as an interval—if a *metric* determines that the distance between two *trajectories* falls within this interval, we accept them as equal.

Trajectory: Time-indexed *data*. A mapping of a time interval to a *variable's* range set. It can be presented as a graphical plot of a *variable* against time.

Transducer: The part of an *experimental frame* that observes the output trajectories of a *model* or *system* and reduces them to *outcome* measures of interest.

Valid Simplification: An operation on a *model* that reduces its *complexity* and results in a *homomorphism*. For example, aggregating *variables* together is a valid simplification if it reduces a *model's* simulation time without affecting its ability to predict the aggregated quantity.

Validation: Testing a *model* for *validity* with respect to a *system* and an *experimental frame*. This process determines the degree to which a *model* accurately represents the real world for the *model's* intended uses.

Validity: Relation between a *model*, a *system*, and an *experimental frame*. Determines how closely the *model* represents the *system* in the *experimental frame*.

The most basic validity is *replicative*, which means the *behavior* of the *model* and *system* agree within acceptable *tolerance* for *experiments* possible within the *experimental frame*. Stronger forms of validity are *predictive validity* and *structural validity*.

Variable (of a *model*): Same as *attribute*—a named slot that can take on a value from its associated range set.

Verification: Making sure the *simulator* of a *model* correctly generates its *behavior*. This process determines that a *model* implementation accurately represents the developer's conceptual description and specifications.

Virtual Simulation: *Interactive simulation* that intends its *models* to seem real to human participants.

Index